The Rise and Fall of
Liberal Government in Victorian Britain

The RISE and FALL of LIBERAL GOVERNMENT in VICTORIAN BRITAIN

Jonathan Parry

1993
Yale University Press
New Haven & London

To Derek Beales

Copyright © 1993 Yale University Press

Library of Congress Cataloging-in-Publication Data

Parry, J. P. (Jonathan Philip), 1957–
    The rise and fall of liberal government in Victorian Britain /
Jonathan Parry.
        p.   cm.
    Includes bibliographical references and index.
    ISBN 0–300–05779–2
    1. Great Britain—Politics and government—1837–1901.
    2. Liberalism—Great Britain—History—19th century.   I. Title.
DA550.P28   1993
941.081—dc20   93-5937
                                                                                      CIP

Set in Linotron Plantin by Best-set Typesetter Ltd., Hong Kong
Printed and bound in Great Britain by St Edmundsbury Press, Suffolk

Contents

Preface

ANY HISTORIAN WHO attempts a book of this scope benefits from consulting the work of a large number of authors. I hope that I have managed to record my debt to most of them in the notes or suggestions for further reading, but this has not always been possible, owing to lack of space. (The notes, by and large, only support specific quotations or pieces of information in the text.) I apologise for any resulting discourtesy.

However, in the course of research, one also accumulates debts to institutions and individuals whose help can be acknowledged with a gratitude untempered by any fear of consequential world-wide forestal destruction. Few can have relied more than I, over the last few years, on the staff of the Cambridge University Library, in whose reading rooms and stacks, corridors and tea-rooms, this book has germinated slowly, discursively and agreeably. It is an incomparable resource, arguably the best working library in the world. Some of the preliminary reading for this book was undertaken in the course of a month's archival visit to the Huntington Library for another purpose, and so I am very grateful to both the Huntington and the British Academy for financial support to allow me to take advantages of the facilities there.

Offering enlightenment on all sorts of matters have been Ian Archer, Justin Barker (who also generously agreed to read a large amount of the book in proof), David Bebbington, Eugenio Biagini, Clyde Binfield, David Cooper, Richard Davis, Simon Dixon, David Feldman, Lawrence Goldman, Peter Gray, Ewen Green, Theo Hoppen, Tony Howe, Bill Lubenow, Peter Mandler, Susan Pennybacker, John Plowright, James Raven, Alistair Reid, Paul Seaward, Geoffrey Searle, Jonathan Spain, Duncan Tanner, David Thompson, John Vincent, Martin Wiener and Philip Williamson. I must thank also the editor of *Parliamentary History* for permission to reproduce material already published in his journal. Successive drafts of this book have grown in range and, I hope, sophistication, as an insular and over-conceptualising Cambridge mind became exposed to the sanity and professionalism of the London University historical scene, between 1989 and 1992; my colleagues at King's College London during that time, especially Peter Marshall, Andrew Porter and Richard Vinen, shaped this book more

vii

than they will probably believe. So, no less importantly, did many of my students, who were polite, but also unrealistic, enough to ask if it would appear in time to be of use to them. The final version owes much, too, to the mixture of congeniality and efficiency established by the Master and Fellows of Pembroke College Cambridge, who have shown what a Cambridge college can and should be like.

I have also been very lucky in the stimulation and encouragement provided over the years by Olive Anderson, Richard Brent, David Cannadine, Maurice Cowling, Peter Ghosh, Patrick Higgins, Terry Jenkins, Colin Matthew, Miri Rubin, Gareth Stedman Jones and Miles Taylor, to all of whom I owe a continuing and substantial debt. The same is true of those who in addition nobly shouldered the burden of reading and commenting on parts of the typescript: Michael Bentley, Peter Clarke, Boyd Hilton, Julian Hoppit, Richard Shannon, Paul Smith and Stephen Taylor; and, above all, Derek Beales, who read all of an earlier draft. Equally characteristic in uncomplainingly accepting the task and in the relentless rigour of its execution, he has the small reward of finding the version that follows a very different, and in parts almost unrecognisable, read.

Pembroke College Cambridge
December 1992

Introduction

LIBERALISM WAS THE dominant political force of Victorian Britain. Gladstone, looking back in 1884, maintained that since the 1830s it had been 'the solid permanent conviction of the nation'.[1] Between 1830 and 1886, a coalition of anti-Conservatives known at various times as whigs, Reformers and Liberals was out of office for scarcely a dozen years and lost only two of fourteen general elections.* They claimed that only they understood how to govern a nation experiencing rapid and unsettling growth and traditionally intolerant of strong central government rule.

This book aims, first and foremost, to be a general account of parliamentary Liberalism during its nineteenth-century heyday. On the face of it, it is astonishing that no satisfactory account exists.[2] The contrast with the Conservatives is striking.[3] Yet the Conservative party was always a more coherent force, more homogeneous, less independently-minded, and usually more amenable to central direction and organisation. Those who define the existence of political parties in terms of a nationwide structure would be hard put to identify a Liberal party until the 1860s (the Liberal Registration Association was founded in 1860) or even 1870s. It was difficult to discipline MPs in the 1840s and 1850s, leading many historians to argue that the Liberal party was not formed until 1859. But discipline hardly became less

---

* For most of this period, 'whig' and 'Liberal' were both used to describe the party, but I have used 'Liberal' from 1835, for reasons explained in chapter 6. I have usually referred to it before 1835 as 'whig', though I have called the government of 1830–4 a 'Reform' government, following contemporary practice. From mid-century onwards, if not before, 'whig' was used principally to distinguish particular tendencies within the party, such as a special attachment to the party's traditions, or membership of the Liberal aristocracy and gentry. I have aimed to use it in these senses from 1835. It is important to note that there was no agreement on what a 'whig' was, and that the 'whigs' were at no time a discrete and easily identifiable section of the party. I have often needed a term to describe the middle ground of the parliamentary party and its propertied extra-parliamentary supporters. I have sometimes employed 'whig' and sometimes other phrases – 'moderate', 'propertied' or 'traditional' Liberal, or 'whig-Liberal' – depending on context or whim.

1

difficult in the 1860s and 1870s; Gladstone regarded MPs as unleadable in 1867–8, as did Hartington in 1874, and in that year Cardwell wrote that the Liberals had 'never been a party, except *ad hoc*, for some special purpose'.[4] The lack of formal organisation, the exuberance and independence of grass-roots Liberals, the variety of local factors behind Liberal electoral success; all these elements make a useful general history of the nineteenth-century Liberal movement almost impossible. One might write a casserole of a book, anxiously including something on every aspect of the Liberal experience. But this would be an indigestible dish, of incompatible ingredients. Far better, then, to accept that there are many valid ways of tackling such diversity and that any coherent one must be partial in scope.

This book is about government and leadership. It examines the ideas and strategies by which the most important Liberal politicians attempted to lead the people, and it discusses the obstacles and crises which frustrated many of their aspirations. So it complements, rather than contributes to, the large amount of recent work which has investigated aspects of Victorian *popular* politics.

Leadership was a particular problem for nineteenth-century politicians. The variety, extent, and fervour of public expectations of central government became altogether novel after about 1800 – as did the legislative ambitions of the governing elite itself. The root problem was unprecedentedly rapid economic development, which heightened social tensions and political awareness at the same time as it eroded the capacity of local hierarchies to restrain discontent and discipline opinion. The pace of European economic and political change from the late eighteenth century onwards threw up a public opinion much larger, more mobile, more politically sophisticated and, it seemed, infinitely more restless than any previous one. The British population rose from 10.69 million to 16.37 million between 1801 and 1831; food imports tripled between the 1770s and the 1820s; there was a great migration of labour to new urban settlements where traditional structures of government were minimal or inappropriate; and overpopulation on the land made paupers of many who could or would not migrate, creating the conditions for rural social tension. The regular recurrence of severe economic depressions intensified the threat to order. Most industry was dependent on volatile but limited home demand, and on fragile credit mechanisms. The cotton industry, the basis of British export strength, relied on foreign raw material and on exports to countries which might well find cheaper supplies in the long run. Until about 1850, the economy, and the social order which depended on it, seemed highly vulnerable, or 'artificial'.[5] Rapid economic and population growth made it essential to discipline the people into an understanding of the benefits and fairness of law, taxation, religious establishments and existing constitutional arrangements. But it also increased public pressure on government. Lop-sided economic development was bound to create grievances among individuals about exploitation or oppression of various sorts – in factories, on the land, and in tax and poor rate burdens – and a demand that they should be rectified. Meanwhile, the feeling that political leaders had a duty to promote the *moral* reformation of society was encouraged by the shock-waves emanating from continental revolutions, by prosperity and broader horizons among the farming, commercial and professional middle classes, and by the spread of evangelical religious fervour which accompanied economic and political ferment. Central government, local magistrates and other professional agencies were impelled to action, partly by fear of losing their authority and partly by a late-eighteenth-century confidence in the power of human intelligence, detailed knowledge and propertied benevolence to dominate nature and to improve society.

This book argues that the whig and Liberal governments in power from 1830 had a more or less coherent response to this situation. Liberals saw government as a matter of integrating and harmonising different classes and interest groups within the political nation. To them, good government involved guiding the people so as to strengthen their attachment to the state and to the firm, fair rule of law, and using policy to shape individual character constructively. Disunity among the diverse individuals, groups and classes which constituted the nation was a worry for them because it heightened the prospect of unrest and perhaps revolution, but also because it failed to realise the potential of man as a communal animal; it encouraged apathy and discouraged the productive application of God-given human energies. Liberals claimed that animosities between land and trade, Church and Dissent, or Protestant and Catholic were not only crippling but unnatural. If nineteenth-century Liberalism meant anything, it meant a political system in which a large number of potentially incompatible interests – whether nationalities, classes, or sects – were mature enough to accept an over-arching code of law which guaranteed each a wide variety of liberties. To accept the rule of law in this way was to demonstrate character, fitness for citizenship. By the 1850s and 1860s, Liberals were confident that their creed was making progress in three senses. The duties and rewards of citizenship were being appreciated by more and more elements of British society; the remit of character-forming law was being extended to more and more aspects of national life; and ever-larger areas of the globe were adopting at least some of the Liberal world-view. The Liberal ideal was to bring as many people as possible under the rule of those principles. This meant binding Scotland, Wales and especially Ireland within a genuinely United Kingdom, spreading progressive commercial and constitutional values internationally, and entrenching those values particularly firmly in the empire.* It follows from this that Liberalism should not

---

* However, because this is a book on governing strategies I have not dealt in any detail with Liberal policy towards Scotland and Wales (before Gladstone's time) in the way that I have with Irish policy. On the whole, Liberals did not have to pay serious attention to specifically Scottish and Welsh demands in framing their policy – except when handling matters such as local government and education, where long-established Scottish structures necessitated a different approach from that taken in England. I have decided, for reasons of space and simplicity of

be confused with nationalism, the principle of national separateness and division. In the Liberal model, self-government for particular geographical regions was to be limited according to the level of citizenship reached by the inhabitants. Their willingness voluntarily to live by Liberal principles would determine the amount of power that could safely be devolved to them.

These assumptions made the Liberal party distinctive in a number of ways from the 1830s onwards. First, whereas the Conservative party was always essentially *English*, the Liberals were a *British* party, a genuinely *unionist* force committed to the integration of all parts of the United Kingdom. Second, whereas the Conservative party remained preoccupied with the defence of government authority, and innately suspicious of popular political activity, the Liberals were committed to open politics, anxious to demonstrate a willingness to respond to popular grievances. Third, whereas the Conservative party never broke free of landed influence, the Liberals were much happier with arguments drawn from political economy, arguments that stressed that different social groups had *common*, not clashing, economic interests. And fourth, whereas the Conservatives remained specifically an Anglican party, Liberals sought to rally public opinion behind a notion of religion as a broad, modern and essentially undogmatic creed, capable of speaking to and uniting the whole nation. Dogmatic differences between sects were to be tolerated, and would naturally diminish as man's understanding of real religion improved. Though Irish Catholic sensitivities often prevented Liberals from making the point quite as explicitly as they might have liked, in general they presented themselves as the party of Protestantism and pluralism, and their faith in the progress of human reason allowed them to deny any incompatibility between the two.

Most of all, Liberals were united by the powerful myth that tories, or Conservatives, offered rule by 'vested interests' – by the aristocracy, the Anglican church, colonial trading interests, local corporations, and sinecure-hunters. The tories seemed a landed, stupid rump incapable of providing government to the general benefit. Liberals defined themselves as opponents of government by class, sect or interest. This was crucial – much more so than historians have tended to recognise. It meant that, while the Conservatives might with justice be called a landed or church party between the 1830s and 1870s, Liberals could not be labelled an urban or Dissenting party in the same way. Liberals' ingrained mythology required them to believe that they offered national, not class, government. Of course individual Liberal leaders had their own prejudices and political requirements,

---

argument, not to discuss these Scottish variations, which would merely be a token gesture. The only exception to this rule is my brief discussion of the Scottish Reform Act of 1832 (see pages 86–7). After 1868, both Wales and Scotland played a more significant part in Liberal calculations, and I hope that I have conveyed something of this in Part IV. Throughout the period covered by the book, Scottish and Welsh popular political activity was very largely concerned with religious issues, and whenever I have used the phrase 'evangelical Dissent', a significant Scottish and Welsh component can be assumed.

and of course they were often capable of manipulating the political situation to suit them. But the need to appear 'disinterested' still affected their behaviour fundamentally. Much of the most valuable historical work on nineteenth-century Britain published in the last twenty years has emphasised the defensive determination of propertied Victorians to protect their privileges from lower-class attack. To some extent, this insight can be applied to nineteenth-century Liberals. But it needs to be qualified. Liberal leadership strategy must not be reduced to a 'conservative' or 'concessionary' mindset, a negative outlook which was primarily anxious to assert 'social control'. All strategies are by definition conservative of something, but political leadership also always involves movement, participation, invigoration and reconciliation. It is about coalition-building, about forming alliances between as many different kinds of passions, principles and interests as possible. This was particularly true of Liberals in our period. It is, for example, unfortunate that the most popular explanation of the 1832 Reform Act presents Liberal leaders as reluctant barterers of small chunks of 'power' to some defined 'middle-class' group outside their narrow charmed circle.[6] In fact, as we shall see, Liberals dealing with parliamentary reform were usually more interested in the distribution of parliamentary seats than in the question of who should vote, and their main concern in discussing the franchise was that defined interests should not appear *excluded* from the constitution. As the composition of the politically-aware nation changed, Liberals altered their perception accordingly. For instance, Lord John Russell equated the 'people' with the 'middle classes' in 1831, but by 1861 he was defining them as the 'working classes'.[7]

To argue this is not to say that Liberal leaders were 'classless' in a late twentieth-century sense. All the party leaders discussed in the text believed that the possession of property, character and wisdom was an invaluable asset in leadership, both nationally and locally. All of them shared the standard nineteenth-century belief that civilisation depended on the maintenance of social ranks. They encouraged individual self-improvement *within* all classes not least because of their ingrained assumption that the class structure was preordained and that men of property were society's natural leaders.

Liberals' distinctiveness came in not believing that possession of property alone made a leader. They assumed that rule by the landed interest, acting as an interest, would almost certainly become selfish, complacent and sectional. Good political leadership required other qualities: breadth of popular sympathy, self-confidence, courage and disinterestedness, and a cultured understanding of the relation between the present and the past, developed through the study of history, literature, theology and perhaps science.*

---

* There was a long whig/Liberal tradition of familiarity with intellectual, scientific and theological thinking and literary and historical culture. The whig salon Holland House, in its heyday in the 1810s and 1820s, brought politicians and men of letters together. Successive generations of leading Liberal politicians

In particular, the good leader needed to be able to respond to social and intellectual change. Liberals believed that politics could not dominate society, which was an immensely complex entity directed by the interaction of millions of wills. The politician needed to understand the intellectual and spiritual drift of national life, so that he could reconcile social evolution with institutional forms. The effective exercise of judgment was his most basic task. All abstract theories of government were too rigid and simplistic to fit the human personality; a flexibility of approach was necessary in order to formulate acceptable laws. Good law regulated passion, suppressed barbarism and encouraged the development of human character; it bolstered true liberty. But legislation which was unsuited or repulsive to the people would, at best, be unable to stimulate their energies, and, at worst, foment class or sectional division in the country because it seemed to favour some group over another. Struck by the force of public opinion, Liberals dismissed out of hand the notion that unpopular law could permanently 'control or govern the people'.[8] Popular acquiescence in legislation was necessary. As Russell wrote in 1839, 'laws and institutions must act gradually and generally in order to be beneficial . . . laws must be respected as well as enacted; the minds of men must be engaged to a willing conformity with the new order of the State'.[9] As more and more social groups came to be included within the loose structure of the Liberal party, it was forced to take account of public opinion all the more assiduously. For example, the speed with which it responded to provincial clamour for Corn Law reform in the winter of 1838–9 is remarkable.[10]

The Liberal party which developed from the 1830s was therefore a different animal from anything which had preceded it in British politics. But it was not born in a vacuum. It owed a lot to the thinking of the whig opposition of the years before 1830. But it was also indebted to the initiatives undertaken by the tory governments of the 1820s, which are discussed in the first two chapters of the book. The emergence of a vociferous public opinion after 1800 forced the tories of the 1820s to make significant changes in the substance and presentation of politics. These changes were particularly associated with Foreign Secretary Canning, who was primarily responsible for establishing the word 'liberal' as British political currency. He claimed that 'liberal' government meant a willingness to listen to public opinion, and that the result was reduced taxes, a more open commercial policy and the encouragement of constitutional principles abroad. However, in practice the 'liberal toryism' of the 1820s was as much tory as liberal. In particular, the bulk of the tory party remained resistant to parliamentary reform and Catholic emancipation. In a sense, this resistance led to the fall of tory government in 1830, when faced with an unusual degree of public clamour. But this book is at pains to stress that the events of 1830 did not

---

patronised worthy debating bodies such as the Society for the Diffusion of Useful Knowledge, the British Association for the Advancement of Science and the Social Science Association. Russell and Gladstone, among Liberal Prime Ministers, were particularly widely-read and prolific authors.

mean that the political nation was as advanced as the incoming whig government on the two issues of Reform and Ireland. Indeed the whig/ Liberal governments of the 1830s eventually foundered because the electorate distrusted their over-responsiveness to popular pressure in general, and Irish Catholicism in particular. Their electoral defeat in 1841 revealed that Liberals had not succeeded in winning the voters who mattered round to their own conception of politics.

It was only after 1846 that Liberals were able to do this. Their strongest weapons were free trade, Protestantism and foreign policy – and Palmerston, who crafted out of them an uplifting vision of national purpose and identity. British prosperity seemed to vindicate Liberals' claim to be able to cater for all major economic interests, while political stability appeared to testify to the superiority of her constitutional settlement. The result was general contentment with Liberal government. Between the 1850s and 1880s, the Liberal coalition spanned an astonishing range of classes and groups, from aristocrats to artisans, industrial magnates to labour activists, and zealous Anglican high churchmen to nonconformists and aggressive free-thinkers. It was strong among merchants and shopkeepers in the large towns of the midlands and north; it relied on the enthusiasm of the Dissenting chapels and the trades unions. Yet it also had a power base in traditional county and market towns, in the literary, legal and academic intelligentsia, and among an important minority of Anglican aristocrats and country gentlemen who not only supplied the party with its parliamentary leadership and its social centres (London salons and country houses) but also influenced the return of MPs for a large proportion of small boroughs and a significant number of county seats.[11] At parliamentary level, it was a loose body of men sitting for a great variety of seats, most of whom stood on their dignity as independent and propertied representatives.

The rest of this introduction discusses in more detail the leadership strategies by which Liberals sought to create and maintain support. Liberals were politicians, and their leadership strategies operated at two levels. They genuinely wished to attack particular obstacles to good government, but they also needed to find cries capable of rallying opinion in and outside parliament, in order to keep the cross-class Liberal coalition functioning effectively and so hold government in place. There were two main components of Liberal political argument, two main areas of common purpose. One centred on a particular model of the constitution: 'parliamentary government'. The other involved a set of initiatives in key policy areas, which aimed to promote certain values and character attributes. In each case, though, there were also tensions within the Liberal ideal which we need to explore.

'Parliamentary government'

Liberals' conception of the integrating function and rational nature of politics required them to idealise parliament as a truly national body, which, under propertied leadership, could succeed in reconciling tensions and subordinating sectional pressures. They often talked of 'parliamentary government'.[12] As late as 1893, the duke of Devonshire (the Hartington of this book) claimed that the constitution dictated 'the direct government of these Islands by Parliament through a Committee', the committee being the cabinet.[13] A well-constituted parliament could represent the national will, the significant interests and opinions of the nation – rather than the oligarchical power of the crown or individual powerful peers, or brute mass force. Its decisions, emerging from free debate among MPs, would be accepted as the closest approximation possible to the settled conclusions of the public opinion represented there. Respectable, respected MPs would be able to lead local constituency opinion to express grievances constitutionally and to accept parliamentary rule. The Liberal constitutional writer Bagehot spoke for many when in 1860 he described the Westminster parliament as 'the most efficient instrument for expressing the practical opinion of cultivated men which the world has ever seen'.[14]

Acclaim for parliament as the nation's grand forum was not an invention of nineteenth-century Liberals. They claimed to be reasserting the constitutional tradition protecting British liberties which had been established by their ancestors in 1688–9 and which had later been eroded by tory corruption and exclusiveness. Nonetheless, parliament probably appeared a more majestic institution in the mid-nineteenth century than at any time before or since. The most striking physical evidence of this is the buildings themselves. In 1834, the old Houses of Parliament – the House of Commons a converted chapel – were destroyed in a fire. The replacement, designed in 1836, built over twenty years, and occupied from the early 1850s, was presented as a 'magnificent Structure, which affords, for the first time', a setting worthy of the free deliberating body of the world's greatest power.[15] The river front is 940 feet long; two towers stand over 300 feet high, one built as the largest and highest square tower in the world; there are 500 rooms and space for 270 statues, sculptures and monuments celebrating past statesmen and their exemplary achievements. The internal decorations are magnificent, especially in the House of Lords, symbolising the pomp and glory of aristocratic leadership. In the niches were placed eighteen large bronze statues of the barons and prelates who witnessed the signing of Magna Carta, the foundation of British liberties. Frescoes at the bar end represent the spirit of justice, religion and chivalry. The decorations everywhere also repeatedly reproduce the heraldic devices and other symbols of the four nations of the United Kingdom, in order to demonstrate the integrating function of the *imperial* parliament. The grandeur – for example in the Central Hall, where MPs were to meet constituents – was clearly intended to overwhelm the visitor with the authority of what, as William Cubitt put it, was 'deservedly termed the New Palace of Westminster'; a palace not for a king, but for the elected and august representatives of a free people.[16]

What should parliament do? One of its functions was to represent a great many specific interests. It was to protect property from attack by government; it was to consent to the regulation of property rights for the general good. But its role as national forum gave it wider duties. Bagehot defined these as the expression of the considered opinion of the people, the political education of the nation, the publicising of errors, abuses and grievances, and the maintenance of government on sufferance of good liberal behaviour.[17] This last role was taken very seriously. All but one of the nine parliaments elected between the 1832 and 1867 Reform Acts dismissed a government during its course, while the Liberal ministries between 1868 and 1886 had their work cut out to preserve what on paper seemed commanding parliamentary majorities. Governments wishing to maintain the power of effective action had constantly to monitor the collective mood of the Commons. In 1861, Prime Minister Palmerston told the queen that on four days per week he had to sit there from 4:30 p.m. until after midnight in order to 'observe and measure the fluctuating bearings of Party and of sectional associations on the present position of the Government and on its chances for the future'.[18]

As this implied, the passage of legislation was a less important parliamentary duty. The ideal was for consent to be given to it only after prolonged deliberation by responsible MPs. Inherent in Liberalism was confidence in the power of discussion and reason. Parliament's assent to bills should not be given easily; it signified that an acceptable degree of consensus had been reached on their merits, so that they fitted the nation's habits.[19] This minimised the possibility of subsequent controversy or repeal, so that, as Gladstone asserted, 'we always progress, never retrace our steps'.[20] Cumbrous parliamentary procedure, dating from the era when significant government legislation was sparse, ensured that powerful groups of MPs could easily block bills.* At times of crisis – 1811, 1833, 1848 – there were minor alterations to procedure, which were aimed at increasing government's power of action. But not until 1882 and in practice 1887 was any serious limit imposed on the latitude given to parliament to discuss questions and hence to talk them out. As so many other examples suggest, the crisis of 1886 struck the real blow to the health of 'parliamentary government'. Not until 1879, and more seriously 1888, were firm rules introduced limiting the duration of the daily parliamentary sittings.[22]

---

* As late as 1884, when the Liberal government had a healthy majority, Joseph Chamberlain, President of the Board of Trade, withdrew his Merchant Shipping Bill with the comment that 'it would be impossible for me to make any progress with this measure unless I have the hearty and general assent, not only of all Parties in the House, but also of persons interested in the matters dealt with in the Bill'. Chamberlain explained that government had introduced amendments to accommodate earlier criticisms of the bill, but that, since opposition persisted from shipowners in the north-east and Scotland, it could be proceeded with only if 'I was able to give a considerable time to its further discussion'. Owing to the state of parliamentary business, this time was not available.[21]

But 'parliamentary government' did not mean that parliament itself was to *govern*. In fact, despite their sensitivity to popular rights, Liberals had a more active conception of the role of executive government than the tories they replaced. 'Parliamentary government', rather, allowed the executive government and the legislature to work together 'with harmony and energy', protecting popular liberties but also maximising the effective power of ministers.[23] Liberals were anxious for the writ of law to run as far as popular consent would allow; they had much more confidence in the ameliorative power of nationwide legislation than British governments had had before 1830. In 1831, Russell criticised the tory notion of politics for its inactivity: 'it is upon law and government, that the prosperity and morality, the power and intelligence, of every nation depend'.[24] Much of this Liberal legislation was founded on another corollary of 'parliamentary government', which again had previously been unfashionable, that 'all public funds and endowments are, in their essence, public property, subject to public inquiry, and if they are unjustly, injuriously, wastefully applied, are a proper field for public interference'.[25] So the Liberals were keen to assert their power of legislative initiative in parliament. Indeed the changes consequent on the 1832 Reform Act significantly *reduced* the ability of back-bench MPs to steer legislation through the Commons independently of ministers. Between 1846 and 1868, years often (though in fact wrongly) reckoned the highpoint of 'parliamentary government', only eight private members' bills were carried against the opposition of the government.[26] Very few amendments were ever successfully carried against government bills.[27] And government was anxious to interfere in the Commons more generally, in order to check intolerance and uncooperativeness there – for MPs were bound to advance sectional interests – and a corresponding polarisation along class or sectional lines outside it. In other words, Hartington's definition of the cabinet as a committee of parliament was misleading in one vital sense, for it was much more a committee of the crown, concerned with the maintenance of law and good order.

This executive activism created a tension within Liberalism, because it threatened to undermine parliamentary freedom of action. How, then, did Liberal leaders seek to balance the ideals of authoritative government and effective parliamentary representation of popular interests? They did so by a particular notion of the nature of political party. When in opposition in the late eighteenth century, the whigs had developed the idea of party as an honourable bond for virtuous men with a common commitment to the protection of popular liberties. In government after 1830, they continued to believe that party was essential: it sustained government momentum, while the constant vigilance of an organised opposition helped to check the abuse of power by ministers. But at the same time Liberals believed that party discipline must be loose. For them, light whipping of MPs was a necessary prerequisite of free debate. It was also inevitable because the Liberal coalition was so heterogeneous. A number of commentators likened it to the Protestant Church in that both bodies were able to measure fairly and flexibly the wants of the nation because of their disdain for rigid hierarchy and their attachment to pluralism.[28] As Gladstone said in 1885, 'Liberalism has ever sought to unite freedom of individual thought and action, to which it largely owes its healthy atmosphere, with corporate efficiency'. But, he went on, this aim 'is noble, but it is difficult'.[29] Party leadership was seen as a fine art, in which the leader's 'character' was all-important. Russell once wrote that it was 'the habit of party in England to ask the alliance of a man of genius, but to follow the guidance of a man of character'.[30] A party leader was given authority by his MPs to advocate their viewpoint without compromising their honour or the national interest. He had to be disinterested, flexible, and yet honourable and moral. Leaders also had to look outside parliament and distinguish between 'true' and 'false' public opinion, between 'matured', 'intelligent', 'permanent' opinion, and passing whims, mostly irresponsible and sectional, which might be ignored.[31] And they had to shape half-formed public sentiments into an effective but responsible rallying-cry. In 1876, Hartington defined political party as 'an engine the object of which is to form the opinion and guide the destinies of the nation'.[32] Liberal leadership meant leadership by example, by advocacy and by initiatives rather than by dictation. Macaulay called parliamentary government 'government by speaking'.[33] To be a successful leader, then, was a laudable ambition. Russell, for example, was intensely anxious to cast himself as a worthy successor to past statesmen of virtue, principally Fox.[34]

However, the Liberals' ideal of consensus through parliamentary debate was often frustrated, and this had important consequences. One frequent obstacle to their plans was the House of Lords. Liberal leaders wanted to demonstrate the benevolence and authority of the landed classes; the new House of Lords was a splendid building; nearly half of each Liberal cabinet sat in it (over half in 1846 and 1855). But its standing had long been affected by the fact that the Commons was the tax-granting House. Even the high tory duke of Wellington said in 1818: 'Nobody cares a damn for the House of Lords'.[35] And most peers did not share Liberal views on how to preserve aristocratic power. Since they could easily defeat contentious measures, there were frequent clashes, such as over parliamentary reform in 1831–2 and 1884, the repeal of the paper duties in 1860, Irish church disestablishment in 1869 and the secret ballot in 1871. Radical MPs came to call for the abolition of the Lords' legislative powers. Liberal leaders often toyed with ways of increasing the weight of reason and Liberalism in Lords' debates, either by increasing the number of peers or by introducing life peerages (floated by Russell and Palmerston from the 1840s).

But the Commons also was frequently more problematic than the Liberal ideal suggested. Liberal ministries' willingness to tolerate parliamentary criticism and defeat of their proposals was bound to lead to complaints – from tories but also from order-loving or doctrinaire Liberals – that Liberal government was too inactive, too weak to safeguard imperial defences, too indecisive to command popular respect, or too lenient to intractable sects and cliques within the Commons. These arguments were regularly deployed

11

against Melbourne, Russell and Palmerston between 1835 and 1865. On the other hand, if governments tried to force on legislation, as Gladstone sometimes did, Liberals could complain that the voice of reason and the process of free debate were under attack. Liberal leaders found it difficult to maintain enthusiasm for their agenda across the range of their parliamentary support. Few Liberal MPs became actively hostile to their governments, but nor were they blindly assiduous in defending their every act.[36] All the governments discussed in this book eventually ran out of steam, largely because their supporters' commitment flagged.

Cornewall Lewis once wrote: 'we seldom legislate when things are prosperous'.[37] This implied that the Commons tended to be too complacent, and was only effectively galvanised by extra-parliamentary pressure. Some Liberals found such pressure distasteful; they had hoped that the 1832 Reform Act would strengthen the power of government and parliament to act independently of outside agitation.[38] The long-serving Liberal cabinet minister George Grey continued to disapprove of statesmen making public speeches and publishing pamphlets.[39] But in fact many Liberals had few qualms about arousing popular feeling, if they could claim also to be educating it. In crises, they were willing to stir parliament to bold action because this demonstrated that it was a responsive body.

Liberals were happy to display their responsiveness to popular political pressure, not least because it helped to stave off calls for further destabilising parliamentary reform after 1832. One gauge of the success of the Liberal governing strategy is that in 1890 Britain had almost the least democratic franchise in Europe. Parliamentary Liberal leaders were *not* enthusiasts for democracy.* After 1832 (and in fact before it), many Liberals disliked the Reform cry, which they associated with controversy, division and unpleasant side-effects. They regarded the 1832 Reform Act as a one-off measure to make parliament truly representative of the key national interests, so that it could regulate property rights more effectively for the general good. In the 1860s and 1880s, some Liberals publicly opposed further Reform, fearing that it would transform the Commons into a swarm of delegates unable to resist mass pressure.

Nonetheless, the failure of parliament to live up to the Liberal ideal created unstoppable momentum within Liberalism for further Reform. Liberal leaders and ideas played the leading role in shaping the three great parliamentary reform packages of 1832, 1867–8 and 1884–5, which increased the number of people voting in Great Britain from under 75,000 at the 1831 general election to over 4 million in 1885. Liberals advocated

---

* Throughout this book, I have tried to abstain from controversy with other historians, but in self-defence must mention E.F. Biagini's *Liberty, retrenchment and reform; popular Liberalism in the age of Gladstone, 1860–1880* (Cambridge, 1992), p. 16, which quotes an earlier book of mine out of context and criticises it for failing to understand that an essential bond between parliamentary Liberal leaders and grass-roots activists was a common commitment to democracy, a charge to which I happily plead guilty.

Reform bills, at various times, for four principal reasons: they offered the prospect of a better integration of opinion under propertied and parliamentary leadership; their passage might galvanise parliament to be more assiduous in passing legislation for the public benefit; their introduction might rally Liberal forces in parliament; and they promised to liberate reforming opinion in the country which the existing constitutional settlement was somehow repressing, so opening the prospect of a more permanent majority for progressive principles. The first two arguments reflected Liberal fears that parliament was failing in its duty of securing popular acquiescence in the conduct of government. The last was a natural response to electoral or parliamentary defeat.

Parliamentary reform appeared irresistible *if* it would stop particular sectional interests from dominating the representative system and obstructing the triumph of reforming principles, reforming legislation and the reforming party. Reformers were anxious to balance the composition of parliament, so that it was controlled *neither* by owners of close boroughs *nor* by demagogues inciting popular support for class-based taxation and law and for the destruction of educational, moralising institutions. Until the 1870s, the rationale for tinkering with the franchise was not so much to reward respectable citizens with the vote (though it inevitably became prized for this reason), as to influence the type of MP elected. Electors, Liberals argued, had the task of assessing the fitness of past and prospective MPs to play their allotted part in parliament. The principal argument against a full democratic franchise was that it would return MPs of no virtue who talked demotic language and adopted unprincipled and sectional attitudes. Conversely, the main argument for parliamentary reform was that many of the MPs returned by the existing arrangements were not disinterested and virtuous enough either.

To repeat, most Liberals were willing to toy with the reform of parliament, but along *representative* rather than *democratic* lines.* Hence Liberals' tendency to oppose extensive schemes of seat redistribution after 1832, which would threaten the social balance of parliament. The future of the Commons as a debating body of men representing the vital national interests seemed to depend on the survival of a substantial number of small boroughs influenced by local property-owners, as well as on the returns from large towns where MPs would be influenced by vocal and often radical popular sentiment. And county seats should continue to represent the interests of property there, both urban and rural. Meanwhile, the right to vote was to remain a privilege conferred on those who demonstrated enough respectability to choose MPs on behalf of the wider community. Ironically, though, each of these strategies for defending the variety of representation was susceptible to differing interpretations, with a striking result. By 1886, the electorate numbered over 5 million. A majority was working class, 4 per

---

* Note the various Liberal definitions of the function of parliamentary representation given in the text, for example those at pages 78, 209 and 213.

cent of voters were illiterate, and voting was now in secret. The small boroughs had been abolished and large towns divided into districts allotted on the basis of population, and the county seats had been chopped into divisions drawn up largely on class considerations. Britain had become a quasi-democracy. This had been done by Reform acts prompted and influenced mainly by the various Liberal principles discussed above. One aim of this book is to explain how this happened.

Issues

The corollary of 'parliamentary government' was that political leadership mainly meant managing MPs. After 1832, Liberal leaders rarely needed to worry about courting the electorate directly. Though they never had a disciplined parliamentary majority in the modern sense, they could usually expect a majority of MPs to work with them if treated sensibly. So they had much less interest in electoral considerations than democratic politicians who are dependent on the electorate for power, while parliament was returned for all sorts of reasons only tangentially connected with decisions at Westminster.

Liberal leaders instead needed to engage the commitment of MPs. Hence, to a peculiar degree, Liberal politics was issue politics. The Liberal movement, inchoate and loosely whipped, could be held together only by promoting policies of common interest. Different Liberals had different enthusiasms and dislikes. But all could identify to a greater or lesser extent with a series of political traditions, or myths, or rhetorics, which together made up a Liberal value-system, and which could be used to inspire followers, to suggest purpose, to underpin constructive legislation, and to keep the Liberal movement in the country in tune with MPs. This value-system was concerned mainly with questions of morals, economy and efficiency. Several aspects of it deserve particular note as they help to define what Liberals meant by good, progressive government.

One, reaching back centuries, was the 'country' tradition. MPs suspicious of the court had long defined their parliamentary duty as that of guarding against the abuse of power by the monarch and his government, in two fields in particular: in expenditure of taxpayers' money, and in legislation affecting civil liberties. By 1830, whig landowners had been in opposition to tory governments almost uninterruptedly for over half-a-century, and so they were bound to see themselves as defenders of popular interests against an exclusive crown which had shut them out of office. After they came to power in 1830, they remained committed to economical, efficient government, and continued to work in harness with radicals, though the latter were much more thoroughgoing in their attacks on the principal objects of expenditure: defence and officeholders' pay. Whig and radical Liberals also shared a dislike of special measures of 'repression', over and above the ordinary process of law. This would smack of failed leadership as well as being divisive and imprudent. From the 1830s, Liberals were united also in wishing to secure a representative structure for municipal government, as a way of institutionalising checks on central power, yet, at the same time, goading property-owners to be more active local leaders. As the century wore on, they extended this interest in decentralisation, in 'self-government', in other ways too.

Linked to the 'country' tradition was a second common denominator: an ethically-motivated anti-clericalism. In opposition, whigs had made contact with the religious minorities which suffered legal discrimination under tory rule. So they took to supporting the grievances of the two principal groups of religious sects outside the established church, Protestant Dissenters (or nonconformists) and (mainly Irish) Roman Catholics. In addition, almost all Liberals objected to the complacency, exclusiveness and inefficiency of the established church, the Church of England, and to its political bias as a bastion of toryism. They sought to reform its grotesquely unfair distribution of wealth, and reduce its political privileges, so that it would be more active in Christianising the nation and less offensive to non-Anglicans. Moreover, most Anglican Liberals and nonconformists were committed to encouraging individual access to revealed religion. They tended to be strong Protestants anxious to popularise a simple, manly religion in which God spoke directly to the believer, unobstructed by ancient pedantry, ritual or other priestly verbiage and condescension. It is difficult to exaggerate the interest of most Liberals (whether orthodox or, in a minority of cases, heterodox in theology) in the spread of religious awareness; they regarded a balanced and developed individual 'character' as the only proper basis of a progressive Liberal state.

So far, so good. But there were points of tension here. Most Anglican Liberals were committed to the belief that the established church, suitably reformed, was a beneficial moral force in guiding the religious and political views of the less educated and bolstering their character development. Most whigs also had relations in the church, for many landed families owned livings. Their views about religious policy were also affected by their commitment to 'parliamentary government': they argued that establishment was a great boon because parliament was the force best able to repress narrow clericalism within the church and ensure that it served the interests of a modernising nation. So they upheld not only establishment but the notion of parliamentary interference in church affairs. This did not please radical nonconformists who pressed for church disestablishment because its complacency damaged the cause of evangelisation, nor the traditionalist high churchman Gladstone, who supported establishment but was anxious to protect church self-government from whig erastianism, that is, from state interference.

The Liberal alliance with Irish Roman Catholics was even more problematical. Neither Anglican nor nonconformist Protestants wanted a seemingly superstitious, bigoted Catholic religion to play too great a role in Irish society. But many Irish people were unwilling to accept British liberal religious values. This was only one dimension of the Irish problem. For much of the century, Liberals believed that Irish grievances came from previous bad tory laws and that their own sympathetic government would eventually secure peace, extend 'middle-class' values of rationality and self-reliance, and encourage economic modernisation and prosperity. But, as time went on, it became more difficult to blame Irish discontent on tory rule. Perhaps Ireland did not fit the Liberal model. Some argued that parliamentary government was unworkable there because 'there is no natural leadership of the people by the squires as there is in England, and they are swayed about between the demagogues and the priests'.[40] But it was politically embarrassing to have to resort to illiberal repression in order to maintain British authority.

Despite the difficulties of assimilating Irish opinion to unionist progressive Liberalism, in general both the 'country' and the anti-clerical Protestant traditions served the party extremely well. No political myth was more deep-rooted in British life than that of the free-born, self-reliant Briton, resistant to tyranny and taxes, and proudly Protestant. The Liberal version of this myth struck chords among all classes. Liberalism therefore articulated the national identity in a self-confident and politically effective form. Superficially internationalist (in its commercial policy) and superficially generous (in encouraging constitutional movements abroad), Liberalism was in fact profoundly chauvinistic, luxuriating in the sense of British superiority to European rivals. The Liberals became the first 'national' party. It was only their errors, late in the nineteenth century, that allowed the Conservatives to usurp that mantle.

Two other strategies of Liberal leadership also merit discussion. One stemmed from Liberals' receptiveness to intellectual debate. We noted earlier how they were attached to the notion of avowedly nationwide and systematic legislation. Their intellectual interests encouraged them to introduce scientific principle into that legislation. Many of their bills aimed to shape society in line with identifiable 'natural laws', so promoting individual character and social progress. This tendency was particularly noticeable in measures to combat pauperism and crime and to reform education, public health and prisons. It was also of significance in dealing with economic questions. But for various reasons discussed in the text Liberals were less doctrinaire about applying political economy in practice than their rhetoric often suggested. So while, after 1846, they gained enormous political benefit from being identified with free trade, they were rarely the prime movers in extending it. More generally, their interest in 'scientific' legislation was always checked by a counter-principle. Most Liberal MPs distrusted the excessive use of state power and the brute application of abstract theory to legislation: hence their concern with decentralisation. Except, perhaps, in crises, Liberals were not in the business of crudely forcing something called 'Victorian values' on recalcitrant subjects. The vast bulk of the rhetorical teaching even of active Victorian politicians like Palmerston, Peel and Gladstone aimed to rouse opinion to attack abuses of power and to safeguard local liberties. Even in the 1870s and 1880s, both political parties aimed to win electoral support more by attacking the dangerous meddling of their opponents than by promising a transformation themselves.

The other Liberal strategy arose from anger at the selfish misbehaviour of the landed interest. This anger could unite most whig landowners and all but the most extreme urban radicals. Most radicals were prepared to accept the notion of the good landlord, the sort of landlord whom whigs admired and believed themselves to be: men who capitalised their estates efficiently, governed their locality dutifully and tolerantly, allowed free voting among their tenants and perhaps permitted them to shoot game. Radicals were more concerned about landlord inefficiency and the lack of opportunity for new men to acquire small estates than with the institution of landownership in itself. And whigs were anxious for the aristocracy not to appear a class apart, with sectional interests. That anxiety explains their onslaught on nomination boroughs in 1832, their attempt to reform the social composition of county magistracies, their ready acceptance of free trade doctrines after 1846, and their willingness to reform landlord-tenant relations and rural local government. But Liberal leaders were also aware that if they pushed too fast in any of these areas, they would probably lose much support among the gentry – as they would if they imposed the hand of central government too heavily on local magistrates' and churchmen's discretionary power over poor relief, education and punishment policy. Lumbering state interference in such matters would fuel resentment among gentlemen *and* radical ratepayers that virtuous local independence was threatened by unscrupulous, impersonal central authorities.

So, while Liberals could find rallying-cries in all these broad policy areas, there was also internal disagreement about how to interpret them and how zealously to implement them. (This pointed up the necessity of parliamentary discussion in the search for compromise.) The 'country' tradition was potent; but many Liberals also asserted the need for some government patronage, and most saw the benefit of strong national defence. Support for religious minorities was genuine, but mainstream Liberals were anxious not to undermine the church establishment in England or the Union with Ireland. 'Scientific' legislation was all very well, and could benefit order and character; but most did not want it to infringe the parliamentary consensus, to hand power to irresponsible extra-parliamentary bodies, or to supersede the magistrates who were charged with maintaining disinterested and moral guidance of their communities. And the vast majority of Liberals, while critical of 'landed interest' selfishness, did not wish to damage landowners' social position. Liberal government involved balancing-acts, sometimes difficult ones.

Approaches

The over-arching theme of this book is that, in the half-century after 1830, there was a coherent Liberal approach to politics, which previous literature has failed to stress. Though its nuances obviously changed over time, reflecting altered political circumstances, there was continuity in fundamental principles. It was an approach which owed most to the whig tradition, but which was influenced also by Canning and the liberal tories of the 1820s. The Liberal constitution aimed to integrate the four countries of the kingdom into a harmonious whole; it allowed parliamentary reform within a carefully-defined framework; and it marginalised those, like Chartists or Irish Nationalists, who complained that the 'parliamentary government' which it offered was repressive (Liberals assumed that critics of the principle of 'parliamentary government' must, by definition, be reactionaries or anarchists). Liberals attempted, by recasting political structures, to supply 'disinterested' and respected rule by a propertied, civilised governing class: by aristocrats and university-educated gentlemen at the centre, by assiduous landowners in the counties, and by the most cultured and respectable merchants in the towns. The leadership offered by this governing class was to be primarily administrative. At the centre, it would check sectional lobbying and corruption in favour of firm economy, yet it would defend Britain's real interests as a modernising commercial, imperial and international power.* Legislative reform would allow reinvigorated local elites to practise rational social administration, while representative local government would prevent central dictation and encourage pluralism and regulated political participation. Parliament would not be force-fed with legislative *programmes* inspired by a party machine or faddist sectional pressures. The Liberal governments of 1830–86 implemented a great deal of legislation, but they did so as part of a strategy, acceptable to most propertied opinion, to use the power of government to strengthen particular moral values in society: hence the importance of economic, religious and Irish measures. So the Liberal political system was didactic, yet also pluralist. It reflected well the dominant culture of the Victorian prosperous classes: bourgeois, manly, individualist, consumerist, Protestant, rational. It appealed to a very wide political constituency. And, by the 1880s, most Liberals had no doubt that fifty years of their rule had assisted enormously in the material and moral development of the nation.[41]

By stressing the power and continuity of Liberal values, this book adopts a different perspective from that in which nineteenth-century Liberalism is normally viewed. Liberal historiography has always been dominated by the figure of Gladstone, and the period of his leadership, from 1868 to 1894, is usually regarded as the climax of Liberal politics. Traditionally, pre-Gladstonian Liberalism is seen as 'whiggism', socially narrow, philosophically ill-defined and politically slippery. Professor Gash criticises Liberals of the 1830s and 1840s for lacking a firm policy.[42] Few historians have much time for Lord John Russell, while hardly anyone has written successfully

---

* However, the text does not dwell much on foreign policy, except where it obviously affected the domestic strategies of politicians. I hope to tackle the subject of Liberal attitudes to the foreigner in more detail elsewhere.

about Palmerston as a domestic Liberal leader.[43] The standard assumption is that the party was always divided between exclusive 'whigs' and aggressive 'radicals', and that the former's role was increasingly to make 'concessions' to the latter (who are broadly equated with the party rank-and-file). Professor Newbould has criticised Liberal parliamentary leaders of the 1830s for their lack of interest in professional provincial party organisation, because it threatened to increase the power of those 'radicals'.[44] In their classic works on mid-Victorian Liberalism, Professors Vincent and Shannon tend to define party primarily in extra-parliamentary terms and so see the 'Liberal party' maturing only when grass-roots enthusiasm was mobilised on a national basis in the 1860s and 1870s.[45] Professor Hamer, the only writer recently to attempt a synthetic history of Liberalism after 1867, asserts that 'Liberals were not held together by any strong sense of common purpose', and places his major emphasis on constituency-based 'faddists' who advocated particular 'sectional policies'.[46] In contrast, this book asserts that the *parliamentary* whig-Liberal tradition was central to British politics, that it was much more fertile than undisciplined radicalism, and that the lack of a professional national organisation added to its flexibility rather than hindering it. Distinctions between 'whigs' and 'radicals' were employed very loosely,* and all Liberals worked from within a common tradition. Despite tensions, only a few radicals wished to set up as a political force separate from landed Liberals; conversely, any Liberal from a whig landed family who hoped for a serious political career knew that he had to work with rather than against MPs from the industrial centres. It was an essential part of the Liberal myth that by joint action each group fertilised the other: 'The process of permeation is reciprocal in its character . . . The Radical is permeated no less than the Whig, as we believe to the great advantage of them both.'[47] The principal problem on the 'left' in the nineteenth century was not conservatism and social exclusiveness on the part of the whig leaders, but the difficulty of rousing the country behind a coherent progressive programme. Liberal leaders were much more adventurous than the political nation. The conservatism of the electorate posed a serious problem in the late 1830s and for most of the 1850s, 1860s and 1870s. The challenges of self-appointed radical firebrands Cobden, Bright and Chamberlain foundered on this apathy.

So this account of Liberalism is organised around the assumption that its success and influence were founded on good parliamentary management, not on excitingly radical bills and populist gestures. The book aims to construct and to connect: to offer a general overview of its subject. It relies

---

* In the text, I have used 'radical' to describe either MPs for the big towns or those who adopted particularly advanced versions of Liberal policies, such as enthusiasm for further constitutional reform, more strident opposition to military expenditure, or more wholehearted attacks on church privileges. By no means all of these MPs expressed 'radical' sentiments on all those issues. For the usage of 'whig', see the footnote on page 1 above. It was not unknown for 'whigs' in that sense to be 'radical' on one or other issue.

on primary (*Hansard*, journals, newspapers) and secondary printed sources of many kinds. It is indebted to several generations of historians. With luck, it may re-establish the merit of older, frequently ignored, work, and provide a meaningful synthesis of the highly fragmented and specialised scholarship of recent years, much of which has been fertile, but which no-one could pretend has clarified the broad trends of nineteenth-century political history. Victorian politics has fallen out of favour with historians, and is thought to be difficult to comprehend and teach. But it is misleading conceptions founded on social class, big bills and the role of popular political organisation which have created that difficulty. If nineteenth-century politics is a giant jigsaw puzzle, the Liberal creed examined in this book is its large central piece.

Moreover, the book argues that Gladstone's influence on the party after 1868 was much less positive than most historians have maintained. Gladstone came not from the Liberal tradition but from the Conservative one which had had difficulty adjusting to Reformed politics after 1832. He was a disciple of the Conservative leader Peel, and had ambivalent feelings about whig-Liberalism – like all Peelites, though they were forced to ally with the Liberal party from the 1850s. As Gladstone grew older, he built on Peel's legacy by developing a number of personal enthusiasms and traits which led him into controversial initiatives after he became Liberal leader. The result was a series of tensions within the party – over foreign policy, devolution, disestablishment and extra-parliamentary faddism, culminating in his proposal of 1886 to grant Home Rule to Ireland. On all these issues Gladstone and his allies seemed to be threatening the older, integration-oriented Liberal tradition. These tensions were exacerbated by other developments of the 1880s, principally the far-reaching 1884–5 Reform settlement and the changed nature of Britain's position overseas. The result was a crippling and permanent split in the party in 1886, for which Gladstone's timing and temperament were most responsible. The Liberal Unionists defected, taking with them crucial propertied support; the rump of the Gladstonian Liberal party became less attached to the principles of 'parliamentary government'; and Liberalism became the shifting programme of a party with an extensive, formal grass-roots organisation, forced to search for votes in the attempt to recover power. The events of 1886 caused the strange death of Liberal England, and dealt a severe blow to the future prospects of Liberal Britain.

PART I

LIBERALISM AND REFORM, 1820–1832

WHY BEGIN A book on nineteenth-century Liberalism with two chapters on tory rule in the 1820s? The answer is that after 1815 two simultaneous processes laid the foundations for Liberal government. The first was the rise of the notion of 'public opinion': the growing belief that 'middle-class' values were now so widespread, and 'middle-class' politicisation so developed, that politicians ignored them at their peril. MPs, conscious of public dissatisfaction with wartime and postwar economic conditions, were very difficult to discipline for constructive work. This damaged the authority of government. Secondly, ministers themselves were increasingly aware that they needed to dismantle much of the apparatus which had been built in the mid- to late eighteenth century to fund and administer Britain's 'rise to greatness': the heavy taxes needed to pay for frequent wars (Britain was at war with European powers for over half the period 1702–1815), and the bloated, ramshackle administrative structure, with its sinecures and pensions, fees and bribes, which had been cobbled together under high pressure in response to military difficulties and opportunities. During the Napoleonic Wars, Britain acquired seventeen colonies, while her military victories enhanced her dominance of world trading routes. By 1818, after twenty years of relentless, ruthless expansion, she controlled most of India. Britain was now the greatest power in the world. Few regretted the achievement. But few, also, were disposed to pay much towards sustaining it; would it not pay for itself? In 1816, parliament refused to renew the wartime income tax. Severe economies and administrative rationalisation were necessary. Thereafter, ministers assiduously reformed salary structures, patronage networks and tariffs, they zealously checked official abuses, and they worked hard to boost exports.

Chapter 1 charts these two processes, and the achievement of the leading tory minister Canning, and his colleagues, in running them together for political benefit. Canning created the myth that the streamlined, economical, open state of the 1820s, aloof from foreign intervention unless in promotion of 'middle-class' causes, was the creation of 'public opinion' itself. By distancing himself from the king, Canning propagated the notion that British ministers were no longer part of an oligarchy, but were uniquely responsive to moral, virtuous, commercial sentiment. The word used to describe this new, apparently disinterested regime was 'liberal'.

This was political sleight-of-hand, because Canning aimed to uphold the constitutional status quo against pressure for Reform. Integral to tory dominance of the Commons were the large numbers of small borough seats, especially of 'close' boroughs which, because they were dominated by one or two landowners, were immune from fluctuations in electoral sentiment. 'Closeness' is a matter of definition, and many details of constituency behaviour have been lost, but a rough estimate suggests that tories held about 187 'closed' English seats in 1790 and 185 before the 1831 election.* In addition, the 45 Scottish seats were overwhelmingly loyal to ministers, since the electorate was extremely small and swayed by a combination of tory landowners and the exertions of a government patronage machine which showered colonial and other appointments on it. Tory rule, then, rested on oligarchy as much as on public support, and it was part of Canning's achievement to disguise this aspect of 'liberal toryism' from those who boasted the power of the 'middle classes'.

Chapter 2 shows how both pillars of tory support collapsed between 1827 and 1830. The institutional power base was eroded; then, in 1830, the confidence of the 'middle classes' was lost. In the process, so also was that of many propertied men anxious about authority. The result was a coalition government which aimed to restore respect for law. It was led by the 'whig' opposition of long standing. This was the beginning of whig, later Liberal, party dominance.

As Chapter 3 explains, the new ministers responded to this loss of government authority by bringing in a far-reaching scheme of parliamentary reform, which became the 1832 Reform Act, and inaugurated the era of 'parliamentary government'. This was not the obvious response; Reform was not a concession to coherent popular clamour. The shape of the Reform Act can only be explained by investigating the whig tradition itself. This had two broad component parts. One was libertarian. Whigs had long charged tories with betraying the principles of the 1688 revolution which had established checks on the power of the crown – with undermining the liberties of parliament and the people, with strengthening the personal influence of the king and the arbitrary power of his ministers, with levying excessive taxation on the people, and with spending much of it corruptly in order to line their own pockets and to secure a compliant parliament by the cunning distribution of official patronage. These charges, which had had point during the French wars, were now, owing to 'liberal toryism', less effective than the second component. This lauded government's potential to

---

* I estimate the number which remained firmly 'closed' at 140 in 1790 and 156 in 1831 (the increase is explained by defections to government during the French wars). I have defined twenty seats as 'closed' in 1790 but opened by the 1820s. Dominant interests can be seen operating in a further number (27 in 1790, 29 in 1830), though since these were large towns, special caution is required here.

take positive action on behalf of the people – to liberate popular energies, to integrate different ranks under the rule of law, to initiate bold and moralising legislation.

Whigs were ambivalent about the tory achievement of the 1820s. On the one hand, they tended to abuse all aspects of the hidebound pre-1832 *ancien régime*. But, on the other, they were to follow many Canningite strategies: the emphasis on economy, commercial expansion and administrative reform; the distancing of ministers from royal power and corrupt patronage networks; the claim to be responsive to virtuous public and parliamentary sentiment. Indeed, many of Canning's followers were to switch sides and became important Liberals. So the 'liberal toryism' of the 1820s was to be a major influence on Liberal history. But, for all that, the nature of Liberalism after 1832 was affected most by the passage of the 1832 Reform Act and the much more active government that it made possible.

CHAPTER 1

Public opinion and 'liberal toryism'

THE OVERRIDING PROBLEMS for tory government between 1800 and 1830 were linked: a rapid growth in the profile of 'public opinion', and parliament's refusal to accept the level of taxation necessary to fund the wartime regime. Public and parliamentary criticism of ministers was expressed particularly forcefully at times of economic or military difficulty. It made the management of affairs extremely awkward just when 'strong' government was most demanded. This chapter traces the emergence of the problem and the success of tories in responding to it in the 1820s.

The problem of public opinion

W.A. Mackinnon's work of 1828 *On the rise, progress, and present state of public opinion* was a typical treatment of what by the 1820s was a commonplace subject, 'public opinion'. Its definition of the phrase was commonplace, too: 'that sentiment on any given subject which is entertained by the best informed, most intelligent, and most moral persons in the community', and 'gradually . . . adopted by nearly all persons of any education or proper feeling'. Mackinnon believed that its growth depended on 'information, proper religious feeling, facility of communication and capital'.[1]

The notion of 'public opinion' owed a great deal to manifest commercial expansion since 1750. The principal beneficiaries of this expansion were urban merchants; prosperous farmers; ex-military or East India Company men who had retired to provincial towns, watering-places or suburban villas; and rentiers, often bachelors or widows, who lived off their holdings in the funds, or who invested in houses, canals, banks and breweries. The expansion of local propertied wealth in turn greatly benefited the professional and upper retailing classes of market-town England, especially those in banking and the law. Each town had its banks, to service local wealth and to channel it into profitable investment. Attorneys' skills were essential in managing corporate and family property, in developing estate resources such as mineral deposits, in arranging clients' investments – in mortgages, insurance companies and private lending – and in elections. As the earl of

Radnor said in 1833, 'One might almost say that England is in the hands of lawyers'.[2]* An immense number of other professions had grown up in order to service the prosperous, such as booksellers and portrait-painters, silversmiths and auctioneers, watchmakers, wine merchants and wigmakers. Shopkeepers imported exotic foods and advertised the latest in London fashions. The number of English provincial newspapers trebled to over 150 between 1780 and 1830. The suburban housing boom of the early nineteenth century required the services of estate agents, property developers, architects, builders and engineers – as well as the omnipresent attorneys. There was a new gentility about education, as long-decaying grammar schools revived and private schools sprang up for young ladies and gentlemen. And the coach trade connected up provincial towns and provided the umbilical cords of the new consumer society.

'Public opinion' was broadly equated with the term 'middle classes'. Brougham defined the 'people' as 'the middle classes, the wealth and intelligence of the country, the glory of the British name'.[3] But the term 'middle classes' tended to mean, not a tightly defined economic or geographical entity, but a coherent set of 'respectable' moral and cultural values: industry, thrift, religion, probity, domesticity and sobriety. The middle classes were idealised as the 'chief . . . depositaries of the piety, the virtue, the knowledge, the industry, the independence, the valour, and the patriotism' of the country. They seemed to offer the strongest assurance for the maintenance of balanced government, the 'best security against the encroachment of arbitrary power on the one hand, and the more degrading tyranny of an ignorant rabble on the other'. As they acquired more intelligence, so they gained 'moral power'.[4]†

These values, then, were not class-bound; they could be held equally well by gentry and the more virtuous of the aristocracy. Landowners as an entity were not under attack. Most market towns continued to rely heavily on the economic, philanthropical and social activity of the local landed elite, whose agricultural profits had boomed with population levels, and on the spending power of local farmers. To the extent that 'middle-class' values were anti-aristocratic, they censured a certain *image* of the aristocracy as idle and decadent – a hostility which was shared, for example, by the duke of Wellington.[6] Similarly, extravagance and corruption in government were

---

* One striking example is Joseph Pitt of Gloucestershire (*c*.1759–1842). As a lad he earned a penny a time for holding the horses of visiting gentlemen; a passing attorney noticed his quickness and apprenticed him. From the law he diversified into brewing, banking and land-jobbing. He bought country houses in Gloucestershire and Wiltshire. From 1793, he was steward to the earl of Carnarvon, and eventually bought enough of his property in Cricklade to return himself as MP from 1812 to 1831. At one time he controlled six seats in the two counties, which he treated as an investment.

† As early as 1799, Canning had praised the 'sober orderly habits' of 'those classes of men, who connect the upper and lower classes of society, and who thereby blend together and harmonise the whole'.[5]

criticised, but not firm rule. In public life, order and purity were both seen as necessary. Decadence, sloth and luxury in rulers and subjects alike were to be condemned as much as vice, blasphemy and lawlessness.

Possibly the most striking attribute associated with the 'middle classes' was religious piety. The perils of threatened revolution, war and unprecedented economic turbulence after 1790 strengthened religion's appeal as an interpreter of upheaval, a support in despair, and a philosophy for survival. It dictated prudence and sobriety, piety and charity, and the respectability that conferred creditworthiness. In the early nineteenth century, traditional religious themes of individual responsibility and virtue, obedience to secular authority, and salvation by faith and works were drummed home by evangelical preachers with a renewed vigour and immediacy. National disaster, as in the 1780s, anxiety for survival, as in the 1800s, or victory in the 1810s all stimulated the fight for Protestant values. The reaction to the French Revolution and the fall of popery encouraged joint missionary enterprise by Anglicans and Dissenters. The major undenominational associations were the London Missionary Society (1795), the Religious Tract Society (1799) and the British and Foreign Bible Society (1804). The same concern had a crucial effect on the provision of elementary education. The Sunday school movement took off all over England from the 1780s; by 1801, 206,000 children were enrolled at them, and, by 1833, 1,363,000, 60 per cent of working-class 5-to-15-year-olds.[7] The leaders of the Bible Society set up a society to found undenominational weekday elementary schools in 1808. High churchmen responded with the National Society in 1811, and the undenominational body became the British and Foreign Schools Society from 1814. The two together quickly dominated the field.

Local 'improving' voluntary associations were another outlet for 'middle-class' values. In 1821, 6,500 clubs and non-circulating libraries were supplying reading material.[8] Literary and Philosophical Societies, or equivalents, were established in most towns in these decades, incorporating libraries, often museums, and lecture-rooms for talks on scientific or sanitary topics.* Hospitals and dispensaries were founded by subscriptions. Between the 1820s and 1840s, 700 Mechanics' Institutes were set up to offer artisans 'improvement' in the form of technical instruction and library and newspaper facilities.

The respectability of the 'middle classes' became an extremely powerful political myth. But in fact the impact of public opinion on Westminster politics was uneven. In practice, it was aroused by economic and political crisis. Mostly, 'respectable' opinion was prosperous and rather complacent, but in turbulent times, it was susceptible to the old 'country' myth that the state was wasteful and corrupt, that metropolitan society was extravagant, artificial and immoral, and that pure values must be reasserted among the

---

* In 1821, members of the Newcastle society decided by a majority of 20:1 that Byron's *Don Juan* was unfit for their library.

influential classes and extended to the poor. Moral and political pressure came in waves. One had struck in the early 1780s, as economic downturn coincided with failure to retain the American colonies.* This movement had lasting effects on the image of government, because its beneficiary, Pitt, was prime minister for all but three years between 1783 and 1806. In the mid-1780s, he symbolised administrative reform and hostility to state corruption. He seemed more disinterested, patriotic, competent, economical and above faction than his opponents.

In the 1800s and 1810s, the power of public opinion seemed to grow remarkably both in scope and in permanence, under the impact of industrialisation and war. During the French wars, the economy was growing so quickly and lopsidedly that it would have created enormous social turbulence even had it not been necessary, at the same time, to fund a 22-year conflict. The annual average value of British exports in the 1810s was almost exactly double what it had been between 1792 and 1799. Yet there was no adequate structure of credit to underpin economic growth, and this, together with the immaturity of domestic and foreign markets and marketing practices, ensured that severe depressions occurred frequently, intensified by the difficulties arising from Napoleon's trade blockade of Britain. The British population rose by 33 per cent between 1801 and 1821, creating unprecedented problems of housing, sanitation and order in towns, and of unemployment in rural areas and in domestic industry, as well as food riots where the supply of corn proved inadequate. The price of a 4 lb loaf in London averaged 6.6d between 1790 and 1794 and 14.6d between 1810 and 1814. Inflation was boosted by the government's need to move off gold in 1797 in order to pay for the war. Even so, a lot of the cost of war had to be paid in loans, with the result that the national debt rose from £238 million in 1793 to £902 million in 1816. The tax take also rose from £19 million to £72 million in the same period, helped by the introduction of a direct tax on income in 1798. It was hardly surprising that consumers and taxpayers should be aggrieved at the profits made by landlords and especially by those who held government stock issued to pay for the war, nor that hostility to war itself should flare up, given the apparent lack of progress. By 1807, after Austerlitz, Jena, Friedland and Tilsit, Napoleon controlled nearly the whole of mainland Europe. Britain stood almost alone against him, and lacked an effective military strategy. A series of unsuccessful British initiatives between 1807 and 1809 fuelled criticism of administrative and military competence and complaints at the wastage of taxpayers' money in a depression. Depression also led to calls for policy changes which might

---

* This stimulated campaigns for parliamentary reform, reductions in government expenditure, the abolition of the slave trade, the reform of prisoners' morals, and the bolstering of Protestant values in the nation through measures such as the repeal of laws discriminating against orthodox Dissenters. Local philanthropy was also mobilised; hence the Sunday school movement and the spread of societies for the prosecution of felons.[9]

restore prosperity: currency reform, national debt revision, tax reductions, even peace were mooted. In 1811–12, provincial merchants, already largely shut out of European markets by Napoleon, lobbied against restrictive aspects of government economic policy, such as the Orders in Council (which were believed to damage trading relations with the USA), and the monopoly over the Indian trade enjoyed by the inefficient East India Company. (As a result, they were abolished in 1812 and 1813 respectively.)

Public irritation spilled over into criticism of government practices. The needs of war forced the administrative machine to expand quickly. This led to an inequitable and inefficient burgeoning of fees in many departments, a growing reliance on sinecures to boost low pay, and increasing and unconstitutional arrears in the civil list. Inflation worsened the strain on administration. The levying of the new income tax made criticism of extravagance inevitable. An inquiry into naval administration led in 1805 to the impeachment by parliament of Pitt's close political associate Melville for mismanagement of government funds. This massive blow to the authority of Pitt's system created the climate for no fewer than fifteen parliamentary investigations into administrative practices, producing over sixty reports.[10] A select committee first established in 1807, under the chairmanship of the evangelical landowner Henry Bankes, revealed the extent of sinecurism. Bankes and disaffected ex-Pittites like Canning pressed for sinecure abolition bills, which passed the Commons in 1812 and 1813. The shortlived Talents coalition of 1806–7 stimulated public expectations of moral government still further by swiftly recognising the justice of the extra-parliamentary demand for the abolition of the slave trade. And the campaign against 'corruption' and for 'open' government was bolstered further by the revelation of more scandals in 1809, in particular the celebrated sexual entanglement of the duke of York, Commander-in-chief of the army, with a woman who made money by telling officers desiring promotion that she would arrange it in return for payment. Parliament's remorseless inquiries forced York's temporary resignation.

Radicals like Sir Francis Burdett and William Cobbett alleged that various corrupt interests had perverted the ideal of a peaceful, moral nation of lightly-taxed smallholders living under the benevolent rule of liberal and disinterested gentry. These, they said, included the serried ranks of borough-owners who seemed to prevent parliament from expressing the views of gentry and public; the fundholders who benefited from high levels of national debt and so used their political influence to squeeze more and more money out of the oppressed taxpayers; and inefficient contractors and idle playboys who won by underhand means lucrative jobs which the taxpayer had to fund. Radicals most commonly called for the abolition of sinecures and of rotten boroughs, a readjustment of the national debt and the reduction of military expenditure. Between 1809 and 1811, groups within the whig opposition in parliament, anxious to exploit public anxieties and yet check the radicals' momentum, instituted campaigns for parliamentary reform. Curwen's bill, aimed at preventing the sale of seats, passed in 1809, and in 1810 Brand collected 115 votes for a motion for triennial parliaments and the abolition of rotten boroughs.

One other aspect of public activity was the anger of particular groups that government did not see them as fully integrated, loyal and respectable. Some were radicals who resented 'repressive' legislation. Many were Protestant Dissenters, who prided themselves on their moral standing in the community, on their support for the war against the infidel Napoleon, and on their superiority of Christian practice to that of many worldly Anglican clergy. In 1811, Lord Sidmouth (ex-Prime Minister Addington, now out of government) introduced a bill which attempted to regulate itinerant preaching by evangelical sects, claiming that some had subversive intentions. This snub to the respectability and patriotism of Dissent prompted a great outcry: 336 petitions were produced against the bill in 48 hours, and it was hastily abandoned. A similar problem, only more intractable, was arising in Ireland, because of the resentment of most Catholics at the avowedly Protestant nature of the regime imposed at the Union. Since George III had refused to accept Pitt's proposal of Catholic Emancipation in 1801, Catholics were forbidden access to high public office. By 1812, with George III declared insane, and anxiety for Irish loyalty considerable, this was once more becoming a major issue in British politics.

If the momentum of the Reform campaign was to be checked, ministers needed to regain the confidence of respectable public opinion. But parliament was very difficult to discipline in the middle and later years of the war. Speaker Abbot estimated in 1813 that the general business of the Commons had risen fivefold since 1760 and by two-thirds since 1801.[11] Concerted opposition to a bill by any significant group of MPs was usually fatal to its prospects. Government legislation could be held up most easily by the presentation of petitions from constituents, which traditionally enjoyed priority over all ordinary Commons business. Because of public disquiet, the number of petitions presented to the Commons, which averaged 880 a year between 1785 and 1789, grew from 1,026 between 1801 to 1805, to 4,498 between 1811 and 1815.[12] Public opinion was too diverse in its enthusiasms for politicians to be able to handle it effectively. In responding to it, between 1807 and 1812, MPs divided into factions, weakening further the prospect of firm government. Boosted by public disquiet, the whig opposition revived to number 150, but it was itself divided over war strategy and parliamentary and administrative reform. Pitt's old coalition was torn apart by quarrels over the conduct of the war and over Catholic Emancipation, and by personal rivalries – most famously the neurotic clash between Canning and Castlereagh, leading in 1809 to a duel which disqualified both of them from government for some time. Government authority in the Commons was rarely secure between 1801 and 1812. In a desperate and vain attempt to strengthen it at a time when the destiny of Europe was in the balance, the crown resorted to dubious constitutional tactics. On three successive occasions (1806, 1807, 1812), it dissolved the Commons and called fresh elections well before the end of the 7-year term which was traditionally seen as integral to parliament's defence of popular liberties against an aggrandising monarch.

It was in this context that Lord Liverpool became Prime Minister in 1812. Liverpool was shortly faced also by the difficulties of adjusting to peace after 1815. The war had cost £1,039 million and had dramatically increased both taxes and inflation. Then the postwar slump led immediately to resentment at high tax levels. In 1816, parliament forced ministers to relinquish £18 million of taxes, refusing to continue the wartime income tax. Yet the government desperately needed money, mainly to pay interest on the national debt. In 1818, such repayments came to £31.5 million out of a total public expenditure of £58.7 million. Mass wartime population growth meant large-scale postwar rural unemployment and hence higher poor rates: poor relief expenditure was £7.87 million in 1818 against £4.3 million in 1803.[13] This hit agriculture, especially since it could no longer expect to benefit from the wartime shortage of grain which had raised prices and extended cultivation to normally uneconomic lands. After the war, government had to try to balance agricultural demands for high tariffs with the need to secure food supplies for the mass of the population, so it maintained an uneasy compromise on the Corn Laws. It had to return to the financial stability of the gold standard (1819), in order to check inflation, yet this was bound to injure interests which had borrowed heavily during the war. And it had to disappoint advocates of Poor Law repeal, from a fear of revolution. High levels of public unrest unnerved magistrates, who demanded repressive government legislation. The murder of Perceval in 1812 and the Cato Street conspiracy to assassinate the cabinet in 1820 were only the most dramatic signs of the fragility of government authority. Liverpool told Peel just before his stroke that never throughout his long premiership had he 'received his letters by the post in the morning without a feeling of anxiety and apprehension'.[14]

Postwar depression also heightened 'middle-class' complaints at the immorality, avarice and political influence of the court. This was symbolised by the Prince Regent's lavish building projects at Brighton and Buckingham Palace, the size of the civil list, and the number of sinecures held by the officeholding aristocracy. Potentially the greatest crisis for the government came in 1820, when George IV succeeded his mad father as king. He immediately sought to divorce his Queen Caroline, and hinted that he would dismiss his government if it did not cooperate. It agreed to set up a secret commission of inquiry into allegations of her adultery, and introduced a bill of pains and penalties against her. But the more it submitted to his bidding, the more it promised to upset public opinion irritated by excessive royal interference in politics and sympathetic to Caroline. She was generally regarded as a wronged woman betrayed by hypocritical and immoral kingly behaviour, and, more implausibly, as a symbol of pure family values. Most 'respectable' opinion was angry at the proceedings, either on those grounds or because minute investigation of her dalliances with Italian gigolos gave the popular prints a wonderful opportunity for disrespectful bawdiness, threatening social hierarchy.[15] When the Lords only narrowly passed the bill, ministers decided not to risk taking it to the Commons.

The combination of these policy embarrassments ensured almost permanent government instability between 1816 and 1822. Severe economic depression revived the belief that government was high-spending and corrupt. A severe reverse followed at the 1818 election: the number of government supporters returned for the 24 most open English boroughs fell from 29 (out of 50) to 15. A commentator noted that most new members did not wish 'to be considered as belonging to Government'.[16] Canning thought that the results revealed the public 'as indifferent' to the success or failure of authority 'as at any period of our history'.[17] MPs were anxious to please constituents by supporting motions for economy and purification, for the suppression of government offices, the reduction of official salaries, the repeal of specific taxes, and the systematic investigation of the estimates. Wellington complained that the country gentlemen acted in concert without supporting the government: 'They profess to support, but really oppose'.[18] One observer wrote in 1822 of 'the clamour of that "ignorant impatience", which calls upon parliament and government to *do something*, often when they ought either to do nothing, or when the right thing to do is that to which the complainants would most object'.[19] The slump in parliamentary confidence badly affected the government's authority and in February 1819 one observer viewed ministers as 'so completely paralyzed, that they dare do nothing'.[20] In May, Liverpool felt that the government's continued existence was 'a *positive* evil' since it could not establish its authority over the public mind.[21] The deflationary trauma, agricultural depression and royal crisis of 1820–2 did not improve matters; Liverpool favoured resignation in the summer of 1821. To one observer, 'authority is gone'; all MPs acted for themselves and even Pitt would have been unable to charm the present-day Commons into submission.[22]

The foundations of 'liberal toryism'

Liverpool's government *survived* because of its institutional advantages – the reluctance of king and parliament to turn to the whig opposition – and because of the return of economic prosperity after 1822. But its emerging *strength* owed much also to its ability to appeal to the 'middle-class' values sketched above, in three crucial areas in particular: morals and religion, taxation and economy, and efficiency in the administration of the law.

First, it benefited in esteem from the unexpectedly quick and decisive victory in war (1814–15), which draped it with the mantle of national saviour. Victory seemed Providential, a statement of divine confidence in British religious and commercial values. The dominant spirit of the 1810s was of expansionist nationalist Protestantism. The Alfred Club, a meeting-place for young politicians like Palmerston, Peel and Robinson, had a powerful conception of the national destiny.[23] Robert Southey, the ex-radical but now tory romantic and the leading writer in the tory secular bible the *Quarterly Review*, enthused about 'making the world English'.[24] Philanthropic societies anxious to spread Christianity mushroomed, seeking to repeat the military victory over the anti-Christ in all corners of the earth, and at home. By 1817, the Bible Society had 236 auxiliary branches and had spent £540,000 in producing and circulating 1.8 million volumes of scriptures in 66 different languages.[25] The spirit of missionary optimism was infectious: preachers discerned the rise of a 'new moral power, which . . . promises to change the face of the universe'.[26]

The government gained 'respectable' support also because its leading ministers were devout advocates of Christianisation. Liverpool himself was a pious churchman who had links with the 'Hackney Phalanx' of leading high church Anglican laymen, who urged reform of ecclesiastical abuses. His two most influential ministers in home policy in the 1810s were Nicholas Vansittart, later Lord Bexley, an actively philanthropical evangelical, and Sidmouth, praised by the anti-slavery campaigner William Wilberforce for his religious devotion.[27] Sidmouth's return to the government as Home Secretary in 1812 brought it a great deal of popularity among country gentlemen and Anglican middle-class opinion, because of his reputation for retrenchment, purity, caution and common-sense English values.[28] India was opened to missionary activity in 1813 and a new see at Calcutta established in the following year. At home, Liverpool was anxious to recognise the virtue of methodists and other nonconformists. Two acts restricting Dissenters' liberty were repealed in 1812. Vansittart described them as 'relics' from the seventeenth century, 'wholly unsuited to times of . . . liberality of sentiment'.[29] A Toleration Act in 1813 repealed the statutes which had excluded unitarians from the benefit of earlier legislation on religious toleration. As for the Church of England, Liverpool took greater pains than those of any eighteenth-century prime minister in selecting conscientious, devout and energetic bishops, such as Blomfield, Howley, Kaye and Van Mildert. He tried to check the damaging tendency of senior churchmen to collect pluralities, by forcing men he promoted to relinquish them. In two acts of 1813 and 1817, the problem of clerical non-residence was tackled. In 1818, the government passed an act setting up a Church Building Commission in charge of £1 million of public money to supplement voluntary subscriptions for the building of new churches for the poor in the expanding towns. Liverpool told the Lords that the bill was 'the most important measure' he had ever submitted to them.[30]

Liverpool was also determined to improve the reputation of government for purity and economy in administration. This was essential in order to sustain public confidence and to balance the books in the absence of a peacetime income tax. A series of measures between 1810 and 1822 abolished large numbers of sinecures at home, prohibited their development in the colonies, and brought in a new system of pensions payments under Treasury supervision to replace sinecures and the old superannuation funds. By 1822 the government could claim that 94 sinecures had been abolished since 1810 and 1,800 public offices in all, at a saving to the public of £580,000. In the 1820s, the process of economy was extended: between 1821 and 1829 4,050 offices were abolished at a saving of £700,974. By 1834 the number of sinecures was minimal. Between 1815 and 1835, the civil service was cut by 14 per cent in size and 26 per cent in cost.[31] In 1816, criticism of royal extravagance was defused by the decision to put certain major items of crown expenditure directly under parliamentary control rather than to hide them in the civil list. In 1820, by tactful pressure, ministers negotiated savings of £200,000 a year in the civil list for George IV's reign. Despite lacking an income tax, the government managed to balance its budgets, and was able to persuade parliament to grant an extra £3 million in taxes in 1819 (in return for an overhaul of debt repayment procedure), and to remit the same amount in 1822. All this was implemented while preserving essentially intact the executive's independence from ignorant parliamentary interference.

Particularly important was the effect that cuts in sinecures and in official expenditure had on perceptions of the government's attitude to the electorate. One of the standard allegations against eighteenth-century governments had been that, lacking confidence in public opinion, they resorted to corruption in order to pack the Commons. Government electoral patronage power fell into two categories: the rewards (in money, places, honours or contracts) which might be given to MPs and boroughowners who supported government, and the normal process of filling up low-level jobs in the localities. Perhaps the first had never been as significant as critics suggested in securing a compliant House of Commons. But by the 1810s, there was definitely little logic in wooing individual boroughmongers by such means. It seemed wasteful of scarce public funds, and ineffective in protecting the Commons from the gales of public sentiment. Most boroughowners had far too little weight to damage the government by withdrawing their support, and had a vested interest in supporting tory governments against whig parliamentary reformers. Liverpool wrote in 1812 that engagements with boroughowners 'rather weaken than strengthen any Government', and refused to enter into any more.[32] He was similarly aware of the benefits of appearing to depoliticise local patronage. In 1821, he transferred control over customs appointments from the Treasury to Commissioners of Customs. The government announced its neutrality in the distribution of patronage for electoral purposes before the 1826 and 1830 contests. This was noted, and the decline in party controversy ascribed to it.[33] Efficiency in the customs was taken further when in 1827 a graduated system of promotion was established throughout the service.

Another crucial development was the government's growing coherence and professionalism. Collective cabinet responsibility and solidarity – a concept denied by Fox as recently as 1806 – was now a reality.[34] It was almost certain that, if Liverpool were dismissed, his cabinet would resign with him. This left the king little freedom of manoeuvre, and made royal interference in politics unwise. From 1823, the cabinet started to meet to preview each parliamentary session and to prepare draft bills and responses to anticipated criticism.[35] Castlereagh was an intrepid and able leader of the House of Commons (1812–22), respected by MPs for his conscientiousness and strength of character, though he was an appallingly inarticulate speaker (he concluded one particularly confused passage with the observation that 'I have now proved that the Tower of London is a Common Law principle').[36] The government employed select committees to help steer parliamentary opinion, especially in the more technical subjects: between 1801 and 1834, 543 were appointed. They often nipped impractical demands from minority groups in the bud, while, if their conclusions *were* translated into legislation, any resulting unpopularity could be shifted away from government to parliament.[37]

Meanwhile, government authority over policy benefited from the accumulation of official knowledge within the administration. The war played the major part in stimulating the collection of information. The first decennial census was taken in 1801, in the hope of estimating food import requirements more accurately and avoiding potential unrest arising from harvest shortages or blockades. Local authorities were required to forward statistics on crop yields, poor relief expenditure and criminal prosecutions.[38] From 1822 the Colonial Office made all colonies supply it with annual statistics of population, taxes, spending and trade. The flow of information was impressive: whereas in 1806 it had sent 902 letters and laid 14 pages of information before the Commons, in 1824 it sent 4,959 letters and in 1826 presented 2,694 pages.[39] This made possible a much greater influence over colonial affairs. Without it, for example, government could not have hoped to mitigate, and eventually abolish, slavery. By the 1810s, a self-conscious administrative elite was becoming confident that it could stamp a more systematic pattern of activity on government. Internal administrative reform created a clearer structure of responsibilities and hierarchy of authority in the civil service. In particular, the division of duties between the political and administrative heads in each department was clarified. Legal advisers, like Henry Hobhouse at the Home Office and James Stephen at the Colonial Office, having been brought in to help draft legislation, codify existing law and give departments advice in the later stages of the war, became permanent fixtures.

Professionalisation and information pointed up areas in which government action might improve its reputation for efficiency, economy and morality. Much of what is sometimes called 'liberal tory' legislation was a product of this. For example, the overhaul of the customs departments revealed a bewildering tangle of duties, complex to administer, discouraging to the trader and an inducement to the smuggler. The consequence was a major consolidation of customs duties in 1825. Over three-quarters of the statutes were repealed, and a new and efficient code for ship registration, warehousing and so on was implemented. Huskisson, President of the Board of Trade, took the opportunity to remove some of the more preposterously prohibitive duties, for example, replacing a duty of up to 75 per cent on imported cotton goods – in which Britain was hardly threatened by foreign competition – with a slightly less absurd one of 10 per cent.

Public pressure for systematisation was greatest in matters of criminal law. In the past, parliament had tended to pass acts of a purely local and temporary nature, without considering the need for overall uniformity or for repealing statutes inconsistent with them. This had caused confusion, expense and executive feebleness. The law's contradictions and inefficiencies had been highlighted by the social strains resulting from massive population growth, rapid urbanisation, poverty, and the churches' failure to reach the expanding population. Since the introduction of regular criminal statistics in 1805, the number of committals for trial in England and Wales had risen alarmingly: 5,146 in 1810, they reached 18,107 in 1830. By the 1820s there were 500 local societies for the prosecution of felons, collecting subscriptions to employ a force of constables to protect property and to help the 'middle-class' campaigns against rowdy games of street football, prostitution, drunkenness, urinating in public, naked swimming and over-affectionate courting couples.[40] Reformers blamed the increased crime rate largely on the lack of efficient deterrence mechanisms, on lax gaol conditions, and on the excessive number of capital statutes (about 220 before 1823). They claimed that jury unwillingness to sentence men to death for minor misdemeanours brought the law into disrepute. Led by the whig Mackintosh, backbenchers pressed for a more liberal yet more effective policy, which would 'bring punishment home, with greater certainty, to guilt'.[41] Anxious to boost the executive's reputation, Home Secretary Peel met this pressure by repackaging its suggestions and calling it Home Office policy. In 1823, government repealed a hundred capital statutes, nearly all of which were redundant,* and passed a Prisons Act requiring magistrates to inspect prisons and submit reports to the Home Secretary. Then, between 1827 and 1830, four statutes were passed which consolidated and codified the law on larceny, damage to property, offences against the person, and forgery, clarified scales of punishment for particular offences and so greatly improved the administration of justice. In 1829, famously, Peel tackled the problem of policing in London – the lack of coordination between parishes and the inadequate numbers of suitable magistrates – by establishing a single constabulary under the control of paid metropolitan commissioners responsible to the Home Office.

---

* The cosmetic nature of these reforms is best shown by the numbers of capital sentences in England and Wales. They averaged 1,039 per annum between 1821 and 1823 and 1,316 between 1828 and 1830 (though few were actually executed). Tories refused to make significant reductions in the number of capital statutes in the absence of an effective system of secondary punishments.[42]

Canningite liberalism

These developments certainly strengthened government in parliament. The most striking evidence of this is Liverpool's ability to remain Prime Minister for nearly fifteen years, though operating from the Lords. No eighteenth-century minister could have survived for so long without being directly accountable to the tax-granting Commons. Liverpool developed the notion of team government; his Commons ministers acquired (greater or lesser) command in their own spheres of excellence. But with important exceptions, such as the cuts in expenditure and patronage, these changes probably had less effect in influencing opinion outside Westminster. The most important steps deliberately taken by ministers to develop *public* confidence in authority came in another field – that of foreign policy – under the guidance of George Canning, who returned to the government as Foreign Secretary and Leader of the House of Commons on Castlereagh's suicide in 1822. Canning's exploitation of foreign issues created a new image for government. The name 'Liberal' was imported into British politics from the Spanish 'Liberales' of the revolutions of 1812 and 1820, with whom Canning sympathised.[43] In 1820, one MP had criticised Liverpool for not attempting to manage 'public opinion, as a mean of Government'.[44] After five years of Canningism, no one could possibly say the same.

The key to Canning's success was his unusual relationship with the 'people'. Until his return to office in 1822, Canning had for twenty years been the coming man of British politics, but had mysteriously failed to arrive, possibly because of his wild temper, cutting tongue, arrogance and willingness to court popularity by playing fast and loose with issues. Canning himself found it useful to imply that it was because he was the son of an actress, a man who had risen by ability alone and who spurned aristocratic connections and the embrace of the court. Canning benefited from his image as a patriot, given him by his early career as Pitt's protégé and a strong supporter of the war. In his quest for public applause, he developed an anti-monarchical edge to his patriotism. His public speeches on the war attributed British military success to the fact that crown influence was balanced by public political participation. The constitution reconciled 'a spirit of democracy sufficient to give energy to a state, with a devotedness to monarchy sufficient to ensure its conservation'. Unhindered, the 'monarchical power' tended to repress those energies; popular representation maintained 'jealous, steady, corrective, efficient control' over it.[45] Canning resigned from the government in 1820 over the Caroline affair, so associating himself with opposition to kingly immorality. Particularly important in distancing himself from monarchical influence was his call to open political offices in Britain and Ireland to Roman Catholics, which George III had vetoed and George IV opposed. Canning had been identified with Catholic Emancipation since Pitt had proposed it in 1801. He worked with the whig opposition in urging it, in 1812–13 and 1821–2, when temporarily out of office. By this means, he could demonstrate the government's subservience to royal pressure, threaten to defeat it in the Commons, and goad the government to woo him back into office on attractive terms.

When he returned as Foreign Secretary in 1822, Canning boosted his and his government's reputation among the 'respectable' public by playing on these ideals. His policy pointed up Britain's divergence from the so-called 'Holy Alliance' of continental autocracies (headed by Prussia, Russia, Austria and France) and from secret policy-making cliques of all kinds. Canning drove a wedge between the Allies in his policy towards Greece in the 1820s, and ignored their condemnations and threats as he moved towards recognising the independence of the Spanish territories in Latin America. He contrasted the secrecy of traditional diplomacy with the openness of his own policy. He made a fetish of distrusting the backstairs negotiations on which foreign policy usually depended, describing it as 'throwing a little dust in the eyes of the House of Commons'.[46] In particular, this meant contrasting the 'cottage coterie' of aristocratic foreign diplomats with whom George IV discussed foreign policy, with the influence of 'middle-class' and press opinion to which Canning claimed to listen in formulating his own *démarches*. In a previous spell in office (1807–9), he had been the first Foreign Secretary systematically to publish diplomatic papers, in order to excite public feeling against Napoleon, and he now continued the practice. By releasing his frosty dealings with continental powers, he was able to gain public affection for the policy – and grind down opposition to it at court and elsewhere.

All this conveyed the message that Canning was on the side of the people against oligarchy. This impression was compounded by his unprecedented activity as a public speaker. Very important here was his stint of over ten years as MP for Liverpool between 1812 and 1823, which gave him claims to speak for the 'people', especially for the business community with its interest in the promotion of foreign trade. In the 1812 election at Liverpool he had delivered 160 speeches. No other cabinet minister cultivated public support in this way, and none sat for a large borough or county, until his protégé Huskisson succeeded him in Liverpool in 1823. In the 1820s, his speeches, though sporadic by later standards, were notorious. His tory critics protested that he made himself 'more ridiculous than enough [sic] by going round the country *speechifying* & discussing the acts & intentions of the Government. This is quite a new system *among us* & excites great indignation.'[47] In 1824 he caused a furore by attending the banquet of the lord mayor of London, a radical supporter of Caroline.[48] He advertised himself as 'one of the people . . . unaccredited by patrician patronage' and standing on 'character' and the support of 'public confidence'.[49] His popularity propelled newspaper editors into the arms of government. Canning once said that he had 'inaugurate[d] the power of the Press by letting it influence affairs', but his other boast, that he 'governed' it, was more accurate.[50]*

---

* It appears that the term 'fourth estate' was used to describe press power from the 1820s: see p. 169n below.

Canning, then, suggested that the era of public influence on policy had superseded oligarchy. He went further: he claimed that three great benefits flowed from this change. The new policy deployed British influence for the general benefit of liberal forces throughout the world, and for Britain's commercial advantage, yet lowered defence costs and taxes.

The first, the promotion of liberal progress against oppression, was implied by Canning's Greek policy and by his recognition of the independence of the three former Spanish republics in Latin America. To the same end, he exploited the anti-slavery issue. He welcomed the formation of the Anti-Slavery Society in 1823 as a restrained pressure group anxious for parliamentary action to promote the education of slaves into useful, moral and aware members of society, the precondition of abolition.* In a pre-concerted response to an Anti-Slavery Society motion, Canning announced an eight-point programme to advance the slaves' well-being. He subsequently published his despatches to the slave colonies. He had a triple purpose: to demonstrate government's moral virtue, to educate public opinion into accepting a realistically slow rate of progress towards emancipation, and to use public pressure, together with the increasing knowledge of colonial society available through statistics, to persuade slaveowners into compliance with this rate of progress. For the government knew that unless it could win the planters round, no reform was possible. It was not feasible to force a policy on them when they were the main agents of British rule, and the only guarantors of the British connection which still helped trade so much.

As for British commercial prospects, they clearly benefited from Canning's Spanish American policy. By befriending the republics, Britain consolidated the economic connection with Latin America which she had been seeking for years. Had she not done so, France or the United States would have gained instead. The benefit to British cotton exports was astonishing: between 1820 and 1840 the number of yards exported to South America grew from 56 million to 279 million, 35 per cent of the total.[52] Meanwhile Huskisson, at the Board of Trade, pushed through reforms in imperial commerce, which aimed to stimulate international trade and good relations, especially in the Western Hemisphere. Huskisson believed that British attempts to restrict the commercial freedom of the American colonies had been the principal reason for their secession, and he was anxious that a similar crisis should not occur in Canada or the West Indies. Similarly, if Britain wished to benefit from trade with Latin America and the United States, she must allow them reasonable access to colonial markets. The legislation of 1822–5 established a much more coherent system of imperial preference, allowing colonial goods preferential treatment in the British market, and vice versa, yet removing the monopolies on the conduct of colonial trade which had previously restricted it essentially to British and colonial shipping. Huskisson argued that prohibitive duties and restrictions

---

* In 1824, Canning warned that immediate emancipation would be like setting Frankenstein's monster loose: a creature with the form and strength of man, but 'in the infancy of his uninstructed reason'.[51]

41

on freedom of shipping obstructed the flow of commerce, 'one of the great means of civilizing and enlightening mankind, of diffusing liberal ideas, and of creating a community of interests between nations for their mutual benefit and improvement'. Similarly, Robinson, the Chancellor of the Exchequer, accompanied cuts in import duties on raw materials for industry, made in his budgets of 1824 and 1825, with ringing declarations that they would 'cut the cords which tie down commerce to the earth, that she may spring aloft, unconfined and unrestricted, and shower her blessings over every part of the world'.[53] In the 1820s, tories became more and more willing to exploit the British empire rhetorically as a purifying, liberating phenomenon: Southey coined the phrase that the sun never set on it.[54] Huskisson averred that 'in every quarter of the globe we have planted the seeds of freedom, civilization and Christianity'. His declared aim was to civilise French-speaking Canada into a system of 'English laws and English institutions'.[55]*

Improved commercial prospects, and Holy Alliance embarrassment, helped to stabilise Britain's international position. Military expenditure fell steadily from £17.7 million in 1818 to £12.3 million in 1824, the second lowest figure of the nineteenth century. This made possible substantial cuts in taxation – £8 million between 1823 and 1825. Yet this was done while Britain's status abroad was apparently rising. Canning seemed to have squared the circle: he could appeal both to postwar triumphalism and to the old tory scepticism about the wisdom of costly and unpredictable aggression unless necessary. It seemed that, owing first to the war, and then to the maintenance of peace and non-intervention in the 1820s, a small island country, blessed by Providence, had gained a position of dazzling power, yet would exercise it to advance the general good, to spread wealth, commerce and moral principles. Canning, building on the great victory of 1815, seemed to have brought Britain material and moral world dominance without the need for heavy armaments or a drastic alteration of her commercial system. Prosperity in the 1820s made it appear that an effective balance had been struck between the agricultural protection and imperial preference which hard-nosed interests required, and the lofty free trade imperialism which ministers proclaimed in their speeches. Britain's long-term economic position now seemed secure enough to satisfy all her creditors. The increase in national wealth and population diminished the real burden of the national debt, and it seemed unnecessary to sacrifice tax cuts in order to reduce it further. So Pitt's sinking fund, established in 1786 as a mechanism for reducing the debt, was run down and then in effect abolished in 1829 – with the further advantage that government was freed from the embarrassment of being seen to be dependent on the City finance houses which had serviced it.

* In 1823 and 1825, the Canningite junior minister Wilmot Horton obtained parliamentary grants to help emigrants settle in Canada, in the hope of reducing the labour surplus at home.

In retrospect, Canning's rhetoric appeared overblown. For most of the 1820s, Britain was both prosperous and unthreatened by any world power. The Spanish, Dutch, Danish and Swedish fleets had been all but destroyed in war; neither the United States nor France were strong enough to challenge Britain, nor was there much cause for them to do so. The changes in tariff policy, meanwhile, were presented as more striking than they were. Huskisson was determined to boost exports to specific colonial and satellite markets, since *prohibition* was obviously stultifying. But a general *protective* system was necessary, because of the 'artificial' nature of the economy, which depended on producing goods which, in theory, other nations could copy, and for which international demand was believed to be limited. Without the help given to the commercial, colonial and agricultural sectors by protection, neither British self-sufficiency in the event of another war, nor the colonial connection, could be guaranteed. Lacking an income tax, the government also needed revenue from duties. Underneath the rhetoric, ministers retained a healthy distrust of the application of 'general and abstract principles of political economy'.[56] A clutch of tariff reform measures between 1822 and 1825 were calculated and cautious, framed on suspicion of other nations' practices rather than a naive attachment to free trade principles. Hardly any countries were yet in a position to exploit the legislation to Britain's disadvantage (restrictions on United States trade had been substantially lifted earlier).

But Canningism had remarkable effects on the political mood. Britain's economic and international strength appeared to be a result of her 'liberalism' – her openness to the moral influence of public opinion and her equal openness in trade. In conjunction with Liverpool's earlier measures, Canning's policy seemed to have shown the benefits of rational and purifying administrative reform, adherence to Protestant values and confidence in the march of mind. Was Britain's power, prosperity and domestic harmony not evidence of the power of human reason? In 1812, Canning had told the Commons that it was inconceivable that 'the settlement of any question, however difficult and complicated, lies out of the province, or beyond the competency of the collective wisdom and authority of the state'.[57] This would have been startling language to hold in the eighteenth century. Canning and friends encouraged the idea that, by tapping public support, an immense addition could be made to the material and moral energy of the state. The Canningite Palmerston suggested in 1829 that, just as a single ship's captain, by using human ingenuity, could steer a bulky vessel through a terrible storm, so could those statesmen 'who know how to avail themselves of the passions, and the interests, and the opinions of mankind ... gain an ascendancy, and ... exercise a sway over human affairs, far out of all proportion greater than belong to the power and resources of the state over which they preside'.[58]

Canning, then, established three key 'liberal' notions: that the state was no longer oligarchical, but rested on public opinion; that public opinion was Protestant, patriotic and liberty-loving (Canning did not merely *identify* with public opinion and 'middle-class' values, but helped to *define* what they were, in ways suited to his own agenda); and that any state which operated on an open political basis and looked to liberate public energies would make great progress.

Together with economic recovery, 'liberal toryism' made the whig campaign for parliamentary reform, and indeed the whigs, irrelevant. By the mid-1820s, the whigs themselves were forced to make light of the dangers to constitutional liberty. In 1826, the whig MP Curwen looked back to the days when it required courage to oppose ministers, for fear of being considered 'an enemy to the State', and praised the Liverpool government for its openness in conducting government.[59] Every year seemed to betoken a yet 'purer spirit of government'.[60] In May 1824, Tierney, the nominal whig leader in the Commons, insisted that the whig party was not pledged to parliamentary reform, and indeed disagreed on it. In 1827, Russell announced that even he had dropped the question because of the 'great lukewarmness on the subject throughout the country' owing to 'the improvement which had taken place in the manner of conducting the government'.[61] Between 1824 and 1829, not a single petition for parliamentary reform was presented to the Commons from anywhere in the country. As the poet Coleridge later said, Canning 'flashed such a light around the constitution that it was difficult to see the ruins of the fabric through it'.[62] The opposition had no option but to applaud Canning's genius and hope to bask in his fame. Morpeth saw his policy as 'inseparably connected with the glory of England and the happiness of the world'; Hobhouse called him 'the terror of tyrants'.[63] Opposition's traditional function of protecting the nation against official corruption seemed redundant: if taxes were to rise again in future, there was no reason to believe that the government, now responsive to public pressure, would not act quickly to remove the grievance. The number of divisions on which government and opposition clashed fell from 88 in 1822 to 20 in 1826. In the provinces, whig club activity declined, as the party lost its sense of purpose and direction.[64] As early as 1823, its leader Tierney believed that the 'party may almost be considered as dissolved'.[65]

In the mid-1820s, Canning dominated British politics. He had marginalised the whig opposition; he had flattered the 'middle classes'; he had saved the regime from the imputation of oligarchy. When, in February 1827, Liverpool suffered a stroke and had to be removed from the premiership, he was the only plausible successor. When he became Prime Minister, Canning slapped down the tory placeman Croker, who had urged him not to forget the importance of the boroughowners, by reminding him that his support rested in 'the body of the people' rather than 'in the hands of the tory aristocracy'.[66] But this was in fact only half-true. Canning intended to continue Liverpool's broad coalition, based on public identification with the principles of economy, efficiency and morality, but also reliant in practice on royal and boroughowner acquiescence. Canning's identification with 'the people' was part of an explicit strategy to stave off political upheaval. He believed that 'we are on the brink of a great struggle between property and

44

population', which 'mild' and 'liberal' politics alone could avert.[67] For him, as for all tories, the unreformed electoral system played a key part in securing property rights; and he had no more intention of undermining it than Wellington or Sidmouth.

Tories and the constitution

Tories generally saw parliament's function as the representation and defence of interests of various sorts, which should form a tacit alliance with government for the defence of authority against anarchy. Crucial in allowing this alliance to operate, the argument went, were the small boroughs on which 'public opinion' did not impinge.[68] The administration itself was benefited by them, since they offered refuge to men of talent who lacked the demagogic appeal and/or money to be returned to parliament for other places. Similarly, they gave the crown and peers influence in the Commons – in 1827 Croker suggested that fifteen tory aristocrats nominated seventy MPs – and so could be credited with preserving harmony between King, Lords and lower House.* Small boroughs also let in informed and independent opinion. There were a large number of merchants only too willing to pay a boroughowner £4,000 or £5,000 for the privilege of sitting throughout a parliament. The number of commercial interests represented in the Commons fluctuated between 130 and 160 between 1800 and 1830 (as against 50–70 in the mid-eighteenth century), and many financiers, such as Alexander Baring, played an important part in the technical debates on commercial questions.[70] Liverpool suggested that the economic interests of large towns could be represented better by local merchants sitting for close boroughs than by popular elections which stimulated 'a permanent spirit of turbulence and disaffection'.[71] Colonial interests in India and the West Indies similarly required representation, if parliament was to assist in governing 'the immense colonial possessions of this extensive empire', with their 'scores of millions of our fellow-subjects'.[72] Also, perhaps a third of all 'close' boroughs were in fact dominated by local country gentlemen who returned themselves or family connections and who, while usually not whig, were also not lackeys of government: such men as Drake, Holdsworth, Bankes, Palk and Dering prided themselves on their independence.

Reform, then, would have a 'most serious effect on the public interests'.[73] To destroy interest representation in favour of MPs returned by popular clamour would weaken security for property and the cause of order. Tories associated the Reform movement with radicals who hoped by it to reduce

* Yet small borough MPs also retained some independence from patrons. Even on a matter of burning concern like Catholic Emancipation, well over half the peers who returned MPs had at least one experience of differing with their MP on a parliamentary vote, and the proportion of MPs who did not vote on the side favoured by their aristocratic patron varied between 25 per cent and 40 per cent of the whole throughout the 1820s.[69]

interest payments on the national debt, lower official salaries, appropriate church property, and diminish protection for colonial and commercial interests. So Reform directly endangered individual property. It also threatened government's power of raising taxes, the most basic test of its authority.[74] Alexander Baring asked how the crown's law officers could conduct unpopular prosecutions if they had constantly to answer to public opinion.[75] The more popular the basis on which the Commons rested, the less tolerant it promised to be of the mixed constitution, and the more unlimited its aggression. Peel warned that all popular assemblies in history had eventually claimed unlimited power; where would this leave executive authority?[76] This view gained particular force in reaction to the French Revolution and the devastating lawlessness, profligacy and sectional antagonism which unregulated public pressure had unleashed. The ignorant and passionate would surely dictate the course of policy. Steadiness of judgment would give way to contradictory, damaging policies determined by the twists of the popular weathervane, urging now protection, now free trade, now war, now savage army reductions, now extravagance to paupers, now a starvation policy.[77] Peel appreciated that, at first sight, the existing arrangements might appear questionable, but explained that the mixed constitution had preserved a greater mix of happiness, liberty and prosperity than any country had known in history. He borrowed Canning's analogy between the constitution and the human body. Man, 'so noble in reason – so infinite in faculties – in apprehension so like a God', nonetheless 'has parts, and performs functions which, if they are to be separately regarded, provoke feelings of abhorrence and disgust'.[78]

But tories also argued that the popular constitution with which Reformers sought to replace the mixed one would be popular in name only, for 'public opinion' could mean anything and nothing. In practice, parliament would still represent interests – whichever interests were able to dominate in the new conditions. Canning, as ever sanguine in public, laughed that determined wealthy interests would still bribe their way in, despite Reformers' pious hopes.[79] Peel, more typically, feared that 'superior intelligence and superior property would be overborne' in favour of 'the very worst and vilest species of despotism – the despotism of demagogues . . . the despotism of Journalism'.[80] In 1820, he defined public opinion as 'that great compound of folly, weakness, prejudice, wrong feeling, right feeling, obstinacy, and newspaper paragraphs'.[81] Tories ridiculed the idea of a mere population test for disfranchising boroughs. In 1831, Sir Joseph Yorke, the MP for Reigate, one threatened borough, avowed that, with nine months' warning, he and his colleague 'the gallant colonel', would have done 'the utmost in their poor power to have increased the population there to the ideal standard of fitness', despite 'the Malthusian principles now in fashion'.[82]

For tories, then, Reform proposals were based on the fallacy that parliament might ever represent 'public opinion' accurately. Good government, they insisted, demanded independence of judgment. Ministers must remain free to distinguish between real, permanent opinion and mere ignorant, temporary popular clamour. Too much, they said, should not be read into particular cries apparently emanating from the 'people'. In early 1831, they suggested that a deliberate and settled popular judgment in favour of Reform had not yet emerged.[83] Rather, it was the obsession of Reform-minded ministers that had 'excited the passions of the people, and spurred their lazy indifference'.[84]

Tories maintained that, while the unreformed electoral system offered the best security for the preservation of order, it also allowed the regulated expression of public opinion. In a bustling, politicised modern society, they argued, popular grievances were easily identified. Large elements of the Commons articulated them, and so gave ministers ample opportunity to judge how far to accommodate them. As the tory minister Spencer Perceval recognised in 1809, government's real strength in parliament depended on it securing the support of MPs from the counties and thriving towns, where public opinion was most developed.[85] As we saw, government was left weak after the 1818 election because of the adverse swing of opinion in the contested elections in the largest seats.*

In demonstrating the responsiveness of the existing system, tories pointed first to the county seats, 82-strong in England, which were traditionally the most highly-prized in the Commons. Aspiring county MPs normally needed to be men of high rank and dignity, yet also 'men of business' who understood the needs of both agricultural and commercial sectors of the county economy. This was because counties had a large and varied electorate. The property qualification was low (ownership of a forty-shilling freehold) and applied equally in urban and rural parts of the county, whether the urban areas returned borough MPs separately or not. In Kent in 1802 32 per cent of the voters qualified from property in towns with more than 100 voters, in Cambridgeshire in 1830 33 per cent, and in Durham in 1820 and Hampshire in 1806 34 per cent.[87] Where substantial settlements returned no borough MP of their own, they were often influential in county elections: by the 1820s both Warwickshire MPs were careful to listen carefully to the sentiments of Birmingham freeholders, and both Staffordshire MPs likewise were anxious to represent manufacturing opinion in Wolverhampton. County MPs were traditionally the most independent of government and the most intolerant of high government expenditure. They were seen as the conscience of the Commons, and exercised influence beyond their numerical strength. In a number of counties, powerful aristocrats had greater control over the representation than squires and farmers might wish – particularly in Westmorland, where the Lowthers retained control, though at vast expense. But in general, influence was kept up only by taking great

---

* In 1829, faced with the need to disprove the argument that public opinion was inveterately opposed to Catholic Emancipation, Peel's test was the voting behaviour of MPs for the fifteen largest counties and twenty most populous boroughs of England, 'a practical and constitutional method of determining the sense of the people'.[86]

pains to construct and maintain alliances of country gentlemen, by flattery, entertainment and judicious lobbying. In turn, both aristocrats and gentry were unwise to coerce their tenants into toeing a particular political line. In many counties, large-scale, prosperous farmers were much the largest single group in the electorate, and they were either owners or, if tenants, tended to be reliable and efficient ones whom the landlord would not lightly risk losing.

Most significant towns also had separate borough representation. Of the 202 English boroughs returning MPs, 65 had more than 600 electors, and 43 over 1,000, including London, Westminster, Southwark, Liverpool, Bristol, Norwich, Leicester, Coventry, Northampton, Nottingham and Newcastle-upon-Tyne. The borough electorate reflected the social composition of the population fairly accurately: 40–50 per cent, typically, were craftsmen, 20 per cent retailers and some unskilled labourers. In the larger boroughs, an average of a quarter, and sometimes – as in Northampton or Canterbury – a half, of adult males, could vote.[88] Wherever substantial numbers of men qualified to vote in another borough lived in one large town, they could combine to influence the election in that borough. So, for example, the Birmingham outvoters usually returned an MP for Bridgnorth. Despite only returning 10 MPs in theory, London and Middlesex electors were particularly well-represented because of the outvoter element in Home Counties boroughs (Maldon, Colchester and St Albans are good examples). Increasing local prosperity meant that boroughowners lost control in a score of boroughs in the early nineteenth century, for example in middle-sized towns like St Albans, Oxford and Boston. The marquess of Stafford gave up the expensive struggle to control returns in the growing towns of Newcastle-under-Lyme and Lichfield in 1825. The marquess of Exeter battled to retain Stamford; the duke of Newcastle fought a desperate contest to discipline the 1,200 electors of Newark.

Nor were tories in theory opposed to all Reform. If parliament represented specific interests, why should individual important towns not gain representation, whenever existing boroughs were disfranchised after proven gross bribery? Croker was unusually ambitious in wanting 33 unrepresented towns with populations of 10,000 to have at least one MP.[89] But political realities ruled out more than the most minor changes: to float any *scheme* of Reform would unsettle Lords and boroughowners and open the floodgates to more radical ideas. Tories relied instead on the argument that parliamentary reform was not necessary, that government could respond to public desires for openness, economy and morality without it. During Canning's heyday, this seemed very plausible.

Canning, then, relied in practice on the unreformed electoral system, but flattered public opinion by attributing to its influence the government's domestic policy of economy and administrative reform, and its high-profile foreign affairs strategy of keeping a distance from oligarchical networks at home and abroad. This worked very well, but was facilitated by the prosperity of the mid-1820s. His legacy was to suggest to the politicians who followed him that 'liberal' policy was necessary to win public confidence, and might well stave off demands for radical constitutional reform. But, by raising public expectations of government so high, he placed his successors in a difficulty, which was to prove particularly acute when economic conditions were not so rosy and dissatisfaction therefore not so easily assuaged.

CHAPTER 2

The collapse of toryism, 1827–30

THE BALANCING ACT of Liverpool and Canning was destroyed between 1827 and 1830. The great tory coalition collapsed in three stages, but the dénouement was by no means inevitable. In 1827–8 the problem was partly Canning's character and partly the Catholic question; in 1829 it was entirely the latter. After the passage of Catholic Emancipation, the government's institutional supports were weakened, but it still had the great asset of widespread public confidence. However, its survival was now dependent entirely on its ability to continue to manage 'public opinion'. In the third crisis, in 1830, it narrowly failed to cope with an unusual degree of public excitement. Wellington's government did not fall because it was an *ancien régime* – in most ways it was no less 'liberal' than Canning's – but because of bad timing.

Shifting foundations of tory support, 1827–9

Between 1827 and 1829 the basis of tory government altered remarkably. This was fundamentally because of a three-way difference of opinion in Liverpool's coalition about how to secure 'strong government'. One strategy was Canning's active engagement with 'public opinion'. But his critics believed that his populist leadership was weakening the authority and independence of the executive. Wellington led those who thought that government could best be strengthened instead by institutional alliances with bodies like the church, the magistracy, the large financial agencies and the army. Many older tories, of the generation personally affected by the French Revolution, shared Wellington's dislike of Canning; in 1824, Sidmouth defined 'liberality' in government as 'cowardice' or 'want of principle'.[1] So did youthful evangelical peers like Newcastle, Winchilsea and Roden, who were very anxious to defend church-state solidarity against the threats of popery and infidelity. A third important strand of toryism had much in common with the second, and also distrusted much of Canning's approach. However, this camp believed that the authority of government must be preserved not merely by institutional alliances but also by a more

50

active *policy* than central government was used to pursuing, particularly in fields where activity could demonstrate government commitment to order and efficiency. This approach came to be associated particularly with the Home Secretary in Liverpool's government, Robert Peel. It implied that, without a firm, cooperative and disciplined majority in the House of Commons, strong government could not be carried on. For Wellington, on the contrary, the prospect of a fragile Commons majority made it all the more important for a government to keep a great variety of other agencies happy, that is the king, the Lords, local magistrates, the City and the East India Company. This in turn made a policy of activity, which might affront many of these bodies, too high a risk.*

But Wellington and Peel worked together in delivering the first blow to tory unity, on Liverpool's retirement in 1827. They told the king that they refused to serve under Canning, since he was known to favour Catholic Emancipation and so there was no security against its passage. In doing so (together, eventually, with five other cabinet ministers), they cut an unfortunate figure: they looked like a faction attempting to dictate a policy and so limiting the king's freedom to choose his ministers. This reminded George IV of Fox's challenge to crown power in 1783, and allowed Canning to present himself, like Pitt in 1784, as the king's servant. Canning claimed to be anxious to carry on a national, rather than factional, government by leaving controversial questions like Catholic Emancipation open. But the dissidents' refusal prevented him from continuing Liverpool's coalition and forced him to become a cross-party man, appealing to whigs for support. This divided whig opinion, too, much of which distrusted Canning. Grey, Fitzwilliam and Bedford of the older generation, Althorp, Russell and Duncannon of the younger, would not support him, though Lansdowne, Tierney, Devonshire and Carlisle joined his cabinet. Canning then died, in August 1827, and his successor, Goderich, was too weak to hold together such a strained coalition. It collapsed in January 1828. Wellington was now asked to form a government, and attempted to reunite the tory party. But after a few months of tension, Huskisson and the three other Canningite cabinet ministers (Palmerston, Dudley and Grant) resigned, and took to criticising Wellington's foreign policy on grounds of 'illiberalism'. (Fortunately for Wellington, the seceding ministers – labelled Huskissonites – were disliked in the Commons as unprincipled and assertive jobbers, and so, despite their ability, their loss was not a fatal blow to government.[2])

So the old coalition had already fragmented, even before Wellington, like Canning before him, had to face the Catholic Emancipation problem. Emancipation had become a political issue originally because of Pitt's desire to integrate Irish Catholics into the United Kingdom during the French wars. It had then been exploited by Canning and the whigs in 1812 and 1821 for political purposes. One reason why Canning liked it was because

---

* This fault-line between Wellington's and Peel's philosophies ran through tory politics between 1827 and 1846.

it symbolised an optimistic view of national destiny. Emancipationists – or 'Catholics' – presented it as the means of regenerating Ireland both economically and spiritually: economically by removing the obstacles to the investment of capital and the modernisation of agriculture and industry, spiritually by allowing the superior truths of Protestantism to be received without prejudice by the Catholic population. Emancipation would remove an artificial impediment and harmonise Irish politics, allowing an integrated respectable opinion to emerge. 'Catholics' argued that the Irish disloyalty to Britain was not inevitable; the cause of disaffection was simply unjust tory law. It was in reference to Catholic Emancipation that Canning had made his remarkable statement of 1812 (see page 43) that the state had the capacity to settle any problem.

Emancipation became so divisive an issue in the 1820s very largely because of Canning's advocacy of it, as one cabinet minister, Charles Wynn, recognised in 1825.[3] Tories who opposed Emancipation condemned his exploitation of the question when in opposition, and distrusted his populist and misleading tone about its benefits. One Wellington supporter complained in 1824 that advocates of Catholic Emancipation and the quick abolition of slavery seemed 'to forget the nature of man'.[4] Canning's 'insight into the real nature of the religious discords of mankind' appeared 'too shallow', even to his biographer.[5] His critics distrusted his judgment in fomenting and manipulating public opinion. Wellington and his friends believed that Canning was not a gentleman; they behaved as they did in 1827 because Canning's character gave them no grounds for thinking that authority was safe in his hands. His principles 'fluctuate every day', he had no 'strength of mind' and his 'actions are decided by the impulse of the moment'.[6] Wellington had been particularly affronted by Canning's manipulation of public opinion to achieve his foreign policy ends. He thought this discourteous to George IV and recklessly offensive to the other European powers whose goodwill was necessary if international peace and order were to be preserved. To him, Canning's 'tricking & shuffling way' of doing business involved avoiding taking a firm line, waiting on events, and keeping information from the cabinet.[7] Wellington ruefully remarked of his discussions on foreign policy with Canning and Liverpool, 'I feel like a man who, going into a crowd, thinks it prudent to button up his pockets'.[8] By 1826, relations within cabinet had become so embittered that they created other bones of contention, such as on the proper levels of corn import duty.

The result of this suspicion of Canning was unfortunate for Wellington and Peel. It made them into the political allies of those who opposed Emancipation on *principle*, primarily legalistic constitutional lawyers and fervently evangelical Protestants. Both these groups rejected Emancipation essentially for the traditional reasons that it might imperil the Protestant succession to the British throne in defence of which so much blood and effort had been spent between 1640 and 1745. This was no longer a serious threat. The more hard-headed reason for opposing Emancipation in the 1820s – which moved Wellington and Peel – was that, in consequence of the passage of the Act of Union with Ireland, it would lead to the presence in the British parliament of a large number of Catholic MPs. Wellington and Peel anticipated that the lobbying of a populist Catholic party from Ireland would inflame sectional discord and probably establish Catholic ascendancy, leading to church disestablishment, land reform and perhaps the repeal of the Union. Both men's experience of Ireland was extensive: Wellington was raised there, while Peel had been Chief Secretary (1812–18).

For both men, then, the key question was how to maintain the authority of government in Ireland, as in Britain. By the late 1820s, both came to feel that this could be better preserved by consenting to Emancipation than by hindering it. Already in 1825 Wellington had toyed with a policy by which it could be granted together with a concordat with the pope to guarantee the loyalty of the priesthood. Most alarming were the activities of Daniel O'Connell's Catholic Association. This was a resolutely consti-tutional body (O'Connell had crowned George IV with laurel when the latter ended his Irish visit in 1821). But by 1828 its local power was much greater than that of traditional law enforcement agencies. Meanwhile, its parliamentary advance – three prestigious county victories in 1826, then O'Connell's return for County Clare in a byelection in July 1828, despite his ineligibility as a Catholic – threatened to be repeated elsewhere. Irish opinion seemed to be deserting the landlords for the priests and mass political meetings. This promised to undermine landed power and govern-ment legitimacy, establishing an alternative focus for Irish loyalties to that provided at Westminster.

Peel in particular was worried about the damage done generally to government authority by leaving the question open. When an Emancipation motion passed the Commons in 1825, Peel, the only 'Protestant' cabinet minister in that House, had tendered his resignation, declaring that a divided cabinet, insulted by a Commons vote, badly lacked dignity. Liver-pool, also a 'Protestant', was only narrowly persuaded not to agree and to resign himself (the Lords then defeated the bill). Recurring tensions of this sort confirmed Peel's view that 'the vigour of the executive government', the one thing which he regarded as essential to properly-constituted politics, was being 'paralyzed' by the continuing failure to resolve the question.[9] Peel's experience as Chief Secretary left him with a clear definition of a reform package which would benefit Ireland, but this required purposeful and unquestioned leadership. Two acts of 1814 and 1822, inspired by him, had attempted to reform the inefficient Irish police force. The latter had established an Irish Constabulary in each of the four Irish provinces, under the Lord Lieutenant. But these reforms had failed to work, because of a lack of coordination between the various bodies. Peel now believed that a force controlled from the centre was a necessary prerequisite of good order. The government had also been unable to establish an undenominational educational system supervised by the state ('the only measure to which Parliament could look for the introduction of habits of industry and morality among the lower orders in Ireland', according to Peel), despite two sets of reports, in 1812 and 1824–5.[10] Nor had it been able to stamp out corruption and negligence among the Irish magistracy. One major cause of incoherent policy-making and administrative tension, he argued, was that Prime Ministers had felt it necessary, ever since 1794, to meddle with the Irish administration in order to maintain a precise balance between 'Protestants' and 'Catholics'. Another was that the Catholic agitation in Ireland had become 'permanent and inveterate'; the rule of law could not be imposed there unless government secured the 'willing moral obedience' of the people.[11] While Catholic Emancipation might lead to the further agitation which he had previously feared, more crucial was the fact that it provided the only circumstances in which a more vigorous executive could hope to impose order and good government on the Irish people.

For these reasons, Wellington and Peel decided in 1828 that their government must itself propose Emancipation. When their bill was introduced in 1829, it was accompanied by two crucial 'wings' to which the two men attached great importance in pacifying Ireland (and appeasing anti-Catholic feeling in Britain). These were the suppression of the Catholic Association, and the disfranchisement of the Association's active supporters, the forty-shilling freeholders, by the increase of the Irish county franchise qualification to a £10 level. Peel was forthright that this would restore to the 'industrious, honest, and independent class' which was heavily Protestant, their 'just weight in the representation', which was at present 'overborne by a herd of voters' sunk in 'poverty and ignorance'.[12] Emancipation also allowed Peel as Home Secretary to formulate his fuller reform programme over the following year (see page 66). This had two prongs: 'to habituate the people to a vigorous unsparing enforcement and administration of the law, criminal and civil', and to introduce 'extensive schemes for the employment, and education, and improvement of the condition of the people'.[13]

Wellington and Peel also hoped that the passage of Emancipation would promote government stability in Britain, by removing the most divisive issue, and by demonstrating effective leadership. This was a gamble, but not an unreasonable one, as the response to Wellington's measure indicated. The bill passed through both Houses of Parliament in little over a month in early 1829. By skill, charm and hard work, Wellington succeeded in winning over both George IV – despite the opposition of the king's brother Cumberland – and the Lords, which passed Emancipation by an extraordinary majority off 104. As Wellington's success became clear, one observer regarded him as 'one of the most powerful Ministers this country has ever seen. The greatest Ministers have been obliged to bend to the King, or the aristocracy, or the Commons, but he commands them all.'[14]

In one sense, the passage of Emancipation clearly damaged Wellington. It was unpopular with a vast number of tories, from both the close boroughs and the shires: 202 MPs voted against the government on at least one occasion during the passage of the bill.[15] Many boroughowners and 'Protestant' squires felt betrayed by their leaders. Some hardened 'ultra'

MPs, led by Sir Richard Vyvyan and Sir Edward Knatchbull, proved irreconcilable. The threat of an 'ultra' reaction was always present in 1829–30. And at the 1830 election, the tory vote in a number of seats was split between pro- and anti-Catholic candidates.

But Wellington's position was changed rather than undermined by the passage of Emancipation. He was determined not to give 'Protestants' any cause for offence and retained two of the three ministers who voted against his bill for this reason. The strength of legalistic and evangelical no-popery was not very great in the political elite; indeed the extremism of most of its leaders (Cumberland, Winchilsea, Newcastle) made it easy to ignore them. Those opposed to Catholic Emancipation on constitutional grounds could not continue their opposition after 1829, for they were bound to support the king and the new law. Even the clergy, who had a special interest in the question, were less unanimous in opposing it than is often thought: 333 clergymen voted for Peel in his celebrated 1829 byelection contest on Emancipation at Oxford University, one of the most reactionary seats in Britain, which he lost only by 755 to 609.[16] Most country gentlemen rejected out of hand the idea of leading a movement of popular protest, as vulgar, disloyal and inflammatory. By 1830, despite hostile motions by Knatchbull and Blandford early in the session, 'ultra' discipline could not be sustained. 'Ultras' differed among themselves on the economic issues dominant in 1830. Their *Morning Journal* folded in May. Perhaps two dozen MPs, probably less, remained interested in following their leader Vyvyan in ranting against Wellington. Most former 'Protestants' supported the government in the 1830 election.[17]

The passage of Emancipation and the emergence of an 'ultra' opposition undoubtedly weakened Wellington's ability to lead a tory party, but it allowed him to approximate more to now-fashionable 'liberal' values. It strengthened government in the Commons – and outside – by minimising the divisions between it, the whigs and the Huskissonites. As Peel had written in 1828, strong government needed a broader base of support than 'the mere Tory party, as it is called'. (By 'Tory' he meant 'Protestant'; what he wanted to rally instead was 'the old party' of Liverpool's era.)[18]

Wellington's 'liberal' reputation was enhanced by the success of his government's financial policy, establishing a reputation for economy and efficiency. Between 1827 and 1830, public expenditure fell from £56.1 million to £53.7 million, two-thirds of the fall coming from military expenditure. Wellington's foreign policy was non-interventionist, so, although anti-Russian, he would not interfere to halt Russia's march on Turkey in 1829. He similarly refused to commit British troops to help the Portuguese constitutionalists, on the grounds that it would bring in the French and Spanish on their opponents' side. Charles Arbuthnot thought him 'the most pacific Minister we ever had'.[24] The sinking fund was in effect abolished in 1829. As for the expenses of civil government, a consensus was forming around the idea that the Treasury should assume control over all the spending departments in order to enforce economies. This was the suggestion of the very influential non-partisan Commons select committee on public income and expenditure (1828), within whose guidelines the Wellington government was happy to work. Another select committee was appointed in 1830 to set the problem of civil list expenditure finally to rest. The government's commitment to retrenchment did not save it from clamour from sectional interests during the severe depression of 1829–30, but until then it was secure in its reputation, especially after an amicable compromise between agriculturalists and tariff reformers in 1828 settled the Corn Law tiff of 1826–7.

Another potential charge of 'illiberalism' was defused when ministers bowed to the whig campaign to abolish the requirement laid down in the Test and Corporation Acts of 1661 and 1673 that holders of public offices should subscribe to Anglican principles. The government mounted a ritual opposition, but 66 tories voted to repeal the acts, and it was quickly decided to concede to the campaign for abolition. In neither the church nor the universities was there significant feeling for the retention of the acts; no bishop voted against repeal, and the bill easily passed the Lords. Peel feared that repeal would increase the number of Dissenting MPs in parliament and generate campaigns for further legislative concessions to nonconformists. This, he thought, might end the 'cordiality' of parochial relations and philanthropical cooperation between church and Dissent, and threaten strife in future.[20] But these arguments were too complex to be popular among MPs anxious to testify to parliament's responsiveness to grievances.

These adjustments meant that, by 1829, there appeared to be no issue on which the opposition could rally for there was no major policy difference between whigs and tories. Indeed many commentators believed that party politics was dead.[21] Whigs were divided on their strategy, with the result that the leaders did not seriously challenge ministers, though they did try to keep up the pressure for economy. With the blessing of the leadership, individual whigs accepted offices in government: Rosslyn in May 1829, Scarlett in June, the Knight of Kerry in March 1830 and Jersey in July. The whig paper the *Morning Chronicle* declared early in 1830 that after the passage of Catholic Emancipation Wellington had ceased to be a party leader and had become a national one.[22] Of course this encouragement was not entirely disinterested: many whigs expected that Wellington would eventually propose a formal coalition.

George IV's death in June 1830 also strengthened the government, by bringing to the throne a much more popular and apparently 'liberal' king, William IV. In contrast to George's aloofness, William demonstrated his common touch, opening St James's Park to the public, restoring the war honours awarded to the radical soldier Sir Robert Wilson but stripped from him for support of Caroline, and wandering about the streets himself, discoursing cheerfully and inconsequentially in the manner of his days as a midshipman. He agreed to a reduction in the civil list (cut by over £300,000 to £510,000 when details were published later) and made a popular speech proroguing parliament, in which he urged further efforts towards peace, retrenchment, and the diminution of taxes, supported Wellington's economic, legal and religious reforms, and looked forward to an era of 'domestic concord and peace'.[23]

In the 1830 election caused by George IV's death, candidates displayed a marked reluctance to take sides for or against the government. Greville commented that none would stand on the government's interest, Mrs Arbuthnot that none definitely opposed it.[24] Helped by his reputation as a military hero, Wellington was attacked by few whigs. Even Brougham, one of the exceptions, nonetheless called for a coalition under him as prime minister.[25] Lord Belgrave was more typical in maintaining that the difference between government and opposition was 'so extremely fine, that it is impossible to distinguish them'.[26] Wellington's retrenchment and reform gained general approval. As the *Times* said, the only sustained attack on him came from a small minority of ultras.[27] In general, it was assumed throughout the 1830 election that the government would survive, by attracting the support of either individual politicians (which the *Times* favoured) or the whigs as a whole. While too weak as it stood, its great advantage over previous governments was that it was not dependent on a 'selfish Parliamentary oligarchy'. Its susceptibility to public pressure was seen as a benefit, since it held out hopes for the implementation of policy changes which had been frustrated, such as the abolition of slavery and the East India Company's monopoly, and further tax and tariff reductions.[28] Whigs like Ebrington declared their support for Wellington as he had demonstrated that he was willing to govern in the popular interest and had sloughed off the old corruption associated with government, such as in the use of crown patronage at elections.[29] There was no contest in many of the largest and most open seats: not in London, Middlesex or Westminster, nor in Coventry or Leicester, all of which had seen famous contests in the very recent past.

In many other constituencies, respectable opinion was anxious to avoid the violence, expense and divisiveness of a contest. By 1830, it was the norm in most boroughs, as in most counties, for the representation to be divided between whig and tory. In 1790, only 36 of the 89 two-member English boroughs not controlled by boroughowners had returned one whig and one tory, but in 1830 the figure in these seats was 55. The aim was to represent all leading interests in the town. It was increasingly fashionable to see the splitting of the borough representation as 'the proper course', because of 'the contrariety of expressed opinions on political questions'.[30] Only if a party overwhelmingly dominated the borough could it return its second-string candidate above the first-choice man of the opposition. So it was difficult to find second-string candidates willing to foot their share of the enormous bill which a contest would entail. By 1830, the prevailing cry, as Holland put it, was 'save me, and save my money'.[31] Splitting the representation also preserved the amity which was thought essential if the borough was to continue to function as a harmonious community for living and trading. In Chester, for example, the animosity of the 1826 election was accused of harming the town's business, and the Grosvenors decided in 1830 to cede one seat to their opponents.[32] In three constituencies recently surveyed, at least one-third, and in one case over one-half, of voters split their choice between parties.[33] The implication of these tendencies for Westminster politics was that there were strict limits to opposition strength; it could not use the electoral system to sweep to office.

Superficially, all these developments indicated Wellington's power. Neither in parliament nor in the constituencies was there much prospect of a coherent movement to overthrow him. As long as the government looked neither unpatriotic nor exclusive, it was almost impossible for the opposition to challenge it successfully. But, lacking strong tory support, Wellington faced another problem. He had to show an ability to deal efficiently and promptly with popular grievances. By 1829, public expectations of government were so high that its survival depended on the continuing appearance of 'liberality'. The question at Westminster was now less one of ideological dispute between government and opposition, than of the responsiveness of government to vigorous popular concerns. As Greville remarked in June 1829, 'if Government have no opponents they have no great body of supporters on whom they can depend'.[34] Wellington had cut loose from traditional moorings and was floating with the current of public sentiment. For someone who despised the manipulative management of opinion, this was an uncomfortable position.

Public opinion rampant, 1829–30

Unfortunately, a severe depression set in in the winter of 1829–30. Public opinion seemed reluctant to follow the guidance of the governing classes. Instead, it appeared splintered and restless. The depression created a heady cocktail of views. It heightened gentry, middle-class and intelligentsia fears of social and moral collapse; it increased clamour for government to respond by legislative initiative, with a view to imposing authority and advancing Christian values; and it highlighted the apathy and selfishness of those MPs who seemed indifferent to the situation.

In early 1830, one London commentator observed country gentlemen returning from their estates, all talking of 'universally prevailing' and worsening distress, 'of the failure of rents all over England, and the necessity of some decisive measures or the prospect of general ruin'.[35] Grey, in Durham, described 'distress so general and intense as was never before experienced; the public, without much distinction of party, calling out with one voice and in a tone that must be heard, for relief'.[36] Agitation took various forms. First and foremost were demands for more economy. There were county meetings of the traditional sort – twenty-two between January and March – held under the aegis of the local gentry in order to press for lower taxes and purer government. Complaints about excessive taxation and high national debt repayments revived resentment, from the gentry downwards, about fundholders, government pensioners and sinecurists. There was also a more specialised campaign by farmers for the abolition of the malt tax, which was said not only to be an unfair burden in itself but also to have cut the consumption of their barley, in order to put some £4.5 million in the pockets of fundholders.

The economic crisis badly affected public psychology. The depression generated considerable insecurity among the propertied, which created a moral panic, a demand for the purification of social values by political action. Even without the depression, one would expect some middle-class anxiety, because rapid economic growth was eroding established notions of social rank. As one commentator wrote in 1829: 'the fluctuations of property is [sic] so rapid, that he who is poor today may be by some fortunate speculation rich tomorrow, & the great capitalist may be at once plunged into poverty'.[37] In 1829 and 1830, apocalyptic tension was particularly liable to affect the religious classes. Perhaps society was in turmoil because God was working out his purpose and was dispensing just punishment to those who failed to abide by divine laws. Few values were more deep-rooted than the idea of the free-born English Protestant, attached to his property and suspicious of 'artificiality' in religion or the economy. Even proposals for small shifts in policy, such as minor differences of opinion among politicians about the proper level of protection for corn, might become sensitive because they appeared to threaten these values. More frightening was the emancipation of Irish Catholics in 1829. It stirred great concern among English Protestants who already felt economically insecure and anxious about national morality in the face of apparently rising crime and pauperism, attacks on abuses in the church establishment, and the growth of religious heterodoxy and infidelity. In general, rural and small-town opinion was unsettled and anxious for reassurance. It is important not to assume that tories would necessarily benefit from such a climate; opinion was more likely to criticise ministers' inaction and to campaign for bold purifying measures.

One area in which tension was rising was between Anglicans and Dissenters, undermining the philanthropic cooperation which had characterised the 1810s. One cause of this was local electoral conflict in the 1820s over Catholic Emancipation, which a lot of nonconformists supported from hostility to state 'repression' of minorities.* Then the church rate issue emerged in several towns in the late 1820s, usually in consequence of the building of 'parliamentary churches' after the 1818 act. Radical Dissenters who did not wish to contribute to the cost of their upkeep argued that the special costs involved in establishing *new* churches (such as the legal costs of enclosing land) should be met entirely by voluntary means. In several London parishes, for example St Pancras, battles over the levying of church

---

* This was not the universal attitude. Dissent was in fact divided and confused, given its unshakeable loathing of the superstitious errors of Papists.

rates for new parish churches led to a campaign against extravagant select vestries.[38]*

The most striking manifestation of unrestrained religious fervour was the growing militancy of the movement for the abolition of colonial slavery. There had been a long tradition of campaigning on slavery, from the late 1780s against the slave trade, and then from the early 1820s against the institution itself. Originally, the Anti-Slavery Society aimed to lead slaves to become more useful, moral and aware members of society, to Christianise them and to make them more aware of their social obligations; emancipation might then become feasible. It was a dignified, even complacent society, drawing strength from a late eighteenth-century humanitarian rationalism according to which slavery was the negation of the attributes of true manhood, the denial of the regulated liberty that allowed men to develop a rounded character and to progress toward the ideal envisaged by God. Its prevailing sentiment until the late 1820s was that by continued pressure on parliament, gradual progress would be made towards a victory for justice. As Dickens wrote, 'charity must have its romance';[39] and the chance to succour and civilise semi-naked bodies suffering under the whiplash in the tropical heat possessed an attraction for propertied philanthropists and their ladies with which the pale, stunted, dishevelled and faintly menacing domestic factory workforce could not compete.

But in late 1829, under the impact of domestic depression, a fervour for 'immediate' emancipation, previously confined to a very small minority of religious enthusiasts, began to take wider root, particularly among the evangelical classes. They superimposed on humanitarian sentiments an anxiety about the divine judgment that awaited a nation too sinful to do its duty in freeing slaves to receive God's message of salvation. The renewed evidence that the economy had not attained a happy state of equilibrium suggested divine displeasure at national and individual sinfulness. Immediate emancipation was urged especially by men who were impatient of the impurities and complacency of institutionalised religion and who attached great importance to the role of the divinely-guided individual in regenerating society. Compromise with corruption merely contaminated the soul. In the words of the leading immediatist agitator Joseph Sturge, 'whenever we take up anything on religious principles, we should act upon it, without reference to consequences'; God would take care of those.[40] In September 1829, the Yorkshire Protestant Dissenters' Association for the Abolition of Slavery was formed with the intention of agitating for an abolition bill in 1830. When parliament assembled in February 1830, the Anti-Slavery Society itself began to change gear, initiating a petitioning campaign and employing a travelling agent to galvanise the provinces into action. Reports

* These campaigns prompted an act of 1831, 'Hobhouse's Act', which allowed ratepayers in any parish of sufficient size to elect a select vestry. But it was hardly used outside London.

of maltreatment of missionaries in the West Indies increased the sense of urgency, and in May 1830 the ASS conference formally adopted the strategy of immediatism. Now was revealed the immense latent power of religious fervour and utopian idealism in the English middle classes, and especially among Protestant Dissenters. For most of the latter it was their first involvement with national politics, their first attempt actively to fight the sinfulness of the depraved, effete, materialist high political world which they had traditionally shunned.

Two developments of 1830 intensified propertied anxiety for social stability. One was rising levels of lower-class radical activity. The Birmingham Political Union, founded in 1829, called for parliamentary reform as a means of attacking the tight currency policy of the 1820s, which it blamed for the depression. This alarmed those who believed that economic prosperity demanded the pursuit of strict principles of political economy. More serious threats were the mainstream Unions founded on old radical arguments about the political rights of working-men, which called for manhood suffrage, annual parliaments and the ballot. The model for these was the Metropolitan Political Union, established in London in March 1830. Such organisations might easily incite popular hostility to irresponsible, effete, 'pantomimical' court and aristocratic government, on the lines most influentially sketched out by Tom Paine in *The rights of man* forty years before.

More disturbing still to respectable opinion was the rise in pauperism as a result of agricultural unemployment. There were three worries: high poor rates, the threat of rural riots as in 1816, and possible economic ruin through the spread of pauperism and its social consequences. Local expenditure from the poor rate rose from £5.78 million in 1823 to £6.83 million in 1830, a level which, given deflation after 1819, matched the all-time high point of 1818. One-third of the population of Preston was receiving poor relief in 1830. The standard myth held by the respectable classes was that the thrifty were being crippled by high rates in order to pay for the pleasures of the self-indulgent indolent, who had no incentive to limit family size. Farmers, meanwhile, tended to employ only labourers in receipt of relief, so reducing opportunities for non-paupers and institutionalising pauperism. Demands for Poor Law reform were expressed frequently at the 1830 general election.

Magistrates were often blamed for their leniency in overruling strict relief levels imposed by local Poor Law officers. In 1832, the mayor of Lincoln ignored three rates granted before the Justices, and refused to levy any.[41] Anxieties about rising crime levels similarly led to grass-roots complaints at the leniency of magistrates' discretionary justice. Again, the desire of JPs to act as mediators between rural classes in order to defuse social tension clashed with the increasing concern about lawlessness expressed by 'respectable' opinion. Magistrates' lassitude was sometimes contrasted (not always fairly) with their eagerness to safeguard their own property by enforcing unduly punitive laws protecting game from poaching gangs. One observer noted as early as 1826 that magistrates' incompetence was leading to a 'pretty general feeling' against the squirearchy.[42] In 1830, when money was tight, this questioning of authority often extended to the parson: the church's demand for tithe was resented by hard-pressed farmers who believed that the church was wealthy enough to do without it and too inactive to merit it.

These tensions were creating something of a consensus among 'thinking men' that more activity was needed from central and local administration. Many younger politicians, tory and whig, were affected by the fashionable science of political economy, which, by interpreting and classifying human behaviour, sought to offer suggestions on questions not just of taxation and tariffs, but also of pauperism, policing and punishment. A great debate about how best to shape individual character was under way among clergymen, philanthropists, politicians and philosophers, in magazines like the *Edinburgh Review* and organisations like the Society for the Diffusion of Useful Knowledge and the Political Economy Club. Here were emerging classic Victorian concerns about government's responsibility to establish more effective mechanisms for securing social order, and to stimulate local initiatives to shape character so that citizens could develop the fortitude and skill to operate within the natural order. Depression brought out the burgeoning intelligentsia's disdain for the genteel, materialist silver-fork values of high society. Literary opinion, from Thomas Love Peacock (*The Misfortunes of Elphin*, 1829) to Thomas Arnold, the new headmaster of Rugby, advocated the leadership of a wise and propertied class. Most of these men believed that that leadership must be founded on devout Christian values. Arnold equated the prevailing toryism with 'indolence and corruption'. He believed that the selfishness of national and local rulers, who attempted to obstruct the law of 'eternal progress', was heaping up divine 'wrath'. His principal solution was the reconstruction of the church as a truly national, integrative and conscientious body which would 'introduce the principles of Christianity into men's social and civil relations'.[43] Rather similar but even more apocalyptic views were being put forward in the periodical press by a vigorous and earnest young Scottish writer, Thomas Carlyle. Like Arnold, he believed that a regenerated aristocracy were the natural rulers of society, the only class which could discipline the passions of public opinion. But he poured scorn on the dilettantism and complacency of current rulers. 'Religion, the *cement* of *society*' was missing. Parliamentary reform would solve little; the 'whole frame of society is rotten'.[44] Also urging '*directive* Government', tapping the 'energy' of the people by utilising 'profound knowledge' of their 'character' in order to supply 'prompt and efficient legislation', were a group of more heterodox young thinkers in London literary circles, who drew inspiration from Jeremy Bentham and James Mill. These included a number of future notable Liberals, from Poulett Thomson, Charles Villiers and Edward Lytton Bulwer to Joseph Parkes, J.A. Roebuck and John Stuart Mill. They pinned their faith in the directing influence of a rational intelligentsia, which they saw imposing systems of education, public health, prosecution, punishment, and poverty prevention.[45]

In short, in the unprecedented turbulence of 1830, we can identify criticism of magistrates and the church, increasing evidence of division between Anglicans and Dissenters and to some extent between agricultural and urban interests, highly-charged anti-slavery activity, clamour for far-reaching reform from Political Unions, and a general expectation that some legislative activity was necessary in order to restore authority and shape social development for good. Between 1827 and 1831, 24,492 petitions were presented to parliament on all these subjects as against 4,498 between 1811 and 1815.[46] It was, then, extremely unlucky for the government that George IV died in June 1830. For all his obstinacy and insults, he never harmed his ministers as much in life as in death. An election had to follow. Almost every candidate for an open seat felt obliged to declare in favour of some ameliorative action; almost every MP returned to parliament pledged to work for economy and purification.

Three aspects of the 1830 election are especially noteworthy. The first, and most important, was the activity in a small number of county seats, traditionally the litmus of public opinion. In all of them, it seemed, 'small gentlemen' and 'independent farmers' were demonstrating dissatisfaction with traditional aristocratic leadership.[47] Particularly striking was the victory of Henry Brougham in Yorkshire. Brougham was the whigs' most extraordinary star, a frenetic, glib, relentless lawyer, who was also educational campaigner, *Edinburgh* journalist and aspiring *savant*: 'if he had known a little law he would have known a little of everything'.[48] He presented himself as a symbol of mind's victory over breeding – in which he was indeed singularly deficient – and sought to sweep the country on that appeal. A true intellectual, his bitter grudge against the aristocracy – his only consistent principle, according to his enemies – alarmed the whig leaders as much as tories. He was nominated for Yorkshire, the most prestigious county seat in England, by the Leeds manufacturers; his principal cry was hostility to slavery, on which he roused the Dissenters. The slavery question dominated other elections from Buckinghamshire to Bristol.[49] In the event, there was no *contest* in Yorkshire. But there were major battles in five county seats, Cambridgeshire, Devon, Norfolk, Suffolk and Surrey. These dominated election coverage because of the clash of issues raised in all of them. The battle lay, not between government and opposition, but between old tory MPs and 'liberal' independents. In all five counties, one candidate – always a whig or an independently-minded tory anxious to please the less wealthy electors – was more or less guaranteed victory, and the struggle was for the second seat. These were between a sitting tory MP, and a new candidate, sometimes whig, but usually the non-partisan candidate of the independent yeomen and/or of the aroused Dissenters hostile to slavery. In all five the issues were much the same: the old tory was accused of being apathetic in conducting his duties, and especially in failing to vote for retrenchment. Some of the tories were smeared with allegations of corruption or complicity in the old order, by virtue of connections with boroughmongers (Manners in Cambridgeshire, Jolliffe in Surrey) or personal place-hunting (Gooch in Suffolk). Some (Wodehouse in Norfolk) refused to pledge to vote for retrenchment, others (Bastard in Devon) for the abolition of slavery. In Norfolk especially, the independent candidate was associated with the farmers' campaign for malt tax repeal. Most squires, yeomen farmers, and small-town nonconformists supported the independent candidates, all of whom declared against slavery and for strict economies, and most for moderate parliamentary reform. Nearly all of them stood free of expense, their expenses being paid for by their supporters. And all five 'independents' won: Adeane in Cambridgeshire, Ebrington in Devon, Tyrell in Suffolk, Briscoe in Surrey and Folkes in Norfolk (the last forced his opponent to stand down before going to the poll). In Huntingdonshire and Leicestershire, similar candidates of the independent squirearchy ran established tory family interests close.[50]

The second interesting aspect of the election was the heightened criticism of 'vested interests'. Opponents of slavery pointed to the pressure of apparently powerful blocs of 'West Indian' sentiment in the Commons. Others demanded abolition of the East India Company's trading monopoly in China, or criticised the influence of 'fundholders' and City interests. At Bridgnorth, battle was joined between 'liberal' Birmingham and Manchester commercial interests and anti-slavery men on the one hand, and a coalition of Indian and protectionist influences on the other. Some whigs fighting urban seats stood on the platform of hostility to particular monopolies of local concern – the Corn Laws, the East India Company, the Bank of England – and sometimes to *all* economic monopolies.

Third, there was anger at borough corporations which attempted to repress public electoral criticism. Corporation control had been exercised in two sorts of boroughs. Some had a franchise limited to members of the corporation itself, which was usually either self-electing or nominated by one or two local patrons. In others, there was a wider franchise, usually a freeman franchise, which the corporation regulated through its powers of nomination and patronage. In the larger towns, corporation power had for some time been weakened by rising general prosperity, by heightened local expectations about politics, and by corporate financial mismanagement. For instance, the corporation interest had been destroyed in Northampton, Reading, Great Yarmouth and Worcester by the 1820s, and was only intermittently successful in Coventry and Leicester. But this meant that corporation attempts to influence elections became all the more notorious, as in Leicester and Northampton in 1826. In 1830, challenges to their influence were made even in small, tightly-managed boroughs, either because of the infiltration of a stranger with money, or simply because of increased resentment and politicisation among the townspeople. The dominant whig interest in Bedford was upset at the hands of a tory brewer. In Queenborough there was a successful challenge to the official candidates nominated by local burgesses who had put the townspeople out of work by arranging the sale of the local oyster grounds for private gain. And in a lot of small boroughs – such as Marlborough, Wendover, Truro, Dartmouth, Hythe, Rye and Hastings – the restricted nature of the franchise was disputed by townspeople who claimed that their electoral rights had been usurped by a corporation or other interest.[51]

The depression, and the bad publicity gained by 'vested' electoral interests, was bound to direct attention to the representative system itself. As in previous economic downturns, calls for government economy were ritually twinned with demands for 'Reform'. Whig and many tory candidates mouthed platitudes about its desirability – as long as the proposals were 'moderate' or 'well-considered'. This meant little. Apart from those individuals long interested in the question, few candidates fleshed out these thoughts coherently, and it is unlikely that most thought of more than the enfranchisement of a few large towns and disfranchisement of a few corrupt boroughs. Parliamentary reform was certainly not the major issue of the election. Only fourteen petitions had been presented to parliament for Reform throughout the 1830 session. But the election did return many MPs pledged to criticise government complacency and incompetence. They wished to see ministers take action to restore social and moral discipline and respect for authority, and they believed that government needed more support in parliament. The 1830 election made it clear that Wellington could not continue otherwise: 'public opinion was never so decided against the Tories, though I think it is in favour of the Duke of Wellington and Sir Robert Peel'.[52] Parliamentary reform arrived on the agenda at Westminster in the autumn of 1830 *not* because popular clamour put it there but because MPs came to see it as a litmus test of the government's willingness to do two things: to take bold, responsive action, and to broaden its basis. How did this happen?

The fall of Wellington

After the election, the government's lassitude and weakness became the major political problem. The 1830 session had already revealed the difficulties which it faced in giving a lead. In almost every field, it faced many demands for action, but the variety of suggestions left it in no position to force legislation through the unreformed, undisciplined but opinionated Commons. In early June, one cabinet minister, Ellenborough, complained that 'with such a Parliament there is no depending upon the carrying of any measure, and Peel is quite disgusted'.[53]

The most urgent need was for further reductions in expenditure and taxation. In March, the government was beaten on a pensions motion. Some tory and whig politicians, interested in political economy and observing the changes in national wealth and revenue patterns, were advocating the introduction of an income tax for a fixed number of years. Peel supported this, thinking that it would provide a steady and adequate revenue immune from parliamentary sniping; it might also allow a more 'rational' tariff policy. All Commons cabinet ministers supported it. But Wellington vetoed it, thinking that it would alienate the bulk of property-owners and the City, thus losing the government backing from both county and close borough MPs, as well as stimulating whig criticism of executive extravagance and 'tyranny'.[54] So government financial policy drifted. Two budgets had to be introduced, one in March and one in June. And ministers' proposed reform of the sugar duties had to be abandoned after it was attacked by Huskisson.

Another great problem was the state of the Poor Law. Abolition was not politically practicable, since many feared that it would prompt revolution.[55] For some time, all sorts of reform proposals had been mooted, such as the abolition of allowances, a recalculation of the liability for the poor rate, the creation of allotments to encourage self-reliance, assisted emigration, and the exploitation of waste lands. But some of these would achieve little, while any effective solution would have unpleasant social and therefore political consequences, and Wellington's government was too weak to dare to stir these up. Peel and Wellington could only apologise that the more the Poor Law was studied, 'the more difficult it was to come to a positive conclusion'; 'it was almost impossible to deal with it successfully'.[56] The government offered no help to any of the schemes for amendment proposed by individual MPs between 1828 and 1830. There was a similar impasse on the proposal that a Poor Law should be introduced into Ireland.

Nor was action forthcoming on Irish or colonial issues. Peel's Irish reform package was blocked. He introduced a bill to establish a national system of armed stipendiary police under the direct control of the Irish government, but it was shot down by whig and gentry opposition, on the grounds that it unduly increased the powers of the state. He planned to impose a national education system very similar to that subsequently established by the whigs, but the Irish Office warned that this would be unpopular among both Protestants and Catholics, and the cabinet believed that reform would inflame the religious question. A bill which allowed the Lord Lieutenant to set up a commission with wide powers to loan money for drainage schemes, with a view to agricultural improvement and the reduction of unemployment, failed on the same grounds as the police bill. Meanwhile, government could not pacify anti-slavery clamour. The West Indian legislatures had obviously failed to obey Canning's eight-point programme of 1823. But an attempt to enforce them more directly would probably incite a movement for colonial independence and perhaps also bloody slave risings. The timidity, inefficiency and poor presentation of Sir George Murray, the Colonial Secretary, made the government look weak. Meanwhile, Wellington prevented action on the future of the East India Company, whose charter was due for renewal in 1833, and whose swollen bureaucracy had caused the accumulation of large debts. Ellenborough, the cabinet minister responsible, wanted the government to take direct control of the administration of India, and to remove the Company's monopoly over the China trade. This would be extremely popular with merchant and manufacturing opinion and would lower prices of consumer goods imported from the East. But Wellington disagreed, believing that the old alliance between the government, the East India Company directors and the City was mutually beneficial to all three – especially to a government anxious not to offend close borough MPs.[57]

Wellington may have been right that, given the turbulent and undisciplined state of the Commons, government could not afford to lose the support of any major elements. But his strategy paradoxically suggested that 'strong' government involved being unwilling to take initiatives. Deaf and isolated, he was amazed at the volume of advice on policy questions constantly flooding into his office from 'nearly every gentleman in England, who has nothing to do but to amuse himself, and is tired of his usual amusements'.[58] Contemptuous of modish 'liberal' rhetoric, he sought refuge in the comforting but flawed idea that the simple maintenance of government dignity would suffice to ride out the storm. Peel had a different, more activist view of government's policy responsibilities, at least on tax, law and Irish questions. But his rigid refusal to bow to gentry pressure for any infringement of pure market principles in currency or poor law matters suggested to most onlookers that he also was fatalistic in response to depression.

Wellington's greatest failing was in not projecting an image of competent, responsive authority. The government badly lacked effective Commons speakers. Wellington was especially criticised for appointing two old army colleagues to replace the departing Canningites of 1828, Palmerston and Huskisson. From then on Sir George Murray and Sir Henry Hardinge were singled out for attack for their inarticulateness, poor image and military connections; some 'likened their minds to cartridge paper'.[59] Herries and Goulburn were also pedantic and uninspiring. Only Peel gave off an air of competence, and this was damaged by aloofness and condescension. The lack of activity in cabinet, Wellington's temperamental dislike of appearing weak in the face of public clamour, and his brusque army style, combined to create an image of his leadership which could be made to seem un-English. It suggested 'an overweening opinion of his own all-sufficiency'.[60] Some said that he aimed to be king in all but name. The radical Durham scorned his 'odious, insulting, degrading, aide-de-campish, incapable dictatorship'.[61] Especially contemptuous of his blundering as 'sole minister' were those intellectual whigs and Benthamites who hoped to tackle the complex issues of government by a systematic application of the discoveries of 'the science of national economy and of legislation'.[62]

Public anxiety mounted as 1830 wore on. One contributory factor was the upheavals on the Continent: the overthrow of Charles X of France at the end of July, and the proclamation of Belgian independence from the Dutch in October. This gave added impetus to the revival of working-class political protest; twenty-seven Political Unions existed by November. But more serious was the return of large-scale rick-burning in parts of south-eastern England badly hit by agricultural unemployment, in October and

November. There had in fact been sporadic outbreaks since August, mainly in protest at the tight administration of poor relief. Although there was in truth little evidence of any link with organised radicalism, the outbreaks caused genuine alarm. One commentator noted in October that the 'whole civilised world seems to be in commotion. All will be for good in *the end*; but I cannot help dreading the *process*.'[63] As the political crisis deepened in 1830–1 (accompanied by a cholera epidemic), there were many outpourings of apocalyptic sentiment that, out of this ferment of unguided opinion there must emerge a reign of 'pure Christianity', of 'justice and religion'.[64] The young Oxford don Mozley was to write that at this time 'almost every middle-class family' believed that, if it could 'have the management of public affairs but for a very short period, it could and would entirely regenerate the world . . . everything was wrong, yet capable of being effectually, and almost instantly rectified'.[65]

By the autumn of 1830, there was anger from all sides at the inability of the government to introduce measures which might inspire respect for authority. 'The effervescence of public opinion' was widely blamed on government weakness.[66] Even a journalist as hostile to parliamentary reform as Southey discerned a general feeling that its 'pitiable manner' in the 1830 session made it 'plainly impossible that the administration could proceed'.[67] But the almost universal hope was, not that Wellington would resign, but that he would display enough political flexibility to welcome the opposition aboard. It had been generally understood that etiquette forbade any offer to Grey while George IV, who had long disliked him, was dying. It was as firmly assumed by many whigs that, on the king's death, Wellington must make him an overture. But none had come. By August there was widespread astonishment that he would not 'open his doors to all who are capable of serving under him'.[68] In his anger at the ebbing authority of his own government, Wellington unbent far enough by October to try to win the small group of a dozen Huskissonites for the government, a task made much less painful by the fortuitous scything down of their generally distrusted leader by Stephenson's Rocket on 15 September. But Palmerston and Melbourne, now heads of this dwindling band, were canny enough to realise that government survival depended on the introduction of whigs as well, and that the only people to suffer, if they joined a sinking ship, would be themselves.

However, Wellington could not face leading a coalition government which included prominent whigs. This was because their presence would strengthen the case for some action on parliamentary reform. Wellington believed that, once a new coalition government began to toy with Reform, it would become powerless against whig pressure for a much more advanced scheme, one impossible for him to accept with honour.

His attitude put whigs in a dilemma. By October Russell remarked that Wellington had lost the greater part of his strength, 'the authority of his name'.[69] Without organised whig help it now seemed impossible to discipline the Commons for the purpose of good government, something which had been alarming Grey since June.[70] One problem was the inflammatory international situation. Wellington had initially reacted with studied moderation to the French and Belgian revolutions, but Grey feared that he might adopt 'Holy Alliance' principles in order to recoup popularity with backbench tories, endangering the state of Europe.[71] At home, government seemed too dependent on the shifting sands of popular sentiment, 'the sport of every breath that blows'.[72] This was quite unacceptable in the context of the riots of late 1830. In later life, Russell vividly recalled the breakdown of rural authority at that time, as labourers were left to poach, loot and fire property and to demand maintenance from the parish for an expanding family.[73] 'Anonymous monopolists of the press' seemed to be leading the people, rather than representatives in parliament.[74] Wellington had secured a spurious independence from public opinion at the price of pathetically 'avoiding defeats by concessions' to odd groups of MPs. This destroyed the legitimate authority of government, which depended on the exercise of rational and honourable judgment.[75] Activist whigs blamed this state of affairs on the collapse of a two-party system at Westminster; that alone could permanently rally opinion under propertied leadership. Holland, even in 1826, had been concerned that the obvious recent decline in party cohesion would lead to a state divided 'between Interests and Countries and religions, grower and consumer, Irishmen and Englishmen, Protestants and Catholicks'.[76]

Whig MPs looked to Althorp for leadership. While other whigs had been lax in criticising Wellington in 1829–30, he had continued to insist on further large expenditure cuts. His strategy, of going on the offensive against the government if it had not strengthened its position by the opening of the new session in November, was now party policy.[77] But, as in the early 1820s, there was no issue on which whigs could successfully threaten the government unless they won the support of MPs outside their ranks. The country gentlemen were dubious allies, not only on Reform, but because William IV still wished Wellington to continue in power. The leading Huskissonites, Melbourne and Palmerston, were unsympathetic to radical Reform (Palmerston had held government office from 1809 to 1828). Russell had floated schemes in the 1830 session, but they were deliberately toned down in extent, because the fluid parliamentary situation still left open the possibility of coalition government. In February Grey had urged his son not to come out strongly for parliamentary reform, since there was no lasting popular feeling on the subject.[78] In the autumn, as the prospect of coalition faded, Brougham threatened to propose a radical Reform scheme, which the leadership feared would marginalise the party. Brougham was firmly told not to advocate any specific plan. Instead, he gave notice that he would shortly move merely for a select committee to investigate the state of the representation. Even this was 'coldly received' in the Commons.[79] When Grey arrived in London in early November, he continued to think that the country was not prepared for parliamentary reform, and supported it coolly, without much expectation of success.[80]

But Wellington also had a dilemma as parliament opened. The government needed to counter the sense of drift, impose its authority, and woo middle-ground and moderate MPs with a symbol of its responsiveness. The most effective gesture would be to offer token parliamentary reform, probably the enfranchisement of a few large commercial boroughs and some minor changes in the conduct of elections. Rumours circulated that Wellington would do this, just as he had dealt firmly and promptly with the Emancipation problem in 1829. But he believed that to announce a plan of moderate Reform would upset some tories while encouraging the whigs to outbid him. A declaration *against* Reform would warn the opposition to drop the subject; if they did not, he probably assumed that Brougham's radicalism would frighten floating MPs into the government's arms and strengthen its own authority.

So on 2 November, Wellington declared, with habitual brusqueness, against all Reform schemes hitherto aired. Unfortunately, his ill-chosen words and inflexible tone had an enormous impact on opinion. They caused general astonishment. The whig MP Campbell thought that 'if Ministers had even remained silent about Reform they would have been powerfully supported'.[81] But his rigid stance seemed to demonstrate his lack of realism about his prospects without fresh support, while the whig motion of inquiry appeared to county MPs to be a better reflection of the country's opinions expressed at the election. Wellington's cabinet colleagues advised him to announce his own select committee into the system, which would buy off county MPs yet be easily controlled by government sources, but he refused.[82] Instead, he submitted a tactical resignation on 15 November, having suffered a symbolic defeat on a lesser issue (the proposed civil list) at the hands of an alliance of whigs, Huskissonites, a section of violent 'ultras' led by Knatchbull and Vyvyan, and a large number of country gentlemen keen on economy and eager to please their constituents; only 15 of 82 English county MPs supported the government. This meant that Brougham's motion, due for discussion the next day, could be avoided.

Wellington must have thought that the whigs would be unable to agree on a Reform scheme and that, failing to form a ministry, they would let him back in with renewed authority and no damage to his character. In retrospect, it is easy to identify his tactical blunders. But the whigs would not have stood a chance of winning power in November 1830 had the radicalism of their Reform Bill been widely anticipated. The problem in 1830 was not clamour for Reform as such, but ministers' failure to offer reassurance that they were capable of bold measures to boost fragile public confidence and social and moral order. So many MPs became willing to see *some* parliamentary reform. It would assist and symbolise government responsiveness to public complaints, and offer the prospect of a broader, more authoritative governing coalition. This did not mean that the propertied classes were radical on Reform. Indeed, the reaction against the effects of the 1832 act was to power the tory revival throughout the 1830s.

Had the whigs been an aggressive opposition in 1830, they would not have been trusted with office. Luck, on their side throughout the year, allowed them to effect a remarkable coup and transform British politics.

CHAPTER 3

The whigs and parliamentary reform

THE MOST IMPORTANT consequence of the change in government in 1830 was the 1832 Reform Act. There are two widely-held, linked assumptions about that act. One is that popular pressure, rather than whig intentions, was the greatest influence on its shape. The other is that it was a 'conservative', defensive measure, a 'concession' to extra-parliamentary forces. These interpretations seriously undervalue the significance of whig Reform principles, which are the subject of this chapter. The 1832 act was a watershed in British politics, a conscious attempt by whig leaders to take advantage of the opportunity of 1830 to make permanent alterations to political structures.

The importance of the events of 1829–30 was that they demonstrated lack of popular attachment to government. This certainly made Reform more widely *acceptable*. In particular, men like the Canningites Melbourne and Palmerston who had previously opposed it, but now accepted office under Grey, argued that only social turbulence had changed their minds.[1] But of course this was the only line that they could take; it does not prove that the act itself was a concession to a coherent public campaign for Reform. The Reform Bill was drawn up by whigs whose interest in the question was not sudden and tactical, but genuine and long-standing. It was essentially the work of six men: Grey, the new Prime Minister, Althorp, the Leader of the House of Commons, and the four members of the government subcommittee charged with preparing the legislation. Most policy at this time emerged from conclaves of a sort, not from the full cabinet. Indeed the 'Committee of Four' contained two ministers from outside the cabinet, Russell and the ex-whip Duncannon (together with Graham and Durham). These men too were affected by the threat to authority revealed in 1830, but this strengthened a pre-existing Reforming outlook. Though they were aristocrats, and naturally wished to preserve the political predominance of the propertied classes, it does not follow that their act had no more radical aims. It went further than most politicians and public opinion believed was necessary, and it profoundly altered constitutional relationships. By a bold redistribution of seats (much more important than its franchise provisions), it gave parliament and indirectly 'the people' the power to overthrow

72

governments on a regular basis. It sought to reconcile the people to government leadership by emphasising the representativeness of parliament as the protector of interests and the expression of the national will. Most importantly, by raising the reputation of parliament in the public mind, it created the conditions for much more active government, and thus it was the precondition for the Liberal politics discussed in the rest of the book.

The whig tradition and the constitution

To say that the whig party had been in opposition to government for nearly fifty years before 1830 is actually to understate the case. The whigs invented the notion of a permanent party of opposition. It was their *raison d'être* to criticise the extravagance, corruption and exclusiveness of the king's ministers. They charged them with conspiring to suppress the liberties of the country, especially during and immediately after the French wars, in three vital ways: by levying unnecessary taxation, by restricting civil liberty through the passage of special repressive legislation, and by discriminating against religious minorities. They set out the possibility of an alternative model of politics in which men like them, bound together by ties of honour and patriotism, would safeguard the liberties and protect the pockets of the people. Argument, allegation and agitation of this sort over fifty years established a series of ineradicable myths about the traditions and function of whiggery. These centred on the heroism of the framers of the 1688/9 constitutional settlement; on the thwarting of their ideals of free representation by subsequent tory abuse of government favours and by the unchecked impact of new, unscrupulous wealth on corruptible voters; and on the duty of those aristocratic families not degraded by crown patronage to restore lost liberties. At the heart of whig thinking was the notion that the aristocracy were the natural leaders and protectors of the people, the peers in the Upper House, their heirs, relatives and connections playing a vital part in the Lower. After the Reform Act was passed, the old whig stalwart Coke of Holkham erected a bas-relief in his house depicting William IV signing it in the guise of King John, with the whig leaders representing the barons of Runnymede. Three aristocratic connections were especially significant in whiggery. The first included eight great landed families, many of whose members had been prominent whigs in earlier centuries and were interrelated many times over by marriage. Their heads – Bedford, Devonshire, Sutherland,* Westminster, Bessborough, Carlisle, Spencer and Fitzwilliam – included some of the greatest peers in the country. The

---

* Stafford until 1833. When the marquess of Stafford was created duke of Sutherland in that year, his became the fourth successive generation of the Leveson-Gower family to be promoted in the peerage (marquess of Stafford 1786, Earl Gower 1746, Baron Gower 1709). The first duke's brother was created Viscount Granville in 1815 and Earl Granville in 1833; his son was also to be an important Liberal.

heirs to these titles were often to play an important part in Commons politics as, respectively, Lords Tavistock, Hartington, Stafford, Grosvenor, Duncannon, Morpeth, Althorp and Milton. The second was the Holland House connection which derived its fame from the whig leader between 1782 and 1806, Charles James Fox. Fox's nephew, Lord Holland, and his wife, ran a famous whig salon. Holland tutored many young whigs into political maturity, most significantly Lord John Russell, a younger son of the sixth duke of Bedford. The third was the family of Charles, second Earl Grey, a radical Foxite in the 1790s and the leader of the whig party from 1806 until 1834. This included his son and heir Lord Howick and his son-in-law J.G. Lambton, created Lord Durham in 1828.

Their traditional hostility to tory exclusiveness made Reform a natural issue for many whigs. But the party as a whole was not, in fact, quick to adopt it. In the 1790s, the party's survival depended on the influence of their great landowners in close boroughs. During the Revolutionary Wars, they stood no chance of getting a parliamentary majority by any scheme of Reform since popular sentiment seemed overwhelmingly tory from either an excess of patriotism or a susceptibility to bribery. They tended to settle for the argument that the best defence of liberty was by the survival, against the odds, of a whig party in the Commons. Party, they claimed, was an honourable bond which allowed common action in order to safeguard libertarian principles. Mutual moral support and pressure helped to prevent individual MPs from succumbing to crown bribes, but so did the existence of small boroughs independent of ministerial pressure. Whigs of Fox's generation talked airily of the liberties of the people, or even, like the duke of Norfolk in 1798, of 'the majesty of the people' – which, in those anti-revolutionary times, earned him the sack as Lord Lieutenant of the West Riding. But it was often not clear what or whom they meant.

However, the early nineteenth century saw a sea-change in the relationship between whiggery and public opinion. On the one hand, many small borough patrons defected to government during the war. On the other, the unpopularity of government, especially after 1806, transformed whig fortunes. The number of MPs giving the party a general support rose from 80–90 in 1801 to 150 in 1812 and just over 200 in 1820.[2] Its social range broadened too. The number of non-tory English MPs who were not primarily landowners rose from 17 per cent to 28 per cent between 1790 and 1831; there came to be 22 lawyers as against 3 in 1790. The whigs' calls for low taxation, opposition to repressive legislation, and criticism of the Regent's extravagance and influence gave them a much higher profile and popularity in the country. The Queen Caroline affair was of particular importance for them in demonstrating the existence of a large body of respectable as well as radical opinion hostile to a government which seemed willing to sacrifice moral principles in order to toady to a profligate monarch. In 1790, 68 per cent of English whig MPs had sat for close boroughs (a higher percentage than of government supporters), but the numbers fell from 123 to 73 (38 per cent) by early 1831, against 177 tories. And 118 whigs, as against 57 in 1790, now sat for English open seats.[3] Whig support in counties, their most popular and prestigious seats, tended to come from independent farmers, the Dissenters, an important minority of gentlemen, and the self-consciously 'town' voters, against the tory aristocratic and gentry estates and their urban connections.* In these seats, even a large estate lacked the ammunition to defeat tories alone. Whigs found it easiest to establish an electoral influence where they could combine a landed base with substantial urban and/or Dissenting support. Fortunately, many great whig families owned land in or near industrial areas: Fitzwilliam in Yorkshire and Lambton in Durham were themselves great industrial magnates, and Sutherland was deeply involved in canals and railways. Carlisle in Cumberland and Yorkshire, Devonshire in Derbyshire, and Grey in Northumberland, were all well situated to capitalise on the urban vote, while other whig grandees, like Coke in Norfolk and Spencer in Northamptonshire, owed their political influence largely to the strength of Protestant Dissent in these counties.†

So, by the late 1810s, whig claims to represent 'the people' had acquired new meaning. It was no longer necessary to live on fading memories of Fox's atypical tribuneship in the borough of Westminster. Many (though not all) whigs revelled in the rhetoric of whole-hearted engagement with popular interests. When Fitzwilliam was dismissed as Lord Lieutenant of the West Riding of Yorkshire in 1819 for vehement criticism of the

---

* Lord John Russell became MP for Huntingdonshire (1820–6) by rousing Dissenters and the whig yeomanry against the duke of Manchester's influence; he blamed his 1826 defeat on 'all the property, all the magistracy, and even the clerk of the peace' being against him. Pendarves, MP for Cornwall, rallied the small gentry, yeomen, tenant farmers and then, from the late 1820s, urban shopkeepers and Dissenters on anti-slavery principles.[4]

† In 1832, Carlisle's son Morpeth, MP for the prestigious West Riding of Yorkshire from 1830, wrote a poem about the great sights of the county, which he defined mainly as whig stately homes and industrial centres. It encapsulates whig confidence in the beneficial moral power of manufacturing. These three verses give a flavour (the subject-matter, in case it is not immediately obvious, is Leeds and its hinterland):

> The muse, less daring than the Argive raft,
> Shrinks from the classic region of the fleece;
> How vain an idle rhymester's idle craft,
> To hymn the trophies of Britannia's peace!
>
> Still, commerce, thine unfettered track pursue,
> Court torrid zephyrs, brave the icy gale,
> Rivet creation's severed links anew,
> With thy light rudder and thy roving sail.
>
> Crowned with the myrtle, vine, and olive leaf,
> Before thy peaceful keel chase gory strife,
> Waft to each want that visits man, relief,
> The lamp of knowledge, and the cross of life.[5]

magistrates' behaviour in the 'Peterloo' affair, he was hailed by other whigs as 'the Father of the People, the Nestor in our day of Freedom'.[6] Lady Cowper wrote in 1821 of the whig peers coming to London 'exulting and triumphant from their country meetings', where they had been 'cheered and drawn and huzza'd'.[7] Lord John Russell's brother wrote to him in 1831: 'I know no sight so grand, as a People roused from their apathy, determined to assert their rights and freedom.'[8] Russell agreed. Nothing distinguished whigs from tories more than the former's willingness to rouse popular agitation. At the 1831 contest, he spoke at a meeting in support of the Reform candidate for the turbulent London borough of Southwark, to tory fury. In October, after the Lords' defeat of the Reform Bill, he caused a much greater outcry when he thanked the Birmingham Political Union for their protest and reassured them that 'it was impossible that the whisper of a faction should prevail against the voice of a nation'.[9] To tories, the faction was the BPU.

Growing popularity, and wartime and postwar discontent, also drew whigs ineluctably into support for parliamentary reform. Brand collected 115 votes for his motion of 1810 (see page 32). From 1819 to 1821, Russell introduced and eventually passed a bill to disfranchise the notoriously corrupt borough of Grampound, exploiting the publicity given to the trial and imprisonment of the bribe-giving candidate Manasseh Lopes – an uneducated second-generation immigrant jewish sugar merchant, and so rather a soft target. Buoyed up by this success, in 1821 Russell introduced four general resolutions on Reform, and in 1822, 1823 and 1826 he brought forward motions with a view to redistributing around a hundred small borough seats to counties and unrepresented towns (the 1822 motion to investigate the question gained 164 votes). By 1821 whig reformers were willing to be seen at the Reform dinner at the City of London, talking with radicals like Burdett.

In the 1820s, Canning frustrated whigs' intentions and undermined some of their arguments. By 1827, the situation appeared so changed that coalition with him, which would certainly not offer Reform, tempted many. These included some who had always been reluctant Reformers (Devonshire, Lansdowne, some whig political economists) but also fiery but inconsistent populists like Lambton, whose reward was a peerage. Yet the coalition failed, and its failure greatly strengthened those who had held aloof from it, principally Grey of the older generation and Althorp of the younger. Grey, a Reformer since the 1790s, had endured decades of opposition, and calumny throughout the war. He had frequently ruled out the prospect of office in a non-Reforming ministry. He could not, then, compromise his honour and hauteur to sit in cabinet under the man he referred to as the son of an actress.[10] For Althorp, Reform was also a necessity: he possessed so intense an aversion to placemen and so strong a zeal for purity as to make compromise with official life a torment even after 1830. The coalition's failure also benefited Russell, who had not taken office and who sought to avert the post-coalition recriminations among divided and embarrassed whigs by raising comforting constitutional questions, first relief for religious minorities and then Reform again. The passage of Catholic Emancipation in 1829 left the whigs bereft of any other ideas; then the discontent of 1830 played into Reformers' hands, and Althorp became Commons leader.

So it was Grey, Althorp and Russell who earned the right to shape the Reform Act of 1832 – and who bore the major burden of its passage. Their attitudes, though, were different, because the basic historical whig principles of liberty and government by consent could be interpreted in various lights by different generations.* Grey's involvement was the legacy of his youth. He had bitterly felt the snub to whig aristocratic honour involved in George III's preference for Pitt as minister. Tory rule, he had argued from the 1790s, was based on political corruption which played on man's natural avarice and sapped public virtue. Pitt had eroded the 'public spirit' and 'independence of mind and conduct' which 'created energy'; the 'strength and safety of the state' depended on the harnessing of 'noble and generous' public sentiments.[11] Calling for the eradication of close boroughs and the recasting of the borough franchise, he argued that the alternative was the decay of national morals, as had happened in the ancient world. As he aged, Grey became pessimistic: 'we were in the old age of our country, everything rotten, corrupt, and worn out'.[12] By the 1830s, the implementation of his long-held Reform principles served mainly to vindicate his honour. He never believed that the act would inaugurate the millennium. When, after its passage, a romantic artist gushed enthusiastically to him about his inspiring leadership on the issue, he was met with an 'inward, sardonic sneer'.[13] Other old whigs like 'King Tom', Coke of Norfolk, were trapped in an outmoded definition of whiggism as a battle against crown tyranny and base, servile aristocrats spendthrift with public money.

The younger Reformers were more positive. They built up that aspect of the whig tradition which envisaged parliament accessing the energy and vigour of the people, so adding to the nation's strength;[14] and they developed a more precise application of the traditional whig idea that the duty of government was to act on behalf of the people. Russell, an avid student of history, remained anxious to defend popular liberties, but he was also aware that government patronage now offered little threat to liberty, while public opinion, so striking in 'bulk and velocity', required more management than did crown power. Affected by postwar nationalist triumphalism, he saw the British constitution as a magnificent achievement which had secured tolerably effective representation and respect for order – the conditions for Britain's astonishing progress in wealth, civilisation, industriousness and

---

* Perhaps for this reason, the whigs' case for parliamentary reform was *not* argued primarily from historical precedent; there was little mention of 1688 in the parliamentary debates (see below, page 82, for an exception, on nomination boroughs). See R.J. Smith, *The gothic bequest: medieval institutions in British thought, 1688–1863* (Cambridge, 1987), pp. 164–70, for interesting though ineffective whig attempts to found the bill's principles on medieval precedents.

morality.[15] His main concern was to further that progress, to use government power to replace bad law, sectional and unnatural, with good.[16] This confidence in the potential benefit of active government was widely held among younger whigs (see page 113). Meanwhile, honest, earnest, rustic Althorp was trusted by both those whigs who remained primarily defenders of liberty against crown power, and those with reforming vision. He was widely read in political economy, but he was also moved by intense 'country' hostility to over-government and over-taxation, and by evangelical anger at the damage inflicted by camp-followers of tory governments – the selfish lay and clerical office-seekers, the monopolists using their influence to gain sectional economic benefits, and the boroughmongers who calumniated aristocratic virtue.

The whig Reform scheme

What did whig Reformers think about the working of the electoral system, and how did they plan to change it? They began with the assumption that the Commons should represent 'the property, the wealth, the intelligence, and the industry of the country'.[17] Like tories, they did not consider parliament's function to be the representation of the population, for such a concession to natural rights theory would unbalance the constitution in favour of the propertyless. Grey was typical in asserting that the people had a right to good government, not to the vote.[18] Parliament was to represent interests, for the obvious reason that legislation and taxation regulated established property rights for the public good. But the whigs' definition of interests was much wider than the tories'. It included more types of specific economic interests but also property in general and that indefinable but vital force, the power of mind. Political intelligence must have an outlet; 'knowledge was power'. The whig MP and *littérateur* Bulwer asserted that the 'genius of a people' could not be suppressed by authority. Russell maintained that the people could no longer be *governed*. Public opinion was too vital to be gainsaid.[19]

The most important aspect of the Reform scheme was the distribution of seats in parliament. In whig eyes, the composition of the Commons should reflect the diversity of national interests. Both specific interests and general opinion should be represented. A rational representative system would increase the real weight of property in the constitution, because it would bolster people's respect for authority. Reform would promote three diverse ends: the defence of the country's real interests, the leadership of a regenerated (whig) aristocracy, and the people's willing acquiescence in the rule of law. Whigs instinctively lauded the power of politics to 'bind firmly and kindly the different classes of society together'.[20] Believing in the potential benignity of Providence, they were confident that political structures could be established which, if worked disinterestedly, were capable of reconciling classes and securing order. So what did they wish to alter about each category of seat?

English county seats had a reputation for returning respected MPs, healthily independent from government pressure yet assiduous in both national and local business. The whigs recognised their industry in promoting the interests of the various classes of property-owners in their constituency, and they seemed effective representatives of both urban and rural opinion.[21] It is no surprise, then, that the whig strategy for Reform in English counties was, first and foremost, to increase the number of seats: in the final act it rose from 82 to 144. Secondly, they aimed to realise more fully the ideal of county representation. This required attention to be given to three matters.

One major aim was to retain and extend the principle that the county franchise should rest on the possession of *property* – which the county MP was charged with protecting. The Reformers of 1832 added new property franchises to the standard forty-shilling freehold qualification. Copyholders and long leaseholders (60 years or more) were enfranchised if their land had a clear yearly value of £10, and short leaseholders too, if the original term of the lease was twenty years or more and the clear yearly value was £50.* This clause was intended to enfranchise 'a great body of yeomen' being short leaseholders on a seven-year renewable lease. A tenure of less than seven years would, whigs thought, expose the improving tenant to the threat of non-renewal and loss of capital, so he would become subject to landlord pressure in voting.[22] In other words, whigs defined the capacity to reason independently on politics strictly by tenure of property; the propertyless, by default, were unworthy of full citizenship. Such thinking was influenced by myth, not reality. It took no account of the changes in the nature of farm tenure. Leases were now not the norm. Large numbers of prosperous farmers, with 400 or even 1,000 acres, mixed in gentry society and attended the local hunt, but were tenants-at-will with no formal protection against eviction – though in practice they had security of tenure.[23] During the bill's committee stage in August 1831, it proved impossible to keep to such a strictly propertied franchise. It left the landlord free to enfranchise or disfranchise voters by granting or refusing leases, and it excluded many of the most politically active farmers.[24] Whig backbenchers, in coalition with tories, forced the enfranchisement of the £50 tenant-at-will, in the so-called Chandos Clause.† Had this just been a tory plot to enfranchise brute and dependent rural voters (as is often said), it would not have passed. It was not this clause but the growing unpopularity of the whigs among landlords and farmers alike which explains subsequent tory domination of county seats.

---

* To qualify for the electoral register, leaseholders had to be in possession for twelve months, freeholders and copyholders for six.
† Compare the 1832 Irish Reform Act, which had no tenant-at-will amendment. As a result, the Irish electorate was very small and landlords could control its size by refusing leases. See K.T. Hoppen, 'Politics, the law, and the nature of the Irish electorate 1832–1850', *E.H.R.*, xcii (1977), 746–76.

A second whig requirement was that the county seat must continue to represent urban as well as rural property. Whigs were well aware of the strength of tory landed influence in the rural backwaters, and were anxious to boost their own electoral chances. But they were also driven by a genuine desire to maintain the unique standing of the county MP as a spokesman for the whole community, and to prevent too sharp a division in the new House between town and country members, which would heighten class tension. Russell warned of the dangers stemming from the emergence of powerful rival lobbies of agricultural and manufacturing opinion.[25] But, though some whigs argued that urban and rural interests were not really opposed,[26] the government also recognised the need for some degree of specific interest representation. Moreover, the political finesse needed to keep urban Reformers happy while minimising opposition from panicky tories meant that, throughout the bill's passage, ministers had to balance benefits to town with concessions to country. In particular, tories were frightened that, after Reform, they would be defenceless against an anti-aristocratic crusade launched by borough MPs, and so ministers had to pledge to reduce urban influence in county seats.[27] In practice, that influence was bound to remain after 1832, since only forty-one new towns were given borough representation, leaving many substantial settlements represented only by county MPs. Where they had a choice, the bill's framers attempted a compromise between the ideal of integration and that of interest separation. Before 1832, freehold property within parliamentary boroughs had given the holder both a county vote and, if the borough franchise qualification was appropriate, a borough one. Now, no one property was to allow the same person votes in both seats. *Either* the freeholder would qualify for a borough vote on the £10 franchise (as most did), *or*, if not, he could vote in the county. An urban copyholder or leaseholder was allowed to vote in the county only if the property did not confer on him *or any other person* the right of borough voting.* Freeholders in the nineteen English and Welsh boroughs which were 'cities or towns of counties' in their own right, independent of the larger county around them, were also given the right to vote in the county at large,† which few had possessed before. For all these reasons, counties continued to have a large urban electorate – as Reformers privately wished. In 1865–6, 100,782 electors in England and Wales, nearly a fifth of the county electorate, qualified to exercise the county franchise by virtue of property situated in parliamentary boroughs.[29]

The third need was to promote the accountability and localisation of county MPs. This meant opening up those counties where political life had

* This was the whigs' original intention with regard to the freeholder vote too, but the four words were removed from the clause in August 1831, provoking tory complaints of anti-rural bias. The issues raised by these clauses have prompted the celebrated but faulty argument of D.C. Moore, that whigs intended to create 'deference communities'.[28]

† Except in the few places where the freehold had previously entitled them to borough voting rights, in which case these rights continued.

been suffocated by great aristocratic influence, but also guarding against the danger that 'strangers' with national reputations might use popularity and wealth to usurp the representation from local gentlemen.[30] The principal problem with the old county representation was that the cost of mounting a challenge to an existing coalition of property-owners was immense, because of the size and spread of most county electorates – typically between 3,000 and 5,000 – and the fact that the poll could stay open for fifteen days of expensive feasting, and could only be held in one place. Voters often needed to be given hospitality at the place of poll for several days while their right to vote was validated. A county contest could easily cost each side £20,000. So it was difficult to unseat an apathetic MP, and most attempts to alter the local status quo were funded by very wealthy interests, often great families with fingers in pies outside the county. The Reform Act split most counties into two divisions, each returning two MPs. This made it easier for locals to stand and also increased the security for the representation of specific interests. In this and other ways, it aimed to cut the cost of contests. The maximum length of the poll was reduced from fifteen to two days.* Polling stations were now to be provided in different centres within county seats. In all seats, county and borough, a register of eligible voters was to be compiled before the election, which would eliminate protracted and expensive legal squabblings during the poll.

The *English boroughs* posed more difficult problems. Large-scale disfranchisement was necessary, in order to attack the economic and corporate vested interests which whigs thought had acquired excessive power, and which had also deprived them of the chance of a parliamentary majority. But redistribution on this scale raised awkward questions. Whigs had no doubt about parliament's right to disfranchise boroughs without compensation: they held that the nomination of MPs by individuals was not private property but a privilege, a moral trust to be exercised for the public good, and removable by law.[31] The problem was to draw up watertight principles for redistribution. Boroughs' claim to return MPs could be asserted on diverse grounds. Many existing boroughs were run by corporations with substantial property concerns and powers of taxation and justice, all of which might entitle them to a voice in promoting and resisting public and private bill legislation. Many unrepresented towns included a large number of private commercial and industrial interests. And many in both categories were also awesome agglomerations of 'intelligence', people with political aspirations and grievances. Reformers also needed to secure order. Russell had blamed the 'Peterloo' riot of 1819 in Manchester on the fact that there 'was no authority to which [the populace] could conform, or from which they could derive instruction'.[32] But a narrow property franchise was unlikely to establish general respect for local hierarchy. In fact, most represented towns enjoyed a freeman, not a property franchise, and this, together with the fact that most sizeable towns had been separately

---

* Then to one day in boroughs in 1835 and in counties in 1853.

enfranchised even in the middle ages, suggested that something like a general representation of town opinion had been envisaged historically. So did the ritual of elections. Traditionally, non-electors – including the ladies of the town – were involved in canvassing and in the process of advertising candidates by their colour of dress, the distribution of handbills and their activity in processions, holding banners, cheering or playing music.[33] No one scheme could reconcile all these requirements, and stand up to buffeting in parliament from continuous radical and tory pressure. Inevitably, the result was compromise.

The heart of the Reform Bill was the attack on the nomination boroughs: the burgage and corporation boroughs, and the freeman and scot and lot seats with small electorates, which were controlled by individuals.* Croker estimated in 1827 that 276 MPs were returned by patrons, 203 of them tories.[35] The 1832 Reform Act disfranchised 55 two-member and one one-member boroughs (in 1830, only 30 or so of their 111 MPs were whigs). Forty-five of the 55 two-member seats had been deliberately created by the Tudors to bolster crown influence.[36] That was bad enough, but the great recent increase in wealth had created a thriving market for a close borough seat, often in order to promote private interests. The land which gave control of some of the most 'rotten' boroughs frequently changed hands for exorbitant sums. Gatton was sold to Mark Wood, former chief engineer of Bengal, for £90,000 in 1801; J.T. Hope, returning himself as MP in 1830, paid double that for it. West India and East India men in particular seemed to gain political influence in this way (as a result of the Reform Act, the number of 'East Indians' in the Commons fell from 65 to 45 between 1826 and 1833, and of 'West Indians' from 40 to 19).[37] Grey dismissed boroughmongers as 'loan contractors or speculating attorneys', Brougham as 'Jew jobbers' and even 'aliens'.[38] Macaulay could see 'no rational principle whatever' in the selection of close boroughs.[39] Jeffrey saw it as 'not a fair influence of any property', but simply a way for individuals to realise gains on money deliberately invested in borough ownership. Arbitrarily-selected individuals, pursuing selfish concerns, gave the aristocracy a bad name by association, and MPs a venal, selfish image, not that of men actively interested in affairs. Public lack of confidence in parliamentary proceedings was understandable, since so many boroughs were 'withdrawn from the natural and benignant influence of property bestowed in acts of kindness and judicious charity'.[40]

However, a line had to be drawn between disfranchised and saved boroughs. Ideally, it would distinguish between *nomination* boroughs and *small* boroughs which, though subject to the influence of local property, could be given an electorate sufficiently independent to goad the property-owner to behave responsibly. Whigs were anxious not to disfranchise the

---

* It was in this context that the whigs sang the praises of the settlement of the 1680s, for laying down that MPs must be freely-elected representatives, not nominated by individuals, especially not by members of the Lords.

latter class, for a number of reasons. They ensured that the Commons reflected a wide variety of sentiment; they helped to bolster the influence of property; many small boroughs did, or might, return independently-minded and virtuous country gentlemen; and those in which the influence of pro-government landowners predominated could be used to secure the return of able ministers and young men of administrative promise who might not be returned by a popular constituency. Political considerations pointed the same way as both Houses had to be persuaded to pass the bill. Many government supporters, even cabinet ministers like Palmerston and Lansdowne, were alarmed at the extent of the government's disfranchise-ment plans. Indeed, the far-reaching nature of the original scheme had stretched the credulity of many observers. To get the bill through, more small boroughs were saved. In the final act, the number of English boroughs to be disfranchised (listed in Schedule A of the bill) was reduced from 60 to 56 and the number losing half their MPs (in Schedule B) from 47 to 30. Even so, 143 MPs were dispossessed. In the end, boroughs were allocated into schedules according to the number of houses in the borough and the amount paid in assessed taxes. The lines between categories were drawn on no set principle, being fixed at the point which would provide the appro-priate number of seats for redistribution. This was inevitably a rough-and-ready arrangement, and many very small boroughs survived. In 1839–40, 21 English boroughs had an electorate of under 300 and 95 more between 300 and 1,000, as against only 71 with over 1,000.[41] At least 41 continued to be controlled by individual proprietors.[42] Grey himself considered the survival of so many very small boroughs to be the weakest aspect of the bill.[43]

About half of the redistributed seats went to newly-enfranchised boroughs, most of which had important economic interests. Twenty-two English towns were given two seats. Most were industrial centres in the midlands and north such as Manchester, Birmingham, and Leeds, the capitals of the three great branches of British manufacture, Sheffield, Stoke and Wolver-hampton. But two seats also went to five London boroughs and to Brighton as a thriving spa town and Devonport as a dockyard borough. Nineteen more places were given one seat, again mainly industrial centres, but including also Frome, a Somerset woollen town, Whitby, for its shipping, the dockyard town of Chatham, and Cheltenham.* Tories jibed that the last, noted for its spas, valetudinarians and young ladies' finishing schools, would represent the opinions of the 'circulating library'.[44] At no election between 1832 and 1867 did Conservatives return even 30 per cent of MPs for these new boroughs.

Russell pointedly explained that these towns were not just selected on the basis of population. Some were chosen because of specific economic interests, some avowedly as a 'selection' from among those 'where there was commercial enterprise and commercial capital, combined with population'.[45]

* Plus Merthyr Tydfil in Wales.

Adding the existing boroughs, this meant, he said, that there would be in all about 180 members representing 'great cities and towns' and their specific and general interests, and over 100 (in the event nearly 150) for towns of 3–6,000 inhabitants, 'who will not perhaps immediately represent any particular interest, and who may, therefore, be better qualified to speak and inform the House on great questions of general interest to the community'.[46]

What of the English *borough franchise*? The aim here was *not* to enfranchise the 'middle classes'. When Reformers talked, as they often did, about bringing the 'middle classes' into the constitution, they envisaged it being done primarily by creating new boroughs, since new ideas and impulses could obviously best be promoted by an alteration in parliamentary personnel, not by a different mix of voters. Though twentieth-century historians have dwelt excessively on the franchise question, it was of distinctly secondary importance in 1831, because it had much less direct an impact on power relationships.* Many middle-class people had had the vote before 1832; the act did not appreciably change the class composition of the electorate.[48] In tackling the franchise, the whigs had two goals: to reduce corruption, and to give a numerous and socially varied body (including all 'respectable' and 'intelligent' opinion), confidence that MPs would listen to their grievances. They aimed to achieve both aims by a borough franchise based on property occupation.

The most common problem in sizeable pre-Reform boroughs was bribery. Poor freemen electors, and those who lived outside the town, were especially prone to regard the vote only as a milch-cow. In freeman boroughs like Stafford, 83 per cent of the electorate were too poor to qualify under the £10 franchise introduced in 1832.[49] Half the electors were non-resident in many medium-sized boroughs, such as Exeter, Colchester, Canterbury and Gloucester. The Liverpool byelection of 1830 was rumoured to cost £110,000. At Penryn, the price of a vote was fixed at £35. At Wallingford, £20 in sovereigns was left at the door of right-minded voters two years after the poll by 'the Miller', picturesquely wearing a leathern apron.[50] Bribery could take many forms. Henry Swann established himself in Penryn partly by getting the contract for the stone to build Waterloo Bridge, half of which he asked local labour to provide. In 1826, Frederick Gye, famous for his ballets and displays of acrobatics and sword swallowing, broke up the

* See, for example, Campbell's speech (*Hansard*, IV, 831, 6 July 1831), in which he saw no threat of agitation for a progressively lower franchise after the act passed, but a real one of the Commons usurping excessive power. Perhaps the most frequently-quoted remark from the Reform debates is Peel's explanation of his opposition to Reform: 'I was unwilling to open a door which I saw no prospect of being able to close'. Professor Gash interpreted this to mean further 'democratization'.[47] Modern historians usually interpret *him* as meaning an extension of the franchise. But in fact the original remark is part of a criticism of the policy of transferring seats from small boroughs to large towns, so weakening the capacity of government to rule independently of shifting opinion.

prevailing interests in Chippenham by offering to subsidise the cloth industry. The one essential, in bribery-driven seats, was to ensure a contest at each election. So the habit evolved of enticing a 'third man' to the constituency, who would be willing to spend his money on treating the voters to food, hospitality and above all drink. This was most efficiently done by a body of non-resident freemen who lived in a large city, like London, and who could attract the attention of ambitious merchants anxious to sit in parliament. Venal attorneys would then ensure that the hapless candidates' purses were all swiftly emptied. Towns like Stockbridge, Sudbury and Seaford defied control by any one interest because the voters realised that they could make more money by regularly switching allegiance to new patrons. Some places, like Honiton, were controlled for many years by the local attornies who arranged the contests. Bankers and attornies often had desires to build up their own electoral influence, as did William Rickford and Joseph Pitt. Hobhouse asked if any individuals had more electoral power than the attornies.[51]

Reformers saw this corruption as doubly evil because 'it produced such demoralizing effects upon the lower [orders]', accustoming them to see politics in terms of material rights alone: the right to clamour for money and beer. This encouraged immorality, and could easily grow until it destroyed any prospect of virtuous politics.[52] Like its close equivalent, pauperism, it was 'a rankling and a consuming ulcer, which, if allowed to continue, will eventually spread gangrene through the whole body of the State'. And it was a grotesque and 'monstrous' perversion of the natural order to argue, as tories did, that this system of 'perjury, and bribery, and corruption' was essential to the representation of 'virtue and knowledge', while an electoral system based on 'public rectitude and intelligence in electors' would lead to the ascendancy of 'vice and ignorance'.[53] Fortunately, there was evidence of increasing anger among the 'respectable' classes at these practices, especially at the hunt for the 'third man', which had not been complained about a decade earlier.[54] In 1820, in Lincoln, there was a successful rebellion by a 'respectable' party against the broker's candidate and in favour of returning a trusted man free of expense. In Wallingford, in 1826, a local tory gentleman challenged the venal whig MP on the same principle.[55] It was said that, if the candidates who had been inveigled in from outside the constituency to scatter their money had been men of substance, they would have been returned in their own locality.[56]

Encouraged by such trends, Reformers aimed to establish a more 'respectable', resident voting force, intelligent enough to resist bribery and numerous enough to resist subjugation to an irresponsible landlord. This meant attacking the rights of the non-resident, the most obvious source of corruption.[57] So, in both surviving and newly-enfranchised boroughs, the act introduced a uniform qualification based on property occupation. Those occupying as owner or tenant any building of an annual value of £10 would be allowed to vote, if they had been in possession for a year and resident for six months, were liable to pay poor rate (where levied), and had paid all poor rates and assessed taxes due. The last was regarded as a vital test of respectability.[58] In boroughs which escaped disfranchisement, existing electoral rights ('ancient rights', that is, in most cases, freemen rights) were to continue for the lives of present holders. But, to qualify for inclusion on each year's register, all such voters had to have been resident for six months in or within 7 miles of the town, and not to have received poor relief within the previous twelve months. (The number of Leicester voters resident outside the borough fell from over 2,500 to 500.[59]) Freemen who acquired their rights after March 1831 were disqualified unless the freedom was acquired by inheritance (in which case the qualification must have existed prior to 1831) or apprenticeship. This extension to future generations was a concession to the bill's tory opponents to facilitate its passage. In 1833, just under a quarter of the electorate were 'ancient rights' voters; in 1865–6, one in ten.*

The new £10 franchise was not a middle-class one, in intention or effect. In London, where rents were high, it was much more generous. Supporters of the bill praised the resulting 'sliding scale' of enfranchisement, which they claimed reflected the degree of economic development. Commercial activity, they said, dictated not only rent levels but also the extent of political intelligence in the community. So, though different *classes* would be represented in different towns, roughly the same level of political awareness would be enfranchised across the country; the franchise would be based on politicisation, not 'rank'.[60] As commerce expanded, the electorate would grow. In this and other ways, the £10 franchise could be presented as an approximation to the ideal. Radicals could be reassured that it was low enough to place the vote within the reach of 'the man of common industry', and so offered an important incentive to hard work, thrift and character, 'providing for the moral as well as for the political improvement of the country'.[61] The Lords were told that it was framed 'on the basis of property' and 'wealth' rather than population, that it would produce a 'respectable and intelligent' constituency, and that it offered 'an adequate Representation of the interests of all classes'.[62]

Finally, the *Scottish* Reform Act of 1832 was a separate measure, but crucial in permitting whig/Liberal domination of Scottish politics. It overthrew the small tory oligarchy which had managed the existing, absurdly narrow, electoral system (see page 24). The nominal electorate before 1832 was about 4,500 (of a population of 2–3 million); sometimes, as in 1826, no elector in the whole of Scotland actually had the chance to vote. The 1832 Scottish Reform Act replaced this system with a £10 household qualification in the burghs and a £10 ownership franchise in the counties. This increased the electorate to 65,000. But the low price of land meant that both franchises were in fact socially restricted; Scottish county politics, in particular, remained the preserve of landowners. In the counties, there was

* See Appendix 1 for more detailed figures.

no significant redistribution of seats, and there continued to be very few contests. Tories regularly took two-thirds of the seats until the 1860s.* But burgh representation was increased by 8 to 23, principally by giving Glasgow (2 seats) and 5 other substantial towns (1 seat each) representation distinct from the old burgh groupings. (These continued: 14 groups of burghs each returned 1 MP. Edinburgh retained its separate representation.) Despite the restricted franchise, Liberals were henceforth undisputed rulers of the Scottish burghs, hardly ever losing a contest between 1832 and 1865. Taking all elections held in Scottish burgh seats between those years, 53 per cent provided Liberals with an unopposed victory, and in 25 per cent more the contest was between two or more Liberal candidates. In only 22 per cent was the main battle between Liberal and Conservative, and tories won just one-sixth of these contests. To Scottish burgh electors, the Conservatives represented an alien force: the Anglican landed interest. Liberalism was the natural vehicle for Scottish urban political expression. So the 1832 Act contributed substantially to Liberal strength at Westminster.

* * *

The fundamental aim of the Reform Act was, by bold means, to strengthen the power of government to locate, and respond equitably to, social tensions, unrest, and grievances, and so secure popular confidence in more active, disciplinary rule. Partly this was to be done by raising the standards of local propertied leadership, by creating a new model aristocracy and gentry. Whigs saw no contradiction in allowing public opinion more chance to speak its mind, hoping thereby to entrench the political position of virtuous local gentlemen. The act struck at those 'who do not live among the people, who know nothing of the people, and who care nothing for them – who seek honours without merit, places without duty, and pensions without service'.[63] Pressure from an aroused electorate would lead MPs to develop 'character', 'kindness and good offices' in order to retain their influence. This would come easily to men of property, because these were natural aristocratic qualities.[64] The aristocracy would lose its association with 'rotten and corrupt boroughs' and be identified solely with 'public virtues'.[65] Local MPs would surely also be more assiduous and disinterested in distributing patronage and promoting local private bills. So the act would 'restore' essential influence to the 'landed interest'. Hobhouse and Palmerston both forecast that the social complexion of the Commons would remain essentially unchanged after Reform, but that the 'motives' of MPs

* From the 1860s, urban and Dissenting Liberal influence eroded tory landed power in both Scottish and Welsh counties (and in previously tory Welsh boroughs), adding further to the party's supremacy in Scotland, and giving it a majority of Welsh seats from 1865.

would be different because election henceforth would be impossible without 'good conduct, morality, and intelligence'.[66]*

But the whigs were not utopian about the disinterestedness of the new House of Commons. They understood that many MPs would speak for sectional interests, such as agriculture or manufacturing. They did not deny that vested interests would continue to be returned; they would just have to work harder. No bill could shut out fabulously wealthy colonial merchants.[68] In practice, many boroughs remained too small to sustain an independent life, while bribery would not rapidly disappear from the many venal seats – especially in places like Coventry and Leicester, where four-fifths of the post-1832 electorate voted on the freeman franchise. The 1832 election at Stafford saw a band entering the town with banknotes stuffed in the musicians' capbands.[69] In the same year, Graham, one of the authors of the act, advised his colleague Palmerston to stand for the county seat of South Hampshire rather than a London borough where the victor would be whoever employed corrupt agents to bribe 'the great unwashed'.[70] Between 1832 and 1850 69 election results were invalidated because of proven corrupt practices.[71] This was probably only the tip of the iceberg. Treating remained the norm. After an election in one town, a tory alleged in the 1840s, hospitals were 'filled with men maimed, and bruised, and maddened with drink'.[72] As Dredge said in *Felix Holt*, the Reform Act had 'brought the 'lections and the drink into these parts; for afore that, it was all kep up the Lord knows wheer'.[73] The Liberal agent Parkes remarked in 1841 that borough results 'generally much baffle previous calculations of both parties'.[74]

But, by diminishing MPs' ignorance of local conditions, Reform would stimulate diversity and debate in parliament. On some issues MPs would promote specific interests, on some they would speak the communal voice. The Commons would be a better guide to the immense national energies which were the true motors of national morality, learning, industry, improvement, trade and so on. So it would protect those energies against assault. It would now be vocal enough to prevent so-called 'strong' government by men who lacked understanding of the popular temper and so used arbitrary law to repress talents. However, policy initiatives would not stem from below; whig leaders did not believe in abstractions like the 'sovereignty of the people'.[75] Sometimes, electors would have to decide directly upon the rectitude of *measures* presented to them, but their main task would be the selection of members in whose character and energy they were willing to place confidence. Representatives would hear the legitimate

---

* The act's effect on the number of contested elections was indeed striking. The immediate increase probably exceeded whig expectations. One half of all constituencies had enjoyed three or fewer contests in the century before 1830, but the numbers of people actually voting in England and Wales increased from 74,638 in 1831 to 390,700 in 1832 (falling back to 272,946 in 1835), and in Scotland from 594 to 43,525. In the three elections of 1832–7, 277, 227 and 251 of the 401 United Kingdom seats were contested.[67]

grievances of the people, but 'in suggesting remedies, those who are called to the business of legislation should follow the deliberate result of their own judgment'.[76] Sometimes the Commons would synthesise the agreed matured will of the community. But often it would reveal a kaleidoscope of views. Then, ministers would have to use their judgment and flexibility to decide on a policy. Reformers did not expect that governments could always gain 'the satisfaction of the whole community'. But, by allowing governments to measure the range of sentiment better, Reform would facilitate the people's 'general acquiescence' in the rule of law.[77]

In particular, government confidence that it understood popular feeling would allow it to respond much more confidently and vigorously to social crises and evils, to pauperism, criminality and so on. It would be 'able to legislate fearlessly for all the interests of this mighty empire'.[78] It would be stronger than pre-Reform governments. It could more safely ignore 'lawless attempts' to undermine the Union with Ireland.[79] The Commons would no longer be 'the mere momentary index of popular will'.[80] Once its 'honour and integrity' were reestablished, the people would 'obe[y] ... its decrees'.[81] They would be more willing to 'support the future burthens of the country'.[82] Public opinion would be both more effective and more effectively regulated. Faced with a sympathetic government, the people would accept that poverty and unemployment were ineradicable, and that the 'greater part of their distresses arise from causes over which Government has no control'.[83] The Reformers had no magic answer to periodic economic distress. It was inevitable 'in the course of human affairs'. But they argued that, before the Reform Act, criticism of the political system was the inevitable consequence of the onset of distress. The public, observing the behaviour and moral quality of MPs, blamed any shortcomings of government, any natural eruption of misfortune, on political corruption.[84] There was no way to rectify this unnecessary source of instability but by Reform.

This review of the whig mind-set suggests how inadequate it is to explain the Reform Act as a sudden concession to popular pressure. The whigs were pragmatic Reformers in that they were not theorists. But their leaders belonged to a powerful political tradition which made them instinctively sympathetic to the idea of measured Reform, in order to restore public confidence in parliament, to emancipate muffled opinion, to prevent bungling interference by ignorant authority, and to strengthen executive power to take tough and necessary decisions. Unwillingness to leave the Reform cause alone was to mark their conduct for most of the next fifty-five years. In 1831 (as later), they talked of Reform as a necessary response to difficult circumstances. But most Reformers who mattered did *not* see popular loss of confidence in government as a short-term problem, to be headed off simply by extending voting rights. They saw it as a long-developing process which required a far-reaching structural remedy.[85] And, as we shall see in Part II, a younger generation of whigs in particular wished to use the increased power of action which the Reform Act promised to transform the range and image of government behaviour.

PART II

FROM REFORM GOVERNMENT TO LIBERAL PARTY, 1830–1841

THE WHIG-DOMINATED government formed in November 1830 lasted, with one short break, until 1841. It had three distinctive characteristics. First, it was a coalition ministry, assembled in response to a perceived breakdown of authority, and determined to restore it. Like the broad-bottom king's governments of the eighteenth century, it initially attracted the goodwill of the bulk of propertied opinion, which looked to it to restore tranquillity, harmony and morality. On the second reading of the first Reform Bill, 51 of the 76 English county MPs who voted supported the government. By early 1831, most grass-roots tories had come to feel that, in the circumstances, some Reform was better than none.[1] Though the tory leadership stayed aloof, the new cabinet was still a mixed bag. Five of its members had been identified as tories for large parts of the 1820s: Melbourne and Palmerston (the two leading Huskissonites, who occupied the prestigious Home and Foreign Secretaryships), ex-Prime Minister Goderich, Charles Grant and an ultra-tory (Richmond). Five of the whigs had served in Canning's cabinet of 1827 (Lansdowne and Carlisle) or actively supported it (Holland, Brougham and Durham). Of the other three, Prime Minister Grey, dignified, remote, and tortured by self-doubt, was scarcely a radical or partisan leader, while Althorp and Graham were both county MPs who were popular with country gentlemen of all camps for their vigorous campaign against extravagance and high taxation. Both disdained faction; Graham had a tory background. Lord Anglesey, Wellington's Lord Lieutenant of Ireland, regained that post.

Second, it adopted two high profile strategies in order to assert that authority: aristocratic leadership and national legislation. The cabinet was 'far more aristocratic than its predecessor'.[2] Only four of the thirteen ministers were not peers of the United Kingdom, and they were Palmerston, an Irish peer, Althorp, heir to an earldom, and Graham and Grant, two large landowners. The cabinet was confident that it could offer benevolent and disinterested guidance. In the words of Lord John Russell – another peer's son, who entered the cabinet in 1831 – 'I thank God we are too [aristocratic] to do anything mean or dirty'.[3] Brougham's threat to land-owner rule was comprehensively destroyed by his vanity when he accepted the Lord Chancellorship and was reduced to delivering his histrionics nightly to stolid tory peers. This was as galling to them as to him, except

93

that they knew that Samson's locks had been permanently shorn. No less striking was the emphasis on national legislation, with bold measures of administrative reform aiming to embrace the whole country, and quell both indiscipline and popular irritation at complacent local authorities. This marked a major change from the timidity of Wellington's ministry.

Third, though a coalition, it was a coalition of those prepared to swallow what emerged as a far-reaching scheme of parliamentary reform. It was a 'Reform' government, and therefore committed to open politics. The 1832 Reform Act allowed a much fuller representation of national interests and created a more active, conscientious and diversified political nation. It required ministers to be more flexible in guiding, interpreting and integrating different strands of public opinion. In particular, Dissenters, Catholics and radicals all became important components of the Reform majority. How were ministers to establish a fruitful relationship with them without antagonising propertied and reluctant Reformers? Also needed was a new definition of party, for the opposition idea of an honourable alliance against tory 'Old Corruption' was no longer relevant. Some whigs hoped that in the new parliament the need for party organisation would decline, as MPs showed themselves to be conscientious, independent and rational. In reality, though, MPs needed firm discipline, or the party might become dependent on sectional radical pressure-groups.

The great problem of Reformed politics was the attempt to reconcile these ideals: authority, aristocracy, legislative initiative and popular involvement. This is the theme of Part II of this book. Chapter 4 is about the most difficult years, 1830-4. They ended in the dismissal of Melbourne, Grey's successor, by the king. Much propertied opinion came to think that the whig strategy for Reformed government meant perpetual political feebleness. The result was a steady tory revival which by 1841 destroyed the massive 'Reform' majority of 1832, while whig leaders had to fall back on urban and Dissenting support. Tories alleged that government was weak in the face of radical clamour, that honourable, independent rule was at an end. These chapters take a different view, especially Chapters 5 and 6. Chapter 5 is about ministers' attempts to impose a set of national administrative structures which would stimulate gentlemen and merchants to provide more assiduous, rational and didactic leadership in their localities, and yet offer the public a representative local government system which would give protection against bureaucratic centralisation. Chapter 6 is more concerned with party politics and the development of an agenda capable of sustaining government momentum in parliament and at constituency level. This agenda had to satisfy the whig drive to promote much-needed moral and social regeneration, yet also had to strike chords with party supporters. Religion, Ireland and free trade were the three issues which emerged as most likely to do both. Though none of the strategies discussed in these two chapters was flawless, it is still possible to discern an effective Liberal party functioning by 1841, with a presentable set of values and a stalwart constituency following. Liberal politics were in the making.

CHAPTER 4

The problem of Reformed politics, 1830–4

No GOVERNMENT BEFORE Grey's had had to survive in parliament without the assistance of the close boroughs; none had had to deal with so many popularly-elected representatives. Yet Grey's task was to reassert ministerial authority. How was his cabinet to tame the Reformed parliament? This question dominated the politics of 1832–4, and dominates this chapter. But it was made more taxing by the struggle to pass the act itself. Grey expected the act to pass quickly and peacefully; he did not want an agitation on it. Instead, there was a long-running crisis over Reform in 1830–2, which raised the political temperature to boiling-point. It implied that threatening vested interests occupied a powerful place in the political firmament, and that only agitation could defeat them. This made political stability look even more remote.

Reform and slavery, 1830–2

Popular expectations were raised simply by the ministers' pledge to legislate on Reform. Petitions increasingly attributed distress 'in great manner . . . to the corrupt state of representation'.[1] In June 1831, one observer commented that the Reform Bill was seen as a 'sort of patent steam-engine miracle-worker' which would supply beef and mutton at 'a penny a pound [and] ale at a penny a quart'.[2] Whereas during the 1830 session there had been only 14 Reform petitions, 645 were presented between Grey's arrival in office and March 1831. Within a month of the presentation of the bill, 23 counties had held meetings to support it.

Though the government wanted to avoid a constitutional crisis, a bill removing the seats of 168 MPs was bound to fail unless public opinion was mobilised in support of it. In April 1831, the government was defeated on a crucial amendment to the bill. Reluctantly, but without hesitation, it persuaded the kind to dissolve parliament – a memorably hot-tempered scene, 'some of the Peers . . . almost scuffling' as he arrived at the Lords.[3] The resulting general election was of immense significance, not only in forwarding the Reform Bill, but in politicising and polarising public opinion.

It was a referendum, not so much on the bill under discussion – since the issues involved were too complicated – but on the abstract principle of Reform (and opposition to slavery). The king's name was frequently invoked by Reformers: he was said to be fighting against an unpatriotic faction of corrupt and parasitic boroughmongers.[4] Only 8 avowed tories were returned for the 82 English county seats, of whom 2 voted for the Reform bill, and 4 more were aristocratic nominees. In many seats there was no point in forcing a contest as leading tories would not stand or put up money in a hopeless cause. In Cumberland, Southey wrote, there was 'literally not a fit person who can be proposed' on the tory side.[5]

In the face of such pressure, the Commons accepted the government's new bill, after a long committee stage. But in early October 1831, the Lords rejected it. This goaded public opinion to an unprecedented display of enthusiasm for Reform. Those who agitated in support of the bill began to turn their wrath against particular targets identified with opposition to it: the Lords, the bishops (who had voted decisively against the bill in the Upper House), corporations, boroughmongering and sinecure-hogging aristocrats, and even, in some quarters, the aristocracy itself. Large numbers of Political Unions were now being formed, 120 by 1832, most calling for manhood suffrage and the ballot. On the whole, popular sentiments were expressed in an orderly way as radicals were determined to demonstrate their respect for law. Plymouth was typical: when news of the bill's rejection became known, shops closed, flags were lowered to half-mast and bells tolled mournfully.[6] But there were also outbreaks of violence which suggested to some that the apocalypse was impending. At Nottingham and Derby, gangs of men went on the rampage, attacking the long-deserted castle in Nottingham and the prison and some centres of local toryism in Derby. In both places it was alleged that the whig corporation, not averse to demonstrating popular fervour for Reform, had been lax in maintaining order.[7] In Bristol at the end of October, Reformers assembled a gang to jostle and jeer a leading tory who had arrived to conduct assizes. Other targets connected with the unpopular corporation were attacked. Assisted by panic and drunkenness, the situation deteriorated badly, especially when troops and constables unwisely withdrew. The soldiers had to reimpose their authority heavy-handedly. Officially, twelve people were killed during the affair; at least one hundred were injured.[8] In November 1831 Ellenborough reported that even villages 'are for the first time invaded by politics and drunkenness'.[9] A hard-headed lawyer, Campbell, thought that 'the world were coming to an end'.[10] Tories began to withdraw money from the funds on a large scale and invest it abroad; Wordsworth seriously considered emigrating to Austria-Hungary. Elizabeth Fry, ever expectant, mixed in circles where it was widely believed 'that the second coming of our blessed Lord is just at hand'.[11]

Over the winter of 1831–2, a third bill was introduced, and passed its second reading in the Lords, but in May 1832 it fell foul of an amendment at committee stage. The king accepted the government's resignation rather than create the forty to fifty peers which it asked for in order to get the bill passed. He called on Wellington, the symbol of opposition to Reform, to form an administration. This was never a serious option, and after Wellington's attempt failed, the government was reinstated and the bill quickly passed. But in the meantime the prospect of tory rule had stimulated more popular activity. Meetings were called in parishes, townships, and vestries up and down the country to defend the bill, and non-payment of taxes was threatened. Much drawing-room bravado was reported: respectable men were said to be talking of refusing to serve as special constables if there was lower-class disorder. Workers were believed to have arms and be willing to march for the bill. One enterprising manufacturer offered to supply the Birmingham Political Union with 10,000 muskets at fifteen shillings apiece.[12] The Unions capitalised on the crisis, organising queues of people to cash in their bank notes in the hope of creating a panic-inducing run on money. An effigy of the archbishop of York was burnt. The king's reputation was damaged by his refusal to create peers. When Althorp told the Commons of it, one observer likened the atmosphere to that in the Long Parliament.[13] The king's whig brother, the duke of Sussex, was banned from court after presenting Reform petitions from Bristol; some thought that he hoped to repeat Louis Philippe's role in France in 1830.[14]

As Sidonia said in Disraeli's *Coningsby*, 'it is not the Reform Act that has shaken the aristocracy of this country, but the means by which that Bill was carried'. Palmerston thought much the same.[15] To an extent which no one had foreseen in 1830, those who had not supported Reform were painted as reactionary and venal. Peel, Wellington and the men of the 1820s suddenly found themselves burdened by the incongruous mantle of obscurantism and vested interest. So, with more justification, did the Church and the Lords. By the time of the first election under the new system in December 1832, the tories were a divided and much-maligned group and less than 150 were returned. The excitements of the last two years had created a new awareness of the possibilities of political action, even in backward market towns, where press activity was stimulated. It divided on party lines, as did banks and hotels in many places. Political Unions had been formed in all major towns (though most did not last). Dissent had been roused to political activity on the Reform (and anti-slavery) side. In Ireland, O'Connell prepared an agenda for agitation. The 1832 general election returned large numbers of MPs who responded sympathetically to popular demands for the abolition of slavery, the repeal of the assessed taxes, strict economy, the abolition of sinecures and pensions, the reduction of the army, the cheapening of the judicial system, church reform, triennial parliaments and the secret ballot.

Government's most immediate problem was slavery, the dominant overall issue at the three elections of 1830–2. In 1831, twice as many petitions to parliament urged the abolition of slavery as parliamentary reform.[16] Before the 1831 election, the Anti-Slavery Society urged its local branches to require candidates to pledge their support for abolition. After it, the Society redoubled its efforts, appointing a special subcommittee – the Agency

Committee – to employ agents to travel the country arousing 'the aid of . . . provincial respectability'.[17] At the end of 1831, 60,000 slaves on Jamaica were caught up in a rebellion, which the planters blamed on the teaching of white missionaries. Chapel-burning and physical attacks on missionaries followed, and these atrocities, publicised by returning missionary preachers, roused evangelicals in Britain to further protest.

How was the government to respond? It was no more inclined than its predecessor to risk insurrection by suddenly emancipating the slaves, nor was it in a better position to force the planters to negotiate. It was divided on strategy. Holland, for example, was a Jamaica estate-owner opposed to swift action. As the cabinet pondered the question gloomily but to no effect throughout 1831, he unleashed his tongue on Brougham who, after 'working up the people to a state of madness on the topick of immediate and unqualified emancipation . . . like other abolitionists, had no plan for carrying their object into practical execution'.[18] In March 1832, the cabinet rejected various proposals 'from a fear either of the Saints [i.e. evangelicals] or the Country Gentlemen'.[19] Indecision forced it to agree to the establishment of a select committee in each House to investigate the question, the one in the Lords requested and dominated by the anti-abolitionists and that in the Commons heavily influenced by their opponents. This did not advance matters much. At the 1832 election, the Anti-Slavery Society bombarded candidates with requests to pledge themselves to vote for abolition. Under the novel pressure of constituency activism on this scale, between 140 and 200 MPs seem to have committed themselves. In the 1833 session, at least 5,000 petitions were delivered, one alone containing 187,000 signatures, all from women.

So to say that apprehension surrounded the opening of the Reformed parliament would be an understatement. Graham, a cabinet minister and one of the Committee of Four, predicted that, if the government 'lose the control in the first session over the reformed House, the Meteor will be hurried into space, and Chaos is at Hand'.[20] Much propertied opinion, critical of the extent of the Reform Act, was now running scared.[21] Such people faced 1833 doubtful that government could direct the popular storm. In December 1832, the tory Lord Aberdeen considered that Britain was 'thoroughly revolutionised in heart, and we must depend on the good pleasure of the leaders of the revolution for semblance of a government'.[22]

But these views were not typical of the whig leadership. Most whigs had not lost confidence in their power and duty to guide the popular mind. Even Melbourne, one of the most conservative of ministers, was (admittedly later) to say that government was the only body in the country capable of creating 'a real feeling and agitation'.[23] The popular cry, 'The Bill, the whole Bill, and nothing but the Bill', had actually been invented by Brougham in order, as Russell put it, to rouse the country 'to the height of [the government's] lofty proposals'.[24]

The Reformed parliament, 1833–4

What was the Reformed House of Commons of 1833 actually like? Brougham noted that MPs were not ' "thick and thin [party] men" in the old sense', but this was a compliment.[25] The Reform Bill had been passed partly in order to end the unthinking partisanship which whigs had discerned operating during tory rule.[26] The act did not much alter parliament's social composition.[27]* Birmingham apart, the new boroughs returned men of great respectability. The most eminent sprang from the most wealthy, gentrified and patrician industrial families: Philips of cotton and Manchester, Wedgwood of porcelain and Stoke, Marshall of flax and Leeds, Guest of iron and Merthyr Tydfil. Some of these MPs symbolised mind, such as the young anti-slaving intellectual Macaulay in Leeds, the whig barrister Parker in Sheffield, and Brougham's lawyer friend Blackburne in Huddersfield. Poulett Thomson of Manchester was a government minister, Chaytor of Sunderland a landed whig baronet.

The most fervent radical pressure came from the turbulent London boroughs and a small lobby of intellectuals, the so-called 'Philosophical radicals'. But neither group was unfamiliar from the unreformed parliament. The most prominent London radicals were Burdett, Tennyson and (from shortly after 1832) Duncombe, Whittle Harvey and De Lacy Evans. They tended to be high-bred romantics applying wealth and honour to battle on behalf of threatened popular liberties, and so upheld a type of politics that the Reform Act was designed to marginalise. Burdett, the archetype, MP for Westminster since 1807, used to ride to parliament from his Wiltshire estate on horseback. Seeking to convince the Reformed Commons how crippling repeated election expenses had been in corrupt days gone by, he revealed that, at one sad juncture, 'Lady Burdett had only one pair of horses to her carriage'.[28] Rigid and vain, he loathed Political Unions as much as boroughmongers, hated the Irish and ended as tory MP for Wiltshire. This was unusual. But Tennyson of Lambeth, a Lincolnshire landowner, prided himself on his descent from the sister of Edward IV, took the name of D'Eyncourt in 1835 to commemorate his links with medieval nobility, and fought a duel with his boroughmonger opponent at the 1831 Stamford election. Duncombe, nephew of a Yorkshire peer, ended up in Finsbury after spending £40,000 on five elections in Hertford against the dominant interest, that of the tory Cecil family. A great dandy and gentleman jockey, he luxuriated in fashionable patriotism; like Durham, he had joined the army at 17 in youthful enthusiasm to slay the tyrant Napoleon. He imbued his many female admirers with the same romanticism; after his defeat at Hertford in 1832, Mrs Henry Tissoe and eight

---

* Over one-third of all MPs sitting between the first two Reform Acts had blood ties with the aristocracy, and at least 71 per cent of those sitting in the parliament of 1841–7 were direct descendants of peers, baronets or gentry families.

hundred other ladies presented him with a plate on which was engraved: 'L'ultima che si perde è la Speranza'.[29] De Lacy Evans was less rich but even more zealously patriotic. He was a distinguished veteran of the Peninsular Wars and Waterloo, and became commander of the British Legion of 10,000 men sent to fight for constitutionalism in Spain in 1835.

Joseph Hume, a self-made East India administrator who battled for forty years against government extravagance, had also been a significant presence before the Reform Act. A genuine public servant, he earned some respect, though he damaged his cause by interminable speeches and pedantry. More novel were the handful of Philosophical radicals. These 'ardent and college-educated young men'[30] were often intellectuals: Molesworth edited Hobbes, Grote wrote extensively on Greece and was described throughout his wife's awe-struck memoir as 'the Historian'. They had supreme confidence in the power of the mind. Following Bentham and James Mill, their politics were didactic. Their main concerns were political economy, emigration, systems of centralised administration, a non-religious London University and the secret ballot. They despised aristocrats as condescending airheads; they spurned party connection as corrupt and limiting; so they never understood the whigs, who they assumed were mere unprincipled nepotists. As a result, they quickly declined into an affronted opposition. They lacked weight because they could not strike a rapport with the people, indeed did not see that this was necessary. Molesworth, the most successful, had to leave two seats in succession (East Cornwall in 1837 and Leeds in 1841) because he offended large groups of Liberal voters with his trenchant and heterodox opinions. At the Southwark byelection of 1845 he was attacked by Dissenters who goaded hecklers to shout 'No 'obbes', under the impression that his writings had atheistic intent. Except for Grote, a banker and City MP, most sat for small boroughs. Warburton, MP for little Bridport (with the aid of illicit expenditure) was typical in caring more for science than popularity, sponsoring the 1832 Anatomy Act which, to working-class horror, allowed the confiscation of pauper bodies from workhouses for dissection. In the 1840s, Molesworth and Charles Buller made their peace with official Liberalism, and prospered; most of the others retired disillusioned.

One predictable major change after 1832 was increased pressure from religious Dissent. Wellington complained that the Reform Act had handed England from Anglican gentlemen to 'the shopkeepers, being dissenters from the Church . . . There are dissenters in every village in the country'; 'the revolution is made'.[31] Though there were less than ten Dissenting MPs in 1833 (scarcely more than in the 1820s), the sects probably now formed over 20 per cent of the total electorate.[32] Politicised by the Reform and slavery agitations, they would naturally look to government for a new purity in administration. They were drawn to political activity also by the need to organise for vestry elections in the major towns in order to prevent the levying of compulsory church rates. Anglican Conservative fear of Dissenting power after the Reform Act was adding to tension between sects, and nonconformists were occasionally even refused marriage and burial in the Anglican church. In 1833 a United Committee of Dissenting bodies was formed, and demanded action to tackle six grievances, including that of church rates, the enforcement of religious tests at Oxford and Cambridge, and the requirement to be married and buried by Anglican rites and to be registered at birth and marriage by the established church.

In general, politically-active Dissent could be expected to work well with Reformed government, because of long-standing whig-Dissenting agreement on two major issues. The first was the traditional civil liberty agenda which had brought them together in opposition. Until the politicisation of the socially more modest evangelical sects, in the 1830s, political Dissent really meant the unitarian (and occasionally quaker) merchant and professional elite in the major commercial centres. These unitarians disparaged orthodox biblical Christianity as superstitious, shared with whigs an interest in intellectual inquiry and the promotion of rational improvement, and regarded Christianity as primarily a matter of good works. The men of great pride and confidence who dominated commercial society liked to celebrate the power of reason, especially their own, and the fact of progress through the rigorous and unshackled application of mind. Though unsympathetic to the selfish, aristocratic church establishment, they disdained a campaign against it as likely to generate ignorant, destabilising popular passions. They assumed that the establishment would naturally sink of its own accord under the weight of obscurantism and irrelevance. Instead, they took up the issues of civil liberty which mattered to them. By far the wealthiest Dissenting group, unitarians stood to benefit most from the formal opening of magistracies to Dissenters, finally won in 1828. They thought most seriously of giving their sons an education at Oxford and Cambridge, still closed in 1830, and were most affronted at having to bow to church practices in baptism, marriage and burial services. So their connection with whiggery was natural. William Smith, chairman of the main lobby group, the Dissenting Deputies, in the 1810s and 1820s, was a long-standing Foxite whig. For their part, whigs had supported repeal of the Test and Corporation Acts as a symbol of national integration and liberty against narrow state exclusiveness, and as a stimulus to religious regeneration. Balancing and integrating diverse groups within the state promised to consolidate the nation's 'intelligence, ingenuity and enterprize' and thus its strength.[33]

Secondly, there was a common whig-Dissenting interest in the moral improvement of the people and in structural reform of urban government. Bound by ties of kinship and trade, the unitarian chapel connections in the leading towns not only ran their own religious affairs but formed a nexus of potentially immense political and cultural power. Before the 1830s, that power was restricted to Improvement Commissions, to philanthropy, and to cultivating the minds of citizens by Mechanics' Institutes (from 1824) for the self-improving artisan, Literary and Philosophical Societies (set up in most towns by the 1820s) for the intellectual classes, and the *Manchester*

Guardian (1821) and similar papers for political reformers. But the overhaul of municipal corporations in 1835, and increased access to the magistracy thereafter, gave elite unitarians a more official and permanent status, and also facilitated the launch of crusades for urban improvement. The principal Dissenting MPs after 1832 were men of this stamp: Philips of Manchester, G.W. Wood of South Lancashire, Bonham Carter of Portsmouth, the congregationalist Edward Baines of Leeds, and the quaker Pease of South Durham. In 1835, Pease carried a bill outlawing cock-fighting, bear-baiting and other acts of bestial cruelty which encouraged animal spirits in the working classes. This was symptomatic of a broad consensus on questions of moral reform among rational and evangelical Dissenters and liberal Anglicans. Particularly potent causes for them were the abolition of slavery, the reform of prison discipline and the attack on tithes and pluralism in the Church of England. Already prominent on such questions were Anglican liberal evangelicals with Dissenting links, such as Fowell Buxton (the great brewer-philanthropist and anti-slavery leader), Evans of Leicester and his brother-in-law Thomas Gisborne.

These various examples indicate that the Reformed parliament was not unmanageable. Most MPs for substantial boroughs were sympathetic to standard popular grievances, but were also men of property and discrimination: James Morrison of Ipswich, the millionaire ex-warehouseman; Ewart the Liverpool educational and law reformer; Strutt of Derby, grandson of Jedediah and substantial landowner; Baillie the free-trading West India merchant at Bristol, and Whitmore, his East India counterpart at Wolverhampton; Fyshe Palmer, the old Foxite whig at Reading. There were also a host of whig scions and established MPs for smaller boroughs hardly affected by 1832, and over one hundred whig gentlemen sitting for English county seats. Charles Wood, government whip, counted 303 steady government supporters and 123 less reliable ones, compared with 34 radicals, 38 Irish repealers and a maximum of 159 tory sympathisers.[34]

Nonetheless, the Reformed parliament posed two important problems of management. One was that increased activity by MPs threatened government control of the timetable. Whereas 241 MPs made spoken interventions in the sessions of 1825 and 1828, 395 did in 1833, attempting, it was said, to please constituents.[35] The Reform crisis had also greatly increased petitioning: 8,900 were presented in 1831. Traditionally, debates were allowed on presentation. Reformers, buoyed by confidence that popular respect for parliament had increased, asked how the Commons could be shielded from this time-wasting process. In 1833, for the first time, restrictions were imposed on the times at which petitions could be brought in, and in the following year debates accompanying the presentation of petitions were forbidden. In 1835, Mondays and Fridays were set aside as order days for government business, crucial if it was to promote its own agenda without interruption. The Speaker welcomed these reforms because they would help to shut out 'the influence of popular feeling' and so allow the House 'to do freely what was right within doors'.[36] MPs' anxiety to protect their image of fearless and independent disinterestedness was further underlined when in 1840 their privilege to speak their minds without fear of encountering judicial action was placed on a statutory basis.

The other problem was that radical borough MPs expected government to conform to certain basic policy positions in supporting economy and religious and moral reform, and in opposing 'repression'. There were also standard radical constitutional demands not conceded in 1832, which MPs did not want to offend constituents by opposing. They would always be likely to vote in force for Grote's motion for the secret ballot and Tennyson's for triennial parliaments. If government showed itself persistently lax in tackling abuses and reducing extravagance, its authority would undoubtedly be badly compromised. Government would always have to *earn* MPs' confidence. Althorp told Grey in January 1833 that 'revolution' was likely unless government took the lead in 'popular measures'. He raised this fear in order to prod Grey into bold legislation on the questions most urgent to MPs, which included church rates, slavery and the Irish church.[37]

However, Grey was unsympathetic to this approach, and in 1833 and 1834 the scope of the King's Speech was disappointing. Partly this is explained by Grey's awareness, as Prime Minister, of the need to conciliate king and Lords. But the main cause was his supercilious vanity and weakness of character. Grey's public actions aimed to maintain the honour due to his name – as Greville put it, to make him 'appear . . . a prudent, sagacious, liberal statesman'.[38] His great asset was the 'measured and stately phraseology' of his oratory in the Lords, delivered with a manly bearing and with the Blue Ribbon and Garter prominently displayed. This distinguished image, 'aristocratic and lofty in the extreme',[39] had kept him at the party's head throughout its long years in opposition, despite his refusal to bear the brunt of day-to-day leadership. In reality, he was fastidious, timid, fatalistic, gloomy and strikingly indecisive; he lacked the energy, resolution, flexibility and moral authority for government. Yet he had to manage a cabinet abounding in prima donnas, ranging from men of high but opposed principle (Althorp, Richmond), through the incompetent (Grant, Goderich) and headstrong (Palmerston, Russell, Stanley), to the downright impossible (Brougham, Durham). To be constantly 'harassed . . . by wrong-headed friends' was more than he could bear.[40]

His instinct before 1830 would have been to retreat to his Northumberland estate, where it was so easy to embody the whig myth of the highbred revered popular mentor. As Prime Minister, something of the same effect could be gained by surrounding himself with family connections: two in-laws as successive chief whips, his son-in-law in cabinet, his son as private secretary, another son in the government, a brother a bishop and so on (appointments which, from a Reformer, raised eyebrows). But Grey could not escape the problem of popular activity which accompanied the new politics. Yet his vanity rebelled against those who presumed on ministerial favour, especially Dissenters and Irish Catholics. In return for entry to parliament by the legislation of 1828 and 1829, both groups had sworn not to use their new status to agitate for overthrow of the establishment. Yet they quickly started to apply what Grey disparagingly called 'constant and active pressure from without', and several colleagues angered him by urging accommodation with their requests.[41]

Commons ministers had to manoeuvre as best they could within the confines imposed by Grey's negativism. They offered two principal approaches to leadership. One was that of Stanley, who was worried by radical and Dissenting pressure but believed that bold policy-making of the right kind could marginalise it and retain gentry confidence. His remarkable achievement in 1833, as Irish and then Colonial Secretary, was to drive the session's three major measures – the Irish Church and Coercion Bills (see page 108) and the abolition of slavery – through the House, placing a conservative stamp on each. To widespread indignation, abolition had not been mentioned in the 1833 King's Speech. Stanley grasped the nettle. His bill upset radicals by setting aside the enormous sum of £15 million in compensation to planters, later increased to £20 million in order to pacify the Lords. Furthermore, though the legal status of slavery would cease in 1834, a lengthy period of apprenticeship, mostly under their former owners, was made mandatory for the ex-slaves, in order to satisfy those who considered this necessary to equip them for freedom.* At the root of Stanley's success was his remarkable power in debate, conveyed most awesomely in his speech on the government's Irish Coercion Bill. Althorp had introduced the bill with embarrassment, Reform and Irish MPs were instinctively unsympathetic, and yet Stanley rescued it from almost certain failure.

But the most influential minister on general questions was Althorp, as Leader of the Commons. Althorp was a strangely unpolitical politician, which was both his strength and his weakness. Aristocratic by descent yet unsnobbishly simple in dress, speech and manner, he had a first-class mind yet was painfully inarticulate. The honest, uncomplaining workhorse who piloted the Reform Bill through interminable sittings, the unremitting opponent of bigotry, repression, complacency or ecclesiastical artifice, the most reluctant of tax-levyers or law-enforcers, he stood the best chance of all Reformers of commanding the confidence of both radicals and country gentlemen. Gladstone, reminiscing, thought him as great as Cromwell.[42] On his death, Greville wrote that, without wit, grace or power of speech, he governed 'the most unruly and fastidious assembly which the world ever saw' better than Pitt, Canning or Castlereagh.[43] But Greville's opinion at the time was less charitable. 'More of a grazier than a statesman', his administrative blunders and 'sluggish . . . vacillating, unforeseeing character' contributed appreciably to the steady erosion of 'the authority of government'.[44]

---

* Another great blow was struck against colonial 'vested interests' in 1833 with the reform of the East India Company: its monopoly over the China trade was removed, and its administrative powers in India were effectively subordinated to government, facilitating the implementation of rational legal and educational reform.

Althorp himself felt that he lacked dignity, which added to his misery at office-holding. But the tory definition of 'authority' repelled him. He hated the practice of party whipping, and discouraged it. He believed that party leadership necessarily involved the superficial indignity of occasional defeat. However, as a supporter said, this encouraged MPs to agitate for particular initiatives in order to influence policy.[45]

The result of Althorp's style of leadership was that, on both economic and religious questions, government only just kept its head above water in 1833–4. Its first financial difficulty had arisen over the 1831 Budget. Althorp, who was also Chancellor, and like-minded junior ministers such as Poulett Thomson and Howick, wanted to impose an income tax on landed and funded property, in order to provide revenue to permit sizeable reductions in tariffs on consumer goods and raw materials. But it was politically impossible for a government backed by gentry, middle-class and radical adherents of a 'country ideology' to reimpose Pitt's hated 'war tax' in peacetime. Instead, therefore, Althorp proposed a transfer tax of ½ per cent on real and personal property, which was aimed mainly to hit fundholders. When told that this proposal infuriated the 'monied interest', one of the great beneficiaries of tory rule, Althorp replied: 'That is its best recommendation'.[46] He planned to gather extra revenue by modifying the wine and timber duties. But the proposals were unacceptable to too many MPs representing City and trading interests. Althorp had to withdraw them.

After the passage of Reform, radical pressure for retrenchment redoubled. Industrial and commercial depression remained severe throughout 1833. Charles Buller reminded the Commons that the Reform Act 'had been brought about for the purpose of lessening taxation'.[47] Urban radicals disliked assessed taxes (taxes on houses and windows) and the fact that government had not abolished the pensions given to government employees of the era of 'Old Corruption'. Rural MPs, however, demanded reduction or repeal of the malt tax, which they claimed was exacerbating agricultural depression and increasing beer prices. Depression also revived calls for the old radical cry of triennial, rather than septennial, parliaments. In 1833 the four major Commons motions on these issues all collected between 150 and 230 votes. The crisis was at its height after the 1833 Budget which, while reducing taxes by £1.35 million, did not alter either the assessed or malt taxes. Amendments urging both were moved, and that on the malt duty was passed in late April. One tory, Thomas Raikes, saw a harbinger of 'revolution': the Commons was beginning to refuse supplies 'as in the time of Charles I'.[48] But Peel rallied tory MPs to support the government and the status quo was restored. The government and Peel also stood together to beat off a call from backbenchers for a review of the currency system. Two select committees, set up to meet discontent at the state of agriculture and manufacturing, were managed so as to scorn ideas for far-reaching currency and taxation reform. Demands for drastic tax cuts continued in 1834, and there was a renewed assault on the system of sinecures and pensions; government had to accept strict limitations on future pension awards.

Althorp had to concede to urban radical pressure for the reduction of the assessed taxes. This meant that, though he wished to repeal the malt tax to help farmers, he lacked the money.

Ministers managed to reduce government spending between 1830 and 1835 from £53.7 million to £48.9 million, the latter being the lowest figure of the nineteenth century. Over £3 million was cut from military expenditure. They reduced public salaries, including their own, typically by £1,000 per annum, in accordance with recommendations of a Commons committee. A government pamphlet boasted that 1,265 offices had been abolished in 1831 and 1832.[49] After a review of the arrangements made for the receipt and payment of public money, the Exchequer was reformed in 1834. These results were impressive, perhaps too impressive. They raised the question of whether public pressure was not too unyielding and indiscriminate. Grey thought so.[50] Would government have the willpower to *raise* taxes when the situation demanded?

As for religious issues, there was no promise of legislation in the 1834 King's Speech to respond to the United Committee of Dissenting bodies' demands. And in the winter of 1833–4 northern towns witnessed campaigns critical of the Committee's moderation and calling for the abolition of church rates. In March 1834 Nottingham Dissenters petitioned Grey for disestablishment, with Hadfield in Manchester echoing the cry. Pushed into action, government's proposals disappointed even moderate Dissenters. It offered to solve the church rates problem by placing the burden on the land tax, but this retained the principle of compulsion to pay. The United Committee declared against the bill and 140 Reform MPs protested against it. A bill on the marriage problem had to be withdrawn after Dissenters complained at the role still envisaged for the Anglican church and minister in the marriage process. A proposed Tithe Commutation Bill did not materialise, while a private member's bill abolishing university tests at Cambridge was defeated in the Lords.

By early 1834, ministers' failure to command the Commons was being severely criticised. Government appeared rudderless. In 1833–4, tories won 10 seats at byelections. Grey's son reflected his father's sentiments when he described the ministry as 'utterly without unity of purpose, and the sport of every wind that blows'.[51] Even Russell thought that at the next dissolution a parliament would be returned 'with which *nobody* could govern the country'.[52] This was striking despondency for an activist whig. It cannot be explained just by the tentative but still productive response on the questions discussed above. The real nemesis lay elsewhere, in Ireland.

The Reformers, Ireland and the crisis of 1834

Support for the right of Irish Catholics to hold political and judicial office had been an article of faith among whigs for many years before its achievement in 1829, because it defended the liberty of the downtrodden against an 'oppressive' state, and provided continuing evidence of the 'illiberality' of tory government. Advocacy of Emancipation also allowed whigs to blame Irish disaffection on tory misrule. Whigs argued that, once justice had been granted, Irish society would become more 'natural' and better ordered. Improved social relations would encourage landlords to reside on their estates; capital would be attracted to industrial investment; diminished police and military expenses would lead to lower taxes for all. There was hope also of religious change. Irish Catholicism was coarse, republican and priest-ridden because it endured 'civil degradation'. Emancipation would give it the option to develop in line with the modernisation and liberalisation of Irish society.[53] In 1826, Russell envisaged that, fifty years after the passage of Emancipation, 'the Catholics would become Protestants – at least . . . less Catholics, and therefore more English'.[54]

But many whigs approached Emancipation in a purely abstract light and for practical purposes were unsympathetic to Irish Catholics. In 1827, Sefton boasted that he 'd[id]n't care a damn' for them.[55] They expected the new Catholic MPs to keep the bargain entered into in 1829 'not to impair or injure the established Church'.[56] It was natural for whig as for tory MPs – and for Dissenters – to feel that Catholicism was an immoral religion which threatened to undermine the free Protestant England of political myth. MPs voted down the first Reform Bill, in April 1831, on a clause decreasing the proportion of British to Irish MPs. So there was potential for discord over Irish *religion*. Nor were whigs clear-headed about Irish *government*. The lack of respectable, respected, resident landlords meant that they had less faith in the benefits of local control than in England. The principal force claiming to represent the Irish 'people' was O'Connell and his thirty to forty MPs who intermittently lobbied for repeal of the Union. Were they representative? And if so, were 'the people' capable of sound judgment? Might not a benevolent authoritarianism do more for the spread of liberal principles? Macaulay proposed the suspension of civil liberties and the despatch of Wellington as Lord Lieutenant.[57] But MPs used to making ritual condemnations of tory 'repression' would hardly be willing to swallow that.

The immediate Irish problem in 1831–2 was disorder, caused by poverty but exacerbated by religious tension. In 1832 there were reported 242 murders and 568 cases of arson. Non-payment of rent, and of tithe to the Anglican church establishment, had become endemic. The irremovable difficulty under which the Anglican establishment laboured was that it served only one-eighth of the population. Most of the rest were Catholic. At Doon in Limerick, the sole Protestant resident, the clergyman, demanded tithe from his 5,000 Catholic parishioners. The Catholic priest's cow was seized and offered at auction under government auspices, protected by a troop of the 12th Lancers, five companies of 92nd Highlanders and two pieces of artillery. But since no parishioner would buy the cow, it remained government property. Such scenes did not engender respect for authority.[58] But divisions within government prevented any attempt to tackle either the status of the church establishment or the spread of poverty. Schemes to pay

Catholic priests in order to encourage their loyalty to the Union were mooted in 1831 but dropped as too controversial. One important step was the national education scheme, established in 1831. A multi-denominational Board of Commissioners was set up to administer schools in which Protestants and Catholics would be taught together for secular subjects and for the reading of selected bible portions; each denomination might in addition teach doctrine to its own pupils. But the government seemed unwilling to do more, clinging to the hope that what Grey called 'a good system of government' would in itself stabilise the situation.[59] The result was paralysis. Stanley wanted coercive legislation but was refused by the cabinet. Government had proclaimed various political societies illegal, proscribed newspapers demanding repeal and arrested O'Connell, but it could not bring itself to try him. In 1832, its attempt to enforce the payment of tithes failed spectacularly and added to popular resentment against it. A legislative package designed to solve the tithe problem was mauled by the Lords so that only the harsher parts passed into law.

By the beginning of 1833, the state of Ireland was a standing affront to whig principles, as Althorp was painfully aware. MPs would no longer tolerate inaction on the church question, which was now the major threat to government survival.[60] The result was Stanley's Irish Church Temporalities Act, designed to make the church establishment more efficient and less offensive to the Catholic majority by severely reducing its size and restructuring its finances. This, he hoped, might make the payment of tithe more palatable. But he insisted on accompanying it with a Coercion Bill, something deeply alien to most Reformers. They passed it only in the expectation of genuine reform in 1834. For them, the litmus test of government sincerity became the question of appropriation, that is, the distribution of any surplus revenue arising from government interference with church funds, not to the church itself but to the benefit of the population as a whole. In 1833, government had deliberately not committed itself on appropriation, and had withdrawn a clause of the Irish Church Bill (Clause 147) when Reform MPs interpreted it in a pro-appropriation light. But the withdrawal had been opposed by 149 MPs. The question was becoming unavoidable.

In 1834, events led the government to accept the principle of appropriation. This was probably the most important single step in the formation of the Liberal party. 'No Reformer could shrink from asserting that principle.'[61] Why was its symbolism so great?[62] First, it asserted the principle that parliament had not only the right but the duty to redistribute the property of the church, a national institution, on behalf of the whole people rather than a sectional group. It signified that an established church was not a corporation of clergymen and patrons but a trust whose funds were intended for the moral and religious instruction of the nation. Appropriation, then, appealed to those who held either or both of these two opinions: that established churches should be upheld as genuinely national institutions, and that their present exclusiveness was intolerable. So it attracted radicals and Dissenters who looked forward to measures to 'unaristocratize' the established church in England too.[63] Furthermore, since Irish church funds were manifestly too large for the needs of the Episcopalian population, redistribution with one eye to the distribution of population had rational, utilitarian overtones, again encouraging to those Dissenters who believed that Anglican numerical preponderance in England was shaky. Appropriation was also a symbol of the responsiveness of the Reformed parliament to Irish needs, while it offered the prospect of the restoration of the natural order. Reformers liked to believe that the Irish were lawless only because they equated British law with tyranny, that past misrule had degraded Irish morals. Reform would secure tithe property and undermine O'Connell's incipient campaign for repeal of the Union, and it would show that whig principles promised order, yet also liberty and brotherhood. But all this would be done without giving Roman Catholics a *sectional* benefit. Rather, the money would go to make them better, soberer citizens, because it would promote the cause of national education, in which Protestant and Catholic were both taught 'those parts of the Christian faith common to all'. This would diminish sectional animosity.[64] Education, especially one in common with Protestants and placing most emphasis on simple undenominational bible-reading, would encourage more rational habits and thought-processes in the Catholic population. Over-enthusiastically, Brougham saw it as education 'within the bounds of the Protestant Church itself', and Russell as offering 'the means of moral control, which may guide the general conduct, and affect the social character of the people'.[65]

This was an idealised picture of the national education system, especially in Catholic parishes where the priest's writ ran unquestioned, but Reform MPs knew little of the true state of Ireland. What mattered was the upbeat combination of activity, integration, liberality and anti-clericalism which appropriation seemed to offer. And Anglicans, Dissenters and Irish MPs could rally on it. It was, then, astute of Russell to announce his approval of appropriation in principle when in 1834 the government brought its inevitable Tithe Bill before the Commons (the bill commuted tithe into a rent-charge, but said nothing about appropriation). A few weeks later, a radical MP, H.G. Ward, asked the Commons to approve the application of the idea of appropriation to Irish church issues. The government knew that it would not be able to persuade its MPs to resist the motion. It met it with the announcement of a commission to investigate the distribution of church revenues, but implied that it would accept redistribution in the likely event of the commission reporting a surplus. This concession to appropriation was, however, too much for four cabinet ministers, Stanley, Graham, Richmond and Ripon (the former Goderich), who resigned.

The resignations were a great turning-point in whig history. The ultimate significance of appropriation concerned its relationship to popular political influence. The crisis revealed that widespread propertied unease about ministers' ability to resist parliamentary pressure was shared by elements within the cabinet itself. Stanley, the most important seceder, refused to accept the new policy because it implied that the property and status of the church, and similar institutions, were to be allocated by the shaky judgment of a fleeting parliamentary majority, including Dissenting sympathisers and other populist-inclined MPs, not by more permanent considerations. This was a difficult case for him to argue. It was tantamount to the high tory doctrine that parliament had no right to regulate church property for national ends, a doctrine which automatically disqualified Stanley from ever leading Reform opinion. So he and Graham were anxious to place the question on as pragmatic a basis as possible and argued that appropriation was unwise because it encouraged agitations against all church establishments and the Union at a time of unprecedented unsettlement in the public mind.[66] They presumably hoped to weaken the government, with a view to creating a political realignment which would rally all the friends of stable government. They achieved the first but not the second, merely worsening the situation.*

The loss of four cabinet ministers was damaging enough. But government had more Irish bog yet to travel. One important aim of appropriation was, by establishing a *natural* 'means of moral control', to relieve government 'from the necessity of adopting acts of coercion'.[68] However, it offered no short-term alternative to the renewal of the Coercion Act, also due in 1834. Here, at least, Grey showed determination. Appalled by the loss of his most right-minded cabinet colleagues, he decided to make a stand against the unprincipled, vulgar, boorish, blustering, abusive O'Connell. This meant renewing the act *in toto*, including the three most controversial clauses, which allowed the Lord Lieutenant to ban public meetings. Almost every Commons member of the cabinet, led by Althorp, strongly opposed this course, doubting if the party would accept it and fearing that it would so irritate O'Connell as to endanger the Tithe Bill and plunge Ireland into worse disorder. A plot developed, perhaps with the ulterior motive of forcing Grey out. The Lord Lieutenant was Wellesley, long an ostentatious supporter of Irish Catholic claims. His Chief Secretary (and son-in-law), Littleton, anxious to pacify O'Connell, was in personal contact with him. Urged by Brougham, Littleton persuaded Wellesley to write to Grey that the controversial clauses were unnecessary. Littleton then secretly told O'Connell that the clauses would be dropped, in order to get his support for the Tithe Bill. Unfortunately, Grey refused to budge. When the uncut bill was introduced, O'Connell entertained the Commons to ranting allegations of betrayal and descriptions of ministerial hands 'stained with blood'.[69] Brought into full light of day were three deeply embarrassing facts: the ministry's secret negotiations with a man generally regarded by propertied

---

* Unfortunately for Stanley, he was incapable of moderation. He overstated his case, and adopted an instant, spiteful and violent opposition to his former colleagues which lost him a lot of character – just as he was to do again after 1846. Greville predicted: 'he will never inspire real confidence'. This was an accurate forecast, and goes far towards explaining the impotence of the Conservative party under his long leadership from 1846 to 1868.[67]

Englishmen as a demagogic ruffian; great divisions in cabinet on the most basic questions of order; and the declaration of the Lord Lieutenant that his Prime Minister's infringement of basic civil liberties was unnecessary. Althorp could no longer defend the bill. He resigned; Littleton resigned; Grey resigned. In the resulting vacuum, there were a number of political options. But the unspoken wish of the Commons won out, and it was Grey, and the public meetings clauses, that did not come back.

Grey's retirement definitively polarised opinion between those for whom Reformed government was sensitively liberal and those for whom it was promoting revolution. On the one side stood most Reform MPs; on the other, the bulk of gentry opinion, the tories, Grey, Stanley and sympathisers, and the king. For most of the second group, Reformers were instinctively unsound, seeking mass approbation: 'to think of governing by agency of that which is to be governed is nonsense'.[70] The king hoped for a new coalition capable of restoring authority, including the Reform leaders, Wellington, Peel and Stanley. He chose Home Secretary Melbourne to try this out. But such a coalition would be dishonourable, and was unacceptable, to all involved.

Melbourne, instead, emerged as head of an exclusively Reform administration. His principal attraction was that he was not Stanley, Althorp, Brougham or Durham. He benefited by being in the right place at the right time – just as in 1828, when he became a leading Huskissonite at a time when stock in centre parties was high, and in 1830, when he was necessary as Home Secretary, both to show that Grey's was not a real whig government and to reassure country gentlemen that order would be maintained (Melbourne had supported the suspension of Habeas Corpus in 1817). Melbourne was now the man most likely to win the confidence of both king and Commons. Firm in repressing disorder and known to dislike the Reform Bill, he lacked altogether the whig penchant for visionary constitutional and religious reform proposals. Popular in society, easygoing and sincere, he yet had great power of energetic administration. Eager for office – his private life was unexacting, owing to a famously disastrous marriage – a mask of flippant detachment only fitfully disguised a stolid conscientiousness. His doctor reported him working all day in his bedroom so that he could send unwanted callers away with the story that he was still in bed.[71] A tough, sceptical political operator and a keen observer of human foibles, he was an adroit judge of political realities, and had the common sense to avoid tricky commitments. 'God help the minister that meddles with art', he told one claimant for public money.[72] This shrewd flexibility attracted Reform as well as conservative opinion. Disdaining religious or intellectual conviction, he never clung to outmoded principle; despising aristocratic frippery, he cared nothing for station or honours; conscientious about patronage, he cut loose from Grey's nepotism. Most of all, however much his manner might have hidden it, he genuinely cared for good, progressive government.

For all the appearance of centrality and sobriety à la Liverpool, Melbourne's ministers were agreed that their government must be more loyal to the Reform majority in the Commons, and less constrained by the Lords, than Grey's had been.[73] Althorp and Littleton returned, with O'Connell in tow; the Lords responded by defeating the Tithe Bill. Melbourne also established a cabinet committee to prepare measures of relief which might be acceptable to English Dissenters. Leading nonconformists were consulted on the marriage, church rate, university and registration questions. The events of 1834 required the new government to be formed on the basis of 'movement'.

But 'movement' implied readiness to concede to pressure, and it became clear that this was unacceptable to the king. The autumn brought a series of abusive letters from O'Connell to the new Home Secretary Duncannon. It also sparked off an embarrassing and protracted row between Brougham and Durham. Durham, who had left the cabinet in 1833, saw his chance to lead a movement of real Reform. In popular speeches in Scotland he urged suffrage extension, the secret ballot and triennial parliaments, and flattered the judgment of Glasgow tradesmen and operatives. He also implicitly attacked Brougham, once the people's favourite, as inconsistent, unprincipled and untrustworthy. At least, Brougham thought this was implied. The Lord Chancellor was insufferably vain and capricious, unable to disguise vaulting ambition or to behave with the dignity that aristocratic reformers expected of their colleagues. He had by now earned a damaging reputation for mad brilliance and a grating, personal manner. He responded in character, in another speechmaking tour of Scotland in which he abused his rivals and implied that he was on terms of easy familiarity with the king. The behaviour of both, apparently drunk on popular flattery, earned derisive comment among respectable opinion and infuriated the king, to whom it was symbolic of the new politics. When Althorp's father died in November, translating him to the Lords as Earl Spencer, Melbourne proposed to replace him as Commons leader with Russell, the harbinger of appropriation. This was the last straw. The king removed his ministers on 15 November.

Though this was within his rights, it boded ill for future stable government. A minority tory government, rapidly formed under Peel, was not going to be strong enough to control the Commons, while its very existence would affront radicals and induce them to agitate for more extensive reforms. But if whigs sought to reassert control of the Reform coach, they could do so only by supplanting Peel, delivering a public demonstration of the king's impotence and entering into open alliance with radicals and O'Connell. And on returning to power, they might well have no more control over the Commons than before, yet would be faced with hostility at court and the Lords' veto on legislation. Where was the evidence that Reformed politics had promoted stability? The situation was almost bound to elicit nostalgia for the rotten boroughs which seemed to have propped governments up before 1830. In 1835, Melbourne fell to reflecting on the Reform Act. 'If it was not absolutely necessary', he wrote, 'it was the foolishest thing ever done.'[74]

CHAPTER 5

Authority and pluralism: the reform of government in the 1830s

THE FEARS FOR government stability so prominent between 1830 and 1834 were a natural response to an unfamiliar political situation. But they give a false impression of the whigs' achievement in the 1830s, as the next two chapters seek to show. Chapter 6 discusses the politics of the Reformers' second term, between 1835 and 1841; here the concern is with their transformation of the practice of government. This institutional transformation was a natural corollary of the Reform Act. The act was passed in the name of more effective, more economical and more respected government. It aimed to strengthen central government in its legitimate functions, and to reinvigorate local propertied leadership, so that both agencies would be better able to foster national progress. It offered to replace arbitrary rule with system and accountability. It sought to create a genuine community of feeling which would underpin the rule of law. The same aims shaped whig attitudes towards local government and social policy. Local leaders had crucial powers, of police, justice, taxation and example. No whig wanted to centralise those powers; but ministers were also aware of the failings of existing local rule, both in its basic function of securing respect for authority, and in the higher aims of moulding lower-class character. The object of the reforms of the 1830s was to bolster local authority and activity, and popular respect for it. This seemed to require the imposition of a more systematic administrative structure.

The younger ministers of the 1830s possessed a novel and striking confidence in government's potential to influence human behaviour for good. Brougham, Russell, Althorp, Morpeth, Howick and Poulett Thomson were only the most prominent of those whigs who read very widely in political economy, history, theology and science, and who were enthusiasts for bodies like the Society for the Diffusion of Useful Knowledge (founded in 1825) and the British Association for the Advancement of Science (1831), which aimed to propagate advances in understanding of the human and natural worlds among respectable public opinion. Their faith in the ameliorative power of law was based on a theologically-inspired rationalism. They had confidence that education, poor law, criminal law and prison reform would improve individual character, as long as reform was founded

113

on what Brougham called 'profound views of human nature'.[1] Rational observation of human behaviour would allow the framing of legislation systematic enough to remove obstacles to a more natural state of society. These obstacles checked or rendered pointless the application of human energies; so too did disorder which made property and capital insecure. But surely a benevolent deity wished to reward human virtue and industry? So the object of government must be to promote order and to encapsulate the fruits of political economy and scientific observation in statutes which would liberate that virtue and industry for its Providential purpose.

This rationalist view was not unique to the younger whigs. Something similar was upheld, for example, by the disciples of the failed lawyer, failed prison reformer, failed politician and impractical polemicist Jeremy Bentham, of whom the most important was Edwin Chadwick, secretary to the Poor Law Commission and later a member of the General Board of Health. Chadwick was a major influence on policy from the 1830s. But he was a rigid centraliser who lacked a sense of the practical and a commitment to liberal politics. Historical over-concentration on the role of Benthamites has disguised from general view the fact that the whig vision of social reform was more realistic and more influential. Whigs were rarely dogmatists. Their inured hatred of arbitrary legislation, their anxiety to promote local accountability, their awareness of the pre-existing constraints on policy, and their appreciation of the complexity of human nature all disinclined them to impose rigid models for human improvement by fiat. Government, they knew, could play only a small part in changing human behaviour. As one of the more dirigiste of them, Howick, said in 1840:

> all that the best laws and the best government can accomplish is by assuring to exertion its true reward, by providing for the security of person and property, by promoting education, and by diffusing religious instruction to encourage the formation of those habits of industry and virtue which alone can be the sources of the welfare and the prosperity either of individuals or communities.[2]

Whigs believed that politicians must not suppress popular criticism and must work with the grain of opinion, because only legislation reflecting some degree of consensus would be taken to heart and hence of real benefit. Russell wrote in 1836 that hitherto institutions 'have been lax, careless, wasteful and injudicious to an extreme . . . We are busy in introducing system, method, science, economy, regularity and discipline. But we must beware not to lose the cooperation of the country.'[3]

Nonetheless, central government needed to act, and act equitably across the country. Here the 1832 Reform Act played its part. It facilitated the orderly expression of grievances, and so boosted government confidence to act decisively on them without fear of popular rebuff. Since only government could take such bold initiatives, the paradoxical effect of 'parliamentary government' was a decline in the proportion of social legislation generated by parliament itself. In its last fifty years, the unreformed parliament had been a very active legislative body. The bills passed were usually local in scope, regulating property rights and the conduct of justice in particular areas in the light of petitions presented by individuals to their MPs. Parliament was required to decide on the most minor matters, such as particular enclosures, the widening of particular roads, and so on. Naturally this took much time, clogging the parliamentary timetable. And, in an unreformed parliament, the pattern of legislation was often arbitrary. Public opinion did not necessarily concur in bills, and consistency of practice across the nation was impossible. When legislation of a more general nature was attempted, either by government or private members, it lacked bite, because of the difficulty of enforcing it, even of reconciling it with the many previous statutes on a similar subject.

From the 1830s, the pace of government activity noticeably quickened, in several respects. One sign was the use of general legislation to plug the deficiencies in the private bill process. For example, the Tithe Commutation Act of 1836 followed 1,200 local acts which exonerated particular places from tithes or commuted them, and so was a valuable, but uncontroversial, exercise in ironing out inequalities between localities and liberating parliamentary time. But there were three other important symbols of the new strategy. One was the Royal Commission. The tories had used Commissions sparingly, setting up on average two a year between 1802 and 1830. But between 1832 and 1841 forty-eight were established.[4] They were invaluable for a government which promised firm action on a consensual basis, because they had power to investigate controversial problems on which parliament spoke with divided voices, and could be stuffed with non-parliamentary 'experts'. They could sit for longer than select committees and collect an intimidating amount of information, away from ill-informed popular or parliamentary pressure. Their conclusions could be made to look unbiassed and intellectually impregnable, essential if they were to lead to major legislation with adverse effects on powerful groups. By 1832–3, Royal Commissions were operating on the factory question, the Poor Law, municipal corporations and the church, all issues raised by popular demand in 1830. They were not, of course, altogether impartial. The Royal Commission on factory labour, for example, was set up by whig ministers anxious to curb the excesses of the Factory Reform movement, whose pressure for reductions in the hours of adult labour they thought damaging to national economic health. So the resulting Factory Act of 1833 did not limit the hours worked by those over 18. It did, however, reduce the maximum number of hours to be worked by children (9–13 years) by nearly a half, and require factory-owners to provide two hours of schooling a day. This new law was to be monitored by a permanent Factory Commission. Though weak, it was one of the earliest central inspectorates charged with regulating local practice. Such inspectorates were the second symbol of the new governing order. The third was the development of elected local bodies charged with governing substantial parts of the country.

As the century progressed and commercial society advanced inexorably (with railways, gas works, schools and the like), these three agencies revolutionised government. In future decades, government departments, associated official bodies and local authorities were all to accumulate more and more powers, previously exercised directly by parliament, in order to regulate property rights in these new and complex circumstances. This allowed greater administrative effectiveness and uniformity, while the otherwise unmanageable growth in private bill business was kept within bounds. Parliament could be freed for its proper tasks: the promotion of genuinely local legislation, and the effective checking of government action which was not in the locality's interest.

In the whig vision, then, sectional parliamentary legislation was to be curbed, Royal Commissions were to suggest major administrative changes, and inspectors were to encourage greater uniformity in local action. Better practice would be instilled into local elites by central leadership, but also by promoting their accountability to local ratepayers. The objective was to reinvigorate a local governing class, to encourage it to use its power to promote moral reform, and to inculcate general respect for its edicts. We need to observe how this strategy affected, first, the functions of local government, and then, the shape of social policy.

Local government

How was government to deal with the shortcomings of local rule, the lack of respect for law, and the lack of constructive activity? The structure of local government was very different inside and outside the towns which had been granted the status of an incorporated borough. The most immediate problems concerned the municipal corporations. Towns had sought incorporation in order to increase their control over their trading and fiscal affairs. It usually led to the acquisition of property and trust funds, and gave three key rights: of levying tolls, dues and other charges; of jurisdiction entirely or largely independent of the magistrates for the surrounding county; and of returning MPs to promote corporate interests. Since by 1800 many smaller corporations existed only to return MPs, and since the larger ones were generally assumed to exert influence in underhand ways to the same end, corporation reform was a logical corollary of 1832. But it was in fact much more necessary because of the apparently alarming consequences of corporations' exercise of their other functions. Reformers had two main objects: to rectify the incompetence of corporations as law-enforcers in potentially turbulent urban centres, and, by removing unpopular corporate privileges, to create a constructive 'community of feeling', as Melbourne put it, between the various classes in the towns.[5] These were duly tackled by the 1835 Municipal Corporations Act, which reformed the governmental structure of the 178 most significant corporations, essentially on lines laid

116

down by the pioneering Royal Commission on municipal government set up in 1833.

Corporation attitudes to law and order probably exercised the government most. They were allowed to nominate their own magistrates. Since their function had historically been essentially to protect corporation property and to promote borough trade, the borough Justices tended to be merchants or other tradesmen; they also tended to be a small, self-perpetuating oligarchy. Government was now worried that they lacked authority, for three reasons. One was that they shared in the disrespect earned by corporations on account of their sectional reputation, for example, because they were an entirely Anglican body (as in strongly nonconformist Leeds), or because they enforced the laws by which tolls and dues only mulcted non-freemen. A second was that they often seemed too remote or complacent to take necessary swift action against disorder. Nothing determined ministers to reform the borough magistracy more than the abdication of responsibility by the non-resident Bristol Justices during the 1831 riots, which allowed looting to get so disastrously out of hand. Third, as the Royal Commission report put it, many magistrates were 'selected from a class incompetent for the discharge of judicial functions', being vulgar and ignorant. The Commissioners revealed that an East Retford JP chatted with culprits brought to court and fought with a prisoner.[6] The solution found in 1835 was to make the council elective. It would send to the crown nominations of candidates for appointment as Justices and the whig government made it clear that it would accept the recommendations. The new system made it likely that nominees would be more respected by the people, and of higher social status. As with the Reform Act, whigs assumed that voters would 'naturally elect the most respectable persons' to the corporation, and that this would ensure that men of 'substance' and 'respectability' became Justices – so necessary in order to earn the 'respectful feeling essential to a due administration of justice'.[7] As in 1832, popular election was a device to secure respect for the natural leadership qualities of the propertied classes.

Authority was further bolstered in 1835 by the requirement that each reformed corporation should appoint a watch committee to manage a paid police force, with penalties laid down for constables' neglect of duty. The committee was to report quarterly to the Home Office, to encourage it to keep the force constantly up to the mark. At a stroke, then, almost every major town in the country was required to appoint an efficient police force.*

Popular but 'respectable' election (as opposed to the freeman franchise) was also the solution to the other source of tension in corporations' affairs identified by the whigs. This was their selfish mismanagement of property and finance, stirring up sectional animosity within the town. At Bristol, merchants blamed slackness of trade on corporation greed in charging high

---

* London was untouched by the 1835 legislation, but the Metropolitan Police were given a wider geographical remit and many extra powers in an act of 1839.

duties on imported goods. Freemen might benefit from corporation policy in various ways. As traders, their imports might not incur duties; sometimes their families gained material or educational benefit from the corporation's charitable trusts, rather than the poor, the church, or other intended beneficiaries. Yet in many towns there was little overlap between freemen and ratepayers. Lack of ratepayer control over corporation finance was held to explain the astronomical levels of corporate debt, which the Commission estimated at £1.86 million. Liverpool had an total bond debt of £792,000 by 1832. More typically, Bristol was in debt by over £86,000 in 1833 and had to alienate some of her estates in 1832. Exeter corporation, which was cleared of malpractice by the Commissioners, was devoting 47 per cent of its total expenditure to debt charges in 1830-1.[8] The act declared that councillors were henceforth to be elected for three-year periods by resident ratepayers of three years' standing.* It abolished favoured individuals' exemptions from dues and exclusive rights of trading, it diverted the management of charitable funds to new trustees, and it required corporations to sell clerical patronage (under supervision) and to give the proceeds to borough funds. Expenditure was limited to specific purposes, corporate property could not be bought, leased or sold without crown approval, and accounts were to be regularly and publicly audited. Thus at last might a 'community of feeling' be created.

The 1835 act did not affect the powers of the other major municipal administrative bodies, generally known as statutory authorities for special purposes. Three hundred of these had been created between 1800 and 1830. In most towns they were called either Improvement Commissions or Paving and Lighting Commissions. These bodies normally applied to parliament for permission to levy rates to pay for establishing a system of town lighting (increasingly by gas, from the 1810s), and often for other basic services such as the provision of a water supply and sewage disposal, and sometimes the collection of refuse. Moral reform was often on the agenda as well. In Alnwick, for example, the lighting and paving of the town was quickly followed by the banishing of the rowdy and traditional annual Shrove Tuesday football game from the streets to nearby pasture. The best commissions were those staffed by a town's more public-spirited merchants, tradesmen, medical experts, philanthropists and educationalists, often from the unitarian elite. Such men sought to respond to the phenomenal population growth of the early nineteenth century, which spawned severe overcrowding, appalling damage to public hygiene, and profound anxiety about theft, assault and occasionally riot. Usually they were upset by the poor state of roads and the resulting congestion, discomfort and timewasting, so damaging to the town's wealth, decorum and reputation. (Macadamization, from the 1820s, was one answer, but was not cheap.) Commissions were

* Successful Lords' amendments perpetuated the freeman franchise and added a class of aldermen, to be chosen by councillors, in order to check the assumed destructive radicalism of popularly-elected members.

often politically (even denominationally) opposed to the self-electing corporations. In Banbury after 1825 a group of reforming Dissenters used the commission to campaign against the influence which a local landowner exerted over a docile and apathetic corporation. In Lincoln a whig latitudinarian doctor, Dr Charlesworth, sought to challenge educational and sanitary inertia, vested interest electoral control, and the status quo on the corporation. In Wycombe, a full-scale battle erupted between the commission and the council, on issues ranging from the council's alleged perversion of its constitution to an ex-mayor's right to plant trees outside his house.[9] Improvement Commissions did not always form a party of reform. Often they were as oligarchical and lethargic as the corporations they were supplementing.[10] But, even so, they undoubtedly tended to increase the pluralism of local political life.

Since separate Improvement Commissions retained their functions in 1835, it is in a sense anachronistic to see the act as aiming at creating a modern system of multi-functional local government. But this is not quite fair. The 1835 Act, like that of 1832, established an open political system which forced its politicians to respond to the expression of any opinion thrown up by events. Whigs assumed that in most towns an openly elected council would be dominated by Reformers – in which they were proved right.[11] So animosity between corporation and commissioners was likely to subside. And the act gave councils power to frame bye-laws for the town's good government, and permitted Commissions to transfer their responsibilities to them. Before the sanitary crisis of the mid-1840s, few did, but then the situation swiftly changed. The act, then, was important in establishing a structure which might subsequently be used for any purposes which local conditions suggested.

The whigs had originally intended to extend the new council structure to the unincorporated boroughs enfranchised in 1832; Brougham had introduced a bill to that effect in 1833. But in these places there was no abuse of corporate property, while their sheer size had forced the evolution of tolerably efficient policing mechanisms. So the prospect of paying rates for a new layer of local government lacked attraction for many substantial inhabitants of the towns, especially since radicals – Cobden in Manchester, Attwood in Birmingham – were agitating for a permanent town council as an avowedly *political* body, to lobby for national policy changes. In these circumstances, there was no consensus for general legislation on incorporation, and instead individual towns were left to ask the Privy Council for it. Birmingham and Manchester were incorporated in 1838, but hardly any other town followed suit before the sanitary revolution transformed urban attitudes to the responsibilities of local government.

Outside the municipal boroughs, the structure of local government could be complex, but the key agencies were two: the parish vestries, which set various rates, most importantly for the relief of the poor and the upkeep of the local Anglican church; and, above all, the county magistrates. They dispensed justice locally at Petty Sessions or informally, but transacted the important business of the county, both administrative and judicial, at Quarter Sessions. Administration was increasingly laborious, and in response to it Quarter Sessions had developed considerable professionalism. The chairman, and an inner core of active Justices, tended to meet regularly to take key policy decisions, while committees supervised the different aspects of business: finance, prison management, bridge repair and the keeping of the peace (mainly under the high constables of the various hundreds and their petty constables). County government created a number of tensions, but Quarter Sessions as an institution largely escaped blame. One major complaint was the perceived insufficiency, apathy and bias of individual Justices, which manifestly lowered respect for the law.[12] The other was irritation at the high rate burden – the county rate, in parts the church rate, but above all the poor rate – especially when the relevant authorities seemed impotent in face of pauperism and crime. The whigs attempted to confront both grievances.

The first was partly tackled by a series of measures reducing individual Justices' powers of summary jurisdiction (the most important of which was their influence over the poor rate: see below). The pattern had been set by legislation which had given publicans right of appeal to Quarter Sessions against the refusal of individual JPs to renew a licence (1828), and had instituted 'free trade in beer' by allowing the easy establishment of beer-shops outside magistrates' control (1830). Greater social tension, though, was created by the game laws. The penalty for illegal killing of hares, partridges and pheasants was a £5 fine until the late eighteenth century, when poaching became commercialised in order to service a booming market. Armed poaching in gangs developed. Landowners sought redress in much more severe statutes, especially against armed group night poaching, which from 1816 to 1828 could earn transportation. As profits grew, fines for run-of-the-mill poaching, tried by one or two JPs outside Quarter Sessions, lost their deterrent value, and Justices resorted to imprisonment. This discretion vested in a local Justice, who might be the suffering owner, created class bitterness on the land and allowed radicals everywhere cheap publicity against landlords. Yet the law still failed to deter, and in the 1820s Quarter Sessions began to press for the sale of game to be legalised. In 1831 the government effected this, and so was able to reduce magistrates' power, setting penalties for common poaching offences (unlawful killing of game, trespassing in bands, intimidation with arms), at the old £5 maximum fine. Similar tension had arisen, especially in Lancashire and Yorkshire, because an act of 1815 empowered two Justices to close any footpath. In the vicinity of fast-growing towns, public rights of way which gave access to the countryside became contested ground between the urban population and local landowners. Again, summary action by interested Justices created great resentment. In the 1835 Highway Act, the power to close footpaths was transferred from Justices to juries in Quarter Sessions.

With exceptions such as these, the reputation of county magistrates had survived much better than that of their borough counterparts, largely owing to their social status. But the need to preserve that status brought another difficulty in that, in the more populous areas of the country, the number of resident Justices was grossly inadequate to maintain order and good administration. Contributing to this, whigs believed, were Lords Lieutenant of counties, who nominated candidates for the magistracy to the crown, and were usually strongly opposed to those with connections with trade.[13] The Duchy of Lancaster was responsible for appointments to the Lancashire bench, but, under tory rule until 1830, it refused to admit cotton manufacturers except in unusual circumstances. Whigs had party political reasons for wishing to redress the balance by selecting substantial merchants and manufacturers, but they were also concerned to create a broad-based, efficient and numerous propertied administrative and judicial elite. Government, helped by zealous lobbying from Lancashire Reform MPs, was appointing cotton manufacturers to the bench on a regular basis by the mid-1830s, and its quality had been transformed. Between 1831 and 1841, the number of active Lancashire magistrates rose from 160 to 282; by 1841, 70 of 94 active Justices in the Salford Hundred, the most industrialised area, were manufacturers or professional men.[14] (The resulting change of tone was especially important since so few Lancashire boroughs were incorporated and thus able to evade the power of the county bench.) Russell, Home Secretary from 1835 to 1839, disliked the tone of many county benches and sought to make similar changes nationwide. He wrote over eighty letters of recommendation to Lords Lieutenant or the Lord Chancellor (who traditionally confirmed the former's nominations), in the hope of persuading them to broaden the social composition of the magistracy.[15] When the Lord Chancellor attempted to make a radical Dissenter a Nottingham magistrate in 1839, the Lord Lieutenant, the high tory Newcastle, protested so vehemently that Russell sacked him, no doubt *pour encourager les autres*.[16] Yet government could not effectively veto county recommendations, and there were few chances to create whig Lords Lieutenant, so its room for manoeuvre was limited.*

Another mechanism by which ministers sought to improve order in counties was by reform of policing arrangements. On coming to power in 1830, they had faced disorder in the shape of the Captain Swing riots, which Melbourne, Home Secretary, repressed energetically. Fearing overtenderness from magistrates, he appointed Special Commissions to try arrested rioters; nineteen were executed and 481 transported. Later, in meeting the Chartist activity of 1838–9, the administration made a quiet and intelligent response, at odds with Chartists' rhetoric of an oppressive government, and so weakening their strongest unifying bond. The decline of the Chartist threat in 1839 justified Russell's confidence that 'the good sense and virtue of the people of England would be fatal to [Chartist]

* Though government was obviously concerned to increase the number of Reform-minded magistrates, it was not merely partisan: more Conservatives than Reformers were appointed to the Lancashire bench between 1831 and 1841.[17]

schemes and objects'.[18] In both cases, order was kept without recourse to special repressive legislation, to which whigs were hostile on principle. But they also disliked having to rely on a standing army, a bumbling yeomanry, and absurdly rigorous discretionary judicial sentences. These legacies of the *ancien régime* seemed illiberal and yet ineffective deterrents to crime. A professional police force, along the lines of Peel's metropolitan force of 1829, was the only alternative. Rural disquiet at the effects of the liberalisation of beer-selling in 1830 and at the increased stringency of municipal policing after 1835 (driving crime into the countryside) provided the opening for a Royal Commission, set up in 1836 to inquire into the wisdom of establishing county forces. This recommended creating a central body of Commissioners in charge of a national system of trained men. But this was unacceptable to the magistrates and to most MPs. In the counties, suspicion of government intervention and its effects – a transfer of power, a hike in rates – ran very high. A Police Bill drafted by Melbourne and Richmond in 1832 had foundered in face of these gut assumptions. But the Chartist scare of 1838–9 concentrated minds and made limited action politically possible. In 1839, Russell pushed through an act which allowed magistrates to establish police forces in their county, under the control of Quarter Sessions, which would decide the strength and efficiency of the forces, and oversee appointments through a chief constable. Salaries would be paid from the county rate. The Home Office reserved power to refuse permission for *extra* constables, though it had no power to demand a *minimum* number. To be seen wantonly increasing the county rate threatened political destruction for whig governments and county magistrates alike. By 1853 onnnly twenty-two of fifty-two English and Welsh counties had established a county-wide force; even the heavily-populated West Riding had not.

Whigs saw criminal law reform as equally important if authority was to be made efficient and respected. In the early 1830s, the death penalty was abolished for coinage offences, for all kinds of forgery, for stealing cattle, sheep and horses, and for larceny in houses. Mostly the result of pressure from whig backbenchers, these, unlike Peel's reforms, had a real effect; 15 per cent of all executions between 1825 and 1831 had been for cattle, sheep and horse stealing. Russell, as Home Secretary between 1835 and 1839, moved matters on. He introduced ten bills based on, but more radical than, the report of the Royal Commission on the Criminal Law (1836). These reduced the number of offences carrying the death penalty from thirty-seven to sixteen. After further changes, the death penalty survived, by 1841, for only a handful of offences; in future, people were executed only for murder and high treason. Whereas an average of 1,316 people had been sentenced to death, and 59 executed, each year between 1828 and 1830, the corresponding figures between 1838 and 1840 were 83 and 9.[19]

The contrast was striking between these simple but effective reforms and the heady rhetoric of Brougham, Lord Chancellor from 1830 to 1834. Brougham, the self-proclaimed people's champion, was anxious to cheapen the cost of justice as a protector for the poor. The legal profession might have been forgiven for quailing at the prospect of combatting his immense energy and power of propaganda. Brougham abolished some sinecures, put the appellate jurisdiction of the Privy Council on a more professional and regular basis, and improved procedure slightly in the notoriously slow-moving Court of Chancery. But legal complexities and long-established privileges prevented him from achieving radical reforms. And vested interests in the Lords blocked his most popular proposal, for the establishment of local or county courts in which suffering tradesmen could seek speedy recovery of small debts. Nor did his Commission of 1833 to codify the criminal and common law have the consequences for which he hoped.

The other local government problem was the rise in the rate burden. County rate revenue had risen from £315,805 to £783,441 between 1792 and 1832, and this was a trifle in comparison to the weight of the poor rate. Anger at these levels led the radical Hume to ask for the financial and policing functions of Quarter Sessions to be transferred to county boards elected by ratepayers. Russell accepted the principle in 1837. But the government could do nothing: to impose county boards would alienate the gentry and win no significant votes. Whigs thought Quarter Sessions efficient and were aware that most county expenditure lay outside magistrates' control (costs of prosecutions, prisons, salaries, bridge maintenance and so on).

Social policy

Ministers were aware of the need to keep some rates low, notably the poor rate, and to enlist ratepayer help in doing so. But they also knew that reducing rates would be difficult and indeed that popular pressure for reduction would endanger another of their major concerns, to which we now turn: the attempt to improve popular morality. How could they combine both objectives? Here again, a *national* approach was obviously needed, and here again it could not be supplied by central legislation alone. Local elite and ratepayer sentiment had to be enlisted in the battle – where appropriate. The three, connected, problems which seemed to demand action most urgently were criminality, pauperism and public health.

The county rate rise owed most to the cost of prosecution and prison management. In 1835, the Treasury accepted half the bill for successful criminal prosecutions. This was a sweetener to local authorities, for in the same year the government began to steer borough and county Justices, the responsible authorities, to incur the expense of prison reform. Various select committee reports in the early 1830s confirmed what advocates of reform had long known, that many local prisons were overcrowded dens of disease and ideal forcing-beds for the corruption of first offenders, debtors and minor thieves at the hands of powerful gangs of hardened criminals. They made reformation impossible. Many gaolers were willing, for a fee, to allow bartering, gambling and even prostitution in preference to operating a regime of hard labour and firm discipline. The mood of reform elsewhere strengthened the determination of aristocratic and middle-class idealists, who were ashamed at official acquiescence in these evils and convinced that prisons might be vehicles of moral reformation, at least of the more impressionable classes of offender. Evangelicals, Benthamites and whigs all held out high hopes of the character-building – and ultimately cost-reducing – effects of a rational policy. Russell was typical in arguing that crime could be tackled successfully only by forcing 'the delinquent into a course of discipline wholly opposite to his habits' – by leading him to industry, abstinence and decorum rather than idleness, debauchery and licence.[20]

The first sign of reform was a Prison Act of 1835 which appointed a centrally-funded prison inspectorate to supervise magistrates. To start with, the inspectors had few teeth, but they tended to be missionaries for scientific approaches to criminal management. In particular, they urged the classification of prisoners into categories of offenders, in order to protect the less depraved from association with evil. Many advocated the use of separate confinement in individual cells for lengthy periods, both as a sharp deterrent and in order to allow convicts to meditate on religion. Their advocacy affected government policy. A more stringent act of 1839 enforced classification into five categories of prisoner, and authorised magistrates to practise separate confinement subject to certain conditions, such as the provision of regular exercise and religious instruction (the appointment of Anglican chaplains was to be compulsory). It laid down a disciplinary code for all prison officials, to be enforced by inspectors. Many prisons would not be able to meet these conditions, and the act was intended to inaugurate a new, more systematic age in prison building. Building plans henceforth required approval by the Home Office, while there were to be two 'model' prisons, Millbank and Pentonville, with separate cells. It was hoped that these would play a crucial part in criminal reformation. In addition, over fifty prisons were rebuilt or remodelled between 1842 and 1850. Meanwhile colonial transportation, previously the standard punishment for the more serious offences, was falling out of favour. Rational thinking suggested that it hindered colonial moral development, while failing to deter future criminals or to improve the transported. Reformers held to a standard myth that it was 'a mere mockery' to call transportation 'a system of punishment'. Instead, it allowed convicts to acquire large tracts of land and stocks of cattle in Australia, like Magwitch in *Great Expectations*.[21] Government planned to abolish transportation to the most civilised Australian territory, New South Wales, and to reduce it even to the wild Van Diemen's Land. But tory MPs protested against this, essentially because they wished to check local spending on prison improvements. Government was beaten on a symbolic motion on the matter in March 1841.*

---

* In the 1840s, governments had to continue to rely on transportation because of the lack of suitable facilities at home. But its cost, the offence it caused to respectable colonists, and the lack of control over the morals of transported

Prison legislation was seen as a bedfellow of Poor Law reform, since pauperism and crime seemed to feed off each other, undermining individual enterprise, removing 'all prudential restraints', and causing 'a rapid deterioration in the moral condition' of the English people.[22] The attack on pauperism was at the heart of whig social reform in the 1830s because it promised at a stroke to cut the bloated poor rate, to teach the labourer individual responsibility, to free the productive energies of labour, to improve consumption, demand and hence wages, and therefore to restore economic viability and reduce social tension and crime. Poor Law reform aimed to restore the natural order of society, in place of a community of 'useless and superfluous members' increasing 'not according to natural laws, but according to artificial contrivance'.[23] The allowance system affronted the rational whig mind because it removed 'all motive for provident forethought' in child-rearing, lowered the value of labour and wasted capital in high rates.[24]

As in other areas, Poor Law reform was delegated to interested cabinet subgroups, and so the more enthusiastic political economists took control, rather than the fatalists like Home Secretary Melbourne. As a result, the Royal Commission set up in 1832 was dominated by thinkers confident that there was no significant natural population surplus and that systematic reform would work. (Advanced magistrates had already been experimenting by abolishing allowances and imposing a workhouse system, apparently with success.) The Commissioners' report became a best-seller, articulating the visionary hopes of a Protestant public. The result was the New Poor Law of 1834. It stripped parish overseers and their supervising magistrates of responsibility for poor relief; they were blamed for misplaced sentimentalism or cowardice and a lack of system in administration. They were replaced by boards of Poor Law guardians, who were to include resident Justices *ex officio*, but were to be mainly elected by ratepayers, on a strongly property-weighted franchise.[†] They were to operate in 667 Unions of town and country parishes, units large enough to bear the cost of building and maintaining a workhouse, and of providing adequate health care for the aged and sick and basic education for pauper children and orphans. Strict limits were imposed on their expenditure, and proper audits of accounts were required. Guidelines were to be laid down by a central Poor Law Commission of three. The Commission's ideal was that no able-bodied man should be relieved except by suffering the indignity of the workhouse, since workhouse relief would be of the most basic kind and the resulting

---

convicts, all signed its death warrant; by 1853, it had been abolished throughout eastern Australia, and in 1867 in western Australia too. In prisons, the progressive stages system became the norm, at the expense of extended separate confinement, which had led to psychiatric disorders and suicides, but rarely reformation.

† The details were complex and changed in 1844. From that year, landowners and ratepayers received one vote for property assessed for the poor rate up to £50, and one vote for each subsequent £50, up to a maximum of six votes for property assessed at £250 or more.

discomfort and moral stigma would drive him to find work instead. Though they were zealous in promoting this, as in disseminating political economy principles, the act did not enforce it, and the Commissioners shrank from imposing it on local bodies. This, not least, was because Poor Law guardians were elected local men. Whigs assumed that ratepayer pressure would combine with Commission influence to reduce extravagance; indeed they saw ratepayer election as a more reliable and proper agent of economy than central bureaucracy. Whatever the cause, poor rate expenditure in England and Wales fell from £6.83 million (1830), through £5.53 million (1835), to £4.58 million (1840).[25]*

The New Poor Law was one of those rare pieces of legislation which, to subsequent generations, defined its era. It was much less controversial in parliament in 1834 (only twenty MPs opposed the second reading) than it became when Unions attempted to apply it to unsuitable urban areas, where its suggestion of government 'repression' of the poor gave a powerful impetus to Chartism. Its significance here, though, is different, and three-fold. First, it is the classic example of legislation so direct and so potentially savage in its effects that no pre-Reform government would have dared to pass it. Second, it established, in boards of guardians, an *elected* authority across the country, separate from the magistrates' bench and more efficient than the parish vestry, which was to bear basic health care responsibilities. The guardians became the natural recipient of the future burdens inexorably devolved on the localities by Victorian systematisers: registration of births, marriages and deaths (1836), free public vaccination (1840), powers to remove insanitary nuisances (1846) and later, greater, powers (see pages 205 and 238). In 1834, tories who criticised the New Poor Law focussed on its excessive centralisation. They missed the point: it struck almost as great a blow for responsible property-oriented local government as the Municipal Corporations Act. Nassau Senior reported from Kent in 1835 that the two together had stimulated 'all sorts of local ambitions'; 'never . . . was any country more thoroughly dug up, trenched and manured'.[26]

Third, and most important, the act established Assistant Commissioners for each region. They were to report to the central Commissioners on guardians' ignorance or incompetence, but also on obstacles to the spread of industrious and self-supporting habits among the poor. As these men, usually earnest gentlemen, began their inquiries, they discovered the immensity of their remit. Crime, education, sanitary conditions, the causes of epidemics, insecurity of employment: all these came within their purview. By the late 1830s, their regular reports to the central Commission were highlighting social defects in a way which no previous information reaching government had done. They created a groundswell of public consciousness capable, unlike any mere legislative edict, of powering a fundamental shift in social attitudes. This was a vindication of whig

---

* The 1834 figure of £6.32 million was not reached again until 1863, by which time the population had risen by 42 per cent.

philosophy. Russell instructed his education inspectors in 1839 simply to 'inspect and report the facts' and let 'opinion do the rest', since 'authority never will'.[27]

One early result of Assistant Commissioners' reports was the 1839 Education Act (see page 138). Another was burgeoning government interest in the vexed question of public health. Their report of 1839 investigated causes of disease in London. Its dramatic conclusions sparked similar inquiries throughout the country. The conscience of the new Home Secretary Normanby was pricked by a personal tour of Bethnal Green. In 1840, the government supported a motion for a select committee on the health of towns. This unveiled to the world the fact that 15,000 people lived in cellars in Manchester without effective drainage or light. In 1841, Normanby introduced bills arising from its recommendations. They sought to impose restrictions on the siting and dimensions of new buildings and regulations for their drainage and ventilation, to be enforced by surveyors of buildings under town council control. But the bills were lost; government was frustrated by its small majority and much local apathy and hostility. Even improving local authorities like Leeds and Manchester found aspects of the bills offensively dictatorial. The whigs had to be content with more indirect stimulus of opinion. Normanby's bill did in fact goad the big towns to promote their own private bills. Successful also, eventually, was the £10,000 subsidy-bribe voted in the estimates of 1840 to whet local interest in providing public walks and parks. Manchester was among the first authorities to respond to it. And in the same year a Royal Commission was set up to investigate children's employment in mines and factories. Its report of 1842 was to hammer another great nail into the coffin of public ignorance of the urban working classes. The 'condition of England' question had been posed, and the whigs had played the major part in posing it.

By 1841 the structural groundwork of Victorian social policy had been laid. Inspectors were reporting, the public mind was exercised, and elected urban and rural authorities were in place to mirror and capitalise on local interest. In the 1850s, 1860s and 1870s, the expansion of this system gave the respectable classes of Victorian England, from the local elite to the body of ratepayers, enormous political influence over decisions that mattered to them. This contributed to political stability, while minimising the amount of further statutory reform needed. Though the 1830s saw a great deal of legislation on the matters discussed in this chapter, this was *not* seen as the precursor of regular bureaucratic intervention, but the fruit of exceptional circumstances. Once the system was established, it could reform itself, until it ran to the satisfaction of the propertied Victorian consumer. The Liberal ideal was a moralistic but pluralistic self-governing order.

CHAPTER 6

The emergence of the Liberal party, 1835–41

MELBOURNE AND THE Reformers returned to office in April 1835. Peel's minority administration had been short-lived. He had called an election at the new year in the hope of gaining enough strength to continue, but though the tories made remarkable gains, Reform forces still had a large Commons majority. They found opposition in such circumstances intolerable: tories were governing in defiance of the people's will. They charged that rule on old tory principles would court mass disaffection and encourage radical agitation, while the only alternative open to Peel, of stealing the Reformers' clothes, would involve losing his honour and degrading the character of public men.[1] But how to remove him? Grey, Howick and Lansdowne, anxious not to undermine constitutional authority, believed that Peel should not be supplanted but reinforced with whigs and Stanley in a stable coalition. They were especially anxious for Reformers not to seem dependent on radicals and O'Connell. In fact, Peel was defeated on so many issues – the Speakership, appropriation, Irish tithes – that his authority was in tatters. He resigned in April 1835, and there was no coalition. Melbourne's new government was a purely Reform government. To its critics, it did not appear – and never became – any more stable than his first. But this chapter argues for a more positive view: the emergence of a more-or-less coherent 'Liberal party', advancing principles attractive enough to supplant mere 'Reform' as a common watchword. This was not a professionally managed party, nor were its principles embodied in regular policy packages. The Liberal party was a liberal party. But it was effective enough. Melbourne did not fall in 1841 because of internal division or government incoherence.* He fell because Liberalism was in advance of opinion among the electors who mattered, those who dictated the result in county and small-town seats.

---

* The government was defeated by one vote on a confidence motion, though many ministers were seeking a dissolution anyway. The confidence motion was preceded by a controversial vote on the sugar duties, on which 33 Reform MPs opposed or abstained (largely county and seaport MPs). But 26 of them then supported government in the vote of confidence.[2]

Tory revival coloured the whole Liberal governing experience after 1835. It stemmed primarily from county gentlemen's disquiet about Liberal ability to defend institutions and provide 'strong' government. Election majorities fell to about 80 in 1835 and 20 in 1837 (including about that number of unreliable Irish Repealers). A major cause of this was simply the drift of sitting propertied MPs or prevailing borough interests: at least 58 MPs who had been Reformers had become tories by 1841.[3] But better organisation by the alarmed local propertied hierarchy was as important, responding to the new need for potential voters to be sought out and registered in advance. Between 1833 and 1837 the registered county electorate rose from 344,000 to 444,000.[4] Peel, determined never again to suffer the indignity of governing without a Commons majority, himself encouraged organisation. In 1841, tories gained 23 seats in the 63 constituencies where most registrations had taken place since 1837.[5]*

Paradoxically, though, the steady drift to toryism was one of the many sources of renewed strength which Melbourne gained in his second government. What were these? The first was that his new cabinet stood on an improved basis. After Peel's unhappy experience in government, for a long time there was no alternative. Knowing this, the king strove, not *always* successfully, to behave politely to his ministers. Then, in 1837, the accession of the 18-year-old political virgin Victoria transformed avuncular Melbourne's standing at court and gave him a unique chance to shape the modern constitutional monarchy. Grey soon ceased to matter; his aloof style quickly dated. Russell's strategy in 1835 of once more rallying Liberals on appropriation tarred Stanley with the most illiberal of brushes and destroyed his dream of leading a central coalition, so he had no choice but to accept a subordinate place on the tory benches. Melbourne exercised to the full the privilege of choosing his own ministers. He refused to tolerate either Brougham or Durham again, and, since neither was in the Commons, their exclusion offered little threat. Wellesley and Littleton, the Irish officers responsible for the 1834 *débâcle*, went too. The prima donna element all but disappeared and there was little jockeying for advantage. Russell was clearly the dominant Commons figure. Melbourne kept his cabinet happy by operating a 'government of departments', with each minister enjoying substantial independence over policy. All in all, 1835 marked the major stage in the whigs' move away from Regency posturing, though not yet to full-blown Victorian industriousness.

The Commons, too, was amenable, not least in reaction to the unpleasant shock of tory government. With Althorp's elevation, the principal exponent

---

* Note also that, as local organisation, and partisanship over national issues, developed, a party could now dominate in many boroughs where previously coalitions of interests had had to share control. Of the 110 English boroughs whose boundaries were not seriously affected by the reallocation of 1832, the number with split representation fell from 55 to 33 between 1830 and 1841, reversing the pre-Reform trend. Split voting among individuals also declined, until the tory split of 1846 increased it again.[6]

of extreme laxity in whipping had disappeared. The new whip, E.J. 'Ben' Stanley, was an effective whip by Reformers' standards, and enjoyed the confidence of radicals. The choice of junior whips also indicated an attempt to bring many types of Reform MP under the government umbrella. They included a big-town representative (Parker of Sheffield), a Scottish radical, and, as Irish whip, two Catholics in succession (More O'Ferrall and Wyse), both of whom were respected both by Englishmen and by O'Connellites. The appropriation issue was an ideal rallying-point. It manifested an abstract desire to placate the Irish, without conceding on the matters which O'Connell or Irish opinion really cared about; it criticised the exclusiveness of religious establishments in a way of which British Dissenters were bound to approve, without offering them anything substantial; while, since it was not very popular in the country, whigs avoided the charge that they had resumed power by whipping up agitation. Tory revival, a small government majority, and electoral defeats for radicals concentrated Reform MPs' minds with the result that hardly any were inveterately hostile.[7] They tended to realise that there was no prospect of a successful agitation for more advanced policies, since there was insufficient 'sound stuff' among the electorate on which to ground a campaign.[8] O'Connell appreciated that he would not get a better Irish policy than ministers were offering. The Reform Club was established in 1836 to provide a common home for whigs and radicals within the party, and 250 MPs, including most cabinet ministers, joined that year, though it never supplanted more familiar meeting-places like Brooks's.

The third gain was the growth of party spirit in the country, an obvious response to registration requirements, tory organisation, and the need to fight the new corporation elections. The church rate conflict was also crucial here, because in many places it politicised vestry elections between church and Dissent and so identified Dissenters with the forces of Reform. In the early Victorian period, then, party developed from the local need to fight elections against a common enemy. Historians of pollbook analysis have identified a general pattern of allegiance in towns. Reformers tended to be merchants, professionals or shopkeepers whose life centred on the town itself, and largely Dissenting; tory supporters were mostly Anglican and had more trading or social connections with surrounding propertied families.[9]

The growth of local popular organisation on the Reform side was of great importance for national politicians. At first sight this is not obvious, because ministers kept their distance from those, like the radical Birmingham solicitor Joseph Parkes, who took the lead in stimulating and coordinating registration activity from the centre. In May 1835 a Reform Association was founded for this purpose, but ministers did not join. It was necessary for them to steer clear of electoral organisation and those who fixed it, in order to preserve their own reputations for independent judgment and dignity – just as it was still not normal for politicians to speak in other men's constituencies. But this does not mean that the parliamentary party was not responsive to public sentiment. For a start, most MPs had joined the

Reform Association by the year's end. Parkes worked with Ben Stanley on registration and discussed progress with Melbourne.[10] More important, the regularity of contested elections after 1832 fundamentally determined Reformers' governing style. None of them could afford to forget the party's popular basis. Each general election was a reminder of it and forced an accommodation with it. As parties diverged, tories rallied round the crown, the church and institutions in general, while Reformers stood on the basis that they sympathised with public anxieties and sought to respond constructively to them. Casting round for a name which would reflect this principle of open, flexible government better than the insipid 'Reformer', politicians began to use the phrase 'Liberal party'.[11]

The increasing adoption of the term 'Liberal party' was important because it symbolised willingness to respond pragmatically to opinion. In most policy areas, it did *not* imply a commitment to particular legislation. In fact, faced with the suspicion of country gentlemen and the Lords, ministers were anxious to play down the role that policy – necessarily contentious – would play in their deliberations. Melbourne emphasised that 'the passing of bills and making laws is only a subsidiary and incidental duty of Parliament'; its main task was to consider and amend the estimates of necessary expenditure, and to correct abuses.[12] On disputed issues, where consensus was impossible, Liberals preferred to leave each minister free to take his own view rather than to force a policy on the party. Maybe this approach was the child of necessity, but it allowed them to contrast their policy of open debate in parliament with Peel's authoritarianism. Spring Rice maintained in 1840 that any party which sought a rapport with public opinion had to respect 'freedom of judgment'. The Liberal party, he argued, was the political equivalent of the Reformed churches: it was founded on the principles of tolerance and encouragement of free inquiry, among independent, respectable and religious men, the only way to increase 'the sum of human virtue, happiness, and freedom'.[13] Jeffrey asserted that Melbourne's government was only 'weak' for the purpose of carrying through speculative and crotchety changes which had not been properly aired and matured. It was strong for its proper functions, of 'maintaining clear rights and demolishing abuses', where it had the support of public opinion.[14] To dictate a course to the people's MPs was distasteful. In 1836 Holland recalled that eighty years previously his grandfather (Henry Fox) 'was nearly impeached for saying he was to *manage* the House of Commons and we are assailed with invective and menace because we do not *command* them'.[15]

However, Liberals *were* also able to agree on particular ideals and policies. For example, we saw in chapter 5 how commitment to representative municipal government, economy and tolerance of Chartist activity united the party. The rest of this chapter shows how, in the late 1830s, two other sets of issues in particular were used to rally Liberal MPs. One, arising out of the great principle of appropriation, concerned religion and Ireland; the other, developing from 1839, was free trade. Both offered a double advantage: they would alter the image of the state in an intellectually coherent whiggish direction, and bolster respect for it among potentially disaffected groups; and they would win the party support from electorally important extra-parliamentary opinion. Both lines of policy were enthusiastically adopted by Russell and indicate the power he now had over party development.

Russell, Liberalism and religion

Between 1834 and 1855, the leader of Liberal MPs, and the most effective interpreter of the Liberal frame of mind, was Lord John Russell. Russell had a stronger sense of history, and hence of personal destiny, than any British political leader except Churchill. His impressive output included a history of Europe from 1713, two books on the history of Christianity, an essay on the French Revolution and another on the development of the British constitution. These books, though not as unsubtly black-and-white as some whig accounts, effectively charted the contrast between insolent, rapacious despotism and constitutional government. Good law secured liberty; liberty promoted reason and progress. Organic reform of political and legal structures, with this in view, was the politician's proper contribution to a more civilised society. In similar vein, Russell also published a full-scale biography of Fox, two editions of correspondence (of Fox, and of Russell's great-grandfather, the mid-eighteenth-century government whig the fourth duke of Bedford), and a life of the fourth duke's grandfather, William, Lord Russell. This was the Russell who led the 'country' party in opposition to Charles II and was executed on a dubious charge of treason in 1683, becoming a martyr to liberty symbolic enough to gain the family a dukedom after 1688. The history of the Russells, especially in the 1640s and 1680s, seemed to uphold two great principles. One was support for popular liberties against government repression, but expressed judiciously and with a view to maintaining order. Lord John wrote that William had spurned the idea of a popular rebellion, while William's grandfather, a moderate parliamentarian, had sought to prevent the Civil War by mediation. The other was hostility to popery and high churchmanship, not surprising in a family with so direct an interest in the success of the Reformation (their lands were mostly royal grants deriving from the dissolution of the monasteries). Lord John's public career was constructed around these principles, suitably updated for the nineteenth century by an Edinburgh University education in the tenets of history and political economy, and practical political tuition from Lord Holland, guardian of the Foxite flame.

Russell was loyal, then, to a set of whig ideals – liberty, retrenchment, toleration, integration, freedom of inquiry, regulated order – and to the notion that, historically, Russells were leading promoters of them. His self-confidence was striking in two respects. One was that institutional reform would advance liberty, the power of reason, and hence national harmony, not only in the sphere of central and local government (worth a wager), but in areas of greater complexity and risk, principally Irish and religious affairs. The other was that Russell himself, seeing this, deserved the lead in bringing it to pass.

Russell's achievement was to fashion from what might easily have re-mained mere whig platitudes a serviceable political creed that pleased the majority of Liberals – whig, Reformer, radical, Dissenter, Catholic – for thirty years. He found ways of cooperating with evangelicals, Dissenters and Catholics on religion, with men of all classes on economy, with intel-lectuals, philanthropists and radicals on law reform. Partly his success in this was the result of the reputation that he had gained by repealing the Test and Corporation Acts and introducing the Reform Bill, both before he was forty. Association with these seminal reforms, though, was not mere luck. It exemplified his greatest asset, his boldness of initiative and his shrewdness of judgment about the measures which opinion could be per-suaded to accept. Russell's fearless adoption of new courses accounted for much of the respect in which MPs held him. He in turn believed in the need for a 'decided course of policy' in order to win the confidence and disciplined cooperation of the Commons.[16] A strong party, united behind a leader of purpose, was in his eyes the prerequisite of good government. Repeal of the Test Acts, parliamentary and municipal corporation reform, appropriation, the Corn Laws in 1841: all these issues were well chosen to rally Liberal sentiment. But he did not think that policy should emanate directly from the popular will. Some of Russell's most striking initiatives concerned issues on which public sentiment was cool, principally educ-ational and Irish reform. In 1844, frustrated by lack of popular sympathy for a campaign to conciliate Irish Catholics, he was reduced to snapping: 'if the people were wrong they ought to be put right'.[17] Leaders knew best; their task was to judge how far the Commons could be guided without disaster ensuing. The talents, character and name of the leader, then, were essential aids in building a suitable rapport with followers. Here Russell had many advantages. He was extremely able: quick in understanding, rapid in action, economical and lucid in speech, phlegmatic in composure. Though not a compelling orator (even if Disraeli was characteristically uncharitable in describing him as 'cold, inanimate, with a weak voice and a mincing manner'[18]), he was adept at making his policy aims appear those which genuine Liberals should want.

But Russell's judgment was no more infallible than anyone else's. His drawbacks were two. One was his lack of stamina. Small, weak, affected by heat and subject to fainting fits, he often failed to carry through his original impulses, and could appear vacillating. More serious was the consequence of his belief that a Russell's place was always at the head. Intensely am-bitious for honourable fame, his attitude to leadership was selfish, a trait compounded by a home-based education and natural shyness. He rarely consulted others, and never flattered subordinates, very often appearing 'cold, short, abrupt, indifferent'.[19] He left it to others to reconcile, or smooth ruffled feathers. This made him appear socially exclusive. In his decline after 1852, petulance at being superseded worsened his unpredictability. But in his long heyday it was different, and if he was sometimes impatient and impulsive, boldness was better than caution in the eyes of most Liberal MPs. The ultimate fact about Russell is that a combination of name, achievement, talent, fearlessness and principle left him without serious rivals as the greatest Liberal statesman of his age.

In the late 1830s, part of Russell's attraction to Liberal MPs was his policy, as Home Secretary, on the questions discussed in chapter 5: the reform of municipal corporations, the severe restrictions in the death penalty, the scientific reform of secondary punishments, and libertarianism in general. In 1836, Russell secured a free pardon for the 'Tolpuddle martyrs' of 1834 and secured first-class passages for their return journey from transportation. He was determined not to repress legitimate Chartist protest, arguing that the people had a right to declare their grievances so 'that they might be known and redressed'.[20] It was idle, he said, to think that force would remove discontent. The cause of Chartism was altogether different. It had arisen because the manufacturing population had grown up in appalling conditions, lacking 'early instruction . . . places of worship' and the chance of having 'their opinions of property moulded by seeing it devoted to social and charitable objects'. It was to 'religious and moral instruction' that one should look to 'knit . . . together the inhabitants and classes' and ensure 'a fair and gradual subordination of ranks'.[21] Russell regarded Chartism as deluded, since it aimed to strike at agencies which he considered essential, the Poor Law Commission, a parliament of independent gentlemen, and a church established in each parish as a moral guide. But the way to demonstrate these delusions was by active promotion of the Liberal alternative, so that reason and virtue were developed. Chartism highlighted a need which to Liberals was already obvious – to supply a system of morality to accompany and enrich the rationalised system of order which we saw being established in chapter 5. The key battle to be fought in order to strengthen the state was the spread of 'enlightened religious and moral principles'.[22] Hence the centrality of religious questions – of church, education and Irish reform – to Russell and like minds.

Whigs had traditionally seen the political function of religion in utilitarian, integrative terms – in the flippant phrase of one of their critics, as 'practically a subdivision of the Home Department for the promotion of morals'.[23] They placed a high value on the maintenance of church establishments, because, however optimistic they were about the *possibility* of progress in suitable moral conditions, they were far from being utopian about human nature. Russell believed that modern man was a 'creature of passion and of imagination', capable of almost as much 'rapacity and . . . ambition' as 'Achilles and Agamemnon'.[24] No equivalent period seemed to have taught more terrible lessons about human sinfulness than that since 1790. Liberty was endangered by infidelity, aristocratic luxury and working-class indiscipline. But establishments were good also because they allowed the state to check that potentially most dangerous of human emotions, religious intolerance. The Church of England, in Brougham's words, was the 'best and most tolerant and most learned' of churches and so the most suited to offer spiritual instruction.[25] Whigs were instinctively anti-clerical, in that they disapproved of the exclusiveness of the tory-church link before 1828, and, more broadly, of the obscurantism, doctrinal pedantry and bigotry which had traditionally disfigured religion and created division and bloodshed in the name of a benevolent God.

These views remained at the heart of the whig-Liberal tradition. But there were generational variations. At the beginning of the nineteenth century, many whigs were well-read Enlightenment sceptics about orthodox religion, while others took their morals from the circles frequented by Fox and the Prince of Wales: gambling, even drinking, were ideological statements of hostility to tory-clerical governing values. This combination of attitudes cast whig anti-clericalism in a distinctive light. Lord King, actually an intellectually serious whig-unitarian, had 'a childish love of mischief and enjoyed plaguing the Bishops and the clergy' by presenting his heterodoxy to the Upper House in 'the shape most revolting to the taste of the audience'.[26] But the next generation of whigs, reared on a diet of international and economic turbulence, political economy, and administrative reform, were profoundly affected by the revival of evangelical seriousness among the propertied classes. To these men – specifically, for our purposes, Russell, Howick, Morpeth and Baring, but the same was true of very many others – religion was a check on the natural passions inherent in sinful humanity, and a way of reconciling a society made fractious by economic and social change, but it was also the key to an urgently-needed moral regeneration. They gained from historical reading a strong sense of the ebb and flow of human societies. Past states, they held, declined into profligacy, vice, materialism, superstition and self-interest when they lost the appropriate values of a pure religion, civilised manners, pride in knowledge, and a devotion to the public weal. The Christian church was a living organism necessary to man's well-being. Religion was essential enough as an ethical code, the basis of public virtue and order, but it was also an inner experience providing man with a sense of something beyond his powers, towards which to direct his development. The Christian personality was the basis of true, securely-established civilisation. Government reform of the church and encouragement of the right sort of education could, like local philanthropy, play an important part in stimulating the spiritual energies of the people.

Some of these men read widely in evangelical theology; others, like Russell, held to a biblical religion, disbelieving even the Thirty-nine Articles. But even the most evangelical were genuine liberals in their commitment to tolerance as between sects and in their confidence that scientific discovery could be reconciled with religious truth. What matters here is their common devoutness – lax old Holland found Howick and Morpeth frighteningly 'serious' on religious subjects in 1839 – and anxiety for the spread of a simple Protestant creed.[27] Lord Suffield had moved in the fastest of sets as an undergraduate and was famed for bending pokers round his neck, but became a sober and pious prison reformer and anti-slaver, a zealous advocate of the Anglican church as 'the most simple and the most rational and the most Christian' of all.[28] Sometimes this earnest commitment to tolerance and brotherhood could become a little wearing, as in the case of Morpeth, MP for the prestigious West Riding until 1841. Morpeth hoped that his public speeches urging class and religious harmony would establish his title to national leadership. But he lacked the determination and incisiveness to rise really high. Defeated in 1841, and banished to the Lords in 1848, he spent the rest of his career disseminating his benevolence in soothing, philanthropic gestures and appeals.

In the 1830s, these younger whigs led the way in forging a legislative programme out of this updated attitude to religion. Religious reform was to follow the lines of parliamentary reform: a genuinely national service was to be put on offer. Exclusive ecclesiastical institutions were to be rationalised, so as to underpin order and to liberate moral energy. Principles of civil liberty demanded that Dissenting rights should be upheld, but the reform of the church establishment would improve its effectiveness as an agent of education, spirituality and pastoral care. This would broaden its foundations and attractiveness, and could not but fail to win some Dissenters over. Government should also play a more direct role in education (as a few older whigs, such as Brougham and Whitbread, had also suggested). The church was too apathetic, exclusive and unpopular to be entrusted with the task of national education. So the state must act, and encourage a system of learning which highlighted the ethical tenets shared by Anglicans and Dissenters, rather than what divided them. Many leading whigs were active in the British and Foreign Schools Society, the major founder of elementary schools outside the Anglican church network, which operated on undenominational principles. And the need to spread similar principles in Ireland made appropriation a key Liberal symbol (see page 108). (Some whigs, like Russell, were prepared to endow the Roman Catholic Church there on the ground that as the people's church it was the best agent of religion and morality.)

Reform of the Church of England had been placed on the agenda by the Reform crisis of 1830–2, which concentrated previously intermittent anger at its misgovernment and complacency. Church leaders themselves woke up to the danger of an anti-slavery-type agitation against it, and in 1832, Grey agreed to their suggestion of a Royal Commission to investigate ways of redistributing church revenue more equitably and productively. Its report paved the way for a standing Ecclesiastical Commission (set up, as it happened, during Peel's brief ministry of 1835), made permanent by the Liberals in 1836. Though parliament would express grievances, lay and clerical experts on the Commission would frame the resulting legislation. Three bills emerging from the Commission's labours were passed in 1836, 1838 and 1840. They greatly reduced the inequalities between the salaries attached to different bishoprics, suppressed certain offices in cathedral chapters, redistributed capitular property which was surplus to requirements to poorer parishes, and restricted the opportunities for pluralism. Meanwhile, an act of 1836 abolished payment of tithe in kind in return for a compulsory cash payment which would depend on the price of corn. This removed a great bone of contention between clergy and parishioners, and also promised more capital investment in agriculture. Such bills did a great deal to improve the church's image.

The church rate issue was much more controversial because it raised the question of the church's privileged status. Even many Liberals wished to uphold the national church's abstract right to levy the rate, though they were happy for local vestries to eschew it. Compulsory rates were levied but fiercely contested in Manchester in 1833 and 1834, and renounced thereafter. In Birmingham and Leeds there were great battles in the mid-1830s, no rate being levied in Birmingham after 1831 and Leeds after 1835. In Leicester the levy had ceased in all but one staunchly Anglican parish by 1837. Local fervour naturally spilled over into national politics. In 1836, there was a major petitioning campaign for (and against) abolition, and the Church Rate Abolition Society was formed in the winter of 1836–7. The issue was disturbing local peace between Protestant sects, and threatened to raise an agitation against the establishment. So the government had to propose a plan, more advanced than that of 1834. In 1837 it proposed to allocate surplus church revenue (acquired by the redistribution undertaken by the Ecclesiastical Commission) to the upkeep of local church fabric. No compulsory rate would be needed. Unfortunately, the Commission refused to admit that internal reform would provide enough revenue, forcing the government to try to raise the money through a separate board charged with the leasing of church property. This outraged the bishops and the tory party, because it meddled with church government. Ministers' suggestion that the church could flourish without rate support was bold, even foolhardy, and many churchmen saw this as a threat to the notion of establishment. An Anglican petitioning campaign arose all over the country. The tories exploited the agitation, significant numbers of MPs became reluctant to support the bill, and the government had to drop it. The fracas stimulated a 'Church-in-danger' cry damaging the Liberals at the 1837 election, and the government declined to tackle the question again. It would have to be decided by the local balance of forces.

The cabinet had more success in meeting other Dissenting grievances. Two acts of 1836 broke the Church of England's monopoly over the registration of births, marriages and deaths and the marriage ceremony. A civil register was set up, maintained by local officials. (This also pleased public health campaigners and others who lobbied for reliable population estimates.) And marriages, if registered with the secular authorities, could be solemnised either in places of worship outside the Anglican church, or in registry offices. After the Lords defeated the 1834 bill to open matriculation and degrees at Oxford and Cambridge to those who refused to swear allegiance to the Thirty-nine Articles, there was no point in more movement on that question. But in 1836 government granted a charter to the London University, where no religious profession was required, so that it could award degrees.

Russell cared most of all for the extension of state superintendance of elementary education. In 1833, the government had given the first, modest Treasury grants to the two voluntary educational societies, the National Society, which ran most schools on exclusively Anglican principles, and the whig-Dissenting undenominational British and Foreign Schools Society. Then whig interest, Poor Law Commission reports, the work of domestic missionaries from the various Christian sects, and the spread of Chartist unrest all highlighted the problem of infidelity in large towns. But the publicity also encouraged earnest young high churchmen in the National Society, including W.E. Gladstone, to urge an expansion of Anglican school-building, in order to monopolise the state grant. Russell, driven by an emotional hostility to the political exclusiveness and doctrinal rigidity of the Anglican priesthood, wanted a very different system. His prime concern was that children of all Protestant sects should study the bible together, and that, if specific Anglican teaching was also to be provided, it would take a secondary place, and Dissenter children might opt out. He hoped that schools would only be funded on these terms – perhaps by the existing state grant, preferably by a more ambitious system of local rating and control. Finally, he wished for state inspection of all funded schools. Roman Catholic schools would be funded for the first time, separately. No matter that they would get a better deal than Anglicans, who would be forced to swallow an essentially undenominational system, and who would regard the scheme as undermining their claim to state protection.

The cabinet, less emotional and more politically realistic, blocked Russell's plans in 1838. His less radical bill of 1839 established an entirely lay Committee of the Privy Council to administer the annual grant to the schools of the two societies. Grants were to be awarded only on submitting to state inspection, but no stipulation was made as to religious teaching. However, setting a marker for a more ambitious future scheme, the Committee would run a teacher-training college and a model school, in which only bible-reading was to be compulsory. Each sect, including Roman Catholics, could supplement this by denominational teaching at set times. The symbolism of this was enough for Anglicans and tories to launch a massive campaign against the bill, as undermining church supremacy. Russell was contemptuous of his former colleague Stanley, now a tory, who 'quoted, in a great speech, a dictum of Henry IV, only four centuries old, assuming for the church the monopoly of education'.[29] But the campaign was very effective. In order to get state inspection accepted, the government had to abandon the college and model school, and later had to agree that all inspectors of National Society schools would be appointed at the discretion of the church and operate on its instructions. This was embarrassing. Brougham thought that propertied alarm at irreligion, Dissent, social change and government weakness after the Reform Act had resulted in a more complete victory for the church than it would have been able to achieve thirty years before.[30]

Liberal unity in 1834-5 had been founded on the promise of sympathy, justice and moral reform in Ireland. Charged with realising this was the new Lord Lieutenant, Mulgrave, a man of disputed ability, but grand, theatrical, indiscreet, romantic (he had written several silver-fork novels) and confident in the popularity of well-publicised aristocratic leadership. In June 1835 he made a triumphal entry to Dublin on a showy charger, wearing a special fancy green uniform, and accompanied by symbols of Irish nationality such as a flag with a cap of liberty. His splendid court in Dublin was meant to encourage landlords to reside on their estates and exercise a paternalist leadership of their tenants. When he attended Dublin's Theatre Royal, he would send an aide-de-camp to invite members of the audience to his box.[31] These gestures were reinforced by policy initiatives designed to convince Irishmen to place confidence in government, and so flesh out the 'Lichfield House Compact' by which O'Connell had indicated his support for the whigs against Peel in 1835. These initiatives owed more to the Chief Secretary, Morpeth, and more still to the Under Secretary, Thomas Drummond, formerly Althorp's private secretary. The 1834 Coercion Act was allowed to lapse. It was replaced by a greatly reformed Irish police force, previously distrusted as corrupt and Protestant, but now placed under an Inspector General who appointed Catholics in large numbers and improved efficiency. Orangemen among the local magistracy were marginalised as far as possible by the appointment of stipendiary Justices in Dublin to superintend them while obstreperous tory magistrates were occasionally sacked. Collection of tithes was rarely enforced by government. Prisoners of good conduct were given early reprieves. Local government reform gave cesspayers some check on expenditure. Disorder diminished. O'Connell ceased to advocate repeal and cooperated with the executive. At least six Catholics were given political office between 1835 and 1841, and Catholics were frequently allocated local patronage, often on his recommendation. Another victory for Mulgrave, and for Home Secretary Russell, was the introduction of an Irish Poor Law in 1838 based on the workhouse system. This, they believed, would force landlords to capitalise agriculture in order to achieve the reductions in pauperism seen after 1834 in Britain. Given also the success of the Irish national education system – 395,000 children were being educated in 3,153 schools in 1843 – Liberals looked on their Irish policy as a major achievement.

Propertied Anglicans in Britain did not see matters like this. To most of them, the government was controlled by O'Connell, was outrageously soft on crime, and turned a blind eye to Catholic religious aggrandisement. Government policy played into the hands of the Lords, which was able to oppose Irish legislation and claim that it was acting in the national interest. Irish Tithe, Municipal Corporations and (voter) Registration Bills were all blocked or crippingly amended in this way. In angry reaction, in 1836,

Russell urged the creation of more peers. In fact, Melbourne created forty-two peers in six years, and Grey before him thirty-six in four, many more than the norm for nineteenth-century Liberal governments.[32] But it made no difference, because, as Russell himself admitted, public support for the controversial Irish legislation was 'very imperfect'.[33] Appropriation was singled out for attack: Tithe Bills which included provisions for it were obstructed in 1835, 1836 and 1837. Eventually it had to be dropped, and the rest of the tithe commutation became law in 1838. The symbol of appropriation had become a major embarrassment. In cabinet, Hobhouse was perhaps typical in seeming 'alarmed at giving it up . . . but . . . yet more alarmed when we seemed to be inclined to bring it forward'.[34] The reform of the oligarchical Irish municipal corporations (only four out of sixty contained Catholics) proved even more awkward. The government wanted to provide more representative and respected local administration. But, although bills were introduced from 1835, it was not until 1840 that the Lords would agree to enact one, and this after amending it so that the franchise level was raised to £10 and fewer than a dozen towns were required to set up corporations – both amendments being calculated deliberately to minimise Catholic influence.

So government policy on religion and Ireland had a divided legacy. On the one hand, it did something to advance Russellite ideals, and it strengthened Liberal bonds with Catholicism and Dissent. Liberal representation in Ireland rose from 33 to 47 between 1835 and 1841, at the expense of O'Connell's Repealers (down from 34 to 18).[35] Among British Dissenters, the general picture is clouded (as throughout the century) by the existence of a small minority of radical evangelical zealots who were prone to react intemperately to almost any state interference with individual religious rights, and were especially vocal in economic depression. For example, the baptist minister J.P. Mursell and the congregrationalist Edward Miall responded to the failure to settle the church rate question by leading a campaign for disestablishment based in Leicester. Most politicised Dissenters, though, were not zealots but worldly men committed to Liberal government and its practical benefits in religious, municipal and legal reforms and in its work against slavery.* They overwhelmingly supported the 1839 Education Bill as an assault on Anglican monopoly; voluntaryism only seriously developed in the 1840s in reaction to perceived tory-Catholic aggression (see page 201). Church rates were not a problem. They were not levied in most big towns by 1840, while the struggle for vestry control had done a great deal to identify nonconformity with the local Reform party. The drift towards free trade pleased Dissenters further (see page 148). In the 1830s, they are recorded as voting Liberal to tory in ratios of around ten

---

*   Slaves were fully emancipated when the apprenticeship system collapsed in 1838 after a high-pressure evangelical-Dissenting campaign led by the Birmingham quaker Joseph Sturge. The crucial impulse in making planters surrender was an abolitionist motion in parliament supported by 215 MPs, including the great majority of English Liberals.[36]

to one.[37] This pattern was equally evident on both sides of the fierce controversy which took place within nonconformity, between unitarians and evangelicals, in the 1830s, over rights to chapel property. (This dispute, incidentally, marked the point at which evangelicals – mainly congregationalists and baptists – ousted unitarians from the leadership of political Dissent, and this fact ought to be born in mind in reading from now on.)

But on the other hand, tories had mobilised propertied opinion against the policies, and blocked many of them. Even some Dissenters drifted towards toryism. These were Wesleyan methodists, the most anti-Catholic of the sects, traditionally less whiggish (because cool on Catholic Emancipation) and least interested in church disestablishment. Smelling popery in the 1839 Education Bill, their leaders lobbied against it.[38] All in all, Russell's religious policy, though significant for party identity, proved more of an electoral liability than an asset. Where, then, to turn?

Depression, economy and free trade, 1838–41

By 1838, government once more badly needed momentum. But its problems then worsened as it ran into the longest and worst depression of the nineteenth century, which lasted until 1842. Bad harvests in 1837 and 1838 intensified a collapse of internal and foreign demand for manufactures after the boom of the mid-1830s. Wheat prices from 1838 to 1841 were the highest between the deflation of 1819 and the Crimean War. This severely depressed domestic purchasing power in non-essential goods. In the early 1840s, manufacturing demand was hit again by foreign trade failure and depression in the investment cycle. Unemployment was severe. From 1838, working-class unrest revived, reasserting the visionary radical tradition that by attacking the bastions of political power a harmonious society of virtuous freeholders could be created. So Chartism was born. In 1838–9, meetings were held in a remarkable variety of places urging the 'Six Points', most importantly universal manhood suffrage, the ballot and annual parliaments. From late 1838 until the summer of 1839, the amount of Chartist-inspired political activity took magistrates by surprise; many became obsessed by fear of disorder. A petition advocating the Six Points was presented to the Commons.

Controversial as this was, it was in fact one of 70,072 petitions presented to the Commons between 1838 and 1842, as against a mere 23,283 between 1828 and 1832.[39] The politicised nation was in full spate, articulating all sorts of grievances – constitutional, fiscal, religious – and demanding redress. The level of political unrest called into question Liberal confidence about the workings of the Reformed political system. But this was merely one of three great embarrassments inflicted on the government by the depression. A second was its inability to meet the traditional 'country' demand in distress, that for tax cuts. Financial crisis categorically ruled them out. Indeed the government needed to find more revenue in order to combat a shortfall in consumption. Between 1835 and 1841 expenditure rose by £4.3 million, to reach £53.2 million, mainly because of international tension – embarrassing to a party which claimed attachment to peace and retrenchment. There were five successive years of large budgetary deficits from 1838 to 1842; in all but one year the shortfall topped £1.4 million. Deficits were guaranteed by the Liberals' refusal to increase taxes in 1838 and 1839. They argued that taxes hit consumption and industrial output and that keeping them low would minimise the extent of the depression.[40] But this approach undermined even further the confidence of country gentlemen worried about the nation's inability to defend itself.

Third, depression increased the restlessness of MPs and so weakened further a government majority which, as a result of byelection losses had all but disappeared. One impassioned critic depicted ministers' noses being 'rubbed in their own filth, as [is done] to dogs when they dung a drawing room'.[41] Radicals pressed for constitutional reform, concentrating on the proposal which would attract most mainstream party support, for the introduction of the secret ballot at elections. This promised to protect voters against tory corruption, and demonstrated to constituents MPs' radical credentials, but it did not unpick the 1832 settlement, so it did not appear too destabilising. The numbers supporting the annual motion rose steadily: 157 in 1837, 198 in 1838, 216 in 1839. There was a respectable whig case for open voting, that it encouraged the elector to act responsibly as a trustee for the general good.[42] But party pressure was so great that the government was forced to make the ballot an open question in 1839, allowing ministers a free vote. (Liberal party discipline was so lax that there had already in practice been a free vote in 1838.) A month earlier, in May 1839, the ministry had temporarily resigned after an unexpected near-defeat on its proposal to suspend the Jamaican constitution (as part of its campaign to protect freed slaves). A few radical MPs opposed suspension on libertarian grounds. They were also critical of apparently authoritarian rule in Canada. Ministers resigned in the hope of rallying support from their MPs by exposing them to a tory alternative. That alternative collapsed even sooner than expected; Peel fell before the first hurdle, since the queen refused to sack her whig Ladies of the Bedchamber. But this made Melbourne's return look like the product of royal whim, a source of support unlikely to strengthen a professedly Liberal government. Peel bade his time, superciliously implying that only his notion of 'strong' government would answer, but privately relieved that he did not have to try it in a minority.

Government weakness in turn had distressing consequences for its legislative authority, as already noted for education policy. It was forced to propose only one-year extensions of the Poor Law Commission's tenure of power in 1839, 1840 and 1841, in the face of pressure for all kinds of conflicting amendments of its functions. This was unfortunate, at just the time when a firm approach to pauperism in the face of Chartist pressure was needed. Howick resigned in August 1839, believing that the government was too weak either to resist ignorant popular pressure, such as for the ballot (which he opposed), or to 'lead and instruct public opinion' in morality, religion and sound economic principles.[43] Activist whigs blamed Melbourne for the impasse; Holland criticised him for mistakenly thinking 'quiet and ease more the aim of a wise Statesman than popularity, authority, or splendor'.[44]

Liberals, then, needed to respond sensibly to public disquiet; to demonstrate to dangerous Chartists the benevolence of the existing regime; to reassert the authority of government in the Commons by bold leadership; and to address economic and revenue problems without unduly increasing direct taxation. What initiative would allow them to do all this? A solution emerged from a depressing statistic. Average wheat prices per quarter, 39s 4d in 1835, were 70s 8d in 1839. The price of bread became a major issue, and with it, the Corn Laws.

The whigs' interest in the free trade cause had traditionally been lukewarm. On the one hand, the discipline of political economy was influential in the party, through the Scottish economists and the whigs' major literary organ, the *Edinburgh Review*. And a number of whigs, when in opposition, had lumped high tariffs, especially on corn, together with high taxes as a selfish imposition on the country by vested interests, counteracting Providential designs of natural bounty. Lord King had argued for repeal of the Corn Laws in 1822 as the only way of acquainting country gentlemen MPs with economic reality and hence with the need to vote for lower taxes all round.[45] On this reading, the Corn Laws were one of the unnatural monopolies which parliamentary reform might remove. On the other hand, really radical changes in tariffs were as problematic for whigs as they had been for Huskisson. It was still generally believed that Corn Law repeal would allow foreign grain to cascade into Britain and swamp domestic agriculture. This would not only be politically and socially unacceptable but would endanger national security in the event of another war and blockade. Outside the intelligentsia, political economy beliefs had little purchase. Whigs did not want to appear a sectional party, discriminating against agriculture. Grey told his son at the 1826 Durham election to steer clear of free trade. It was 'a ticklish subject' as it split opinion.[46] Althorp, a member of the Political Economy Club, did not declare against the Corn Laws publicly until 1843. Most whigs attached more importance to political structures than to economic laws. If any force was destabilising the natural harmony of society, they preferred to blame tory government rather than landowners.

So the party was uncommitted on the question. When sympathetic radical MPs (centred on Wolverhampton) brought forward motions to consider the Laws, junior ministers were allowed free votes from 1830, and the cabinet from 1835.[47] Meanwhile Poulett Thomson, Manchester MP, Russian merchant, and President of the Board of Trade, pursued an unspectacular policy of gradual tariff reductions.

In the course of the 1830s, acceptance of 'natural' economic arrangements like free trade was greatly furthered by shifts in the intellectual climate.

Particularly significant was the apparent success of the New Poor Law in lowering rates and checking pauperism. The railway boom encouraged confidence in the effects of an ever freer, ever quicker flow of goods. Proposals to tamper with the currency lost their former popularity. The talk now was of the benefits of an unobstructed Providential economic system. Statistical inquiry helped here; the Statistical Department of the Board of Trade was established in 1832. A select committee on import duties of 1840 was a vehicle for Board of Trade propaganda about the need to distinguish between tariff duties which brought in significant amounts of revenue, and those which were merely protective. It publicised the Board's findings that, of 862 articles on which duties were charged in 1838, 17 provided 94½ per cent of the total revenue, yet that tariffs as a whole raised prices to the consumer substantially.[48]

So the return of economic depression from 1838 inevitably led to calls to dismantle obstructions to a 'natural' economic order. One problem was surplus labour. Russell, now Colonial Secretary, set up a Colonial Land and Emigration Commission in 1840 to supervise emigration, not least by acting as agent for the sale of colonial lands in such a way as to attract investment and labour. Another perceived obstacle to prosperity was the lack of an international trade; Britain seemed to suffer from too narrow a range of export markets (mainly colonies and traditional satellites). Faced with increasing continental competition, Foreign Secretary Palmerston believed that 'it is the business of the Government to open and to secure the roads for the merchant', especially in extra-European countries. Hence his interest in China, Arabia and 'the countries on the Indus'.[49] The 'opium war' with China (1839–42) was one product of the pressure placed on Peking to open up the China trade. The Anglo-Turkish Convention of 1838, driven by a similar search for export markets, removed internal monopolies hindering trade with Turkey, established a modest non-discriminatory tariff on imports instead, and led to Britain overtaking Russia in Turkish trade.

In this context, high bread prices in the winter of 1838–9 were bound to prompt a campaign for reduction or repeal of the tariff on corn imports, headed by northern commerce. The MPs who presented petitions were anxious to stress that this was not just a sectional matter since lobbying was coming also from the 'the most reflecting portion of the working classes' – from operatives, handloom weavers and artisans suffering from lack of work.[50] In parliament, these MPs claimed that high prices caused manufacturing distress, because they checked demand, at home and abroad. Foreign countries, unable to pay the high cost of British goods, increased their own production. This, they said, permanently threatened British exports – as did Britain's exclusion of foreign corn at normal prices, which encouraged those countries to retreat behind tariff walls. The favourite example was the Prussian commercial league. Advocates of Corn Law reform denied, though, that it would lower wage levels, since these were dictated not by the price of bread but by the demand for labour, which would be stimulated by lower bread prices and by less crippling foreign manufacturing competition.[51]

Official Liberals' response to this pressure was remarkable. In March 1839, every significant government minister in the Commons supported a motion to consider – in effect to amend – the 1828 Corn Law.* This was lost by 195 votes to 342.[†] Most Commons cabinet ministers – Russell, Morpeth, Thomson, Hobhouse – had in fact supported an 1838 motion for inquiry into the Laws. But at that time only 95 MPs had supported it. Since then, national petitioning had swelled Liberal interest and virtually committed the government to reform. This all took place *before* the decision to form a national Anti-Corn-Law League (a response to the motion's defeat, in fact). As Whittle Harvey said, the government was far in advance of mainstream sentiment.[52]

Why were ministers so prompt? The rational whig mind found the Corn Law indefensible when attacked. This was not because it was convinced by the petitioners' simplistic explanation for the rise of foreign competition. What struck ministers forcibly was that agitation against the Law followed inevitably from a rise in bread prices. The Law was acceptable only when conditions did not require it. Such a statute was unworkable, and inspired anything but respect for authority. The Corn Law, first and foremost, was a political question. Amendment might soothe and rally middle-class opinion and steer 'the better portion of the working classes' away from 'the guidance of the visionary, the fanatic, the revolutionist, and the incendiary'.[53] It was an attractive issue for ministers *both* because many of them genuinely believed that free trade was a 'beautiful mechanism' which was 'obviously designed' by 'unerring wisdom and divine benevolence' for 'regulating the supply of food'[54] *and* because action helped to convince middle- and working-class opinion that economic policy was being regulated by natural laws rather than by selfish vested interests.

The free trade argument also allowed ministers to invoke a broader, cross-class appeal. They claimed that farming too would benefit from it, that agricultural and manufacturing interests were similar. Ministers argued that farmers clung to the Corn Laws because of low prices which they feared repeal would lower. But, with population rises abroad, there was no longer a corn surplus in Europe waiting to swamp British produce.[55] Rather, the present lack of profit in farming was unnatural. It was caused by domestic over-production in order to supply a rapidly rising population even through bad harvests, and by merchants' dislike of operating in the excessively fluctuating international corn trade. So the Corn Laws, paradoxically, kept prices artificially low in most years. Moreover, they

---

* Of British ministers, as far as I can see only Robert Gordon, Secretary to the Board of Control, opposed the motion.

† Plus 34 tellers and pairs on each side. *Hansard* records that 33 ministerial MPs were absent. A handful of Liberal county MPs, and substantial numbers of Irishmen, opposed the motion.

raised them at times of dearth, because they excluded imports at most prices, which discouraged potential importers from trying to trade, so that when prices rose high enough for ports to open, no extra supply was available. And the lack of a regular trade in corn with other countries, exacerbating price fluctuations, discouraged the investment of capital, energy and intelligence in domestic agriculture, which was the prerequisite of effective competition.[56] Many farmers were reported to be criticising the unreliability of the sliding scale, and wanting a change.[57]

Liberals had to argue this because they could not be seen to be acting on a class basis. But they probably also believed it. They looked back with nostalgia to the broad alliance of 1831 which included gentlemen and farmers as well as urban opinion, based on support for open, low-tax government. Since then, Reformers had progressively been driven from the counties, the Blue Riband of the representative system. Already at the 1835 election they only won a bare majority of English county seats; in 1837, they had only 47 to the tories' 97. Russell, Howick, Palmerston and Morpeth had all sat for large county seats early in the 1830s, but Russell and Palmerston were defeated in 1835, and Howick and Morpeth in 1841. Liberals did not *want* to be exclusively reliant on urban support. Even Wood, a friend of free trade and northern commerce, talked of 'that silly anti-corn law league'. Corn Law reform might educate the gentry out of irrational protectionist fears, woo them from toryism and raise popular respect for them.[58] So the new policy had a curious double value: it pleased the specifically urban supporters on whom Liberals were reliant, but, by holding out the hope of destroying the identification of landowners with a 'landed interest', offered the prospect of the eventual recovery of county support. At any rate, it could not do much harm. The Liberals' leading election agent believed that the 16 English county seats lost in 1841 were doomed before the introduction of the Corn Law question, which would have little electoral consequence one way or the other.[59] This was because results were determined largely by the comparative organisational and financial strength of the two sides over months or years, especially as it affected their ability to register supporters. So the continued swing of 1841 to the tories probably owed as much to the ongoing electoral effects of the 'church-in-danger' cry of the 1830s as to the newer question of free trade.

However, the manifest hostility of the bulk of the Commons to Corn Law reform made action on it with a view to legislation pointless. Melbourne also disliked the idea of such a controversial policy. So there was no further initiative. But then, in April 1841, the government changed tack. Russell declared that it would propose a moderate fixed duty (8s per quarter) in place of the 1828 Law, the reform which he personally had advocated since January 1839.[60] The fixed duty meant that more revenue would be raised more predictably than by the existing Law; so it would also help to solve the revenue difficulty without recourse to direct taxes, which might please landowners. But what Russell had said in 1840 still held true. Government could only act constructively on the Corn Laws if there was a general disposition to alter them, and this still did not exist.[61] So why did the government change tack in 1841?

Partly the change was forced on the government by budgetary requirements. This requires some explanation, for Baring, the Chancellor of the Exchequer, objected to introducing theoretical questions into his budgets, and was sceptical that general tariff reductions would greatly help revenue yields. The need for money had led him to impose an extra 5 per cent on the vast mass of tariff duties in 1840, in order to spread the extra burden as lightly and generally as possible. In 1841, faced again with the need to increase the revenue, the government rejected the option of further loans or a politically-controversial income tax. It plumped instead for a reduction in the high differential between duties on colonial and foreign sugar and timber, which had prohibited foreign competition from entering the British market. This revived a plan of Althorp's from 1831. It was attractive because it struck a blow against West Indian sugar planters and Canadian merchants who were generally seen as part of a tory network of colonial interests hostile to the general good. The ingenuity of the scheme was that, by reducing the differential, more foreign sugar and timber would be imported, displacing an equivalent amount of colonial produce but yet boosting receipts because the former would still pay a higher duty than the latter. So reducing duties would benefit the revenue, the British consumer and, indirectly, the colonial trades themselves, forcing them to be more competitive. It nodded to free trade theory, but did not undermine protection in practice. However, the reduction in the duties on sugar, a necessity of life, directly affected the poor; it was unavoidably a political issue. So it made a lack of action on the more popular corn question too embarrassing to countenance. Russell made the corn announcement on the day of the budget, so that the government could appear to be making a general attack on high tariffs.

But budgets were less important than politics in prompting Liberal action. The major aim of the corn declaration was not to allow legislation but to woo electoral opinion. Government was defeated on the sugar duty reduction, but Russell announced that it would press on with the corn proposal. Though Peel, desperate to avoid that discussion, headed it off with a no-confidence motion which government lost by one vote, the result was what Commons ministers were working towards anyway, a dissolution and an election fought on the proposal to lower unpopular tariff duties. Melbourne opposed the dissolution, but then Melbourne was not a real whig, and Melbourne was outvoted.

This strategy marked a seminal development in Liberal politics. To place so directly before electors a question of direct financial significance to them was a great constitutional innovation. Peel, disgusted, saw it as an open bribe and an incitement to class hatred. But for Liberals, it was not only legitimate but necessary in order to guide agitation and demonstrate government responsiveness.[62] It highlighted Liberals' self-perception as rational defenders of popular rights and interests. It showed urban Britain how sensitive to its demands ministers were: Palmerston claimed that the 'country' – that is, 'all those persons who are engaged in carrying on . . . industry and commerce' – had 'spoken', and its views were 'too strong to be resisted'.[63] It indicated to Chartists and other working-men that government was alive to their grievances and that Chartist reform was not necessary. And it galvanised urban radicals and Dissenters, much more effectively than the ballot would have done, by portraying free trade as a Providential policy. 'The gracious designs of Providence' arranged that shortages of food and raw materials in any one part of the globe were made up for by abundance elsewhere; man's ingenuity in devising means of communication enabled him to exploit 'the beneficence of the Creator', and it was foolish to allow 'unjust' – indeed unChristian – legislation to stand in the way of its realisation.[64] In the 1841 election, many Liberal MPs invoked the language of the Reform crisis again, and talked of the Corn Laws as surviving symbols of corrupt, vested interest government which it was their duty to sweep away in order to purify the economic order. Tories were painted as 'monopolists', as men who would pay no heed to legitimate public aspirations, legislate for vested interest at the expense of the nation, and pit sect against sect and class against class.[65]

At this election, then, the Liberal leaders were not the effete and exclusive aristocrats of legend – any more, in fact, than they had been throughout the 1830s. In the parliament of 1841, seven of the nine Liberal ex-cabinet ministers in the Commons sat for an urban seat with a population of over 35,000. Prominent among them was Russell, who won in the City of London. This was a well-chosen seat, popular but respectable, with a reputation for radicalism in days gone by but also for protectionism. A heroic struggle against 'interests . . . most strong, and . . . combinations most formidable' was on offer.[66] (In fact, Russell scraped home by nine votes, bottom of the four winning candidates and beaten by two tories.) The 1841 contest allowed a combination of the old whig cry of the reconciliation of interests under the impartial rule of property, with the new exhilaration of struggle, with popular help, against monopoly. Bolstered by their religious, Irish and financial policy, Liberals had a strong urban following. They still lost; tories had a majority of 87. But it was a victory won in rural areas and small towns. Tories took 123 of 144 English county seats (compared with 42 of 82 in 1830); 21 of the 23 boroughs which they gained between 1835 and 1841 had electorates of less than 1,000. This was a legacy of Reformers' failure to disfranchise enough small boroughs in 1832 and, above all, of the unprecedented swings to toryism in the counties, which reflected the new issue politics of the 1830s. The county and small-town electorate had proved less advanced than the brief apocalyptic fervour of 1830–2 had suggested. The tory reaction had destroyed the momentum of Liberal government and emasculated its policy; now it deprived it of office. For the first time, Liberals had struck some popular chords on free trade, traditionally a technical question. Poulett Thomson congratulated Russell on being the first man to 'elevate the subject and excite the feelings of the

People' on it.[67] But even this was not enough. Similarly, education and Ireland had left the propertied electorate cold. Charles Wood's retrospective, many years later, summed up Liberal views on the 1830s: 'the people generally were ignorant . . . and the old Whigs were far in advance of the people'.[68] Or, as Thomas Arnold put it in 1836, in characteristically intellectual vein: 'vulgar minds never can understand the duty of reform . . . and the mass of mankind . . . will always be vulgar-minded'.[69]

PART III

THE AGE OF RUSSELL AND PALMERSTON, 1841–1867

IN THE 1830S, Liberalism acquired political and intellectual coherence but fell foul of too many propertied voters. Part III tells a more positive story. It is about emerging Liberal political dominance between 1846 and 1866. It differs from traditional accounts, which see 1859 as the significant date in the formation of a popular Liberal party. Certainly, the formation of Palmerston's second coalition government in that year was an important moment; it confirmed a return to two-party politics, after the confusion of the 1850s, and from then on indiscipline on the Liberal benches was less damaging. But that indiscipline did not disappear, Palmerston was frequently defeated in the Commons, and a general parliamentary division along party lines had in fact persisted all through the 1850s. In order to explain the emergence of a powerful Liberal political force, we need to look at other factors.

One, obviously, was the destruction of the tory alternative which Peel had built up in his government of 1841–6. This self-inflicted wound, Peel's greatest legacy to Liberalism, is explained in chapter 7. But even more important was the process charted in chapter 8. It shows how the Liberals' handling of financial, administrative and foreign policy, and of parliament, established respect for them across a range of classes and groups of which Melbourne, in the late 1830s, could only dream. Administrative overhaul, and skilful presentation, removed the aura of whiggish social exclusiveness which clung to the party leadership as late as 1850. The retention of the income tax, a tory tax reintroduced by Peel in 1842, was rendered acceptable to radicals by persuading them that a disinterested state machine would not misuse it. So MPs were cajoled into tolerating higher defence spending, and this, together with Palmerston's Canningite strategy of manipulating foreign policy for public advantage, made Liberal leaders seem reputable guardians of the national interest. Meanwhile, Palmerston's administrative conception of politics, and his flexible, masterly reading of the parliamentary situation, allowed him to create a consensus following at Westminster. Liberals were greatly assisted in these achievements by Peel's other legacies of free trade and a band of young followers who proved good and economical administrators. Under Palmerston, Liberals stood not for controversial legislation but for competence and class-free economics.

At the same time, they continued to develop the agenda of moral improvement which we saw them sketching out in chapters 5 and 6. Chapter 9 shows this operating in Ireland, religious and social policy, and local government. Didactic progressive elitism was married, if a trifle uneasily, with the extension of popular involvement. This balancing-act was particularly associated with Russell, and he sought to demonstrate it also in taking up the cause of moderate parliamentary reform. Liberal involvement with this issue before 1867 was, accordingly, limited and cautious. It is paradoxical, then, that it led, by a bizarre process, to the passage of a much more radical Reform Act in that year, which seemed to endanger the high-minded, administrative yet popular Liberalism painstakingly promoted over the previous two decades, and usher in an era of unrestrained mass influence.

CHAPTER 7

Peel's legacy, 1841–6

By 1841 IT was clear that the electoral system established in 1832 could still be dominated by the social elite. If one party could win the confidence of most of the propertied classes, it could establish a prolonged dominance in parliament. Peel's strategy as tory (or Conservative) Prime Minister after 1841 was to ensure that the natural ruling party would be his. He sought to recreate the situation of the 1820s in which radical threats were seen off easily, and the whig/Liberal opposition marginalised. In that prosperous decade, government had combined firmness, economy and morality and so had realised 'middle-class' values. Tories still saw themselves as representing the 'best portion of the entire Community', a 'great preponderance of property, of learning, of decent manners and of pure religion'.[1] The 1841 election result seemed to suggest that Conservatives had regained the natural majority among the permanent interests of the country which had evaporated in the Reform crisis. There were only 188 contests in the 401 United Kingdom seats, as against 251 in 1837; in 1847 there were to be only 164.[2] The initial enthusiasm for registration activity seemed to be petering out; challenges to established electoral interests appeared likely to go on diminishing.

Peel aimed to restore the principles of the 1820s, of strong government, offering efficient administration and sound financial management, and of independence for local magistrates, the Anglican church and other institutions. This approach had three legacies for the Liberal party, which this chapter examines. Peel's rule highlighted the weakness of government in the 1830s, and suggested that any future Liberal ministry would have to appear more competent in finance and more reassuring on religion and defence. His response to economic and social crisis, in particular his move to free trade, fundamentally shifted the prevailing consensus about the role of government and the definition of 'vested interests'. And his failures as a leader destroyed his hard-won position and let the Liberals back into power in 1846, in fraught circumstances.

*   *   *

Peel was not the flaccid 'moderate' of the text-books. He had contempt for Liberalism, for government by consensus and popular flattery. The Reform

Act made him more determined than ever to assert the principles of firm executive rule. In the 1830s, this was an effective rallying-cry against ministers. But it was also a personal psychological need, a product of his unshakeable self-confidence in his impressive administrative powers, his inability to suffer fools gladly, his very restricted experience of 'the world' (an MP at 21, he had held senior office from the age of 24), and his unwillingness to take advice from those who had more knowledge of it.[3] He magnified the indignity which the Reform Act had delivered to government authority. He remained preoccupied with securing to ministers the freedom of manoeuvre necessary to permit the dispassionate administration of the law, the safeguarding of institutions, and the pursuit of an effective financial and defence policy. He feared that, unless government was left free to regulate taxation, defence expenditure and foreign initiatives in line with a disinterested appraisal of national interests, sectional pressures would derange spending plans and distort economic activity.

Fluent, plausible, dignified, wonderfully businesslike and clear-headed, Peel established complete ascendancy over his party in the 1830s. His basic charge was that Liberal government had failed the cause of efficient authority on almost all counts. His speeches staunchly defended the rule of law, the maintenance of a constitutional balance between the queen, the Lords, the Commons and local magistrates, and the influence of religious establishments in Britain and Ireland, as the safeguards of individual responsibility and development.[4] He opposed further constitutional reform – such as the secret ballot or shorter parliaments – because he feared that the simplistic slogans of the ignorant and passionate would crush personal independence and responsibility. He claimed that those attributes, nurtured by religious establishments, defeated stagnation and corruption and led to material and moral progress. So he could exploit fear of Catholicism, Dissent and infidelity. Only an alliance with Protestantism, he stressed, could provide the state with the 'new source of strength' which it needed. He alleged that the Liberals' Church Rate Bill undermined the church's authority, while Liberal educational policy damaged the only body capable of providing the moral education which the nation desperately needed. Such arguments also struck chords with tories who were horrified by Chartism and government weakness in finance. One tory vicar asked: 'What is Chartism but opposition to all human government?'[5] In the late 1830s, a number of Conservatives voiced fears for the survival of civilisation. Wellington warned that Britain was coming 'very fast' to the 'natural state of man, plunder'. Abinger urged that the way to preserve liberty, property and civilisation was by 'discountenancing all vice, immorality, and impiety'. Graham thought that Britain was 'almost ungovernable'.[6]

This tory sensitivity to the need to preserve the firm rule of law and religion encouraged Peel to define Conservative party philosophy in a particular way. For him, Conservatism meant above all the preservation of the independent judgment of national leaders, what Gladstone called in 1844 the 'principle of an individual conscience in governors, which is to actuate them in the work of governing'.[7] This, Peel thought, was the principle of Pitt and Wellington. In 1841, he appealed to this vision in making it clear that he would not endure 'a servile tenure', carrying 'other men's opinions into effect'. He demanded the 'liberty of proposing to parliament those measures which I believe to be conducive to the public weal'.[8] Peel developed an authoritarian view of party as a body of MPs willing to support the minister in his views. This was both reactionary and revolutionary. In 1845 he refused to admit that a minister owed 'any personal obligation to those Members who have placed him [in government]'.[9] After his experience with the Catholic question in the 1820s, he refused to weaken government authority by allowing major policy questions to remain open within the government. One of his main concerns remained the 'neutralizing' of the 'mischievous energies of the House of Commons'.[10] In 1835, he had feared that weak government would lead to the 'great public evil' of the Commons usurping 'many of the functions' of 'Executive Government'.[11]

Gladstone said later that Peel had been 'Prime Minister in a sense in which no other man has been it since Mr. Pitt's time'.[12] He familiarised himself with the work of all departments and he controlled the cabinet agenda. His conception of government was administrative much more than legislative. It was in fact he, not the Liberals, who founded his governing style on the old whig adage of 'men not measures'. He did this primarily by the pursuit of 'efficiency' in financial management. He saw his major task on entering government as being to re-establish budgetary solvency. This would provide more flexibility of response in case of foreign attack – no unlikely situation after Palmerston's irresponsible foreign policy – as well as securing a firmer base for economic recovery and boosting the parliamentary dignity of government. In 1842, the annual deficit was £2.4 million. Balanced budgets could be restored only by an unprecedented demonstration of executive power, the imposition of an income tax in peacetime. Peel accompanied this by the removal of tariff duties on hundreds of items, most of which had been shown by the 1840 select committee to produce only a tiny revenue. Import duties on raw materials were to be cut to 5 per cent or less, and on finished manufactured articles to 20 per cent or less. His foreign and colonial policy was deliberately low-key and low-cost. The quarrels of the late 1830s with France and the United States were made up. By 1846, Britain enjoyed good relations with every major power. The negotiation of peace in Afghanistan in 1842 was a great relief to Peel (though Governor General Ellenborough's subsequent 'forward policy' in north-west India was not always appreciated in cabinet). Treasury control over colonial expenditure remained very strict. Meanwhile, Peel's taxation policy helped to restore the budget to health. In 1844 there was a surplus of £1,443,000 and in 1845 of £3,356,000. Wheat prices stabilised at the desired levels, at a steady average of about 51s per quarter between 1843 and 1845.[13] With the tariff reductions 'surpass[ing] all his expectations', Peel took advantage of commercial prosperity to reduce duties in his 1845 budget by three times the amount taken off in 1842.[14] All export duties on

British goods were abolished, and import duties were removed on 430 articles, mainly on raw materials for industry. This gave him the authority to renew the income tax for three years, in order to meet necessary increases in defence expenditure. The crisis of order in Ireland had led to an increase of 7,000 in army strength in 1843, while incidents with France in Tahiti and Tangier in 1844 put an extra £1 million on the naval estimates. By 1845, Peel's authority in financial matters was so great that a potentially fractious parliament readily consented to the renewal.

Peel's administrative achievement was outstanding. He changed the image of toryism single-handedly. In doing so he won the confidence not only of many propertied gentlemen but also of a very talented band of young politicians who could not be ignored after his death, and helped to perpetuate his style of government. In the short term, he marginalised the opposition; Russell could not find a strategy for Liberalism. Peel had shown that tory government did not unleash the reign of vested interests, exclusiveness and corruption that Reformers' rhetoric had prophesied. Some Liberals were impressed by Peel's authoritative style of government. Others were embarrassed by his superior efficiency in financial management. Liberals were particularly divided about the wisdom of action on the three issues on which the government was potentially vulnerable: Ireland, Corn Law repeal and the lack of franchise reform. Their occasional attempts at an initiative on Ireland in 1843–4 merely served to unite the tories all the more. As Peel said, contemptuously, in July 1843, Russell had lost all control over his party: 'they act in bands'.[15] New questions – primarily the condition-of-England question – cut across parties. For most of 1845, it still looked as if Peel would remain in power for a dozen years or more.[16] The climate of the mid-1820s had apparently returned.

But Peel's image of easy confidence did not tell the full story. Conservative government was unable to place a firm stamp on large parts of its agenda, largely because its authoritarianism was distrusted by Liberals and many anti-centralising Conservative MPs. Graham, Peel's Home Secretary, became a particularly suspect figure, because his neurosis led him to over-react to what he called the 'mad insurrection of the working classes' of 1842.[17] He offended county tories by his indifference to their independence and character as governors of the localities. He favoured appointing paid lawyers to Quarter Sessions to check what Peel called 'irresponsible' magistrates and to improve the administration of justice. A splenetic cabinet response aborted the idea.[18] Peel had to restrain him from dismissing magistrates in large numbers for incompetence. His support for a County Courts Bill ensured its rejection in the Commons. His use of the Post Office to open the private correspondence of potential troublemakers, which previous Home Secretaries had done as a matter of course, provoked a full-scale constitutional row because he was found to be opening Mazzini's letters at the request of the Austrian Ambassador, yet refused to release details to the Commons. A thriving market developed in envelopes and seals with such mottoes as 'not for Sir James Graham'.[19] The bill of 1842 to give extra powers to the Poor Law Commission was butchered. His attempt to insert into the 1843 Factory Bill clauses for factory education on the rates, but with the schoolmaster effectively appointed by the local Anglican clergyman, foundered on a mass provincial Dissenting petitioning campaign against it. On social questions, meanwhile, the doctrinaire resistance of Peel and Graham to anything less than a twelve-hour legal limit to the factory working day, and their lukewarmness on the subject of sanitary legislation, seemed to many tory and Liberal MPs an inadequate response to the Royal Commission reports of 1842–3 on the sanitary and employment conditions endured by the labouring population.

All governments promote some measures which fall between stools. But Peel and his acolytes seemed unusually insensitive to Commons opinion. Most awkwardly, it became apparent that Peel's conception of Conservatism was different from that of many rural tories. He saw Conservatism as a particular style of *government*, and his party as a necessary bulwark, in a hyperactive Reformed parliament, of that governing style. They saw it as a defence of particular *values*: law and order, low taxes, local magistrate autonomy, Protestantism, and other cultural symbols of landed predominance. Propertied supremacy, they thought, was best maintained not by executive assertiveness but by the rule of men of character. This difference of opinion was to prove fatal. Why?

* * *

At the grass-roots, the Conservative revival of the 1830s was based on perceived threats to Anglican and propertied dominance. In this respect it paralleled and built on revived church activity. Between 1832 and 1851 over three times as many new sittings were provided in Anglican churches as between 1818 and 1832; 2,029 new churches were built, at a cost of over £6 million.[20] In 1838–9, the National Society founded twenty-four diocesan and subdiocesan boards of education. In opposition, many tories built up exaggerated fears for popular morality and exaggerated hopes about the prospects of improving it by firm, inspiring tory leadership. Tory Anglicans, instinctively hostile to Liberal pluralist church policy, and aware that no coherent definition of the church-state relationship had previously been necessary, countered with tightly-structured theories of church-state relationships, of which the Oxford movement's was the most famous and young William Gladstone's *The state in its relations with the Church* offered the most hostages to fortune. Similarly, they contrasted the turmoil of Chartism with a vision of an equally cosy and coherent paternalist social order. The tory judge Abinger sunk his hopes in 'the spirit, the zeal, and the energy of the gentry of England'.[21] Charlotte Elizabeth, probably the most famous of evangelical writers of the 1830s, editor of the *Christian Lady's Magazine*, hoped to defend 'sacredly English' values by bolstering the 'manly bearing of a bold, an independent and a peaceful peasantry, the humblest of whom

159

knows that his cottage is a chartered sanctuary, protected alike from the aggression of civil and of ecclesiastical tyranny'.[22] Lord John Manners, one of the leading lights of the romantic tories who called themselves 'Young England', toured the textile districts in 1841 and decided that 'nothing but monastic institutions can Christianise Manchester'.[23]

In 1841, tories had high hopes that Peel's return to office would restore the values under threat in the 1830s. Imagine, then, their bewilderment at the continuation of social unrest; 1842 was the worst year of the depression, and perhaps the grimmest of the nineteenth century. The church's failure to Christianise the large towns was looming larger in their minds year by year. So was the apparent prevalence of materialism and indifference to depravity.[24] The publication of the reports of the public enquiries of 1840–3 about the conditions in which the urban population lived and worked provoked an outpouring of horror about social prospects. The Scottish literary tory Lockhart summed up the prevailing mood when he discerned a 'cancer at the bottom of our social condition'.[25] Chartist agitation for suffrage reform revived under the umbrella organisation of the National Charter Association led by the mob orator O'Connor. A national petition for the Charter, presented to the Commons in May 1842, was alleged to contain over three million signatures. In the summer of that year, there was a wave of strikes to protest against wage reductions. An alarmed public exaggerated the degree of coordination between the strikes – the nickname 'Plug Plot' was coined – and assumed Chartist involvement. The economic and social situation and the tories' return to office revived crusading, Dissenting middle-class radicalism too, in three particularly alarming forms: the moralised and fervent Anti-Corn Law League (see page 163), the evangelical quaker Joseph Sturge's Complete Suffrage Union of 1842, and the Anti-State Church Association of 1844, led by Edward Miall. Miall argued that the existence of a wealthy, lazy, politically conservative state church was a 'tremendous obstacle to the progress of divine truth' since it checked proselytising zeal and encouraged men to acquiesce in high taxation, militarism and commercial monopolies.[26]

The disestablishment campaign was encouraged by three measures of Peel's government which antagonised evangelical nonconformists: the educational clauses of the 1843 Factory Bill, the Dissenters' Chapels Act of 1844,* and the increase in the Maynooth grant of 1845 (see page 162). At just the time when the populace seemed most to need the message of the church establishment, its authority and financial and legal privileges in England, Scotland and Ireland were under assault on several fronts. One development which alarmed tories (and encouraged the disestablishment campaign) was the acrimonious split in the church establishment in Scotland in 1843, after a decade of rising tension. Scottish evangelicals refused to

---

* This confirmed the right of long-settled unitarian congregations to the ownership of their places of worship, against the opposition of the evangelical sects from which unitarians had seceded and who claimed still to own the property.

countenance the power of propertied, often irreligious lay patrons over appointments to parish livings: it seemed to obstruct the idea of religious brotherhood and the work of spiritual regeneration. The government refused to alter the law and, in 1843, the Non-Intrusionists broke away to form the Free Church; 451 ministers seceded. The 1851 census confirmed the obvious fact that only a minority of Scottish churchgoers now attended the Established Kirk. At a stroke, the political authority of the church establishment north of the border had collapsed.

In England, many Anglicans, especially evangelicals, were angered by the Dissenters' Chapels Act, because it recognised the rights of a heterodox anti-Trinitarian sect; 106 Conservative MPs voted against it. They were also upset by the evolution of the high church Oxford movement of the 1830s (the Tractarians) into a substantial intellectual force within the church, bent on undermining the doctrines introduced into the Church of England at the Reformation. It seemed to evangelical critics that 'popish' principles were being assiduously cultivated in the traditional seminary of Anglicanism and that this would soon revolutionise the character of parochial preaching. The presence of high church Oxonians in Peel's cabinet – such as William Gladstone, from 1843 – seemed equally alarming. In the eyes of Protestant tories, Tractarians, by casting doubt on the Englishness of the church, added much weight to Dissenters' campaign for disestablishment. A final, connected misery for supporters of Anglican values was the emergence in 1843 of a repeal movement in Ireland, led by O'Connell and egged on by a new generation of politically active, ultramontane Catholic clergymen.

So, by 1843, tories were beset by threats to church establishments in all parts of the kingdom, by the fear that pro-Irish sentiment might undermine the Union and create problems in Canada, and by the rise of utopian radicalism in Britain and the prospect of continuing economic decline and perhaps revolution. Peel's private secretary was assassinated in 1843 by a man who mistook him for the Prime Minister. Attempts were made on the queen's life. The survival of government authority, and of civilised society, seemed in the balance. Gladstone was typical in his despair about 'the growing impotence of government for its highest functions'. In 1843, he wrote in frustration: 'When will anybody govern anything?'.[27]

The effect of this crisis was to make Conservatives desperately anxious to bolster the values which they thought crucial to maintaining civilised society. But this pulled Peel and many of his followers in different directions. Peel's solution was a bolder executive style, in order to demonstrate government's power, efficiency, and decisiveness, and he expected the party to support it in the name of authority. Yet his very activity seemed to many MPs further to undermine the values needed to restore morality and order. They were already irritated by his craving for party discipline. In 1844, he attempted to stamp out Conservative support for two minor amendments to government proposals on sugar duties and factory labour, by threatening to resign if he were defeated. Nothing approaching this degree of dominance over backbenchers had previously been attempted by a party leader, and even Gladstone, a strong supporter, thought his conduct on the sugar question dictatorial and insulting to tory dignity.[28] But the real difficulties emerged in the two fields in which Peel sensed that firm action was most necessary: Ireland and finance.

Peel believed it imperative to 'break . . . up the Roman Catholic combination for repeal' in Ireland, in order to enforce the law and to be able to 'look . . . foreign powers in the face'.[29] He was also aware that Irish issues were the ones on which it was easiest for the opposition to attack, as in 1825 and 1835. In 1844, he proposed a Royal Commission on the tenure of land, a reform of the law on charities, and more money for the national education system. In 1845, he introduced a plan to recast Irish higher education so as to build loyalty to the Union among the burgeoning professional classes. This included an increase in the annual grant to the Catholic seminary at Maynooth, awarded since 1795, from £9,000 to £26,000, in the hope that its improved status would attract recruits of a higher class and encourage a more conciliatory frame of mind in the next generation of priests.[30] By such means, the British state might also build up enough credit with the Catholic Church to be able to establish a concordat with Rome. (This was not, then, a new style of toryism in action, but a variant on Wellington's plan of 1825–6 to stabilise Ireland.)

But the Maynooth proposal stirred up an unprecedented degree of Conservative opposition, because it highlighted the incompatibility between the requirements of practical policy and the religio-political values to which tories were clinging with increasing tenacity and desperation. It was the strength of tory reaction, not Peel's policy, which was new. On the third reading, 149 Conservatives voted with Peel and 148 against; the bill was carried by the support of a large majority of the Liberal party. Part of the reason for tory backbench hostility was the memory of Peel's volte-face to support Catholic Emancipation in 1829. Peel was thought to be demanding a blank cheque for the future. Many believed that he was planning, or would be forced to concede, the establishment and endowment of the Catholic Church. This interpretation was helped when leading Liberals like Russell advocated Catholic endowment as the logical consequence of Peel's proposal, and Peel refused to pledge not to do this in future.[31] Tory memories of 1829 mattered also because Emancipation was by now so widely perceived to have been a mistake. As Melbourne said of the crusty 'two bottle a day' men who had opposed it in 1829, 'the worst of it is, that the fools were in the right'.[32] Emancipation seemed to have helped to destabilise British and imperial politics, and had encouraged the growth of illiberalism in the Catholic priesthood. Some Anglicans who had supported it in 1829 in the belief that it would pacify Ireland and encourage conversions to Protestantism regretted their error and voted against the Maynooth proposal.[33] The principle of the Maynooth grant had come under increasing attack within the tory party since the 1830s because of the spread of dogmatic evangelicalism – in hostility, not least, to the growth of Tractarianism in the English church. One observer thought that men were 'alarmed at the doctrines not of Maynooth but of Oxford'.[34] More generally, the proposal touched a raw nerve among grass-roots tories who held their defence of 'Protestantism' dearly in consequence of the turbulence of recent years. It seemed to threaten the tighter definition of state-church relations to which they clung, and dealt a devastating blow to the idea that the state was a religious force, its powers sanctioned by God, and that it had a Providential duty to spread Protestant values. This blow affected different Tories differently. Some, like Gladstone, realised that it was henceforth foolish to argue for the maintenance of Anglican privilege explicitly on the ground of the religious identity of the state, since this would damage Anglicanism more than help it, by stirring up Dissenting animosity. But others treated the Maynooth vote as an aberration. Most Anglican evangelicals continued to emphasise the sacred nature of the church-state link, defining it in explicitly anti-Catholic terms. And traditionalist high churchmen, though less vehemently anti-Catholic, upheld the connection tenaciously as the most effective way of spreading true Christianity.

Tory anxiety was still in full spate when in the autumn of 1845 it became clear that most of the Irish potato crop would be inedible through disease. Famine portended. The result was an even more fundamental clash between Peel's administrative activism and mainstream tory values, on agricultural protection.

Peel had been a bitter critic of the Liberal strategy of fighting the 1841 election on Corn Law reform. But this was not just because it seemed a shoddy bribe and a class-divisive policy. It also boxed him into a difficult corner. Most tories were instinctive protectionists; the Corn Law appeared to offer security in a hostile world; it was all they knew. But it had not been a front-rank political issue before the Liberal and Anti-Corn Law League free-trading pressure of 1839–41, especially the attack on 'monopolists' at the 1841 election itself. In reaction to this, tories began to define protection as a seminal part of their creed. 'Of a sudden the Conservative party as they crowded the benches of the new House of Commons found themselves Protectionists.'[35] This was unfortunate because for Peel the adjustment of tariff levels was just the sort of technical issue on which he expected the party to follow ministers' judgment.

The political crisis of 1841–3 demonstrated what Peel may already subconsciously have felt: that the Corn Laws were indefensible. Economic misery stimulated the Anti-Corn Law League's energies and allowed it to blame 'insolent feudal tyranny' for interposing a 'busy, bungling hand' to wreck the machinery designed by benign Providence to spread resources fairly among God's peoples.[36] Its leading spokesman, Richard Cobden, became a major figure, while hundreds of evangelical nonconformist ministers were active in its campaigns, transforming its style and appeal.[37] They argued that aristocrats were slothful parasites on the state, raising the price of the people's bread unfairly in order to help the landed interest and to add revenue to state coffers which could be used for the anti-Christian purposes of corruption and foreign war. In 1842, Peel amended the Corn Laws by altering the sliding scale, in an attempt to do what the 1828 law had failed to do, to keep prices as stable as possible and give 'protection to the producer at low prices, encouragement to supply as they rose'.[38] But this failed to satisfy the League. In July 1842, at a League meeting, R.S. Bayley, a Sheffield nonconformist minister, referring to threats to kill Peel, said that few would weep at his death. Meanwhile, John Bright was privately urging employers to lock men out in order to create an economic crisis of such proportions that Peel would be forced to give in and repeal the Corn Laws.[39]

Peel's decisions to alter and then, in 1846, to abolish corn duties were both economic and political ones. He believed that repeal was of benefit to the economy, that it held out the prospect of stable and perhaps slightly lower food prices, which would minimise artificial and damaging trade and currency fluctuations and stimulate demand in all economic sectors. It would offer a better guarantee of future food supplies from abroad, and it would stimulate investment and competition in domestic agriculture. But it was just as much a political decision. In the light of Chartist, League and Irish unrest, the state had to show that it was doing all that it could responsibly do to stave off misery for the people. Peel needed to demonstrate that his party was not in thrall to vested interests. He also needed to teach the people the limits of the state's responsibility for the condition of the economy. Peel was a pessimist about future economic prospects. He believed that British prosperity was artificial since it was based on industrial profits which would decline with increased international competition. In 1847, after repeal, he was still predicting a 'cataclysm which shall cumber the surface of our western world' because of the industrial system which doomed millions to labour, suffering and declining prospects.[40] So he expected depressions and unrest to return; the state could only try to minimise the bad effects. If all those laws which led public opinion to blame human agency for economic failings were abolished, then people would be more likely to accept that future depressions were beyond political cure. The Corn Laws were ideal for this purpose since they were both the most hated and the least effective of such laws.

These views were alien to most tory landlords, and to the tenant-farmers to whom county MPs were now so accountable. But Peel's original strategy was to use prosperity gradually to show them that their fears were unfounded. In the winter of 1845, though, he took advantage of the Irish famine and suddenly changed tack to urge quick and total repeal. So his tory enemies could allege that he ignored the sentiments of his party, the sentiments which had made him prime minister in 1841. This was not quite fair. Lacking support in cabinet for his repeal plans, Peel had resigned in December 1845, but, though Russell had come out for total repeal – and a public agitation for it – the month before, he failed to form a Liberal government. This was largely because a group of influential Anglo-Irish whig landowners resisted total and immediate repeal, though Russell was also personally irresolute, lacking confidence that Peel would give him the support necessary to govern in a minority. Fortunately the cantankerous Howick (who had just succeeded his father as third Earl Grey) refused to serve in a Liberal cabinet with Palmerston as Foreign Secretary, and so could be made the scapegoat for Russell's failure. Peel resumed office. His supporters now claimed that he formed the last bastion against democracy and chaos. As Wellington put it, the question was now 'not one of Corn Laws – it is one of *Government*'.[41] Faced with the responsibility of action, Peel could not resist portraying himself as a bold leader who could control his backbenchers. He boasted to Gladstone that he could carry repeal through and keep the party together.[42] He was adamant that the question was for parliament to decide and should not be put to the voters.[43] In turn, parliament – because of party discipline – would respect the wishes of government. The government had much 'more extensive information and a deeper insight . . . than superficial and irresponsible observers' in parliament and outside. How could 'those, who spend their time in hunting and shooting and eating and drinking', compete with that insight, and how could they expect government to concede 'to the prevailing and popular feeling of the day its own convictions'?[44] Only Stanley (now in the Lords) had resigned from the cabinet. In the Commons the advocates of Protection seemed leaderless. Peel could not have predicted the emergence of Disraeli and Bentinck, that most unorthodox, ill-matched but unflagging pair, the one romantic and ambitious, the other a choleric defender of a social order. But they could build on grass-roots tory feeling forcefully expressed in byelections. Peel, displaying a Canute-like executive arrogance, ignored that fact, trying to deny the basic premise of the Reform Act, that governments relied ultimately on constituency approval. Peel repealed the Corn Laws, but with Liberal support. Only 114 Conservatives voted for the third reading and 241 opposed it. Disraeli and Bentinck then turned Peel out of office by allying with Liberals in opposition to an Irish Coercion Bill. The Peelites seceded and took up a position in the political centre, leaving protectionists, led by Stanley, Disraeli and Bentinck, as the most numerous body of opposition to Russell's new Liberal government.

The events of 1846 created a double legacy. On the one hand, the repeal of the Corn Laws was a very great asset to political stability. Whereas the whigs had sought to establish the state's openness primarily in *constitutional* terms, from 1846 onwards British opinion was led to judge politicians also by their distance from *economic* vested interests. Subsequent government success in conveying the impression of disinterestedness in financial matters was one of the keys to popular confidence in it. So it is a major turning-point of British political history. But Peel's other legacy was to ensure that only Liberals would benefit. The Conservative party of Stanley and Disraeli remained the principal opposition, retaining almost intact the strength which Conservatives had built up in counties and small towns in the 1830s. But Corn Law repeal made it look like a disreputable gaggle of vested interests, a group of stupid country gentlemen rather than the inheritor of a long tradition central to British politics. It presented the softest of targets to opponents. It seemed alien to the spirit of the age. Liberal hegemony was the fruit of Peel's hatred of tories who balked him, but it was not what he had intended. Peel loathed the Liberal-radical dynamic. In 1846, with the repeal passing through parliament and his government heading for disaster, he refused a coalition with Liberals on free trade principles. That course would 'make the future formation of a strong Government, on sound Conservative principles more difficult, if not impossible'.[45] Peel's commitment was still to the maintenance and revival of a 'really Conservative party' in opposition to a Liberal-radical one.[46] But these hopes were destroyed by the loathing of most protectionists for his character and obstinacy, by the continuing attractiveness of protection itself when agricultural prices were depressed in 1849–52, and by the success of protectionists in articulating Conservative principles more persuasively than Peel, with the result that there was a steady drift of 'Peelite' MPs back to the mainstream party. Peel's behaviour in 1845 and 1846 made permanent enemies of his erstwhile followers. They found him arrogant in his supercilious refusal to consult his party, dishonourable in overthrowing the principles which were his basic title to govern, cowardly before class-based agitation, despicable for abusing as selfish 'monopolists' the agriculturalists whose support he had exploited over a career of thirty-seven years' duration, and childishly and vulgarly spiteful to them in his canting declarations of warmth to Cobden and to those who 'earn their daily bread by the sweat of their brow'.[47] In the end, the small elite of Peel's ex-ministers who remained loyal to him had no option but to join with the Liberals, donating their administrative ability to keeping in power men whom, by and large, they despised, and with whose views on the constitution, religion and Ireland they were never particularly happy. The great beneficiary of the Corn Law crisis was the Liberal party which eighteen months before had seemed bankrupt, divided and almost irrelevant.

CHAPTER 8

Coming of age, 1846–66

By THE LATE 1850s, the Liberal party had become the natural, respectable ruling force in Britain. It had reassured the bulk of propertied opinion that it could administer affairs responsibly and defend national interests forcefully, yet it had drawn the sting from radical criticism by suggesting that vested interests had lost all influence over policy. Its tone no longer appeared narrowly aristocratic, its foreign, financial and religious policy struck many chords with the provincial rank-and-file, and it had secured a seemingly permanent majority in the House of Commons. This chapter seeks to show how that was done.

One great boon was the Conservative split of 1846 which brought Russell to the premiership and left the main opposition in the hands of men who claimed still to be protectionists. This gave anti-Conservatives a valuable basic point of agreement. They now definitively adopted the phrase 'Liberal party'. Nearly all candidates newly elected in 1847 used it in preference to any other designation.* For years to come, the basic rhetoric of Liberalism

---

* The following table summarises the affiliations of all non–Conservative United Kingdom MPs recorded in *Dod's parliamentary companion* for the relevant years:

	1838 total	1843 total	1847 reelected	1847 newly elected	1847 total
Whig[†]	99	70	41	11	52
Moderate reformer	17	8	5	0	5
Reformer	85	56	26	4	30
Radical reformer	34	23	13	7	20
Liberal	35	67	70	105	175
Repealer	22	18	14	6	20
Other	6	4	2	1	3
No entry*	41	33	17	1	18

[†] includes 'moderate whig' and 'independent whig'
*   mostly government ministers, and some radicals, like Cobden, Bright and O'Connor.

Halévy, *History of the English people 1830–1841*, p. 183n, also suggested that the title 'Liberal' was adopted officially in 1847.

attacked monopolies, promised a politics responsive to public opinion rather than to vested interests, and lauded 'self-government' (that is, *both* local government autonomy *and* individual responsibility). At its heart was free trade. Free trade could be presented as a solution to unnatural economic depression, a boon to world consumption and prosperity, a prerequisite of international peace, and an equitable, natural and peaceful regulator of social relationships. Economic fluctuations were revealed as awful and wonderful displays of God's handiwork; the state could be absolved of blame for them.

From the early 1850s, economic progress seemed to validate this liberal language. The *Times* wrote in 1852: 'We have committed ourselves to the general laws of Providence, and Providence now rewards us with a vista of social improvements, and unexpected blessings, which men had not dreamt of ten years ago.'[1] Britain found a more secure base for industrial development, less dependent on an over-producing cotton industry and an immature credit structure. Many jobs were created in mining, metalwork and transport, and the great capital goods industries – coal, iron and steel, shipbuilding – consolidated their position as national staples. Exports rose by 350 per cent between 1842 and 1873, and as the variety of markets expanded, the vicissitudes of each had less power to inflict suffering on the economy. The number of bankruptcies fell; capital investment sharply increased. Working hours began to shorten and wages increase, as the benefits of marrying labour to advanced machinery became more apparent to manufacturers. Slowly improving real wages benefited domestic consumption of goods. It began to seem that elements of the factory workforce shared the 'respectable' values discerned among shopkeepers and artisans.

Well might Palmerston boast in 1856 that 'progressive improvement is the law of our moral nature'. Such improvements 'more and more qualify man to fill the dignified position which his Creator destined for him in this world'.[2] Liberals made clear, though, that individual effort, rather than government intervention, was the key to greater prosperity and inter-class cooperation. Morpeth explained in 1863 that the 'Supreme Disposer' sets the 'energies of man' to 'strive' with nature but gives him 'the final mastery' of it.[3] Palmerston agreed: 'it is only movement, contending and conflicting movement, which keeps the course of nature healthy and active'; 'everything in nature that is still and stagnant becomes vitiated and corrupt'.[4]

Such language became a regular feature of Liberal speeches. Classic examples were the tours of Gladstone down the Tyne (1862), Palmerston along the Clyde (1863) and both men to Lancashire and Yorkshire in the early 1860s. Both explained that free trade and 'assiduous' government policy had restored peace and harmony to the country.[5] But they also warned that governments could play only a minor role in stimulating industry; men must cultivate their own energies. At Sunderland, Gladstone insisted that governments should not interfere with functions which 'they are totally unable to discharge'.[6] Both men praised human skill and stressed the need for class harmony in order to draw it out. No opportunity was lost of expressing feelings of 'admiration' and 'wonder' at the effects of genius and exertion in overcoming natural obstacles. At Bradford, for example, Palmerston marvelled that a 'barren moor' had been converted into a great commercial town.[7] They emphasised the natural harmony of different interests, declaring that agriculture and peace would both benefit from scientific progress and international trade (Palmerston described the Bradford Exchange as 'a temple of peace'). Capital and labour must work in harmony for each depended on the other's skill and energy.[8] The more prosperity a community enjoyed, the greater 'the union of the various classes of the community'. Gladstone rhapsodised that 'mistrust and alienation' were 'gradually fading away like mists before the rising sun'.[9] At Sheffield and Glasgow, Palmerston celebrated the ingenuity of skilled labourers as well as entrepreneurs, and told the 'sturdy and honest working classes, the strength and stamina of the country', that by hard work, aided by free institutions and free trade, they might come to be 'possessed of riches'.[10] Every honest worker, then, was part of the Liberal community. As Palmerston arrived at Sheffield, the 'horny hand of many a smiling but grimy-visaged artisan was spontaneously extended to his Lordship, and shaken by him with . . . heartiness and . . . bonhommie'.[11]

As Gladstone wrote in 1862, in a country 'so largely endowed with the power of self-government', public opinion must always be the arbiter of policy.[12] Liberals liked to boast of their receptiveness to the powerful onward movement of public opinion. The 1850s witnessed general awe at the power of the free circulation of information, generated by technology and rapid railway communication. Buoyed by the defeat of Chartism and the emerging evidence of artisanal respectability, Liberals were confident that it would be well directed. Hence the symbolism of the repeal of the stamp duties in 1855. Milner Gibson advocated it on the grounds that a cheap press would be in the hands of 'men of good moral character, of respectability, and of capital', who could be relied on to educate 'the minds of the working classes'.[13] The repeal resulted in a further massive increase in the circulation of political intelligence. The number of English provincial newspapers rose from 234 in 1851 to 394 in 1858, 743 in 1860 and 916 in 1874, and the papers were Liberal to Conservative in a ratio of about two to one.[14] Faced with press criticism of the management of the Crimean War (criticism which led the Liberal journalist W.R. Greg to assert the surpassing power of the press as a 'fourth estate' of the realm), Palmerston countered with the view that newspapers had no power independent of 'the feelings and opinions of the mass of the nation', to which they had to adjust.[15]★

This Liberal rhetoric caught admirably the burgeoning confidence of the age, yet also its sense of the fragility of prosperity, resting as it did in the hands of Providence.[16] It was also very useful politically. Particularly

---

★ The phrase 'fourth estate' was in common use in 1855. In that year a correspondent in *Notes and queries*, 1st ser. XI, 452 (9 June 1855), held that Brougham had probably first applied the phrase to the press, in 1823 or 1824.

important, in suppressing radical moves for *franchise* reform, was the assertion that the state was purely administered and that *economically* Britain was a productive community of all classes. But all this talk was vague, and did not go far to solve Liberals' practical political problems. The electoral system was still sufficiently biassed towards counties and small boroughs to give Conservatives (including Peelites) half of MPs in 1847 and 1852. And the majority which non-protectionist forces usually managed to scrape together was split and difficult to manage. This was true especially in the late 1840s, because of economic instability, and the mid-1850s, because of excessive political confusion. The question therefore was how to unite these forces for good work. The rhetoric discussed above established only a basic framework. This chapter will see three broad strategies emerging. One was identified with Russell: a bold, legislative policy of constitutional and religious reform to unite a Liberal-radical coalition. The second was that advocated by cautious Liberals, distrustful of radicals and of Russell's impetuosity, and anxious to ally with Peelites on a programme of economy and good administration. This would bow to Cobdenite free trade principles, while defeating organic radical reform and offering reassurance to a conservative electorate. The third was that of Palmerston, who disliked both Russellism and Peelism. His alternative strategy was the most successful in rallying the whole coalition, so that he was prime minister for all but sixteen months between 1855 and his death in 1865.

The problem of Liberal disunity, 1846-59

On becoming Prime Minister in 1846, Russell told the Commons that, though Peel had for a time succeeded in government by enforcing great 'identity of conduct' on his party, to continue the attempt was unlikely to be either successful or 'advantageous to the country'.[17] But many Liberals felt that Russell was in power by 'accident', not popular demand, and that Peel's firm administrative government – men, not measures – had been too successful for the country to tolerate anything else. This was particularly the view of centrist political economy Liberals, administrators rather than populists, most significantly Clarendon and Wood. Clarendon believed that old-style whig government would agitate unpopular issues and yet seem too 'aristocratic' for the middle classes. Instead, a government was needed 'fairly representing the industrial mind and conservative progress of the country'.[18] Russell took his advice; he offered cabinet places to three Peelites and to the leading anti-corn law activist Villiers (Clarendon's brother), and dangled an offer in front of Cobden.* But none accepted, though Cobden's

---

* Russell had in fact offered Cobden, without success, the Vice-Presidency of the Board of Trade when trying to form a government in December 1845, and now intimated that he could have a cabinet post if in future he were to change his mind about joining government.

subordinate Milner Gibson, MP for Manchester, did take office as Vice President of the Board of Trade.

Widespread unwillingness to be committed to a minority Liberal administration in a Conservative-dominated parliament was awkward, because Russell faced economic, religious and constitutional tension, which in one form or another persevered throughout his premiership. The terrible severity of the 1838–42 slump was followed by another major manufacturing depression in 1847–8, and a run on the banks. Depression prompted the return of unrest in England, from the Chartists, and even more seriously, in famine-hit Ireland. In 1848, the Chartists presented a National Petition for their six constitutional demands to the Commons, while in Ireland an abortive insurrection was being prepared, forcing the government to arrest a number of leading agitators for making seditious speeches. Then, in 1849–50, prosperity revived, but agricultural glut cut average wheat prices, stable between 50s and 55s per quarter between 1843 and 1846, to 44s in 1849 and to 38s–41s between 1850 and 1852. Inevitably, angry farmers lobbied for protection.

Russell itched to respond to Chartist grievances, to the revelations of inner-city squalor emanating from the official reports of the mid-1840s, and to the religious crises of the same period. Unfortunately, the fragmentation of the old two-party system in 1846 made a coherent Liberal response on these fronts almost impossible. The 1847 election gave the Liberals a single-figure majority over Peelites and protectionists combined. The Peelites (initially numbering about a hundred, but soon hit by defections to protectionism) would not guarantee to support Russell except on free trade. Personally and symbolically, Peel was a threat to Liberal government. How was Russell to assert the superiority of the Liberal vision of parliamentary government by men of character, strong through public confidence in their fairness, tolerance of open debate, and responsiveness to genuine grievances? Among the other components of the shaky Liberal majority were 64 Irish MPs and a fluctuating number of English radicals, at least 26 of whom were avowed supporters of church disestablishment in England.[19] The Maynooth affair in particular created electoral tension between radicals and mainstream Liberals. A number of the latter, such as Macaulay, were defeated at the 1847 election because of nonconformist irritation at their support of the Maynooth grant in 1845. So concerted Liberal action on religious questions was fraught with danger – yet the religious crisis seemed to demand urgent attention if establishments were to be defended and liberalised.

Some radicals demanded further parliamentary reform because – like many other Liberals – they were riled by the increasing selfishness of protectionist gentry and farmers, and by Liberal failure in the counties (they won 15 per cent, 27 per cent and 20 per cent of English county seats in 1841, 1847 and 1852). The consequence was radical criticism of 'the landed interest'. Yet, as in the 1830s, Liberals had to please the forces of property if they were to sustain the image of a national government. As Wood told Palmerston in 1846: 'the character we have to acquire and maintain as a government is that of being prudent, steady people'.[20] And if the Liberals fell, the likely alternative was a protectionist government with a bigoted economic and religious policy. This in turn would incite radicals to wage class warfare against the landed interest and would lead inexorably to far-reaching democratic parliamentary reform and the triumph of urban radical sentiments.[21]

On financial matters, the government was threatened by an unofficial radical-protectionist combination. The sudden shift to free trade left it dependent for revenue on the income tax, a tax historically unacceptable to radicals. Protectionist Conservatives were also willing to attack it as a symbol of executive oppression and fiscal stupidity, dampening demand and checking industrial and agricultural production. But if the government was to fund an even semi-credible army, finance the country's institutions, defend free trade and retain any reputation for political and economic management, the retention of the income tax was essential. Without it, the deficit would be over £3 million; in the absence of tariffs, this meant an almost insuperable financial crisis and crippling damage to government authority. The taxation question greatly damaged Russell's government between 1846 and 1852, making it look inefficient and yet unable to allay radical irritation. Continuing Chartist unrest, and utopianism about world peace in the wake of free trade, intensified the hostility of radicals to the tax burden in its current form.* Parliament's consent to the tax had to be renewed in 1848. This was bad timing, since expenditure had gone up substantially, owing to the enormous loans of 1846–7 to Ireland and a brief war scare in late 1847. Meanwhile revenue was declining because of economic depression – which, at the same time, naturally intensified calls for tax reductions in order to boost consumption. Throughout the spring and summer of 1848, radicals, Irish MPs and protectionists were unmanageable on financial questions, creating a mini-version of the continental upheavals of the same year. Before satisfying the Commons, the government had to present no fewer than four budgetary statements to MPs, to accept lower military estimates, and to appoint two select committees to investigate ways of finding further economies. In return, the tax was eventually renewed, at the old rate.

Meanwhile, radicals were reviving the campaign for parliamentary reform, with fifty of them adopting the 'Little Charter' (household suffrage, the secret ballot, triennial parliaments and more equal electoral districts). In 1848, their ballot motion won a majority of five, against cabinet opposition. Thereafter, government was always at the mercy of MPs critical of the income tax or particular items of expenditure. A motion to cut official salaries was successful in 1851, and the budget of that year was mauled, the

---

* Some wanted 'differentiation', by which some sources of income, particularly salaries, would be taxed at a lower rate than other (inherited) sources. But radicals were divided about this: see P.R. Ghosh, 'Disraelian Conservatism; a financial approach', *E.H.R.*, xcix (1984), 275.

income tax eventually being renewed for a year only after the government briefly resigned. But Liberals could not cut spending on defence; the consensus was rather that an increase was urgent.

Despite these great problems, Russell *was* successful at rallying Liberals on a number of issues. Above all, his policy on religion, education, Ireland and public health is important and is considered in the next chapter. Another unifying success was the destruction of the 'old colonial system': the removal of the preferences enjoyed by colonial produce, and the abolition of the shipping restrictions on colonial trade. In 1846, foreign slave-grown sugar was still charged a duty of 63s per cwt compared to 14s per cwt on colonial sugar. Within a few weeks of returning to office, the Liberals announced that they would equalise all types of duty at 14s by 1851, giving time for the colonial interests to become competitive (in 1848, the plan had to be altered to equalisation at 10s by 1854). Later, colonial preference was abolished on timber and coffee. In 1848, at the height of its problems, the government, looking for an issue to demonstrate its liberality, committed itself to move against the Navigation Acts, which were repealed in 1849. The ships of other nations were now conditionally allowed to compete for the carriage of goods to and from Britain (except for the coastal trade), in the expectation that this would give the British consumer more and cheaper choice. The 1849 settlement repealed duties on goods imported into the colonies and no nineteenth-century parliament again imposed taxes on the empire. These reforms testified to traditional whig dislikes: the shipping, Canadian timber and West Indian sugar interests had been three of the major lobbies in the unreformed Parliament. It was politically attractive as well as economically sound to argue that open competition would benefit international trade, lower prices for consumers and force once-protected industries – especially slackly-managed West Indian plantations inured to abundant slave labour – to become more efficient. The issue allowed Russell to display his 'classless' credentials, gain the confidence of radicals upset with inaction in other policy areas, and polarise Commons opinion between him and the opposition, to the benefit of good government and to the detriment of tories tarred with defending 'vested interests'.

Simply surviving for nearly six years was another achievement. Nonetheless, by 1850–2 there were three major complaints against Russell's government, which were to prevent his returning as premier throughout the 1850s. One was his failure to be 'sufficiently Prime Minister', as his brother told him – compared, of course, to Peel, who had been killed falling from his horse in 1850 and had acquired instant martyrdom.[22] His government seemed always to be withdrawing and revising its proposals in line with factional criticism, whether on budgets, the sugar duties, the navigation laws, encumbered estates in Ireland, hours of factory labour or public health legislation. This was hardly surprising when so many groups had to be conciliated. But it was also true that Russell did not have Peel's interest in administration, and was not a firm Treasury overlord of other departments.[23] The Peelite elite of ex-ministers promised that they, having imbibed the tory administrative tradition with their mother's milk, could offer more efficient government than Russell's 'feebleness and . . . extravagance'.[24]

Russell's difficulties encouraged a second strand of criticism, the traditional one of whiggish social exclusiveness. In 1846 he had appointed a heavily aristocratic cabinet: eight peers (including his father-in-law), an Irish peer and an heir to an earldom sat in a cabinet of sixteen. But this was a conscious attempt to demonstrate the relevance and responsiveness of aristocratic government in turbulent times. Despite it, Russell relied heavily on expert advisors, in the shape of Royal Commissions on specific subjects, bureaucrats like Edwin Chadwick, or junior ministers in direct touch with 'commercial' sentiment such as H.G. Ward (Admiralty), James Wilson (India), Milner Gibson (Trade) and Benjamin Hawes (War and Colonies). Still, his critics argued that his apparent reluctance to consult outside a small family circle was to blame for his poor record on economy and other matters. To young intellectuals, whiggery appeared the exclusive creed of 'a cousinhood remarkable more for the antiquity of their race than for the freshness of their intellects', and Russell its 'Last Doge'.[25] More damaging to Russell was the gloss put on such beliefs by his Foreign Secretary Palmerston. Palmerston's conduct of foreign policy during and after the 1848 revolutions played to the popular gallery in an effort to rally radicals to Russell's government and so fob off the probable consequences of its defeat – either protectionism or democratic constitutional reform. However, it infuriated the pro-Austrian court, and Russell's vanity was inflamed by complaints that he could not keep his Foreign Secretary in check. In 1851 Palmerston broke ranks by telling the French that he approved of Napoleon III's *coup d'état*. Russell, worn down, sacked him, but looked to be doing the court's bidding. Palmerston's successor, Granville, was seen as an aristocratic stooge, not a man of the people, and within two months Palmerston had played the major part in Russell's final parliamentary defeat.

Russell's third offence was impulsiveness. He was affronted by radicals' criticism. How could they charge a Russell with extravagance and remoteness? His natural response was to regain their respect by bold action. He attempted two initiatives, but both, by definition, would be controversial within the cabinet, so Russell sidestepped opposition there. One involved a religious matter. In October 1850, the press drew attention to a papal brief establishing a Catholic hierarchy of bishops in England. This generated much popular anti-Catholic hostility. Russell was also angry, on the erastian grounds that the brief encroached on state sovereignty in religious matters (the government was not notified in advance), and because of his own intense hostility to Tractarianism in the Church of England, which he saw as an advance guard for Romanism. So, without consulting the cabinet, he published the so-called Durham letter, attacking both papal policy and Tractarianism, and then introduced an Ecclesiastical Titles Bill to fine any cleric from outside the established church who assumed a territorial title. He hoped to exploit popular hostility, to rally Dissenters disaffected by the Maynooth grant and by his own education initiative of 1847 (see page 202), and to embarrass the Peelites (who included Tractarian sympathisers) by reminding the public of their religious illiberalism. Up to a point the strategy worked: the bill gained large majorities. But it was impulsive because it antagonised the Peelites and the Irish, two constituents of the informal coalition which kept the government afloat. In cabinet, friends of both groups disliked it.[26]

The second initiative, even more offensive to 'centrist' Liberals, was Russell's conversion to the cause of parliamentary reform. Three imperatives swayed him. One was the need to rally Liberal forces in and outside parliament behind a bold invigorating cause. A second, post-Chartism, was to demonstrate Liberal concern to reassure the respectable working classes about the constitution. A third was to arrest the ugly class division between land and trade caused by the emergence of a 'selfish' party of the landed interest, in tension with equally sectional bodies such as the Anti-Corn Law League. Russell was very anxious to maintain a cross-class support for Liberal leadership, and to divert ignorant sentiment on both sides away from utopian and destabilising expressions of class hostility.[27] But 'landed interest' control of the counties had deprived Liberals of a parliamentary majority. To play the Reform card in response had many attractions. It offered the prospect of boosting Liberal strength in parliament at the expense of protectionism. It promised to prevent the Peelites, who loathed the idea, from taking the initiative on the anti-protectionist side of politics. It re-established Liberal credentials in the eyes of radicals who were upset by Chartism, increased taxation and government expenditure on defence and religious education. It countered criticism that the government lacked sympathy for the people, it appealed to grass-roots Liberals who were enthusiastic for the principle of 'self-government', and it implied that the Liberals' definition of the 'people' was expanding with economic development. Russell attempted to persuade the cabinet to accept a Reform scheme for 1849, but was unable to commit himself to it publicly before 1851. Introduced in 1852 (to cabinet displeasure), it died with Russell's ministry.

After Russell's final fall in February 1852, these three failings created a groundswell of opinion among his colleagues that his governing style was politically dangerous. But as intolerable to them was the minority Conservative government under Stanley (now Derby) which followed, and which made gains at the 1852 election. Centrist Liberals and Peelites argued for a new style of Liberal government reflecting the conservative mood of the Commons, based on sober administration, on men not measures. Firm adherence to the principles of political economy would hold the line against agitation for subsidies to Irish landlords, excessive outdoor relief and uneconomic cuts in the working day. Administrative reform and low taxation would improve government's reputation for efficiency and hence check demands for constitutional change. (Gladstone, for instance, regarded civil service reform as '*my* contribution to parliamentary reform', that is, an alternative to it.[28]) And Palmerston's removal from the Foreign Office would guard against meddling and please cost-conscious radicals and country gentlemen. This conception was what Wood called 'centre' government and the leading Peelite Aberdeen 'Conservative progress'.[29] General support for it led to Derby's defeat and his replacement in December 1852 by a coalition led by Aberdeen, including four former Peelite ministers and the three leading centrist Liberals, Wood, Clarendon and Lansdowne. Palmerston was denied the Foreign Office and was made Home Secretary. Russell had to be given the lead in the Commons, because no one else *could* lead it, but most of his old colleagues, Grey, George Grey, Carlisle, Maule, Labouchère and Seymour, were excluded.

Despite the Peelites' carefully constructed reputation for efficiency, any hope that the Aberdeen coalition would provide the answer to Liberal disunity were quickly dashed. Russell believed that Aberdeen had promised him the quick reversion of the premiership. When this did not materialise, he rocked the boat by launching another Reform Bill, for the 1854 session. Palmerston resigned in protest, in December 1853 (he soon came back). But this was a well-timed resignation: it indicated further his distance from foreign policy-making and hence from blame for the Crimean War, into which Britain was sucked in early 1854. Unprecedented, harrowing press reporting exposed the subsequent indecisive military actions: the bloody battles of Balaclava and Inkerman, the year-long siege of Sebastopol, and the awful death-toll from disease. The Peelites, doubtless in the interests of executive efficiency, had taken *all* the cabinet posts most responsible for the conduct of the war. They now got more than their deserved comeuppance. Public opinion rounded, in particular, on Aberdeen and the hapless Newcastle at the War Office. Russell demanded a 'reconstruction', designed to winkle Peelites out and embarrass Aberdeen. But little was done. So by the beginning of 1855, the government was wide open to parliamentary censure. Unwilling to oppose the radical Roebuck's motion for a committee of inquiry into war management, Russell resigned, pulling the plug on the government. The motion was carried overwhelmingly and Aberdeen and Newcastle were forced out. But Russell – tarred with the radical Reforming brush – got no support as a wartime Prime Minister. Stock in Peelism was also low; in fact the other three leading Peelites soon followed Aberdeen in resigning. Neither Graham, long neurotic about the sanctity of government authority, nor Gladstone, blind in adulation of masterful Peelite government, would tolerate the new government's acceptance of Roebuck's motion, which, to an indignant Gladstone, was 'the most revolutionary proceeding of this our day'.[30]

So, to the regret of the court, the premiership had to go to Palmerston, the 'voice of the country', the only man who could convince foreigners that British war policy 'rested on the public feeling'.[31] How differently, he implied, would affairs have turned out if the English mastiff, rather than weak Aberdeen, had been allowed to shape foreign policy in 1853! Now he alone could prosecute the war boldly, quickly and successfully. Palmerston's governing style was designed to head off Russellite radicalism and anaemic, low-spending Peelism. His men were solid centrist administrators: Clarendon and Wood from before, joined by Cornewall Lewis, Vernon Smith and, of those dropped in 1852, George Grey, Maule and Labouchère.* Meanwhile the Peelites split, with Argyll staying in the cabinet, and two other efficient but undoctrinaire and unfussy ex-tories joining, Canning and Harrowby.[32] Over the next two years, Palmerston presided over the destruction of Peelism as a separate political entity. Those Peelites who left could not agree on a line towards him, and their group was smashed when they were perceived as hostile to the two most fashionable nostrums, Palmerston and parliamentary reform, at the 1857 election. Only those men of ability whose claim to office was unshakeable had a future; and, for us, that means Gladstone.

Russell's fate was different. He was persuaded to accept a place under Palmerston, but more humiliation visited him when, as British representative at the Vienna conference (spring 1855), he supported the peace terms discussed there. The cabinet, fearing popular hostility to them in Britain and France, overruled him. Palmerston persuaded him not to resign and thereby reveal his support for the proposals. So Russell condemned them in the Commons. The Austrians leaked news of his former support and he had to go. He seemed to have no future. But he still knew best how to rally the Liberal benches in the Commons. In 1857 and again in 1858 he, with radical, tory and Gladstonian help, brought down Palmerston for infringing Liberal principles. And his advocacy of parliamentary reform gave him a famous victory at the 1857 City election. His reputation for egocentric restlessness now prevented him from being able to form a government, but he could destroy them at will. Most Liberals instinctively trusted him over Palmerston. His prominence in Palmerston's new government in 1859 was a *sine quâ non* of its survival, and he won cabinet offers for the radicals Cobden (who declined) and Milner Gibson and Villiers (who accepted). At 74, Palmerston might just be a stopgap for him.

Support from Russell, radicals and Gladstone made Palmerston stronger after 1859 than before. One impetus behind coalition unity was another minority Conservative government in 1858–9, which appeared alternately weak and dangerous at home and abroad. Disraeli apart, tories lacked front-bench speaking ability. Though they had dropped the inflammatory demand for a return to agricultural protection after 1852, they were still branded as sectional by Liberals if they tried to defend landed economic interests, while, if they did not, there seemed little point in a Conservative government. It was incapable of resisting majority Liberal pressure aimed at humiliating it. In 1858 it had to take up the jewish emancipation question and accept the abolition of the property qualification for MPs (the first

---

* George Grey had actually returned in 1854, and Labouchère did not come back until November 1855. Maule was now Panmure. Of the other casualties of the Peelite incursion in 1852, Carlisle became Lord Lieutenant of Ireland, while two more, Clanricarde and Seymour (now duke of Somerset) were brought back by Palmerston in 1858 and 1859.

Chartist proposal to reach the statute-book). 'The fact is Lord John Russell is governing', one backbencher wrote in April 1858.[33] The same happened in 1859 over parliamentary reform. Radicals were innately suspicious of the Conservative government, and Bright worked up a campaign for Reform. This threatened to incite the Liberal opposition to unite in favour of a Reform bill; so the ministry introduced a weaker one of its own, despite disquiet from its backbenchers. But the Liberal majority defeated it as a partisan measure. Government feebleness cast widespread doubt on its ability to conduct foreign policy firmly yet peacefully, at a time when the Italian question threatened European stability. Tory rule, in short, seemed weak and unprincipled. Derby himself concluded that the best security for traditional interests lay with a strong Conservative opposition restraining a responsible Palmerstonian government.[34] By 1859, Palmerston was the most conservative Prime Minister available.

The basis of Liberal stability, 1855–65

The Palmerstonian period (1855–65) strengthened the basis of Liberalism in three crucial ways, which must now be investigated. First, it consolidated its reputation for efficient, fair administration. Second, it established a successful compromise between the needs of a national foreign policy and the pressure for economy. And third, in consequence, it marginalised traditional radicalism and created a more constructive definition of Liberal governing purpose, which a great variety of groups could accept. In short, it managed to approximate to the uplifting, integrative rhetoric discussed in the first section. It seemed as if Liberalism really did come as close as human nature allowed to disinterested national government.

* * *

Belying the blustering, devil-may-care image which he latterly liked to project, Palmerston spent the first nineteen years of his political career (1809–28, as Secretary at War) essentially as an official, not a party man or orator. He remained, true to those liberal tory roots, an immensely hard-working administrator. He was not a party animal; he believed in being in power. It was the only end of political life for him, both duty and pleasure. Clear and unpretentious in speech and on paper, he expected the same from others, hence his difficulties with Gladstone. His tireless industry as Foreign and Home Secretary was notorious.[35] As Prime Minister, therefore, his agenda was primarily administrative. He offered competence, safe management of national affairs, inquiry into abuses, and purity of administration. Legislation was not contentious but worthy and necessary. Bagehot – admiringly – called his regime 'dull government', dovetailing with the needs of a practical, successful manufacturing country.[36]

Integral to it were administrative Liberals (aided by the Peelite remnant after 1859) who set the tone of his domestic policy. None were partisan men. These Liberals included the two most important members of the old Grey connection, Sir George Grey (nephew of the ex-Prime Minister) and Sir Charles Wood (son-in-law). There were also Sir George Cornewall Lewis and his brother-in-law the earl of Clarendon, and Henry Labouchère, brother-in-law of the ex-whig Chancellor Baring (like *his* mentor Althorp, Baring disliked office and withdrew after 1852). All were clever gentleman-politicians: Wood and Grey had taken firsts at Oriel College Oxford, Lewis wrote on history and philosophy. Grey, the linchpin, was Home Secretary for fourteen years. Wood was Chancellor of the Exchequer under Russell, at the Admiralty for three years in the mid-1850s, and in charge of Indian policy for the other ten years.* Cornewall Lewis was Chancellor 1855–8, and later Home Secretary and Secretary for War. Had he lived, he, not Gladstone, would perhaps have led the party. Clarendon, an ex-diplomat, was a good Foreign Secretary (1853–8, 1865–6), more emollient abroad than Palmerston. Grey and Wood were the cabinet's main links to the queen and Prince Albert; another Grey, Charles, was private secretary to Albert and then Victoria (1849–70). They also helped to appease the third Earl Grey, equally able but dogmatic and difficult as a colleague and, as a peer, dispensable from cabinet after 1852. And they, with Clarendon, employed the universal respect of their colleagues to become the great reconcilers of cabinet differences.

Their administrative governing style was the more important because of the criticism of government practice, welling up in 1855, that had made Palmerston Prime Minister. The Crimean War embarrassments prompted a public campaign for the wholesale application to government of 'middle-class' values of practical management and technological know-how. Mrs Gaskell's novel *North and South* (1855) was a text for the times, as was Dickens' *Little Dorrit* (1855–7). The 'efficiency' movement at this time was broader than any one organisation, marrying traditional 'country' criticism of state exclusiveness with the hardheadedness of the business elite, the anti-aristocratic animus of the literary intelligentsia, and the manly Christianity of some representative upper-middle-class gentlemen. The Turcophile archaeologist-politician Layard made a melodramatic attack on the conduct of the war. The nonconformist businessman Samuel Morley headed a more restrained campaign for administrative reform. But the problem was wider than the 1855 furore suggested. Shoddy preparation of legislation and insufficiently rigorous parliamentary discussion had been causing disquiet for some time, most clearly expressed in that previous year of turbulence, 1848. It had led Trevelyan to propose competitive examinations for the civil service, and others to suggest different changes.[37] In the *Edinburgh Review*,

---

* He presided over the establishment of efficient civil government and a rationalised financial system and legal code in India. In his famous despatch of 1854, he sketched out a comprehensive system of Indian education to university level.

Lewis had sketched out his ideal 'liberal system of government' as 'the old whig party of England, improved and enlarged by modern speculation, particularly in questions of public economy and jurisprudence'. But he had warned that a rational policy on pauperism, punishment, law reform and so on would emerge only from a more vigorous executive, capable of framing effective solutions to parliamentary grievances without weakly waiting on opinion or responding to arbitrary and undisciplined clamour.[38]

These tensions suggested the need for administrative reform, but also for a lesson to idealists in the limits to the power of any government. Wood, Grey and Lewis were very anxious about the survival of propertied rule, which they considered necessary to uphold impartial law and sound economical principles. (All of them were serious-minded political economists, sensitive to commercial opinion: Wood sat for Halifax; Clarendon was brother of the anti-corn-law activist Villiers; Lewis was a Chancellor after the City's heart; Labouchère carried Navigation Act repeal.) They also saw propertied rule as an essential safeguard of the spread of morality (both Wood and Grey were devout liberal evangelicals and strong supporters of the established church). They set out to make critics of government understand that many matters would always remain outside the reforming capacity of mankind, that the call for 'middle-class' values in administration was utopian and sentimental, and, in practice, would mean characterless bureaucracy. The 'efficiency' campaign was potent, they thought, for two reasons: because the urban middle classes lacked political experience, and because of the apparent incompetence of existing leadership. What was the solution? Upper- and middle-class education must be improved, to underpin good government, and manufacturing men must learn the craft of local administration. Authority must remain as decentralised as possible, so as to give a fair field for middle-class local activity and provide 'as few fields for attacking the government of the country as we can help'. The stability and prosperity of the country would depend on the rule of 'men of independent character, of independent mind, and independent fortune'. 'Self-government', Wood said in 1849, must remain 'the rock upon which the stability of all the institutions of this country rest'.[39]

As a result, Palmerston's governments strengthened existing practices in a number of ways. For a start, to counter parliamentary lethargy, more use was made of Royal Commissions than ever before or since: 152 were set up in the twenty years 1852–71, as against 101 in the twenty years before or after.[40] These grew in number in the 1860s, and, since they took years to report, much of the Liberal legislation after 1868 was founded on these Palmerstonian inquiries. But in most cases their purpose was administrative, not legislative. For instance, commissions were appointed to improve army and navy recruitment, to secure good management of the new Volunteer force, the Royal Academy and the Ordnance Survey, and to plan the Thames Embankment and National Gallery.

One major problem that they addressed was that of upper- and middle-class education, a hotly-debated topic after the Crimean War. Some public schools had spectacularly reformed their teaching and character in line with Victorian seriousness, but most had not. Most of the 700–800 ancient grammar schools and church-foundation secondary schools were tied by the terms of their endowments to an inappropriately narrow syllabus or a much-restricted catchment area. Though a series of acts in 1853, 1855 and 1860 established a permanent Charity Commission to review the statutes of charitable bodies, its powers to rectify the situation were limited, in the face of strong local opposition from the beneficiaries of the statutes. In the 1860s, two Commissions met, presided over by Clarendon and Labouchère (now Lord Taunton). Clarendon's was set up in 1861 to investigate syllabuses at the nine leading public schools. Clarendon himself was aware of the 'immense national importance of the education of the upper classes', yet the inferiority of their schooling in science, modern languages and mathematics to many in strata below them. His Commission aimed to help schools to 'mould . . . the character of English Gentlem[en]' so that they could 'govern others and control themselves', developing 'vigour and manliness of character' and a 'strong but not slavish respect for public opinion'.[41] An act of 1868 allowed the governing bodies of seven of the schools to make necessary changes and established special commissioners to do so for them if they dallied. But the greatest impact of the Clarendon Commission was in encouraging upper-grade endowed schools which it did *not* investigate to aspire to the status of a high-class public school. It also paved the way for the more ambitious Taunton Commission of 1864, which looked at all endowed schools. The Taunton report (1868) advocated ending free entry in favour of competitive examinations, and establishing a permanent body of commissioners with many powers to reform school statutes and to sweep away restrictive regulations. Above all it asserted the need for a tripartite division of secondary schools, some to be high-class establishments providing education for gentlemen and the upper professions until the age of 18 or 19, some, for lesser professions, finishing at 16, and some concentrating on technical education and finishing at 14. So each class would benefit from a systematic education, improving standards for all yet entrenching the existing social order. These were heady and revealing ideals. The resulting legislation was controversial, though of limited effect (see page 264). But the wider publicity which the reports gave to the cause of secondary school reform was of unparalleled significance, in essence creating the late-Victorian public school system.

Palmerston was also more interested than the Russellite whigs in civil service reform. The old whig-radical tradition distrusted the power and secretiveness of bureaucracy and believed that the best security against abuse lay (rigid economy apart) with the promise of 'character' offered by the traditional appointments system. But time was outmoding these views. Two adjustments were needed. The first was to recognise the increased complexity of government business. It was no longer practicable to expect ministers to carry the proportion of departmental administration that the young Palmerston had done. No more of an answer, in an age of parliamen-

181

tary assertiveness, were the non-parliamentary and unaccountable boards which had traditionally done much of the work. In 1847 the old Poor Law Commission, unaccountable to parliament and hence distrusted, was replaced by a Poor Law Board chaired by a responsible minister. This satisfied the Commons, yet in practice greatly strengthened the power of the Board's permanent officials. It pointed to a changed conception of government, in which the departmental minister, aware of parliamentary feeling, was to criticise and correct the work of his permanent staff, rather than to conduct the administration himself. The second adjustment, to reinforce the weight of gentlemanly ability within administration, followed from this. The patronage system attracted too many incompetents and crammer products to government service. From the 1850s, competitive examinations were generally seen as the answer. While appearing to respond to anti-aristocratic critics, they would not subvert gentlemanly dominance of national institutions but, though the agency of the pioneer reformed public schools, entrench it. In 1853 competitive examinations were introduced for the Indian Civil Service; in 1857 and 1858, after the Crimean disaster, entry to the military academies at Woolwich and Sandhurst was opened to competitive examination. In 1855 the Civil Service Commission was established to certify the fitness of nominees for domestic civil posts. But, because of suspicion from the old whig-radical school, competitive examinations were as yet only introduced at the margins. Before the further reforms of 1870, less than one-third of certificated candidates sat one. However, Palmerston was extremely strict in matters of patronage, seeing it as 'a trust imposed on me for the public advantage'.[42]

He was anxious more generally to build an image of disinterested government. He followed Peel and Russell in creating very few peerages, baronetcies or knighthoods.[43] In 1856 he tried but failed to introduce life peerages, in order to improve the quality of the Lords as a legal body. He attempted to add several great manufacturing families to the peerage, though it was difficult to find suitable and interested men and only the Strutts passed scrutiny. He refused to award Privy Counsellorships 'except in virtue and by reason of official position'.[44] And in 1855 an important reform in the arrangements for handling private bills in the Commons prohibited MPs from sitting on committees to discuss controversial bills affecting their own locality.[45]

Meanwhile, Grey, Wood and Lewis brought to the upper reaches of Liberal cabinets administrative ability of a very high order. Unfairly neglected in historical writing, they played a crucial part in the redefinition of the Liberal governing ethos. They were not orators but displayed the 'Grey' qualities of 'good official efficiency with parliamentary ability sufficient for daily use'.[46] They were clear-headed, hard-working, practical, straightforward, resolute, patient and sincere. Some saw Grey as 'really Prime Minister in all internal affairs' under Palmerston.[47] Moreover, they, Clarendon and Palmerston sought to banish fears of aristocratic unwillingness to govern, by training up a generation of modern-minded, serious, conscientious and dutiful young peers. By the early 1860s, four of these were important ministers at under 40: Baring's son Thomas (the future Lord Northbrook), Lord Dufferin, Lord Wodehouse (later earl of Kimberley) and Earl de Grey (Goderich's son, later marquess of Ripon). All were serious Christians with a social conscience. De Grey was a Christian Socialist, much influenced by Maurice and Kingsley, and the other three, at Christ Church together in the mid-1840s (Wodehouse took a First), had been particularly affected by the social crisis of the 1840s and imbued with the latitudinarian moral earnestness which swept Oxford in reaction to the excesses of the Oxford movement. Wodehouse and Dufferin were tested on diplomatic missions by Palmerston and Clarendon and then given office. All four served under Charles Wood at the India Office and imbibed his sense of Britain's duty as a progressive imperial power, which they were later to employ to crucial effect in proconsular posts in India, Ireland and Canada. Like their mentors, they were not primarily interested in party politicking. They aimed to validate one of the great claims of Victorian Liberalism: that it offered rule by high-minded men of property and unshakeable character, disdainful of reputation, short on vanity or personal ambition, and anxious to demonstrate the willingness of the aristocracy to serve the people by laborious administration. Much of this was also true of another young Liberal junior minister of the same generation, Lord Hartington. Hartington, though, was less religious and more of a party political animal; he was to be Palmerston's greatest heir (see page 260). By contrast, the more theatrical whig leadership style, unsuited to a practical commercial society, disappeared with men like Normanby, and his 'Turveydrop-like pomposity',[48] and earnest but innocent, indecisive and inept Carlisle, formerly Morpeth. Carlisle was sent to Ireland as Lord Lieutenant, for which his 'heartfelt flummery' was perfectly suited.[49]

Palmerston's appointments also nodded to the vogue for social science and political economy, most noticeably in the case of the duke of Argyll and successive education ministers, Robert Lowe and H.A. Bruce. In 1856, Argyll and Lowe launched a twenty-five year truculent defence of extreme political economy principles with joint authorship of the bill to abolish limited liability. They defended it by applauding the superiority of that 'natural law', that 'infinite sagacity', by which man's behaviour was ruled and which kept 'the great machine of society . . . oscillating to its centre'.[50] Both were also genuinely interested in using the power of government to improve education and health (see pages 202–7).

* * *

By 1865, Palmerston felt confident enough of his ministry's disinterested and efficient image to ridicule the anti-aristocratic radical Cobden as an impractical inverted snob, like 'a shop apprentice in a back alley in the City'.[51] Traditional-style radical criticism of his government had been spiked also by its attractive financial and foreign policy. The great failing of Liberal government before 1852 had been its inability to convince radical MPs that government deserved adequate, regular tax revenue, and as a result, respectable opinion had blamed government for lax national defence. To change this was the achievement of Palmerston and his Chancellors. It brought immense benefits, adding to government stability and bolstering Britain's international standing. Palmerston's role was not to incite jingoism, as historians sometimes say; it was rather to rein in parliamentary pressure for low spending.

Government's success in persuading Liberal MPs of the need to levy taxes in fact stemmed from the combination of the two quite different financial strategies of Liberal Chancellors. One was that of Wood (1846–52) and Lewis (1855–8), operating within the undoctrinaire fiscal tradition of Althorp and Baring. The other was that of Gladstone (1852–5, 1859–66), operating from within the Peelite tradition. The difference was revealed in tariff and taxation policy. Wood and Lewis were both well-read in political economy, but they did not share the drive of Peel and Gladstone for tariff reductions. In line with whig dislike of strong government, they tended to believe that the promotion of trade was only a marginal concern of the Treasury, whose job should be to raise revenue as fairly and uncontentiously as possible. They held that the most successful fiscal policy was a flexible one which reacted quickly and pragmatically to the shifting burdens borne by different social groups. It was not a suitable arena for the application of long-term theories and stratagems which were bound to be falsified by unpredictable events. In other words, Liberal fiscal policy continued to display a hand-to-mouth quality at which apostles of 'strong government' jibbed. Gladstone, on the other hand, had a much more high-profile conception of budgets. He proposed an active policy of checking spending. To demonstrate the state's zeal in keeping expenditure down would, he believed, convince radicals of the moral necessity of remaining taxes, while encouraging taxpayers publicly to oppose further increases. This would marginalise demands for constitutional reform, and, by keeping strict limits on expenditure, reduce the danger of loss of government authority through a lack of income in recessions. This policy allowed him to take up the old tory cry of whig financial incompetence, yet appealed to radical irritation at heavy spending. For a third-party politician not clear where to look for political bed-fellows, this was astute. His celebrated budgets of 1853 and 1860 reduced the number of articles liable to customs duty from 466 to 48, of which only 15 were of significance; none were on raw materials, basic foodstuffs or manufactured goods. His proposal, in 1860, to repeal the excise duty on paper had particular political benefits because the Lords rejected it. Radicals wanted a tussle with the Lords on the issue, Palmerston did not. Gladstone improved his radical credentials by incorporating paper duty repeal in the provisions of his 1861 budget, which the Lords deemed it prudent to accept.

But Gladstone's strategy meant challenging Palmerston and Lewis on the income tax. In his 1853 budget, he had set out a plan to cut spending and to abolish the tax by 1860 and lowered the wage threshold at which it became payable from £150 to £100. His aim had been to stir up popular pressure for lower taxes. But this strategy was blown out of the water by the outbreak of the Crimean War in 1854 and the evidence of the war's popularity. After Gladstone resigned in distress in 1855, he opposed Palmerston's continuation of war, high military expenditure and high taxes. This enhanced his reputation among radicals like Cobden and Bright who had opposed the war from the beginning, and all other expensive foreign undertakings, because they imposed fresh burdens on the taxpayer. But while Gladstone's concern was economy, Palmerston and Lewis were exercised about political stability, and so stalwart defenders of the tax. They believed that it reduced class animosity by demonstrating a commitment to taxing property,* while, since it was more productive every year, it bolstered government authority over expenditure. After the embarrassments of the late 1840s, parliament must be taught that, once it had approved policies which necessitated expenditure, it had a moral obligation to grant funding for them.[52]

In the mid- to late 1850s, Gladstone attacked Lewis's tax policy as extravagant. When Palmerston astutely made him Chancellor again in 1859, he half-fought in public with the premier over expenditure. Palmerston wanted to increase defence spending, and had an unanswerable case. The long-standing inadequacy of national defences, as a result of continual parliamentary pressure on spending, had caused alarm, even without the war and the subsequent international tension, exacerbated by Napoleon III and Bismarck. Developments in technology (such as ironclad ships) required new spending, while criticism of the war's conduct heightened pressure for military reorganisation. Palmerston demanded more ships and extra fortifications against France. He ridiculed Gladstone's strategy: if war came, the lack of ships, arms and defences 'would be ill made up for by the fact that some hundreds of merchants and manufacturers had made large fortunes'.[53] Palmerston got his way and twenty-four ironclads were in or ready for commission by 1865; fortifications were built in nine dockyards. Defence expenditure rose by £8.4 million between 1859 and 1862. Yet Gladstone's public calls for economy maintained his semi-radical credentials. The government enjoyed the best of both worlds, because the buoyant economic position then kept revenue high, international tension relaxed a little (by 1866 defence spending was nearly back to 1857/8 levels), and substantial reductions in both indirect and direct taxation became possible. Income tax fell from 10d to 4d, and tea duties from 1s 5d to 6d a lb, between 1860 and 1865.

Government's skilled ambiguity changed radicals' relationship with taxation. Gladstone succeeded in convincing them that the fight for economy

---

* Similarly, Wood in 1851 had replaced the unpopular and insanitary window tax with a tax on inhabited houses above £20 annual value, in proportion to that value.

no longer had to be conducted *against* the state. Liberal governments could link up with the people in an ongoing crusade for pure administration. Cobden himself favoured the government with his assistance in 1859–60, when he helped to negotiate a free trade treaty with France. Confidence in government's willingness to lower expenditure was boosted by the imposition of institutional checks on extravagance. In 1856, Baring moved for a select committee on public monies, which he chaired. It proposed a series of administrative changes, leading to the creation in 1861 of a Public Accounts Committee, chaired by him, which allowed the Commons for the first time to examine the reports of the Audit Board as to how public money had been spent. For its work to be effective, all departments would first have to submit appropriation accounts – explaining what money was needed for – to the Commons. The committee of 1856 urged this and it was done in stages over the next decade, with Treasury backing. The Exchequer and Audit Departments Act of 1866 regularised the procedure by bringing all departments under the scrutiny of the Audit Board and strengthening its powers. Also in 1866, a parliamentary standing order invalidated all backbenchers' motions for extra expenditure opposed by government. This checked the considerable pressure to compensate farmers affected by the cattle plague.

A deft merger of potentially incompatible traditions was also the secret of government foreign policy. Despite tensions, that merger was usually successful enough to create a bond between Liberals and a reassuring public image.

The radical tradition in foreign policy had stressed the innate power of public opinion in spreading constitutionalism, peace and prosperity to foreign parts, especially when complemented by open trade. Military and diplomatic effort seemed to radicals an expensive hindrance to this process, not a help. They inherited the long-standing distinction in 'country' ideology between the army and navy: the one potentially repressive at home as well as abroad, the other enjoying the freedom of the seas and inculcating a liberal patriotism in its servicemen; the one a great burden on the taxpayer to the benefit of idle aristocratic offspring, the other an agency by which British values (and goods, in the case of the merchant marine) could be carried all over the world. Radicals tended to subscribe to the agreeable myth that Britain's geographical and trading position allowed her the luxury of constructive influence in shaping a liberal world without the hard-pressed taxpayer having to pay for it. To them, aristocratic diplomats, manoeuvring to maintain a chimerical 'balance of power', were, like soldiers, a sinister, reactionary, blinkered vested interest. Their role seemed to be merely to help prop up despotic continental regimes, and to stimulate artificial international rivalry, even war. The most famous radical jibe about the 'balance of power' policy was Bright's of 1858, that it was 'neither more nor less than a gigantic system of outdoor relief for the aristocracy of Great Britain'.[54]

These notions, in stronger or milder form, were popular among the Liberal and radical MPs on whom Palmerston depended for his majority. Only a minority, inspired by Cobden, carried their principles so far as to advocate non-intervention abroad on a general basis, but the infectious optimism unleashed by 1846 created a general predisposition to trust to the spread of free trade and constitutional principles rather than to cliquish diplomacy. Palmerston had to tap such sentiments in order both to legitimise his own standing as a Liberal leader, and to prevent the reassertion of *domestic* constitutional radicalism in the Commons. He was aware of the importance of rallying popular opinion behind authority in a liberal state, especially after the 1848 revolutions. Like his mentor Canning before him, he saw manipulation of foreign issues as of benefit not only to his own career but also to the preservation of political stability. Moreover, again like Canning, he believed that British policy could best be promoted among the hostile courts of Europe by showing them that it rested squarely on popular approval, and so must be treated with more respect than a purely diplomatic manoeuvre.[55] And he had one further aim: to convince hard-headed businessmen of his anxiety to promote their interests. As noted above, he was determined to increase spending. Yet he could do so only by selling his policy to the Commons and commerce, by convincing penny-pinchers in and outside parliament that Britain's dominance of world trade, and her power to negotiate tariff reductions (such as with France in 1860), depended on a strong navy.[56]

So Palmerston had to play to the public gallery. But, as his anxiety over defence suggests, he also knew that radical principles could never be the basis of an effective foreign policy. Britain's self-interest required a traditional, compromising, balance-of-power stance. Lacking a large standing army, she was incapable of asserting her position in Europe except in concert with other powers. The greatest threats to her came from her traditional rival, France, and from Russia's ambitions to expand southward into the Mediterranean and Ottoman Empire (disrupting Britain's sizeable market there) and towards India. So Britain had a vested interest in propping up not only Turkey but also the Austrian Empire as a counterbalance to her two rivals. Yet Austria's was not a constitutional regime, and was suppressing the aspirations for self-government of the Italians and Hungarians, two of the nationalities most earnestly defended by radicals. Only Russia was more unpopular with radicals than Austria, largely because of her oppression of the Poles, yet Britain had no power to help the latter, and indeed was willing to tolerate Russian ambitions there in order to divert her from her southward aspirations. Moreover, Palmerston believed that peace, currency stability and an open road for the merchant, Britain's basic needs in Europe, were best promoted by a general policy of maintaining the constitutional status quo. In particular, doubtful about Britain's ability to resist attack from France, Palmerston was consistently keen to pacify her, though this frequently offended Liberal opinion.

Palmerston's goal, then, had to be to reconcile the radical and pragmatic foreign policy traditions. He could do so only by bluster. He repeatedly expressed Britain's determination to promote constitutional, commercial and anti-clerical values as an antidote to despotism and reaction all over the world, even though his actual policy was much less wholehearted. Palmerston revived all Canning's tricks. He persuaded the Commons of his liberality by holding frequent foreign policy debates in which he not only made all the right noises but also published an unprecedented number of diplomatic despatches, so as to contrast his openness with the behaviour of the continental powers.[57] Clearness and determination of aim made him widely fêted as 'masculine', '*English* to the backbone', the 'true English mastiff'.[58] Cobden sneeringly called Palmerston's performance as 'vigilant guardian of the national safety' a 'fantasy'.[59] But it had a striking effect. To Cobden's intense annoyance, total government spending increased from £54 million to £67.1 million between 1852 and 1865, and radical critics were powerless to stop it. Palmerston marginalised them by appropriating the old radical language of patriotism. Popular radicalism had once articulated a powerful critique of both British and foreign governments for using taxes and repressive legislation to undermine freedom. Now Palmerston hijacked that critique, asserting that the British people and the liberal British state were united in a determination to free foreigners from despotism, but that to be taken seriously abroad, Britain required a large naval force.[60]

Palmerston's achievement in winning higher defence expenditure was generally applauded by the governing classes. But this did not mean that they all approved of his tactics for getting it, or of his general policy. Many of them considered him dangerously populist. The political divide on foreign policy in the 1850s was the same as on domestic policy in the 1830s and 1840s. On the one hand, there were the men of the Reform Act, those confident with 'public opinion', and, on the other, the Peelites and tories, who believed that foreign policy was a technical business best left to knots of expert diplomats. The tradition of Castlereagh and Aberdeen was one of patient, pragmatic negotiation with other powers in order to maintain good relations in a flawed world. The main obstacle to peace with the autocratic continental regimes, they maintained, was inconstant but turbulent public pressure at home, now hot against 'tyrants', now unreasonably economical about defence. These views, and consequent distrust of Palmerston, were also vocally expressed by the court.

So all the major rows about Palmerston's foreign policy concerned his blustering, undiplomatic, meddling manner, which appeared to place a higher value on courting British popular liberal opinion than on smoothing international relations. One source of tension was his reaction to the European revolutions of 1848. The queen and the tory-Peelite lobby were stalwart defenders of continued Austrian control in Italy and Hungary. Palmerston did not want to destabilise Austria (though he wanted political reform in the Austrian territories in Italy), and gave no significant practical support to the revolutionaries. But this did not mollify his critics. They alleged that his speeches to the radical gallery fomented uprisings all over Europe, alienated foreign courts from Britain and weakened her long-term influence abroad. After 1859, the impetuosity of British policy seemed to double, because Russell had to be found major office and Palmerston was determined that he must not lead the Commons. So Russell became Foreign Secretary, interpreting his role as the promotion of national independence against the 'foreign yoke'.[61] The 'two dreadful old men', as the queen called them, needed firm reining in: first on the Italian question, where their unwillingness to prevent Napoleon from intervening alarmed the queen and many cabinet colleagues, worried that it might lead to a French attack on the Rhine frontier; and then in 1864, because Palmerston had threatened to assist Denmark against Prussian aggression on the Schleswig-Holstein affair, a bluff which Bismarck then called.[62] On both occasions, the cabinet managed to moderate their zeal.

Palmerston's words, not his actions, were usually the problem. It is striking that on the two occasions when government *action* was most controversial, it was naval action, aimed at soft targets, Greece and China, which could not effectively retaliate against British power. These were the Don Pacifico furore of 1850 and the bombardment of Canton in 1856 (the latter ordered, without the premier's knowledge, by a Palmerstonian governor of Hong Kong, in response to Chinese interference with British traders; Palmerston had no choice but to defend it). In both cases, Palmerston had to counter charges in parliament that British 'swagger' had lacked all proportion and had degenerated into bullying insensitivity. He did so by asserting the superiority of British law over that operating in corrupt countries such as Greece. Where law lacked character, Britain must reserve the right to interpose her own higher standards in order to protect her citizens. This, he argued, was a continuation of his 'policy of improvement and of peace' during the 1848 revolutions. Those who voted against him would be damaging Britain's ability to uphold those principles, and indicating an indifference to the claims of constitutionalism.[63] In 1850 he convinced the Commons; in 1857 he failed, but the result was a general election which he won convincingly. The 'peace party' was vanquished: Cobden, Bright, Miall and Milner Gibson all lost their seats.

Palmerston's success in cultivating an image as a defender of British interests, liberal values and restrained economy would not have been possible without luck: the conjunction of prosperity (apparently caused by free trade), of British naval and trading dominance, and of the *independent* success of 'liberal' movements on the continent. In particular, the process of Italian unification lifted Liberal hearts and was much exploited by government, though it occurred with the minimum of expensive and diplomatically-controversial British intervention – except, of course, at the verbal level. Britain's identification with it reached its zenith with Russell's famous despatch of October 1860 to the British minister in Turin, in response to the continental powers' censure of Garibaldi's invasion of southern Italy. Russell's declaration of support for 'a people building up the edifice of their liberties', and his equation of the rising against the Bourbons with the whigs' 1688 revolution in England, were published (as Russell surely intended) in every major newspaper in Italy and indeed Europe. Italians were reported to be 'weep[ing] over it for joy and gratitude in the bosom of their families, away from brutal mercenaries and greasy priests'.[64] Similarly, Palmerston's great parliamentary speech on the Polish crisis of 1863 ('almost worthy of Tacitus or Livy. It . . . must raise the House of Commons in the estimation of the world') condemned the 'barbarous' behaviour of Russia, the great radical bogy, yet reassured MPs scared of intervention that a unanimous expression of condemnation, no more, would be a most constructive proceeding.[65] (Unfortunately, it was not.)

Palmerston's ability to mobilise radical libertarianism, yet maintain a traditional balance-of-power policy, reached its height over the Crimean War of 1854–6, Britain's only European war between 1815 and 1914. The war was the product of escalating tension between Britain and France on the one hand and Russia on the other. Russia occupied the Danubian Principalities in 1853. In considering a response, the Aberdeen coalition split on predictable lines. Aberdeen wished to conciliate Russia by behind-the-scenes diplomacy while Palmerston (and Russell, who was anxious to rally MPs so that they would urge the reversion of the premiership to himself) demanded a popular but risky course of uncompromising resistance to Russian aggression. The result was indecision, and Britain drifted into war. Thereafter, Aberdeen's lack of public relations skill was no match for Palmerston. Once war began, it became in the public mind a libertarian struggle against Russia's 'vast military empire' and ecclesiastical despotism.[66] Though Russia quickly withdrew from the Principalities, public opinion in Britain and France would not consider a negotiated settlement. But only this would end the war. Eventually, in 1856, diplomacy secured peace, hardly punishing Russia except by the (unsustainable) neutralisation of the Black Sea. Her despotism was scarcely winged. As Aberdeen had foreseen in 1855, the people would accept from Palmerston terms which, had he proposed them, would have brought talk of 'cutting my head off'.[67] Having taken his opportunity in 1855, Palmerston remained premier and master of the situation until his death – except briefly in 1858–9.

The occasion of his overthrow in 1858 is instructive. His anxiety to pacify France had led to controversy before (after Napoleon's coup in 1851 and after the Vienna talks of 1855). Now a bomb made in England by an Italian nationalist nearly assassinated Napoleon; he demanded British action to prevent a similar occurrence. The result was a government attempt to strengthen the law against conpiracy to murder. This gave Russell, Bright and other critics of Palmerston the perfect opportunity to defeat him; he seemed to be sacrificing British civil liberties in order to bow the knee to continental dictatorship. Palmerstonian rhetoric, then, had become a stronger political force even than Palmerston.

So Palmerstonianism was an extremely powerful element in British politics. Palmerston's embarrassment in the Danish crisis of 1864 is frequently misunderstood as a turning-point in Liberal attitudes to foreign policy, towards non-interventionism in Europe.[68] This is not true. Britain's position remained the hard-headed one that intervention was impossible without partners. What had collapsed was the old balance-of-power system, as a result of the Crimean War. Defeated Russia was unable to restrain the dramatic rise of Prussia between 1864 and 1870, and Austria and France were incapable of cooperating effectively against it. The major difference between Palmerston's foreign policy and Gladstone's in office after 1868 was one of presentation. Gladstone urged his party to support limited international intervention in European disputes, using different rhetoric and with a greater emphasis on economy. But his policy was less successful; it appealed to fewer aspects of the multi-faceted, not to say contradictory, Liberal outlook on Europe. Palmerston managed to convince Liberals that he was promoting economy and morality but that at the same time he was strengthening real British interests and British pride, while his firmer grasp of *realpolitik* made him more acceptable to diplomats. Palmerston understood that even most radical MPs, though they talked of peace and low taxes, were anxious for Britain and her interests to be well to the fore internationally. Roebuck, Osborne and De Lacy Evans were among those who succumbed most publicly to the charms of Palmerstonian policy. Most MPs were happy to sanction Palmerston's demands on the taxpayer. The real loser in the 1860s was not 'interventionism' but Cobdenism. Palmerston gave promising provincial radicals like Forster and Stansfeld junior office in the 1860s in the knowledge that they regarded it as dead: 'impractical and un-English'.[69] Forster represented that increasingly important strain in northern commercial opinion which hoped that the Foreign Office and Board of Trade would actively promote commerce, rather than relying on 'natural' forces.[70] Unlike Cobden's internationalism, Palmerston's did not appear to endanger 'national' ends; he rallied men of all classes behind him by suggesting that there was no difference between British interests and moral principles. By promoting them, the country could feel not only virtuous, and united, but also superior to other nations. To his great benefit, Palmerston appeared cosmopolitan and chauvinist at the same time. He set out an uplifting vision of national identity and purpose.

So, in administrative, financial and foreign policy, Palmerston squared the circle. He presided over a far-reaching change in the image of the state. To a much greater extent than before, its ministers seemed disinterested, its taxes justifiable, its fiscal stance neutral as between interests, its success in promoting liberal commercial, constitutional and religious values cheap at the price. The sting was drawn from radicalism; it sought increasingly to participate with dutiful aristocrats in sober administration. Liberalism came to look responsible. Again much more than in the 1830s, the 'permanent interests' of the country could place trust in it. Where national and propertied interests were concerned, Palmerston seemed to have as safe a pair of hands as one could expect in a liberal age. His parliamentary management was the final element in providing that reassurance.

* * *

Palmerston was an insider; he had an unrivalled understanding of the workings of the political system. He was a parliamentarian, not a mob orator. He hardly addressed the public during the Crimean War. When he did speak in the provinces, he dealt in principles and apparent confidences, not in demagoguery. His purpose was to demonstrate popular approval of him and so consolidate respect for him in parliament. He knew that parliament, not the electorate, usually determined his fate. He did not seek to use elections to crush parliamentary opposition. Since local issues dominated elections, spiced by grass-roots radical enthusiasm in some areas, this was wise. The defining fact about Palmerston's rule is that he governed nearly throughout with parliaments elected under, and relatively sympathetic to, previous short-term tory governments (those of 1852 and 1859). He preferred this to seeking a new mandate for Liberalism. When he was forced to call an election in 1857, parliamentary reform and Liberation Society principles were unleashed in too many places for comfort, and MPs in the new parliament proved susceptible to the counter-appeals of Russell and Bright. Palmerston was dethroned within a year and learned his lesson on returning to power in 1859.[71]

Thus, Palmerston's tenure of power depended on his management of parliament. He was Liberal enough for most Liberals but also offered Conservatives stronger and less destabilising government than could their own leaders. Palmerston came closer than anyone to realising the principles of parliamentary government implicit in the 1832 Act. He steered the ship of state by gently drifting in the water yet keeping a deceptively firm grip on the tiller and a canny sense of prevailing winds. His greatest asset was lack of vanity. Sooner or later, other political leaders would over-reach themselves, making an impetuous but miscalculated grand gesture in pursuit of immortal fame or at least the flattery of the highbrow periodicals. Palmerston was all but immune from this; he kept power not least by laughing at himself. He bowed willingly to inevitable Commons reverses and humiliations: between 1855 and 1865 government was defeated 112 times.[72] But he laughed also at the public and parliament; 'he took them all in as regularly as the newspapers'.[73] Looking in later years 'like a retired old *croupier* from Baden', he disguised reversals of position, ignorance of detail and occasional outright lies by his 'racy, buoyant & facetious' manner, 'scoffing, gay and airy'.[74] With self-confidence, good humour and bluster – but also intellectual force – he manipulated the foibles of all classes.

Palmerston succeeded in this because he was an administrator, not a legislator. He disliked radical change and believed it unpopular, but also knew that if the parliamentary climate were to change to favour it, Liberal MPs would prefer Russell over him as his executor. So his doctrine was that parliament's function was, by debate, to reconcile interests, persuading doubters about the utility of any proposed change, until some degree of consensus was reached: 'improvements must be the result of a general concurrence . . . all counter opinions must be reconciled'. By this means, legislation only emerged slowly, but it was accepted as permanent, the national will.[75] In 1861, he rejected a select committee recommendation to curtail private members' rights to obstruct progress by moving amendments on going into supply, arguing that legislation was not the only duty of the Commons, which was 'the mouthpiece of the nation; the organ by which . . . all complaints . . . which may arise among the people at large, may be brought to an expression'.[76] Maintaining that party in the old sense of 'slavish' and 'jobbing' partisanship was dead, he was adept at adapting his policy to fluctuating parliamentary opinion.[77] The most striking sign of this was his government's concession to Conservative and evangelical Liberal sentiment on questions of order. In 1862, by exploiting alarm at rising rural crime statistics, a Conservative backbencher got a Night Poaching Prevention Bill passed, which gave new powers to policemen to search for poachers. Most Liberals disliked it, seeing it as subsidising a new class of gamekeepers from the rates and giving them legal authority. The government agreed. Similarly, it criticised the 1863 Security from Violence Act which introduced more severe punishments for violent robberies (a panic response to a well-publicised sequence of them). Nor was it keen on the 1865 Prison Act, prompted by a harsh Lords' select committee report of 1864. The act listed over a hundred regulations for local prisons to follow, including the provision of separate cells and particular rules for the discipline and treatment of prisoners. If prisons failed to comply, they could be closed. But, despite government coolness, all these measures passed.

Palmerston's easy-going style of government did not please everyone; the lack of big bills was one cause of subsequent interest in parliamentary reform (chapter 9). Nonetheless, his dominance was overpowering. Younger radicals could not effectively deny that government was more of a force for good than for evil. When one of them, Stansfeld, accepted office, he declared that refusing to take 'due share in the supreme management of affairs' was no longer a symbol of 'independence' but of 'moral cowardice'.[78] His was a new, constructive, public-spirited Liberalism. Most northern 'radical' MPs were men of great moderation, philanthropy and respectability: Thomas Bazley of Manchester, William Brown (of Brown, Shipley and Co.) of South Lancashire, J.C. Ewart of Liverpool, Grenfell of Preston. The 1859 Liberal cabinet was the strongest to face the Commons in many decades. Palmerston, Russell, Gladstone, Grey, Wood and Lewis were joined by Milner Gibson and Villiers as radicals and the most efficient Peelites, Herbert and Cardwell. Palmerston's price for securing this was low: a commitment to Russell to bring in a minor Reform Bill, which he could rely on parliament not to want, and permission to Gladstone to repeal the paper duties.

Yet the prize was great. For the next thirty years, heirs to great whig estates, intelligent gentlemen, public school City men, lawyers and upwardly mobile northern and Welsh employers were to rub shoulders in Liberal cabinets without embarrassment or condescension. The Liberals seemed to be both the national and the popular party. In each of the three elections of 1857, 1859 and 1865, Liberals gained solid majorities of between 60 and

100. Moreover, this majority acquired a permanent air, since the number of election contests fell to very low levels: 383 United Kingdom MPs were returned unopposed at the 1859 election. Split voting in such contests as did occur also fell, with one estimate indicating a decline from 19 per cent to 8.5 per cent between 1857 and 1865.[79] The Liberals' electoral base seemed unshakeable. The main reason for this firming of support seems to have been urbanisation. As growing towns overspilled the old borough boundaries, the number of artisans and shopkeepers with a vote for the county increased, while local Liberal organisations began to pay more attention to harnessing the urban vote in counties.[80] By the 1860s, Liberal support in English county seats had stabilised at about the 1837 level again, giving the tories only a 45–50 seat lead there as opposed to the 87-seat average lead of 1841–52. More Liberal county victories benefited landed influence in the party, while, in the wake of returning agricultural prosperity, progressive landlords' self-confidence was manifest in capital investment, better estate management and more effective use of advanced techniques. Landowners like Ramsden, Morpeth, Goderich, Milton and Lord Frederick Cavendish were returned for the prestigious industrial West Riding seat. The party's profile did not become appreciably less landed, just more diversified as men of property gained wider experience of commerce, industry and professional life. In 1865 there were 31 more Liberal MPs than in 1847 (360 as against 329). By one estimate, the number among them who owned land was 207 (against 195), while the number with financial interests was 123, the number with manufacturing interests of various sorts 116, the number with interests in railways, shipping and transport 108, and the number of lawyers 61 (against 44, 74, 69 and 45 respectively).[81]

The constitutional writers of the early 1860s were convinced that Britain had attained an enviable degree of political stability.[82] Liberal dominance reflected that. Liberals succeeded in the trick of reflecting the diversity and maturity of mid-Victorian society. They were the party of aristocratic leadership, business sense, moral integrity and administrative efficiency. Herbert said in 1859: 'society is strong and dominates the government set over it'.[83] As long as this was generally believed, Liberals were set fair to be the natural ruling party. Liberal leaders brilliantly encapsulated the ambiguities within their creed between order and liberty, state activity and individual responsibility, establishment and free-thought, vigorous national defence and unsparing economy, and, above all, between aristocracy, efficiency and popularity. Disaster would have ensued had anyone tried to resolve those tensions. As it was, most of the political classes became convinced that good work was being done and that Liberalism was the creed of all good men. Palmerston was the defining political personality of his age. Raw power exuded from his every letter. On his demise in 1865, well might Gladstone write: 'Death has indeed laid low the most towering antlers in all the forest'.[84] Palmerston bound together the 'great bundle of sticks' that comprised the Liberal party and made it the supreme political force of the nineteenth century.[85]

CHAPTER 9

Liberalism and the people, 1846–67

IN THE 1850s and 1860s, Liberalism did not just mean efficient administration and a strong foreign and financial policy. It also seemed to offer the best route to the moral improvement of the people. Liberals claimed to be advancing the integration of sects and classes under the firm rule of law, and to be allowing men more scope to develop talents in line with scientific progress. This was also compatible with a gradual, regulated extension of popular political involvement. For their part, most provincial Liberals appeared to accept the good intentions of the leadership. Liberal leaders were able to secure high-minded government in several policy spheres, without surrendering power to mass working-class opinion. This balancing act in Irish, religious and local government policy is the subject of this chapter. While Palmerston was most involved in the matters discussed in chapter 8, the most active and influential Liberal in these fields was Russell. Russell also committed the party to further, carefully limited, parliamentary reform, which was designed to demonstrate politicians' faith in popular respectability, and goad parliament to better work, while maintaining elite political dominance. Neither in this area, nor in local government, did democracy feature on the agenda. Nonetheless, Liberal commitment to parliamentary reform was to have unforeseen democratising consequences. This also requires explanation.

Ireland

One good quarter in which to observe Liberal ideas about social development is Ireland, about which they knew little in the way of inconvenient fact to disturb their planning. This period saw the most unqualified application of British definitions of liberal progress to Irish society.

Like O'Connell, Russell assumed that tory rule after 1841, almost by definition, eroded popular confidence in the law. In 1844 he declared that Ireland was 'occupied, and not governed', ruled by force, not affection.[1] In government from 1846, Russell prepared two strategies to encourage Irish assimilation. One was the involvement of the Catholic Church in the political order by a series of readjustments of church-state relationships, in particular the payment of Catholic priests by the state, which might dissuade them from fomenting the repeal movement, and might improve their moral influence over the young. The other was the active encouragement of economic modernisation, in particular the capitalisation of estates to eliminate the gross inefficiency in agricultural organisation which left the country so pauperised, vulnerable to famine, and discontented. If landlords resided, bore the full cost of poor relief during natural disasters, or sold out to those who would do both, they would have an incentive to sink their capital in agriculture and manufacturing, and so relieve unemployment, diversify Ireland's economic base and expand the professional and retailing middle class.[2] The problem was that to move on the religious front would be very unpopular with English public opinion, while the attempt to evolve a more 'natural' state of society in Ireland, based on the principles of individual responsibility and of local landed leadership, would require a revolution in Irish social structure, and expose ministers to charges of gross inhumanity to the peasantry.

Theoretically, the terrible famine of 1845–7 allowed the government the clean slate that it needed for this plan. In practice, though, strict application of the principles of political economy was politically impossible. The reality of mass starvation forced ministers to intervene, if only, as Russell said, to stop the Irish people becoming 'the prey of cut-throats and incendiaries'.[3] In August 1847, three million Irishmen were being fed at the public expense. Some continuation of Treasury aid to Irish landlords to help them bear the brunt of famine relief was politically inevitable, despite criticism of 'communism' from English opinion and a pervasive belief that irresponsible and selfish landlords were milking the situation for their own benefit. In 1847, the Irish Poor Law was amended, extending the principle of outrelief to the able-bodied, against opposition in both Houses of Parliament. Severe financial constraints in Britain in 1847–8 were mainly to blame for the lack of more aid: the Commons was mutinous about granting necessary expenditure even on the mainland.

The return of Irish political agitation in late 1847 was another blow, with the number of committals at Irish courts rising by 227 per cent between 1846 and 1849.[4] In 1846, Russell had appointed Bessborough, a resident Irish landlord and a friend of O'Connell, as Lord Lieutenant, but on his death in 1847 he replaced him with Clarendon, who lacked sympathy with an activist reform policy. He took to wearing dark glasses and demanding coercive measures. The cabinet, lacking knowledge and anxious to avoid 'tory' repression, were very reluctant to agree. But the emergence of a fully-fledged repeal campaign in the spring of 1848, culminating in Smith O'Brien's rising in July, forced it to agree to suspend Habeas Corpus. The unrest, and the abrogation of civil liberties, had the predictable consequence of encouraging Russell to urge a programme of remedial measures to win the affection of the people. He placed before the cabinet a package of proposals, including the payment of Catholic priests from the proceeds of a land tax. But the bishops' hostility prevented any progress with it, to the relief of other ministers who knew that, after the Maynooth crisis, the Commons would not accept it. Many of Russell's other plans were also blocked by lack of interest in cabinet or party. One had been to grant long-serving tenants retrospective compensation upon eviction, designed to regulate land clearances and to encourage investment; another was a large-scale scheme of assisted emigration. The goal of regeneration by legislation had receded.

Nonetheless, Russell was still responsible for three major pieces of Irish legislation in 1849–50. One, the 1850 Irish Franchise Act, reformed political relationships. It increased the Irish electorate, notoriously corrupt and in any case reduced by the famine and emigration. Registration had been a farce, and the application to Ireland in 1832 of a leasehold county franchise had in practice given power to landlords to determine the nature of the register by their selection of tenants. The 1850 Act was significant because registration was now to be conducted officially, while a new *occupation* franchise was introduced based on Poor Law valuation (£12 in counties, £8 in boroughs). The electorate rose from 45,000 to 163,000. It gave tenant farmers as a body a powerful electoral voice for the first time.

The government also passed two acts aimed at developing Liberal economic and intellectual principles and 'middle-class' values in Ireland. In 1850 the three undenominational colleges established in 1845 were incorporated into a new Queen's University with degree-giving powers. This promised to make them more attractive to the Catholic middle classes, and so give influence over higher education to minds more rational and less bigoted than those of the priesthood. In 1849 the Encumbered Estates Act facilitated the sale of bankrupt estates to new owners (many, it was hoped, English[5]) who might invest capital in much-needed improvements and consolidate tenancies into more efficient units.

These two acts were the cornerstone of Liberal policy in Ireland – such as it was – between Russell's fall in 1852 and his return as Prime Minister in 1865. They indicated the power of two great Liberal myths. One was that the education of Protestants and Catholics in the same institutions – the national system at elementary level, and the Queen's University – would diminish sectional bitterness and spread morality and respect for the Union. The national schools, Lord Lieutenant Carlisle believed, approximated to 'the fulfilment of that great Christian commandment of loving one another'. By establishing 'a serene temple of knowledge' barred to the 'rivalries of creeds and parties', they seemed to be advancing an undoctrinaire under-standing of science, the motor by which Irish society would naturally improve.[6] The second belief was that the application of investment and agricultural science to Irish land was the key to greater prosperity, and that the two preconditions for this were for government to supply property with security and peace and for landlords to reside on their estates. Palmerston (an improving and respected Irish landlord) insisted that landlord and tenant must be left free to draw their own contracts, including any local customs which they wished to recognise. For the state to concede to tenants' demands for fixity of tenure was 'communistic'. An Irish Land Act of 1860 wrote freedom of contract into the statute books; another, in the same year, encouraged tenants to raise capital for improvements and confirmed their right to compensation for them – if the landlord consented.[7] Palmerston approved of emigration (1.5 million people left Ireland between 1849 and 1860) and the trend towards bigger estates.

These natural law assumptions found their perfect advocate in Carlisle, Palmerston's Lord Lieutenant between 1855 and 1864. He presided at meetings of agricultural societies and the Social Science Association, and urged an increase in pasturage, reliance on drainage and the building of railways so as to benefit commerce ('What the Piraeus of old was to Athens . . . Queenstown is, and will be, to Cork').[8] Moreover, reliance on Providence seemed to work. Irish shipping tonnage more than doubled in the ten years after 1853, while pauperism and crime were severely checked. Carlisle encouraged the importation of another English habit, cricket. He loved to score at matches, had a cricket ground built at the Viceregal Lodge, and under his impetus clubs sprang up in many parts. Unfortunately they did not quite have the Anglicising effects that he doubtless intended. He would have been distraught at the later career of one of County Wicklow's finest cricketers of the late 1860s, Charles Stewart Parnell.

Despite his reputation for insipid benevolence, Carlisle had no difficulty justifying the firm rule of law in Ireland. For him, as for Palmerston, a professional police, the strict application of the Poor Law, and the encouragement of rational punishment reform were all English importations essential to the regulated modernisation of Irish society. (The income tax was extended to Ireland in 1853.) Even the Protestant established church in Ireland, though much less defensible, was a symbol with which Palmerston would not tamper. According to Gladstone, many years later, he attempted to prop it up in 1864 by a legal move which Gladstone and Russell resisted.[9] British ministers avoided conciliating Irish Catholics by legislative initiative. There was no need: after O'Connell's death in 1847, Irish MPs were essentially divided and leaderless. A tenant-right party emerged in 1852, but it soon foundered on disputes, office-hunger and the apathy which accompanied the growth of prosperity. To English opinion, Palmerston seemed to have solved the Irish question, not by concessions to Catholics but by applying common-sense economic and moral principles. This belief powerfully shaped British attitudes to Ireland for a generation. When the more activist Russell returned to the premiership in 1865, he toyed with land and university reform. But he was obstructed by the lack of guidelines as to what new departures English, Scottish or Irish opinion would accept.[10] He was not prepared to break decisively with Palmerston's 'progressive' consensus. Gladstone was to be bolder – though not necessarily politically wiser.

Religious policy

Notions of integration and undenominationalism had an equally powerful effect on religious policy in England. Most Liberals – especially Russell – disliked the polarisation which resulted from the tensions of the 1840s: the rise of dogmatic high church Tractarians on the one hand and of extreme radicalism in Dissent (Miall and the Anti-State-Church-Association), allied with old London-based radicals hostile to state corruption, on the other. Such developments threatened the standing of the English church establishment as a nationally-accepted, doctrinally broad force for moral and social discipline. The 1851 census revealed the extent of the church's loss of authority. It showed that 40 per cent of churchgoers in England and a majority elsewhere attended non-Anglican churches, while in the great cities fewer than 10 per cent of the population seemed to be going to church at all. Russell's planned response was to use ecclesiastical and educational policy to rally a coalition of broad and low church Anglicans, Protestant Dissenters and free-thinkers against the exclusiveness and apathy of Anglican institutions. Reform of the Church of England would make it more open, more tolerant, more responsive to modern needs, yet still an entrenched force in each parish. The result would be a more spiritual, less intellectually meretricious religion and a more harmonious and elevated national mood. Better educational provision would also promote morality and integration, the more so if it was unsectarian.

Liberal reform of religious institutions was designed to improve their effectiveness. Anxiety to develop Anglicanism's ability to combat infidelity led government to establish the new see of Manchester in 1847. In 1850, aided by pressure from anti-clerical backbenchers, Russell, with George Grey, reformed the structure of the amateurish and unwieldy Ecclesiastical Commission, giving most of its powers to a small full-time professional sub-committee, in the hope that this would make church management more efficient.[11] In the same year, he launched a crusade to modernise Oxford and Cambridge. Advances in biblical and archaeological studies increased his anxiety to see the universities discussing the truth of all received dogmas in the light of modern critical and scientific discoveries. Instead, they seemed hidebound, lifeless bastions checking the development of a more spiritual and relevant religion. He believed that the fault lay in the stranglehold exercised by the petty-minded colleges over university teaching. So he set up Royal Commissions dominated by liberal-minded clerics and Fellows. Their reports duly urged structural reform to increase the power of professors and open up college Fellowships to nationwide competition, though conservatives drew much of the sting from the plans before the legislation reached the statute books in 1854 and 1856.

The enemy for Liberals was high church exclusiveness and intolerance. A major battle for control of the church erupted in 1850 when the lay-dominated Judicial Committee of the Privy Council overruled a bishop who had refused to institute an unorthodox evangelical to a Devonshire living (the 'Gorham judgment'). This was a blow struck by state edict for a more tolerant broad church, a basic principle of whiggery. Russell had already deliberately infuriated high churchmen by his appointment of R.D. Hampden, celebrated for his critique of orthodox dogmas, to be bishop of Hereford in 1847. He supported Hampden as an 'active' upholder of 'Protestant doctrines' against the errors of the Oxford movement.[12] High churchmen now demanded that bishops, not a lay-dominated committee, should pronounce on doctrinal matters. They called also for the revival of church self-government (in the shape of Convocation, the synodical assemblies suspended by crown fiat since 1717). Russell refused. It was this high church agitation, in turn, which drove him to the Durham letter of late 1850, which stigmatised Tractarians as proto-Roman Catholics attempting to undermine the church's title to nationality (see page 174). In 1857, Palmerston removed church control over divorce and subverted the theological principle of the indissolubility of marriage, against the opposition of high churchmen such as Gladstone. Full divorce had only been possible before by the very costly process of private bill legislation. Ecclesiastical courts had been able to grant judicial separations, but these did not permit remarriage during the spouse's lifetime. Now both jurisdictions were swept away and a secular Court of Divorce was established in London, which could grant full divorce and permission to remarry.

These attacks on high church obscurantism were designed, among other things, to reassure Dissenters about the church's Protestantism and so to increase their regard for it. In Liberal eyes, both Anglicans and Dissenters shared an 'ardent spirit of attachment to the Protestant faith', and reconciliation on this basis should be encouraged.[13] Liberal policy encouraged Anglican-Dissenting accommodation. An act of 1860 required trustees of (Anglican) middle-class schools to admit, but not to indoctrinate, children of adherents of other denominations. This anti-clerical policy was the fruit of Liberal backbench pressure. So were the amendments to the university legislation of 1854 and 1856 which removed the requirement that candidates for first degrees at Oxford and Cambridge should subscribe to the Thirty-nine Articles.* In 1862 and 1864, Liberal backbenchers introduced bills to abolish oaths for higher degrees and fellowships at the two universities; similar bills gained a second reading in 1865 and 1866 (but failed). Similarly, Palmerston's church appointments policy aimed to improve nonconformist trust in the Church of England. He promoted a string of liberal evangelical bishops – such as Tait, Bickersteth and Baring – who were keen to cooperate with Dissent and were anxious to remove any hint of exclusiveness in politics or dogma. The appointments were suggested by his wife's son-in-law, the philanthropic evangelical earl of Shaftesbury, who boasted that they would bring many Dissenters into the church.[14]

Accommodation with Dissent was assisted by developments in Liberal

---

* Candidates for higher degrees at Cambridge were similarly exempted. In neither university were theology degrees opened to non-subscribers.

attitudes to church rates. A court judgment of 1853 opened the way to a successful countrywide agitation by nonconformists against the principle of the rate. Parishes were increasingly reluctant to court trouble by attempting to levy it, while the growth of private philanthropy made it less important. The struggle against the compulsory rate turned the Anti-State-Church Association (renamed the Liberation Society in 1853) into a major national force. Anglican Liberals already worried by the 1851 census came to accept that to uphold the principle of compulsory rate liability would damage the church establishment. For all these reasons, from 1855, the Church Rate Abolition Bill proposed each year by a Liberal backbencher regularly secured a second reading. Palmerston and Russell moved to support it. And from 1859, abolition became a standard rallying-cry for Liberals, while Conservatives opposed it fiercely in an attempt to mobilise sentiment fearful for the church establishment itself. Palmerston used the issue to keep Liberal spirits up, and a necessary degree of two-party antagonism alive, while the strength of tory opposition prevented it from actually passing. The compulsory rate was finally abolished on Gladstone's initiative in 1868. But the whig principle of a national church open to all survived abolition, because whig and tory peers amended the bill so as to stop what they saw as a high church plot to prevent non-ratepayers from interfering in church affairs in future. Wood argued that the sons of leading Dissenters who involved themselves in parochial government frequently joined the church.[15]

In order to please provincial Liberal opinion, Palmerston also had to nod to evangelical-Dissenting desires on thorny matters like the 'Sunday problem'. In 1855 the aristocratic evangelical Liberals Lord Robert Grosvenor and Viscount Ebrington introduced a bill which forbade almost all Sunday trading. The government, aware of Dissenting pressure on MPs, thought it prudent to support it. But it proved unpopular among the working classes, for whom it seemed to threaten access to fresh food and drink. The result was mass meetings in Hyde Park, symbolically aimed at preventing gentle-folk driving their carriages there on a Sunday. Seventy-two people were arrested; a policeman attempting to clear a path was hit by a large eel from the Serpentine. The bill had to be withdrawn. Nonetheless, in 1856 similar considerations forced Palmerston to oppose a motion to open the National Gallery and British Museum on Sundays.[16]*

The principal obstacle to Liberal-Dissenting cooperation was the attachment of some Dissenters to the voluntary movement which rejected all state grants for education. This became a serious political problem at the 1847 election, mainly in reaction to the consolidation of the Maynooth grant in 1845. The voluntary temper threatened the success of the extension of state aid for religious education, about which Russell cared very much. He believed that educational deficiency led directly to vice, crime and economic

---

* However, the right to hold public meetings in the Park, previously questioned, was henceforth practically established.

and social discord.[17] One of the first acts of his 1846 government was to introduce Education Minutes which transformed the basis of the state grant. Previously grants had gone only to subsidise new buildings, where local demand was already evident. This limited the amount disbursed and did little to improve the content of education in the schools. Now, the training of selected pupil-teachers in normal schools was to be subsidised, facilities for training were to be offered to teachers already *in situ*, and higher salaries were to be given to teachers judged to be qualified. This, Russell believed, would attract more intelligent teachers and stimulate the imaginative inculcation of moral feeling.[18] It gave inspectors extra power over both teachers and apprentices, while teachers were to act 'as a guide and example in the formation of the character of the apprentice'.[19] Schools were also given grants for the purchase of books and educational apparatus. In 1847, both Wesleyan and Roman Catholic schools became eligible for grants. But, at the 1847 election, several Liberals who had voted for the education grant were defeated by Dissenting activity, such as Macaulay at Edinburgh, Hawes at Lambeth, and Williams at Coventry. Voluntaries argued that the state aid degraded Christianity into the servant of civil government.*

In fact, though, voluntaryism as such soon ceased to be a major problem. Dissenters were divided. Though many evangelical congregationalists and baptists adopted the voluntary cause, others, especially the unitarians, wanted more state intervention. Manchester unitarians were prominent in the Lancashire (later National) Public Schools Association, which introduced a bill to establish a network of schools funded by a local rate. However, this solution was politically impracticable because it gave insufficient security for religious education (its parliamentary sponsor, W.J. Fox, was prepared to see purely secular teaching, with denominations coming to school at fixed times to teach their own creeds). Many progressive propertied Liberals feared that if penny-pinching or irreligious ratepayers were given power to determine the extent of religious teaching, securities for effective moral education would end.[20] The obstacles to a more systematic state educational policy were many: almost all religious sects were suspicious of extended central or local government power, while public opinion right across the political spectrum was disquieted by the ballooning educational grant. As a result of the reforms of 1846–7, and the award of capitation grants to schools from the 1850s, it grew from £75,000 in 1845 to £1.3 million in 1862. Between 1839 and 1862, the state spent £3.9 million on salaries; by 1859, 12,600 men and women had been awarded certificates.[21]

Despite these difficulties, most Liberal leaders wished to go further, partly because the system provided a patchy service, especially in poorer areas, and partly because it gave too much unregulated power to the National Society. Russell, in particular, wanted to allow boroughs to levy

* The extension of the grant to Roman Catholics was not announced until after the election.

rates to assist schools or build their own. In 1856, when in opposition, he tried to capitalise on the post-Sebastopol mood of 'national efficiency' to advance this idea, but failed. The government compromised: it established a special Education Department under the aegis of the Privy Council. Then, in 1858, it set up a Royal Commission, the Newcastle Commission, which proposed a national, economical, decentralised education system. It suggested that the state grant might continue on a capitation basis, but that Quarter Sessions in counties, and town councils, should establish lay-dominated boards to levy a rate to fund schools on the basis of pupils' examination performance. However, local rating was unacceptable to many Dissenters (since in rural areas tory churchmen would control the schools) and other ratepayers. In 1862, in the 'Revised Code', Robert Lowe, the education minister, altered the basis of the central government grant, so that it was awarded only to schools with certificated teachers, on the basis of children's examination performance and attendance. This greatly increased the power of inspectors and struck at church schools offering poor secular teaching. So did the department's decision not to give grants to National Society schools in single-school areas which did not excuse Dissenter children from denominational instruction. This forced the schools to limit denominational teaching to fixed points on the timetable. Grant levels fell, yet between 1863 and 1869 a thousand new schools were opened and an extra 300,000 children attended. Though progress was slow, Liberal education policy was corroding Anglican exclusiveness and leading both the sects and public opinion to appreciate the benefits of state aid. This laid important foundations for the future.

Local government

Tension between Liberal leaders' desire for improvement and the resistance of powerful local interests to rate expenditure was particularly marked on educational questions because of the dislike of paying for the propagation of other men's religious opinions. But in fact the problem was more widespread. In all their dealings with local government, Liberals were faced with the need to promote rational progress without trampling on local autonomy – which would raise insuperable political obstacles from Conservative squires, from parliamentary representatives of local vested interests, and from radicals defending ratepayer rights. Yet inaction was impossible because of the emergence of the condition-of-England question. Existing whig interest in it was magnified tenfold by Chartism, by the Royal Commission reports of 1842 and 1845, by Peel's non-interventionism and by the return of cholera in 1848–9. Scientific ignorance about the spread of disease notwithstanding, it was obvious that primitive sewerage, water supply and burial practices, in the midst of massive overcrowding, were largely to blame for the shocking mortality rate in large towns. Russell's government was bound to act after 1846.

The solution adopted was the statutory devolution of powers to elected local authorities. Before 1846, the standard way of promoting sanitary improvements was for individual authorities to prosecute private bills allowing them to levy rates for certain purposes. This was extremely expensive and time-consuming. In 1846, Liverpool was alleged to have spent over £100,000 on this in ten years.[22] Most authorities had neither the money nor the inclination to proceed in this way, and even the better private acts were often badly drafted and limited in scope. Liberals now sought to give life to effective local sanitary authorities with a common and extensive set of powers. This was the purpose of Morpeth's Public Health Act of 1848, the first major piece of compulsory public health legislation.

The act established a structure of elected authorities – local boards of health – to administer all aspects of public health in most urban areas. A General Board, accountable to parliament, was to act as a supervisory body.* This General Board had the power to force localities to form a local board where mortality rates were particularly high, or where one-tenth of ratepayers demanded one (even against the opposition of a local authority). Alternatively (in fact more usually), municipal councils could apply to acquire the extensive powers of a local board, without the need to initiate a private bill. Boards were to enforce the installation of privies in new houses; all houses were to be connected by drain to an appropriate outlet; the building of cellars for accommodation was to be prohibited. Boards were given powers to construct and control sewers, drains and a water supply, to plan and manage highways, to prevent or regulate 'nuisances' (slaughter-houses, cesspools, any insanitary trade), to provide or close burial grounds, to lay out public parks, and to make byelaws. They were also allowed to borrow against the rates for up to thirty years, for purposes of sanitary improvement. The 1848 act marked the key stage in the development of the distrusted municipal corporation into the proud Victorian civic authority. Nearly all Improvement Commissions surrendered their powers to the new elected boards. The act had been adopted in 219 places by 1858. And in that year, with the abolition of the General Board, the procedure for establishing a local board became much easier – no central approval was necessary, and authorities other than town councils might choose to apply – while the range of powers available increased. By 1864, 268 more places had established boards. Borrowing against the rates for local government expenditure rose by 244 per cent between 1848/58 and 1858/71.[23] Boards' powers were soon further extended. The 1866 Sanitary Act, sold to the Commons at a time when the return of cholera created a heightened concern for health, allowed central government to discipline negligent authorities

---

* The creation of the General Board was the least significant of the act's provisions, so its demise in 1858, a victim of anti-centralising tory and radical pressure, did not do much damage. The Benthamite civil servant Edwin Chadwick, incidentally, did not want sanitary powers to be given to local elected boards but to crown-appointed local commissions.

and to enforce minimum sanitary standards, and increased local authority discretion to inspect insanitary dwellings. The central health inspectorate (of professional engineers) established in 1848 continued to supply local authorities with technical assistance and advice, for example in treating sewage. John Simon, the medical officer to the old General Board, was responsible for much of the government advice. An act of 1859 secured his position by placing his medical department under the Privy Council, removing him from periodic scrutiny by a penny-pinching House of Commons, and giving him increased powers of publicity.

Local authorities were stimulated to act in other ways. George Grey's measure of 1846 allowed them to levy a rate to build public baths and washhouses, and Ewart's Acts of 1850 and 1855 permitted them to establish public libraries on the rates. Manchester, the first authority to do so, reported that 138,000 volumes had been issued in 1853 – though the historical work in most demand was not exactly Macaulay, but an anonymous compilation of *Shipwrecks and disasters at sea*.[24] Between 1845 and 1847, eleven 'model' or 'Clauses' Acts greatly facilitated the future passage of private bills and extended their scope by codifying a standard set of regulatory powers to be acquired by authorities which petitioned to adopt the relevant act. They covered such matters as gas and water supply, cemeteries, paving and cleansing, police and land-purchase.

So by the late 1860s, elected authorities in all urban areas of significance were working within sanitary guidelines laid down by expert opinion. The counties followed, more slowly. In 1846 and 1848, boards of guardians had in effect been designated sanitary authorities in areas without boards, by the Nuisances Removal and Diseases Prevention Acts, which empowered them to instruct magistrates summarily to remove the causes of pollution. In 1855, they, like boards of health, were obliged to appoint a sanitary inspector with powers to enter premises. Meanwhile, the Poor Law Board had become more adventurous by the 1860s. It had appointed a central medical officer, and was encouraging guardians to build public hospitals and dispensaries providing outpatient treatment, both of which were to be made available to non-paupers in the belief that this was the best security against a much more numerous decline into pauperism.*

Whether boards of health or boards of guardians, all sanitary authorities outside municipal corporations were elected on a ratepayer and property-

---

* In other respects local county government preserved most of its independence from central government; Quarter Sessions remained the most powerful body. But in 1856 George Grey took advantage of the absence of the army in the Crimea to persuade the Commons to require all counties to establish a police force. These were to be controlled by magistrates but subject to (loose) Home Office inspection in return for a subsidy of one-quarter (later one-half) of the cost (the same applied to borough forces). Highways Acts in 1862 and 1864 empowered Quarter Sessions to combine parishes into highway districts, run by a board comprising resident Justices and elected parish officers.

owner franchise heavily weighted by property value (see page 125).*
This was quite deliberate. The greatest obstacle to sanitary progress was
democracy. The penny-pinching economy movements of small ratepayers,
which emerged in the 1850s in many provincial towns, lowered the social
composition of councils. London MPs, still anxious about state 'tyranny',
managed to exempt London from the 1848 legislation altogether (various
acts of the 1850s tried to make amends). Except in towns where boards
were dominated by knots of sanitary enthusiasts, administrative standards
remained low. By 1864, only 33 boroughs and parishes had adopted the
Baths and Washhouses Act and only 24 the Public Library Acts.[25] Of
the local authorities whose police forces were still adjudged inefficient by
the inspectorate in 1870, nearly all were medium-sized boroughs. The 1866
Sanitary Act allowed government to compel local authorities to enforce
standard byelaws on sanitation in dwelling-houses, but only 7 of 38 London
parishes were doing so in 1876.[26] Such lapses were hardly surprising: when
Leicester town council adopted the Public Health Act in 1848, the borough
rate rose in a year from 9d to 2s 3d.[27]

It would be a fallacy to expect *parliament*, as opposed to government, to
do much against this popular economy movement. Parliament, traditionally
enough, saw its function as being in large part to check centralising
measures. Bright and other radicals conducted a series of skirmishes against
the Highway Bills of the early 1860s, arguing that the proposed new boards
would effectively be controlled by county magistrates appointed by the
crown, and would themselves be liable to jobbery.[28] When parliament did
consent to legislation, it was on a haphazard basis, the consequence of
isolated enthusiasms or panic. Much legislation bore no relation to the
ability of the state to enforce it, or to its zeal in doing so.[29] So it was not
always a happy experiment. (For example – in a different policy field –
medical pressure, supplemented by military zeal for a more professional
bachelor armed force, led to a bold but crude attempt to stem the rapid rise
in sexually-transmitted diseases among soldiers and sailors in 1864: the
Contagious Diseases Act allowed the compulsory examination and if necessary hospitalisation of prostitutes in garrison towns.†)

Popular zeal for economy did not encourage high-minded Liberals to
think well of radicals' constructiveness, any more than did voluntaryism in
religion. This discouraged many Liberal ministers from considering further
parliamentary reform; the conduct of the existing parliament on social and
educational questions seemed sufficiently wretched. In 1857 Lowe dismissed
parliament as venal and superficial and called for an expanded adminis-

* And numbers of municipal corporations did not materially increase: only thirty-
  one towns were incorporated between 1835 and 1865.
† The Social Science Association had been trying to focus public attention on the
  prostitution problem for some years: hence Russell's complaint at the 1858
  conference of the irresponsibility of the *Times* in publishing a letter from 'a
  woman who was leading an abandoned life, who spoke of it in glowing terms': 16
  October 1858, p. 8.

trative elite, 'true votaries' in central regulatory agencies.[30] In 1858 Russell told the Social Science Association to lead an informed agitation for reform on health and prison discipline, since parliament was ignorant.[31] Yet Russell *was* an advocate of further Reform, for it was equally plausible to argue that it would give parliament the familiarity with urban conditions necessary to underpin useful legislation. Parliamentary reform, then, was not a subject on which Liberals were likely to agree.

Parliamentary reform

Liberal interest in parliamentary reform was the main cause of the great change in the franchise effected by the 1867 Reform Act. In seeking to account for this, we need to avoid imprecise romantic explanations, such as that Liberals – especially Gladstone – came to appreciate the good moral sense of respectable artisans, or that there came to be an identity of interest between middle- and working-class Liberalism. There is *some* truth in these arguments, but the 1867 Reform Act was an accident. So, in a sense, was Liberal commitment to any significant measure of parliamentary reform. Liberals remained much more interested in improving the lower classes than in redistributing power in parliament towards popular representatives.

One cause of Liberal interest in Reform was the desire for more improving legislation than Palmerston had provided. His claim to the premiership was his unique ability to dominate a parliament which was too fractured to accept rule from anyone else. So his governments appeared permanently fragile, without direction. The result was an apparent lack of social scientific progress. By 1865, despite expert lobbying and an unprecedented number of Royal Commissions, policy on education, religion, Ireland and land was treading water. Administrative and army reformers had made little headway since the Crimean War crisis. On Palmerston's death, Lowe, a typically 'scientifically-minded' minister, complained that he had 'left his party without tradition, chart or compass, to drift on a stormy sea on which their only landmark was his personal popularity'.[32]

Many young Liberal intellectuals, taking their lead from John Stuart Mill, demanded parliamentary reform in the hope that the presence of a larger electorate would goad the 'rich and powerful' to be more assiduous leaders, demonstrating more 'energy and intellectual eminence'. Such men argued that MPs must strive to teach the poor that they were valued members of the community; this would enlarge the common man's 'sense of vision and . . . sense of responsibility'.[33] MPs' duty was to respond to working-men's genuine grievances conscientiously and scientifically; only Reform would force them to do that. Mill artfully headed off discussion of what these grievances might be by pointing out that, if they were already known, there would be no need for Reform, but he conceded that parliament needed to pay more attention to solving strikes, pauperism, crime and disease.[34] He stressed that God gave men faculties to be cultivated to the utmost, and that man must work towards a community in which everyone both laboured, and developed his character, to the best of his ability.[35] By involving all elements of the nation in its discussions, the state would tap the maximum amount of energy and virtue.*

Under Palmerston, parliament also seemed to have become complacent and susceptible to sectional financial pressures. MPs seemed uninterested in checking spending, and too many had their own costly projects to advocate. In 1863, Trelawny wrote that 'Parliament teems with great contractors' anxious to earn money at the public expense. 'They are little better than politician soldiers and sailors, who almost always support proposals involving more cost. We are governed by cliques. [T]he working classes are not represented . . . except that Government condescends to spend their earnings.'[36] Palmerston could be blamed for bamboozling parliament away from its proper duties, by alternately using his powers of rhetoric and popularity to ride roughshod over its anxieties, and by demeaning and insouciant concessions to its passing whims in order to curry favour.[37] In 1860, the Russellite Liberal MP Bouverie blamed government inertia for 'a factious populace, eluded laws, luxurious nobles'.[38] Cobden charged Palmerston with undermining party enthusiasm, constantly shifting the basis of his parliamentary support so that, instead of standing on principles, he had become a 'despot'.[39] His deliberately cavalier manner, designed to counteract the impression that government might do everything, upset earnest Liberals who believed in guidance of the public mind. 'His fatal fault was in not being able to distinguish between true and false public opinion.'[40] To Bagehot, the ideal Prime Minister should be 'the greatest teacher of all in Parliament . . . the great elevator of the country'. Palmerston, though, had encouraged existing tendencies towards materialism in national life.[41]

However, these arguments alone could not motor a Reform bandwagon. They signified inflated intelligentsia expectations of what could be achieved in politics. Most government activity had traditionally been unsystematic, but this had been disguised by Liberal agreement about defined 'vested interests' within the old state which could be attacked. Unfortunately, in proportion as the state succeeded in appearing to purify itself, so the number of such targets declined. Also, many of those most anxious for scientific legislation were hostile to further, necessarily more democratic, Reform. Commentators like Greg and Fitzjames Stephen wanted more 'permanence' in government, so that it could demonstrate administrative and scientific competence.[42] Greg, in retrospect ambivalent about the effects of the 1832 Act, was willing to consider a further instalment of

---

* Gladstone followed this line of argument, for example when speaking in Flintshire in 1864. He asserted that 'God did not give us any portion of our constitutions for nothing': *Times*, 7 January 1864, p. 7. In 1866, he unfurled a vision of post-Reform politics in which parliament would no longer be dominated by the 'influence of separate classes' and would recognise more 'the public interest properly so called': *Hansard*, CLXXXIII, 144, 27 April 1866.

Reform, if it was really 'philosophical' and added to parliament's legislative and intellectual capacity, if it allowed it to 'reflect and understand all those interests, feelings, opinions, and classes of character, which constitute the permanent elements of the nation'.[43] This was unlikely. Such men were very hostile to increasing the weight of ignorant urban opinion. Lowe, one of them, bitterly opposed franchise extension in 1866. Other intellectuals, like Mill and Thomas Hare, wanted to attack landed power and to increase the confidence of the working classes in the system, but to offset the direct effects of democracy by proportional representation, which promised to safeguard the rule of the educated.

However, arguments for more legislative activity *could* engender a wider Liberal interest in Reform, when connected with another, more important but more mundane fact: the impact of artisans, shopkeepers and even factory workers on local Liberal politics in the 1850s. Liberalism's close ties with urban community life meant that it was directly affected by increasing popular politicisation and pluralism. Affiliation to trade societies, nonconformist chapels, cooperative movements and friendly societies (membership 1.5 million in 1850, 4 million in 1872) all provided avenues by which the more prosperous working-men could become involved in local Liberal politics. So did the Anti-Slavery League (1841), the peace movement (rejuvenated in 1848), the Liberation Society (1853) and the temperance body, the United Kingdom Alliance (1853). Among the doctrines to permeate borough Liberalism by these means was diluted Chartism. Provincial Liberal artisans pressed for franchise extension in order to secure recognition as independent and respectable citizens and in order to strike at over-government. Faced with their demands, Liberal borough MPs could not help affirming artisans' increasing political intelligence and rationality.[44] To acknowledge their respectability and fitness to vote was politically astute, and often necessary, but in any case borough MPs were usually optimistic about the steady growth of popular political common sense. For whatever reason, few of them were willing to go on record resisting an extension of the borough franchise.[45] In 1861, Russell defined the 'people' to mean the 'working classes' and maintained that they would bring more intelligence to the representation.[46] Liberals portrayed the respectable artisan as a man of thrift, sobriety and self-respect, a product of prosperity and the spread of education, and 'an efficient power in the State' by virtue of his power of combination.[47] Such a figure seemed to meet Gladstone's 1864 definition of the qualities necessary to exercise the franchise well: 'self command, self control, respect for order, patience under suffering, confidence in the law, regard for superiors'.[48] Cobden and Bright propagated the myth that, in contrast to complacent MPs, artisans were zealous supporters of their own low-spending, low-tax radicalism. In the 1866 Reform debates, Liberals suggested that, if the more intelligent working-men were included in the political order, the *variety* of views among them would be revealed, militating against the emergence of artificial but destructive notions of class solidarity.[49] Forster, the employer, and Goschen, the banker, both scorned the idea that labour organisations could ever break away from their dependence on capital; property would maintain its just influence. Only exclusion from the franchise would create a shared grievance.[50]

Russell was astute, then, in floating his Reform Bills of the 1850s and 1860s. Their main thrust was to lower the borough franchise qualification (from £10 to £6 in 1854 and 1860), and hence to win the support of the bulk of Liberal borough MPs. No matter that the £6 level would be as arbitrary in its workings as the £10 one of 1832; it was the best way by which MPs could endorse the 'respectability' of vocal artisans. But their political reluctance to be seen *resisting* Reform proposals should not be mistaken for a general *enthusiasm* for Reform. Palmerstonian Liberalism had seriously enfeebled radical zeal for the old cries of triennial parliaments, household suffrage, even the ballot. Most old-style London radicals had retired, often to be replaced by representatives of dubious morality.[51] They might be aldermen protecting insanitary vested interests, or bribe-giving businessmen such as the lead smelter MP Roupell of Lambeth, whose money was obtained by forging deeds. His reward was life imprisonment. Most Lancashire manufacturing MPs did not press for Reform.[52] One whimsical Member wrote that Palmerston 'retarded a Reform Bill by shaking hands in the lobby with Radical representatives, and asking their wives to Saturday *soirées*'.[53] The Reform Bills failed because reaction in the country was apathetic. Popular feeling was weak in 1854, in 1860 (when even Palmerston was willing to settle the question by a moderate franchise extension, had support been forthcoming), and in 1866, when *Punch* printed a cartoon of John Bull, his wife and their dog all falling asleep from boredom while trying to read speeches on Reform.[54] But since Liberal activists remained interested in borough franchise extension, the situation was difficult, and perhaps best summarised by Granville in 1857: 'The country does not care a great deal about it, but would be very angry if it was thought that the Government was anti-reforming'. So a moderate gesture was necessary.[55]

This ambiguity was indicated also by the strange position occupied in Liberal hearts and minds by Cobden and Bright, the old Anti-Corn Law League warhorses straining but always failing to recreate what nostalgia fallaciously suggested had been their great popular triumph of the 1840s. Bright campaigned for radical Reform after 1858, especially for the redistribution of seats, principally from hostility to the aristocracy. He abused Palmerston's parliament as 'a sham', dominated by 'class prejudices' and vested interests. 'Justice is impossible from a class'; the rich could no more legislate for the poor than could the poor for the rich.[56] He fulminated against 'justices' justice' and the monopoly power of rural landlords in county seats. Cobden believed that, if tory landed dominance there could be broken, a lot of 'healthy radicalism' in small towns and villages could be tapped.[57] Reacting to the 1861 census revelations that landed proprietorship was restricted to only 30,000 individuals, he campaigned for land reform, but it failed to win interest in the industrial north.[58] Bright resented the 'inveterate flunkeyism' of the commercial classes and blamed it largely on Palmerston.[59] Encouraging the thirst for wealth at the expense of morals, Palmerston seemed to have blunted the middle classes' independence, zeal for economy, and political activity.[60] His Volunteer Corps allowed them to rub shoulders with local landowners, and, when elected to parliament, they consorted with idle younger sons of peers and were admitted to whig salons. Fiery young radicals developed this critique, alleging that a 'vast cousinhood' of five hundred landowning MPs was stifling progress, and that the aristocracy was 'destroying our glorious England' by attempting to corrupt the working-man into 'base, tuft-hunting, subserviency'.[61]

The significance of these arguments is that they articulated the Liberal conscience. Liberal MPs sympathised with Bright's moral appeal, drawn from the earnestness of provincial nonconformity, and his image as attacker of what an acute American observer called 'the whole fabric of sham religion, sham loyalty, sham aristocracy, and sham socialism'.[62] Liberal landowners entertained him in their country houses, willingly enduring his abuse of propertied selfishness.[63] Yet it was obvious that there was little support in the party for his proposals.

This ambivalence in the Liberal mind is crucial in explaining the nature of Russell's and Gladstone's interest in parliamentary reform. On Palmerston's death in 1865, they became the two leading Liberals. Parliamentary reform was important for them as a symbol of their anxiety to restore a clean-cut party division after Palmerston's conjuring-tricks. Each man had additional reasons for adopting the cry. Russell's long-standing interest is explained partly by genuine emotional commitment; when his 1854 bill was lost he submitted to a 'hysterical fit of crying' on the floor of the Commons.[64] As noted above (page 175), he wanted to arrest the division between land and trade and to subvert Chartist and radical criticisms of Liberal government. And, throughout the 1850s, he needed to find an issue with which to rally Liberal MPs against Palmerstonianism. Building on borough MPs' unwillingness to vote against Reform, he agitated the question regularly from 1852. So many MPs talked of it at the 1857 election that Palmerston was forced to promise a measure in the 1858 Queen's Speech. His resignation that February required the incoming Conservatives to take it up, and their proposal, which did not involve lowering the borough franchise, was so unacceptable to Liberals that the question was again prominent at the 1859 election. So, though Russell's measure of 1860 foundered on apathy, he was determined to drive a Reform Bill through in 1865–6, his first session as Prime Minister after Palmerston's death. Many MPs had again called for Reform at the 1865 election.[65]

Gladstone was driven to favour Reform from a desire for more active, economical government. He was worried lest executive complacency stimulated unstoppable radical pressure for organic constitutional reform; the result, he feared, would be a monolithic democratic central government flattening the church, the Lords and other institutions in its way.[66] The financial extravagance of Palmerston's parliaments particularly alarmed

211

him. At Manchester in 1864, Gladstone tried an appeal to the public to call MPs to account, pointing out that 'temptation in the administration of public money' could be checked only by public pressure.[67] Gladstone maintained that poor voters could be brought to see that their natural interest lay in checking extravagance, so parliamentary reform would restore the Commons' traditional function as an effective check on government expenditure, which Palmerston's despotism had destroyed. In other words, Gladstone was convinced by Cobden's vision of artisanal zeal for economy. He also needed to consolidate a reputation as the coming man of Liberal politics, attractive to radicals and propertied Liberals alike. (Hence his cultivation of provincial nonconformists in a series of meetings with leading preachers.[68]) Reform was a valuable card to adopt for this reason as well.

But Russell and Gladstone were not *radical* on Reform. A limited borough franchise extension was insignificant, if *not* accompanied by the large-scale redistribution which Bright demanded in order to increase the number of MPs representing urban popular opinion. Borough franchise extension apart, Russell and Gladstone advocated Reform for two reasons. Like Bright, though on different grounds, they wanted to attack the notion that good leadership necessarily depended on landownership, and to open up the tory counties to Liberals. But, unlike him, they wanted to bolster the weight of 'legitimate' property interests by limiting the extent of redistribution. Both strategies require elaboration.

The emergence of a solid phalanx of Conservative MPs manifestly landed in tone and bias encouraged Liberal dislike of landed *privilege*. But this was not a view confined to radicals. It allowed *propertied* Liberals to continue to argue that property owners who were sympathetic to the people should exercise power. It was the unthinking tory association between landownership and the right to power which they rejected. Developments after 1846 distanced Liberals from the instinctive assumption of early-century whigs that effective leadership went hand-in-hand with the possession of local land. In 1849, Lewis argued that the majority of the people possessed the common sense and virtue to accept the leadership of the wise minority even without being connected to them by property.[69] Indeed the celebrated Liberal journalist Bagehot maintained in the 1860s that because counties tended to elect only *local* landowners, this guaranteed that county MPs would be 'stupid'.[70] Meanwhile the need to undermine tory rural power forced Liberals to a change in attitude to the county franchise that was ultimately to prove revolutionary. They rejected the principle of the 1831 Reform Bill that county voters should be property-owners; they now proposed to counter the weight of property with a much more generous occupation franchise. The 1850 Irish Franchise Act was the first government proposal to reflect this switch (see page 197).* In 1851, the Surrey

---

* Of course the first county occupation franchise was imposed by the Chandos clause of 1831, which ministers had opposed.

Liberal MP Locke King proposed to equalise the English county and borough franchise at a £10 level. He represented many urban £10 house-holders who, unlike their borough counterparts, could not vote. Lowering the county franchise was also attractive to Cobden, whose Anti-Corn Law League had tried to 'liberate' the counties from tory control by encouraging qualified urban freeholders to register for a county vote. Cobden pointed to county seats like North Staffordshire and Bedfordshire which returned protectionists but whose respectable inhabitants were Liberal free traders.[71] Russell's bill of 1854 proposed a £10 householder franchise in counties (though a lower borough franchise: he disliked a uniform franchise as a step on the road to a democratic representation). The principle of lowering the county franchise became very important to Liberal MPs, and 179 voted for Locke King's motion in 1857, against 192 tories and Palmerstonian ministers.

The county franchise, then, was to include population as well as property. When Liberal leaders defined the objects of representation in the 1860s, they talked of balancing the interests of 'population, property, and intelligence' – a slight adjustment of the language of 1832, in order to accommodate lower-class interest in the right to vote.[72] But Reform for them was still conservative, in that they wished to preserve the influence of a genuine variety of propertied interests in parliament. Indeed, Russell's bills of the 1850s even toyed with various gimmicks to increase the respectability of the Commons. His 1854 bill, for example, proposed to give seats to the Inns of Court and London University, to introduce the minority vote in 3-member seats,* and to extend the franchise to all university graduates and to salaried men who earned £100 a year, received £10 per year from stock dividends, or had £50 in the Savings Bank. This was the sort of considered, philosophical Reform of which Palmerston and Wood approved.[73] But by 1866, such 'fancy franchises' looked too insulting to the mass of voters to appeal to Liberal MPs, and they were dropped.

The crucial fact continued to be that Russell and Gladstone remained staunchly opposed to organic Reform, that is to the extensive redistribution of seats.† Neither man wished to attack the small boroughs. In the 1850s, they had both defended them staunchly with a modified version of the traditional argument that these were nurseries of statesmen and experts who might not otherwise find seats.[74] Russell argued that the Commons was a uniquely powerful body among the world's legislatures, so must remain able

---

* By this arrangement, each voter would have only two votes, so making it likely that the minority party would return one MP. This promised both to increase Liberal county representation and to keep down the number of urban radical MPs.

† In the 1860 bill, only 25 seats were to be redistributed, and no borough altogether disfranchised. The largest redistribution planned in any of Russell's bills was in 1854, when 62 were to be reallocated, but the introduction of the minority vote and specific interest group representation was presumably a deliberate compensation for that.

to debate a great range of questions, and that it must be able to work with the crown and the Lords and so preserve 'the balance of the constitution'.[75] By 1866, Liberal leaders were more prone to admit that small boroughs added little of distinction: they were no longer necessary boltholes for men of promise, since, as a number of MPs asserted, thriving urban communities would elect men of common sense, intellectual or commercial distinction and broad interests as their representative.[76] But Liberal leaders still refused to sacrifice the notion of variety in the representation. They wished to perpetuate 'the great middle class of constituencies' neither agricultural nor manufacturing.[77] The fast-rising young political economist Goschen defended the 'old principle of communities', which safeguarded parliament's independence from direct mass pressure.[78]

The 1866 Reform Bill was moderate, reflecting this approach and the desire not to offend anti-Reforming Palmerstonian Liberals. The borough franchise was to be lowered, but only to £7, adding only about 200,000 voters from the working classes, who would remain in a minority of borough electors. (Gladstone in fact claimed that the percentage of working-class voters had fallen substantially since 1832.[79]) The occupation franchise in counties was to be lowered to £14, enfranchising an estimated 172,000 largely middle-class and urban voters.* Meanwhile the bill made hardly any provision for extending borough boundaries. This meant that continuing urbanisation would steadily weaken the rural character of many county seats, a process encouraged further by the Liberals' decision to create very few new boroughs in their redistribution. Forty-nine seats were to be released by diminishing small borough representation. But no boroughs were to be disfranchised (8 were to lose one seat and 63 were to be grouped to return 22 MPs), while 26 of the extra seats were to go to English counties and only 6 to new one-member boroughs.†

Despite its moderation, the 1866 bill failed to calm enough worried Liberal MPs. Lowe opposed the bill, and articulated the views of many intellectual Liberals when he protested against any step which would undermine what he saw as the disinterestedness and variety of the existing Commons. He pointed out that no other legislature had as much power, and the Commons was already an obstacle to strong scientific government. If it lost its *representative* character and became dominated by delegates

---

* In their Reform bill of 1859, the Conservatives had attempted to make county seats safer for their party by equalising the county and borough suffrages and transferring borough freeholders' voting rights from the county to the town seat. The 1866 bill, on the contrary, retained the freeholders' right of county voting. It also reaffirmed Liberals' commitment to a mixture of urban and rural influence within county seats by allowing the small class of urban copyholders and lease-holders the county vote on the same terms as the freeholders, ending the distinction introduced in 1831.

† Plus 4 new seats for London boroughs, 5 more for big English towns and 3 for big Scottish towns. (Also, 3 went to Scottish counties, one to London University and one to the Scottish universities.)

advancing class interests, all confidence in good government would disappear. Lowe was particularly sensitive to this because of his commitment to political economy. He feared working-class pressure for a redistribution of taxation on class lines, rather than the steady reduction of taxation on all classes, and he feared also the erosion of the state's power to discipline paupers strictly through the Poor Law, and of its neutrality in the market against trade union pressure for sectional benefits in law.[80] Perhaps more typical of dissident Liberal opinion in the Commons was the less intellectually rigorous dislike of Russell's haste and zeal expressed by the many Palmerstonians who would have preferred a less active Prime Minister. By now Russell was widely distrusted for leaning 'too much on the Radical leg', while Gladstone seemed completely baffling to the whig mind.[81] Russell had rejected the proposal of a Royal Commission to plan the ground for a consensus measure.[82] Impatient for a last draught of fame, he intended to settle the question promptly, but his rapidity antagonised MPs who baulked at another quick and expensive election. The Palmerstonian secession was led by respected whig names, Grosvenor and Lansdowne, and the bill was defeated. But Russell's resignation in June 1866 ensured the advent of a minority Conservative government led by Derby. To keep power, it would have to bring in its own bill.

The Conservative Reform Bill of 1867 had four objectives. It sought to defuse agitation for Reform permanently by *ostensibly* adopting the principle for which urban radicals had long lobbied, male household suffrage. Second, it sought to limit that idea in practice by a series of restrictions. Not only must the voter be rated for the relief of the poor, and have paid his poor rates and taxes, but there was to be a two-year residence requirement, while those whose landlords paid rates on their behalf would have no right to vote. The bill also proposed 'fancy franchises': a vote would be earned by the payment of twenty shillings a year in direct taxes, by appropriate educational qualifications, or by substantial holdings in the funds or savings banks – so this would give a 'dual vote' to a large number of mostly propertied men. Critical Liberals estimated that there would be 260,000 extra propertied votes, while the number of working-class voters would hardly be greater than in the 1866 plan.[83] Third, in order to maintain Conservative influence in the counties – where it mattered – the occupation franchise was set relatively high (£15) and the Boundary Commission was instructed to reduce many county boundaries, transferring urban areas to boroughs. For example, they proposed that 30,000 voters should be moved from Warwickshire to Birmingham. Finally, the extent of redistribution would be very small with only 27 seats losing one MP. So, even if the borough electorate did increase in future years, thousands of votes would pile up in large seats without significantly affecting the tone of the Commons.

The second and third of these objectives, in particular, were unacceptable to most Liberal backbenchers. With the government lacking a majority, the bill was radically amended under their pressure. But Liberals were undisciplined and at odds throughout 1867, the more so because the Peelite Gladstone was not trusted as Commons leader, especially on matters of constitutional reform, while Bright had launched a ferocious radical campaign for Reform in the winter of 1866–7. These pressures, added to Liberals' own image of their relationship to the people, meant that many MPs were unwilling to accept any provision which appeared to question their commitment to a wide borough franchise. The key development was the refusal of 48 MPs, conscious of constituency pressure for household suffrage, to follow Gladstone in his attempt in April 1867 to reinsert a property qualification for the borough franchise. This was the so-called Tea-Room revolt. Though this revolt established that the basis of the bill would remain *household* suffrage in boroughs, Liberals were still determined to strike out the objectionable 'fancy franchises'. They complained that they discriminated between classes and were irrational; on both counts they would create tension and not settle the question. They also pointed to the unfairness of the ruling on the personal payment of rates, since in some towns parish officers chose not to demand personal payment as a qualification for the electoral register.[84]

So was wrought the most unintentional revolution in the history of British politics. The bill was amended in line with Liberal thinking in these areas, *but* from the baseline of borough household suffrage. The tory duke of Buccleuch complained that the only word in the final act surviving from the original bill was the first 'Whereas'. The county occupation franchise was lowered to £12 (a compromise: most Liberals wanted £10).* Disraeli had tried to abolish the county voting rights of borough freeholders, but these were maintained. The Boundary Commission's proposals for the extension of fifteen borough boundaries were rejected by the Commons, by Liberal demand – though boundaries had to be redrawn in the counties which gained extra seats in redistribution, and this was done broadly in Conservative interests, so that at the 1868 election they secured a net gain of 25 seats in those counties.[85] In the boroughs, the dual vote was abolished, the residence requirement was reduced to one year, a £10 lodger franchise was introduced, and, most famously, 'Hodgkinson's amendment' was passed, rating the occupier not the owner and abolishing the practice of rate-compounding by the landlord. So all occupiers who paid rates personally would qualify for the register. But this arrangement offended occupiers (since landlords often did not reduce rents to reflect the transfer of the rate burden from owner to occupier). Rating authorities also found compounding convenient, and in 1868 many continued to allow it and to register compound householders for the vote. For the sake of fairness, in 1869, the right of compounding was restored. Now *all* compound householders were to be eligible for the vote, a major change.

The effects of Reform in 1867 were contrasting. In many senses they were very limited. The Liberal – and Conservative – leadership had attained

* And the £10 ownership franchises of 1832 were lowered to £5.

the major objective of restricting the extent of redistribution. Liberals could not be seen to restrict it quite as far as the original bill proposed, so the number of small English boroughs to lose one member rose to 35 (those with a population below 10,000), while 3 two-member and 5 one-member seats were disfranchised (with a population below 5,000). But only 9 new one-member English boroughs were created. Four large boroughs were given a third member,* but the minority clause would operate in these boroughs and in 7 three-member counties, as a sop to worried Conservatives and to intellectual Liberals. Overall, the structure of parliament was hardly different in 1868 from in 1865. In 1881, 72 United Kingdom boroughs with a population of less than 10,000 returned MPs; 40 per cent of all borough MPs sat for seats with a population of less than 20,000. In 1872, 27 English boroughs had an electorate of less than 1,000 and 77 under 2,000.[86] Moreover, the £12 county occupation franchise did not have the liberating effects that Liberals intended, since suburban middle-class voters came to display propensities as strikingly tory as those of old voters.[87]

On the other hand, the English borough electorate rose from 500,000 to 1.25 million between 1866 and 1871. This seemed a revolutionary change. Male household suffrage on a one-year residence qualification was virtually established in the boroughs, and Britain had, it appeared, become a democracy. Liberal as well as Conservative observers were understandably apprehensive about the behaviour of what Bagehot called the newly en-franchised 'ignorant multitude'.[88] Russell's prolonged tinkering, followed by 'two years' weak and reckless' tory government, had altered the situation beyond the worst fears of the average propertied Liberal.[89] Neither Russell nor Gladstone had wanted such extensive constitutional change; neither were democrats. The question was, whether borough household suffrage would improve the prospect for high-minded, improving Liberalism, or turn the Liberals into an explicitly popular party, motivated by grass-roots hostility to the land, the church and the taxation of the poor.

* As was Glasgow in Scotland, while the City of London gained a fourth.

PART IV

THE GLADSTONIAN LIBERAL PARTY, 1868–1886

The consequences of 1867

THE BOROUGH FRANCHISE revolution of 1867–9 had a profound effect. In particular, it increased the political weight of the electorate. In a great novelty, governments defeated at the polls in 1868, 1874 and 1880 resigned without meeting parliament. Power to select and dismiss ministries moved from Westminster to the constituencies. This meant that their fate rested on small numbers of votes. After the 1880 election, Salisbury calculated that the Conservatives could have won had a mere two thousand electors across the country voted differently. So effective party organisation in each seat was now crucial. Parties were no longer content to allow the traditional compromises of local politics to survive. Until the 1860s, most elections were not fought at all; 383 United Kingdom seats were left uncontested in 1859. But the number of uncontested seats fell from 302 in 1865 to 212 in 1868, 109 in 1880 and 43 in 1885 (only 10 were in England).[1] Local parties developed a professional organisation in order to access a much enlarged electorate, to put their supporters on the register, to keep them there against opposition objections, and to keep track of the subsequent movement of population.

Moreover, political organisation was a potentially valuable agency in integrating new electors into the town's communal life. Local party clubs came to be a natural extension of the old philanthropic agencies by which elites had demonstrated their concern for the less wealthy. They offered leisure and sporting facilities, newspaper rooms and libraries, smoking concerts, lectures and debates, partly, at least, in an attempt to deepen the values of citizenship. In the boroughs, by the 1870s and 1880s, almost every aspect of local life was politicised; friendly societies and working-men's clubs supported different parties, just as the banks and attornies had after 1832. Another powerful integrating force was political image. In the 1870s, the growth of the mass market made possible a cult of the leader as a symbol of virtue, largely through the proliferation of the Liberal provincial press (see page 169) and its increasing circulation, but also owing to a thriving industry in artefacts idealising individual politicians. As leader of the party from 1867–8, Gladstone was particularly worshipped. His image was reproduced on ash-trays, plates, tea-spoons – and Conservative-made

221

chamberpots. In the 1880 election, posters of Gladstone the woodman cutting down Beaconsfield the upas-tree appeared in a number of constituencies.[2] Gladstone's name was a rallying-cry from 1868. One candidate in that year explained that, whenever he was lost for words on the hustings, he bought time by saying ' "Gladstone", and then they are sure to cheer'.[3] In late 1871, Gladstone reflected that he and other prominent Liberals had 'over-stumped' that autumn, owing to a flood of local speaking invitations.[4]

All this stimulated discussion of national political issues. MPs now found themselves speaking regularly in their constituencies each autumn. In the past, most voters had acted from loyalty to local communal ties, to deferential bonds with landlords or employers, to religious denominations, to friendly societies, or to particular publicans. But now, voting was influenced more and more by the perception that particular interests would be damaged or promoted by government action. It is probable that these perceptions mainly affected local activists such as property-owners, church and Dissenting ministers, publicans, attorneys, trade unionists and so on. But their enthusiasm was the key to electoral success: it mobilised less politicised voters who otherwise would have stayed at home. Historians of elections have discerned an increasingly uniform national pattern to swings in voter allegiance from the 1870s.[5]

The rise of issues and organisation threatened to alter the relationship between the MP and his constituency. One of the most widely-expressed fears among the propertied classes after 1867 was of 'sectionalism'. 'Wire-pullers' in constituency parties, with the power to deliver or withhold large numbers of votes, were said to be using that power over the candidate to force him to pledge to vote for particular 'sectional' proposals, so destroying his fabled independence of mind. In the 1870s, there were four particular lobbies from which pressure was feared. One was from the National Liberal Federation of Joseph Chamberlain, and his earlier organisation the National Education League, which are discussed below (page 275). But immediately after 1867 three other pressure groups caused more concern. Two were Dissenting-based bodies: the United Kingdom Alliance, the temperance organisation which advocated legislation to allow local referenda on the number of public houses, and the Liberation Society, which campaigned for the abolition of church rates as a preliminary to disestablishment of the Church of England. Both these bodies, benefiting from the organising capacities of local agents and the enthusiasm of radical Liberals, had been trying to bludgeon Liberal candidates into pledging support for their proposals since the early 1860s. They claimed much success, though this was undoubtedly exaggerated.[6] Their campaigns were part of a wider revival of radical Dissenting activity in the early 1860s, stimulated by the failure of the Liberals' church rate bills and by the 1862 celebrations of the bicentenary of Dissenters' ejection from the Church of England. The most striking consequences were in Wales, where in 1868 the dormant Dissenting majority was mobilised to break the hold of the old Anglophile gentry in a number of seats.[7] It seemed very likely that both groups would gain great

222

strength as a result of the Reform Act. The same was true of the third force, the trade councils, forums for organised skilled workers, which were being established in the major provincial towns as a way of increasing living standards through arbitration and cooperation, but which also had legislative objectives because of the unsatisfactory state of trade union law.

The fear of popular pressure – on these matters and on questions of taxation and foreign policy – was always present in Liberal politics after 1867. But most Liberal MPs, proud of their judgment as interpreters of local public opinion, were in fact able to resist too many concessions to these potentially unrepresentative organised groups. Nor can we discern an increase in the policy-making influence of a Liberal 'party machine'. The Liberal commitment to open debate, and the great variety in constituency size and type before 1885, ensured that no central party organisation could claim to represent the sentiments of the party as a whole. Local, not national, organisation remained the key to electoral success. Power to return MPs lay with Liberal property-owners and their agents in many small boroughs and in Liberal counties; with all-powerful industrial magnates in many of the newer boroughs; with the traditional turbulent mix of propertied, Dissenting, shopkeeping and artisan influences in mid-sized towns like Oxford and Banbury; and with highly-organised caucuses only in a few large boroughs with otherwise unmanageable electorates.

So the importance of *organisational* changes on high politics was limited and mainly psychological, for it fuelled *fears* about the survival of propertied MPs' freedom of judgment. But the growing interest in *issues* had a much more direct influence. Between 1868 and 1872, an all-time record 101,573 petitions were presented to the Commons, bearing an annual average of 3,125,350 signatures (as against 1,371,578 between 1863 and 1867).[8] The question for Liberal leaders was how to lead such an aroused body of sentiment – to *lead*, because as Hartington said in 1879, public opinion was now too advanced and diverse to be *governed*.[9] Part IV examines this quandary.

Introductory summary

The major problem for the Liberal party after 1867 was how to marry its two traditions: how to remain the party of wisdom, property and rational parliamentary debate, and yet also the party of the people. For the Liberal myth dictated that popular sentiment was not to be followed blindly. In 1885, one writer argued that an 'ideal Liberal . . . will love the approval of his own conscience more than the approval of the conscience of the people'.[10] Essential to grasp from the outset is that there was no great cleavage between sections of the party as to how to tackle this problem. Most general accounts of Liberal politics institutionalise a division in the party between negative, obstructionist 'whigs' and positive-thinking 'radicals'. Some, principally Professor Hamer, see party leadership as a question of humouring different 'sections' of the party by organisational strategies which allowed as much radical reform to be passed as possible. The division of 1886 which eventually split the party is often portrayed as a battle almost entirely between Gladstone and the excitingly interventionist radical Chamberlain, whose loss to the party is thus seen as tragic. Alternatively, the defection of 'the whigs' in that year is noted, but explained as an overdue, natural, class-based revolt by anachronistic figures. Ireland, it seems, merely provided a helpful excuse. The defection, indeed, can be seen as assisting the party by removing obstructions to the development of a popular programme of 'reforms' aimed at 'the working class' (as if the Liberals either wanted or needed to become a class party). These three chapters aim to refute all these interpretations.[11] Liberals saw themselves as the party of reasoned, economical, efficient and energetic government. Neither 'sectionalism' nor the search for working-class votes distorted leadership behaviour, at least before the catastrophe of 1885–6 destroyed the party's status as the natural governing body of the world's greatest empire. Most Liberals were neither whig grandees nor obstreperous, visionary radicals. They were a mixture of landowners (in 1874 43 per cent of Liberal MPs were of great landlord or landed gentry family), industrialists and professional men, nearly all of whom were of studied moderation and loyal to the leadership.[12] Even at the beginning of 1886, 110 of 339 Liberal MPs were from the landed classes, 164 were professional men, 142 were active businessmen, and 12 were from the 'working classes'.[13]

Chapter 10 shows the Liberals adapting the bulk of their domestic policy very well to conditions after 1867. They managed to bind propertied and working-class supporters in favour of a more assiduous agenda of social and moral improvement, without subverting traditional economic principles. This was the golden age of Liberal reform. Even in the 1880s, there was *no* coherent 'radical' challenge to the official Liberal agenda, *no* concession to a 'programmatic' conception of politics driven by grass-roots sectionalism. There is, then, no substance in the widely-held belief that class tension between 'whigs' and 'radicals' on economic or social policy was the real cause of the division of 1886. There was much more legislation after 1868 than before, but it mostly aimed at improving local administration and popular morals.

However, chapters 11 and 12 reveal that greater tensions developed within the party about how to lead the people in other fields. As we have seen, previous Liberal practice was to assert that popular acceptance of the rule of law, at home and in Ireland, needed safeguarding by maintaining certain institutional and religious constraints on individual licence. In the 1870s and 1880s, these constraints seemed increasingly threatened by mass activity, of three particular types: by campaigns from evangelical Dissenters calling for church disestablishment, from populist agitators demanding that foreign and imperial policy should be shaped by 'sentimental', anti-militaristic and penny-pinching considerations rather than a hard-headed appraisal of national interests, and from Irish 'Nationalists' who claimed that they represented a coherent movement for self-rule. Faced with these crusades, how far should Liberal leaders trust popular morality, judgment and capacity for self-government?

The issues raised in these campaigns were the very ones on which Gladstone had particularly strong views, and these views fitted ill with traditional Liberalism. This is not to say that he was a bad leader, for in other respects he was extremely effective in mobilising a broad coalition of support. His Peelite administrative outlook, mercantile origins and successive 'popular' constituencies (in south-west Lancashire, Greenwich and Midlothian) symbolised commercial efficiency; his marriage into a Flintshire landed family, his Conservative past, and his high churchmanship did something to reassure different schools of non-radicals; and his oratorical fire, religious zeal and eye for self-advertisement struck chords with provincial Liberals. And, on becoming leader in 1867–8, he swiftly rallied Liberals to a great victory. Though in opposition to Disraeli's minority Conservative government, he led the Commons to pass resolutions hostile to the Irish church establishment. The disestablishment issue was the Liberals' prime rallying-cry at the 1868 election. It was well chosen to unite the party, because Irish church appropriation had been the defining symbol of common Liberal purpose in 1834–5. Gladstone spoke several times a week in his Lancashire constituency, mainly on Irish questions; the speeches were reported across whole pages of the *Times*. The result was a Liberal majority of 110, Disraeli's resignation, and the swift disestablishment of the Irish church.

From 1868, then, Gladstone stamped his moral power on the party and added greatly to its reputation as a popular yet disinterested agency. But his leadership was never uncontroversial. His personality prompted suspicion in a wide variety of Liberal minds. He remained unsympathetic to organic constitutional reform, to anti-clericalism, and to those who tolerated the drift of parliamentary debate, yet these were the three staples of the Liberal tradition. He loathed Palmerstonianism for its blustering defence of national interests and its primarily administrative conception of politics, yet it was these aspects that had reassured so many propertied voters about Liberalism. Gladstone was a Peelite; a religious enthusiast; a man of colossal, restless energy; a relentless advocate of retrenchment; and a populist who convinced himself that he understood the public conscience and that he could mobilise it to cleanse the state of arrogant, wasteful misgovernment. He inspired Liberals on many occasions and for many reasons but, ultimately, large numbers of them proved no more willing to accept his emotive, authoritarian, evangelical, sentimental, unpredictable leadership style than the Conservatives of 1846 had tolerated Peel's. In 1886, Gladstone broke up his party almost as single-handedly as his mentor had done forty years before. The Liberal party did not fall apart because of 'sectionalism' or whig 'inflexibility' but because of Gladstone's distance from the Liberal tradition.

CHAPTER 10

Liberalism exuberant, 1868–85

LIBERALS' RESPONSE TO the 1867 Reform Act was to fashion a new political order. The party believed that only it could make working-men feel respected members of the community, yet integrate them into a political system dominated by an solid, civilised and civilising phalanx of public-spirited landowners, 'expert' intellectuals and leading provincial merchants. This cross-class propertied and wise elite was capable, they thought, of operating a rational and ethical politics designed to uphold the rule of law, to promote moral values and to provide low-cost efficiency. This chapter discusses the success of this ideal.

The new Liberal party

Two symbolic Liberal causes offer a useful way in to understanding this new politics. Both were in part a response to the anxiety of the 1860s about the spread of materialism in all classes: luxury and extravagance in the upper classes, money-grubbing in the middle, and improvidence, brutality and atheism in the lower. The flower of the mid-Victorian intelligentsia – Carlyle, Mill, Matthew Arnold, Kingsley, George Eliot, Huxley – debated what to do about this problem. The Liverpool unitarian William Rathbone, shortly to be a Liberal MP, described in his tract *Social duties* (1867) how industrialisation and class segregation in growing towns had replaced personal ties between rich and poor with ignorance and sensualism on both sides. (His influential solution was a more systematic organisation of charitable aid, leading to the creation of the Charity Organisation Society in 1869.)

The first of our two causes, one dear to Rathbone, was research into 'the science of society'. Scientific inquiry had built up a vast amount of knowledge about the natural world and about the human body. It was an affront to Victorian rationality to assume that similar progress could not be made in understanding the laws of social development. It was comforting to believe that social disorder and disequilibrium must always be the fruit of 'some ignorance or of some rebellion' against God's natural laws. The giddy prospect loomed of curing such misfortunes by 'larger knowledge and a

227

better will'.[1] An important organisation, the Social Science Association, had been set up in 1857 just after the Crimean War, in order to promote debate and inquiry, and to educate provincial opinion. It was divided into five departments of inquiry, covering the law, education, penal reform, public health and social economy. It became something of a cliché in the 1860s to talk of the need for 'a Social Science policy . . . the day of expedients is passed, and the reign of principles begun'. In this climate, 'every institution must justify itself at the bar of public opinion'.[2] Aristocratic incompetence – *any* incompetence – would be rooted out. Rigorous investigation of the efficiency of institutions would stimulate a higher social unity. Government legislation could then harmonise more with divine intentions for social development. One important Liberal cabinet politician, the duke of Argyll, published *The reign of law* in 1867, which celebrated the growing awareness of the place of natural laws in politics and society. Edward Denison, a Liberal social science enthusiast, urged government to 'come out clearly and boldly as the great mediator, to draw to itself the hearts of the people as the one power capable of saving them from themselves; to let them see that Law really is the ideal king, the Arthur of real life'.[3]

The second, a corollary of the first, was the movement for the abolition of all religious tests at Oxford and Cambridge universities. This old whig cry took on a wider significance in the 1860s. Its prominence reflected the urgency of forging cultural links between the Dissenting manufacturing elites of the North and the propertied Anglican establishment. In 1865, Goschen and Forster urged university tests abolition on the Commons in order to improve respect among the manufacturing classes for the church and for universities. University tests reform promised a number of benefits. It would reduce the social and ecclesiastical exclusiveness of two power-ful institutions. It would expose narrow-minded trainee clergymen to an increased 'lay element'. It would educate young aristocrats and rich Dissenters' sons together, 'leavening' both by broadening the horizons of each. Manufacturing philistinism – satirised in Matthew Arnold's *Culture and anarchy* (1869) – would be diminished by access to a classical education that would teach Dissenters, as it traditionally taught landowners, the need to demonstrate civic responsibility in their own public sphere. A common cultural code adopted by a broadened social and intellectual elite would supply a much improved 'tone and character to the intellect and feeling of the nation'.[4] It would secure enlightened rule at central and local level. The abolition of all university tests became one of the great symbols of propertied-latitudinarian-business-Dissenting-intellectual integration in a Liberal coalition. It was achieved in 1871.

It is no accident that Goschen and Forster were two of the leaders of this campaign. They were precisely representative of the new Liberalism of the 1860s, vital figures to understand if one is to comprehend both the achieve-ments and the tragedy of Gladstonian Liberalism. For these two men became open enemies of the Gladstonian style of politics by the late 1870s, yet in the mid-1860s were seen as radicals, because they were able, industrious, middle-class critics of institutional and aristocratic inefficiency. This was the new agenda, and their zeal in promoting it facilitated a meteoric rise; Goschen, an MP at 32 in 1863, was in cabinet by 1866, and Forster, elected in 1861, by 1870. Goschen was the son of an immigrant German merchant who established a City firm. Sent to Rugby to become a 'typical British boy',[5] he imbibed Arnoldian religion from headmaster Tait and political economy from Bonamy Price. Rugby, like his double First at Oriel College Oxford and directorship of the Bank of England at 27, was merely a preparation for a career of public service planned by his upwardly mobile father. Goschen represented the City, a large commercial seat. Forster sat for Bradford. Forster's father was a quaker minister and anti-slavery propagandist. The anti-slavery cause was one of his entrées, as a successful Bradford worsted manufacturer, into national politics. Forster and Goschen were both symbols of moralised commercial efficiency, of the class that Bagehot identified in the 1860s as 'coming up trained to thought, full of money, and yet trained to business'.[6] To snobs, they appeared ungentlemanly. Forster's nickname was 'Gorilla'; Goschen's friend advised him to take elocution lessons. But in fact they both had a strong commitment to the firm rule of law, to the value of a classical university education (which Forster so much regretted not having had), and to undenominational religion as a moralising agency and a means of integrating Anglican and Dissenting values. Both were Arnoldian Anglicans; Forster was expelled from the quakers for marrying Arnold's daughter. Both imbibed from Palmerston a determination to uphold Britain's role as a strong, moral force in international relations. Forster, a founder of the Bradford Chamber of Commerce, wanted the Board of Trade to play a larger role in boosting British exports and became an enthusiast for Imperial Federation. This was not Cobdenite radicalism, nor was it Gladstonian. Rather, it was self-consciously masculine, national efficiency stuff. Both were enthusiasts for parliamentary reform in the 1860s, because it would allow commercial MPs to act as disinterested trustees for the public interests. But both despised the 'wirepulling' lobby groups of the 1870s, with whom Forster fought fierce battles in Bradford.

In Gladstone's 1868 government, Goschen was put in charge of local government, and Forster of education. Another 'middle-class' social science enthusiast, the Welsh gentleman-mineowner Henry Bruce, was Home Secretary. No clearer indication could have been given of the government's determination through domestic policy to develop a new bond with the people in partnership with men of wealth and science. Yet the cabinet could not do this alone. The most striking development in the Liberal parliamentary party after 1867 is the emergence of a class of earnest backbenchers, great commercial spokesmen, with the same values: Mundella of Sheffield, Samuel Morley, the Nottingham stocking millionaire, in Bristol, William Rathbone of Liverpool, Charles Reed the print magnate of Hackney, and Jacob Bright of Manchester. Like Goschen, Forster and Bruce, they all sat for populous constituencies, and quickly emerged as the leading parliamentary interpreters and guides of urban working-class opinion. These were not old-fashioned radicals suspicious of 'tyrannical' government legislation. Rather, they had a businesslike impatience with the 'rather profitless discussions' in parliament which frustrated a constructive legislative programme.[7]

In fact, they were all legislators themselves and were among the most active of MPs in promoting private members' legislation after 1868. The number of private members' bills introduced rose from 66 in 1864 to 82 in 1869, 98 in 1871 and 113 in 1873, as MPs developed a concern for positive action.[8] Their legislative contribution was by no means insignificant.* Nor were they hidebound political economists. The average small master of the 1830s and 1840s had endured fragile profit margins and frequent overcompetition for unstable domestic markets; this had made him resistant to any measures to increase working-class wages, reduce hours of work or increase national taxes and so depress domestic consumption. But these men were wealthy, freer from competition worries, and saw themselves as benefactors and reconcilers in their localities. They were openly sympathetic to trade unions (because they offered the prospect of a stable forum for industrial negotiations), to high wages, and to the extension of working-class education as a route to winning workmen's confidence and commitment and improving their productivity. Though Dissenters (except for Mundella), they were all enthusiasts for a universal system of state-aided undenominational education, and cared nothing for the sectarian scruples of radical voluntaryists. Morley withdrew from the Liberation Society when it campaigned for disestablishment, not integration, after 1868. Rathbone and Morley refused to give pledges to constituents and disliked mass lobbying.

Other MPs followed their active solicitude for working-class morals.[†] Two may be selected as representative of this mixture of property, high-

---

* In 1872, Mundella steered through the Arbitration Act and helped to pass the Borough Funds Act. Candlish and Hodgkinson, two other big city Liberal MPs, introduced the municipal franchise bill in 1869, which Jacob Bright amended to introduce women's suffrage; Bright was responsible for the 1870 Married Women's Property Act and Lubbock for the Bank Holidays Act of 1871. All these statutes are discussed in the text below. In addition, Reed's Act of 1869 exempted Sunday and ragged schools from the poor rates; he later got postmen exempted from Sunday labour. Muntz and Dixon of Birmingham were responsible for the act of 1872 which tightened penalties for adulterating food and drugs.

† The succession of the Irish literary whig Torrens to the critic of state power Duncombe in Finsbury is symbolic of the sea-change in MPs' attitude to social activity; Torrens was a campaigner for better urban housing, water supply and open spaces, most famous for his 1868 Artisans' Dwellings Act. MPs' assiduousness as legislators did not stop with humans. Two private members' acts of 1869 and 1872 were the first to protect sea birds. Auberon Herbert, the promoter of the 1872 bill, rested his case 'on the ground of right feeling and compassion towards those who, though they had no power of agitating in their own behalf, yet . . . possessed so many of the qualities the presence of which we so much respected in men and women': *Hansard*, ccxi, 1652, 12 June 1872.

mindedness and popularity: Tom Hughes, author of *Tom Brown's school-days*, and Sir John Lubbock, a banker, Kentish baronet and prolific amateur natural historian (*Ants, bees and wasps*; *Flowers, fruits and leaves*). Both were involved with the Christian Socialist movement and committed to working-men's improvement. Lubbock recommended to them a hundred best books, including Epictetus, Spinoza, Descartes, the Mahabharata and the Nibelungenlied as well as Aristotle, Plato, Bunyan, Goethe and Samuel Smiles.[9] Both believed in 'wise and strong government' by men of strong living faith teaching the mutual responsibility of all classes.[10] *Tom Brown's schooldays* (1857) had proposed a straightforward manly unsnobbish and unpriggish leadership by flawed, decent, educated upper-middle-class gentlemen. It was Hughes's contribution to the critique of the failings of aristocratic government, so widespread in the mid-1850s.

As some of these examples suggest, the outlook of the parliamentary party was affected also by educational developments, by changes in the tone of instruction offered to young men at Oxford and Cambridge in the 1840s and 1850s. Rising to political prominence in the 1860s were university graduates from those years who had been exposed to high-minded teaching by earnest Christian Socialist, latitudinarian or high church dons. And young academics like Harcourt, Fawcett and Trevelyan entered politics confident of the power of intellect to promote rational progress. Also raising the tone of debate was the explosion of high/middle-brow journals catering for well-read Victorian gentlemen interested in politics, literature, science and theology, such as the *Saturday Review* (1855), *Fortnightly Review* (1865), *Contemporary Review* (1866), *Macmillan's Magazine* (1859) and *Cornhill Magazine* (1860). John Morley, editor of the *Fortnightly* at 29, Oxford scholarship boy, son of a Blackburn surgeon, and agnostic positivist, was a particularly active exponent of new Liberal departures. He sought to develop the arguments of the revered Liberal philosopher John Stuart Mill (himself briefly MP for Westminster, 1865–8) that for the first time Liberals could properly represent 'the nation' as a whole, as opposed to 'a class'. The awakened zeal of the people must be harnessed to provide invigorating yet consensual government, 'force and energy and smooth rapid movement' in contrast to the 'dead-lock' under Palmerston.[11]

All this suggests that the Liberal ideal of disinterested service by propertied but unsnobbish leadership was perhaps closer to reality at this point than at any previous time. As the local duties of an MP became more engrossing, the role became less attractive for those who had sought a seat primarily to raise their social status (a tendency greatly furthered by the passage of the 1883 Corrupt Practices Act). MPs' attendance and voting records were monitored by activists. An extremely full analysis of MPs' sessional voting records by T.N. Roberts, secretary of the Liberal Registration Association, revealed the solemnity with which some MPs took their duties as spokesmen and guides of the expanded electorate. John Candlish, MP for Sunderland (1866–73) voted in all but one of 404 divisions in the 1869 and 1870 sessions.[12]

It was, then, the period after 1868 which saw the zenith of a style of government influenced by the free association of a wide variety of different popular forces represented in parliament and disciplined by MPs. *Dirigiste* whipping of MPs was ruled out, as before. Leaders had to attend almost constantly in the Commons in order to convey the moral authority of government. Gladstone sat on the front bench from 4.30 p.m. to about 1 a.m. on nights when government business was being done (minus a relaxed dinner-hour), and sometimes until 3 a.m. Liberal MPs' loyalty to the party whip improved after 1868, but was still lax by twentieth-century standards.[13] The party saw itself as a virtuous free-acting body of disinterested trustees of the people's conscience, exemplars of public service, and respectful of property if it did its duty. It was significant that when Gladstone first retired from politics in 1875, his successor as Commons leader was *elected* by MPs for the first time. It was scarcely less significant that the victor was the heir of a duke.

For the party considered itself to be representative of all classes. It was more varied in composition than ever before. One survey of Liberal MPs in 1868 lists among them 197 with a landowning interest, 32 with army and navy links, 124 with a financial interest, 76 with a railway connection, 63 merchants, 70 lawyers, 32 men of letters and academics, and a total of 112 other interests in manufacturing.[14] Young, clever Liberal peers like Camperdown and the earl of Morley, recently graduated with Firsts at Jowett's Balliol, took junior office in 1868. Their leader in the Lords, Granville, married the feline urbanity, tact and judgment of a diplomatic family with simplicity of dress and speech, a marked absence of snobbery, and a willingness to go any lengths with Gladstone. On the first day of the 1869 session he walked hand-in-hand from cabinet to parliament with John Bright, in order to demonstrate the mutual confidence between the Liberal aristocracy and the Liberal conscience. Bright had been so affected by the atmosphere of Liberal purity that he agreed to give Gladstone's 1868 cabinet his seal of approval by shackling himself to it as President of the Board of Trade. This was a mistake: he quickly discovered that the administrative work so patiently borne by aristocrats was boring – and so *difficult!* – and that even the purest of governments unaccountably seemed to get into scrapes that he had always attributed to landed selfishness and arrogance. A radical tribune could not be expected to sully his reputation in this way for long; he resigned in 1870, pleading ill-health.

The Liberals survived this blow. The rest of this chapter examines their developing agenda for virtuous government. It is mainly concerned with strengthening the power of local government to moralise working-men. But it would be unfair to paint this merely as 'social control'. MPs were anxious to demonstrate their accommodation with constituents' needs. A large number of statutes between 1868 and 1874, the product of backbench pressure, aimed to demonstrate parliament's responsiveness to the requirements of new electors.

The most significant was legislation affecting working conditions. Pressure for trade union reform came from both workmen and 'New Model' masters. From the 1850s, emphasis on the place of 'natural laws' had made magistrates more willing to take a narrowly free-market view of employment contracts, to declare unions' activity to be in restraint of trade, and to debar them from legal protection of funds. This culminated in the *Hornby versus Close* decision of 1867 against the Boilermakers' Society. The Trades Union Congress was formed in 1868 to lobby for a change in the law; so did Mundella, Hughes and other parliamentary friends of the unions. The result was the Trade Union Act of 1871, which protected union members and their funds from the threat of prosecution for restraining trade. At the same time, the Criminal Law Amendment Act confirmed that threatening or obstructive behaviour by masters or workmen was an offence. This was interpreted by some magistrates as outlawing peaceful picketing; seven Welsh women were imprisoned for saying 'Bah!' to a blackleg. In reaction to such decisions, Liberal pressure for further change built up in 1873, but no action was possible before the dissolution of January 1874. So peaceful picketing was not legalised until 1875 (that is, by a Conservative government, but this, contrary to received wisdom, was not significant).[15] Mundella's Act of 1872 regulated arbitration procedure and bound both sides to honour certain types of agreement. The 1872 Mines Regulation Act established a detailed code of regulations covering safety, age and conditions of employment, and education of boy workers (minimum age 12). It was accompanied by an increase in the powers and a doubling in the number of inspectors and was the first act in this area to be effective.[16] The same was true of the 1870 Factories and Workshops Act. In the 1870s, full-time child employment was in practice outlawed, as was women's labour above ten hours a day. Meanwhile, Lubbock's Act of 1871 introduced four annual Bank Holidays (in England).

The emergence of trade unions as political bodies also facilitated the settlement, in 1872, of the long-standing radical demand for the secret ballot in parliamentary and municipal elections. This was a ritual demand of the new MPs: in 1868, 151 election addresses had urged it. The ballot appealed for two contrasting reasons. It seemed to safeguard the purity of the voter against Conservative dictation in the counties or the temptation of treating in the corrupt smaller boroughs, which flourished during the abnormally long preparation for the 1868 election. But it also diminished the danger of intimidation of inexperienced voters in the larger towns by powerful trade unions. And the indiscriminate lowering of the borough franchise in 1867 weakened the main argument against it, that electors were privileged trustees for the well-being of the community, and that scrutiny and guidance of their behaviour by non-electors were legitimate.*

Liberal backbench pressure was also responsible for the first concentrated

---

* Many Liberals, including Gladstone, were reluctant converts to the new principle, which implied that the electoral process was henceforth to be a free-for-all among competing selfish interests.

attack on discrimination against women. One grievance was the archaic state of common law, which did not recognise a wife's separate right to her personal property (the census of 1861 revealed that there were 839,000 married working women). Another was the lack of proper professional education for middle-class women, and a third, the need for enfranchisement at national and local level. These issues had been lobbied at the Social Science Association, and by local groups, most importantly that around the Liberal MP for Manchester, Jacob Bright, and his wife. Under pressure from them, in 1867, the SSA prepared a bill to give a married woman the same legal rights over property as an unmarried one. The problem affected poor women especially, since those with sufficient property to make it worthwhile could use the rules of equity to protect their property by trust. The question had been discussed in parliament before, in 1857, but between 1868 and 1870, in the new political climate, it received much greater press discussion. Jacob Bright's 1870 bill, supported by government, passed into law. It specified three important types of property which women could own separately, and so did not interfere with the principles of common law. Once the Judicature Act of 1873 had reformed the legal code, establishing the supremacy of equity over the common law, a more thoroughgoing reform could be passed by the next Liberal government, in 1882. This allowed all married women an equitable marriage settlement preserving their separate title to all existing and subsequently-acquired property. In 1872, private members anxious about the incidence of rape and infanticide secured the passage of the Bastardy Laws Amendment Act. This aimed to relieve single mothers from bearing the cost of supporting their children, by greatly increasing the rights of JPs to force fathers to contribute to their maintenance and education.

In 1869, Jacob Bright amended the Municipal Franchise Bill to give unmarried women the vote on the same ratepayer franchise as men; in 1872, 109,000 women were on the municipal register, 12 per cent of the total.[17] In 1870, they were given the vote on school boards, while, amid much petitioning, his Women's (parliamentary) Suffrage Bill passed its second reading, though this was the highpoint of the women's suffrage cause until the 1880s.* In 1869, a backbench amendment to the Endowed Schools Bill allowed the Commissioners to allocate ancient endowments to girls' schools as well as to boys'. The Taunton Commission had been scathing about the inadequacy of girls' education, and over ninety girls' schools were created

---

* In 1883, it was defeated by only 16 votes (114:130), but Gladstone (an opponent) suppressed a move to include it in the Reform settlement of 1884 on the grounds that it would endanger the whole package. His 1880s governments saw other steps being taken on women's issues, though. The Contagious Diseases Acts were repealed in moves culminating in 1886, both because they offended now-powerful women's activists and because medical opinion had recognised their futility in tackling venereal disease. The Matrimonial Causes Act of 1884 protected women from having to comply with a decree for the restitution of their husband's conjugal rights.

under the terms of the act. Reform of girls' education was advocated on the grounds that middle-class women existed 'in affluence and idleness . . . wasting their lives in luxurious drawing-rooms' and often 'sunk in abject and frivolous superstition'. If educated, they would be better and more efficient members of the community, would diffuse 'intellectual culture and moral elevation' among the family, and would sustain their menfolk in a necessary 'rational manly piety'.[18]

The other notable backbench campaign for working-men's interests was the open spaces movement. Following an inquiry into the status of Wimbledon Common, Liberal MPs and intellectuals were to the fore in founding, in 1865, a society to restrict the enclosure of commons. Cowper-Temple and Shaw-Lefevre were the two leading lights; Hughes, Mill and Fawcett were influential early members; Lubbock, Harcourt and Samuel Morley were prominent subscribers. Some were just anxious to promote the health and recreation of the working-man. Others, like the writer Leslie Stephen, an early Secretary of the Society, were intellectual stoics for whom exercise celebrated the individuality and energy of mankind, a theme equally prominent in the Alpinist craze of these years. The Commons Preservation Society fought court cases to vindicate the rights of commoners in such places as Hampstead and Plumstead. It won a series of cases against enclosure-minded Lords of the Manor, but these were expensive. In 1866, Cowper-Temple's Metropolitan Commons Act facilitated the process of preservation. As a result of this and private acts, Blackheath, Hampstead Heath, Clapham Common, Wormwood Scrubs and a number of other London parks were secured for the people between 1870 and 1880. The major demonstration that this was a cause dear to Liberal backbenchers' hearts came in 1871, when Cowper-Temple led a revolt against the stringent economy of Gladstone and Lowe at the Treasury, which was threatening public access to Epping Forest. In the 1840s and 1850s, crown forestal rights over most of the land were sold so that the owners could inclose it for productive gain; the area of forest was reduced from 9,000 to 3,000 acres between 1793 and 1870. In 1870 Lowe announced plans to release 2,400 more acres for sale and to keep just 600 for recreation. The backbench revolt of 1871 defeated this plan. Cowper-Temple explained that 'in Bethnal Green alone there are no fewer than eight entomological societies, consisting of working men, who found in the Forest . . . new and beautiful species of butterflies'.[19] Instead, a Royal Commission met, legal battles were fought, the inclosure of 3,000 acres over the previous twenty years was declared unlawful, and in 1878 the Corporation of London, which had already bought much of the enclosed land, was required to buy and manage the rest for the public (it had secured 5,530 acres by 1884). After 1868, Liberals turned their attention also to rural commons. Legislation was not possible until 1876, and that was a compromise, but, in the meantime, Liberal pressure from Fawcett and Cowper-Temple secured the suspension, from 1869, of all enclosure schemes.[20]

In these respects, Liberals sought to demonstrate their responsiveness to the new electorate. Yet, even here, that electorate was more the recipient than the creator of the Liberal agenda.* The rest of this chapter examines the great expansion in the powers of local government, where that was more explicitly the case. Here we see the application of a coherent Liberal programme of education, social science, economy and devolution. The object was to develop what was called 'self-government' and 'self-development' in a moral, rational, pluralist political society. These were the most recurring aspirations in Andrew Reid's 1885 collection of responses by famous men on the subject, *Why I am a Liberal*. No quotation more elegantly encapsulates the 'heart of Liberalism' at this time than L.T. Hobhouse's retrospective definition of 1911:

> to foster the development of will, of personality, of self control . . . Liberalism is the belief that society can safely be founded on this self-directing power of personality, that it is only on this foundation that a true community can be built, and that so established its foundations are so deep and so wide that there is no limit that we can place to the extent of the building.[21]

For nearly all mid-Victorian Liberals, 'personality' was conceived in specifically Christian terms. Had it not been, their mission to extend 'self-government', and their confidence in the safety and propriety of doing so, would have lost almost all power, meaning and logic. Liberals of the 1860s and 1870s increasingly expressed an incarnationalist confidence in the divinely-instilled potential of all humanity and the possibility and duty of creating a true human brotherhood. But this was perfectly compatible with an underlying insecurity about working-class morals and a strong commitment to the use of law to regulate human liberty in ways consonant with progress. Defence of 'the reign of law', and confidence in its conseqences, was a Liberal commonplace. One of Hughes's objections to Palmerston's slack, jokey, 'devil-may-care leadership' was that it gave a 'shake' to the 'old reverence for law'.[22] Liberals were committed to reform of local government powers because it promised to strengthen order, accountable elite leadership, and popular Christian development all at the same time.

Moral, social and local government reform

From 1868, the pace of Liberal legislation noticeably accelerated. A number of factors came together to ensure this: the Royal Commission reports of the 1860s; the constructive pressure of new MPs; Gladstone's energetic, restless

---

*　One radical pundit claimed that the Gladstone government did not tackle matters of direct concern to the working classes: the landlord-tenant question, the repeal of the Criminal Law Amendment Act, the difficulty of gaining really cheap divorce, and so on. See T. Frost, *Forty years' recollections: literary and political* (1880), pp. 312–13.

conception of executive government; and the influence of men like Forster, Goschen and Bruce in cabinet. The appointment in 1869 of Henry Thring as the first parliamentary counsel to the Treasury also helped. This office became responsible for preparing all government bills, its brief being to prevent departments from introducing shoddy, inconsistent or unbudgeted legislation. 'Efficient' institutional reform was applied to the civil service when, in 1870, Gladstone and Lowe opened most posts to competition by examination.*

The most pressing problem after 1867 was working-class education. This was an issue attractive to all parts of the party. It was a necessary defence mechanism after 1867, a vehicle for working-men's liberation and character-formation, a challenge to the church's complacency in its provision of schooling, a pathway to improved national efficiency, and a means of assaulting improvidence, vice and crime. Russell, Hartington and Lowe all urged swift action. Voluntaryism quickly lost support; leading noncon-formists Edward Baines and R.W. Dale renounced their traditional ani-mosity to state aid. In 1867 Bruce and Forster's bill renewed the attempt to give ratepayers the power to establish local boards to create and run schools where existing provision was deemed inadequate. In 1868 their bill included provisions to force boards on recalcitrant localities.

The Elementary Education Act of 1870, establishing a national system of education, was the legacy of this general concern. Like so many of the social reforms of the first Gladstone government, it was essentially a cross-party measure. It could pass only if it safeguarded the position of voluntary schools (something regarded as crucial both by Conservatives and Glad-stone). There was a protracted and complex debate, mainly on religious grounds, over the details (see page 263), but this should not detract from the massive significance of the act, nor disguise the satisfaction in the party at its passage. It provided that, where existing voluntary provision was deemed insufficient after a short period of grace, locally-elected school boards would be established to build and maintain schools and to fund them from the rates. As intended, this gave a great fillip to church activity. The number of children attending denominational schools rose from 1.15 to 1.98 million between 1870 and 1880 (as against 770,000 in board schools), and Anglicans had raised £12¼ million for educational provision by 1883.[23] But the act also presaged an inexorable extension of state and local funding and supervision in future years. Local boards and (from 1876) attendance com-mittees in areas without boards were empowered to enforce attendance, though with mixed results, especially in rural districts. In 1880 the new Liberal government made education compulsory as part of its attack on sloppy county administration. Successive 'codes', issued by the Education Department, specified and widened the nature of the curriculum: by 1876

---

* Demurring departments could opt out; the Foreign Office did. Civil service reform also removed one of the few remaining sources of patronage available to the chief whip, so demonstrating further the 'neutrality' of the state.

this might include algebra, Euclid, botany, animal physiology and English literature.[24] In 1882 the 'New Code' encouraged a further broadening, with the teaching of subjects from cooking to chemistry being subsidised. It also sought to stimulate higher grade schooling. By 1885 the annual education grant stood at £5.1 million, over three times the 1870 figure.

Forster had originally intended the school boards to be appointed by town councils and parish vestries, but backbench pressure at the dawn of urban democracy forced direct ratepayer election instead.* This had great implications for political participation, especially in the towns. The school board election contests turned on questions of real local and denominational significance. Interest in local government was boosted. So was national electoral organisation, since the elections trained thousands of party activists.

The advent of elected school boards was one more step towards the establishment of an efficient pluralist political order. Another was provided by the Local Government and Public Health Acts of 1871 and 1872. In 1871, the Poor Law Board and the medical department of the Privy Council were amalgamated into a new Local Government Board. The new department was to be responsible for the Poor Law, public health, and most other local government matters. A comprehensive network of local sanitary authorities was created under it in 1872, each with specific obligations and a medical officer. In towns, the existing agencies (municipal councils or boards of health) were to be rechristened urban sanitary authorities; elsewhere boards of guardians were required to form rural sanitary authorities. Their powers were codified in consolidating legislation of 1875. The object was to decentralise: to improve local professionalism rather than add to state power.[25]

The function of the Local Government Board was twofold: to check unsound behaviour by local authorities – so protecting the interests of ratepayers and inspiring confidence among lenders in their management of capital – and to facilitate the acquisition of local powers. From 1868, it and its predecessor audited local authorities directly. This gave security for a massive expansion of local expenditure and borrowing. Sanctioned loans to local authorities had been £7.4 million between 1858 and 1871; between 1871 and 1884 they totalled £31.5 million.[26] The LGB presided over a vast growth of the system of Provisional Order legislation, which went very far to replacing altogether the traditional cumbrous private bill procedure. Local authorities submitted schemes to it. If approved, these were embodied in Provisional Orders, which became law either after a fixed period or if confirmed by parliament, in schedules, usually on the nod. Typically, Provisional Orders altered local authority boundaries and hence fiscal burdens, or gave authorities additional public health powers, control of gas and water works or (from the 1880s) power to supply electricity. The LGB

---

* The cumulative vote was chosen in order to protect religious minorities. It gave voters as many votes as there were vacancies; they could allocate as many as they chose to one candidate.

checked byelaws issued by local authorities and issued model byelaws as a guide.

This new structure, together with the increasing activity of urban leaders after the Second Reform Act, gave a massive boost to municipal powers. The fashion of the 1870s became to municipalise civic gas and water supplies, with the number of urban districts providing some supply of water rising from 250 to 413 between 1871 and 1879.[27] Forty-three local authorities adopted the Public Library Acts in the 1870s, as against 34 in the previous twenty years.[28] The most famous advocate of dynamic local government in the 1870s, Joseph Chamberlain in Birmingham, was less a pioneer than a typical exponent of liberating local energies for such purposes. The Birmingham town council under his leadership overhauled sanitation, sewerage and paving. (Less typically, it also bought up 90 acres of slum property to develop for commercial purposes.) Helped by developments in education and sanitation, local government expenditure country-wide rose from £27.3 million in 1870 to £55.5 million in 1882. Death rates were cut by one-third between 1870 and 1900. The most obvious symbols of this new civic confidence were the great municipal buildings of the north and midlands: the Gothic town halls of Manchester (1868–77), Bradford (1869–73) and Rochdale (1866–71), the Renaissance council house, museum and art gallery in Birmingham (1874–85), the Walker art gallery and Picton reading room in Liverpool (1874–9), the Leeds municipal buildings (1876–84), and the many magistrates' courts, public libraries and so on in smaller towns.

This assertiveness in policy and architectural matters can be seen as a demonstration of the power of provincial commercial leaders. Their local profile needed heightening not only because of the importance of educating the electors enfranchised in 1867 but also because of the need to check the rise of economy movements on local councils which endangered the sanitation and other expenditure necessary to create more harmony between classes. So the 1860s saw the development of the civic gospel: the ideal of social service, class harmony and religious brotherhood in municipal life, aimed at persuading ratepayers to condone higher spending and merchants to play their due and benevolent part in local government.[29]* The Birmingham Dissenting preacher R.W. Dale urged commercial leaders to join the town council and board of guardians on the grounds that 'the man who holds municipal or political office is a "minister of God"'. In this he followed George Dawson, Birmingham's unitarian pastor who did most to create the vision of the town as 'a solemn organism through which should flow, and in which should be shaped all the highest, loftiest and truest ends of man's moral nature', in which 'sectarianism' and harsh 'political economy' would be forgotten and 'brotherhood' found.[31]

* One great advantage of municipalisation, in fact, was that it helped to solve the rating problem: the Birmingham gas works made the council an annual profit of about £25,000–£30,000.[30]

Central government and revitalised local authorities worked together after 1867 to improve popular morals – an agenda which was the more attractive to local bodies because most were still elected on a plural-voting propertied franchise.* One component of this agenda was a series of reforms in the Poor Law. Increased poor rates had led to public irritation at what seemed an increasing and character-sapping lack of discrimination by reckless alms-giving and inefficient or sentimental local authorities. From the late 1860s, the Poor Law Board mounted a campaign against outrelief. The workhouse labour test was extended, while, as noted above, more stringent sanctions were applied against fathers of illegitimate children. Between 1868/9 and 1873/4, the Poor Law rate per head of population fell from 7s 3/4d to 6s 6d, and the percentage of adult male paupers receiving workhouse relief rose from 21.8 per cent to 28.6 per cent.[32] Meanwhile Poor Law medical services were expanded to cater for the sick poor by the building of general and specialist hospitals. Authorities were encouraged to separate infirmaries and dispensaries from the stigma of the workhouse so that the respectable classes could make more use of them. So state guidance would encourage more suitable treatment for the deserving and tighten discipline on the undeserving. Similar thinking led to a new victory for hard-line prison reformers. The Habitual Criminals Act of 1869 placed twice-convicted criminals under supervision for seven years after discharge and made them liable to detention if they were found in suspicious circumstances, even in the absence of evidence of ill-doing. Home Secretary Bruce promised government 'assistance and encouragement to the reclaimable' but to hunt 'the hopelessly irreclaimable . . . down without mercy'.[33] The extension of education, meanwhile, would increase the proportion of 'reclaimables' in future generations.

Against drunkenness, also, moral superintendence was increased. The institution of free trade in beer, from 1830, had always had its critics, not least because 25,000 new beershops had opened in the six months after the act passed. In the 1850s, 'respectable' pressure for the return of licensing control to magistrates was strong, but defeated by the prevailing free-

---

* Boards of guardians, and boards of health outside municipal boroughs, retained a property-weighted plural voting franchise until 1894. In municipal boroughs the ratepayer franchise of 1835 was retained until 1918. However, a backbench bill of 1869, which the government could hardly resist, lowered the qualification period for ratepayers from $2\frac{1}{2}$ years to one year. It also established the right of compound householders in all towns to vote (in some the right had already been given by an act of 1850). Together with the enfranchisement of unmarried women ratepayers, this meant that 13 to 18 per cent of the population now enjoyed the municipal franchise. The property qualification for councillors was abolished in 1882, but Liberals had not wanted it even in 1835. As a result, there was a slight increase in trade union membership of municipal councils, especially among gasworkers and dockers keen to safeguard their interests as a result of the municipalisation of services. In the 1890s, 5–6 per cent of Birmingham council were trade unionists or skilled workers.

market climate. As in so many areas, the raised working-class political profile after 1867 brought swift action at local level – prosecutions for drunkenness rose by a quarter in the last half of the 1860s – and then nationally. A cross-party private members' act in 1869 returned beershops to magistrates' control; they could refuse renewal of licences on an inspection of the character of applicants. The government's 1872 Licensing Act then established more systematic licence renewal procedures for public houses. This, too, was a cross-party measure rather than a victory for puritan extremists. Liberals did not give into temperance pressure to reduce the number of public houses, which they thought would merely increase publicans' monopoly profits. The act's real significance was to establish compulsory opening hours and to increase penalties for drunkenness and for publicans who encouraged anti-social behaviour. Magistrates had the power to shut public houses which carried on a disorderly trade. The 1869 and 1872 acts greatly extended police surveillance of drinking places. Prosecutions for drunkenness rose by a half in the five years after 1872.

Among the many attractions to Liberal leaders of devolving powers to local bodies in this way, one noteworthy one is often forgotten: that it diminished radicals' ability to criticise central government. This was particularly noticeable during the controversy about the 1870 Education Act. Radical Dissenters' complaints about Clause 25 (see page 264) were solved by local school board elections, allowing them to continue to vote Liberal at national level. It also neutered the other great provincial Dissenting group, the temperance lobby. They demanded 'local option' on the number of public houses allowed, and their ideal was for complete 'local veto' by plebiscite. But the local veto was unpopular with libertarian intellectuals, Liberal brewers, working-men for whom moderate drinking was a symbol of self-discipline, and the floating but thirsty voter. However, support for some sort of local option – which might mean merely control of licences by elected councillors rather than by unelected magistrates lacking public confidence – was compatible with Liberal doctrine on self-government. So in 1883, Gladstone and Home Secretary Harcourt, previously a proponent of libertarianism in licensing, voted for the temperance group's vague 'local option' motion, which passed decisively (288:141). Prohibitionist expectations were high; Gladstone was toasted in lemonade; but nothing happened. It became known that the cabinet would treat the question as part of their general review of local government, which was never completed.

Not surprisingly, local government was attractive to all elements of the Liberal party: it looked popular and devolutionary, yet strengthened government authority and limited the scope of sectional Westminster radicalism. When, in 1886, Hartington claimed that the 'extension of popular self-government all over the country' was a firm Liberal principle, he was agreeing with Chamberlain's view that 'the most fruitful field before reformers at the present time is to be found in an extension of the functions and authority of local government'.[34]

Liberals also turned their attention to the reform of county government. But their main concern was not, in fact, the unelected nature of Quarter Sessions, though that was a significant consideration for some radicals. After all, tenant-farmers would be the biggest beneficiaries of a ratepayer franchise, and they were as tory as, and less public-spirited than, the squires. The real problem, rather, was that there was little drive for social improvement in counties, because the rate burden was already too big for ratepayers' comfort. Throughout the century, central government imposed more and more duties on county magistrates (particularly in matters of police and prisons), yet subsidy from central coffers did not improve as much. This caused resentment, especially since rates were levied only on real property and so bore unduly heavily on farmers and other small occupiers, as against industrial and commercial profits. So ratepayers lobbied for lower, not higher, rates. Yet, compared to the boroughs, administration appeared backward in providing sanitation, education, communal open spaces, libraries or baths. In the 1870s, a strong cross-party movement of tory and Liberal county MPs, and the powerful Central Chamber of Agriculture (founded in 1865), protested against further burdens on the rates. A number of government bills in 1871 and 1872, which would have imposed charges on county ratepayers for vaccination, the militia, election expenses and so on, were withdrawn or defeated in consequence. So Liberals who wished to improve county government were trapped. They doubted if setting up councils elected by ratepayers would generate more enlightened leadership. But they could not accept the demands of what became known as the local taxation movement, to subsidise county rates from central government revenue, because this meant subsidising the rule of unelected JPs. Also, many radicals accused magistrates of rating landowners too leniently.

Though Liberals tinkered with county government reform, they could not satisfy both the advocates of lower rates and the demands of social reformers. Between 1869 and 1871, Goschen, the responsible cabinet minister, drew up a massive restructuring of local government and finance. He planned elected county boards, and a reform of the rating system, in order to make the burden of local expenditure fall more heavily on local landowner-JPs, so that their rule would become less extravagant. But landowner-local taxation opposition in the Commons forced the scheme's withdrawal. The CCA claimed to support county financial boards, but only if rates fell less heavily on property. Conservative victory in 1874 then sharpened Liberal hostility to tory landowner domination in rural areas. Agricultural depression in the late 1870s increased social tension. It augmented tenant-farmer irritation at high rating levels, and indicated to Liberals the need for a benevolent, solicitous county government, capable of restoring good relations between classes. This, Liberals maintained, could not be done without elections. In opposition, Liberals developed a commitment to elected county boards and a reform of the rating system so as to make authorities truly 'responsible to the ratepayers'.[35] But, though the issue was heavily publicised in the 1880 campaign, Gladstone's second government, suffering from an overcrowded legislative programme, made no progress on it. This was partly because there was division about how to apportion the rates. The local taxation movement continued to press for the rating of personal property, which many Liberals would not accept, and in fact was partly responsible for the government's final defeat in 1885. There was also a dispute about how direct election should be, since a simple ratepayer franchise would probably give fewer securities for order and social enlightenment than the gentry and the permanent professional officials who ran the Quarter Sessions committees. County government reform was never central to Liberal thoughts, and was too socially divisive. So it was left to the Conservatives to establish county councils in 1888.*

In fact, Liberals were less interested in county government reform than in extending rural landownership. This became a major question in the 1870s, especially with the onset of severe agricultural depression. Radicals were irritated at the revelation, in a parliamentary return of 1874, that a quarter of the land in England and Wales was owned by 710 people, and nearly three-quarters by 5,000.[36] 'Monopoly' and complacency could be blamed for inadequate investment. Propertied Liberals preferred to put the point differently. Hartington, the Liberal leader in 1880, assured depressed tenant-farmers that sorely needed capital application to agriculture was being frustrated, not by the selfishness of the landlord, but by the encumbrances of mortgages and jointures, and other restrictions, which prevented him from realising his wealth. At that election, Liberals united in urging the extension of the principles of free trade and efficiency to the land market: the abolition, where practicable, of legal restrictions on the sale and development of large blocks of land – of what Hartington called 'all artificial obstructions [to] the scientific cultivation of the soil'.[37] However, this alone would not satisfy tenant-farmers, who were irritated by their lack of formal rights over the land. They argued that investment was impracticable without greater security for a return on crops, which the land and game laws frustrated because, in the name of 'freedom of contract', tenants were forced by landlords to renounce customary rights.

Liberal land legislation in the 1880s responded to all those grievances. Gladstone's 1880 budget abolished the malt tax, something desired by landlord and tenant for fifty years, and converted it into a beer duty. This repealed a tax on a raw material, unfair on the farmer who was exposed to the savage winds of open international competition.[38] The 1880 Ground Game Act invalidated all agreements which landlords extracted from tenants

---

* With the same constitution as the municipal boroughs of 1835. There were several significant exemptions from elected council control: powers of justice and licensing stayed with magistrates, and they shared responsibility for the police with a council committee. Moreover, towns with 50,000 people were normally made county boroughs, with completely separate powers, so the county councils had relatively little taxable wealth and – before the transfer of education in 1902 – uncontroversial powers: over highways, lunatic asylums, livestock disease regulation and so forth.

by which the latter agreed to leave hares and rabbits to ravage their crops while fattening as game for landlords. Landlords and tenants were now to have concurrent rights to kill such game, while landlord privileges to shoot airborne game remained intact. The 1882 Settled Land Act aimed to give life tenants as much freedom to sell, lease or improve their estates as was compatible with the survival of the idea of family settlements (by which the descent of landed property was normally regulated). It freed land from most of the fetters of entail without abolishing the principle. It sought to encourage capital improvement by life tenants previously fearful that they would not realise their investment. It was a major piece of land reform, yet was uncontentious (it was a cross-party measure introduced by a Conservative). The 1883 Agricultural Holdings Act gave the tenant the right to compensation for specified types of temporary or, if permitted by his landlord, permanent improvements to his land. The aim, again, was to assist tenant investment in improvements, while safeguarding landlord control over general estate policy.

All these bills won general party approval, because they talked the language of efficiency, capitalisation and the spread of ownership and responsibility for land. A small minority pointed out that the Ground Game and Agricultural Holdings Acts offended against the principle of freedom of contract and thus the pure milk of political economy (so did the 1880 Employers' Liability Act, which made an employer liable for personal injuries sustained at his works as a result of negligence by other employees). Such measures raised eyebrows in two sections of the Liberal party, the 'scientific' intelligentsia represented by men like Lowe, Argyll, Goschen and rising men like Leonard Courtney, and those whose economic interests seemed threatened by it. The latter included landowners, but also employers and railway directors, such as Sir Edward Watkin. The Liberty and Property Defence League was set up in 1882 in order to lobby against legislation of this sort. Founded by Lord Elcho, an ex-Peelite Liberal and a leading anti-Reformer in 1866, it was backed by prominent whig political economist peers like Grey, Halifax, Fortescue, Somerset, Lyveden and Sutherland. A government bill of 1884 to increase protection for merchant seamen foundered against hostile lobbying from shipowners and LPDL supporters.[39]

It is wrong, though, to give propertied whig fears about a shift by government towards discriminating in favour of the poor much political significance, as those who write about the subsequent splits in the party often do.[40] Most Liberals who broke with Gladstone in 1886 continued to vote with their old party on questions of land reform in Britain and Ireland (as on questions of local government and franchise reform).[41] Commons criticism of the 1880–3 bills was confined to isolated Liberal MPs, like H.R. Brand on ground game. The measures were moderate, designed to preserve landlord rights wherever possible, and encourage the free flow of capital. Game law reform solved one of the most socially contentious issues for Liberal candidates in rural areas in the 1860s and 1870s. The supporters of the 1880 act argued that, in reality, it upheld freedom of contract by giving a pragmatic protection to a tenant who was otherwise unable to bargain effectively against his landlord.[42] Ministers pointed out that previous legislation – such as truck and merchant shipping acts – had frequently restricted freedom of contract on similar grounds.* For the tories, Salisbury frequently said in the 1880s that freedom of contract was indefensible when incompatible with morality or true commercial interests.[43] Gladstone and his ministers explicitly ruled out advanced measures of land reform, such as fixity of tenure or a court for the revision of rents.[44]† In 1885, Argyll told Gladstone that no significant defection of Liberal landowners had yet taken place.[46] In fact, Liberal anxiety about property in the 1880s was prompted mainly by Chamberlain's radical plans, which involved giving local authorities power to acquire land compulsorily to let out to labourers as allotments and smallholdings at a 'fair rent'. The notion of a 'fair rent' set by a directly elected body anxious to bid for support alarmed many Liberals, not just landowners (since there was no reason why the same principle should not be applied to urban rents or indeed wages). They thought it utopian to imagine, and dangerous to pretend, that local bodies could establish a happy peasant proprietorship by such means. Instead, landowners should be encouraged to provide allotments and smallholdings voluntarily.[47] However, Chamberlain's ideas were not widely held where it mattered in the party.‡

In this chapter we have noticed that policy in a number of fields after 1867 increasingly shunned purist definitions of political economy. This should not surprise us; politicians were faced with the need to respond to the mass electorate, and they compromised accordingly. The fact is that Liberals were never the party of doctrinaire political economy, but the party of integration. They were a political, not an economic force and the requirements of political reconciliation came first. Few Liberals who mattered found this drift of policy alarming, and in any case it affected the Conservative party as much. Friction on political economy may have contributed a little to the tense atmosphere within the Liberal party in the mid-1880s, but questions of economic principle were not important enough to cause a major split. Liberals were committed to using the powers of central and

---

* So far was the 1880 Ground Game Act not a novel concession to radicals that the government of 1831 had wished to vest the legal right to kill game with the occupier unless the lease specifically reserved it to the landlord – but the Lords amended the clause.

† At Midlothian, Gladstone had even defended large landed estates as better than a multiplication of ownership.[45]

‡ So fear for property rights was a factor in the split of 1886 only in the sense that it was one among many topics on which seceding Liberals might worry that Gladstone might at a future date make an unprincipled bid for sectional radical support. Chapters 11 and 12 explain why this view of Gladstone as an unpredictable populist arose; but it was always much more implausible that he would strike at property rights than at the other contentious interests discussed in those chapters.

local government pragmatically and constructively, so as to secure order, economy, free-market conditions and self-improvement. Between 1868 and 1885, this agenda was strikingly successful, and it could have continued to supply fruitful work for many years after then. It was a primarily administrative and elitist agenda; it made no real concessions to class interests, nor was it a programme driven by constituency organisation. There is no substance in the argument that 'whigs' and 'radicals' were unable to agree on a domestic policy in the 1880s. The development of 'self-government' had been found compatible with the extension of moral guidance and the preservation of class harmony. Social policy had helped to tackle the key Liberal task in a quasi-democracy, to promote rather than to damage civilised values – the values of law, property, religion and economy, underpinning the extension of true liberty. But Liberals also had to do this in other policy areas. There, they were not so united or successful. Chapters 11 and 12 discuss why this was. It had much to do with the role of one man: William Ewart Gladstone.

CHAPTER 11

Gladstone's Liberalism and its critics

GLADSTONE CONDONED MOST of the agenda set out in chapter 10. But hardly any of it was his. It arose from within the whig-Liberal tradition, updated to cope with political needs after 1867. Gladstone was not from that tradition; he was a Peelite. In essentials, Gladstone's aims remained conservative: he passionately upheld the legitimate authority of government and the Church, and believed in rule by property and in the superiority of traditional constitutional arrangements. But he had a distinctive approach to achieving these ends: he worked to restrain the arrogance of government, moralise the aristocracy, and shelter the church from the dangers involved in association with politics and political controversy. He sought to win popular respect for the existing order by associating men of property with a system of pure, low-spending, efficient government. This urge was intensified by his extraordinarily strong sense of corruption and of man's duty to struggle against it. His public speeches from the 1860s displayed extreme sensitivity to the responsibilities of modern government. He stressed that to rule Britain and her empire in the complex modern world was so great a burden that it 'altogether transcends and exceeds human strength'.[1] He felt that only by arousing the popular consciousness was it possible to check abuses of government power and other manifestations of class-preference or class hostility in public life. So he turned politics into a combat with complacency and vested interests. He sought to create and maintain a self-questioning, evangelised and ever-alert political society.

The theme of the rest of this book is that the conservatism of Gladstone's *ends* gives an inadequate impression of the destabilising effect on the party of his *means* of achieving them. His particular political concerns were with finance, religion and the immorality of coercive or careless government; everything else in politics was to him just mundane administration. His economising zeal, his foreign policy, his instincts about Ireland, his hostility to clumsy parliamentary interference with the doctrine and discipline of his beloved Church of England, all took the form they did because of his drive to eradicate incompetent, boastful over-government. The problem for the Liberal party was that these attitudes could be very controversial, because of Gladstone's own forcefulness in promoting them, and because they meshed, or seemed to mesh, so well with the intemperate agitations by provincial Liberal groups for severe retrenchment, religious radicalism, 'sentimental' foreign policy, or Irish self-government. It was in these areas that the Gladstonian party came to look so different from Palmerston's. This chapter examines Gladstone's outlook, the abstract criticisms levelled against it, and the history of religious, Irish, financial and foreign policy during his first government.

Gladstone and the Liberal party

Central to Gladstone's public life was his intense religious consciousness. To him, man's innate sinfulness was 'the great fact in the world'.[2] He convinced himself that politics involved a battle against the 'grievous and overwhelming mass' of 'sin' and 'sorrow' which misgovernment and man's nature inflicted on humanity.[3] Public life opened up so grand a 'field for the natural man' that 'ideals . . . are never realised'. Final victory over evil was impossible, but man's duty, nonetheless, was to struggle with as much 'energy' as possible against it.[4] Even his face, deeply lined, was 'more indicative of struggle than of victory', to one observer.[5] This conception of public life as a great burden of responsibility marked all his doings.

Gladstone believed that the fight against corruption depended on the vigour of national religion. Traditional Christian doctrine alone could show man his duty to seek redemption through struggle; it was the fundamental safeguard of human happiness.[6] By the 1860s and 1870s, he identified three great threats to its transmission. These were the materialism and complacency of a worldly modern society; the rationalising tendencies within the intelligentsia which offered 'quack' remedies for man's ills by suggesting that goodness could be propagated simply by moral precepts, rather than by surrender to the divine spirit; and anti-clerical whiggish interference with the purity of religious dogma and practice. The move towards democracy from 1867 placed a yet higher value on evangelisation. In response, Gladstone came to admire all those Christians, Anglican or Dissenter, whose zeal and reverence for God's message might 'keep in a state of freshness the heart and conscience of man'.[7]

As a young tory in the 1830s, Gladstone had invested high hopes in the church-state relationship as the supreme evangelising influence on public life. Indeed, this conception allowed him to devote his career to politics – which offered a fairer field for the expenditure of his massive reserves of energy and ambition – rather than to the church, as his conscience would otherwise have dictated. In the 1840s, Gladstone had been stunned to realise that the church-state connection was not doing its job in combatting moral and social chaos. Having discovered that government did not have the 'moral powers' to sustain a Christian society, he concluded that only public opinion could.[8] In the 1850s and 1860s, Gladstone awoke to the immense and evolving power of public opinion, and the duty of the politician to adjust to it in order to train its energies to effective ends. The orator's 'choice', he wrote in 1858, was to be 'what his age . . . requires in order to be moved by him; or else not to be at all'.[9]

Gladstone's movement into the Liberal party in the late 1850s was caused ultimately by his belief in most tories' inability to engage with shifting opinion so as to sustain efficient, moral government. His theology told him that, if humanity was afflicted by sin, it was also the greatest creation of the divine. God manifested himself in the power of 'Good attached to Personality'.[10] There was ample material here to be shaped for good.

From then on, Gladstone's political task, at its most abstract level, was to help to draw out the goodness within the human personality, in a crusade against selfishness, materialism and apathy wherever it occurred. In later life, one of his most constant refrains was the damage caused by the rise of a plutocracy, deficient in Christian feeling and morality. He blamed the worship of wealth for the social irresponsibility of the new rich, the damage their influence inflicted on social harmony, the desertion of selfish middle-class voters to a sectional Conservatism, and the decline of the quality of the Commons as landowners and administrators ceded dominance to 'the money power'.[11] In 1868, he ascribed the 'diminished watchfulness' about national expenditure to the recent rapid growth of wealth.[12] It was by arousing popular fervour as a counterbalance to moneyed apathy that Gladstone did most to change the image of British politics. In 1883, one Liberal remarked that it was chiefly owing to him that 'there never was a time when drawing-rooms, and snobberies of all kinds, had less practical influence than now'.[13]

Gladstone did not see this mobilisation of popular sentiment as in any way hostile to the maintenance of propertied government; rather the reverse. He systematically promoted Liberal aristocrats – Hartington, Rosebery, Spencer – to prominent positions in order to demonstrate to the people the suitability of landed families for popular leadership. In 1869, he wished to expand the numbers of administratively able peers in order to improve the Lords' tone, intelligence, responsiveness and reputation.[14] In 1871, he tried to send the dissolute Prince of Wales to Ireland as the queen's representative, in order to strengthen respect for the monarchy and to help form his 'character'.[15] As for the distribution of parliamentary seats, he remained a staunch defender of the small boroughs, which bolstered the representation of the landed and administrative classes. It was, he wrote, the 'natural condition of a healthy society' that the 'leisured class' should be the main rulers.[16] Gladstone idealised the aristocracy, perceiving it as willing to share his own mission to purify state administration against vested interests out for personal gain.

The people, then, were to press propertied rulers to campaign against abuses and vested interests. Meanwhile, the governing classes were to lead the electorate away from the temptation of selfish campaigns, and to encourage their innate 'sense of right and wrong . . . of humanity and justice'.[17]

In this way the Liberal party would bind together the marquesses and the masses. The goal of his leadership was to maintain the party as a cross-class machine for the development of a higher national unity. Gladstone, like most politicians bred in the early nineteenth century, believed that, while in a technical sense a two-party system was necessary to make government in parliament work, there was a natural ruling party with superior claims to reconcile all elements within the nation. He devoted much effort to keeping propertied Liberals in the party, in order to prevent the balance of opinion within it from shifting in favour of destructive policies urged by a particular class or sect. This also affected his attitude to toryism. Having invested Liberalism with the mantle of Peel, he was incapable of seeing his own Conservative opponents in any light other than 'factionalists' trading on 'class-preference'.[18] Modern Conservatism seemed to have lost its old judicious 'reverence' for authority and antiquity and to have been reduced to 'class-interest', bolstered by vile 'Tory democracy' which aimed at 'inflaming public passion' and teaching bad principles about foreign policy and finance.[19] It thus sought to hurry on the rule of plutocracy, to encourage popular ignorance, and, sooner or later, to create conditions in which assertive radicalism would have cause to mount a destructive campaign against institutions. Gladstone was taken aback by the revival of this bastard toryism as a real party of majority government between 1874 and 1880 and he was outraged when Disraeli started to pass legislation, in 1874, repealing previous Liberal measures, as in abolishing the Endowed Schools Commission.[20]

* * *

Though, on the face of it, Gladstone's strategy was conservative, the religious zeal with which he promoted it distanced him markedly from the integrationist, rational and parliamentary whig temper. The whigs believed in organic institutional reform, and open debate in parliament, in order to win popular confidence in political and religious institutions. Gladstone disliked institutional reform, abhorred anti-clericalism and, at times of stress, had little respect for 'parliamentary government'. This had crucial consequences for his politics.

Gladstone was profoundly hostile to whig erastianism and to other attempts to regulate the religious spirit by political institutions. Hence, for example, his opposition to the 1857 Divorce Act and the 1874 Public Worship Regulation Act. He disliked the anti-clerical whig/Dissenting alliance for its attempt to alter the teaching and status of church schools or Anglican universities, institutions whose survival he regarded as essential to the future of civilisation. Hence his reluctance to sanction the abolition of university tests and his lack of interest in the cause of state education. Both moves, he thought, would encourage more damaging interference with

Anglican teaching. Conversely, he lacked altogether the whig commitment to national establishments as agents of popular moralisation. Of course he greatly valued the church establishment, a unique parochial organisation. But he was attached to it as a branch of the Church Catholic, the trustee for historic church doctrine, and was willing to see disestablishment rather than political meddling with that doctrine, which he considered a much more powerful Christianising force than the church's temporal status. He had no faith in the ability of institutions to guide public opinion; hence his complete lack of interest in the defence of Protestant privileges in innately Catholic Ireland.

In short, Gladstone's prescription for the spread of right feeling was simple, but most unwhiggish: religion, not political institutions. In 1874, he remarked: 'as to its politics, this country has much less, I think, to fear than to hope; unless through a corruption of its religion – against which, as Conservative or as Liberal, I can perhaps say I have striven all my life long'.[21] If religious truth survived, Gladstone had an unqualified confidence in popular receptivity to it. In other words, Gladstone had a striking absence of doubt about the inherent moral capacity of 'the people'.

Nothing was more distinctive about Gladstone's Liberalism than his invocation of the moral worth of the 'people'. His rise in the Liberal party in the 1860s owed almost everything to his ability to suggest that he had a purchase on extra-parliamentary opinion, that he should head the party because he alone spoke the language to which they were willing to listen. His peculiar combination of fervent morality and crushing assertiveness convinced even Cobden and Bright that he had his finger on the pulse of small master, shopkeeper and artisan sentiment. They were not alone. Gladstone, whose failing was never lack of self-confidence, developed an extraordinary notion of his role, nay duty, as an instrument of God's will. He was to mould public opinion to noble ends. If Providence had entrusted him with a 'striking gift', he wrote in extreme old age, it was 'an insight into the facts of particular eras, and their relations one to another, which generates in the mind a conviction that the materials exist for forming a public opinion, and for directing it to a particular end'.[22]

So Gladstone's definition of the 'people's will', like that of his father's hero Canning before him, bore a remarkable resemblance to the values which he himself wanted to propagate. Though he would often talk of the superior wisdom of the 'popular judgment', this was because it seemed so responsive to his appeals.[23] His aim was to build on the biblical language of justice and sinfulness with which working-men were familiar, with a view to stimulating political virtue – while leaving the technical questions of which government mainly consisted in expert hands.[24] His populist political campaigns took the form that they did because of two particular qualities which his antennae claimed to discern in the public mind. One was the anxiety for economy and peace which Cobden and Bright kept saying were staunch beliefs of shopkeepers and artisans. The other was the commitment to the 'laws of eternal righteousness' which the leading Dissenting preachers

– who, he presumed, had a devoted popular following – expounded in the sermons which he read and approvingly scored.[25] Gladstone came to convince himself that he could lead the 'people' to oppose extravagance and immoral government. To him, this was conservative work. It would guide popular sentiment away from institutional radicalism, for his religious strategy promised to undermine hostility to the state-church link, while his financial plans would remove any anger at the existing distribution of political power. By the 1880s, he had supplanted the traditional language of radicalism with the suggestion that the primary purpose of political activity was to demonstrate the spiritual power of humanity itself, 'collective as well as individual man'. His rhetoric combined the evangelical language of struggle against corruption with an invocation of the potential of human brotherhood. Humanity, he asserted, had revealed powers and resources which offered the possibility that the Christian civilisation would escape the decline suffered by all its predecessors.[26] In 1886, a supporter described Gladstone's speeches as offering the 'Promised Land flowing with milk and honey'.[27] Such language probably struck chords with many working-men; it certainly did with sentimental intellectuals like John Morley who, rejecting orthodox Christianity, believed that men regenerated their 'moral energy' by 'spiritual contact with the mass of men'.[28]

Gladstone, then, was the man most responsible for developing the myth of 'the people' as a moral force, sharing essentially Christian sentiments, bound together in a spiritual campaign against injustice, and collectively charged with making responsible judgments about broad principles of government. He used this conception to batter parliament into doing good work. Like Peel, he never believed the whig myth that parliament could be properly representative of the people. Ever the good Peelite, he remained critical of the 1832 Reform Act for destroying the old constitutional equilibrium. In his eighties he startled even the Fellows of All Souls by insisting that 'in point of ability and efficiency . . . the country had never been better governed' than before 1830.[29] As an institution peopled by sinful men, parliament's tendency would always be to apathy and obstruction. In 1867, Gladstone asserted that 'agencies out of doors' which sought to form public opinion were the 'legitimate expressions of the people, by which bad legislation is to be corrected'.[30] Gladstone removed the moral centre of Liberalism away from parliament. Previous Liberal leaders had seen 'the people' as an aggregate of discrete elements reconciled by parliamentary debate. But, for Gladstone, parliament's main aim was to refine and process a continuous round of corrective, purifying legislation emanating from an executive anxious to satisfy a roused and coherent popular conscience that good was being done. Like Peel, he believed that the 'machine' of government needed constant oiling if it was to retain its perpetual, healthy, ordered motion, capable of stimulating all parts of the nation to useful and competitive labour. He gained immense satisfaction from taking personal charge of a large policy question and surmounting the obstacles to the formulation of a coherent, hard-hitting and defensible bill, such as the Irish bills of his first government.* His zeal for purification, superimposed on his Peelite inheritance, created a new conception of politics organised around an endless agenda of business. In 1877 he declared that the 'vital principle' of the party was 'action'.[32] This was news to most Liberals.

Crusader politics had many advantages: it helped to give the party a common aim, it strengthened Gladstone's credentials among provincial nonconformists, and it helped to educate the people into the benefits of political participation on class-free lines. But it was also essential temperamentally. Gladstone's reserves of energy were matched only by his constant need to burn them up in active endeavour and his sometimes manic frustration if the available outlets to do this proved insufficient. The perpetual drive to find these outlets – administrative, oratorical, sexual, spiritual – dominated his life. It inspired his rescue work, his recourse to flagellation, his hot-tempered parliamentary tirades, his urge to dominate large crowds, his tree-felling, and his series of vehement, whirlwind and unpredictable interventions on the political stage. Aberdeen once said of him: 'You must keep that damned fellow always in office, give him plenty to do, else he is sure to do mischief'.[33] To Spencer, he was 'governed by the most intense impulsiveness and enthusiasms'.[34] John Morley described him in 1886 as 'vehement and masterful beyond belief'.[35]

* * *

Gladstone's intention was to reorientate the Liberal cross-class alliance in pursuit of goals different from those of Palmerston or Russell, though not fundamentally so. Economy and propertied rule were to be defended by rousing public opinion to political participation under aristocratic leadership. Regulated franchise extension was beneficial, because it trained people 'for the habitual hereditary discharge of public duty' and increased 'the sum total of the public energies'.[36] The liberal and non-aggressive aspects of Palmerston's foreign policy were to be continued, but its triumphalist tone was to be replaced by a warning against corrupting, extravagant, unrestrained power; while still greater economies in defence were to be attempted. The whig-Dissenting anti-clerical coalition was to be succeeded by an alliance of earnest spiritual Anglicans (such as Frederick Temple and James Fraser), intellectuals and Dissenters against complacency and in favour of piety. His exercise of church patronage, about which he cared very greatly, was designed to show the church as a genuine and pure-minded spiritual force; this would help to defuse Dissenting hostility to its established status, and both bodies could then promote evangelisation in

---

* Gladstone's political appeal among the intellectual classes was largely founded on this ability to draft and explain complex legislation; it seemed an essential component of the rational and progressive politics which they believed Liberalism was promoting, and so partly compensated for his other defects.[31]

friendly apolitical rivalry. Gladstone also changed the balance within the Liberal coalition by exciting the consciousness of the Celtic peoples. He wrote in 1870 that Liberal policy was now to raise all the countries within the United Kingdom to 'the highest level of intelligence and civic energy'.[37] The Midlothian campaign of 1879–80 was a landmark in demonstrating to Scotsmen that they were an integral part of the British political community. In 1870, he appointed the first Welshman to a Welsh see since 1715; in 1881, he set a precedent by bowing to Welsh MPs' pressure for separate legislation for the Principality (characteristically, a Sunday Closing Act). And Gladstone sought to alter Liberal priorities on Ireland. Russell had urged restoring Irish Catholic *civil* rights as the way to get beneficial English economic and religious values accepted. But Gladstone wished to move away from the whiggish preoccupation with modernisation through political economy and mixed education; he wanted to show Irishmen that government recognised the customary rights of Irish tenants and the *spiritual* independence of Irish Catholics.

This conception of Liberalism as a joint and zealous struggle for economy, self-government and Christianisation was massively powerful and massively influential. Gladstone probably did more to moralise the people than any political leader in British history. But it had a number of flaws. The first was that it imposed a strain on traditional Liberal notions of progress through easy-going gentlemanly cabinet and parliamentary discussion. The combination of an extensive legislative programme and a personal popular appeal gave Gladstone greater power over his cabinet than that exercised by any previous Liberal leader. Gladstone interpreted opinion and his cabinet colleagues could then decide for themselves whether to follow him. Gladstone said that he never backed down from a course of action in deference to a colleague, preferring to 'leave behind those who can't keep up with me'.[38] Harcourt, on behalf of the 1880 cabinet, claimed that Gladstone 'regards the rest of us as children . . . by whose opinion he is not likely to be guided'.[39] Meanwhile, Gladstone became more and more irritated by the failure of parliament to set aside enough time for his ambitious legislative programme. Even in the 1870s, before Irish obstruction became serious, his legislative record was actually less effective than Palmerston's or even Russell's, because too much of it was too controversial.*
One answer was to give a majority of the House (if large enough) power to close debates and take a snap division; this was the famous 'closure' of 1882. The closure, however, was hardly used before 1886 (though it became standard practice thereafter), partly because Gladstone never thought it of

---

* I have analysed the fate of government bills introduced into the Commons for four different pairs of sessions: 1847–8, 1849–50, 1863–4 and 1871–2. The numbers passing were 195, 159, 178 and 152; the numbers withdrawn, 27, 18, 24 and 48; the numbers defeated 8, 26, 2 and 1; and the numbers sent to the Lords but not passed, 4, 9, 3 and 9. So the percentages passing were 83.3 per cent, 75 per cent, 86 per cent and 72.4 per cent.

much legislative benefit.[40] He was increasingly attracted by the more radical solution of devolving discussion of whole classes of legislation to other bodies or regional assemblies.

He found devolution attractive because it addressed his extreme sensitivity to the excessive burden of modern government.* This was a second source of tension because it cut across traditional Liberal notions of trusteeship, especially as regarded Ireland. He came to believe that disorder in Ireland was the consequence of a 'miserable & almost total want of the sense of responsibility for the public good & public peace'. As a result of that irresponsibility, Britain had to govern Ireland 'unaided by the people', an 'enormous weight', which was inevitably resented by the Irish peasantry.[42] Throughout the 1868 campaign Gladstone poured out his distaste at the 'painful' and 'shameful' state of Irish political culture, the failure of the British to secure 'love' for the law, and the urgent 'responsibility' on British voters, if they called themselves 'a Christian people', to work to create that love.[43] His solution, he announced in 1867, was to govern Ireland by 'Irish ideas'.[44] Major legislative surgery was needed to dissolve bitterness and restore the condition of a properly-regulated society, in which civil and proprietary rights were upheld, 'governing functions' were restored to 'the leisured class', and each man was guaranteed 'security for the fruits and the results of his industry' and education 'according to the discipline' of his own church. By the latter he meant the Catholic Church, the 'Church of the Nation', the 'Church of the poor'.[45] Gladstone did not believe that modern Protestant religion was intellectually and morally superior. Instead, his theological heritage taught him the necessity of defending the traditional religion of each national culture, as the guardian of the fountain of hope, happiness and virtue for the local people. But he did not want Irishmen to surrender their judgment to ultramontane priests. Gladstone hoped by church disestablishment and education reform to destroy the unnatural influence gained by priests over lay Irish Catholics; the reforms would help establish a self-reliant, Catholic, but not Romanist, middle class capable of sharing political power. Similarly, he was anxious to wean Irish landowners and farmers off grants in aid of local expenditure and other state handouts, and to teach them their social responsibilities to their own poor.

Devolution eventually became a vital element of Gladstonianism. But the third problem was that Gladstone was fascinated as well as repelled by the power concentrated in the modern state. He had to dominate. His crusades were the product of the clash between his religious conscience and his obsession with power: power to dictate events, power to smash opponents across the floor of the Commons, and power to sway a vast audience. Gladstone could not let power go. Unable to believe that anyone not of his own cast of mind could offer virtuous government, he could not tolerate

---

* See above, p. 247. Gladstone adopted this theme from remarkably early in his career: in 1859 he was already warning that 'the demands of the British empire surpass and transcend the powers of any assembly'.[41]

defeat. By the 1880s, it seemed that on three crucial occasions when cast into opposition Gladstone had revealed his lack of self-control, of 'character', by adopting destructive principles in order to recover power: his campaign of 1868 against the Irish church establishment, his destabilising onslaught on Disraeli's foreign policy from 1876, and his conversion to Home Rule in 1885–6.[46]* He was also prone to lose his temper whenever thwarted by opposition, especially from the House of Lords (despite his professions of respect for it). When it attempted to amend the 1869 Irish Church Bill, he had to be restrained by cooler heads from breaking off negotiations and appealing to the country. A similar problem occurred after it rejected the 1884 Reform Bill. Gladstone embarked on a speaking tour of Scotland intending to dissuade the Liberal rank-and-file from agitating for reform of the Upper House, but emotion soon overcame him and he talked of the Lords as an 'irresponsible power' which might need to be disciplined.[48] Backbench Liberal indiscipline in the Commons also irritated him, and his heavy legislative agenda was largely a response to the humiliation he endured whenever Liberals would not follow his lead, as in 1867–8.[49]

But where would this restlessness lead him? In 1860 Clarendon forecast that Gladstone's 'insatiable desire for popularity' and 'fervent imagination' would drive him to 'subvert the institutions and the classes that stand in the way of his ambition'.[50] His politics depended on the conviction that vested interests 'never slept' and 'made a night of it' whenever public vigilance was relaxed.[51] Incapable of retiring to the life of religious contemplation which his conscience sought, all his political actions had to be moralised into a war on those who could be portrayed as hostile to the people's interest. But this necessarily meant offending more and more men from the 'classes' and relying more and more on the myth of the superior morality of 'the masses'. Gladstone's motto in his last election campaign, in 1892, was 'trust the people'. They were 'least disqualified' by the 'great disabling causes' of 'selfishness and passion' from understanding a just cause when it was put to them.[52] But almost anyone who crossed Gladstone might qualify as 'selfish'. What were his criteria? Whereas Russell's activism sought to demonstrate the good sense of a propertied parliament, Gladstone's seemed dangerously lacking in principle.

Gladstone's fundamental problem was that he idealised the aristocracy and idealised the people. Both errors were the product of his own arrogance. Believing that he had correctly identified what the people should want, he assumed that he could mobilise them to demand it, and that the Liberal propertied classes would unquestioningly accept his reading of the situation. When they did not, he accused them of class selfishness and antagonised them further. Gladstone did not intend to be a divisive politician, but he was not a coalition-builder by temperament. His was the politics of conviction not consensus. Meanwhile, he misinterpreted popular reverence

---

* His friend Wilberforce ascribed his attack on the Irish church to 'the unconscious influence of his restlessness at being out of office'.[47]

for him. Many trade unionists, Dissenters and Celtic radicals did indeed follow his banner wherever he took them. Men walked immense distances to hear his speeches, and thronged to Hawarden to watch his tree-felling, as the steady disappearance of ferns and plants from his garden indicated. But often they did not quite want what he wanted. They wanted a symbol of their own respectability, their dignity as fully-fledged citizens, and their capacity for self-government. 'Gladstone' was that symbol because his manipulation of the new mass media created the illusion of direct communication, and because his election campaigning style was deliberately personal and flattering (for example, at Midlothian he said that each elector must ask his conscience whether to accept responsibility for tory extravagance, expansionism and over-government). Some of his followers also wanted to interpret his politics as a statement of hostility to aristocratic privilege, or to the church establishment which attempted to shackle their freedom of thought; others, in Wales and Scotland, as a celebration of their distinctive cultural identity; while others simply wanted lower imposts. Gladstone's tragedy was that, while he hoped to recast the Liberal coalition but to retain its unique breadth and diversity, his relentless zeal eventually left him with a very much smaller group. This was leavened, as ever, by unreflecting party men and ambitious timeservers, but its driving force was composed of evangelical Dissenters, parochial Celtic revivalists, sentimental intellectuals, and self-improving class-conscious working-men: an alliance of outsiders who had invented their 'Gladstone' just as surely as Gladstone had invented his 'people'.

Gladstone's critics

Most Liberals valued Gladstone's leadership for most of the time. They did so for several reasons. They approved of his ethical language and his ability to communicate with and to elevate the people. His cabinet colleague Carlingford wrote admiringly: 'What power he has! What influence over public opinion and action! – generally well used'.[53] Many felt that only he could lead radical opinion and draw its sting. His financial and administrative ability was much admired. So, frequently, were his conservative intentions. His temperamental shortcomings created a curiously schizophrenic effect: restless beyond measure when deprived of power, he seemed more sound when in office. Even his religion was in some ways a reassuring symbol. Goschen, one of the earliest to fall out with him, nonetheless conceded in 1882 that Gladstone was 'the great link to the traditional Christianity and culture', after whose departure he feared 'chaos'.[54]

It was also difficult for Liberals who disliked his populist mode of leadership to say so, since they were historically the party of the people and not altogether averse to agitation. Furthermore, the more vehement of his critics were unrealistic in their political expectations. Much of their jumpiness was a response to increased working-class politicisation after

1867. They contrasted the new political order with a former state in which MPs had been high-minded, independent trustees of the national interest, never swayed by constituency pressure; but this was idealised hindsight.[55]

Nonetheless, there was an increasingly coherent criticism of Gladstone, and its coherence was supplied by the whig-Liberal inheritance. Traditional Liberal values – commitment to the rule of law, to church establishment, to the political influence of property and to the parliamentary idea – seemed all the more important after 1867. Liberals were bound to ask how many of these values Gladstone shared.

Gladstone's background as a tory high churchman was one obvious source of disquiet. The party's broad churchmen, liberal evangelicals, and progressive intellectuals shared a contempt for clerical dogma; its erastians, Palmerstonian landowners, and irreverent worldly 'society' sceptics agreed in distrusting clerical enthusiasm. All these groups had traditionally been able to unite on a platform asserting the duty of *parliament* to preserve the church's national basis against narrow-minded clerical influence, so that it could act as an educational and moral agency and spiritual support.[56] The more advanced whig-Liberals also wished to harmonise the church with the political development and spiritual needs of the nation by bringing its parochial activities 'under the effective control of local government'.[57] Gladstone's lack of interest in extending state education, and his reluctance to repeal university tests, were symbols of his distance from their tradition. Moreover, they were self-consciously Protestant, and compared the Liberal party to Protestantism – a house of many mansions, flourishing through open debate but owing common allegiance to the principles of order and freedom.[58] They disliked 'Romanising' high churchmen, lacking in intellectual breadth, who seemed to want to foist outdated dogma and perverting ritual on congregations, and would prevent the church from moving with the intellectual and spiritual drift of national life.[59] They were liable to see Gladstone as emotional and irrational.

His apparent religious failings compounded a feeling that his judgment was untrustworthy. In the late 1850s and 1860s, it was common among the Liberal establishment to argue that Gladstone lacked stability, common sense and proportion.[60] Granville wrote of his 'states of morbid excitement', his fearsome forcefulness and his tendency to bully his colleagues.[61] Some thought that he would soon be fit for 'a mad-house'.[62] For all his subsequent successes, these charges never disappeared. He seemed unable to 'command his own intellect'; he was the lynchpin of a 'strange alliance between Radicalism and Ritualism', a 'passionate, impulsive, unreasoning instrument'.[63] Liberals who believed in government by reasoned debate and the search for consensus were taken aback by Gladstone's obsessiveness and hastiness. In 1877, Lord Houghton, hearing Gladstone, in characteristic mode, claim that he had 'been in a hurry for forty years', thought that that 'must account for many of his shortcomings'.[64] Even former Peelites agreed. Selborne complained that Gladstone had 'no consistent or settled respect for law'.[65] By 1874, J.D. Coleridge, though still an admirer, was alarmed by his 'impulsiveness' and '*wince*[*d*] under his want of dignity, not of manner only, but of character'.[66]* Gladstone's friend Argyll found him uniquely susceptible.[67] This was not *manly* Liberalism; self-control was lacking. Harcourt, Gladstone's most effective 'Protestant' Liberal critic, once suggested that Gladstone was 'so like a woman'.[68] Elcho wrote in 1866 that Gladstone showed 'the impulsiveness of woman without her instinct'.[69] Was this the straightforward leadership which a great empire needed?

Gladstone's deficiencies of judgment seemed so serious because, like his mentors Canning and Peel, he seemed to deny the need for real parliamentary government. Yet, like them, he lacked the stability of character necessary to assess what 'true' public opinion was. Gladstone seemed susceptible to popular pressure, especially from the organised intimidatory groups of the 1870s. Many Liberals doubted if he had fixed principles.[70] His mode of leadership was frequently painted as a combination of authoritarianism and populism, a determination to set the agenda by assessing the state of popular forces and plumping for one of the most vocally-agitated causes, which he would then impose on the whole party by fervent advocacy, however inconsistent such a course was with his own previous sentiments on the subject. Much was made of his convoluted speaking style. His mode of argument was condemned as 'Jesuitical' because it seemed capable of justifying any course of behaviour.[71] Whig-Liberal thinking suggested that, while the people *could* be led well, their passions might easily be directed to immoral ends. Gladstone sometimes seemed minded to bring out their worst aspects.

In 1865, the Conservative Lord Stanley perceptively criticised Gladstone's 'dictatorial' and 'dogmatic' frame of mind and the 'fundamental difference' between him and the 'sceptical', 'oligarchic' and group-minded whigs.[72] Gladstone's whig cabinet colleague Kimberley noted in 1873 that Gladstone was 'not the man to govern without "measures", nor is he at all suited to lead a party in difficulties. He must have a strong current of opinion in his favour.'[73] After sitting in his cabinet, Lord Chancellor Selborne wrote in 1874 that Gladstone's lack of 'sense of proportion, and breadth', made it 'hardly possible for him to be Minister, except when it is the time for some "heroic" measures': he was incapable of 'harmonis[ing] and regulat[ing other men's] action in the manner necessary for ordinary good government'.[74] To the typical whig or Liberal mind, these were stinging rebukes, since the whig-Liberal tradition demanded that good leadership involved the skill to respond flexibly and inspiringly in unpromising circumstances, integrating opinion by hand-to-mouth means. Gladstone seemed to lack the character, tact and temper necessary to lead a party responsibly, except by threatening

---

* Both these Peelites were lawyers, significantly. Gladstone's seeming disrespect for law was symbolised by the Collier affair of 1871, in which he appointed his own Attorney General to a puisne judgeship for a few days only, merely in order to render him technically qualified for a paid judgeship on the judicial committee of the privy council. This manoeuvre narrowly escaped censure in both Houses. A rather similar case arose over the appointment of a rector of Ewelme.

it by rousing opinion from out-of-doors. Bouverie in 1866 claimed that he was 'neither honest, moderate or gentleman enough . . . to be the whig minister'.[75] Gladstone's high church religion, toryism and temperament were thus of a piece; so, to some whigs, was his arriviste social background.*

These criticisms need to be introduced here because they became important. But they became important because of Gladstone's handling of specific emergencies. There was no revolt against him on general grounds. Liberals were not innately distrustful of active popular leadership or popular fervour in a good cause. The point is, rather, that the whig-Liberal tradition held to key ideals: integration, establishment, reason, consensus, law, parliamentary government. At various times, different Liberals concluded that under Gladstone's leadership these values were, or might be, under serious threat.

*　*　*

Lord Hartington, heir to the seventh duke of Devonshire, became the symbol of a Liberal alternative to Gladstonian politics, both before and after his election by Liberal MPs to be their leader on Gladstone's first resignation in January 1875. Hartington once explained his differences with Gladstone by saying 'he was a Peelite, and I was a Palmerstonian'.[77] Hartington modelled himself very successfully on Palmerston's leadership style, but added two other qualities which Palmerston had lacked: a great social position, and a less outrageous parliamentary manner. Had he ever been able to head the party on his own terms, Hartington might well have been its greatest leader.

Hartington's principles were very simple. He wanted to maintain the Liberal party as the country's natural ruling body, and the whig aristocracy as its leaders. His aim was to retain enough support from the gentry, the rising plutocracy and the propertied middle classes to secure a permanent electoral majority for the party and to marginalise radicals who might threaten the rule of property and law. All Palmerston's principles were his. Firm support for Britain's responsibilities as a modernising imperial power was twinned with a commitment to the rule of law and the defence of the Protestant minority in Ireland (the Devonshires owned 60,000 acres in Cork and Waterford). Hartington believed that self-government in Ireland should only be extended very slowly, as respect for law, educational standards and prosperity permitted. Loyalty to free trade and to good progressive administration at home was instilled not just by Palmerston but also by his father (and teacher); the seventh duke was earnest, scientific and devout, a great agricultural improver and educational benefactor, Chancellor of London

---

* In 1860, Emily Eden criticised his 'parvenuism . . . something in . . . his way of coming into the room that is not aristocratic'.[76]

University for twenty years and of Cambridge for thirty-five (in which post Hartington succeeded him).

Hartington was like Palmerston also in his astuteness about how to keep the Liberal coalition together. He traded on the innate respect for social rank held by most Liberal MPs and a large swathe of middle-class public opinion. He gambled and shot with the Prince of Wales and was a fixture at Newmarket. His isolated upbringing away from school encouraged a disdain for the feelings of others which could be used to create an idiosyncratic aristocratic hauteur; 'he would leave the card-room at the Turf Club only just in time to be late for dinner, however exalted the rank of his host'.[78] Whereas Gladstone despised the new plutocracy and its mores, Hartington played bridge with them at country houses and got the Rothschilds and Ernest Cassel to reinvigorate his family finances on the stock market. His self-indulgent, very private life with his mistress the duchess of Manchester was known in these circles but not to earnest provincial Liberals. Philistine himself, and proud of it, he knew how to play on the snobbery and fears of worthy Dissenting brewers and bankers; unlike Gladstone, he did not believe that the way to win their respect was to excite their consciences. Not a man of deep spirituality, and yet committed, like all good Liberals, to the extension of state education on undogmatic, practical lines, he considered Palmerston's sedate anti-clericalism the best route to party unity and intellectual progress. Devoid of strong principles on minor questions, he found it easy to make common ground with the bulk of MPs. The radical Dilke said of him in 1876: 'quite fearless, always goes with us when he thinks it safe for the party, and generally judges rightly'.[79] His earthiness, lack of social grace, indifference to fame, and simplicity of dress pleased radicals; he wore the Order of the Garter upside down at court and took his collie to the Commons. His manner of speaking and administration was equally straightforward and was, after his name, his greatest asset. He appeared massively dependable: stolid, resolute, fair-minded and clear-headed, a man of manifest public integrity. He was genuinely able, more able than he usually cared to reveal. Sir Henry James was astonished, when accompanying him on an election campaign and unexpectedly discovering that reporters were following them from venue to venue, to hear him give three completely different, clear-minded and very well-informed speeches off the cuff in a row.[80] His characteristic Commons performance, described by Lowe as 'all good sense and no earnest nonsense', bore favourable comparison with Gladstone on both counts.[81] Slow and careful in making up his mind, but responsible and firm in executing policy, he epitomised the good Liberal aristocrat. He worked hard and apparently selflessly. 'His ability and industry would deserve respect even in a man; in a Marquis they command admiration' was the comment of *Vanity Fair* in 1869.[82] Hartington did indeed have a strong sense of duty, but he knew also that nothing better secured the title of the aristocracy to govern the empire, leaving Dissenters and radicals the short straw of municipal government, than for its leading representatives to project this impression. In fact, the image of weary, dutiful self-sacrifice was a pose in one respect. His one-time private secretary remarked in 1886 on his love of politics; that apart, he had 'no *real* interest in life'.[83] All in all, Hartington succeeded phenomenally well in gauging the tenor of respectable public opinion. Asquith was not just eulogising when he observed, on Hartington's death, that he commanded 'in a greater degree than perhaps any other public man the respect and confidence of men of every shade and section of opinion in this kingdom'.[84]

Gladstonianism in practice, 1868–74

The far-reaching franchise extension of 1867 redoubled propertied anxiety that popular morality should be effectively regulated, and so questions of religious policy moved centre-stage. But the Reform Act also threw a great spanner in the works, because one of the great beneficiaries of the increase in urban politicisation was universally assumed to be the Dissenting radicalism of the midlands, the north and the Celtic regions. The Liberal majority in Scotland, Wales and Ireland rose from 13 to 83 between 1859 and 1868, and the number of Protestant nonconformist MPs doubled between 1865 and 1868. Sixty-nine Dissenting MPs sat through the 1868–74 parliament, of whom two-thirds were supporters of English church disestablishment, together with about 50 other MPs from urban areas. This was the heyday of the Liberation Society. Disestablishment became the major radical cry because it symbolised the struggle against complacent authority, and allowed a coalition with the Irish and also with working-men who saw the church as a symbol of social control. To Liberal working-men, the disestablishment cause was a mark of their dignity; support for it demonstrated confidence in innate popular respectability. But most Anglican Liberals profoundly opposed it, and were similarly concerned to defend the principle of religious teaching in schools. They wanted to extend the role of the state in education, and to teach an undogmatic religious creed, but not to undermine the church's place in national life, because it would have adverse consequences both morally and politically.

The religious compromise embodied in the 1870 Education Act was in line with this whig-Liberal thinking. Voluntary schools, which in most areas meant church schools, would continue to be funded by central government (the grant was increased by one-half). But, wherever inspectors found a deficiency in voluntary educational provision, locally funded, managed and elected school boards were to be established. In a major coup for whiggish principles, the Cowper-Temple amendment, forced on the government by the party, laid down that no distinctive denominational teaching was to be provided in these schools, a blow to Anglican assumptions of privileged status which would have been inconceivable before 1867. Gladstone was outraged at the symbolic castration by parliament of Anglican dogmatic vitality. But it was the only way in which the bulk of the party would tolerate continued official sanction of religious teaching.

However, there were three problems with the 1870 compromise. It allowed school boards to offer the 'secular' solution if they so wished – by which board schools would not teach religion at all but would set time aside for the various denominations to come in and teach their own creeds to the children of those parents who requested it. Led by Welsh Dissenter Henry Richard, 62 MPs had voted to make this compulsory in 1870. Gladstone preferred it to the Cowper-Temple compromise. It was the nearest sustainable approximation to the old Dissenting voluntaryism, the best available symbol of resistance to state-church oppression and of applause for popular morality. Permission for the secular solution was then made explicit in the terms of the 1872 Scottish Education Act. In practice, hardly any board offered it. But since boards were to be popularly elected, Dissenting activists could easily take control in the large towns. Birmingham became the first major board to go secular in 1873, perhaps setting a trend.

Second, local Dissenting activity, fear of secularism, and the deliberate curbs on denominational teaching in board schools drove tory clergymen and laymen into a strident church defence campaign. Also worried were some propertied Liberals for whom guaranteed religious instruction was essential in the new political climate: men such as Thomas Hughes and Edward Akroyd, MP for Halifax, publicly encouraged the campaign. The regularity and intensity of the school board elections forged an even closer link between politics and religious issues than was usual in this period. At the 1874 election, Conservatives benefited greatly from the fierceness with which the church defence campaign had been mounted in many places at the school board elections in late 1873, particularly in London where the number of tory parliamentary seats rose from 3 to 10 (out of 22) in 1874. Liberals once again learned the lesson that it was unwise to rouse the antagonism of the church, which seemed as powerful as ever: the number of Anglican clergymen rose from 17,320 to 21,663 between 1851 and 1881, and more clergymen acted as magistrates in 1873 than in 1831. Though detailed local work has not been done on the 1874 election, the Liberal defeat can be blamed mostly on the defection or abstention of substantial numbers of influential property-owners because of the threat to the church.[85]

The third consequence of the 1870 act also fuelled the tory campaign in 1874. Voluntary and board schools had to be funded by different mechanisms because provincial Dissenting activists would not fund church and Roman Catholic teaching on the rates. But an obscure clause of the act, Clause 25, permitted payment of fees to church schools from the rates in particular circumstances. This was hardly ever implemented, but hostility to it became a useful rallying-cry for nonconformists who wanted to create a broad Liberal coalition in favour of further attacks on the power of the church in education and elsewhere. The Birmingham-dominated National Education League attempted to turn Clause 25 into a major question; its driving spirit, Joseph Chamberlain, used it to advance his own career and to help to lever radical nonconformist candidates into Liberal seats. Historians' respect for Chamberlain has led them to take at face value his claim that this

263

campaign indicated general nonconformist anger at Gladstone's government which contributed significantly to the 1874 defeat.[86] This was not so. Anti-clerical whigs and moderate Liberals as well as nonconformists saw the repeal of Clause 25 as a useful cry on which to unite the party, so it indicated hostility to the church, not to official Liberalism. The Clause 25 cry helped to get nonconformist-dominated school boards elected, which they were in most towns by 1873; so the clause would never be implemented in such places. For this reason, the Dissenting grievance was minuscule. Furthermore, in many areas, radicals and nonconformist activists were steadily infiltrating local constituency party organisations and taking control. A striking example was the enforced replacement of the old whig George Grey at Morpeth by the miners' candidate Thomas Burt, while neither Hughes nor Akroyd, for instance, could find a seat. So many Liberal candidates in the north of England and Scotland had a generally radical approach to religious problems by 1874 that it would have been irrational for nonconformist voters to desert the party, and there is scant evidence that they did. Few Dissenters thought disestablishment a practical short-term possibility; most admired Gladstone's moral fervour. Chamberlain's National Education League was largely a failure and in August 1873 had to suspend its aggressive policy of putting up candidates against official Liberal ones.

The problem was rather that the campaign against Clause 25 was another indication of the Liberal party's tendency to upset the church, and was readily exploited by tories. As Disraeli said, 'we all go down to our con-stituents and say that the Constitution depends upon it, and we none of us know what it means'.[87] In 1873, Mundella lamented that the 'middle classes are everywhere becoming more and more Ecclesiastical and Conservative'.[88] The church defence campaign was boosted also by the consequences of the Endowed Schools Act of 1869. This was a response to the Taunton Commission. It established an Endowed Schools Commission to reform middle-class schools, according to a three-category blueprint: public schools, schools for the professions, and schools teaching practical skills to small farmers and tradesmen. In some cases the ESC sought to raise the status of a school, in others to lower it. Its new schemes aimed to make schools more financially viable by making them charge fees (many had given free education to the children of favoured local parents), and imposed regulations for their future management. They also sought to remove religious tests for masterships and reconstitute governing bodies which had fallen under vested interest control. All this caused great animosity. Clause 19 of the act gave church schools exemption from interference with the result that many schools claimed exempt status, usually unsuccessfully. The combination of concern for status and for religion drove school managers to appeal to the Lords against Commission schemes. One of the first acts of the incoming Conservative government of 1874 was to abolish the ESC.

Underlying the church defence movement was fear of disestablishment, for which aroused Dissenters were now calling. Annual Commons motions for it each collected about 100 votes. Whiggish Liberals sought to head this off by resurrecting the old anti-clerical alliance. Hence their commitment to the repeal of Clause 25, to the abolition of university tests in England and to a Protestant solution of the contemporaneous Irish university problem, and their anxiety to marginalise well-publicised ritualist practices and other high church activity within the establishment by various measures of minor church reform.* Another aspect of this strategy was their support for the Public Worship Regulation Bill introduced by the archbishop of Canterbury in 1874 (after the Liberal defeat) to give parliamentary sanction to his campaign against ritualism. Yet this strategy was anathema to Gladstone, and so was stillborn; the result was stalemate and irritation within the party. Infuriated by the Cowper-Temple clause, he had refused to budge on Clause 25, believing that, though insignificant in itself, it would lead the anti-clerical alliance into a stronger attack on the privileges of church schools. He vehemently opposed the Public Worship Regulation Bill. Riled by Harcourt's taunts, he came close to calling for disestablishment in order to safeguard church independence. Radical nonconformists were delighted at this row and at Gladstone's position, and redoubled the campaign to make disestablishment the next page in the Liberal programme. Gladstone did not want this; the Bulgarian agitation of 1876 had the not insignificant consequence of drawing nonconformist energies away from the disestablishment campaign. By portraying Anglicans in a purer light, he hoped to convince Dissenters that disestablishment was unnecessary. But in fact his powerful example made leading nonconformists like Dale the more convinced that a moralised disestablished church, and Dissent, could both flourish and work together to 'make the political life of England . . . more religious'.[89] Whig-Liberals found this reasoning absurd, but feared that Gladstone's commitment to the politics of mission and struggle, his hostility to anti-clerical parliamentary interference in religion, and his need to rally the provinces against Disraeli, might lead him to disestablishment as 'the best card to play, both for the leadership of the Liberal party in politics and for the resistance of Liberalism in ecclesiastical affairs'.[90] When church establishments came under threat again in 1885, many Liberals were to doubt Gladstone's loyalty to them.

*   *   *

These quarrels mattered also because they had resonances for the Irish question. Gladstone wished to govern on 'Irish ideas'; but, in a tense political climate, how compatible would this be with whiggish anxiety about

---

*   For example, Cowper-Temple, Hughes and Harcourt backed such measures as the reform of church patronage, the promotion of lay preaching and increased lay involvement in parochial government, and relaxation of the Anglican rubric by deleting the Athanasian creed from services.

law and Protestantism? There were in fact two Irish questions in the late 1860s. One, the most practical, concerned the rights of tenant-farmers (see page 292). The other turned on the demands of Catholic bishops and laymen for changes to the religious status quo. They demanded the disestablishment of the Anglican Church, which served only one-eighth of the population. They also called for more recognition of Catholic denominational teaching in the state-supported university colleges and the national education system. That is, they wanted to undermine the mixed education system which the whigs and Peel had constructed between 1831 and 1850 in the hope of modernising Ireland out of the clutches of the Catholic priesthood. No Catholic higher education institution was allowed to grant degrees. Middle-class Catholic laymen as well as priests believed that Irish youth ought to be allowed to receive a full university education in an explicitly Irish and religious environment. So did Gladstone.

Irish church disestablishment was not a problem for Liberals. Opposition to the Irish establishment's exclusiveness had been the motor of party activity in 1834–5, the first symbol of its 'Liberalism', and memories of the alliances of the 1830s played an important part in cementing Gladstone's coalition of 1868. The church was a minority imposition, and hopelessly unsuccessful. It was complacent in the use of its generous revenues, gained largely by a tithe rent-charge on the Catholic population. It seemed the greatest obstacle to popular acceptance of the benefits flowing from the British connection. In 1865, Wood had called it an 'abomination', but he and Palmerston thought disestablishment 'madness' because of the popular anti-Catholicism which tory defenders of establishments might stir up against it.[91] Gladstone's achievement in the 1868 election campaign was to steer most of Protestant Britain to a more mature attitude. Was this not evidence of the good sense of the new electorate? In 1869, the Irish Church Act put the principle of state neutrality between Protestant and Catholic on a new basis. All state grants, including that for Catholic Maynooth, were abolished.

However, two additional reasons for Liberal unity on Irish disestablishment were less reassuring for the future. First, an important segment of the party had believed in 1868 that Gladstone's resolutions left open the prospect of concurrent endowment of the three main Irish religions rather than complete disendowment. Concurrent endowment symbolised a continuing determination by the state to support Protestant values in Ireland and religion everywhere, and to keep potentially seditious priests under its thumb. So it was favoured by whigs like Russell and Grey, who had proposed schemes to this effect in 1866–7. It was in fact whig peers' anxiety to insert this principle into the bill in some way which was responsible for the clash with the Lords in 1869; tories would not have risked a quarrel alone.*

Second, other representative Liberals were willing to disestablish the

---

* Gladstone was prepared to accept some form of concurrent endowment in principle, but rejected it in deference to provincial Dissenting hostility.

Irish Church on the grounds that it was the *last* necessary act of justice to Ireland, in order to secure formal equality between Catholic and Protestant. The removal of this grievance, they argued, would defuse irritation with British rule and allow Liberal educational and economic principles to operate *more* successfully in modernising the country. To them, it was a boon to the unhindered spread of Protestant and other 'British' values. Political economists like Lowe and Argyll argued this strongly. They had also consented to disestablishment not least from horror at the alternative. When Disraeli became Prime Minister in February 1868 he attempted to preserve the church establishment by buying off the Catholics, promising a state charter for a Catholic University, with a hint of financial support. It was this proposal which allowed Gladstone to reunite the party in favour of disestablishment. Neither Lowe nor Argyll saw any need for Liberals to ally with Irish Catholics after 1869.[92]

Their belief in the integrative benefits of education free from clerical control led such men to create a symbol out of the motion of the Liberal intellectual Fawcett for the repeal of university tests in the Protestant Trinity College Dublin. In their eyes, the tests were the last obstacle to a genuinely mixed education system at university and elementary level, which they saw as essential to the liberalisation of Irish culture. So modernising Protestants like them had no sympathy with the Irish Catholic educational grievance. Some old whigs like Wood (now Halifax), Grey, George Grey and Russell had a slightly different view. They wanted concurrent endowment for the university system, so that the state supported (and so improved) the education given in selected Catholic institutions but also safeguarded the financial future of Trinity College. This was on the principle of reform in Ireland which Russell articulated when he warned Gladstone that, while one should take note of Irish opinion in ruling, it should always be 'in such a manner as to foster their virtues and to repress their vices'.[93] What neither group wanted was Gladstone's emotional commitment to Irish Catholicism. The result of this three-way clash of prejudices (for no group had much knowledge of Irish education) was a comic drama which lasted for years. Between 1871 and 1873 Gladstone fought against massive inertia in the party in order to bring in a bill. He planned a state-supported federal degree-giving university examining body, to which Trinity would, and Catholic institutions could, affiliate, but with no state funds going to colleges. For the bulk of those Liberals who concerned themselves with such issues, this proposal had two flaws. In order to make the federal university structure work, there were to be no examinations in vital subjects such as modern history or philosophy, in order to avoid discrimination against Catholic dogmas. This was hardly a university worth the name in the eyes of intellectually-aware Liberals. Second, it was possible for small-town Catholic colleges to join the structure in such numbers that they would dominate it, undermining the future intellectual freedom of the venerable Trinity College. Hartington, the Irish Secretary, almost resigned in opposition to the scheme. Despite numerous promises of concessions by

Gladstone, enough liberal-evangelical whigs, intellectuals and Scottish anti-Catholic Liberals refused to support the bill that in March 1873 it was defeated – since in addition it was opposed by most Irish MPs, voting on the instructions of the Catholic hierarchy who demanded *endowment* for the denominational colleges.*

This crisis was significant in a number of ways. It led to the government's temporary resignation (though Disraeli refused office) and long-term loss of momentum. It encouraged the growth of the Home Government Association, and the 'home rule' movement took 59 Irish seats at the 1874 poll. This had been foreshadowed by success at byelections from 1869, which turned on dissatisfaction with British policy on the land laws, religion and the imprisonment of nationalist agitators. Gladstone's commitment to university reform had mounted in part in reaction to this evidence that his previous Irish policies had not reduced ill-feeling. Hence also his successful battles in cabinet to release all the civilian Fenian prisoners from jail, and his eventually unsuccessful opposition to proposals from Hartington to introduce coercive legislation in disordered parts of the country. His intensity of feeling, on questions of both order and now religion, further exasperated his critics. The Irish University question was not of first-rate importance, but the point was that most Liberals did not think that it should be a question at all; there was no interest in it in the party, and strong private opposition in many quarters. The ingratitude of Irish MPs had shown how impossible it was to satisfy them. Palmerston's Irish strategy seemed vindicated. The affair had prevented the development of an anti-clerical policy to solve the English religious problem. Gladstone's policy, moreover, gave Disraeli the opening which some *whigs* had wanted to brandish the Kulturkampf banner. He now criticised Gladstone's indulgence of papist pretensions. In widely-reported speeches in 1872 and 1873, Disraeli charged the Liberals with being the party of hostility to established religion and, in Ireland, of support for clericalism against civil liberty and for anarchy against the law. At Glasgow in 1873 he urged England to take 'a stand upon the Reformation' and so 'guard civilization alike from the withering blasts of atheism and from the simoom of sacerdotal usurpation'.[94] These arguments must have helped to influence the 1874 election result. It seemed that Gladstone was too anarcho-populist in some ways, and too clerico-authoritarian in others.

* * *

Disraeli was also able to exploit other weaknesses of Gladstone's government: its handling of the linked questions of foreign, defence and financial policy, and its 'harassing' legislative programme.

---

* It is a common error to suppose that English Dissenting MPs were hostile to the scheme. It approximated to the secular solution. What is true is that opposition to the idea of *endowed* Catholic education, which they wrongly feared that Gladstone would favour, had greatly stimulated their campaign for secular education in both England and Ireland.

Throughout his first two premierships, Gladstone was the dominant figure in financial policy, though Lowe (1868–73) and Childers (1882–5) shared the Chancellorship with him. His financial administration remained one of the principal unifying factors in Liberalism. During his first government, he aimed, as before, to reduce public expenditure, so demonstrating the benevolence and class neutrality of the state, and disciplining the new voters into accepting the tenets of political economy. One remarkable achievement was to reduce the unredeemed public debt. Having hovered at just below £800 million from the 1830s to the 1850s, it fell under his stewardship from £809 million in 1859 to £654 million in 1885. Formal Treasury supervision of the estimates was established in 1869. Helped by economising 'middle-class' politicians Cardwell, Childers and Goschen at the defence departments, Gladstone and Lowe cut £4 million from defence expenditure between 1868 and 1873, despite the cost of abolishing army purchase and of the defence scare which accompanied the Franco-Prussian War. In 1873, defence spending was at its all-time lowest since the Crimean War. Direct and indirect taxes were remitted to the tune of £9½ million: the income tax was cut from 6d to 3d between 1868 and 1873; the corn registration duty was abolished in 1869; the sugar duties were halved in 1870 and again in 1873, and the coffee duties in 1872.

Even so, this policy caused some tension in the light of the perceived increase of popular pressure after 1867. Some was the fault of Lowe, a politically inept and stunningly uncharismatic Chancellor. His crass attempt to make up a revenue shortfall by imposing a tax on matches in 1871 led to a march of Bryant and May match-girls on Westminster with Lowe taking shelter in the underground tunnels. He then withdrew the tax and put the whole revenue burden on income tax, not impressing property-owners anxious about government weakness before class-based pressure. His insensitive 'cheeseparings'[95] were doubly controversial because the international situation was no longer as rosy as in the early 1860s. In 1870, the Franco-Prussian War created a new German threat, while England's bogy Russia rose again, moving its ships into the Black Sea in defiance of Palmerston's Treaty of Paris of 1856. Naval cuts attracted unfortunate attention when three ships sank in a blaze of publicity, including an ill-designed prototype turret-ship. But Gladstone's obsession with economies did not abate. Criticising Lowe as 'wretchedly deficient' in controlling spending, he took charge of the Exchequer himself in 1873 and tried to force through £1 million more in defence cuts in order to go to the 'people' with a plan to abolish income tax.[96] The defence departments resisted, so Gladstone impulsively decided to appeal over their heads to the voters, but the election of February 1874 was lost. The whole affair alarmed whigs, not least because they did not want income tax abolition and believed that Gladstone could only make up the shortfall by taxing property, such as by death duties.

At a time of continental tension and incipient doubts about Britain's international standing, Gladstone's over-zealous defence cuts were bound to paint an unattractive contrast with Palmerston's redbloodedness. So was his foreign policy, which seemed not only anaemic, but also ineffective in spreading liberal values abroad. Palmerstonians like Otway and Layard criticised Gladstone's Russian policy, though in reality this was another casualty of the collapse of the European balance of power. Most damaging was the premier's perceived weakness towards the United States. In an unPalmerstonian gesture towards world brotherhood, the cabinet agreed to submit to international arbitration American claims for damage done to Union forces during the civil war by the *Alabama*, a Confederate warship which had been allowed to leave Liverpool. Whig critics, led by Russell (Foreign Secretary at the time), capitalised on the long-drawn-out dispute and the eventual award of £3¼ million in damages against Britain, which even Gladstone later privately admitted was enormous.[97] The British arbitrator, Lord Chief Justice Cockburn, publicly protested against the government's acceptance of the award.

Liberal dissidents saw in such a policy a lack of manliness and an obsession with expenditure cuts to win lower-class approval. Grey charged the government with over-reliance on the 'fleeting public opinion of the hour', pointing to the decision to cut the army by 26,000 men in 1869, and then to increase it by much the same amount in 1870 in reaction to the Franco-Prussian War.[98] In 1871, in the Lords, Russell and Grey supported tory peers in defeating the government bill to abolish the system of awarding army commissions by purchase, also on the ground that it was precipitate.* Grey had been pressing for a well-considered reform of military organisation since the 1830s, and blamed popular indifference for its failure. He considered Cardwell's proposed regular force too skimpy and inexperienced (owing to reliance on short-service); he believed that the great expense of purchase abolition would disincline parliament from funding further needed increases; and he thought that whereas purchase encouraged the less competent officers to sell out, abolition would perpetuate a stagnating but large officer class, a separate vested interest, all anxious to please an omnipotent Commander in Chief, and so constituting a potential threat to liberty.[99] But the government simply abolished purchase by royal warrant. This made Lords opposition to the idea of the secret ballot, the following month, inevitable. Russell and two of Palmerston's cabinet ministers, Somerset and Lyveden, opposed the Ballot Bill, because it had been insultingly presented to them at the end of the session, implying that they had no revising function, and because there was no evidence of public demand for it. They maintained that the Commons should 'instruct the country in the formation

---

* Criticism of the purchase system had been evident since the Crimean War panic. It was a vehicle for meritocratic attacks on aristocratic influence and incompetence in public life. High demand for commissions had driven their price up; 5–6,000 officers had £8–10 million invested in the system. In 1871, the government bought the commissions up.

of its political opinions' rather than make major changes just in order to please radical MPs.[100]

In these ways, whig peers joined forces with the young tory Lord Salisbury in developing the doctrine that the Lords had the power, indeed duty, to refer hasty, slipshod or controversial bills, not discussed at a previous election, to the people at a subsequent poll, before passing them.[101] This was a natural reaction to Gladstone's overstuffed legislative programme of 1868–74. In 1871, for example, Goschen's massively ambitious local government and finance reform, Bruce's badly-drafted Licensing Bill, and other major legislation, from Royal Parks to Scottish Education, had to be withdrawn after parliamentary criticism. The legislative burden was too much for Childers and John Bright, who suffered breakdowns and had to leave the cabinet. By the late 1870s, Cardwell was insane. Of Gladstone's Commons cabinet ministers, only Hartington and Goschen enhanced their standing, and they were increasingly critical of Gladstone.

In private, Gladstone recognised that loss of power in the Lords was one of the major reasons for the collapse of government authority.[102] But his public reaction, typically, was to make a speech at Whitby describing the Ballot Bill as 'the people's Bill', before which the Lords should yield (they did, in 1872). This invocation of popular fervour was the more offensive to whigs who disliked Gladstone's frenetic style of government.[103] Such developments led the anti-democratic intelligentsia, over-sensitive to popular influence on government after 1867, to allege that Gladstone was presiding over the disintegration of a once broad and central party into a collection of disparate groups 'of extreme opinions and of crazy crotchets'.[104] Henry Maine was typical in maintaining that the problem with democracy was lack of self-restraint; it was thus, by turns, unprogressively inert and rashly over-exuberant.[105] Fitzjames Stephen lamented the decline in independent executive power under the new electoral dispensation, and warned against treating public administration as 'an educational process' for the citizen rather than a job for the informed.[106] One disaffected MP claimed that he and colleagues were being harried by a bevy of populist pressure groups, from the Liberation Society to the republican movement, the United Kingdom Alliance, the National Education League, and the opponents of the game laws and the Contagious Diseases Acts.[107] Similarly, political economists in particular were worried by the large number of strikes for shorter hours or higher wages which followed the 1871 Trade Union Act, of which the most famous was that of 9,500 Tyneside engineers for a nine-hour day, which secured the new terms in all the country's chief engineering firms. Wood ventured the thought that sentimental Liberal government might have encouraged an assertion of trade union power at the expense of national productivity.[108]

Others fell back on a different aspect of the whig tradition and criticised Gladstone's illiberalism. These were led by Harcourt and Fawcett, two intellectual MPs (both were Cambridge professors) with radical connections but also (in Harcourt's case) a claim to speak for whig values. They formed a powerful lobby below the gangway, backed by the *Daily News*. While Fawcett was eccentric and had the Liberal whip withdrawn, Harcourt's broad libertarianism had a wider appeal within the party. He hoisted 'the good old Whig flag' in a series of criticisms of Gladstone's 'wild proposals . . . flighty nature', 'sudden impulses . . . unintelligible policy' and domination of cabinet.[109]* Gladstone blamed this dissident whig-radical group in part for his loss of governing momentum.

Most damaging of all was the ebbing electoral confidence, revealed in byelections, as the tories gained 23 seats between 1871 and 1873. At the 1874 general election, the Liberals lost 73 seats in England and 15 in Scotland. The Conservatives won an overall majority of 48. This staggering turnaround – the first Liberal defeat since 1841 – was clearly caused by propertied Anglican disaffection; there were major losses of county seats in England and in the anti-Catholic Scottish Borders, and of borough seats in London and the home counties. Liberals now held only 27 of 170 English county seats. Ironically the extension of the county franchise to suburbia in 1867 assisted the decline. Locke King, the unintentional father of villa toryism, was defeated by it in East Surrey.

Too many electors believed that vociferous Dissenters, 'Little Englanders' and Irish Catholics had excessive power over the party, and that Gladstone had not done enough to keep these provincial pressures in check. This feeling was an understandable response to the great change of 1867. Though Gladstone should carry *some* of the blame for it, for pursuing an idiosyncratic agenda, in large part the defeat was beyond his control. He was politician enough to know that he had to sustain a conservative image during these years: he opposed disestablishment, he made few extra-parliamentary speeches, and he did not deal directly with Irish leaders. Even so, his peculiarities grated on much of the liberal establishment, and when, of his own volition, he retired as leader in early 1875, there was a revival of interest in 'whig principles' of the sort espoused by Hartington – whom Harcourt recognised as 'far the best constitutional sovereign in the party after the fall of the despotism'.[110] Since 'the Country wants repose', many Liberals assumed that the 'moderate section of the Liberal party' must regain ascendancy if the party was again to 'become powerful'.[111] Hartington, Forster, Goschen and Harcourt took control. Hartington's leadership – initially reluctant, but soon confident – aimed to vindicate the role of reason and steady progress in politics. He offered financial rectitude, anticlericalism, a strong foreign policy, Unionism, and a diet of scientific but *considered* legislation. By this means the left could be disciplined, the centre revitalised, and the anti-democratic gentlemen and intellectuals on the right reassured. In other words, the answer to Liberal problems seemed to be a reassertion of *parliamentary* government. There would inevitably be some

---

* Harcourt identified dictatorship in the Licensing Act, the secret ballot, apparent limitations on the right of public meeting in the parks, and excessive estimates.

differences of opinion about the proper pace of reform on land, local government, franchise, education and church questions, but, as the Liberal intellectual Brodrick argued in 1877, there was general agreement on underlying principles in all cases. Would not time and free debate in parliament see a consensus emerge?[112] Superficially, this whiggish logic was undeniable. In practice, though, events did not unfold quite as predicted.

CHAPTER 12

Traditional Liberalism under attack, 1874–86

THOUGH A MORE parliamentary Liberalism was much in demand in 1874, the defeat of that year put a spoke in the wheel, because it required Liberals to confront the suggestion that they were no longer the popular party. For most of them, this was an unsustainable proposition. But, in that case, parliament was no longer representative of public opinion. Activity, even agitation, was necessary to release that opinion.[1] Between 1874 and 1880 Liberals developed three new strategies to this end. One was the establishment of the National Liberal Federation, which aimed to organise and speak for grass-roots opinion. The second was the emotional moral crusade to rouse the people – exemplified by the Bulgarian agitation and Gladstone's Midlothian campaign. The third was the agitation for household franchise in the counties, to liberate a lost 'people'. This chapter begins by charting the development of those three strategies. But it also argues that the first two could be accommodated with traditional Liberal practice without too much difficulty, so that the 1880–5 Liberal government was in essence traditional. The third new strategy led to the far-reaching Reform settlement of 1884–5. On top of some background economic anxieties, this created tension in 1885 among cabinet Liberals between the most truculent aristocratic 'whig', Hartington, and the self-appointed leader of popular Liberalism, Chamberlain. But this tension played little part in the break-up of the party in 1886. The cause of this, rather, was the quite separate quarrel between Hartington (and Chamberlain) in one corner, and a rejuvenated Gladstone in the other, on questions of Irish and imperial policy, crippling in themselves, and doubly so because they highlighted fundamental differences about how to preserve the rule of law and didactic leadership in face of sometimes passionate popular activity.

Agitation, 1874–80?

The most important development in popular Liberal party organisation after 1874 was the creation of the National Liberal Federation by Joseph Chamberlain in 1877, as a forum for popularly-elected constituency associations. The intended purpose of the NLF was twofold. It would encourage Liberal organisation, especially in seats lost in 1874 because of apathy (usually in counties) or internal division (usually in boroughs). But, by refereeing a policy debate among activists, it also promised, unlike the Westminster parliament, to realise a genuine popular moral impulse. Chamberlain saw it as 'a really Liberal Parliament . . . elected by universal suffrage, and with some regard for a fair distribution of political power'.[2] He hoped that it would demonstrate forcefully to Liberal MPs the strength of provincial support for advanced rallying-cries, such as county franchise reform and disestablishment.[3]

The NLF was a controversial body. Its critics claimed that it promoted machine politics, or democracy, both of which would narrow the party's appeal and undermine the ideal of policy emergence through free discussion by a representative range of parliamentary opinion. In the late 1870s, there was much apprehensive criticism of 'wirepullers' and the 'caucus'.[4]

Criticism took three forms, but each was overblown. One was the fear that local officers from each association, themselves elected by only a small proportion of members, might dictate terms – radical terms – to prospective parliamentary candidates. In fact attempts to impose a policy – which were in any case not new to the period after 1867 – were rare, and success rarer; MPs could easily ignore or fudge commitments, or indulge in them knowing that defeat for the matter in question was inevitable.[5] Local factionalism spawned a few highly-publicised conflicts between activists and MPs, famously that involving Forster in Bradford, but these were nearly always resolved amicably.[6] Even angular intellectuals like Leonard Courtney continued to be able to find congenial small or Scottish borough seats. The second anxiety stemmed from the behaviour of Chamberlain's Birmingham association. It operated a highly-marshalled canvassing system which instructed voters on the combination in which to cast their votes. This was a consequence of the minority vote clause of the 1867 act, which left Birmingham with three MPs but its voters with only two votes. Such instruction appeared dictatorial, but the minority vote clause only applied in a dozen constituencies, and the imbalance of party strength did not usually make direction necessary even there. Third, it was believed that Chamberlain would use the NLF to impose a policy agenda on party leaders. But this was also implausible. The NLF could not look representative. In 1884 only eighty-eight English boroughs and a dozen other associations were affiliated to it, and these included Manchester and its satellite associations, bodies traditionally jealous of Birmingham's role in provincial Liberalism. Associations from London, Scotland and nearly all the small boroughs and counties saw no merit in joining. Its policy programme was slight and predictable, being the standard radicalism of the big towns. Where Liberals disagreed, so did the NLF.

So both Gladstone and Hartington could afford to be indulgent towards the NLF, which if anything increased rather than diminished the chaos of opinion on the backbenches. Hartington naturally disliked the fact that it was 'outside the control of the official element of the party', but, in 1879, he welcomed its contribution to party organisation, warning only that the caucus structure was not suited to many smaller constituencies and must remain representative in large ones.[7] Both leaders adopted the easygoing but impeccably Liberal line that, where the party was divided, such as on Scottish disestablishment or local option, opinion must be left to 'mature'.[8]

In fact, most intellectual Liberal animosity to the NLF was the result of its association with the two other developments of the mid-1870s, the growing interest in county franchise reform and the apparent malleability of popular sentiment on foreign policy questions. Chamberlain was a convenient bogy, but the more dangerous man was Gladstone, who, though nominally retired, raised many eyebrows by addressing the inaugural conference of the NLF with apparent and alarming enthusiasm.[9] Gladstone, typically, blamed the defeat of 1874 largely on the lack of opportunity of 'stirring the country'. He spent the years in opposition looking for a 'virtuous passion'. In 1876, he seemed to find it.[10] The Bulgarian agitation of that year was a grass-roots movement, heavily reliant on nonconformist (and some high church) enthusiasm, which demanded autonomy for the Christian provinces of the Ottoman Empire in response to atrocities against their inhabitants. It opposed the tory government's pro-Turkish policy. Russia used the atrocities as grounds to mobilise for war against Turkey, and the agitators feared that jewish Disraeli would lead Britain into an Eastern war against the Tsar. Gladstone's fervent participation brought the agitation much publicity; his pamphlet *Bulgarian Horrors* sold 200,000 copies within a month. But many Liberals found the agitation's aim of provincial autonomy impracticable and damaging to regional stability. Thinking that diplomacy was best conducted by those whose interpretation of the national interest was unsullied by religious fervour, they disliked the canting, clerical nature of the agitation.[11] To them, it was one more sign of how far from Palmerstonianism Gladstone was, and how much less responsible. The whig duke of Sutherland called him a Russian agent in public. The unwisdom of founding action on Gladstonian notions of popular morality seemed to be demonstrated when by 1878 public opinion had expressed itself decidedly hostile to the old liberal bogy Russia. Disraeli wrapped himself in Palmerston's mantle; the Conservative party established a studiously respectable 'Patriotic Association' to exploit Liberal anger at Gladstone's appeasement of Russia. The affair badly split Liberals and weakened further the faith of many in Gladstone's judgment and patriotism. Bryce believed that many gentry left the party for good over it, and the City clearly preferred tory policy.[12]*

Gladstone's barnstorming anti-tory campaign through his newly-adopted constituency of Midlothian in the months preceding the 1880 election

---

* In the City seat itself in 1880, the three Conservative candidates scored nearly twice the number of votes polled by the three Liberals, in a seat dominated by the Liberals until 1874.

similarly unsettled a range of Liberal opinion. Some disliked the prospect of his return to the political stage. Some were taken aback by the rapid developments in political communication and by Gladstone's exuberance in exploiting them. Midlothian completed the process by which hero-worship of Gladstone became a cult. People came from the Hebrides to hear him speak. On his journeys to and from Scotland thousands would assemble at railway stations to watch his train come past. The *Times* published an estimated 250,000 words spoken by him in six months in 1879–80. Gladstone's mode of address, his root-and-branch assaults on 'a whole system of government', stirred the evangelical zeal of provincial noncon-formity and of a minority of Anglican high churchmen, both of whom gloried in the 'romantic and religious glamour' surrounding Gladstone's attack on those 'strongholds of Anti-Christ', 'the obscene empires of Mammon and Belial'.[13] The amount of zeal summoned up could not but give the impression that popular fervour – or 'King Mob', as Fitzjames Stephen put it – was being summoned to overthrow, not only a government, but also the traditional style of politics, including the Liberal parliamentary leadership.[14] There was distaste for Gladstone's use of pious cant – notably when he appealed to the ladies in the audience to assess Disraeli's govern-ment by its callousness towards noble, patriotic South African Zulus who had 'offered their naked bodies to the terribly improved artillery and arms of modern European science', and towards women and children in Afghan hill-villages sent forth to 'perish in the snows of winter' as a result of British action.[15]

However, Liberals were ambivalent about these tactics because they almost all approved of the ends for which Gladstone was striving in 1880. Nor was his performance an affront to Liberal reverence for reason. Very many more people read his speeches in close-set newspaper reports than were swayed by his charismatic oratory. In fact, his arguments were very similar to those of Hartington, the official Commons leader. The point about the 1880 election, often neglected by concentration on Gladstone, is that Hartington's strategy of restoring the confidence of large numbers of propertied Liberals succeeded. He united the party by stressing the validity of traditional Liberal themes in the fight against Disraeli. In a high-profile campaign in which he made twenty-four major speeches, he attacked the extravagance and ineptitude of tory financial and foreign policy between 1874 and 1880 as strongly as Gladstone.

The 1880 election was fought in a severe agricultural depression.[16] Both Gladstone and Hartington claimed that Disraeli had contributed to this by muzzling parliament, preventing it from checking abuses in policy. By 1880, income tax had been raised to 6d, in order to pay for wars in Afghanistan and South Africa which Liberals considered unnecessary and immoral. Disraeli's government, supported by a disciplined and unbreak-able Commons majority, had been able to raise large votes of credit for its foreign initiatives. Most war expenditure was met from loans and added to the national debt, at a time when depression reduced revenue. Heavy annual deficits over three years created a deficiency of £8 million by 1880, a sad contrast to the £6 million inherited from Gladstone in 1874. Liberals were angered by parliamentary impotence. Tory ministers, they said, had given into class-based pressures for increased military estimates and had been responsible for scandalous jobs in the civil service.[17] Yet government had been defeated only 8 times between 1874 and 1879, compared to 50 defeats between 1868 and 1873 and 60 between 1862 and 1867.[18] Hartington pledged that Liberal government would restore the 'authority' of parliament which Disraeli had unforgivably 'lowered' in the 'mind of the country'. Another consequence of restoring parliamentary self-confidence was that, by open discussion in the Commons, a well-matured and generally acceptable social and administrative policy would emerge. This would allow 'a gradual but constant progress in the moral and material condition of the people'.[19] Under Disraeli, in contrast, parliament had failed in its duty of responding calmly and continuously to national problems. Despite his majority, he had not offered a healthy diet of bills.[20] He had failed to legislate on landlord-tenant relations or county government, while his measures on education and the army were reactionary and that on agricultural holdings inadequate.[21]

But Lowe's reference to the 'docility of an "imperial" parliament' pointed up the worst danger of a neutered Commons: that it allowed irresponsible jingo bluster to conceal a secretive, sinister, ill-conceived foreign policy. Disraeli's government was lamentably 'personal'.[22] Hartington pointed to Disraeli's early romantic writings criticising representative government as a 'popular fallacy' and his lack of interest in rational education of the electors.[23] As Lowe put it, 'thinking men' were upset by 'the feeling that there is nothing which the combined ignorance, vanity, and audacity of one man may not attempt'.[24]

By such approaches, Liberals could forget their earlier disagreements over Bulgaria, and turn foreign policy to their advantage. They charged that, in all international spheres, tory initiatives had been undertaken without adequate parliamentary consultation, and had revived 'the principles of Lord Bolingbroke and the system of Lord Bute'.[25] The decision to send Indian troops to Malta in 1878 raised the spectre, however fanciful, of the repression of domestic discontent at some future period by imported Asiatic force.[26] Almost all Liberals could now agree that Disraeli's desire to cut a dash at the peace conference of 1878 had forced Britain into defending a rash and unsustainable settlement in the East. The new Anglo-Turkish Convention and the annexation of Cyprus implied a commitment to uphold the integrity of the Ottoman Empire which was potentially catastrophic for British interests and which threatened to surrender Balkan sentiment into Russian hands. Moralists and balance-of-power pragmatists in the party united in criticism of this attempt at single-handed policing at a time when Germany, Austria and Italy were all stronger than in 1854 and shared an interest in preventing Russian aggression.[27] They charged, moreover, that drifting, incompetent cabinet policy had allowed 'prancing pro-Consuls' to commit Britain to brutal, expensive and morale-sapping wars in Afghanistan and South Africa, in opposition to traditional Liberal policy in both theatres.[28] This foreign policy was not, Hartington insisted, Palmerstonian. Instead, it was like 'the bastard imperialism of the Second Empire'.[29] Liberals viewed Disraeli's jingoistic speeches and empty, monarchical, imperial symbols (such as the title 'Empress of India', conferred on Queen Victoria in 1876) as an attempt to delude ignorant, irrational voters into giving a clamorous support for reckless adventures: he sought to inflame their 'warlike passions'.[30] The central question posed in the Liberals' campaign was whether, parliament having failed to stop tory mismanagement, the 'people' were also willing to shoulder responsibility for it – so admitting their degraded and passionate nature – or whether they would show themselves thinking men worthy of the franchise.[31] The 1880 campaign was a hymn to the rationality of the Liberal electorate.

The result was a triumph for cross-class traditional Liberalism. Helped by the NLF's *organisational* strength, the Liberals won a sound majority of 52 (over tories and Irish together) in 1880. Most importantly, 38 seats were gained in English and Scottish counties (both Gladstone and Hartington deliberately stood for, and won, county seats). Though the Farmers' Alliance president James Howard was returned for Bedfordshire, county success in general was a result less of tenant farmer enthusiasm for the party's programme than of the revival of landed whigs' commitment to the party, their organisational and financial support, and an aroused urban Liberal vote.[32] The county results significantly boosted the propertied element on the Liberal benches: of 346 MPs, 41 were heirs, sons or brothers of peers, 28 more were baronets, and there were 71 other great landowners or landed gentry.[33]* Hartington wisely rejected the queen's offer of the premiership, believing that Gladstone would be a safer proposition at the head of the government than outside it.

As a result, the 1880–5 government was never in thrall to radical pressure. Gladstone's ardour was satisfied and his conservatism came to the fore. At the top of the Liberal agenda was Peelite restorative work on national finances. Gladstone's influence here guaranteed fairness between classes and so appeased both radical critics of inevitably increased expenditure on imperial defence, and Palmerstonians who would have liked yet more ships but who cavilled at the graduated income tax that Chamberlain might have demanded in order to pay for them. The domestic agenda was mapped out in advance by the rural depression and the resulting commitments to taxation, local government and land reform (see pages 242–3). Backbenchers were also kept happy by symbolic measures abolishing flogging in the army and allowing Dissenters to conduct their own services at burials

---

* English counties returned, among others, representatives of the following great Liberal landed families: Ashley, Beaumont, Brand, Carington, Cavendish (three), Cowper, Egerton, Fitzwilliam, Foljambe, Grey, Howard, Lambton, Leigh, Moreton, Portman, Ramsden, Russell, Spencer and Vivian. Tory support kept up in the south-east and East Anglia, but declined in most other counties.

in parish churchyards (both passed in 1880). Potentially divisive bodies like the Liberation Society and the parliamentary committee of the TUC were mute; the United Kingdom Alliance was easily fobbed off. Liberals could claim to rest on general public support, not the self-interested weight of organised lobbies. Gladstone's various foreign policy campaigns had invigorated radicals and marginalised those like Chamberlain who had hoped to use the period of opposition to win widespread support for an advanced policy programme; Gladstone astutely muzzled him in a low-profile cabinet post at the Board of Trade. The government was not dependent on the Irish, so moderate Liberals need not worry unduly about Gladstone's unpredictability in that quarter. The 1880–5 ministry was remarkably free from internal Commons dissension. It was the last of the old-style Liberal ministries.

Parliamentary reform again

In the long term, the most important of the three post-1874 Liberal quests to recover support was the commitment to electoral reform. One important fruit of this was the 1883 Corrupt Practices Act, provoked by anger at tory victory in 1874, and the first effective blow struck against bribery. Strict limits were imposed on permitted campaign spending, some sorts of expenditure were banned altogether, bribery and treating became imprisonable offences, and public inspection of accounts was established. Official election expenses fell by three-quarters between 1880 and 1885.[34]

Most significant, though, was the Liberal pledge to equalise the county and borough franchise on the basis of household suffrage. This in turn necessitated a complete overhaul of the representation of seats. The result was that by 1885 the long-standing representative system was in tatters, and Britain had taken the essential steps on the road to democracy.

The fundamental reason for this was that Derby and Disraeli had badly mishandled the parliamentary reform settlement of 1867. It created illogical arrangements which had no claim to 'finality' and which made further change irresistible. Disraeli had hoped to preserve propertied rule in the counties by giving the appearance (but not the reality) of household suffrage in the boroughs. Liberals had no choice but to force him to concede the reality instead. This made the county franchise settlement unsustainable.

This was, first, because much enthusiasm was aroused for the idea of popular political participation. After 1867, many Liberals were keen to stress the virtue of the popular judgment. Also, the large extension of the borough franchise seemed to invalidate the traditional 'trustee' theory of representation and to strengthen the argument that voting was a right, a means of self-protection; hence the swift introduction of the ballot. But these changes made the second consequence of 1867 much resented. This was the massive inequity set up between men of the same class, situation and outlook who happened to live on either side of a line dividing borough and county seats. Artisans and even some shopkeepers who lived in small unenfranchised towns in county constituencies lacked the vote. So did large numbers of miners, as in Northumberland and Durham where only 10 per cent were said to be enfranchised.[35] In 1873, G.O. Trevelyan estimated that there were at least 3 million dwellers in county seats who were townspeople in habits and circumstances but deprived of the suffrage.[36] Worse, economic change had destroyed the idea that boroughs and counties were coherent geographical communities which had separate interests. With urban sprawl, it was increasingly difficult to argue that county communities were in principle different from borough ones.[37] The logic of a high county franchise, which property could dominate, had been that county areas depended on landowner investment and patronage for prosperity and homogeneity. This was no longer true.[38]

Though many Liberals were interested in county franchise extension before 1874, the election defeat, followed by heightened agricultural depression, sealed its success; Hartington declared in its favour in 1877. The election was not lost in the boroughs for the Liberals won 180 British borough seats to the Conservatives' 143. But they took only 50 county seats, compared to 169 Conservative ones. Liberals could rationalise the defeat as being the verdict not of the 'people' but of a small class who intimidated some voters and benefited from the exclusion of others. Meanwhile, economic tension was straining the relationship between landlords, tenants and labourers. Landlords and tenants quarrelled over levels of rent, access to land through the market, compensation for improvements, and the right to shoot game. The Agricultural Labourers' Union, formed in 1872, demanded better wages and living conditions, and shorter hours. Inevitably, Liberals used the same argument in support of enfranchising agricultural labourers as they had on behalf of the urban artisan: unless they had the vote, parliament would lack the knowledge or incentive to respond to their grievances.* Radicals complained that much existing social legislation – on artisans' dwellings, truck, child labour – did not apply to rural areas or small towns, and that even where it did, the neglect of unelected magistrates made it a dead letter. Master and servant, liquor, land, education, sanitary and church reform would all, therefore, be helped by county franchise extension.[39] As landlords and labourers emerged as separate and important 'interests', the idea that one should rule unchecked and the other be deliberately *excluded* from the franchise was unacceptable to most Liberals.[40]

---

* There is little evidence of Liberals' *sympathy* for the Agricultural Labourers' Union; they were not a rural party. The 1872 strikes were suppressed partly by the use of troops to gather the harvest. It is better to see Liberal interest as an attempt to prevent the recurrence of tension. In any case, the Union collapsed in the late 1870s, and most labourers had never been involved in it. See J.P.D. Dunbabin, 'The "revolt of the field": the agricultural labourers' movement in the 1870s', *Past and Present*, xxvi (1963), 68–97.

Implicit in this argument was a wider assumption that landlords, unless made responsible to the people, were unfit to govern their localities. So county franchise reform meshed well with the local government and land reform ideas which we have already seen Liberals mooting in the run-up to 1880 (pages 242–3). The restoration of social harmony, administrative efficiency and Liberal representation in the counties seemed to go hand-in-hand. This was a clever tactic because it appealed both to those radicals who disliked landlord power and to the bulk of moderate Liberals who believed that greater economic and political efficiency by the landed classes would regenerate rural society. While county MPs might remain 'the same men . . . they will be actuated by new ideas and new motives'.[41] They might also be more Liberal; Hartington said in 1880 that there was no reason why not, since counties had the same interest in efficient and cheap government as boroughs.[42] Jacob Bright drew a distinction between borough MPs, generally Liberal and anxious to represent the interests of all classes in the constituency, and county MPs, passive men, sitting by virtue of landowning connections, and removed from 'an atmosphere of discussion'. It was not surprising that they represented 'political ignorance and political selfishness'. A final argument was that a proper representation of boroughs *and* counties would make parliament 'a self-acting, self-indicating machine' fully alive to national interests. So it would stabilise the state by making extra-parliamentary agitation against abuses superfluous.[43]

After the Liberals returned to government, this commitment evolved into the 1884 Reform Act, which extended the household and lodger suffrages of 1867 to the counties. It increased the British electorate by two-thirds; 4.4 million could vote in England and Wales in 1886, compared to 1 million in 1866. A few doctrinaire Liberals, principally Lowe and Goschen, had consistently opposed the extension of the county franchise. They argued that there was no security for good government if the executive was dependent on the whims of a House of Commons elected by voters ignorant of basic principles, particularly of political economy.[44] But so overpowering was the reasoning behind county franchise extension that in 1880 even Lowe surrendered to fashion and renounced his opposition. In 1884, there was a remarkable roll-call of the whig peerage in support of the principle of the third Reform Bill: 146 voted for it, including querulous spirits such as Somerset, Fitzwilliam, Fortescue, Norfolk, Minto, Argyll and Elcho (now Lord Wemyss).

So the logic of the act was irresistible, despite the enormity of the consequences. Moreover, logic also dictated a large-scale scheme of constituency redistribution. This was necessary for three reasons. First, the great increase in the county electorate (250 per cent in England and Wales) made existing seats impossibly large and heterogeneous. Rural labourers, small-town artisans and suburban clerks all needed representation, along with that of local property. The question for politicians was how far to recognise, and how far to suppress, that mixture of influences within individual seats. Liberals had for a long time been anxious to avoid making too rigid a distinction between urban and rural areas, which would aggravate class tension.[45] On the other hand, many felt that unless *some* attention was paid to the representation of specific minority interests, those interests would be swamped by the weight of new voters. As the range of government activity increased, elements in each party naturally feared the socially destructive influence of sectional groups on the opposing side, when in government.

Redistribution was urged, secondly, because after 1867 the electorate, not parliament, now chose and dismissed governments. But voters in big towns were grossly under-represented by the old model of representation. In 1867, for example, the number of voters in Birmingham had risen from 10,823 to 63,909, but the number of representatives only from two to three. It was said that, if Manchester and other similar towns had their fair share of representation, national government would no longer be in the hands of incompetent tories, allowing Liberals to revive agriculture and improve employment and wages.[46] In the 1880 campaign, Hartington himself called for redistribution to give fair weight to great urban centres.[47]

Thirdly, the importance placed on representing opinion accurately cast the spotlight on the small boroughs, traditionally justified on the grounds that they represented 'minorities'. Was this an effective representation of the right minorities, or merely a now-glaring abuse? Not all Liberals wanted to abolish small boroughs, the traditional safeguard of property and intelligence and the boltholes for unpopular ministers. But small boroughs witnessed most of the corruption which remained in the system, and were still heavily influenced by individual patrons or by purely local squabbles. They also favoured the Liberals disproportionately, which disinclined canny Conservatives to defend them. Yet if most small boroughs were merged into counties, this would make the new 'county' seats even more urban.

So the redistribution settlement had to recognise that the old notions of interest representation – through small boroughs and through equal standing for towns and counties of widely varying sizes – were outdated. A tolerably fair indication of the numerical distribution of voters was required. Yet this pointed up the need also to protect minorities against swamping by the 'masses', and hence to recast interest representation on a new, more efficient basis.

How were these ideals to be reconciled? One favoured solution of Liberal intellectuals was proportional representation. From the 1860s, various such schemes were mooted, of which the single transferable vote had come to be the favourite by the mid-1880s. Much of the initial pressure for proportional representation had come from intellectuals like J.S. Mill who were sceptical of the reasoning capacities of a mass electorate and wished to see a mechanism for securing the presence in the Commons of intelligent men who they believed would not win favour with majority opinion in a large territorial constituency. But it was also attractive in that it promised a real democracy, a more accurate representation of working-class opinion itself. Also, the 1884 act extended household suffrage to Ireland, so threatening to alter the balance of representation between loyalists and Nationalists there. In 1884–5, in discussions on the Redistribution Bill, a number of Liberals argued that the most effective way of preserving the political influence of intelligent principles and of the loyal Irish minority in the new democracy was by a system of proportional representation rather than single-member districts. In March 1885, an amendment for the transferable vote was proposed by two academic Liberals, Sir John Lubbock and Leonard Courtney (a former professor of political economy at University College London, who resigned from the government on the issue). Their argument was that democracy had usually failed in past societies because of the opportunity which it gave to extreme men to accumulate excessive power. This could be avoided only by a system which preserved the influence of minorities, which the single-member system did not properly do.[48] Lubbock feared that the new Irish representation would 'tend to break up the Empire'. Courtney was quite explicit about the prospect that, henceforth, 'political economists would . . . be driven from the House', that the principles of the poor law and of free trade would be endangered.[49]

But these were unfashionable ideas: only 12 British Liberals joined Lubbock and Courtney in the lobby (with 4 Irish Liberals and 15 Tories, 7 of whom also sat for Irish seats). This was partly because radicals like Chamberlain detested any form of proportional representation, on the grounds that it would allow the forces of obstruction to defy the popular will.[50] But just as important were those who thought that it would boost caucus-type party organisation, as it required a greater disciplining of each party's supporters than a straightforward vote.[51] To them, in a highly organised national party system, proportional representation threatened to highlight, not representative voter sentiment, but one of two sorts of organised minority opinion. One was a minority political party; this would interfere with the need for a firm majority for the governing party in parliament if it was to exercise authority. The second was whichever policy cliques within each party happened to have captured the local organisation. This threatened to clog the parliamentary timetable on behalf of unrepresentative, unscrupulous sections. MPs could rely for election on the votes of organised faddists, groups such as opponents of alcohol sales, vaccination or vivisection.[52] Proportional representation would damage MPs' ability to speak for the country as a whole. Liberals preferred the simple system of majority voting in single-member seats, on the ground that it secured effective executive government, and because it forced the MP to find a modus vivendi between the opinions of various local elements and his own views, out of which a higher synthesis, 'what is best and soundest', emerged.[53] The basic flaw of proportional representation was that, in an attempt to reflect with mathematical accuracy the diversity of opinion within a constituency, it ascribed to voters a more precise set of views than in fact they possessed. It offended against the traditional notion that 'character' in a well-rounded MP was the best way to reflect the variety, flexibility and incoherence of local opinion. The MP's job was to mature and reconcile the half-formed sentiments of the whole community, which the constitution recognised as 'an integral quantity'.[54] The Liberal mainstream believed that the best defence of threatened minority interests – as in Ireland – was provided not by one or two extra MPs but by the 'liberal character of the Legislature' as a whole, as Hartington put it.[55] Hartington had no time for intellectuals' anxiety that the new electors would be ignorant of the great principles of political economy, pointing out that most of the old electors had been as well.[56]

But how to secure a balance of opinion within the traditional majority voting system that would continue to smoothe over social divisions and minimise the effects of voter ignorance? The answer adopted in the Redistribution Act of 1885 reflected Conservative attitudes as much as Liberal ones, because of the astuteness of the Conservative leadership in 1884. Led by Salisbury, the tories initially blocked the Franchise Bill in the Lords and won a place in negotiations over redistribution as the price of letting it through. So the 1885 act was a compromise between many contributors: Gladstone and Salisbury, but also Hartington and Dilke, two of the other negotiators, defending whig and radical interests within the Liberal party. None of them got quite what they wanted. But the pace of borough disfranchisement was set by the Conservatives, who pressed for the suppression of large numbers of small boroughs in order to create as many single-member suburban and county seats as possible, to the irritation of both Gladstone and Hartington, who tried but failed to limit small borough disfranchisement to the 10,000 population level. Tory logic was avowedly class-based: to create pockets of middle-class urban and suburban influence, and to reduce the size of county seats and with it the cost of elections and the chance of external challenges to local gentry predominance.

The 1885 Redistribution Act created a system of overwhelmingly single-member seats, apportioned roughly on the basis of population, but each also constructed with a view to interest representation. All counties, and all boroughs with a population of over 165,000, were to be divided into a number of one-member districts, to be determined by population (the minority vote clause of 1867 was abolished where it had operated). So these areas gained many extra seats: 62 in English counties, 37 in London, 26 in the 12 multi-district big towns.* Those seats were found by merging 76 small boroughs with a population below 15,000 into county seats, and reducing 35 others with a population below 50,000 to single-member status. This left just 21 English and 6 other two-member boroughs. The effect on the Commons was remarkable. In 1879, 192 of the 282 English borough seats represented towns with a population of under 50,000; in 1886, 73 of 226 did. In 1879, 200 MPs sat for English boroughs which had returned members before 1832; in 1886, 67 did (whole boroughs only). The most significant effect of redistribution in 1885 was the death of the small borough.

* See Appendix 2 for more details.

In retrospect, the redistribution of 1885 marks the crucial step towards the modern system of socially ill-defined constituencies dominated by the party machines. The great growth in the county electorate damaged landed influence and made more professional constituency organisation essential. So did the emergence of more democratic local government – and hence more regular elections at all levels – in the counties in the 1880s and 1890s. Added to falling rent-rolls, this delivered a major blow to aristocratic power. The number of local landowners returned for county seats declined dramatically, to be replaced by local businessmen and professional political outsiders.[57]

However, not all of this was predictable in 1885. Much of it was caused by the collapse of landed influence in the Liberal party as a result of the 1886 crisis. After that date, those few landowners who remained Liberals continued to win county seats if they had the money and organisational backing to do so. Though the new county electorate was more urban and hence more independent of landed influence than before, it remained true that a combination of prestige, money and organisation won county and market town elections. This is why the defection of a relatively small class of propertied men had so disproportionately damaging an effect on Liberal fortunes from 1886 onwards. In that respect, though the decline in small borough seats certainly reduced the number of propertied Liberal MPs, it was not clear that the advent of single-member county seats would; some predicted that it would compensate them, by perpetuating local influence and reducing the cost of election fights.[58]*

Liberals certainly argued that single-member county seats were the best hope, among a choice of evils, of securing 'representation of minorities . . . representation of separate interests and pursuits' and 'large diversity' in the electoral system.[60] The Boundary Commission was told, as was traditional, to base divisions on recognised local traditions and with regard to 'the pursuits of the population'. In consequence, some divisions in Liverpool were twice as populous as others. Where possible, urban areas of counties were to be placed in the same division: hence the creation of the Jarrow division of Durham, for example.[61] Accordingly, the new divisions were

---

* One long-held assumption about 1885 is that the virtual demise of the two-member borough seat reduced the number of 'whig' MPs because they had previously been allowed one of the two seats by radical constituency caucuses. In fact, most borough seats already returned only one member before 1885, and the seats which lost one of their two members in 1885 were generally substantial 'county towns' which then swung not to the radicals but decisively to the Conservatives. In 1880, Liberals took 74 per cent of these seats, in 1886, 11 per cent. See Appendix 4, category D for a full analysis and list. This extraordinary change, never to my knowledge noticed before, is worth investigation, but at first sight it seems an excellent indication of the hostility of the 'respectable' classes to the new Liberal departures of 1885–6. (À propos of the long-held assumption, above, it should also be noted that the radical NLF disliked the single-member idea, especially for London, where Liberal organisation was so weak.[59])

subject to an interesting mix of influences. Of the three Hampshire divisions, one was urban, suburban and dockland in character, one very agricultural, and one agricultural and military (owing to the Aldershot garrison). The influence of miners, framework-knitters and ironworkers made Mid-Derbyshire a Liberal seat; the combination of less mining, more agriculture, and the Cavendish influence was to make West Derbyshire Unionist. Agriculture and the Taunton suburbs turned Somerset West tory despite the Liberal slate-quarry influence; but scattered small cloth manufacturing towns, a heavy Dissenting presence and the influence of Liberal gentry secured that party victory in Somerset South.[62] This attempt to mix influences can also be discerned in a rearguard action on behalf of the old whig talisman, the borough freeholder vote in counties. Despite having to accept the extension of over thirty borough boundaries and hence the addition to borough seats of 366,368 urban voters who would otherwise have influenced the county, Gladstone and Hartington succeeded in defending the right of men owning freehold property in the boroughs to vote on that franchise in the appropriate county, even if qualified elsewhere and even if non-resident. Half a million votes qualified on the ownership franchise in 1886. Radicals were astonished at this defence of plural voting. Not until the sea-change of 1886 did the Liberal leadership reject it.

The immediate significance of 1885 lay not in boosting 'radical' over 'whig' strength in the Liberal party, but in increasing general concern for the future influence of property and intelligence against the power of uncontrollable, unpredictable mass pressure. Though the logic by which democracy had arrived was flawless, the swiftness and extent of the change was jarring. As Home Secretary Harcourt – not a cowering reactionary – wrote in December 1884, the new legislation was 'a frightfully democratic measure which I confess appals me'.[63] The Reform Act did not make whig-Liberal politics impossible. But it did create a heightened sense of insecurity about threats to the traditional Liberal governing ideals prominent throughout this book. The Liberal party fell apart in 1886 not because these ideals were now outdated but because of a disagreement between two different approaches to defending them in the turbulent circumstances which 1885 created.

The tensions of 1885

Anxiety about the effects of the Reform settlement was compounded by the state of the economy. In the towns, the 1880s brought increased unemployment – and greatly increased awareness of it – and some riots in large towns, most strikingly in Trafalgar Square in February 1886. In the countryside, rent rolls on great estates were badly hit by the effects of cheap international competition in basic foodstuffs. Malthusian fears about the pressure of population on resources revived. The existing distribution of property seemed threatened by political and economic developments.

287

Economic uncertainty also led to concern about the future of Britain's export trade in the face of international competition. The heightened colonial activity of other European powers suggested that Britain's foreign possessions and naval supremacy were under attack. And would the new democracy be willing to sanction the taxes necessary for efficient defence and to tolerate 'expert' control of international diplomacy?

The peculiarity of Liberal history in 1885–6 is that 1885, unusually, was a year of tension between 'whig' and 'Chamberlainite' factions. But this was manageable and had very little to do with the crisis of 1886. An election was due after the passage of redistribution and was held in November–December 1885. The timing suited Chamberlain particularly because the Liberals had by then been defeated and replaced by a minority Conservative government, which increased his freedom of manoeuvre. He had long been planning to exploit the advent of an increased electorate by floating a programme of advanced legislative proposals. Its main points were the extension of local government powers to acquire land at a fair price to let as allotments, smallholdings and artisans' dwellings; the establishment of elected authorities in counties; free and efficient elementary education, funded by higher taxes and/or by church disestablishment and disendowment; and graduated taxation, in order to reduce the burden on the poor and (though this was rarely stated) to maintain adequate levels of defence spending. As his later career was to reveal, Chamberlain's concern was with 'strong Government and an Imperial Government'. He believed that the traditional justification for parliamentary independence, that of checking the abuse of power held by a small class, now unfortunately led to it 'meddl[ing]. . . . far too much' with an executive which was founded on popular approval.[64] He hoped by active leadership of mass opinion to overhaul inefficient government practice. He sought to rally middle-and working-class opinion behind this policy by targetting an aristocratic enemy. He talked of the 'natural rights' of men, the 'excessive inequality in the distribution of riches', the benefits of 'socialism', especially at local level, and the 'ransom', in the shape of high taxes and rates, which men of property should expect to pay in order to safeguard their advantages.[65]

Chamberlain hoped to convince Liberals that only he could interpret the views of the new electorate; this would create momentum behind both his programme and his career. But his strategy had three flaws. First, most constituency radicals were distant from his thinking, belonging rather to the party's moralistic-economy wing whose confidence Chamberlain had never really commanded, as the failure of the National Education League had shown. They thought that Chamberlain, who had no rapport with evangelical religion, lacked 'moral fibre'.[66] Disappointed by the financial record of the 1880–5 government, most of them hoped that Reform would facilitate further economies. Second, respectable opinion disliked his apparent threat to market principles and the church establishment. Third, he, no more than anyone else, had much idea of what policies would appeal to newly-enfranchised rural labourers. So, though he gained a great deal of publicity in 1885, set the political agenda, and worried traditional Liberals, he failed. As Liberals had done so often, he overestimated the radicalism of electors. By the summer, he realised this, and tried to relegate his more damaging ideas – further constitutional reform and disestablishment – to the distant future. But, despite his efforts, disestablishment became a major issue in the election, especially in Scotland, where it was made a test question in a number of constituencies. The Conservatives fanned the flames by launching a 'Church-in-danger' campaign, and the formidable energies of the clergy were enlisted in the fight.[67] The whigs became alarmist; an anti-disestablishment manifesto was published in the *Times*, bearing the names of such peers as Westminster, Bedford, Somerset, Fitzwilliam, Selborne and Grey.[68] Moderate Liberals criticised Gladstone for failing to give a lead, both against disestablishment and in disciplining Chamberlain.[69] Gladstone was finally forced to declare that disestablishment was impracticable at present and should not be made a test question. But the electoral damage was done. Though in the counties the Reform Act allowed Liberals finally to tap the urban Dissenting and artisan opinion, and rural labouring sentiment, which had been suppressed for so long, Chamberlain's aggression led to heavy losses among the middle classes in the boroughs, especially in Lancashire, London and the market towns. The result was that, while Liberals had an 84-seat majority over the Conservatives, Parnell's Nationalists, who had swept southern Ireland, held the balance of power with 86 MPs, and kept Salisbury in power.

The reverse badly embarrassed Chamberlain and highlighted his subordinate role in the party. Hartington was still the leader-in-waiting most capable of synthesising the parliamentary and popular tradition within the party. When Gladstone retired, Goschen and Forster would return, Chamberlain and Dilke could be promoted, and a Palmerstonian foreign policy would unite the party. The new parliament was *not* hostile to property; it was packed with 'new men, in deadly earnest' for sober and rational reforming measures to continue the work of social and moral improvement.[70]* The Liberals still seemed likely to be the majority party for many years.

For all the tension of 1885, domestic questions were not seriously at issue between Liberals. They could agree on extending the powers of local government and supplying a steady stream of administrative improvement, along the lines charted in chapter 10. The more controversial questions centred on defence and Ireland. And these revealed once more the old truth that, if the glint in Chamberlain's monocle sometimes appeared threatening to propertied Liberals, it was as nothing compared to the unnerving gimlet stare of Gladstone.

Gladstone had been a destabilising factor since 1880. His insistence

---

* The average number of private members' bills introduced rose from 131 in 1881/4 to 226 in 1885/8 and 256 in 1889/92. I have taken these figures from the annual returns in *Parliamentary papers*.

that he was about to retire to contemplate religion made rational policy discussion difficult within the cabinet, and forward planning almost impossible. Uncertainty for the future greatly increased tension. Both Hartington and Chamberlain were driven onto the defensive, acting as protectors of sectional interests within the party. Yet both were forced to defend Gladstone's continued leadership, for fear that if either took the blame for pushing him out, the succession would favour the other. It is symptomatic of the confused relations within cabinet that both men at times believed that they individually stood alone against their colleagues.[71] The bizarre result was the simultaneous emasculation of all the leading Liberals of the day, and a style of government far removed from the decisive, purposeful yet reassuring Liberal ideal. Yet this also encouraged Gladstone to stay. It allowed him to argue that only he could unite the party – and save it from Chamberlain, whose 'socialism', irreligion and class language he abhorred.

Discussion of imperial and defence policy was particularly affected by these uncertainties, and by the hostility of Gladstone and the party's moral-economy wing to a Palmerstonian strategy of national assertion. Led by the court, the advocates of the latter strategy were increasingly vocal; to them, firm defence of British markets and territorial interests seemed all the more necessary in reaction to domestic economic difficulty and international imperial rivalry. After the Bulgarian agitation and the Midlothian campaign, they worried about Gladstone's failure to provide clear, hard-headed leadership. He seemed to lack purpose, except in his propensity to 'sentimentalism' about popular rights. One Liberal imperial administrator found Gladstone ignorant yet dogmatic on foreign questions and believed that his rambling, unintelligible speeches were the consequences of that lack of command.[72] Moreover, the Conservatives were now very interested in exploiting propertied Palmerstonian disquiet at Gladstone's 'unpatriotic' policy. An assertively 'national' approach, articulating Britain's identity as a self-reliant, Protestant power, was urged by most of the metropolitan press, while historical works like J.A. Froude's *History of England*, presenting Britain's sixteenth-century history – the Reformation and struggle with degenerate Catholic Spain – as the doorway to national greatness, made possible by the government's hard-headed control of popular religious passions, became more popular than when originally published in Palmerston's heyday. Gladstone, for his part, was increasingly impatient with his critics: by November 1881 the moralistic Little-Englander Morley-Stead *Pall Mall Gazette* was 'the only paper he can now be got to look at', and earlier that year he had announced his belief in a 'great conspiracy against the nation . . . which lives and works among the heads of the military class'.[73]

This clash of views made overseas affairs particularly contentious between 1880 and 1885. One area of permanent tension was the administration of India by Gladstone's 'sentimental' Viceroy Lord Ripon. Ripon sought to win the confidence of the natives by repealing his predecessor's restrictions on the vernacular press, decentralising certain public duties to popular local bodies, and allowing non-European judges to try cases involving European settlers. All were bitterly contested by the bureaucracy in India and at home, on the ground that they applied the principles of English Liberalism to a people not yet fit to practise them, and so weakened respect for European rule. The first had to be repealed (by Morley, of all people, in 1910), the second failed and the third was substantially withdrawn after a fierce argument.

In 1880, controversy quickly arose over the Transvaal, which had been annexed under the aegis of Disraeli's government. At Midlothian, Gladstone had criticised this but, on coming into office, the Liberals were advised that the annexation was in fact acceptable to the Boers and offered the oppressed local Zulus essential protection. Reluctantly, tory policy was continued, in fact of much moral Liberal criticism in parliament. The advice was faulty. The Boers rose up, and an unwise British military initiative led to an embarrassing defeat at Majuba Hill in early 1881. Gladstone's response was to haul up the white flag: the Pretoria Convention in August replaced annexation by a declaration of British 'suzerainty' over the Boers. This elegant term disguised the reality of what was in fact withdrawal, a position which was confirmed in 1884. To the 'national' public, this weak-willed climbdown damaged Britain's world standing. The queen was furious, and Gladstone, speaking at Leeds in October, was forced to pledge that he was 'devoted to the empire'.[74]

In these circumstances, the government was wise to intervene in turbulent Egypt in 1882 (behind the quickly crumbling figleaf of 'Concert of Europe' action). The defence of the Suez Canal and British financial interests made action imperative. In the process, however, Alexandria had to be bombarded, which offended 'sentimental' Liberals, and Bright once again enjoyed the luxury of a conscience-stricken resignation from cabinet. Gladstone was not distressed by the logic of defensive imperial intervention, especially in order to restore financial probity in Egypt (a Baring was dispatched to pummel finance and administration into shape in 1883). But he was angered by any financial burden beyond strict necessity; the crises abroad were preventing a repetition of the economies of his first government. So, when Moslem rebellion proved ineradicable in the vast wastes of Egypt's dependency the Sudan, he was unsympathetic to calls for the British army to stay to fight it. In a public outburst he described the Moslems there as a people 'rightly struggling to be free'.[75] But General Gordon, driven by evangelical missionary zeal, disobeyed the orders he had been given to evacuate British troops in the Sudan. When the rebels cut him off, cabinet whigs demanded the despatch of a rescue force. Gladstonian obstinacy and cabinet infighting postponed the decision to relieve Gordon for too long. When the news of his heroic death was received in London, the 'Grand Old Man', the G.O.M., became the M.O.G., 'Murderer of Gordon', in the eyes of the tory press. Gordon became a Christian martyr. No single episode before 1886 did more damage to public confidence in Liberal government. It revived the bitter allegations in propertied circles that Gladstone was not to be trusted in the most basic duties of government, the protection of life, property and territory. His Foreign Secretary, the gouty Granville, was much criticised for his procrastination and insufficiently sombre attitude to crises. Most cabinet peers wanted the government to resign; only Gladstone kept it alive.[76]

At the same time, the government had to face more expenditure demands. Defence spending rose by £4.5 million between 1880 and 1886. Increased ship-building by other powers, especially France, led to a campaign in 1884 from the services and the press for naval expansion. Then the Russians advanced on Pendjeh in 1885 and another Afghan war threatened. The government was forced to withdraw its troops from the Sudan – despite Hartington's Commons pledge to avenge Gordon's murder – and to ask for £11 million in a vote of credit. To meet the deficit (£15 million in all), income tax had to be raised from 5d to 8d, and death duties and beer and spirit duties were increased. The financial package was not popular. The government's opponents rallied, too many Liberal MPs abstained and the government was defeated and resigned in June 1885.

The short-term crisis apart, this vote was not a sign of disunity in the party. But it did point to one worrying problem. The defeat, and Salisbury's accession to office, was caused largely by the opposition of the Parnellites en bloc. This was the result of recent quarrels about Irish policy (which also placed Chamberlain in a problematic position and led him and his supporters to hope for government defeat). A combination of imperial and Irish issues had led nine cabinet ministers to tender their resignations in the month before the government fell. The Irish question, that most dangerous of issues for Liberals, had returned. And it had returned at a time when overseas problems had already spawned a coherent critique of 'sentimental' Gladstonian policy from the court, the military and most of the aristocracy and plutocracy, who were wondering if the principles of imperial integration were safe in his hands.

Ireland and Home Rule

There were in fact three Irish questions in the 1880s. Land, coercion and local government posed separate difficulties.

The Irish land problem had worsened markedly in the late 1870s, in reaction to the agricultural depression, which created great social tension. Liberal attempts of 1849 and 1860 to strengthen freedom of contract principles in Irish land tenure arrangements had been flawed, because those principles did not fit the reality. Many Irish tenants, especially in Ulster, understood themselves to be partners in ownership with the landlord, customary freeholders, with recognised rights, such as the right to remain in possession if they paid rent, and to transfer their occupancy to another tenant. Many landlords in the south accepted the first of these claims; they were less happy with the second. Evictions were not common, except during severe economic tension in 1845–50 and later in 1879–82. Nonetheless, Irish tenants naturally hoped for legal protection for these customs. They also relived eras of alien confiscation of land with a peculiar intensity. In 1865 the Irish radical Dillon told a commission that there had been 'very recent . . . and very extensive confiscations', but when pressed on this said that they had occurred 'in the time of Cromwell'.[77] Gladstone's Irish Land Act of 1870 had nodded to tenants' views without explicitly granting fixity of tenure. It recognised Ulster tenant right and other customary rights wherever landlords had previously acquiesced in them. It confirmed all tenants' right to compensation for improvements, and compensation for disturbance (eviction) for causes other than the non-payment of rent. By this means it sought to discourage evictions. But Gladstone also articulated the views of some economists that tenant security would benefit agricultural investment. This bill was criticised more by doctrinaire political economists Lowe and Argyll in the cabinet than by the Commons, where only 11 MPs voted against second reading.

But the agricultural depression of the late 1870s made it superfluous. Irish harvests were extremely poor from 1877 to 1879, causing rent arrears and evictions on a large scale. Nationalist leaders Davitt and Parnell exploited tenant anger by stitching together a mass (though unwieldy) campaigning organisation, the Land League, which fought evictions with agrarian outrages. The solution of the incoming Liberal government of 1880 was a Compensation for Disturbance Bill, which aimed to check evictions by temporarily extending compensation for disturbance to those evicted for non-payment of rent. To British landowners, this was a staggering proposal, because it tore up the prescriptions of political economy, responded to violent lawlessness by giving a class boon even to untrustworthy tenants, and could not be withdrawn, once introduced, without prompting massive social unrest. Lansdowne resigned from the government in protest; 21 Liberal MPs voted against it in the Commons, and it was routed in the Lords by 282 to 51, with a majority of Liberal peers opposing it. But this was not a sign of impending secession from the party. It was, instead, an indication of the Liberal peerage's willingness to use the Lords as a revising chamber for obviously hasty and slipshod legislation.[78] The government's response, the 1881 Irish Land Act, was much more acceptable; it followed the recommendations of a Royal Commission. A judicial machinery was set up to fix fair rents. The historic right of most tenants to fixity of tenure and the right to sell their interest (assuming payment of the judicial rent) was confirmed. Argyll resigned from the cabinet in protest, but in general the revolt of the political economists was muted. Gladstone reassured them by arguing that freedom of contract was inappropriate in Ireland only because the normal relationships of a commercially-developed society had not yet been forged. Again Liberals asserted that the best route to that developed state was through giving tenants sufficient security to invest capital, which would also reduce Ireland's dependence on the Exchequer.[79] The 1881 act was irrelevant to marginal farmers in the west unable to pay their rents, but an Arrears Act of 1882 allowed them to apply for reductions, and this did a great deal to reduce agitation.

So Liberals could just about reconcile Irish land legislation with models of economic progress under the Union. The political difficulty now became not land, but coercion. Much of the difficulty here was caused by the bad judgment of Forster, the Irish Secretary (1880-2), called 'the pendulum' by the Dublin Castle administration on account of his vacillation. Anxious to live up to his tough stage Yorkshireman image, Forster forced through a Coercion Act in 1881 conferring on the Lord Lieutenant power to arrest on warrant persons suspected of acts of violence or intimidation. This offended the libertarian instincts of Liberal backbenchers and failed to achieve its purpose of destroying the Land League. The Land Act split the League (as Gladstone intended), but Parnell, in an attempt to regroup his forces, edged towards a populist campaign in which he seemed to be arousing tenant feeling against the Land Act. This led the government to intern him in Kilmainham Gaol; nothing was more likely to make him a martyr in Irish eyes. Gladstone, having hoped to smash him and build up the constitutionalist wing of the Irish party, now came to appreciate his power as a popular educator. In the spring of 1882 he had him released in return for a pledge that he would exert his authority to quell discontent. The extraction of such guarantees was normal on releasing suspects, and Parnell had not been convicted. Nonetheless, an overwrought Forster resigned, alleging that the 'Kilmainham Treaty' damaged the authority of law. In fact, the government realised that it was politically essential to accompany the release with another, less arbitrary, coercive measure, the Crimes Act, which established a special tribunal, without jury, to deal with cases of treason, murder and other important crimes for which an impartial trial by ordinary judicial process seemed impossible. It also extended summary jurisdiction for some minor crimes. The logic of the Crimes Bill was reinforced by the assassination of Forster's successor, Lord Frederick Cavendish, on arriving in Dublin in May 1882.

Under the intelligent rule of the Lord Lieutenant, Lord Spencer, the Crimes Act regime broke the Land League and brought some measure of government authority back to the Irish countryside – helped, of course, by the stabilising rent reductions of 1881-2. Spencer reorganised the police forces and rejuvenated the magistracy. It is vital to understand that in the mid-1880s most Liberals had not lost confidence in their ability to govern Ireland essentially on their own terms. British law remained tolerably effective in all key areas. It maintained a court which aimed to arbitrate fairly between landlords and tenants. It upheld an education system which, by asserting the principle of non-denominationalism, offered some security to Protestant communities. It continued to enforce 'British' institutions such as the poor law. Liberals sustained a framework in which Catholic and Protestant, landlord and tenant, had to tolerate each other. Opposition was fragmented; Parnell had great difficulty in constructing a 'Nationalist' alliance in 1879-80 and, even so, had only 35 regular followers in the 1880 parliament. Parnell's 'nationalism' appeared to be merely manageable economic grievances dressed up in new clothes, so many Liberals refused to see him as a representative political leader.[80] Liberals prided themselves on their 'character' and determined impartiality as administrators. Northbrook was typically phlegmatic in 'much doubt[ing] whether the difficulty of governing Ireland is not exaggerated'.[81]

The Irish difficulty in the mid-1880s came instead from the application to Ireland of the constitutional assumptions which Liberals were developing for use elsewhere in the kingdom. One was the extension of the county franchise, which promised to be a great boon to Parnell. But no less important was Liberal interest in county government reform in Britain. This made it impossible for Gladstone or Chamberlain to deny that the establishment of elected county authorities in Ireland would develop habits of responsibility and orderliness among the population. Gladstone maintained that it would teach Irishmen the value of low taxes and good communications, and stimulate local schemes for land purchase and agricultural improvement which would bind tenants and local landlords together in mutual respect. The problem in 1885 was that, with the Reform Act passed, there was no longer an excuse not to proceed with local government reform. Chamberlain demanded it as his price for tolerating the renewal of the Crimes Act, which also expired in 1885. He proposed elected county boards, which would also nominate a central board which would administer education, the poor law and public works. Hartington and the cabinet whigs succeeded in blocking this proposal, fearing that the board would lobby for separation. Instead, the cabinet agreed to renew the Crimes Act for one year, to the anger of Chamberlain and Dilke, and to the greater anger of Parnell. Hence his part in the government's defeat – which also saved Chamberlain from having to decide whether to support the Crimes Act or resign.

Parnell then kept the minority tory government in power, even after the 1885 election – at the price of leaving the Crimes Act unrenewed, to tory backbench anger. To Gladstone, this alliance with the 'demoralised & dangerous' tories was a corrupt bargain, entered into against the wishes of the electorate. It would be 'an abdication of primary duty' not to give vent to the people's will by supplanting it.[82] Furthermore, in opposition Chamberlain and Dilke were becoming more undisciplined on policy in general, to Gladstone's irritation.[83] Gladstone convinced himself that one last service was demanded of him before retirement. He began to prepare a scheme of Irish devolution. This carrot persuaded Parnell to ally with him and to defeat Salisbury in January 1886. In April 1886 Gladstone's new government brought in a Home Rule Bill.

Gladstone saw Home Rule as a conservative measure. He was anxious to restore proper social and political relationships in Ireland, establishing responsibility, upholding the influence of property, and marginalising lawbreakers and politically-obsessed priests. The 1885 election, in which Parnell's followers won 85 Irish seats, sweeping all but Ulster, persuaded him that the Irish 'people' had definitely pronounced in favour of self-government and the Nationalists. This was a remarkable propaganda coup for Parnell, who had only turned the Land League into a 'National League' three years before. Gladstone's sudden discovery that 'Nationalism' was the deeply-held belief of the Irish 'people' was treated with enormous scepticism by critics who surmised that Parnell's crucial leverage over British politics might be the more important factor in his thinking. As he read about Ireland (he had only been there for a month, in 1877), Gladstone became obsessed with the notion that the Irish people formed an organic whole through a shared national identity. He romanticised the Nationalist crusade, in reality a bitter, divisive affair, as a solvent of social and religious tension and a means of upholding the leadership of men of property, like the late eighteenth-century Irish nationalist campaigns described in his history books. In this light, the policy of coercion seemed immoral and doomed to failure. In late 1885, Gladstone convinced himself that Ireland was on the verge of anarchy.[84] He dramatised the situation as 'one of those crises in the history of nations when the path of boldness is the path, and the only path, of safety'.[85] The idea of a great crisis, requiring swift *action*, provided the justification, for which Gladstone was subconsciously looking, not to renounce the political arena. His bill seemed to offer the prospect of restoring propertied influence by establishing two 'orders' in an Irish parliament; one would consist of 103 peers and other large property-owners. By reviving respect for the natural rulers of Ireland, it promised to diminish the influence of nationalist agitators and ultramontane priests.

In the debates of 1886, the fundamental argument used by supporters of Home Rule was that it was a natural development of the principle of popular, responsible self-government, the only way to rally Irish opinion on the side of the law. They claimed that divisions of class and religion in Ireland stemmed from the abdication, by the natural leaders of Irish society, of their responsibility to 'direct and control' popular effort.[86] Jealousy and hostility between landlord and tenant, and Catholic and Protestant, were owing, not to Irishmen's temperament but 'to the system under which they have been governed'; 'Irish human nature is no worse . . . than other human nature'.[87] If thrown together in one parliament and saddled with the alarming responsibility of raising a revenue, imposing order, maintaining a system of national education, settling agrarian discontent, attacking pauperism and attracting capital investment, Irishmen would have no choice but to suppress sectional differences and learn the art of self-government.[88] Once the unifying factor of hostility to British-made law had evaporated, the Nationalists would lose their power and a more natural political state would emerge, in which diverse local enthusiasms would be reconciled by propertied central leadership. Home Rule Liberals claimed that there were only two options: self-government, or brutal repression denying political rights.[89] They accepted that the government of Ireland under Forster and Spencer had driven Irish discontent underground, but claimed that good government should have higher aspirations, to bind hearts and minds and abolish discontent 'bag and baggage'.[90] Burt hoped to replace the sham union at the level of parliamentary decrees with a 'real and genuine union between one people and another'. Such language was particularly attractive to those like Burt (a miners' MP) who articulated the *British* working-man's desire for self-government. Cowen, another northern radical, defended Home Rule on the principle of allowing each nation to work out its own 'individuality'; political participation would educate and enrich the labourer, would 'wreathe his face in smiles'.[91] Home Rule, in other words, was a declaration of support for the dignity and good sense of the popular conscience everywhere.

Gladstone was also keen to encourage devolution from the imperial parliament for procedural reasons. He wanted to remove the block to legislation caused by the obstructive tactics of the Irish Nationalist MPs, and, more generally, to relieve the Commons of an unmanageable legislative burden. Home Rule might be the first in a series of concessions of power to local bodies which, far from diminishing the dignity of the imperial parliament, would strengthen it for the purpose of regular and cleansing legislative action. Gladstone insisted that decentralisation tapped local vigour more effectively, adding to the unity and strength of the empire.[92]*

But the problem about Home Rule was that while it appeared in line with some Liberal ideals, it directly contravened other, even more powerful, Liberal myths – those of national and imperial integration under the rule of law, and the responsibility of the propertied for the maintenance of order and extension of morality. So it left Liberals with an excruciating dilemma. Those who found it unacceptable tended to be those most defensive of the rule of law, most strenuously attached to church establishments, most respectful of the power of mind, and most concerned about the maintenance of a 'disinterested' economic policy.[†] Ninety-four Liberal MPs, led by Hartington, voted against the second reading of the Home Rule Bill in June 1886, defeating it and leading to a general election which they fought as a separate body of Liberal Unionists. Defectors also included the overwhelming majority of the Liberal peerage (including Peelites and political economists like Argyll, Lowe (now Sherbrooke) and Selborne), an incalculable number of Liberal gentry, the cream of the Liberal intelligentsia and an unquantifiable but vast amount of general propertied opinion. Liberal Unionist MPs included whigs like Viscount Baring, city men like Goschen and Rothschild, laissez-faire zealots like Watkin, and intellectuals like Courtney and Lubbock. But the seceding MPs were also

---

* Unsurprisingly, the Home Rule policy was attractive to the small but growing and vocal band of Welsh and Scottish devolutionists.

† In the party as a whole, there was a strong correlation between opposition to Home Rule and to church disestablishment motions, but no significant correlation on questions of imperial or foreign policy, or agrarian or social reform. See W.C. Lubenow, 'Irish home rule and the great separation in the Liberal party in 1886: the dimensions of parliamentary Liberalism', *Victorian Studies*, XXVI (1982–3), 161–80.

distinguished by the support of Chamberlain, with a few supporters, and Bright. Some influential nonconformist ministers also left the party, mainly non-evangelicals (quakers, like Bright, or unitarians, like Chamberlain), or anti-Catholic Wesleyans, and so more resistant to Gladstone's emotional appeals. Chamberlain's secession was significant not in terms of numbers of adherents – the NLF rallied with tremendous force behind Gladstone – but because it helped to disguise the whig-Liberal nature of the secession, and perhaps made it easier for moderate Liberals with radical constituents to dare to leave the Gladstonian fold.[93]

The fundamental criticism of these men was that the scheme did not maintain the supremacy of the imperial parliament as Gladstonians claimed, and that disastrous practical consequences would follow. This was partly because it could not be a final settlement. It encouraged the Nationalists to agitate for complete separation.[94] Defence, foreign affairs and trade were to be left in the hands of the imperial parliament. Ireland was expected to contribute towards necessary costs in these areas, and a sum of one-fifteenth of the needs of the imperial exchequer was fixed as her contribution. But Irish MPs were not to sit at Westminster – though Gladstone said that he would consider accepting an amendment that they might do so. Either way, the position was unsatisfactory; if at Westminster, the Nationalists could still wreck business until they won complete independence, and if excluded, the cry of 'no taxation without representation' would be a perfect one on which to launch an independence campaign. And how would the imperial levy be collected?

Liberal Unionists claimed that in practice the bill surrendered all power to the Irish parliament, in violation of the principles of integration and efficiency. It gave it control over internal law and order and taxation and it placed the appointment of judges, magistrates and the civil service with the Irish executive. In these circumstances, the safeguards retained by imperial government became irrelevant. The crown would not dare to exercise its legislative veto, not having done so against the British parliament for generations. Nominally, the imperial parliament reserved the right to reassert the powers which it was to delegate to the Irish assembly. Similarly, the Judicial Committee of the Privy Council had the power to determine whether the Irish parliament was exceeding its responsibilities. But in practice, how could these bodies combat an Irish executive which enjoyed popular support and control over the judiciary and the 'revolutionised civil service'?[95] As Hartington said, in practice British rule could be reestablished only by martial law, but armed conquest was unacceptable to him as to all Liberals.[96] Unionists asserted that Westminster's incapacity to act in Ireland was all the more obvious because of the exclusion of the Irish MPs (though of course retaining them would create an equally intractable set of problems). Some Gladstonians came close to admitting that, in the event of unacceptable behaviour by the Irish, the imperial parliament did indeed have no real safeguards, but denied that a crisis was a serious possibility.

However, to Liberal Unionists such a crisis was all too likely. Their defence of imperial rule over Ireland was that it provided a fair field for all interests. It held the ring between Protestant and Catholic, landlord and tenant, law and liberty, ratepayer and pauper. They believed that the main agency of social harmony was the rule of law, guaranteeing the liberties of all groups. They did not believe that a local parliament, suddenly faced with all the burdens of governing a backward and violent country, could do this job as well as the British. In practice, it would be dominated by sectional influences, in particular the mob-orator Nationalists and the Catholic bishops and priests. They would not maintain the liberties of those opposed to them, the liberties of the progressive, propertied Protestant minority, the best safeguard of Irish modernisation.* They would not attract capital or promote liberal learning (the more doctrinaire political economists among the seceders were especially keen to point out that peasant prejudices would ensure the spread of distress, pauperism and superstition).[97] Their leadership would necessarily be wrong-headed. Several Unionists claimed that the real cause of Irish discontent was not Parnell's nationalist figleaf, but simple agrarian discontent. The ultimate reason for this was the world agricultural depression, and the expertise of the imperial parliament was best suited to provide solutions to that. But the Irish had persuaded themselves that the land laws in all civilised societies were wrong.[98]

Unionists believed that the only *raison d'être* of an Irish parliament was that it would pass laws – especially on land – which the imperial parliament would never pass. So the question became whether to agree to slough off the responsibility of governing Ireland to such a body. To Hartington, this was quite unacceptable. Government was about maintaining the 'undisputed supremacy of the law', and about exercising judgment, based on communion with parliament and people, as to when and how to amend it to the general benefit.[99] Unionists denied that coercion was repression. Rather, it involved taking pains to defend the same basic values of civilisation that were voluntarily accepted in the rest of the nation.[100] Home Rule struck a devastating blow at the notion of the supremacy of a truly national supra-factional parliament. To the quaker Unionist Leatham, hardly had this system reached its full flowering, with the passage of the 1884 Reform Act, than it was proposed to destroy it.[101] James maintained that unity meant, not the mere acceptance of the same monarch, but subordination to one legislative body which upheld a common legal code.[102] Goschen insisted that no other parliament in history had as many duties, privileges and responsibilities as that of Britain, and that current MPs were merely life trustees charged with perpetuating its authority. The principle of parliamentary government was that anti-social minorities of any sort were to be resisted.[103] To give in on this point would set a bad example at home and,

---

* Note that Liberals played the *Protestant* card – the card of individualism and modernisation – very much more than the specific *Ulster* card – the card of bigoted minority Orangeism.

especially, in the empire, at a time of severe international competition. It would suggest that Britain had lost 'the old capacity for governing'; it would shake British authority in India.[104] The imperial parliament had deliberately and rightly weakened the landed and religious ascendancy of the minority which it had found in power at the time of the Act of Union and parliament had a corresponding duty not now to abandon that weakened minority.[105] A fly-by-night success for an ostensibly 'nationalist' force in the 1885 election indicated, not that Liberals must slavishly accept Parnell's demands, but that they should redouble their efforts to supply good government to Ireland. It was from the elected government-in-parliament of the United Kingdom, not from Parnell, that the answers to political problems must come.*

Liberal Unionists differed about their own constitutional prescriptions. Hartington believed that Irish unfamiliarity with government dictated that any extension of responsibilities should be slow, an organic outgrowth of existing institutions, supervised by local landlords and developing in line with the level of Irish education. He had also long advocated that economic modernisation in Ireland be promoted by the state, such as by lending money for the construction of a railway network, a scheme vetoed by Gladstone on Peelite free-market principles.[106] Bright wanted a variant of the 1885 central board scheme. Chamberlain was anxious for the imperial government to retain vital powers over the appointment of judges and magistrates, and taxation, as well as over foreign and defence policy. But, keen to demonstrate his continuing sympathy for popular control within an imperial context, he floated the idea of devolving specifically reserved powers to separate legislatures in Ulster and the southern provinces, and to England, Scotland and Wales, with a Supreme Court to legislate on the limits of the legislatures' powers. This scheme – the Americanisation of British politics while retaining a strong imperial government – was unacceptable to nationalists and to almost everyone else.[107]

Liberal Unionists also charged that Gladstone had betrayed the principles of parliamentary government in another sense. He had demonstrated his authoritarianism and contempt for the opinion of party-in-parliament and the doctrine of free parliamentary discussion which had allowed Liberals to combine great legislative force with the free play of individual opinion.[108] Gladstone had suppressed free debate and exploited 'popular idolatry' of himself, in order to impose his policy.[109] He had not openly avowed his support for Home Rule before his government was firmly established. But

---

* It is important to note that this whig-Liberal intellectual framework, placing empire, Union and progress centre-stage, was so powerful that advocates of Home Rule had to try to work within it. For example, a cartoon in the *Pall Mall Gazette* depicted Gladstone's policy for Ireland as the British lion and the Irish pig peacefully and harmoniously pulling 'the Imperial plough', while, when steered by the tory leader Salisbury, the same plough ran aground because the two animals were pulling in different directions: *Pall Mall Gazette*, 29 June 1886, p. 1. It is difficult to see this convincing many voters.

he told all those who were not convinced Home Rulers to be quiet in public, lest they commit themselves to views which might later handicap them.[110] He had then encouraged wavering Liberals to join his government and to contribute to a process of ostensibly open-minded dialogue about the Irish situation. Hartington asked: 'Did any leader ever treat a party in such a way as he has done?'[111] Gladstone knew that Hartington and many of his followers were bitterly opposed to self-government for Ireland, but he assumed that, since Chamberlain's agenda was worse, they could be bulldozed into compliance with it by Gladstonian verbal manipulation backed up by aroused popular fervour (just as, in the face of such fervour, Gladstone was sure that the Lords 'would not dare' to oppose the bill).[112] He told Harcourt that he was prepared to proceed on Home Rule without support from Hartington, Chamberlain or indeed anyone.[113] Hartington refused to join the 1886 government, thinking that to be trapped into the process of 'developing opinion' would damage his character. Chamberlain and Trevelyan did join, but soon resigned when it became clear that Gladstone was pulling all the strings and that no one else in the cabinet was willing to dissent from his proposals.* Bright sneered at MPs who surrendered 'judgment and conscience' to the 'sudden changes' of Gladstone, or became mere 'delegates' of constituency associations which worshipped his infallibility. 'They remind me very much of those gentlemen who go out as tourists with Mr. Cook. They enjoy great security, because they are personally conducted.'[115] Hartington declared himself 'a Protestant in politics as well as in religion', claiming 'for myself and for my friends the right of private judgment and of individual opinion', and contrasting this with the new Liberal doctrine of swallowing contradictory opinions 'not by the force of argument . . . not by any gradual process of reasoning, but by the simple order and injunction of one man'.[116]

Gladstone's mode of proceeding seemed doubly objectionable because it was irresponsible. Was his Home Rule initiative not another example of his inability to renounce power, whatever the cost to the country? It was unlikely that he would have been in a strong enough parliamentary position to form a government had voters known, at the 1885 election, that he would propose Home Rule.[117] His return to office in January 1886 required an alliance with Irish Nationalists; what prospect did this offer of strong government? Unionists were sure that it was Parnell's ability to make him prime minister in 1886 which had led to the Home Rule policy.[118] Gladstone had subverted the constitution in order to win the favour of a gang of men

---

* For his part, Gladstone was contemptuous of Chamberlain's attempts to find a compromise on Home Rule. He regarded Chamberlain's manner as overbearing and untrustworthy, his grievance as being the blow Home Rule intentionally delivered to his own policy ('it withdraws a great amount of factitious support from Radicalism'), and his strategy as fundamentally flawed because it depended on possessing, what Gladstone was confident he himself possessed, a rapport with 'the *people*'. At every stage in negotiations in 1886–7, Gladstone sought to humiliate and marginalise Chamberlain.[114]

who had demonstrated contempt for justice and human life, 'who defy the supremacy of the law'.[119] Hartington quoted Gladstone himself saying, in 1881, that the Nationalists' principles were 'plunder'. And once such a reckless offer had been made to the Irish, would they ever accept anything less?[120] His behaviour after 1886 struck his critics as even worse, as fomenting parliamentary obstruction, in alliance with Parnellites, against the decision of an elected House of Commons to pass coercive legislation for Ireland which was milder than his own of 1882. He defended boycotting as the 'only available weapon' of 'the Irish people, in their weakness and in their poverty . . . against the wealthy and the strong'.[121]

Gladstone's impetuous response to the defeat of his bill was to dissolve parliament and appeal to 'the people', believing that he would 'sweep the country'.[122] This, to Unionists, was the final irresponsibility. In his frustration, he used mass meetings to vent his rage – most famously at Hengler's Circus in Liverpool in June 1886, where he talked with terrifying force of 'a combination of the classes against the masses', and urged 'the nation' to overbear 'the resistance of the classes', since on matters concerning 'truth, justice, and humanity . . . all the world over, I will back the masses against the classes'.[123] Where, now, was the idea of cross-class collaboration? And the act of dissolution itself was a 'grievous wrong', since it institutionalised the division within the party, and mischievously identified 'true' Liberalism with Home Rule and with Gladstone's continued leadership.[124] Resignation in favour of Salisbury would have allowed Liberals time to regroup in the obscurity of opposition – and time for Gladstone to retire, with dignity, but definitively.

It was the determination of Gladstone to stay in charge and to redefine Liberalism around Home Rule that caused so many crippling defections from the Liberal party. Neither Hartington and his followers, nor Chamberlain and his, wished to leave. Few of them were enamoured of the Conservatives' apparently irrational, prejudiced, unintelligent governing style. The departure of each group was at first provisional; they stayed in the wings throughout 1886 and 1887, hoping that Gladstone would retire or that the party would turn its attention elsewhere. After all, most of those Liberals who remained loyal to Gladstone probably did not care much for Home Rule. They took their stand on personal admiration for their leader, confidence in his popular rapport, cowardice in the face of the rank-and-file, or a hope that the new policy would be only a temporary aberration.

The division of 1886 was an accident, not a long-expected socio-economic combustion. But it was also more than a personality quarrel. At root, it was, unsurprisingly, about Ireland. But, to a lot of Unionists, it was also about the moral dimensions of political leadership in a proto-democracy. Gladstone's commitment to Home Rule was the most convincing demonstration imaginable that his priorities were at odds with those of the mainstream nineteenth-century Liberal tradition. Defecting Liberals did not share his need to promote an endless agenda of business in order to satisfy restless energies. They did not believe, as he and his evangelical Dissenting supporters did, that politics was a heroic struggle against the sinfulness of natural man: that it involved crusades against the selfishness of those who served the state, and, in particular, a perpetual battle against those who were responsible for securing national defence. Liberal Unionists were suspicious of Gladstone's desire to be memorialised on the walls and mantlepieces of humble cottagers the length and breadth of the country, and disliked his increasing habit of depicting the masses – whether in Britain, Ireland or the empire – as 'the sole source of authority, justice, and right'.[125] Unionists distrusted leaders who displayed excessive enthusiasm, arbitrariness, clericalism, class-obsession and cant, and Gladstone could be arraigned on all counts. They had lost confidence in his ability to distinguish between the matured wishes of reasoning opinion, and unconsidered sectional clamour, and so they came to feel no security for the future conduct of politics in his hands. This was not surprising. In 1886, Gladstone *did* spectacularly misinterpret and idealise the will of the political nation. Unionists were able to ignore his call for Home Rule not only because their judgment pointed in that direction, but also because a mass popular movement for it never materialised. Indeed, two of the most high-profile Liberal tribunes, Chamberlain and Bright, were on the Unionist side. Gladstone's relentless crusader politics alienated the bulk of those who believed in an administrative, rational, didactic, consensual and parliamentary conception of Liberalism – who believed in it both for its policy results, and as the best way to keep a loose but invincibly large coalition of propertied and popular sentiment together under cultured leadership. Gladstone's impulsive, sentimental, evangelising, over-active political temper was a much greater threat to that conception than Chamberlain's 'socialism', because it could strike many more chords with provincial Dissenters and Liberal working-men. Crude class interpretations have no place in explaining the division of 1886. When Liberal Unionists merged with Conservatives, they did so in defence of manly, progressive, considered imperial administration by 'the property, the wealth, the intelligence, and the industry of the country' – the very forces that the whig Reformers had sought to represent in parliament fifty-five years before.

Epilogue

THE MAINSTREAM LIBERALISM analysed in this book aimed to offer authoritative but well-regulated government. It aspired to see central and local affairs administered by a propertied but socially diverse, rational and civilised elite, assiduous in promoting economy and developing Christian and industrious qualities in the population at large. It sought a constitutional system which would perpetuate the dominance of those groups and values while imposing checks on arbitrary rule and winning the confidence of the politicised nation. Meanwhile it attempted to secure open trade and respect for British influence in important regions overseas, which would benefit the country's economic interests, project an inspiring image of national purpose and rally a wide range of domestic opinion to government.

Elements of this Liberal worldview were present in the 'liberal toryism' of the 1820s, but the whig coup of 1830, taking advantage of economic crisis which undermined confidence in tory government, was necessary to establish its full parameters. In 1830, many whigs still possessed an opposition mentality suspicious of government and so were unprepared for power. But the younger whig generation provided the impulse for a series of institutional, religious and Irish reforms in the 1830s, with integration the dominant theme. These reforms profoundly reshaped the political system and defined the essential framework of nineteenth-century Liberalism. But too many property-owners were offended by the government's willingness to court public opinion in general and Irish Catholicism in particular. The county seats, once the scourges of 'Old Corruption', moved decisively into the tory camp and the Liberals were defeated in 1841. However, over the next five years the tories failed to adjust to Reformed politics. Returning in 1846, Liberals established something approaching political hegemony. They offered free trade, a strong, economical, 'patriotic' foreign policy, the rule of law, efficiency in domestic administration and the extension of local responsibility. In economic and social matters, crucially, they made the state look disinterested as between classes. Under Palmerston's astute and easygoing leadership, Liberalism became the natural ruling force. Old anti-state radicalism was neutered; new middle-class politicians emerged, committed to constructive manly efficiency at home and abroad. Urbanisation consolidated Liberal parliamentary dominance.

From the 1850s, this administrative Liberalism met less and less op-position from 'vested interests'. From the 1860s, the pace of improving legislation quickened, not as part of a 'programme' imposed by a popular party machine, but because of increased conscientiousness within parlia-ment itself. At local level, pluralism was extended, yet did not under-mine the cultural dominance of property. But the unintentional borough franchise revolution of 1867, and the accompanying changes in electoral organisation, fuelled worries about gathering popular pressure; so did the urgent, emotional politics of the new leader Gladstone. Gladstone had many assets as a Liberal leader, but his Peelite executive arrogance, sense of Providential mission, suspect temperament, and overt veneration of 'the people' alarmed many. His first government ended in a collapse of pro-pertied electoral support greater even than had happened in 1841. But Disraeli's Conservatism failed to impress administrative Liberals and by 1880 a remarriage of propertied and popular sentiment within the party had taken place. Gladstone's second government was remarkably untroubled by problems of parliamentary management, considering the range of difficult decisions that it faced abroad. There was intra-party jockeying for ad-vantage in expectation of Gladstone's retirement, but in 1885 hardly anyone doubted that Hartington would be the next leader, that he would successfully revive Palmerstonian politics, and that Chamberlain would cooperate with him in a 'national' foreign policy and a judicious extension of local government powers.

It cannot be overstressed, then, how sudden and how dramatic was the split of 1886. That division was not about the role that the state should play in regulating property or in handling the economy. At issue, rather, was the question of popular control. How far should those who roused the 'popular conscience' be followed, if a hard-headed view of 'national' interests sug-gested that that conscience was misguided – or, indeed, that it did not represent the settled view of rational public opinion? No Liberal could deny the principle of involving the 'people' in politics, but the party's traditional view had been that the interests of civilised elite rule required that great care should be taken to monitor that involvement and to keep the lid on demagoguery and temporary popular enthusiasms. The immediate, and primary, cause of the division of 1886 was Gladstone's commitment to Irish Home Rule. Liberals had traditionally invested much effort in modernising Ireland, and many whigs had land there; both interests were endangered by Gladstone's sudden decision to grant self-government to the Irish peasantry. But the Home Rule crisis had a broader significance too. It confirmed all the doubts about Gladstone, and the Dissenters and working-men who formed his power-base within the party, which had been circulating for twenty years. Gladstone was increasingly seen as an unpredictable, irrational leader, prone to mount zealous crusades against misgovernment and extravagance from a self-deceiving notion that he was marshalling a sympathetic public conscience in the cause. So to his critics he seemed a soft touch for any well-organised minority who could persuade him of their morality. His temperamental bonds with evangelical Dissenters threw into question his loyalty to the church establishment and his remorseless opposition to government expenditure seemed to threaten the defence of British interests abroad. The latter was especially worrying in the 1880s, because of evidence of challenges to British economic and strategic superiority. This created a powerful body of 'national' opinion anxious to maintain Britain's foreign and imperial position. The manner of Gladstone's commitment to Home Rule suggested that, in his conception of Liberalism, passion had triumphed over reason; separation over assimilation; populist appeals over parliamentary discussion; mob values over manliness; distaste for authority over responsible leadership; sentimentalism over science; 'government by average opinion' over didacticism.[1] The result was the revolt of the Liberal Unionists, who defected into an eventual and reluctant alliance with the Conservatives. Liberal Unionists reassured themselves that at least the new Conservative leader Salisbury might make a better fist of defending endangered values than the unprincipled, irresponsible, un-English Disraeli.

Gladstone's behaviour in 1886 turned the Liberal party from a great party of government into a gaggle of outsiders. From then on, its attachment to the principle of popular control became increasingly monotonous – hence Gladstone's motto, 'trust the people', at the 1892 election. Its critics satirised the canting sanctimonious uplift generated by Liberal platform orators who talked of 'Goad's people'.[2] In order to win Welsh and Scottish sympathy for Irish self-government, Gladstone chose to pander to those Celtic Liberals who were most conscious of the cultural distinctness of their countries. At Swansea in 1887, he announced that 'Welsh nationality is as great a reality as English nationality', and in 1891 he finally committed himself to Welsh church disestablishment.[3] Though he was not foolish enough to call for Home Rule for Wales and Scotland as well, such declarations generated more distrust of him in England, especially among those most anxious for Great Britain to play a forceful international role. His approach to cultivating Welsh and Scottish sentiment was certainly very different from the anti-clericalism and periodic anti-Popery associated with Russell and Palmerston, which had allowed Celtic Dissenters to expend their political energies in a self-consciously *British* cause.[4] More generally, whereas Palmerston and Russell had used Protestantism and constitutional and fiscal liberty to construct a notion of Britishness which large numbers of men in all classes found sympathetic, and which bound them to Liberalism, Gladstone became less and less successful, as time went on, in his attempt to redefine that Britishness. Concepts such as devolution, church-state separation, local democracy, passionate moral crusades and non-assertion abroad were inspiring to many diverse groups, but they lacked the breadth of appeal necessary to hold the centre-ground of politics. Too many people saw the aged Gladstone's religious, Irish and foreign policy attitudes as unmanly, a betrayal of the attractive national identity constructed by his Liberal predecessors.

So, from 1886, the Liberals' electoral base was badly damaged. After the election of that year, the party found itself in a clear minority in English boroughs *and* English counties for the first time since 1830, and now became identified in the public mind very largely with the 'Celtic fringe'. At just the time when new constituency structures and changes in funding (as a result of the 1883 Corrupt Practices Act) demanded greater attention to organisation, Liberals lost much of their most influential support. One estimate sees the number of landed Liberal MPs falling from 159 to 59 between 1880 and 1886.[5] Granville, Spencer and Kimberley headed a very small rump of loyal peers.

Gladstone lamented that 'nine-tenths of our wealth is gone'; he later doubted if Liberals 'now hold more than one acre in fifty'.[6] The propertied defection was so marked that it led to serious embarrassment at local level, where, by 1892, only about 15 per cent of county magistrates were Gladstonians.[7] In 1886, 1895 and 1900, the Unionist coalition won 119, 133 and 163 United Kingdom seats without a contest, as against the Liberals' 40, 10 and 22. Not surprisingly, the Unionists won all three elections. Organisational failure depressed turnout and so contributed further to defeat. From 1891, in a desperate search for funds, Liberals began to entice rich businessman MPs like the linoleum manufacturer James Williamson to donate with a view to receiving a peerage. The ennoblement of men like 'Lord Linoleum' did little for his party's moral reputation.[8]

Liberals came to look increasingly sectional and democratic. They lost their place in 'society'; the queen led the ostracism of the few peers, like Spencer, who remained with Gladstone. In the whip's office, the seceding Lord Richard Grosvenor, son of the country's wealthiest duke, was replaced by the Dissenting manufacturer Arnold Morley. The 1885–6 crisis significantly speeded up emerging tendencies towards disciplined party voting in the Commons, with dramatic consequences for the distribution of power within Liberalism.[9] As the country gentleman element declined, and NLF influence in candidate selection grew, MPs became more 'careerist', more concerned with promotion within the party and more willing to receive instruction from the whips. So it was easier to impose a legislative programme on parliament. The NLF, now suddenly the party's backbone, was the great beneficiary of this. Organisational changes in 1887 made it more attractive to Welsh, London and Home Counties associations; Birmingham, the only important association to defy Gladstone in 1886, was recaptured by his forces in 1888. In 1886 255 local bodies were members of the NLF, in 1888 716.[10] A Liberal Publications Department was set up in 1887 to spread propaganda. In return for the NLF's organisational assistance, leaders had to patronise its functions regularly and accept the bulk of the increasingly detailed policy agenda agreed at its annual meetings. It adopted Welsh disestablishment and the abolition of the Lords' legislative powers in 1887, one man one vote and the taxation of ground rents in 1888, and Scottish disestablishment, the payment of MPs, the power of local veto over alcohol sales, and the abolition of duties on all basic items of household food in 1889.[11] These meetings culminated in the construction of the 'Newcastle Programme' of 1891, which was widely taken as a statement of the next Liberal government's policy intentions. The strength of sectional pressure groups and democratic principles meant that the Liberal government narrowly elected in 1892 broke decisively with previous policy practice. Its proposals were many and predetermined, and most of them upheld the principle of popular control: not only Irish Home Rule, but the disestablishment of the minority Welsh church, local referenda on the prohibition of liquor licensing, and the abolition of plural voting in national and local elections. The last proposal, the most significant aspect of the local government reform package of 1894, democratised boards of guardians and health. Working-class pressure for increased outrelief burst forth and contributed powerfully to the near-doubling of poor relief expenditure by 1906. This in turn created a local government financial crisis which impelled the 1905 Liberal government to ease rate burdens by introducing old age pensions and national health insurance. Had he lived, Gladstone would not have liked that. As it was, he bridled at most of the 'sectional' 1892–4 reforms, and accepted them only in the delusion that Liberal footsoldiers could be marshalled to fight for Home Rule.

Opposition to sectionalism and populism allowed Conservatives and Liberal Unionists to coalesce after 1886 around the familiar assumption that government should be carried on by individuals of wisdom, flexibility and rounded character whose judgment was matured by traditional socialising institutions. Unionists claimed to be a national force, with great reserves of character and intellect, willing to pursue dispassionate investigations into all aspects of the life of the people in order to promote consensual legislation. Thus might popular respect for the rule of law and affection for the beneficial rule of Parliament be restored.[12] In contrast, they said, Liberals had rejected the tradition of guidance by propertied and educated men steeped in the parliamentary culture. They were undermining the 'strength of the parliamentary tradition', in which politicians of 'experience and judgment', 'trained from their youth in the methods of ruling', held the political nation together by 'sober discussion' in a 'really deliberative assembly'.[13] Was not the Newcastle Programme a manifesto by which an alliance of Liberal constituency party associations could dictate a policy to the country if given a majority of seats, whatever the arguments levelled against it? Alternatively, it seemed to involve the 'passionate submission of both conscience and intellect to the will of Mr. Gladstone'. Either way, it was 'political Popery' which depended for success on 'widespread political ignorance'.[14]* Unionists claimed that, while their coalition defended *na-*

---

* So some Unionists, like Dicey, advocated the use of the referendum, in order to reveal the unpopularity of specific Liberal policies, most obviously Home Rule. But others, like Arthur Elliot, rejected the idea as a 'deathblow to parliamentary government'. See J. Meadowcroft and M.W. Taylor, 'Liberalism and the referendum in British political thought 1890–1914', *20th century British history*, I (1990), 48.

tional causes, their opponents were a 'mongrel political combination of teetotallers, Irish revolutionists, Welsh demagogues, Small Englanders, English separatists, and general uprooters of all that is national and good'.[15]

Conservative success in propounding these ideas meant that the party was able to establish a monopoly of real power after 1886. This was the heyday of Unionist principles. Salisbury used his inbuilt Lords majority to block any Liberal legislation which had passed the Commons without clear evidence of matured, considered public support. This applied particularly to Home Rule, which the Lords defeated by 419 votes to 41 when it came to them in 1893, but also to a host of other 'sectional' bills between 1892 and 1895 and 1906 and 1909. Salisbury's justification was that the slender Liberal majority of 1892 rested on the votes of 150 electors in eight constituencies, collected by offering many different policy bribes. This was no mandate for a Newcastle Programme.[16] Faced with the return of Liberal government in 1906, the Unionist leader Balfour felt justified in declaring that it was his party's duty, 'in office or out of office, to continue to control the destinies of this great Empire'.[17] In the constituencies, Unionists had been able to exploit working-class animosity to Liberal faddism to considerable effect since the 1880s. One Unionist target was the hypocrisy of the middle-class nonconformist who sought to suppress the poor man's right to beer and spirits while himself privately taking sustenance from well-stocked wine cellars.[18] Another was the hysterical provincial nonconformist drive against prostitution, arising out of the campaign against the Contagious Diseases Acts. This drive was spearheaded by local branches of the National Vigilance Association, founded in 1885 to take advantage of the new law facilitating private prosecutions of brothels. On average 1,200 were prosecuted each year from 1885 to 1914, compared to 86 between 1875 and 1885. The NVA also exposed the names of brothel clients, and campaigned against simulated nudity in music-hall *tableaux vivants* and the bare arms and legs of Zoe the acrobat at the Royal Aquarium. Even in Cheltenham, there were mob riots in 1887 against NVA activity.[19]

Not until 1905 did the Liberal party recover from the damage caused by sectionalism and populism. Then it was saved only by the bogy of a tariff-reforming Conservative party, together with international factors which caused a marked (but temporary) lull in the now near-permanent anxiety about inadequate defence spending. For a change, the Liberals looked the sound party at the 1906 election: the party of 'disinterested' free trade, offering the attraction of low taxation *and* sound defence. Thereafter, Liberals also benefited from the supercilious intellect of their emerging leader Herbert Henry Asquith, who mounted a great struggle to break Unionist hegemony. Asquith despised 'the small fry, the *whitebait*, of the Liberal party'[20] and carried on the marginalisation of the NLF which had begun after the disastrous defeat of 1895.[21] A former 'Liberal Imperialist', he saw the vital importance (electoral and otherwise) of keeping defences strong; he also put Home Rule on the backburner. For him, politics was about accustoming the masses to the beneficent rule of meritocratic Liberal mandarins. If the principle of pluralism in the localities was upheld, he and his friends in the liberal intelligentsia assumed that the 'people' would accept guidance at national level by high-powered, independent-minded men such as themselves. Asquith himself had three invaluable skills: extraordinary efficiency in the despatch of business, great deftness in conducting political negotiations, and the ability to use sonorous, optimistic rhetoric to disguise policy fudges and maintain an unshakeable command over Liberal MPs and pundits.

But, despite Asquith's mandarin approach, he did not alter the two fundamentals of post-1886 Liberalism. After 1905, Liberal administrative pride stimulated a vast increase in the amount of legislation introduced, compared to the Unionist ministries. And the realities of Liberal party politics necessitated regular dealings with the various interest-groups which comprised the governing coalition. As a result, the leaders had to make major concessions in public to trade unionists, nonconformists, suffrage activists and, after 1910, Irish Nationalists. So Liberal government had two controversial consequences. One was a packed policy programme, comprising items which might be unpopular, but which were rammed through the Commons by an inbuilt party majority and new parliamentary procedures.* This was unacceptable to the Lords, and led to five years of bitterness between the two Houses. The second was a great extension of popular involvement under the umbrella of a pluralistic state: by granting self-government to Ireland (and planning Home Rule for Scotland too); by giving power to the trade unions (through industrial arbitration mechanisms and the right to raise a political levy) and the friendly societies (under the national health insurance scheme); and by retaining popular control of the poor law. The Liberals' opponents were able to associate popular control with ever-increasing, but often badly directed, central and local expenditure on the poor, which they said also jeopardised the state's ability to increase taxation suddenly in a crisis of imperial defence.[22] The prewar 'national efficiency' movement gained its real strength from right-wing and Fabian criticism of the adverse consequences of populist politics for Britain's standing as a military and economic power.

So neither of these two new Liberal fundamentals was accepted by Unionist forces. The consequences were very serious. The real threat to Edwardian Liberalism came not from the left (since Liberal populism

---

* Party professionalism and the divisiveness of Home Rule together account for the major changes which took place in parliamentary procedure after 1886. In 1887 the closure was used for the first time against the main opposition party, and from then on it came to be applied between fifty and sixty times a session. In the same year the more controversial 'guillotine' was first used. This fixed times for the closing of discussion on the various sections and stages of bills. Tories applied it on five measures between 1887 and 1905, but Liberals used it on the 1893 Home Rule Bill, one bill of 1894, and twenty-one measures between 1906 and 1912. For detailed figures, see *Parliamentary papers*, 1907, LXVI, 93, and 1912–13, LXVII, 91.

consigned Labour to a slow advance through local politics) but from the right. Liberals' governing practice created an acute constitutional crisis, which mounted between 1906 and 1914. In 1914, both of their big principles were still being contested. Throughout that time, ministers remained clearly on the defensive, fighting the great weight of the political and social establishment and the millions of voters who respected its title to govern, or who simply disliked rate and tax increases. British history to 1914 shows that the nineteenth-century administrative, propertied, economical, individualist, unionist, 'national' tradition cast a long shadow. Indeed one may wonder if it lost its power even then. One party continued to rely on it for much of its appeal; and it is perhaps not accidental that the Conservative (and Unionist) party has been the dominant political force of twentieth-century Britain.

Chronology

1812 General election; Prime Minister Perceval assassinated; Liverpool Prime Minister
    Anglo-American war (until 1814)

1813 Napoleon defeated at Vitoria and in 'Battle of the Nations'

1814 Allies enter Paris; Napoleon abdicates

1814–15 Congress of Vienna

1815 Final defeat of Napoleon at Waterloo
    Corn Law: free importation permitted only over 80s a quarter

1816 Spa Fields riots
    Income tax not renewed
    Canning rejoins government as President of Board of Control

1817 Blanketeers march; suspension of Habeas Corpus (until 1818)

1818 General election: obvious government losses

1819 St Peter's Fields meeting, Manchester ('Peterloo'); Six Acts

1820 Cato Street conspiracy discovered
    Death of George III; Prince Regent becomes George IV; general election; bill to deprive Queen Caroline of royal title introduced, later dropped; Canning resigns

1821 Death of Caroline
    Grampound disfranchised; seats given to West Riding of Yorkshire

1822 Castlereagh commits suicide; Canning becomes Foreign Secretary and Leader of House of Commons

1823 O'Connell founds Catholic Association
    Criminal law and prison reform

1824 Repeal of Combination Acts against trade unions

1825 Catholic Emancipation passes Commons; crisis; is defeated in Lords

1826 General election: no-popery victories

1827 Liverpool incapacitated by stroke; Canning Prime Minister; seven cabinet ministers, led by Wellington and Peel, refuse to serve; some whigs join government; death of Canning; Goderich succeeds as coalition Prime Minister
    Britain, France and Russia sign Treaty of London to protect Greeks against Turks; Battle of Navarino defeats Turks

1828 Fall of Goderich coalition; Wellington Prime Minister; coalition whigs return to opposition

Huskisson and three other Canningite cabinet ministers resign after mix-up over minor seat redistribution proposals
Corn law: sliding scale of duties instituted
Repeal of Test and Corporation Acts
O'Connell wins County Clare byelection
Greek independence recognised

1829 Catholic Emancipation
Metropolitan Police founded
Birmingham Political Union established

1830 Death of George IV, June; William IV king; general election in depression; French revolution brings Louis Philippe to throne, July; death of Huskisson, September; Captain Swing riots; fall of Wellington, November; Grey Prime Minister of whig-dominated coalition pledged to parliamentary reform

1830–2 Cholera epidemics

1831 Reform Bill introduced, March; obstructive amendment to it passed, April; parliament dissolved; Reform principles triumphant at general election; Commons passes second Reform Bill; Lords defeat it, October; protest and rioting
Britain and France guarantee Belgian independence
Game Act

1831–3 Irish tithe war

1832 Third Reform Bill introduced; passes second reading in Lords, then obstructed; king refuses government request for large-scale creation of peerages; Grey resigns; 'Days of May'; Wellington unable to form government; Grey returns; Reform Bill passed; general election on new system produces great Reform majority

1833 Abolition of slavery
Irish Church Temporalities Act; Irish Coercion Act
Factory Act
Abolition of East India Company monopoly over China trade agreed

1834 New Poor Law
Quadruple Alliance with France, Spain and Portugal to protect constitutional regimes in Spain and Portugal
Government breaks up over Irish Church appropriation, June; Grey resigns over Irish coercion, July; Melbourne Prime Minister; king dismisses his government, November; Peel Prime Minister of minority tory government

1835 General election; tories make gains but still in decided minority; Peel defeated and resigns; Melbourne Prime Minister
Ecclesiastical Commission set up
Municipal Corporations Act

1836 Tithe Commutation Act
Registration of births, marriages and deaths, and liberalisation of marriage laws, agreed
Government grants charter to non-religious London University
Reform Club founded

1837 Death of William IV; Victoria queen; general election: further tory gains
French-Canadian rebellion

1838 Afghan wars (until 1842)

Irish poor law; appropriation abandoned; Irish tithe question settled
Apprenticeship for ex-slaves abolished

1839   Government signals need for corn law reform; Anti-Corn Law League formed
Chartist convention meets; petition for People's Charter presented to parliament
Education Act
Prisons Act; County Police Act
Jamaican constitution suspended to deal with ex-slave unrest; government resigns; 'Bedchamber crisis' means Peel fails to form government; Melbourne returns
'Opium War' with China (until 1842)

1840   Union of Upper and Lower Canada
Penny post introduced; adds to government financial troubles; general rise in tariffs

1841   Ministers propose 8s fixed duty per quarter of imported corn; government defeated on sugar duties and then on vote of confidence; parliament dissolved; tories gain majority at general election; Peel Prime Minister

1842   Income tax introduced; sliding scale of duties on imported corn lowered
Second Chartist convention and petition
Mines Act; first report of Royal Commission on sanitary conditions

1843   Disruption in Church of Scotland
O'Connell agitates for repeal of Union

1844   Dissenters' Chapels Act
Irish initiatives; Devon Commission on land tenure appointed

1845   Maynooth grant increased; Queen's colleges set up
Income tax renewed; abolition of many import duties
Annexation of Punjab; Sikh wars (until 1849)
Severe Irish potato famine; Peel proposes corn law repeal; cabinet unwilling; government resigns; Russell fails to form Liberal alternative; Peel returns

1846   Repeal of corn laws; Peel defeated on Irish coercion by Liberals and rebellious Protectionist tories; Russell becomes Liberal Prime Minister; Peelite frontbenchers secede from body of tory MPs, initially with backbench support, which slowly fades away back into the main body, led by Stanley

1846-7 Irish famine continues
Education Minutes

1847   Poor Law Board replaces Poor Law Commission
Ten Hours Act
General election: Liberals continue with shaky majority

1848   Budget crises
Irish rising; suspension of Habeas Corpus there
Third Chartist petition presented
Palmerston, Foreign Secretary, sympathises with continental revolutions
Cholera epidemic; Public Health Act

1849   Repeal of Navigation Acts
Encumbered Estates Act in Ireland

1849–50   Don Pacifico, British subject resident in Athens, with claims against Greek government, has house burned down; Palmerston sends squadron and Greeks eventually comply with British demands for redress; parliamentary controversy over this, June 1850

1850   Irish Franchise Act; Queen's University established
Death of Peel; Aberdeen, Graham, Newcastle, Herbert and Gladstone now the significant Peelites

1850–1   Durham letter and Ecclesiastical Titles Act

1851   Budget crisis; radicals defeat government on county franchise; government temporarily resigns
Russell plans Reform Bill for 1852
Palmerston assures French of his approval of Napoleon III's coup d'état, without cabinet authority; he is dismissed

1852   Government defeated on Militia Bill, with Palmerston's help; Russell resigns; Stanley, now Derby, forms minority tory government; it makes gains at general election but still lacks majority; it is defeated on Disraeli's budget by Liberal-Peelite coalition; this coalition takes office under Aberdeen; Peelites take nearly half the cabinet places, displacing many whigs and relegating Russell and Palmerston

1853–4   Crimean crisis leads to British and French declaration of war on Russia, early 1854; battles of Alma, Balaclava and Inkerman; siege of Sebastopol; graphic press reporting

1854   Oxford University Act
Russell's Reform Bill withdrawn

1855   Roebuck instigates motion for committee of inquiry into war management; Russell resigns and supports it; it is accepted; Aberdeen and War Secretary Newcastle resign; Derby refuses office; Palmerston becomes coalition Prime Minister; he accepts committee of inquiry; other leading Peelites resign; government continues on essentially Liberal basis, though with continuing difficulty
Administrative Reform Association activity; Civil Service Commission established
Vienna peace talks fail; Russell resigns; Sebastopol falls, September

1856   Treaty of Paris ends Crimean War; Britain, France and Austria guarantee Turkish independence; Black Sea declared neutral
Education Department established; Cambridge University Act
Police Act: county forces compulsory

1856–7   'Arrow War' against China; bombardment of Canton; Palmerston is censured by Russell, radicals and the tory opposition over this, 1857; defeat leads to general election; strong Liberal gains; Palmerston remains Prime Minister

1857   Indian Mutiny
Matrimonial Causes Act facilitates divorce

1858   Palmerston defeated by Liberal-radical-tory opposition to Conspiracy to Murder Bill; Derby forms minority tory government
Government of India Act: all political powers of East India Company ceded to government
Jewish MPs allowed to sit in Commons
Newcastle Commission on elementary education

1859   Tory Reform Bill introduced and defeated by Liberal opposition to disfranchisement of borough freeholders; parliament dissolved; government gains at general election are insufficient to provide tory majority; Derby defeated on vote of confidence; Palmerston Prime Minister again with Russell Foreign Secretary, Gladstone Chancellor of Exchequer; the absorption of Russell and the remaining Peelites under Palmerston means that two-party politics is in essence restored, though the government side of the Commons remains undisciplined

1860   Cobden-Chevalier Anglo-French Commercial Treaty
Liberal Reform Bill withdrawn
Garibaldi conquers Sicily and Naples: this gives powerful impetus to Italian unification

1861   Repeal of paper duties
Clarendon Commission on public schools

1862   Revised Education Code

1864   Britain fails to stand by Palmerston's promise to help Denmark to prevent Prussian move on Schleswig-Holstein
Taunton Commission on endowed schools

1865   General election: strong Liberal majority; death of Palmerston; Russell Prime Minister (in Lords, since taking earldom in 1861, so Gladstone becomes Leader of House of Commons)

1866   Sanitary Act
Liberal Reform Bill defeated; Russell government resigns; Derby Prime Minister of another tory minority government

1867   Tory Reform Act passed: household suffrage in boroughs
Transportation abolished; Canada gains dominion status

1868   Abolition of compulsory church rates
Trade Union Congress founded
Last public execution
Derby retires, February; Disraeli Prime Minister; Russell retires as Liberal leader, succeeded by Gladstone; Gladstone defeats government on Irish Church resolutions; when new registers are ready, general election is held and Liberals win strong majority; Disraeli resigns; Gladstone Prime Minister, December

1869   Irish Episcopal Church disestablished
Endowed Schools Act

1870   Franco-Prussian War; Britain does not intervene, but defence spending is increased temporarily; Russia repudiates Black Sea neutralisation of 1856
Elementary Education Act
Irish Land Act; Home Government Association founded by Isaac Butt; several byelection victories, 1871–3, show that the movement for Irish Home Rule is attracting support
General institution of competitive examinations for civil service entry

1871   Trade Union Act
Creation of Local Government Board
Abolition of university tests
Abolition of practice of purchasing army commissions
Bank Holidays introduced
Peace Preservation Act, Ireland, allows partial suspension of civil liberties in proclaimed districts

316

1872   Secret ballot instituted
Licensing Act
Settlement of *Alabama* controversy with United States, by international arbitration
Foundation of Agricultural Labourers' Union by Joseph Arch

1873   Irish University Bill defeated; government resigns temporarily

1874   Gladstone proposes abolition of income tax; dissolves parliament; tories gain majority at general election; Gladstone resigns; Disraeli Prime Minister
Public Worship Regulation Act

1875   Gladstone 'retires' as Liberal leader; Hartington elected to succeed him (i.e. as leader in Commons; Granville continues as leader in Lords)

1876   Queen Victoria pronounced Empress of India by Disraeli government
Turkish killings in Bulgaria; Gladstone's pamphlet incites Bulgarian agitation

1877   National Liberal Federation founded by Joseph Chamberlain

1877–8   Russo-Turkish War; Treaty of San Stefano; Congress of Berlin

1878–80   Afghan War

1879   Zulu War

1879   Land League formed in Ireland; Parnell prominent; 'Land war' begins

1879–80   Gladstone mounts two high-profile speaking campaigns in his new constituency of Midlothian

1880   Disraeli dissolves parliament; Liberals win healthy majority at general election; Disraeli resigns; queen asks Hartington or Granville to form government, but both recommend Gladstone; Gladstone Prime Minister
Ground Game Act
Employers' Liability Act
Compulsory elementary education
Burials Act

1881   Death of Disraeli; Salisbury effectively becomes tory leader
Afrikaner revolt in Transvaal and Orange Free State against Cape domination; British defeated at Majuba Hill; substantial independence conceded to Afrikaners by Treaty of Pretoria
Irish Land and Coercion Acts; Parnell arrested

1882   'Kilmainham Treaty': Parnell released; Forster resigns as Irish Secretary; his successor, Lord Frederick Cavendish, assassinated in Phoenix Park; Crimes Act and Arrears Act end 'Land War'; Parnell recycles 'Land League' as 'National League'
Occupation of Egypt; but Mahdist rebellion in Sudan

1883   Agricultural Holdings Act
Corrupt and Illegal Practices Act

1884   Third Reform Act: household suffrage in counties

1885   Redistribution Act
Death of Gordon at Khartoum
Pendjeh crisis with Russia
Cabinet quarrels over the future of Irish government
Government defeated, with Parnell's help, on budget; Salisbury forms tory minority government, supported by Parnell, in return for non-renewal of Crimes Act; at general election, Parnellites just rob Liberals of

overall majority; news emerges of Gladstone's willingness to grant Ireland Home Rule

1886   Salisbury defeated by alliance of Liberals and Parnellites; Gladstone forms Liberal government on basis of considering Home Rule; Hartington and others decline places; Chamberlain resigns from cabinet, March, as Home Rule plans firm; Government of Ireland Bill introduced and is defeated by revolt of 94 Liberal MPs; Gladstone calls election; Hartington, Chamberlain and other anti-Home Rule MPs fight as Liberal Unionists; Gladstone is defeated and Salisbury forms tory government with Unionist support; Goschen becomes first Liberal Unionist to take office, December, as Chancellor of Exchequer.

Biographical notes

ABERDEEN, fourth earl of (1784–1860): ed. Harrow, Cambridge; ambassador extraordinary at Vienna, 1813; tory; Foreign Secretary, 1828–30, 1841–6; Secretary for War and Colonies, 1834–5; Peelite, and led the group from 1850; Prime Minister, 1852–5, but resigned when vote for committee of inquiry into management of Crimean War passed.

ALTHORP, Viscount (third Earl Spencer, 1834) (1782–1845): ed. Harrow, Cambridge; MP Northamptonshire 1806–34; devoted huntsman; became Foxite; threw himself into politics after his wife's early death in 1818; student of political economy; leader of whig opposition in Commons, 1830; Chancellor of Exchequer and Leader, House of Commons, 1830–4; reluctant office-holder; retired to country pursuits on inheriting peerage.

ARGYLL, eighth duke of (1823–1900): ed. privately; succeeded to dukedom, 1847; loosely associated with Peelites; long tenure in cabinet as Lord Privy Seal, 1853–5, 1859–66, 1880–1, Postmaster-general, 1855–8, Secretary for India, 1868–74; resigned in opposition to 1881 Irish Land Act; fierce Liberal Unionist from 1886; active religious controversialist (Scottish Presbyterian) and enthusiastic scientist and natural historian; a favourite at court; his son married Queen Victoria's daughter.

ARNOLD, Thomas (1795–1842): ed. Winchester, Oxford; Fellow, Oriel College, 1815; pioneering headmaster of Rugby, 1828–42; added mathematics, modern history, modern languages to the syllabus; distinguished theological writer and historian; advocate of broad church reform to make it of service to the whole nation; immensely influential on a string of later-famous pupils and young teachers at Rugby; appointed Regius Professor of History, Oxford, in the last year of his life.

BAGEHOT, Walter (1826–77): ed. Bristol, University College London; son of shipowner and banker, and briefly worked in the family business; journalist and economist; son-in-law of owner of *Economist* magazine, and its editor from 1860; philosophical Liberal; *English Constitution* published 1867.

BAINES, Edward, elder and younger (1774–1848; 1800–90): congregationalist family; the elder founded the *Leeds Mercury* and was a leading local whig activist and MP for Leeds 1834–41; the younger, ed. New College Manchester, edited *Leeds Mercury* from youth, was also a Liberal activist, a leading educational voluntaryist in the 1850s, MP for Leeds 1859–74, and later a Liberal elder statesman; knighted, 1880.

BARING, Sir Francis Thornhill (created Baron Northbrook, 1866) (1796–1866): grandson of founder of Baring Brothers; ed. Winchester, Oxford (1st); Hampshire country gentleman; MP, Portsmouth, 1826–65; junior Treasury office, 1830–4, 1835–9; Liberal chief whip, 1834–5; Chancellor of Exchequer, 1839–41; First Lord of Admiralty, 1849–52; then chose to retire. For his son, see NORTHBROOK.

319

BESSBOROUGH: see DUNCANNON

BRIGHT, Jacob (1821–99): brother of John, below; ed. quaker school, York; chairman of family cotton firm in Rochdale; MP, Manchester, 1867–74, 1876–85, Manchester South, 1886–95 (Gladstonian); active campaigner on women's issues.

BRIGHT, John (1811–89): son of Rochdale millowner, worked in family firm; quaker; rose to local attention by opposition to levying of compulsory church rates, 1830s; treasurer, Rochdale branch, Anti-Corn Law League, 1840, later campaigned nationally for the movement; MP, Durham, on repeal principles, 1843; MP, Manchester, 1847–57; advocate of financial, land and parliamentary reform; opposed Crimean War; defeated at Manchester, 1857; MP, Birmingham, 1857–85 and Birmingham Central, 1885–9; supported Northern cause in American Civil War; proposed reforms in India and Ireland; entered Gladstone's cabinet, 1868, as President, Board of Trade; resigned, pleading ill-health, 1870; accepted sinecure post of Chancellor, Duchy of Lancaster, 1873–4, 1880–2, but resigned again, in opposition to bombardment of Alexandria; fierce Liberal Unionist from 1886. One of the great Victorian moralists; orator to the puritan classes.

BROUGHAM, Henry (created Baron, 1830) (1778–1868): ed. Edinburgh; lawyer; cofounder, *Edinburgh Review*, 1802, and voluminous contributor to it; whig MP from 1810, for various small boroughs; attorney-general to Queen Caroline, 1820, and defended her at her trial; advocated commercial, educational and legal reform; founder, Society for the Diffusion of Useful Knowledge, 1825, and co-founder, University College London, 1828; after several attempts to oust the Lowther interest in Westmorland, was elected MP for the prestigious county seat of Yorkshire, 1830, mainly on anti-slavery, commercial and legal reform principles; claimed to be the popular hero; astonished the political world by accepting Grey's bait of the Lord Chancellorship and a peerage, November 1830; instituted some legal reform, 1830–4; not reappointed Lord Chancellor, 1835; never held political office again; President, Social Science Association, 1857; author of historical works, eccentric memoirs and many other polemics; made Cannes fashionable.

BRUCE, Henry (created Baron Aberdare, 1873) (1815–95): inherited lucrative coalmining land in Aberdare valley; ed. Swansea; barrister, 1837–43; stipendiary magistrate, Merthyr Tydfil and Aberdare, 1847–52; Liberal MP, Merthyr Tydfil, 1852–68, Renfrewshire, 1869–73; junior office, 1862–4, Education minister, 1864–6, Home Secretary, 1868–73, President of Council, 1873–4; first President of University College Cardiff, 1883, and first Chancellor, University of Wales, 1894; patron of geographical and historical research.

BRYCE, James (1838–1922): son of Scottish geologist and schoolmaster; Presbyterian; ed. Belfast, Glasgow, Oxford; Fellow, Oriel College Oxford, 1862–89; achieved fame with *Holy Roman Empire*, 1864; mountaineer; assistant commissioner, Taunton Commission; advocate of university extension; Regius Professor of Civil Law, Oxford, 1870–93; Liberal MP, 1880–1906; authority on Near East and United States; co-founder, *English Historical Review*, 1886; keen advocate of Irish Home Rule; cabinet office, 1892–5, 1905–6; ambassador to Washington, 1907–13; Viscount, 1914; leading advocate of League of Nations. Quintessential manly self-made Gladstonian Liberal intellectual politician.

BURDETT, Sir Francis (1770–1844): ed. Westminster, Oxford; married a Coutts; radical MP from 1796; MP, Westminster, 1807–37; aristocratic popular tribune; imprisoned twice on political charges; self-proclaimed Queen Anne tory; ended a Queen Victoria tory, as MP for North Wiltshire 1837–44, anti-Catholic and farmers' friend.

BUXTON, Thomas Fowell (1786–1845): Essex family; mother a quaker; ed. Trinity

College Dublin; married a Gurney; partner in mother's family brewery, 1808; evangelical Anglican philanthropist; active in Bible Society, Spitalfields missions, and the prison discipline movement; MP, Weymouth, 1818–37; succeeded Wilberforce as leader of the parliamentary agitation against slavery, 1823–33; created baronet, 1840; ill-fated venture to civilise the Niger, 1839–43, damaged his health. His son Charles and grandson Sydney were both active Liberal MPs.

CANNING, George (1770–1827): son of barrister, raised by banker uncle; ed. Eton, Oxford; MP from 1794; early disciple of Pitt, and held government office under him 1796–1801, 1804–6; Foreign Secretary, 1807–9, resigned after duel with Castlereagh, whose war policy he condemned; MP, Liverpool, 1812–22, then Harwich; dangerous political floater; rejoined cabinet as President of Board of Control, 1816, but resigned again, 1820, in support of Queen Caroline; nominated Governor-general of India, 1822, but accepted instead the succession to the dead Castlereagh as Foreign Secretary and Leader, House of Commons; Prime Minister, 1827.

CARDWELL, Edward (created Viscount, 1874) (1813–86): son of Liverpool merchant; ed. Winchester, Oxford; tory MP 1842–6, thereafter Peelite-Liberal MP until 1874; junior Treasury office under Peel, 1845–6, and became devoted free-trader; edited Peel's memoirs; President, Board of Trade under Aberdeen, 1852–5; natural bureaucrat, institutional reformer, retrencher; Secretary for Ireland, 1859–61, Chancellor, Duchy of Lancaster, 1861–4, Colonial Secretary, 1864–6, Secretary for War, 1868–74; lengthy cabinet office left him prey to insanity; ended in care.

CARLISLE: see MORPETH

CARLYLE, Thomas (1795–1881): son of Dumfriesshire mason; ed. at parish school, Edinburgh University and auto-didactically; schoolmaster; became tutor to Edinburgh University pupils; voluminous and trenchant author on literary, historical, philosophical and political subjects; contributor to *Edinburgh Review* and many other magazines; moved to Chelsea, 1834; mixed in intellectual circles there; J.S. Mill accidentally burnt much of first draft of his *French Revolution*; notwithstanding this, it made his reputation, 1837; many other works; much-caricatured Victorian sage; critical of sentimentalism, materialism, democracy; advocate of strong leadership; enormously influential as mentor and hate-figure.

CAVENDISH, Lord Frederick (1836–82): younger brother of Hartington; ed. Cambridge, where his father was Chancellor and an enthusiast for scientific progress; married a Lyttelton and hence into the extended Gladstone family; MP, West Riding of Yorkshire, 1865–82; junior office, 1873–4; Secretary for Ireland, 1880–2, where his father held extensive estates; assassinated in Phoenix Park.

CHAMBERLAIN, Joseph (1836–1914): London unitarian family; left school at 16; joined Birmingham screw-manufacturing firm, 1854; retired wealthy at 38; chairman, National Education League from 1870, pressing for a national, unsectarian, preferably secular education system; self-consciously dynamic mayor of Birmingham, 1873–5, demolished much of city centre to improve civic image; MP, Birmingham, 1876 onwards; founder, National Liberal Federation, 1877; his energy, and apparent representativeness of extra-parliamentary Liberalism, made his rise to cabinet unstoppable; President, Board of Trade, 1880–5, and author of much technical reform there; advocate of strong foreign policy and national efficiency at home; set himself up as leader of the new voters, 1885, with his 'Unauthorized Programme'; President, Local Government Board, February–March 1886, but resigned in opposition to Gladstone's Home Rule Bill; leading Liberal Unionist; controlled much of West Midlands politics; Colonial Secretary in Salisbury's Unionist government, 1895–1903; resigned in order to advocate tariff reform, 1903; a stroke, 1906, largely incapacitated him. He came nearer than anyone before Lloyd George to destroying the dominance of the traditional governing classes; but he failed.

CHILDERS, Hugh (1827–96): ed. Cambridge; administrator and politician in Australia, 1851–7; MP, 1860–92; junior Treasury office under Gladstone, 1865–6, which influenced his subsequent financial policy; First Lord of Admiralty, 1868–71; broke down under strain of family bereavements; Chancellor, Duchy of Lancaster, 1872–3, but resigned again; Secretary for War, 1880–2, Chancellor of Exchequer, 1882–5; businesslike, but deemed insufficiently economical by Gladstone, so Home Secretary, 1886; an important early convert to Home Rule in 1886.

CLARENDON, fourth earl of (1800–70): Canningite family; diplomat from 1820; ambassador to Madrid, 1833–9; succeeded to peerage, 1838; wooed by both parties; joined Melbourne's cabinet as Lord Privy Seal, 1839–41; President, Board of Trade, 1846–7; Lord Lieutenant of Ireland, 1847–52; an urbane and successful Foreign Secretary, 1853–8, 1865–6, 1868–70; angry at having to make way for Russell, 1859; Chancellor, Duchy of Lancaster, 1864–5, to boost government strength in Lords; Queen Victoria found his levity disrespectful.

COBDEN, Richard (1804–65): son of Sussex farmer; entered calico business; settled in Manchester, 1832; free-trade polemicist from 1835; effective leader, Anti-Corn Law League, 1838–46; MP, Stockport, 1841–7, West Riding of Yorkshire, 1847–57 (defeated), Rochdale, 1859–65; advocate of international arbitration and domestic economy; negotiated 1860 commercial treaty with France; refused office, died young, hence won reputation as exceptionally high-minded; a venerated symbol of free-trading Liberalism for generations, though a failure in business, and twice required financial support from massive public subscriptions.

COKE, Thomas (created earl of Leicester, 1837) (1754–1842): succeeded, 1776, to large Norfolk estate of Holkham, bleak cradle of agri-economics; pioneer breeder of sheep, cattle, pigs etc.; MP, Norfolk, 1776–1806, 1807–32; self-appointed 'Friend of Liberty' and 'King Tom of Norfolk', but insignificant outside; publicly ridiculed Castlereagh's sexual powers; nine children; insufferable.

COWPER, William (COWPER-TEMPLE from 1869) (created Baron Mount-Temple, 1880) (1811–88): son of fifth Earl Cowper; nephew of Melbourne; stepson of Palmerston; inherited Palmerston's Hampshire and Irish estates, 1869, on his mother's death; ed. Eton; army, 1827–35; MP from 1835 (South Hampshire, 1868–80); private secretary to Melbourne, 1835; junior office, 1841, 1846–52, 1852–5; President, Board of Health under Palmerston, 1855–8 and, in addition, first Education minister, 1857–8; author of the compromise on religious teaching in the 1870 Education Act; Vice-President, Board of Trade, 1859–60; First Commissioner of Works, 1860–6, becoming interested in provision of parks for public; first President, Commons Preservation Society, 1867; friend of Ruskin.

DALE, Robert (1829–95): Congregationalist minister in Birmingham from 1853; great following; published numerous theological works.

DE GREY: see RIPON

DERBY: see STANLEY

DILKE, Sir Charles (1843–1911): of distinguished metropolitan literary family; ed. Cambridge; advocate of 'Greater Britain'; MP, Chelsea, 1868–86; radical intellectual, protégé of Fawcett, republican; junior office, 1880–2; cabinet as President, Local Government Board, 1882–5; better placed than Chamberlain to capitalise on the new political situation created by the 1885 redistribution settlement (for which he was most responsible); but career ruined by adultery scandal, 1885–6; defeated as MP, 1886; MP, Forest of Dean, 1892–1911.

DUFFERIN, first earl of (originally Irish baron; created UK baron, 1850, promoted earl, 1871 and marquess, 1888) (1826–1902): great-grandson of the dramatist Sheridan; mother a great society beauty; ed. Eton, Oxford; at court, 1849–52, 1854–8; attaché to Russell at Vienna, 1855; official inquiry into Levant massacres, 1860; junior office, 1864–6; Chancellor, Duchy of Lancaster, 1868–72; Governor-general of Canada, 1872–8; ambassador to St Petersburg, then Constantinople, 1879–84; Viceroy of India, 1884–8; ambassador to Rome, then Paris, 1889–96. The most glittering of all diplomatic careers.

DUNCANNON, Viscount (fourth earl of Bessborough, 1844) (1781–1847): Irish whig family; ed. Oxford; MP from 1805, pocket boroughs until Nottingham, 1832–4; whig chief whip in opposition, 1820s; member, Committee of Four on Reform Bill; First Commissioner of Woods and Forests, 1831–4, 1835–41; called to Lords as Viscount Duncannon, 1834; cabinet as Home Secretary, 1834, and Commissioner, above, 1835–41; on good terms with O'Connell; Lord Lieutenant of Ireland, 1846–7, the first resident Irish landlord appointed for many years.

DUNCOMBE, Thomas (1796–1861): ed. Harrow; army, 1813–19; MP, Hertford, 1826–32, Finsbury, 1834–61; presented Chartist petition, 1842; member of council of 'Friends of Italy', 1851; man of fashion.

DURHAM, first earl of (J.G. Lambton, created Baron Durham 1828, promoted earl 1833) (1792–1840): Durham landed family, made immensely rich by coalmines; army, 1809–11; MP, Durham county, 1813–28; populist; member, Committee of Four, Reform Bill; Lord Privy Seal, 1830–3, resigning owing to ill-health and family bereavements; ambassador extraordinary, 1832, 1835–7; sent to Canada to restore order after the 1837 rebellion, but resigned after controversy about his behaviour; the 1839 report which bears his name is widely seen as the foundation of the modern Canadian state.

ELLICE, Edward (1781–1863): ed. Winchester, Aberdeen; Canadian fur trader and influential lobbyist; MP, Coventry, 1818–26, 1830–63; government chief whip, 1830–2; Secretary at War, 1832–4, co-founder of Reform Club, 1836; *eminence grise*.

EVANS, George De Lacy (1787–1870): army from 1806; Peninsular and Anglo-American wars, and Waterloo; MP, Rye, 1831–2, Westminster, 1833–41, 1846–65; commanded British legion against the Spanish Carlists, 1835–7; KCB, 1837; unflagging advocate of army reform; GCB, 1855, for role in Crimean War.

FAWCETT, Henry (1833–84): ed. London, Cambridge; lost eyesight in shooting accident, 1858; extreme political economist, follower of J.S. Mill, advocate of proportional representation, opponent of clerical education; Professor, Political Economy, Cambridge University, 1863–84; MP, Brighton, 1865–74, Hackney, 1874–84; zealous proponent of reform of Indian finance; Postmaster-general, 1880–4. His wife, Millicent Garrett, was leader of the women's suffrage movement and a campaigner for women's education and property rights.

FORSTER, William (1818–86): son of quaker minister, philanthropist and abolitionist who was connected by marriage to the Gurneys; ed. at quaker schools; woollen trade at Bradford from 1842; married daughter of Thomas Arnold, 1850, and left quakers; MP, Bradford, 1861–86; junior office, 1865–6; Education minister, 1868–74 (in cabinet from 1870); candidate of the national efficiency business wing for Liberal Commons leader, 1875, but withdrew in favour of Hartington's more general appeal (his chances were in reality always slim, but were not helped by the abuse, by extreme Dissenters, of his 1870 Education Act compromise, and his robustness in subsequently defending it); battled with Miall and local 'wirepullers' in his Bradford seat, 1874–80, with similar robustness; Secretary for Ireland, 1880–2; resigned in opposition to Kilmainham Treaty; robustness now his fixed mode of self-presentation; first Chairman, Imperial Federation League, and opponent of Gladstonian foreign policy; dying, 1886, promised robust opposition to Home Rule.

FOX, Charles James (1749–1806): ed. Eton, Oxford; son of arch-ministerialist Henry Fox, but became attached to whig opposition during American war; Secretary of State, 1782, 1783–4, but removed by successful royal and Pittite manoeuvre; MP, Westminster from 1780, and emerging popular tribune; elevated opposition to Pitt into an art form, 1784–1806; drinking and gambling friend of the Prince of Wales; Foreign Secretary, 1806, after Pitt's death, but died in same year. His personality and personal following were gigantic, but his ideological legacy was blurred, or perhaps slurred.

GLADSTONE, William (1809–98): son of upwardly-mobile West Indian merchant and slaveowner; ed. Eton, Oxford, where he acquired an arriviste's deep admiration for aristocracy and church; Oxford friendship with the future duke of Newcastle gave him pocket borough entry to parliament as high tory, 1832; junior office, 1834–5; published earnest theocratic works, 1838–40, to Peel's incomprehension and regret; Vice-President and President, Board of Trade, 1841–5, where he became fascinated by the technicalities of finance; enthusiastic convert to free trade, and Peelite from 1846; frustrated by third-party status and lack of political employment, 1850s, and took to reclaiming prostitutes and self-flagellation; Chancellor of Exchequer, 1852–5, 1859–66, which formalised his move into Liberal party; great financial reform schemes and set-piece battles with Palmerston; cultivated publicity, and symbolism of tree-felling, from 1860s; fortuitous destruction of his political cohort left him unchallenged Liberal leader, 1868; Prime Minister, 1868–74, 1880–5, 1886, 1892–4.

GODERICH, Viscount (Frederick Robinson; created Viscount, 1827, promoted earl of Ripon, 1833) (1782–1859): son and grandson of ennobled politicians/diplomats; ed. Harrow, Cambridge; tory MP, 1806–27; junior office, 1804–6, 1809, 1810–12; Vice-President, Board of Trade, 1812–18, and President (in cabinet), 1818–23; Chancellor of Exchequer, 1823–7; Secretary for War and Leader, House of Lords, under Canning, 1827; Prime Minister, 1827–8; joined Reform government as Secretary for War, 1830–3, Lord Privy Seal, 1833–4; resigned over Irish Church appropriation; reverted to tory party; President, Board of Trade, 1841–3, President, Board of Control, 1843–6.

GOSCHEN, George (1831–1907): son of immigrant London banker; ed. Rugby, Oxford; moved in intellectual circles there; entered family bank; director, Bank of England, 1858; clever, dogmatic, hyper-assiduous, political economist; MP, City of London, 1863–80, and other seats, 1880–6, 1887–1900; junior office, 1865, cabinet, 1866; President, Poor Law Board, 1868–71, First Lord of Admiralty, 1871–4; opposed county franchise extension, 1877, uneasy at developments in popular Liberalism; declined Viceroyalty of India, Gladstone's comically inappropriate one-way ticket out of domestic politics, 1880, ditto Speakership, 1883; critic of Gladstonian foreign policy; early and decided opponent of Irish Home Rule; the threat he posed, as a floating politician, was realised by his acceptance of Salisbury's offer of Chancellor of Exchequer, 1886–92, in Unionist government; First Lord of Admiralty, 1895–1900; created Viscount, 1900; advocate of university extension; ecclesiastical commissioner, 1882. He symbolised the marriage of administrative intelligence, City finance and manly progressive religion, and its move away from Gladstone.

GRAHAM, Sir James (1792–1861): ed. Westminster, Oxford; whig MP, 1818; political economist; member, Committee of Four, Reform Bill, 1831; First Lord of

Admiralty, 1830–4, resigning over Irish church appropriation and the general threat posed by popular pressure; moved with Stanley into tory party; Home Secretary, 1841–6, again demonstrating anxiety about disorder; free trader and Peelite from 1846; refused office from Russell, but came to advocate coalition with Liberals; First Lord of Admiralty, 1852–5; resigned in opposition to parliamentary inquiry into war management. Some questioned his moral fibre.

GRANVILLE, second Earl (1815–91): grandson of first marquess of Stafford; son of ambassador at Paris (1824–41), created earl 1833; ed. Eton, Oxford; MP, 1836–46, when succeeded to title; junior office, 1840–1, 1848–51; Foreign Secretary in place of Palmerston, 1851–2, and again, 1870–4, 1880–5; other cabinet office, 1852–8, 1859–66, 1868–70, 1886; Liberal leader, House of Lords, 1855–65, 1868–91; refused premiership, 1859 and 1880; confidant of Gladstone and smoother of tempers and differences; indispensable, though latterly notoriously unbusinesslike; Chancellor, London University, 1856–91; known as 'Pussy'.

GREG, William (1809–81): son of Manchester merchant and Cheshire millowner; distinguished, learned and philanthropical unitarian family; ed. Bristol, Edinburgh; in business, but failed, 1850; much interested in literary and speculative criticism; his *Creed of Christendom* (1851) was a critique of theological orthodoxy; prolific journalist and polemicist from 1852; appointed (by Lewis) to Commissionership of Board of Customs, 1856, restoring his financial independence; official posts until 1877; remained voluminous pundit; hostile to democracy and Gladstone.

GREY, second Earl (1764–1845): son of ennobled general (Seven Years' War; American war; West Indies 1794); ed. Eton, Cambridge; MP, Northumberland, 1786–1807, when succeeded to title; Foxite, and member of Society of Friends of People, 1790s; First Lord of Admiralty, 1806, Foreign Secretary after Fox, 1806–7, but otherwise held no office until 1830; regarded as whig leader in opposition, but rarely at Westminster; Prime Minister, 1830–4.

GREY, third Earl (Viscount Howick, 1807–45) (1802–94): son of Prime Minister, above; ed. Cambridge; moved in intellectual circles; MP, 1826–45; junior office, 1830–4; energetic Secretary at War, 1835–9, but resigned, discontented at lack of legislative output and efficiency; zealous, 'crotchety' free trader, like his brother-in-law Charles Wood; blamed for Liberal failure to form government, 1845, owing to his attempt to veto Palmerston as Foreign Secretary; this incident characteristic of his career, in gaining him opprobrium for saying undiplomatically what most intelligent critics thought; active Colonial Secretary, 1846–52; never held office again, a victim first of Peelite office-hunger, and then, unlike other displaced whigs, of Palmerston's enmity; became vociferous cross-bench critic; tiresome, verbose, but intellectually powerful, influential at court, and arguably the father of Liberal Unionism; still operating behind the scenes against Gladstone in 1886.

GREY, Sir George (1799–1882): nephew of Prime Minister; ed. Oriel College Oxford under Whately (1st); MP, 1832–52, 1853–74; junior office, 1834, 1835–41; Chancellor, Duchy of Lancaster, 1841, 1859–61; Home Secretary, 1846–52, 1855–8, 1861–6; Colonial Secretary, 1854–5; he, Charles Wood and Henry Brand, Liberal chief whip 1859–66, were Palmerston's '*corps d'armée*', influential, discreet and effective party managers.

HALIFAX: see WOOD

HARCOURT, William (1827–1904): grandson of archbishop of York, 1807–47; son of scientifically-minded rector; estates; ed. Cambridge; successful barrister; active journalist, 1850s and 1860s; became expert on international law; Whewell Professor of International Law, Cambridge, 1869–87; MP from 1868; tireless critic of Gladstone; bought off with Solicitor-generalship, 1873–4, hence knighted; vigorous opposition to Disraeli, 1874–80, cemented his political fortunes; Home Secretary, 1880–5; despite initial uncertainty, joined Home Rule cabinet; not uncoincidentally, his way to the leadership seemed clear; Chancellor of Exchequer, 1886, 1892–5; but, too bullying and candid, he was passed over for Rosebery as Prime Minister, 1894–5, and resigned Commons leadership, held since 1894, in 1898. One of the last parliamentarian-aristocrats, yet one of the first modern political professionals.

HARTINGTON, marquess of (eighth duke of Devonshire, 1891) (1833–1908): son of seventh duke, intellectual, scientist, philanthropist; but none of these; ed. privately, Cambridge; MP from 1857; junior office, 1863–6; Secretary for War, 1866, 1882–5; Postmaster-general, 1868–70, Secretary for Ireland, 1870–4; Liberal leader, Commons, 1874–80; not agitated about Bulgaria, 1876; refused premiership 1880, and again 1886 and 1887; Secretary for India, 1880–2; leading opponent of Home Rule and founder Liberal Unionist party, 1886; independent supporter of Salisbury, 1887–92; President of Council, 1895–1903; resigned in opposition to Chamberlain's tariff reform scheme.

HATHERTON: see LITTLETON

HERBERT, Sidney (created Baron Herbert, 1860) (1810–61): son of eleventh earl of Pembroke; ed. Harrow, Oxford; MP, South Wiltshire, 1832–60; junior office, 1834–5, 1841–5; Secretary for War, 1845–6, 1852–5, 1859–60; tory, then Peelite; assiduous administrator, damaging his health.

HOBHOUSE, John Cam (created Baron Broughton, 1851) (1786–1869): son of independent Sidmouthite MP and the daughter of a unitarian minister; ed. Westminster, Cambridge, where he became intimate friend of Byron; literary radical; advocate of Greek independence; MP, Westminster, 1820–33, Nottingham, 1834–47, Harwich, 1848–51; Secretary at War, 1832–3; Secretary for Ireland, 1833, but resigned on government failure to abolish house and window tax, and lost his seat as well; in cabinet as First Commissioner of Woods and Forests, 1834, President, Board of Control, 1835–41, 1846–52.

HOLLAND, third Baron (1773–1840): succeeded to title, 1774; nephew of Charles James Fox, who largely brought him up; ed. Eton, Oxford; opposed Union with Ireland; married divorcée, 1797, after fathering her child; she inherited extensive Jamaican estates; Lord Privy Seal, 1806–7; mixed with Napoleon; supported the cause of international revolution; travelled very widely; ran a vivacious salon for literary and political speculation, at Holland House; Chancellor, Duchy of Lancaster, 1830–4, 1835–40.

HOWICK: see GREY, third Earl

HUGHES, Thomas (1822–96): ed. Rugby, Oxford; barrister; Christian Socialist; cofounder of Working-Men's College, Great Ormond St, 1854, and Principal, 1872–83; MP, Lambeth, 1865–8, Frome, 1868–74; county court judge, 1882–96; *Tom Brown's schooldays* (1857) was followed by other fiction and works of history.

HUME, Joseph (1777=1855): self-made man; entered medical service, East India Company, 1797; returned to England, 1807, very wealthy; MP briefly, 1812, then 1818–41, 1842–55; radical; principally responsible for repeal of combination laws; tireless opponent of government extravagance; critic of Corn Laws.

HUSKISSON, William (1770–1830): son of minor country gentleman; ed. in Paris; private secretary to British ambassador there; government official from 1793; his ability noticed by Pitt; MP from 1796; resigned with Pitt, 1801; junior office again, 1804–6, 1807–9; now follower of Canning, resigned with him 1809, and succeeded him as MP for Liverpool 1823–30; office again from 1814; cabinet from 1823, as President, Board of Trade; advocate of freer trade and imperial preference; Colonial Secretary, 1827–8; resigned from Wellington's government, 1828, after wrangle over redistribution of seats from two corrupt boroughs; killed by Stephenson's Rocket at opening of Liverpool and Manchester Railway, 1830. Indecisive in this as in much else, but highly influential on economic policy.

JEFFREY, Francis (created Baron Jeffrey, 1834) (1773–1850): ed. Edinburgh; Scottish barrister; co-founder, *Edinburgh Review*, and editor, 1803–29; made it the leading whig journal; Lord Advocate, 1830–4; MP, 1831–2, and for Edinburgh, 1832–4; retired from politics to become Judge of Court of Sessions, 1834–50.

KIMBERLEY, first earl of (1826–1902): ed. Eton, Oxford (1st); succeeded grand-father as Baron Wodehouse, 1846; under-secretary, Foreign Office, 1852–6, 1859–61, and minister at St Petersburg, 1856–8; Lord-Lieutenant of Ireland, 1864–6, for which he gained earldom, 1866; cabinet office, 1868–74, 1880–5, 1886, 1892–5; Liberal leader, House of Lords, 1891–4, 1897–1902; Chancellor of London University, 1899–1902. A clever man; the ablest Gladstonian peer after 1886.

KING, Peter Locke (1811–85): son of seventh Baron King (see page 135); ed. Harrow, Cambridge; MP, East Surrey, 1847–74; responsible for the abolition of the property qualification for MPs, 1858; advocate of county franchise reform and the abolition of compulsory church rates.

LABOUCHERE, Henry (created Baron Taunton, 1859) (1798–1869): ed. Winchester, Oxford (1st); MP, 1826–59; junior office, 1832–4; Vice-President, Board of Trade, 1835–9, and President (in cabinet), 1839–41, 1847–52; Secretary for Ireland, 1846–7; Colonial Secretary, 1855–8. Baring's cousin and brother-in-law.

LAMBTON: see DURHAM

LANSDOWNE, third marquess of (1780–1863): son of the Lord Shelburne who was Prime Minister, 1782; inherited an interest in political economy; ed. Westminster, Edinburgh and Cambridge; MP 1803–9, when he succeeded to the marquisate; whig Chancellor of Exchequer at 25, 1806–7, as Lord Henry Petty; thereafter a leading whig, but mostly behind the scenes; influential in creating the whig coalition with Canning, 1827, and took cabinet office, 1827–8; honorific cabinet office, 1830–4, 1835–41, 1846–52, 1852–8; Liberal leader, House of Lords, 1842–52. No man has served so long and left so little mark. His son and heir, the fourth marquess, played a key role in defeating the 1866 Reform Bill, but died that year.

LAYARD, [Austen] Henry (1817–94): born in Paris; worked in solicitor's office in London, 1833–9; travelled in Turkey and Persia, collecting information for British government; gained celebrity as archeologist, searching for Nineveh, 1845–53; attaché to embassy at Constantinople, 1849–51, under Stratford Canning; after his accounts of his excavations were published, he was lionised in London, a good springboard for a political career; MP from 1852; Turcophile, and sought to use Crimean War failings to browbeat governing elite, not least into giving him a job; in fact his immoderation damaged his prospects; junior office, 1861–6; intemperate First Commissioner of Works, 1868–9; left for ambassadorships in Madrid and Constantinople, 1869–80, complaining of lack of self-expression possible in domestic democratic politics; fervent (as in most things) Protestant.

LEATHAM, Edward (1828–1900): quaker; son of Yorkshire banker; ed. University College London; in family firm; Bright married his sister; also connected to Gurneys and Barclays; published a novel, 1858; MP, Huddersfield, 1859–65, 1868–86; Liberal Unionist.

LEWIS, Sir George Cornewall (1806–63): son of earnest country gentleman administrator, first chairman of Poor Law Commission; ed. Eton, Oxford; various official inquiries, 1830s, including Poor Law Commissionership, 1839–47; MP from 1847; junior office, 1848–52; out of parliament, and editor of *Edinburgh Review*, 1852–5; succeeded to father's baronetcy (1846), 1855; Chancellor of Exchequer, 1855–8,

Home Secretary, 1859–61, Secretary for War, 1861–3; wrote rather turgid books. Uncharismatic, but an efficient gentleman-intellectual.

LITTLETON, Edward (created Baron Hatherton, 1835) (1791–1863): ed. Oxford; succeeded to Staffordshire estates, 1812; married Wellesley's illegitimate daughter; Canningite/Wellesleyite MP, Staffordshire, 1812–32, and South Staffordshire, 1832–5; a Reformer, 1830; Secretary for Ireland, 1833–4 (not in cabinet).

LIVERPOOL, second earl of (1770–1828): son of leading Pittite politician; ed. Charterhouse, Oxford; Pittite MP, 1790–1803, when he was summoned to Lords as Baron Hawkesbury (succeeded father, 1808); Commissioner, Board of Control, 1793–9, Master of Mint, 1799–1801, Foreign Secretary, 1801–4, Home Secretary, 1804–6, 1807–9, Secretary for War and Colonies, 1809–12, Prime Minister, 1812–27, when incapacitated by stroke. The ultimate insider.

LOWE, Robert (created Viscount Sherbrooke, 1880) (1811–92): ed. Winchester, Oxford; hung around Oxford as private tutor in order to earn money; barrister and politician, Australia, 1842–50; returned to London as leader-writer, *Times*, 1850, in which role he acquired political influence; MP from 1852; junior office, 1852–5; Vice-President, Board of Trade, 1855–8; Education minister, 1859–64; first MP for London University, 1868–80; Chancellor of Exchequer, 1868–73; Home Secretary, 1873–4; albino; very bad eyesight; cultivated reputation as self-made man; believer in rigid economy and rigidly-assessed education; opponent of democracy.

LUBBOCK, Sir John (created Baron Avebury, 1900) (1834–1913): grandson of leading banker; son of distinguished mathematician, first Vice-chancellor of London University; ed. Eton; left early for career in family bank; MP from 1870 (London University, 1880–1900); polymath; enthusiastic populariser of science, natural history and good literature.

LYVEDEN: see SMITH

MACAULAY, Thomas Babington (created Baron Macaulay, 1857) (1800–59): son of evangelical anti-slavery activist; ed. Cambridge; wrote for *Edinburgh Review*; MP, 1830–2, Leeds, 1832–4; Commissioner, and Secretary, Board of Control, 1832–4; member, supreme council of India, 1834–8; returned to London; began *History of England*, 1839; MP, Edinburgh, 1839–47, 1852–6; swift cabinet placing as Secretary for War, 1839–41, Paymaster-general, 1846–8; resigned in order to write.

MACKINTOSH, Sir James (1765–1832): ed. Aberdeen, Edinburgh; barrister and author in London, 1790s; recorder and judge, Bombay, 1803–11; MP, 1813–32; advocate of criminal law reform; Professor of Law at Haileybury, 1818–24; author of various historical works; Commissioner, Board of Control, 1830–2.

MELBOURNE, second Viscount (1779–1848): born William Lamb; ed. Eton, Cambridge; married Lady Caroline, 1805; she attempted to elope with Byron, 1812; marriage quickly deteriorated, though formal separation only took place 1825; lukewarm whig MP, 1806–12, 1816–26, 1827–8, when he succeeded to title; appointed Secretary for Ireland by Canning, 1827–8, resigned with Huskisson from Wellington's government; Home Secretary, 1830–4; Prime Minister, 1834, 1835–41.

MIALL, Edward (1809–81): congregationalist minister, Leicester, 1834; agitated against church rates and establishment; founder and editor, *Nonconformist* magazine, 1841–81; advocated cooperation with Chartists, 1842; founder, Anti-State Church Association, 1844, which became Liberation Society, 1853; MP, Rochdale, 1852–7, Bradford, 1869–74, but defeated in challenge to Forster, 1874; proposed disestablishment motions, 1871–3.

MILL, John Stuart (1806–73): son of Benthamite philosopher, historian and Indian administrator, James Mill; ed. by him in utilitarian tenets; Indian administrator,

1823–58; forceful pundit, philosopher, political economist; his later works – *On Liberty, Representative government*, etc. – written in seclusion from society in un- orthodox ménage with Harriet Taylor, 1850s, and display dislike of social con- formity; their high-minded anti-materialist classlessness acquired for Mill a great aura among middle-brow Liberals; MP, Westminster, 1865–8; advocate of propor- tional representation and women's rights.

MOLESWORTH, Sir William (1810–55): of wealthy baronet family; expelled from Trinity, Cambridge, for attempting a duel with his tutor; ed. Edinburgh; MP from 1832; started *London Review*, 1835; edited Hobbes, 1839–45; advocate of colonial self-government and abolition of transportation; in cabinet as First Commissioner of Works, 1853–5, Colonial Secretary, 1855.

MORLEY, John (1838–1923): son of Blackburn surgeon; ed. Cheltenham, Oxford; journalist, 1860s; influential editor, *Fortnightly Review*, 1867–82; moved in positivist circles; rationalist historical works; campaigned with Chamberlain for national edu- cation system, 1870s, but differed with him over foreign policy; editor, *Pall Mall Gazette*, 1880–3; MP, 1883–1908, then created Viscount; Secretary for Ireland, 1886, 1892–5, and leading influence on Home Rule policy; became confidant of Gladstone, and his biographer, 1903; Secretary for India, 1905–10, Lord Privy Seal, 1910–14, resigned in opposition to war, 1914. The conscience of Gladstonian Liberalism; nicknamed 'Priscilla'.

MORLEY, Samuel (1809–86): son of Nottingham hosiery manufacturer; worked in family firm, became immensely wealthy; congregationalist; philanthropist; treasurer, Home Missionary Society, from 1858; paid for many Dissenting chapels; lobbyist for voluntary education; co-founder, Administrative Reform Association, 1855; teetotaller; encouraged working-men to stand for parliament; proprietor, *Daily News*; MP, Bristol, 1868–85; member, London School Board, 1870–6; assisted Agricultural Labourers' Union; refused peerage, 1885. His son Arnold became Liberal chief whip, 1886, and served in the 1892–5 cabinet.

MORPETH, Viscount (seventh earl of Carlisle, 1848) (1802–64): son of sixth earl, whig grandee who joined Canning's cabinet, 1827–8; ed. Oxford; MP from 1826 (Yorkshire, 1830–2, West Riding 1832–41, 1846–8); Secretary for Ireland, 1835– 41, in cabinet from 1839; First Commissioner of Woods and Forests, 1846–50, in charge of public health (cf. 1848 Act); Chancellor, Duchy of Lancaster, 1850–2; Lord Lieutenant of Ireland, 1855–8, 1859–64.

MULGRAVE, second earl of (promoted marquess of Normanby, 1838) (1797–1863): son of Pittite general, politician and military adviser, a patron of art; ed. Harrow, Cambridge; moved in literary circles, silver-fork novelist; MP from 1818, succeeded to title, 1831; Governor of Jamaica, 1832–4; Lord Privy Seal, in cabinet, 1834; Lord Lieutenant of Ireland, 1835–9; Secretary for War and Colonies, 1839, Home Secretary, 1839–41; ambassador at Paris, 1846–52, where he was involved in Palmerston's 1851 indiscretion about Napoleon's coup; minister at Florence, 1854– 8. Lacked gravitas.

MUNDELLA, Anthony (1825–97): Nottingham hosiery manufacturer; set up concili- ation machinery with workers, 1866; MP, Sheffield, 1868–85, Sheffield, Brightside, 1885–97; much involved with factory, trade union and education legislation; cabinet as Education minister, 1880–5, President, Board of Trade, 1886, 1892–4.

NEWCASTLE, fifth duke of (1811–64): son of evangelical high tory fourth duke; ed. Eton, Oxford, with Gladstone; tory, then Peelite MP, 1832–51, when succeeded to title; Secretary for Ireland under Peel, 1846; divorced his wife, 1850, after she eloped to Italy with her lover, and after Gladstone, disguised as a guitarist, procured the necessary evidence from a villa near Lake Como; Secretary for War and

Colonies, 1852–4, and for War, 1854–5, resigned over Roebuck motion for inquiry; Colonial Secretary, 1859–64.

NORMANBY: see MULGRAVE

NORTHBROOK, second Baron (promoted earl of Northbrook, 1876) (1826–1904): son of Sir Francis Baring and nephew of Sir George Grey; ed. Oxford; MP, 1857–66, when succeeded to title; junior office, 1857–8, 1859–66, 1868–72; Viceroy of India, 1872–6; First Lord of Admiralty, 1880–5; Liberal Unionist; retired to run Hampshire.

O'CONNELL, Daniel (1775–1847): ed. Catholic institutions in France; very forceful Irish barrister; early advocate of Catholic Emancipation; killed a Dublin merchant in duel, 1815; formed Catholic Association, 1823, and renamed it, 1826, after law suppressed it, 1825; by mass meetings he created a great political movement, widely seen as the stimulant of Irish national feeling; MP for County Clare, 1828–30, and for other seats, 1830–47, though ineligible to sit until Catholic Emancipation, 1829, of which his election was the immediate catalyst; supported as MP by annual tribute from Ireland; arrested, 1831, on account of political activity, but prosecution dropped; gave unpredictable support to Reform governments, 1834–41; lord mayor of Dublin, 1841–2; founded Repeal Association, 1840; seriously advocated repeal from 1843; arrested, 1843, for inciting disaffection; imprisoned but released on appeal, 1844.

PALMER: see SELBORNE

PALMERSTON, third Viscount (Irish peerage) (1784–1865): Hampshire estates; ed. Harrow, Edinburgh, Cambridge; tory MP 1807–28; Canningite, then whig, MP, 1828–65; junior office, 1808–9; Secretary at War, 1809–28; resigned with Huskisson from Wellington's government, 1828; attacked Wellington over foreign policy, 1829; Foreign Secretary, 1830–4, 1835–41, 1846–51, when dismissed; Home Secretary, 1852–5, though temporarily resigned, December 1853, over Reform; Prime Minister, 1855–8, 1859–65.

PARKES, Joseph (1796–1865): son of Warwick manufacturer; disciple of Bentham; unitarian (married Joseph Priestley's daughter); widely connected in London and Birmingham radical circles; Birmingham solicitor, 1822–33; member, Birmingham Political Union, May 1832, when he talked of rebellion; moved to London as Secretary to Royal Commission on municipal corporations, 1833–5; became influential parliamentary solicitor, dealing with registration etc.; effectively first national agent for Liberal party, until 1847; co-founder, Reform Association, 1835, and Reform Club, 1836; Taxing-master in Chancery from 1847; historian of the Chancery bar. Hilaire Belloc's grandfather.

PARNELL, Charles Stewart (1846–91): of county Wicklow landed Protestant family; ed. Cambridge; MP from 1875; pursued obstructive tactics in Commons from 1877, and quickly eclipsed Isaac Butt as effective leader of the Irish party; used 'Land War' to knit together broad coalition in the Irish Land League, 1879–80; elected chairman, Commons Home Rule party, 1880; very dynamic and skilful leader, disguising the heterogeneity of his supporters; advocate of 'boycotting', 1880; imprisoned, 1881–2; released by the 'Kilmainham Treaty'; renamed the Land League the National League, 1882; from 1886 was in alliance with Gladstonian Liberals; smeared by *Times* articles, 1887, and, on vindication, became a Liberal hero, 1889; named in adultery scandal, 1890, and became a Liberal villain; career destroyed; forced out of National party leadership.

PEEL, Sir Robert (1788–1850): son of rich calico-printer, MP and new baronet; ed. Harrow, Oxford; tory MP from 1809; junior office, 1810–12; Secretary for Ireland, 1812–18, Home Secretary, 1822–7, 1828–30; defeated as MP, Oxford University (since 1817), on passage of Catholic Emancipation, 1829; Prime Minister, 1834–5, 1841–6; killed riding, 1850. Consummate administrator and financial reformer.

PHILIPS, Mark (1800–73): eldest son of gentrified Manchester manufacturer with Warwickshire estates; unitarian; MP, Manchester, 1832–47; Sheriff of Warwickshire, 1851.

RATHBONE, William (1819–1902): eldest son of distinguished Liverpool merchant family; unitarian with strong notion of public duty; partner in family firm, 1841; philanthropist; active in domestic missionary and charitable work; leading spirit behind establishment of training schools for nurses, and of Charity Organisation Society, 1869; MP, Liverpool, 1868–80, and for Carnarvonshire seats, 1880–95; remained Gladstonian, 1886; President, University College, Liverpool, from 1892, and University College of North Wales, from 1891.

RIPON, first marquess of (created 1871; Viscount Goderich, 1833–59; Earl de Grey and Ripon, 1859–71) (1827–1909): born, 10 Downing St, while his father, Viscount Goderich, was Prime Minister; family wealth came from state service; ed. privately; Christian Socialist and political radical as youth; lectured on entomology to working-men, 1852; MP, 1853–9, when he succeeded father and uncle to two different titles; junior office, 1859–63; Secretary for War, 1863–6; Secretary for India, 1866; President of Council, 1868–73; gained marquessate for role in settling American claims against Britain, 1871; controversially 'sentimental' Viceroy of India, 1880–4; First Lord of Admiralty, 1886, and supporter of Home Rule; further cabinet office, 1892–5, 1905–8; Liberal leader, House of Lords, 1905–8. Grandmaster of the Freemasons, he caused much astonishment by converting to Roman Catholicism, 1874. For Earl of RIPON, his father, see GODERICH. His uncle was Peel's Lord Lieutenant of Ireland, 1841–4.

ROBINSON: see GODERICH

ROEBUCK, John (1801–79): son of civil servant in India; ed. in Canada; unsuccessful barrister and QC; disciple of Bentham, associate of Philosophical radicals, and always contemptuous of whigs; MP, 1832–7, 1841–7, and for Sheffield, 1849–68, 1874–9; fiery radical, of strong but often inconsistent views; known as 'Tear 'em', and 'the Diogenes of Bath'; abuse of editor of *Morning Chronicle*, 1835, led to duel; advocate of strong foreign policy under Palmerston and later Disraeli, yet also criticised lacklustre administration of Crimean War, hence his role in overthrowing Aberdeen, 1855; supported Austrian rule in Italy and Southern cause in American civil war; criticised trade union activity and denounced working-men as wife beaters. His popularity fluctuated.

ROMILLY, Sir Samuel (1757–1818): Huguenot family; largely self-educated; lost Christian faith and turned to Rousseau; remained deist; moved in international Enlightenment circles; barrister; Solicitor-general to whig government, 1806–7, and knighted; MP, 1806–7, 1808–18; zealous advocate of criminal law reform; committed suicide on death of wife.

RUSSELL, Lord John (created Earl Russell, 1861) (1792–1878): son of sixth duke of Bedford; ed. Westminster, Edinburgh; MP, 1813–61; urged parliamentary reform unsuccessfully, 1820s, and repeal of Test and Corporation Acts, successfully, 1828; Paymaster-general, 1830–4, in cabinet from June 1831; introduced all three Reform Bills, 1830–2; called for Irish Church appropriation, 1834; his appointment as Liberal leader in House of Commons, 1834, led William IV to dismiss Melbourne government; he held the leadership, in and out of office, until 1855; Home Secretary, 1835–9; Colonial Secretary, 1839–41; Prime Minister, 1846–52, 1865–6; Foreign Secretary, 1852–3, 1859–65; cabinet without office, 1853–4, President of

Council, 1854–5; plenipotentiary at Vienna, 1855, and briefly Colonial Secretary, but resigned after details of Vienna talks released; historian.

SELBORNE, first earl of (Roundell Palmer; created Baron Selborne, 1872, promoted earl 1882) (1812–95): ed. Rugby, Winchester, Oxford; devoted high churchman associated with Oxford movement (his brother, ditto, seceded to Rome, 1855); barrister and QC; MP from 1847, nominally tory, in fact Peelite; Solicitor-general, 1861–3, Attorney-general, 1863–6; declined office, 1868, in opposition to Irish church disestablishment; Lord Chancellor, 1872–4, 1880–5; responsible for 1873 Judicature Act; vehement critic of Home Rule.

SHAW-LEFEVRE, George (1831–1928): son of government official and Vice-chancellor, London University; nephew of Liberal Speaker of Commons, 1839–57; ed. Cambridge; MP, 1863–85, 1886–95; co-founder, Commons Preservation Society, 1865, and virtually permanent chairman of it; junior office, 1866, 1868–74; First Commissioner of Works, 1881–5, 1892–4 (in cabinet from 1884); extended public access to Regent's Park, threw open Hampton Court Park and Kew Palace; strong supporter of Home Rule and economy; served on London County Council, 1897–1912; created Baron Eversley, 1906. High-minded administrator, but lacked charisma.

SIDMOUTH, first Viscount (created 1805) (1757–1844): born Henry Addington, son of well-connected London doctor; ed. Winchester, Oxford; Pittite MP, 1784–1805; nominated Speaker, House of Commons, by Pitt, 1789–1801; chosen as Prime Minister and Chancellor of Exchequer on Pitt's resignation, 1801–4; pursued a peace policy, leading to Treaty of Amiens, 1802; resumed war, May 1803, but ensuing crises rallied opposition to his fragile government, and Pitt ousted him; cabinet under Pitt briefly, 1805, and in Talents, 1806–7; critic of war, 1807–9; returned to cabinet, 1812; Home Secretary, 1812–22, cabinet without office, 1822–4.

SMITH, Robert Vernon (created Baron Lyveden, 1859) (1800–73): son of 'Bobus' Smith, wit, made immensely rich by Indian service; nephew of Sydney Smith; ed. Eton, Oxford; MP, 1829–31, and for Northampton, 1831–59; junior office, 1830–4, 1835–41, 1852; cabinet as President, Board of Control, 1855–8.

SOMERSET, twelfth duke of (Lord Seymour until 1855) (1804–85): son of eleventh duke; ed. Eton, Oxford; MP, 1830–1, 1834–55, in which year he succeeded to title; junior office, 1835–41, 1849–51; cabinet as First Commissioner of Works, 1851–2, and First Lord of Admiralty, 1859–66; theist.

SPENCER, fifth Earl (1835–1910): ed. Harrow, Cambridge; MP, 1857, but succeeded to title in same year; Lord Lieutenant of Ireland, 1868–74, 1882–5; in cabinet, 1880–5, 1886, 1892–5, surprising most by supporting Home Rule, having previously opposed Gladstone over coercion and Central Board scheme; Liberal leader, House of Lords, 1902–5.

SPRING RICE, Thomas (created Baron Monteagle, 1839) (1790–1866): Anglo-Irish gentry family; ed. Cambridge; whig MP, Limerick, 1820–32, Cambridge, 1832–9; junior office, 1827–8, 1830–4; cabinet as Secretary for War, 1834 and unpopular Chancellor of Exchequer, 1835–9; fluent and genial but lacked effectiveness; withdrew from political life to take post in Exchequer, 1839–65.

STANLEY, Edward (Lord Stanley, 1834–51, fourteenth earl of Derby, 1851) (1799–1869): son of thirteenth earl, whig and natural historian; ed. Eton, Oxford; whig MP from 1822; junior office, 1827–8; Secretary for Ireland, 1830–3; Colonial Secretary, 1833–4, but resigned over Irish church appropriation; joined tory opposition, 1835; Colonial Secretary under Peel, 1841–5; elevated to Lords, 1844; resigned in opposition to proposed repeal of Corn Law; tory leader, 1846–68; Prime Minister, 1852, 1858–9, 1866–8; failed to form governments, 1851, 1855; classical scholar; gambler; Chancellor of Oxford University, 1852–69. His son, Lord STANLEY,

1851–69, fifteenth earl of Derby, 1869 (1826–93), was ed. Rugby, Cambridge; tory MP, 1848–69; earnest social and sanitary reformer; one of the very few young tories respectable to the Liberal metropolitan and intellectual worlds; said to be fitted to be 'perpetual President of a Social Science Association'; Colonial and Indian Secretary in his father's government, 1858–9; Foreign Secretary, 1866–8, 1874–8; after repeatedly giving signals that he was in the wrong party, resigned in opposition to Disraeli's warlike policy, 1878; joined Liberals, 1880; Colonial Secretary under Gladstone, 1882–5; Liberal Unionist, 1886, and their leader in Lords; Chancellor of London University, 1891–3.

STANLEY, 'BEN' (Edward Stanley; created Baron Eddisbury, 1848; second Baron Stanley of Alderley, 1850) (1802–69): son of Cheshire whig gentleman, ennobled 1839; ed. Eton, Oxford; MP, 1831–2, and for North Cheshire, 1832–41, 1847–8; junior office, 1833–4, 1841, 1846–52; Liberal chief whip, 1835–41; cabinet office, 1855–8, 1860–6. Sarcastic: 'Ben' was short for 'Benjamin Backbite'. His Irish wife, a great salon influence in the party, was an ardent Liberal and promoter of women's education. Their children, famously unorthodox, included a Catholic priest, the Moslem 3rd Baron, the radical educationalist and polemicist Lyulph Stanley, Bertrand Russell's mother, and the women's rights campaigner and prohibitionist Rosalind, Countess of Carlisle.

STANSFELD, James (1820–98): son of Halifax lawyer, judge and confidant of Wood; unitarian; ed. University College London; independent means; close friend and admirer of Mazzini; MP, Halifax, 1859–95; junior office, 1863–4, 1866, 1868–71; President, [Poor Law Board and] Local Government Board, 1871–4, 1886; not offered cabinet office, 1880; parliamentary leader of campaign to repeal Contagious Diseases Acts; Home Ruler.

STEPHEN, James FITZJAMES (1829–94): son of Sir James Stephen, Colonial Office civil servant, evangelical, anti-slaver, later Professor of Modern History at Cambridge; ed. Eton, London, Cambridge; barrister; anti-sentimental anti-clerical journalist, baiter of Liberal intellectuals; legal member of council in India, 1868–72; judge of High Court, 1879–91; other official posts. His brother LESLIE (1832–1904) was fellow of Trinity Hall Cambridge, 1854–67, but resigned tutorship and later relinquished holy orders on losing his faith; athlete and Alpinist; friend and biographer of Fawcett; great practitioner of the higher journalism in London; editor, *Cornhill Magazine*, 1871–82; historian; first editor, *Dictionary of National Biography*, 1882–91.

SYDENHAM: see THOMSON

TAUNTON: see LABOUCHERE

THOMSON, Charles Poulett (created Baron Sydenham, 1840) (1799–1841): son of London Russian merchant; worked in family firm in London and Russia, 1815–30; MP, Dover, 1826–32, Manchester, 1832–9; Vice-President, Board of Trade, 1830–4, President, 1834, 1835–9; founder, Statistical Department of Board of Trade, 1832; Governor-general of Canada, 1839–41, supervising the Union; fatally injured riding.

TIERNEY, George (1761–1830): merchant family; ed. Eton, Cambridge; barrister; MP, 1789–90, 1796–1830; whig; co-treasurer, Society of Friends of People; opposed Foxite secession from parliament, 1797; fought duel with Pitt, 1798, over naval augmentation; drifted away from whigs; Treasurer of Navy under Addington, 1803–4; President, Board of Control, 1806–7, on Fox's death, and thereafter with whigs in opposition; active party organiser and tactician; chosen party leader in Commons, 1818–21; withdrew after divisions on Caroline affair; accepted cabinet office under Canning and Goderich, 1827–8. Extreme pragmatist; never fully trusted by whig grandees.

VILLIERS, Charles (1802–98): brother of Clarendon; not rich; ed. Haileybury (under Mackintosh), Cambridge; moved in Benthamite circles in London, 1820s; barrister; assistant commissioner on Poor Law, 1832–4; legal post, 1833–52; MP, Wolverhampton, 1835–98; parliamentary leader of Anti-Corn Law movement; Judge-advocate-general, 1852–8; in cabinet as President, Poor Law Board, 1859–66; received ex-minister's pension thereafter; Palmerstonian in foreign policy; Liberal Unionist, but never spoke in parliament after 1885.

WELLESLEY, first Marquess (second earl of Mornington, 1781 (Irish); created Baron Wellesley (UK), 1797, Marquess (Irish), 1799) (1760–1842): eldest brother of Wellington; ed. Eton, Oxford; British MP, 1784–97; Commissioner for Indian affairs, 1793–7; expansionist, controversial Governor-general of Bengal, 1797–1805, and one of the outstanding makers of British India; Foreign Secretary, 1809–12; failed to form coalition government, 1812; like Canning, supported Catholic Emancipation, and tried to exploit the issue, 1810s, in order to gain high office; Lord Lieutenant of Ireland, 1821–8, 1833–4; wrote the letter which was responsible for the crisis of July 1834; household office, 1830–3, 1835. Wonderfully forceful administrator, but his love of autocracy and pomp made him unfit for English politics.

WELLINGTON, first duke of (Arthur Wellesley; created Viscount Wellington, 1809, promoted earl of Wellington, 1812, marquess, 1812 and duke, 1814) (1769–1852): younger son of Irish earl; army from 1787; Irish MP, 1790–5; commanded in India, 1797–1804; UK MP, 1806–9; Secretary for Ireland 1807–9; commanded in Peninsular War, 1808, 1809–13, invaded France, 1813–14; field-marshal, 1813; ambassador to Congress of Vienna, 1814–15; commanded at Waterloo, 1815; cabinet, 1818–27, when he refused to serve under Canning; Commander-in-chief, army, 1827–8, 1842–52; Prime Minister, 1828–30; failed to form government, May 1832; Chancellor, Oxford University, 1834–52; briefly Prime, indeed sole, Minister, 1834, while Peel returned from Italy; Foreign Secretary, 1834–5; cabinet, 1841–6; tory leader, House of Lords, 1828–46.

WODEHOUSE: see KIMBERLEY

WOOD, Sir Charles (created Viscount Halifax, 1866) (1800–85): son of Yorkshire baronet (succeeded, 1846); ed. Eton, Oriel College Oxford with George Grey (1st); married second Earl Grey's daughter, 1829; MP, 1826–32, 1865–6, and for Halifax, 1832–65; Liberal chief whip, 1832–4; junior office, 1835–9, when he resigned with Howick; cabinet as Chancellor of Exchequer, 1846–52, President, Board of Control, 1852–5, First Lord of Admiralty, 1855–8, Secretary for India, 1859–66, Lord Privy Seal, 1870–4.

Appendix 1
The electorate and electoral qualifications, 1833–86

Electorate	1839–40	1865–6	1871	1883	1886
England/Wales					
counties	495,946	540,271	800,314	966,721	2,538,349
boroughs	329,426	514,026	1,250,019	1,651,732	1,842,191
Scotland					
counties	46,851	49,979	79,750	[b]99,652	315,267
boroughs	35,680	55,515	171,912	[b]210,789	235,564
Ireland					
counties	[a]60,607	172,010	175,149	[b]165,997	631,651
boroughs	[a]31,545	32,655	49,025	[b]58,021	106,314

England/Wales county electorate (main categories)

	1839–40	1865–6	1871	1883	1886
40s freeholders	316,775	358,526			
Copyholders	54,304	22,320		514,226 owners	508,554 owners
Leaseholders					
Others/joint	12,042	40,989	558,311 owners/tenants		
£50 tenants	112,562	116,527		92,934	2,020,650 occupiers
£12 occupation			242,003	356,344	
Householders					
Lodgers					8,937

England/Wales borough electorate (main categories)

	1839–40	1865–6	1871	1883	1886
£10 occupation	236,679	452,484	1,200,800	1,592,225	1,749,441
Householder					
Lodger			5,257	21,918	57,684
Ancient rights	77,371	49,847	43,962	37,589	35,066

a = 1833   b = 1882

Source: *P.P.* 1844 xxxviii 427 (1839–40); *P.P.* 1866 lvii 121, 838, 845, and 1867 lvi 443 (1865–6); *P.P.* 1872 xlvii 389, 395 (1871); *P.P.* 1883 liv 369 (1883); *P.P.* 1886 lii 569 (1886). Figures for the Irish electorate, 1833 and 1866, are from C. Cook and B. Keith, *British Historical Facts 1830–1900* (1975), p. 115, but official figures for the Irish electorate before 1850 are particularly unreliable.

Appendix 2
Redistribution 1832–85 and the old boroughs of England

	1830	1833	1879	1886[a]
No. of enfranchised boroughs returning MPs before 1832	202	146	131	54
No. of seats occupied by them	403	260	200	67
Total no. Eng borough seats	403	323	282	226
Total no. Eng borough/county seats	485	467	454	460

Fate of 195 2-member boroughs of 1830 (plus Weymouth, 2-member from 1832)

55 were disfranchised 1832

30 lose 1 member 1832 (Schedule B) (of which 5 were disfranchised 1867/8)

10 were disfranchised 1844–70 (1844 (1), 1852 (1), 1865–70 (8): 3 for being too small, 7 for corruption)

35 lose 1 member 1867/8 (Schedule A) (population less than 10,000)

2 in London (Southwark, Westminster) survive 1832–85, and are then divided (see below)

64 others survive until 1885[b], of which, in 1885:
   13 are merged into counties (population less than 15,000)
   35 lose 1 member (population 15,000–50,000)
   12 remain as 2-member (population 50,000–165,000)
   4 are divided into 19 single-member districts (population over 165,000)

City of London (4 member) becomes 2-member 1885

Fate of 1-member traditional boroughs (5 until 1832, 4 of which survive, plus 30 from Schedule B 1832, 25 of which remain after 1867, and 35 from Schedule A 1867):

6 survive 1885 as 1-member boroughs: 1 from pre-1832, 4 from Schedule B 1832, and 1 from Schedule A 1867

All others were merged into counties in 1885

New boroughs created

In London: 5 2-member 1832
                2 more 2-member 1867

Elsewhere: 17 2-member 1832
                 19 1-member 1832
                  1 extra 1-member 1861
                  9 extra 1-member 1867[c]

In 1885 these were treated as follows:

London, outside City, was divided into 57 1-member districts

Elsewhere: 2 2-member (1832) were merged into counties
                  3 1-member (1832) were merged into counties
                25 1-member remain 1-member
                 8 2-member remain 2-member
                 8 2/3/-member (see [c]) were divided into 39 1-member districts

and 7 new 1-member boroughs were created[d]

a   As integral seats, not divided into districts.
b   Liverpool gained a third seat in 1867. Sandwich was due for disfranchisement for corruption discovered in 1880.
c   Also, in 1867, 4 additional seats were given to individual boroughs which had been created in 1832, making one extra 2-member seat and 3 3-member seats.
d   These seven seats include two seats in West Ham which in the text have been treated as additional London borough seats. Two other seats sometimes described as 'new boroughs' of 1885 were Hanley and Aston Manor, but I have instead grouped them in with the single-member districts created out of old multi-member large boroughs, Stoke and Birmingham respectively. Had this not been done, Stoke, a 2-member seat created in 1832, would be counted as losing one member in 1885.

Appendix 3
Profile of the Liberal forces in parliament, 1830–86

Numbers of non-Conservative MPs returned at each general election 1830–86 (except 1831)

The table should be read vertically; total numbers in each category change over time

	1830	1832	1835	1837	1841	1847	1852	1857	1859	1865	1868	1874	1880	1885	1886 L/LU
A	30														
B	25	19	19	17	14	17	14	18	14	15	13	8	14	3	1/2
C	46	82	62	56	43	52	56	68	58	54	38	30	36	1	0/0
D	37	57	38	39	28	39	41	47	47	44	50	38	52	15	4/3
E	16	25	19	18	20	24	26	27	24	23	24	15	25	23	16/3
F	6	17	18	17	15	17	16	18	18	18	20	12	14	23	11/2
G	–	46	37	38	39	38	41	42	41	42	57	42	52	49	28/11
H	12	28	16	9	3	13	8	17	14	13	15	6	7	11	3/4
I	14	33	23	12	6	7	6	14	11	10	11	7	12	41	13/15
J	8	28	21	13	5	7	5	12	12	15	11	5	16	37	14/12
K	7	15	13	10	7	12	10	11	9	13	10	9	19	45	34/4
L	160	226	193	185	159	187	194	220	202	196	202	145	193	114	61/21
M	41	104	73	44	21	39	29	54	46	51	47	27	54	134	64/35
N	11	33	29	30	28	30	30	32	32	34	39	36	41	39	29/9
O	13	29	23	15	12	13	15	21	22	25	34	23	39	50	38/10
[P	c45	75	68	73	62	64	65	59	50	58	66	70	78	85]	

For definitions of Categories A–P, see pp. 340–1.

Appendix 4
Strength of Liberal parliamentary forces, analysed by different types of seat

(Appendix 3, recalculated as percentage of available seats in each category)

	1830	1832	1835	1837	1841	1847	1852	1857	1859	1865	1868	1874	1880	1885	1886 L/LU
A	27														
B	42	63	63	57	47	57	47	60	47	52	52	32	56	[75]	[25/50]
C	38	68	52	47	36	44	48	59	50	49	58	46	55	[50]	[0]
D	53	82	54	56	40	56	59	67	67	63	72	54	74	43	11/9
E	50	78	59	56	63	75	81	84	75	72	73	46	76	53	37/7
F	[75]	95	100	95	83	95	89	100	100	100	91	55	64	39	19/3
G	–	87	70	72	74	72	77	79	77	78	85	63	80	59	34/13
H	57	76	43	27	8	35	24	46	38	35	35	14	16	20	5/7
I	58	79	55	29	14	17	14	33	26	24	23	15	25	73	23/27
J	36	68	51	32	12	17	12	29	29	37	22	10	33	67	25/22
K	50	62	54	42	29	50	42	46	37	48	31	28	59	67	51/6
L	39	70	60	57	50	58	61	69	63	63	72	51	69	50	27/9
M	50	72	51	33	15	27	20	37	32	35	27	16	31	57	27/15
N	41	89	78	81	76	81	81	87	87	92	95	88	100	93	69/21
O	31	64	51	33	27	29	33	47	49	56	72	49	83	86	66/17

[ ] = sample less than ten

For definitions of Categories A–O, see pp. 340–1.

Categories in Appendices 3 and 4

A   *Disfranchised boroughs 1832* (55 2-member and 1 1-member boroughs in Schedule A, 111 seats)

B   *Small boroughs 1: Schedule B boroughs*, losing 1 seat 1832 (60 seats 1830, 30 1832–59, 29 1865, 25 1868–80, 4 1885–6)

C   *Small boroughs 2: other old boroughs*. These comprised the 4 old 1-member boroughs surviving after 1832, 10 2-member boroughs disfranchised 1844–70, 35 Schedule A boroughs 1867 (boroughs with a population of under 10,000 in 1861, which lost one of their two seats), and 13 seats, 2-member until 1885, which were then merged into counties, having a population of under 15,000. One of these 13, Weymouth, had 4 MPs until 1832. Total number of seats: 122 1830, 120 1832–7, 118 1841–7, 116 1852–9, 110 1865, 65 1868–80, 2 1885–6.

D   *'County towns' et sim*, 35 old 2-member boroughs surviving until 1885 and then losing 1 member because their population was between 15,000 and 50,000. Seats: 70 1830–80, 35 1885–6. (Bedford, Boston, Bury St. Edmunds, Cambridge, Canterbury, Carlisle, Chester, Colchester, Coventry, Dover, Durham, Exeter, Gloucester, Grantham, Hastings, Hereford, King's Lynn, Lincoln, Maidstone, Newcastle-under-Lyme, Oxford, Penryn and Falmouth, Peterborough, Pontefract, Reading, Rochester, Salisbury, Scarborough, Shrewsbury, Stafford, Taunton, Warwick, Wigan, Winchester, Worcester.)

E   *Sixteen old large boroughs outside London*. All had a population of over 50,000 in 1885 (32 seats 1832–65, 33 1868–80, 43 1885–6). (The 1885 and 1886 figures include 1 Irish Nationalist, returned for a Liverpool seat, as a Liberal.)

F   *London boroughs*. Seats: 8 1830, 18 1832–65, 22 1868–80, 59 1885–6.

G   *New boroughs, outside London, created 1832–85*. Seats: 53 1832–59, 54 1865, 67 1868–74, 65 1880, 83 1885–6.

H   *Twelve Home Counties* (Beds, Berks, Bucks, Essex, Hants, Herts, Isle of Wight, Kent, Middlesex, Oxon, Surrey, Sussex). Seats: 22 1830, 37 1832–65, 43 1868–80, 56 1885–6.

I   *Twelve other southern counties* (Cambs, Cornwall, Devon, Dorset, Gloucs, Hunts, Norfolk, Northants, Rutland, Somerset, Suffolk, Wilts). Seats: 24 1830, 42 1832–65, 48 1868–80, 56 1885–6.

J   *Eleven Midlands counties* (Cheshire, Derby, Hereford, Leicester, Lincoln, Monmouth, Notts, Shropshire, Staffs, Warwicks, Worcs). Seats: 22 1830, 41 1832–65, 49 1868–80, 55 1885–6.

K   *Six northern counties* (Cumberland, Durham, Lancashire, Northumberland, Westmorland, Yorkshire). Seats: 14 1830, 24 1832–59, 27 1865, 32 1868–80, 67 1885–6.

L   *All English borough seats*

M   *All English county seats*

N   *Welsh/Scottish borough seats*: 27 1830, 37 1832–65, 41 1868–80, 42 1885–6.

O   *Welsh/Scottish county seats*: 42 1830, 45 1832–65, 47 1868–80, 58 1885–6.

[P   *Ireland*. I have included these seats in Appendix 3 for a rough comparison, but they are problematical in several respects and so I have not transferred them to Appendix 4. The figures for 1832–85 come from K.T. Hoppen, *Elections, politics and society in Ireland 1832–1885* (Oxford, 1984), p. 264, supplemented by Craig, below, for 1835 and 1841. These do not distinguish between Liberals and Repealers/Independents/Home Rulers/Nationalists, not least because it was often difficult to make the distinction at the time. The 1830 figure is little more than nominal, based on crude estimates by me done for another purpose. Party affiliations were fluid at that time and much more research would be needed to arrive at a convincing figure. Throughout the period, Irish MPs' day-to-day attendance was less reliable than that of British MPs.]

Source: F.W.S. Craig, *British parliamentary election results, 1832–1885* (Aldershot, 1989 edn), and *British parliamentary election results, 1885–1918* (1974). For 1830, I have used H.S. Smith, *The parliaments of England from 1715 to 1847*, ed. F.W.S. Craig (Chichester, 1973 edn), supplemented by my own material. Again, it should be stressed that it is unwise to be too dogmatic about party affiliations in 1830, which were often either unformed or shifting.

It is particularly important to note that I have followed Craig's description of party affiliation, and that Craig lists Peelites as Conservatives until he thinks that it is clear that they had become Liberals. This is another area where precision is impossible.

Where election results were declared void on petition, I have based the figures on the rerun poll, except in the case of two seats in Category D in 1880 where an investigation for bribery meant that there was no rerun. The table at this point includes the original, void, result, but, if these results are excluded, the number of Liberal MPs in that category for 1880 falls to 49 of 66.

Notes

All books are published in London unless indicated otherwise.

Introduction

1. J. Morley, *The life of William Ewart Gladstone* (3 vols., 1903), I, 128.
2. Only two modern books even approximate to this description, and both are avowedly thematic: D. Southgate, *The passing of the whigs, 1832–1886* (1962); I. Bradley, *The optimists: themes and personalities in Victorian Liberalism* (1980). R.B. McCallum, *The Liberal party from Earl Grey to Asquith* (1963) is thin.
3. See R. Blake, *The Conservative party from Peel to Churchill* (1970); *The Conservative leadership 1832–1932*, ed. D. Southgate (1974); N. Gash, D. Southgate, D. Dilks and J. Ramsden, *The Conservatives: a history from their origins to 1965* (1977) and B. Coleman, *Conservatism and the Conservative party in nineteenth-century Britain* (1988).
4. T.A. Jenkins, *Gladstone, whiggery and the Liberal party 1874–1886* (Oxford, 1988), p. 40.
5. For Peel's use of this phrase, see e.g. B. Hilton, 'Peel; a reappraisal', *H[istorical] J[ournal]*, XXII (1979), 601.
6. There is a good short summary of the historiographical debate about the 1832 Act in J. Milton-Smith, 'Earl Grey's cabinet and the objects of parliamentary reform', *H.J.*, XV (1972), 55–7. See also R.W. Davis, 'The whigs and the idea of electoral deference: some further thoughts on the Great Reform Act', *Durham University Journal*, LXVII (1974–5), 79–91.
7. See p. 209.
8. Lord J. Russell, *Hansard['s parliamentary debates, 3rd series]*, III, 802, 22 March 1831. All references to *Hansard* debates in these notes are to the 3rd series unless indicated.
9. Lord J. Russell, *Letter to the electors of Stroud, on the principles of the Reform Act* (1839), p. 29.
10. See p. 145.
11. See the analysis of Liberal seats in Appendices 3 and 4.
12. See e.g. Henry, third Earl Grey, *Parliamentary government considered with reference to a reform of parliament: an essay* (1858; 2nd edn 1864), and, for a modern discussion of the concept, A.B. Hawkins, '"Parliamentary government" and Victorian political parties, *c*.1830–*c*.1880', *E[nglish] H[istorical] R[eview]*, CIV (1989), 638–69.
13. *The parliamentary debates 4th series [Parl. Deb. 4]*, XVII, 34, 5 September 1893.
14. *The collected works of Walter Bagehot*, ed. N. St. John-Stevas (15 vols., 1965–86), VI, 43.
15. *A descriptive account of the palace of Westminster* (1852), p. 5.
16. *Hansard*, CXI, 346, 24 May 1850.
17. W. Bagehot, *The English constitution* (1963 edn), pp. 150–3.
18. *The letters of Queen Victoria: a selection from her majesty's correspondence between the years 1837 and 1861*, ed. A.C. Benson and Viscount Esher (3 vols., 1908 edn), III, 446–7.
19. Bagehot, *English constitution*, pp. 153–4.
20. At Liverpool, *Times*, 14 October 1864,

342

p. 7. See similar sentiments by Palmerston, quoted at p. 192 below. On the success of this system in stopping the repeal of existing legislation, see T.E. May, *The constitutional history of England since the accession of George the Third 1760–1860* (2 vols., 1861), I, 430.

21. *Hansard*, CCLXXXIX, 1889–90, 3 July 1884.

22. A.L. Lowell, *The government of England* (2 vols., 1908), I, 302–3.

23. Grey, *Parliamentary government*, esp. p. 17 (1864 edn).

24. *Hansard*, IV, 345, 24 June 1831.

25. For G.O. Trevelyan, speaking at Manchester in 1885, this was 'the broad principle of the Liberal party': *Times*, 11 February 1885, p. 10.

26. For figures, see G.W. Cox, *The efficient secret: the cabinet and the development of political parties in Victorian England* (Cambridge, 1987), pp. 49–50. I suggest in chapter 10 below that parliamentary activity was greater after 1868.

27. See the table in Lowell, *Government of England*, I, 317.

28. See pp. 131, 258, 301 in text below.

29. *The Gladstone diaries*, ed. M.R.D. Foot and H.C.G. Matthew (11 vols to date, Oxford, 1968–90), X, li.

30. D.O. Maddyn, *Chiefs of parties, past and present, with original anecdotes* (2 vols., 1859 edn), II, 205.

31. See e.g. W. Empson, 'Open questions', *E[dinburgh] R[eview]*, LXXI (July 1840), 514; W.R. Greg, 'The expected Reform bill', *E.R.*, XCV (Jan. 1852), 233.

32. At Keighley, *Manchester Guardian*, 4 November 1876, p. 8.

33. In his article of 1859 on Pitt the younger, 'the greatest master of the whole art of parliamentary government that has ever existed'; *The miscellaneous writings speeches and poems of Lord Macaulay* (4 vols., 1880), II, 131–2.

34. On this theme in whiggery, see A.D. Kriegel, 'A convergence of ethics: saints and whigs in British anti-slavery', *Journal of British Studies*, XXVI (1987), 427–31. For the Conservatives, Peel also talked of his desire for 'honourable fame' in *Hansard*, LIX, 555, 17 September 1841.

35. E. Longford, *Wellington: pillar of state* (1972), p. 58.

36. The latest estimates of loyalty rates within the party show remarkable consistency from 1836 to 1875: Cox, *Efficient secret*, p. 23.

37. *Letters of Sir George Cornewall Lewis to various friends*, ed. Sir G.F. Lewis (1870), p. 329.

38. See pp. 102–3.

39. M. Creighton, *Memoir of Sir George Grey* (1901 edn), pp. 86–7.

40. Lecky, quoted in *Journals and letters of Reginald Viscount Esher*, ed. M.V. Brett and Viscount Esher (4 vols., 1934–8), I, 66. See p. 107 below for the advocacy by Macaulay and others in the 1830s of a benevolent dictatorship over Ireland.

41. This was true even of Gladstone, who was unusually aware of the burden of sin in the world. See his 'Locksley Hall and the jubilee', *Nineteenth Century*, XXI (Jan.–June 1887), 1–18, and 'Universitas Hominum: or, the unity of history', *North American Review*, CXLV (1887), 589–602.

42. N. Gash, *Reaction and reconstruction in English politics 1832–1852* (Oxford, 1965), pp. 199–200.

43. An interesting exception is P.M. Gurowich, 'The continuation of war by other means: party and politics, 1855–1865', *H.J.*, XXVII (1984), 603–31.

44. I. Newbould, 'Whiggery and the growth of party 1830–1841: organization and the challenge of Reform', *Parliamentary History*, IV (1985). See also Matthew in *Gladstone diaries*, X, li.

45. J.R. Vincent, *The formation of the Liberal party, 1857–1868* (1966); R.T. Shannon, *Gladstone and the Bulgarian agitation, 1876* (1963).

46. D.A. Hamer, *Liberal politics in the age of Gladstone and Rosebery: a study in leadership and policy* (Oxford, 1972), esp. p. xi.

47. A. Elliot, 'Three Reform bills', *E.R.*, CLXI (Apr. 1885), 582.

Chapter 1

1. [W.A. Mackinnon,] *On the rise, progress, and present state of public opinion, in Great Britain, and other parts of the world* (1828), pp. 5, 15.

2. *Journeys to England and Ireland by Alexis de Tocqueville*, ed. J.P. Mayer (1958), p. 58.

3. *Hansard*, VIII, 251, 265, 7 October

1831. See Althorp's definition of the 'people' as 'the great majority of the respectable middle classes of the country', at ibid., II, 1143, 1 March 1831.

4. J. Miller, 'Past and present state of the country', *Quarterly Review*, XXXII (June 1825), 186–7; *Speeches of George Canning delivered on public occasions in Liverpool* (Liverpool, 1825), pp. 286–7; Morpeth, in *Hansard's parliamentary debates 2nd series [Hansard 2]*, XXII, 879–80, 23 February 1830.

5. See N. McCord, 'Some difficulties of parliamentary reform', *H.J.*, X (1967), 377–80.

6. *The journal of Mrs Arbuthnot 1820–1832*, ed. F. Bamford and the duke of Wellington (2 vols., 1950), II, 282.

7. T.W. Laqueur, *Religion and respectability: Sunday schools and working class culture 1780–1850* (New Haven, 1976), p. 44.

8. H. Ritvo, *The animal estate: the English and other creatures in the Victorian age* (Cambridge, Mass., 1987), p. 9.

9. See J. Innes, 'Politics and morals: the Reformation of Manners movement in later eighteenth-century England', in *The transformation of political culture: England and Germany in the late eighteenth century*, ed. E. Hellmuth (Oxford, 1990), pp. 57–118.

10. On this, see J.R. Breihan, 'Economical reform, 1785–1810', Cambridge Ph.D. thesis (1977), esp. p. 256.

11. *The House of Commons 1790–1820*, ed. R.G. Thorne (5 vols., 1986), I, 334. The annual number of entries of business in the Commons journal rose from 3,453 to 8,350 between 1790 and 1808: *P[arliamentary] P[apers]*, 1810, II, 552.

12. L. Radzinowicz, *A history of English criminal law and its administration from 1750* (5 vols., 1948–86), I, 528.

13. B.R. Mitchell and P. Deane, *Abstract of British historical statistics* (Cambridge, 1962), p. 410.

14. Peel, *Hansard*, XXXIX, 877, 8 December 1837.

15. *Journal of Mrs Arbuthnot*, I, 44; C. Wynn, in Duke of Buckingham and Chandos, *Memoirs of the Court of George IV 1820–1830 from original family documents* (2 vols., 1859), I, 58; L. Davidoff and C. Hall, *Family fortunes: men and women of the English middle class, 1780–1850* (1987), p. 153.

16. C. Wynn, in Gash *et al.*, *Conservatives*, p. 40.

17. J. Bagot, *George Canning and his friends* (2 vols., 1909), II, 82. For similar sentiments among Sussex yeomen, recorded by Huskisson, see J.E. Cookson, *Lord Liverpool's administration: the crucial years 1815–1822* (1975), p. 143.

18. In 1822: Buckingham, *Court of George IV*, I, 292.

19. *Letters of the earl of Dudley to the bishop of Llandaff*, ed. E. Copleston (1840), p. 302.

20. W.H. Fremantle, in Duke of Buckingham and Chandos, *Memoirs of the Court of England, during the Regency, 1811–1820, from original family documents* (2 vols., 1856), II, 301.

21. H. Twiss, *The public and private life of Lord Chancellor Eldon* (3 vols., 1844), II, 329.

22. E. Phipps, *Memoirs of the political and literary life of Robert Plumer Ward* (2 vols., 1850), II, 88.

23. See W.D. Jones, *'Prosperity' Robinson: the life of Viscount Goderich 1782–1859* (1967), pp. 29–31.

24. In 1811: G. Carnall, *Robert Southey and his age: the development of a conservative mind* (Oxford, 1960), p. 125.

25. W. Canton, *A history of the British and Foreign Bible Society* (5 vols., 1904–10), I, 318. Between 1810 and 1820, membership of the venerable Society for the Propagation of Christian Knowledge rose spectacularly, from 3,560 to 14,530: W.K. Lowther Clarke, *A history of the S.P.C.K.* (1959), p. 148.

26. Robert Hall, Baptist, speaking at the Leicester auxiliary of the Bible Society in 1817: *The works of Robert Hall* (6 vols., 1832), IV, 383.

27. R. Furneaux, *William Wilberforce* (1974), p. 218.

28. See e.g. the view of Wellington, in Buckingham, *Court of George IV*, I, 172–3.

29. B. Semmel, *The Methodist revolution* (1974), p. 133.

30. *Hansard's parliamentary debates 1st series [Hansard 1]*, XXXVIII, 709, 15 May 1818.

31. Cookson, *Lord Liverpool's administration*, p. 345; *Hansard*, IV, 530, 30 June 1831; S.E. Finer, 'Patronage and the public service: Jeffersonian bureaucracy and the British tradition', *Public*

Administration, XXX (1952), 329–60.

32. *Sir Robert Peel from his private corre-spondence*, ed. C.S. Parker (3 vols., 1891–9), I, 42–3. Matthew Russell, the earl of Caledon, J.F. Luttrell, the Bullers, Christopher Savile and Mark Wood were among those persistently demanding places and honours, to very little effect: see J.P. Parry, 'Constituencies, elections and members of parliament, 1790–1820', *Parliamentary History*, VII (1988), pp. 152–3.

33. J. Galt, *The member: an autobiography*, ed. I.A. Gordon (Edinburgh, 1975 edn), p. 105; *Times*, 23 July 1830, p. 5. Of course much patronage remained in government hands – including 17,000 sub-postmasterships in 1885 – but there are many examples to show that ministers and MPs found its distribution a great bore. See e.g. H.J. Hanham, 'Political patronage at the Treasury 1870–1912', *H.J.*, III (1960), pp. 75–84; (Peel) *The correspondence of Charles Arbuthnot*, ed. A. Aspinall (1941), p. 234; (Gascoyne) J.R. Dinwiddy, 'The "influence of the Crown" in the early nineteenth century: a note on the opposition case', *Parliamentary History*, IV (1985), pp. 197–8; Morley, *Gladstone*, I, 649–50.

34. See A. Aspinall, 'The cabinet council, 1783–1835', *Proceedings of the British Academy*, XXXVII (1952), 214–24.

35. P. Fraser, 'The growth of ministerial control in the nineteenth-century House of Commons', *E.H.R.*, LXXV (1960), 454n2.

36. John, Earl Russell, *Recollections and suggestions 1813–1873* (1875), pp. 26–7; C.J. Bartlett, *Castlereagh* (1966), ch. 6.

37. For government manipulation of select committees, see e.g. B. Hilton, *Corn, cash. commerce: the economic policies of the tory governments 1815–1830* (Oxford, 1977), p. 135.

38. D. Eastwood, ' "Amplifying the province of the legislature": the flow of information and the English state in the early nineteenth century', *Historical Research*, LXII (1989), 282–4; D.V. Glass, *Numbering the people: the eighteenth-century population controversy and the development of census and vital statistics in Britain* (Farnborough, 1983), pp. 91, 97–8, 106–13.

39. D.M. Young, *The Colonial Office in the early nineteenth century* (1961), p. 245.

40. See M.J.D. Roberts, 'Public and private in early nineteenth-century London: the Vagrant Act of 1822 and its enforcement', *Social History*, XIII (1988), 273–94.

41. The quotation is from C.E. Dodd, 'Amendments of the criminal law', *Quarterly Review*, XXXVII (Jan. 1828), 148.

42. Statistics are taken from D. Beales, 'Peel, Russell and reform', *H.J.*, XVII (1974), 879.

43. E. Halévy, *A history of the English people 1815–1830* (1926), p. 81.

44. *Memoirs of Plumer Ward*, II, 71.

45. L.T. Rede, *Memoir of George Canning late premier of England* (1827), pp. 280, 371, 373.

46. A.N. Porter, *The origins of the South African war: Joseph Chamberlain and the diplomacy of imperialism, 1895–99* (Manchester, 1980), pp. 8–9.

47. 1823: *Journal of Mrs Arbuthnot*, I, 275.

48. *The Croker papers: the correspondence and diaries of the late John Wilson Croker*, ed. L.J. Jennings (3 vols., 1884), I, 266–7.

49. Rede, *Canning*, pp. 358–9.

50. H. Temperley, *The foreign policy of Canning 1822–1827: England, the neo-Holy Alliance, and the New World* (1966 edn), p. 314.

51. *The speech of George Canning in the house of Commons, on the 16th day of March, 1824* (1824), p. 21.

52. E. Hobsbawm, *Industry and empire* (Harmondsworth, 1969 edn), pp. 146–7, and E. Hobsbawm, *The age of revolution: Europe 1789–1848* (1973 edn), p. 381.

53. *The speeches of William Huskisson with a biographical memoir* (3 vols., 1831), III, 664; Robinson, in B. Gordon, *Economic doctrine and tory liberalism 1824–1830* (1979), p. 14.

54. R. Southey, 'State and prospects of the country', *Quarterly Review*, XXXIX (Apr. 1829), 516. See also J. Barrow, 'Political importance of our American colonies', ibid., XXXIII (Mar. 1826), 412.

55. *Speeches of Huskisson*, III, 287–8.

56. Huskisson in *Hansard 1*, XXVII, 920, 16 May 1814; Jones, *'Prosperity' Robinson*, pp. 56–7; N. Gash, *Lord Liverpool: the life and political career of Robert Banks Jenkinson second earl of Liverpool 1770–*

1828 (1984), pp. 117–18, 158.

57. *Substance of the speech delivered in the House of Commons, by George Canning, on Monday, June 22, 1812* (1812), p. 6.
58. *Hansard 2*, XXI, 1668, 1 June 1829.
59. *Times*, 20 June 1826, p. 2. At this election a number of whigs contrasted the present liberal behaviour of ministers with past tory practice; most argued their case by reference to Canning's foreign policy. See ibid., 17 May, p. 3 (Leonard), 12 June, p. 3 (Howick), 13 June, p. 2 (Palmer) and 19 June, p. 1 (Lambton).
60. Arnold, in 1824, cited in A.P. Stanley, *The life and correspondence of Thomas Arnold* (2 vols., 1881 edn), I, 65–6.
61. *Hansard 2*, XI, 721, 11 May 1824, XVII, 543–4, 3 May 1827. In 1826 and 1827, Althorp and Russell were still proposing minor legislation to cut down the expense of county elections and to diminish opportunities for corruption at contests.
62. 11 May 1830: *Specimens of the table talk of Samuel Taylor Coleridge* (3rd edn, 1851), p. 70.
63. D.D. Olien, *Morpeth: a Victorian public career* (Washington D.C., *c*.1983), p. 41; Lord Broughton, *Recollections of a long life* (6 vols., 1909–11), III, 212.
64. A. Mitchell, *The whigs in opposition 1815–1830* (Oxford, 1967), pp. 56–7, 183.
65. M.S. Hardcastle, *Life of John, Lord Campbell* (2 vols., 1881), I, 416.
66. Jennings, *Croker*, I, 368.
67. A.G. Stapleton, *George Canning and his times* (1859), p. 350.
68. Where not separately attributed, the material in the following paragraphs is based on a reading of tory speeches on the 1831 Reform bills.
69. See J.J. Sack, 'The House of Lords and parliamentary patronage in Great Britain, 1802–1832', *H.J.*, XXIII (1980), 923–30.
70. For figures, see G.P. Judd, *Members of parliament 1734–1832* (New Haven, 1955), p. 89.
71. C.D. Yonge, *The life and administration of Robert Banks, second earl of Liverpool* (3 vols., 1868), III, 137–8.
72. Sadler, *Hansard*, III, 1540, 18 March 1831; Malcolm, ibid., IV, 738–9, 5 July 1831.
73. Wellington, ibid., III, 854–5, 24 March 1831.
74. Peel, ibid., IV, 885, 6 July 1831.
75. Ibid., III, 1802, 21 April 1831.
76. Ibid., III, 904–5, 24 March 1831.
77. J. Fullarton, 'Parliamentary reform', *Quarterly Review*, XLIV (Feb. 1831), 557–8, 570; *Sermons on several occasions, and charges, by William Van Mildert, late bishop of Durham, to which is prefixed a memoir of the author by Cornelius Ives* (Oxford, 1838), pp. 125–6.
78. *Hansard*, II, 1340, 1351, 3 March 1831.
79. 1820: Rede, *Canning*, p. 436.
80. *Hansard*, III, 1673, 1821, 19 and 22 April 1831.
81. Jennings, *Croker*, I, 170.
82. *Hansard*, III, 235, 8 March 1831.
83. North, ibid., III, 155, 7 March 1831; Praed, ibid., III, 244–5, 8 March 1831.
84. Peel, ibid., II, 1337–8, 3 March 1831.
85. *Memoirs of Plumer Ward*, I, 259–60.
86. *Hansard 2*, XX, 737, 5 March 1829.
87. J. Cannon, *Parliamentary reform 1640–1832* (Cambridge, 1973 edn), pp. 293–8.
88. F. O'Gorman, 'The unreformed electorate of Hanoverian England: the mid-eighteenth century to the Reform Act of 1832', *Social History*, XI (1986), 39.
89. In 1819: Jennings, *Croker*, I, 136–7. Southey recommended giving seats to large towns, in his *Quarterly Review* article of 1816 on parliamentary reform, but the editor struck it out: Carnall, *Southey and his age*, p. 222.

Chapter 2

1. G. Pellew, *The life and correspondence of Henry Addington first Viscount Sidmouth* (3 vols., 1847), III, 471.
2. Edward Law, Lord Ellenborough, *A political diary 1828–1830*, ed. Lord Colchester (2 vols., 1881), II, 12; Broughton, *Recollections*, III, 272.
3. Buckingham, *Court of George IV*, II, 269.
4. *The diary and correspondence of Charles Abbot, Lord Colchester*, ed. 2nd Baron Colchester (3 vols., 1861), III, 341.
5. *Some official correspondence of George Canning*, ed. E.J. Stapleton (2 vols., 1887), I, 363.
6. Wellington's sentiments, reported in Rede, *Canning*, p. 539, and *Journal of Mrs Arbuthnot*, II, 88.

7. *Journal of Mrs Arbuthnot*, I, 328, 341–2, 352–3.
8. Ibid., I, 284.
9. *Hansard 2*, xx, 735, 5 March 1829.
10. *Hansard 1*, xxxi, 878, 16 June 1815.
11. *Hansard 2*, xx, 733, 735, 748, 5 March 1829. See also Wellington's sentiments, in Ellenborough, *Political diary*, I, 352.
12. *Hansard 2*, xx, 772, 5 March 1829.
13. Parker, *Peel*, II, 122–4.
14. *The Greville memoirs: a journal of the reigns of King George IV, King William IV and Queen Victoria by C.C.F. Greville*, ed. H. Reeve (8 vols., 1896 edn), I, 180.
15. *Three early nineteenth-century diaries*, ed. A. Aspinall (1952), p. xxiv.
16. N. Gash, *Pillars of government and other essays on state and society c.1770–c.1880* (1986), p. 76.
17. N. Gash, 'English reform and French revolution in the general election of 1830', in *Essays presented to Sir Lewis Namier*, ed. R. Pares and A.J.P. Taylor (1956), pp. 266–7, 277–8; G.I.T. Machin, *The Catholic question in English politics, 1820–1830* (Oxford, 1964), pp. 153–5; E. Jaggard, 'Cornwall politics 1826–1832: another face of Reform?', *Journal of British Studies*, xxii (1982–3), 87–91.
18. *The private letters of Sir Robert Peel*, ed. G. Peel (1920), p. 104.
19. Aspinall, *Charles Arbuthnot*, p. 123.
20. Ellenborough, *Political diary*, I, 39; *Hansard 2*, xviii, 747, 26 February 1828.
21. *Greville memoirs*, I, 216; P.C. Scarlett, *A memoir of James, first Lord Abinger* (1877), pp. 133–4; Gash, *Reaction and reconstruction*, p. 119.
22. D.C. Moore, *The politics of deference: a study of the mid-nineteenth century English political system* (Hassocks, 1976), pp. 215–16.
23. *Times*, 24 July 1830, p. 2.
24. *Greville memoirs*, II, 20; *Journal of Mrs Arbuthnot*, II, 381.
25. *Times*, 7 August 1830, pp. 1–2.
26. Ibid., 28 July 1830, p. 3.
27. Ibid., 14 July 1830, p. 3.
28. Ibid., 5, 7, 12 July, 7 August, 1830, pp. 2, 3, 4, 1–2.
29. Ibid., 16 August 1830, p. 3.
30. Wilmot Horton: S.M. Hardy and R.C. Baily, 'The downfall of the Gower interest in the Staffordshire boroughs, 1800–30', in *Collections for a history of Staffordshire 1950 and 1951* (Kendal, 1954), p. 296. See also *Times*, 10 June 1826, p. 4.
31. A.M.W. Stirling, *Coke of Norfolk and his friends* (2 vols., 1908), II, 378. See K.J. Atton, 'Municipal and parliamentary politics in Ipswich, 1818–1847', University College London Ph.D. (1979), p. 304.
32. H. Hughes, *Chronicle of Chester: the two hundred years 1775–1975* (1975), p. 87.
33. J.A. Phillips, 'The many faces of Reform: the Reform Bill and the electorate', *Parliamentary History*, I (1982), 123.
34. *Greville memoirs*, I, 216.
35. Ibid., I, 272.
36. *The life and times of Henry Lord Brougham written by himself* (3 vols., 1871), III, 21.
37. A.H. Eyre, quoted in P.B. Munsche, *Gentlemen and poachers: the English game laws 1671–1831* (Cambridge, 1981), p. 168.
38. F.W.H. Sheppard, *Local government in St. Marylebone 1688–1835: a study of the vestry and the turnpike trust* (1958), pp. 275–98.
39. C. Dickens, *The life and adventures of Nicholas Nickleby* (1839; Oxford, 1982 edn), p. 215.
40. H. Richard, *Memoirs of Joseph Sturge* (1864), p. 89.
41. Sir Francis Hill, *Georgian Lincoln* (Cambridge, 1966), p. 207.
42. *Journals and correspondence of Sir Francis Thornhill Baring after Lord Northbrook*, ed. earl of Northbrook (2 vols., pr. pr., 1902–5), I, 49.
43. Stanley, *Arnold*, I, 243, 249–51, 307.
44. J.A. Froude, *Thomas Carlyle: a history of the first forty years of his life 1795–1835* (2 vols., 1882), II, 92, 95.
45. The quotations are taken from Edward Lytton Bulwer's major work, *England and the English*, ed. S. Meacham (1833; Chicago, 1970 edn), pp. 396–9.
46. Radzinowicz, *English criminal law*, I, 528.
47. Le Marchant: *Journals of Sir Francis Baring*, I, 66.
48. A celebrated jibe: *The complete peerage by G.E.C.*, ed. V. Gibbs, II (1912), 341n.
49. Viscountess Knutsford, *Life and letters of Zachary Macaulay* (1900), p. 454; R.W. Davis, *Political change and con-*

tinuity 1760–1885: a Buckinghamshire study (Newton Abbot, 1972), pp. 77–8; *Greville memoirs*, II, 30.

50. See the extensive *Times* reports of these contests. Unfootnoted material in subsequent paragraphs comes from the same source.
51. See *Times* reports of these contests.
52. Scarlett, *Abinger*, p. 126.
53. Ellenborough, *Political diary*, II, 264.
54. Ibid., II, 210–13.
55. Canning had famously argued this: see J. Hamburger, *James Mill and the art of revolution* (New Haven, 1963), p. 19n3. The *Quarterly Review* suggested the same: see the articles in vols. XXVIII (Jan. 1823), 349–65, XXXIII (Mar. 1826), 429–55, and XXXVIII (July 1828), 53–84.
56. *Hansard 2*, XVIII, 1544, 17 April 1828, XXIII, 533, 18 March 1830.
57. See Ellenborough, *Political diary*, passim, for these impasses, and G. Broeker, *Rural disorder and police reform in Ireland, 1812–36* (1970), pp. 199–200.
58. *Despatches, correspondence and memoranda of Field Marshal Arthur duke of Wellington*, ed. second duke of Wellington (8 vols., 1873), v, 184 (October 1828).
59. Sir H. Lytton Bulwer, *The life of Henry John Temple, Viscount Palmerston: with selections from his diaries and correspondence* (2 vols., 1870), I, 286.
60. *Greville memoirs*, I, 272.
61. *Brougham's life and times*, III, 44.
62. [Henry Brougham,] *The country without a government: or plain questions upon the unhappy state of the present administration* (2nd edn, 1830), p. 1.
63. *The diaries and correspondence of James Losh*, ed. E. Hughes (2 vols., Durham, 1962–3), II, 98.
64. Ibid., II, 131; *The Christian Observer*, XXI (1831), 187–8, 639.
65. T. Mozley, *Reminiscences chiefly of Oriel College and the Oxford movement* (2nd edn, 2 vols., 1882), I, 273–4.
66. *Greville memoirs*, II, 78.
67. R. Southey, 'Moral and political state of the British Empire', *Quarterly Review*, XLIV (Jan. 1831), 315.
68. *Greville memoirs*, II, 25.
69. Mitchell, *Whigs in opposition*, p. 236.
70. *Correspondence of Princess Lieven and Earl Grey*, ed. G. Le Strange (3 vols., 1890), II, 8.
71. Ibid., II, 92–3, 102–4.
72. Brougham, *The country without a government*, p. 22.
73. Russell, *Recollections*, pp. 63–6.
74. Lord Holland, cited in Davis, 'Whigs and electoral deference', 81.
75. *Lieven-Grey correspondence*, II, 62, 102–3, 119.
76. L. Mitchell, *Holland House* (1980), p. 69.
77. Mitchell, *Whigs in opposition*, p. 228.
78. M. Brock, *The Great Reform Act* (1973), p. 76.
79. Ibid., p. 117.
80. *Hansard*, I, 37, 2 November 1830. See third Earl Grey to Viscount Halifax, 17 October 1884, Hickleton papers, Cambridge University Library, A 4 55.
81. Hardcastle, *Campbell*, I, 486.
82. Ellenborough, *Political diary*, II, 426, 433.

Chapter 3

1. See e.g. Melbourne, *Hansard*, VII, 1176, 4 October 1831.
2. Mitchell, *Whigs in opposition*, pp. 60–1.
3. My estimates.
4. Russell, *Times*, 22 June 1826, p. 1; E. Jaggard, 'The parliamentary reform movement in Cornwall, 1805–1826', *Parliamentary History*, II (1983), 126–7; Jaggard, 'Cornwall politics 1826–1832', 93.
5. *The viceregal speeches and addresses, lectures and poems of the late earl of Carlisle*, ed. J.J. Gaskin (Dublin, 1866), p. cxxxiv.
6. E.A. Smith, *Whig principles and party politics: Earl Fitzwilliam and the whig party 1748–1833* (Manchester, 1975), p. 351.
7. *The letters of Lady Palmerston*, ed. T. Lever (1957), p. 67.
8. *Early correspondence of Lord John Russell 1805–40*, ed. R. Russell (2 vols., 1913), II, 19.
9. *Hansard*, VIII, 599, 12 October 1831.
10. P. Dixon, *Canning: politician and statesman* (1976), pp. 280–1.
11. E.A. Smith, *Lord Grey 1764–1845* (Oxford, 1990), pp. 49, 208.
12. 1823: Broughton, *Recollections*, III, 22.
13. *The diary of Benjamin Robert Haydon*, ed. W.B. Pope (5 vols., Cambridge, Mass., 1960–3), IV, 195.
14. See e.g. Smith, *Grey*, p. 49 (cited

above), and Fox in *House of Commons 1790–1820*, ed. Thorne, III, 816.

15. Lord John Russell, *An essay on the history of the English government and constitution, from the reign of Henry VII to the present time* (2nd edn, 1823), pp. 423, 461; and his speech in *Hansard 1*, XLI, 1103–5, 14 December 1819.

16. See quotation at Introduction, p. 10 above.

17. Althorp, *Hansard*, VII, 424, 21 September 1831. Grey's equivalent term was 'the respectability, the wealth and the intelligence': ibid., VII, 934, 3 October 1831.

18. Ibid., I, 38, 2 November 1830.

19. Lansdowne, Radnor, ibid., VII, 1349–50, 1396, 5 October 1831; Bulwer, ibid., IV, 757–60; Russell, ibid., III, 802, 22 March 1831.

20. Russell, ibid., III, 800, 22 March 1831.

21. Stanley, ibid., III, 1649, 19 April 1831; Althorp, ibid., V, 676, 3 August 1831.

22. Althorp, Denman: ibid., VI, 201, 204, 280, 299–300, 17 and 18 August 1831.

23. G.E. Mingay, *English landed society in the eighteenth century* (1963), pp. 170–1; R.J. Olney, *Lincolnshire politics 1832–1885* (Oxford, 1973), pp. 32–48; F. O'Gorman, 'Electoral deference in "unreformed" England: 1760–1832', *Journal of Modern History*, LVI (1984), 407.

24. Althorp, Hughes Hughes: *Hansard*, VI, 280, 287, 18 August 1831.

25. Ibid., IX, 984, 27 January 1832.

26. Milton, ibid., VI, 344, 20 August 1831. Althorp claimed that there was at least no division of interest between *small-town* opinion and surrounding rural areas: ibid., VI, 562–3, 24 August 1831.

27. The most remarkable ministerial statement was Brougham's admission that in a proper representative system the urban influence which had returned him for Yorkshire in 1830 should not have been able to overbear the squires as it had: ibid., III, 1063, 28 March 1831.

28. See Milton-Smith, 'Earl Grey's cabinet', 68n78, and Brock, *Great Reform Act*, pp. 222–30, 369–70 for comments on Moore. The most developed statement of Moore's view is *Politics of deference*.

29. *P.P.*, 1866, lvii, 15; a few divisions made no returns.

30. Althorp, *Hansard*, V, 1227, 11 August 1831.

31. Mulgrave, ibid., IV, 104, 21 June 1831; Mackintosh, ibid., IV, 674–85, 4 July 1831.

32. *Hansard 2*, V, 615, 9 May 1821.

33. See F. O'Gorman, 'Campaign rituals and ceremonies: the social meaning of elections in England 1780–1860', *Past and Present*, CXXXV (May 1992), 79–115.

34. Russell, *Hansard*, III, 795, 22 March 1831; Grey, ibid., VII, 943, 3 October 1831; R. Grant, ibid., III, 170, 7 March 1831.

35. In the UK as a whole: Jennings, *Croker*, I, 371–2. See detailed estimates in Sack, 'House of Lords', 919.

36. Russell, *Hansard*, IV, 326, 24 June 1831.

37. B.W. Higman, 'The West Indian "interest" in parliament, 1807–1833', *Historical Studies*, XIII (1967–9), 3.

38. *Hansard*, VII, 954, 3 October 1831, VIII, 240–1, 7 October 1831.

39. Ibid., II, 1194, 2 March 1831.

40. Ibid., III, 65–7, 4 March 1831.

41. *P.P.*, 1844, XXXVIII, 427.

42. N. Gash, *Politics in the age of Peel: a study in the techniques of parliamentary representation 1830–1850* (Hassocks, 1977 edn), pp. 438–9.

43. *Hansard*, VIII, 325, 7 October 1831.

44. C. Seymour, *Electoral reform in England and Wales* (Newton Abbot, 1970 edn), p. 70.

45. *Hansard*, III, 1519, 18 April 1831.

46. Ibid., IV, 337–8, 24 June 1831.

47. Gash, *Politics in the age of Peel*, pp. 7–8. Peel's comment is at *Hansard*, IV, 890–1, 6 July 1831.

48. O'Gorman, 'The unreformed electorate', 44–6.

49. Ibid., 47.

50. E.A. Smith, 'Bribery and disfranchisement: Wallingford elections, 1820–1832', *E.H.R.*, LXXV (1960), 622.

51. *Hansard*, II, 1292, 3 March 1831.

52. Denman, ibid., III, 770, 22 March 1831.

53. Hobhouse, ibid., II, 1294–5, 3 March 1831.

54. Denman, ibid., II, 1244–5, 2 March 1831; Palmerston, II, 1321, 1328, 3 March 1831.

55. Hill, *Georgian Lincoln*, pp. 227–8; Smith, 'Bribery and disfranchisement', 623–6.

56. Sudbury, *Times*, 6, 19 June 1826, p. 3; Reading, ibid., 12 June 1826, p. 2.
57. Ebrington, *Hansard*, II, 1180, 2 March 1831.
58. B. Keith-Lucas, *The English local government franchise: a short history* (Oxford, 1952), pp. 46–7.
59. A.T. Patterson, *Radical Leicester: a history of Leicester 1780–1850* (Leicester, 1954), p. 192.
60. Campbell, *Hansard*, IV, 830, 5 July 1831; Bulwer, ibid., VI, 608, 25 August 1831; Hawkins, ibid., VII, 198–9, 19 September 1831.
61. Russell, ibid., II, 1083, 1 March 1831; Morpeth, ibid., II, 1218, 2 March 1831; Johnstone, ibid., III, 152, 7 March 1831.
62. Grey, ibid., VIII, 327, 7 October 1831.
63. Russell, ibid., II, 1086–7, 1 March 1831.
64. Stanley, Lord Dudley Stuart, Graham, ibid., III, 52, 135, 225, 4, 7, 8 March 1831.
65. Grey, ibid., IV, 119, 21 June 1831.
66. Hobhouse and Palmerston, ibid., II, 1293, 1327–9, 3 March 1831.
67. D. Beales, 'The electorate before and after 1832: the right to vote, and the opportunity', *Parliamentary History*, XI (1992), 146, 148; Gash, *Politics in the age of Peel*, p. 441.
68. Grant, *Hansard*, III, 173, 7 March 1831; Althorp, ibid., IV, 788, 5 July 1831.
69. Hardy and Baily, 'Downfall of the Gower interest', 300.
70. K. Bourne, *Palmerston: the early years 1784–1841* (1982), pp. 536–7.
71. D. Beales, *From Castlereagh to Gladstone* (1971 edn), p. 111.
72. Pakington, *Hansard*, CII, 1044, 21 February 1849.
73. G. Eliot, *Felix Holt, the radical*, ed. P. Coveney (1866; Harmondsworth, 1972 edn), p. 223.
74. N. McCord, *The Anti-Corn Law League 1838–1846* (2nd edn, 1968), p. 60.
75. See e.g. Grey's refusal to bandy this phrase about: *Hansard*, IV, 122, 21 June 1831.
76. Russell, ibid., II, 1065–6, 1 March 1831.
77. Lord John Russell, 'Earls Grey and Spencer', *E.R.*, LXXXIII (Jan. 1846), 257.
78. Morpeth, *Hansard*, III, 1088, 28 March 1831.
79. Grey, ibid., III, 1161, 30 March 1831.
80. Hawkins, ibid., III, 1623, 19 April 1831.
81. Palmerston, ibid., II, 1329, 3 March 1831; Grey, ibid., III, 1077, 28 March 1831.
82. Russell, ibid., II, 1089, 1 March 1831.
83. Graham, ibid., III, 231, 8 March 1831; Jeffrey, ibid., III, 76–7, 4 March 1831.
84. Mackintosh, ibid., IV, 681, 4 July 1831.
85. As many MPs said: e.g. Ebrington, Morpeth, ibid., II, 1181, 1217, 2 March 1831; Bethell, ibid., III, 237, 8 March 1831; Duncombe, ibid., III, 315, 9 March 1831.

PART II: INTRODUCTORY SUMMARY

1. See e.g. (East Kent tories) G.R. Gleig, *Personal reminiscences of the first duke of Wellington* (Edinburgh, 1904), p. 63; (Bradford tories) D.G. Wright, 'A radical borough: parliamentary politics in Bradford 1832–41', *Northern History*, IV (1969), 137; (Marquess of Hertford) Jennings, *Croker*, II, 98–100; (Lord Grenville) Duke of Buckingham and Chandos, *Memoirs of the Courts and cabinets of William IV and Victoria: from original family documents* (2 vols., 1861), I, 146; Southey, 'Moral and political state', 317.
2. Buckingham, *Courts of William IV*, I, 151.
3. G. Blakiston, *Lord William Russell and his wife 1815–1846* (1972), p. 282.

Chapter 4

1. The quotation is from a petition from Lewes: Phillips, 'Many faces of Reform', 120.
2. Earl of Lytton, *The life of Edward Bulwer first Lord Lytton* (2 vols., 1913), I, 410.
3. *Hansard*, III, 1808, 22 April 1831.
4. C.G. Forrester, *Northamptonshire county elections and electioneering 1695–1832* (1941), p. 130; B. Trinder, *Victorian Banbury* (Banbury, 1982), p. 48.
5. *New letters of Robert Southey*, ed. K. Curry (2 vols., New York, 1965), II, 365–6.
6. R.A.J. Walling, *The story of Plymouth* (1950), p. 200.
7. M.I. Thomis, *Politics and society in Nottingham 1785–1835* (Oxford, 1969),

pp. 226–8; Mozley, *Reminiscences of the Oxford movement*, I, 255–65.
8. See M. Harrison, *Crowds and history: mass phenomena in English towns, 1790–1835* (Cambridge, 1988), pp. 289–314.
9. Aspinall, *Three diaries*, p. 154.
10. Hardcastle, *Campbell*, II, 2.
11. *A portion of the journal kept by Thomas Raikes from 1831 to 1847* (2 vols., 1856), I, 50, 83; *Memoir of the life of Elizabeth Fry with extracts from her letters and journal*, ed. K. Fry and R.E.C. (2 vols., 1847), II, 140.
12. Sir D. Le Marchant, *Memoir of John Charles Viscount Althorp 3rd Earl Spencer* (1876), p. 433.
13. Aspinall, *Three diaries*, p. 255.
14. Broughton, *Recollections*, IV, 234–5.
15. B. Disraeli, *Coningsby or the new generation*, ed. T. Braun (1844; Harmondsworth, 1983 edn), p. 246; Bourne, *Palmerston*, p. 522.
16. S. Drescher, 'Public opinion and the destruction of British colonial slavery', in *Slavery and British society, 1776–1846*, ed. J. Walvin (1982), p. 27.
17. Sir G. Stephen, *Anti-slavery recollections: in a series of letters addressed to Mrs Beecher Stowe* (1854; 2nd edn, 1971), p. 160.
18. *The Holland House diaries 1831–1840: the diary of Henry Richard Vassall Fox, third Lord Holland* (1977), p. 208.
19. Ibid., p. 158.
20. *Russell's early correspondence*, II, 38.
21. See on this: Bourne, *Palmerston*, p. 506; Broughton, *Recollections*, IV, 161; (Birmingham) D. Cannadine, 'Birmingham evidence and Westminster reaction', *Bulletin of the Institute of Historical Research*, LII (1979), 196.
22. M.E. Chamberlain, *Lord Aberdeen: a political biography* (1983), p. 259.
23. *Lord Melbourne's papers*, ed. L.C. Sanders (1889), p. 517.
24. *An anecdotal history of the British parliament from the earliest periods, with notices of eminent parliamentary men, and examples of their oratory*, ed. G.H. Jennings (4th edn, 1899), p. 238.
25. C.S. Parker, *Life and letters of Sir James Graham 1792–1861* (2 vols., 1907), I, 170.
26. One important piece of government propaganda celebrated the effect of the act in undermining 'private interest and party feeling': *The Reform ministry, and the Reformed parliament* (4th edn, 1833), p. 107.
27. See J.V. Beckett, *The aristocracy in England 1660–1914* (1986), pp. 432–3.
28. M.W. Patterson, *Sir Francis Burdett and his times (1770–1844)* (2 vols., 1931), II, 668.
29. T.H. Duncombe, *The life and correspondence of Thomas Slingsby Duncombe* (2 vols., 1868), I, 130.
30. As Parkes dismissed them in 1838: W. Thomas, *The Philosophical radicals: nine studies in theory and practice 1817–1841* (Oxford, 1979), p. 445.
31. Jennings, *Croker*, II, 205–6.
32. R. Anstey, 'Parliamentary reform, Methodism and anti-slavery politics, 1829–1833', *Slavery and Abolition*, II (1981), 221.
33. Lady Spencer 1828, quoted in R.W. Davis, 'Toryism to Tamworth: the triumph of Reform, 1827–1835', *Albion*, XII (1980), 135.
34. Kriegel, *Holland House diaries*, p. 461.
35. Cox, *Efficient secret*, p. 53.
36. Morley, *Gladstone*, I, 150.
37. Kriegel, *Holland House diaries*, p. xxxvii.
38. *Greville memoirs*, III, 75.
39. Hatherton: Smith, *Lord Grey*, p. 326.
40. *Lieven-Grey correspondence*, III, 6.
41. Smith, *Lord Grey*, p. 305.
42. Sir A. West, *Recollections 1832 to 1886* (2 vols., 2nd edn, 1899), II, 40.
43. *Greville memoirs*, V, 303.
44. Ibid., III, 3, 61–2, 65.
45. Ibid., III, 67.
46. Aspinall, *Three diaries*, p. 9.
47. *Hansard*, XX, 176, 30 July 1833.
48. *Journal of Thomas Raikes*, I, 183.
49. *Reform ministry and Reformed parliament*, p. 23.
50. Smith, *Lord Grey*, p. 306.
51. Ibid., p. 303.
52. *Greville memoirs*, III, 212.
53. W. Empson, 'The last of the Catholic question – its principle, history, and effects', *E.R.*, XLIX (March 1829), 237–8, 258.
54. *Times*, 16 June 1826, p. 4.
55. *The Creevey papers: a selection from the correspondence and diaries of the late Thomas Creevey*, ed. Sir H. Maxwell (2 vols., 1903), II, 117.
56. Bathurst, cited in G. Best, 'The whigs and the Church Establishment in the age of Grey and Holland', *History*, XLV (1960), 112.
57. *Greville memoirs*, II, 371. Durham wanted a reformist dictator installed: S.J. Reid, *Life and letters of the first earl*

of Durham 1792–1840 (2 vols., 1906), I, 316–17.

58. C. Mahony, *The Viceroys of Ireland* (1912), pp. 235–6.

59. A.D. Kriegel, 'The Irish policy of Lord Grey's government', *E.H.R.*, LXXXVI (1971), 26.

60. E.A. Wasson, *Whig renaissance: Lord Althorp and the whig party 1782–1845* (New York, 1987), p. 307.

61. [R. Grant,] *Random recollections of the House of Commons, from the year 1830 to the close of 1835, including personal sketches of the leading members of all parties* (1836), p. 200.

62. This paragraph is based in particular on the following speeches of Russell: *Hansard* XXIII, 666, 6 May 1834; XXIV, 796, 23 June 1834; and XXVII, 361, 30 March 1835.

63. Ewart, ibid., XXIV, 45, 2 June 1834.

64. *Selections from speeches of Earl Russell 1817 to 1841 and from despatches 1859 to 1865* (2 vols., 1870), I, 432.

65. Brougham, *Hansard*, XXIV, 304, 6 June 1834; Russell, ibid., XXIV, 797, 23 June 1834.

66. See Stanley, ibid., XXIV, 34, 2 June 1834; Parker, *Sir James Graham*, I, 196–9, 240–1.

67. *Greville memoirs*, III, 103.

68. Russell, *Hansard*, XXIV, 797, 23 June 1834.

69. Ibid., XXIV, 1246, 7 July 1834.

70. Lord Beauvale, Melbourne's brother (!), writing in 1839, cited in Mabell, Countess of Airlie, *Lady Palmerston and her times* (2 vols., 1922), II, 37–8.

71. A.R. Ashwell and R.G. Wilberforce, *Life of the right reverend Samuel Wilberforce* (3 vols., 1880–3), I, 326.

72. P. Ziegler, *Melbourne: a biography of William Lamb 2nd Viscount Melbourne* (1978 edn), p. 178.

73. Ibid., p. 175.

74. *Russell's early correspondence*, II, 153.

Chapter 5

1. Isaac Tomkins, Gent. [Lord Brougham], *Thoughts upon the aristocracy of England* (1835), p. 11.

2. *Hansard*, LI, 778, 29 January 1840.

3. To Chadwick: A.P. Donajgrodski, 'Sir James Graham at the Home Office', *H.J.*, XX (1977), 103; see quotation at Introduction above, p. 6.

4. H.D. Clokie and J.W. Robinson, *Royal Commissions of Inquiry: the significance of investigations in British politics* (Stanford, 1937), pp. 58–9, 76–8.

5. *Hansard*, XXX, 495, 13 August 1835.

6. *P.P.*, 1835, XXIII, 39.

7. E.P. Hennock, *Fit and proper persons: ideal and reality in nineteenth-century urban government* (1973), pp. 308–12.

8. *P.P.* 1835, XXIII, 98, XXIV, 1194, XXVI, 2718; R. Newton, *Eighteenth-century Exeter* (Exeter, 1984), pp. 149–50.

9. Trinder, *Victorian Banbury*, pp. 12–13, 38–48, 161; Hill, *Georgian Lincoln*, pp. 216–17, 231–4, 252–3, 277–81; L.J. Ashford, *The history of the borough of High Wycombe from its origins to 1880* (1960), pp. 247–50.

10. See A.T. Patterson, *A history of Southampton: volume one: an oligarchy in decline 1700–1835* (Southampton, 1966), pp. 106–7, 138–41; Atton, 'Ipswich', 141–7. In Ipswich, Bristol and many other towns their membership was very similar to the corporation's.

11. For some figures, see D. Fraser, *Urban politics in Victorian England: the structure of politics in Victorian cities* (Leicester, 1976), p. 124.

12. See quotation from Baring, pp. 61–2 above, and S. and B. Webb, *English local government from the Revolution to the Municipal Corporations Act: I: the parish and the county* (1906), pp. 556 ff.

13. For instance, the tory duke of Beaufort, Lord Lieutenant of Monmouthshire, refused in 1827 to recommend the younger son of a newly landed ironmaster: ibid., p. 582.

14. D. Foster, 'Class and county government in early-nineteenth-century Lancashire', *Northern History*, IX (1974), 48–61.

15. R. Foster, 'Wellington and local government', in *Studies in the military and political career of the first duke of Wellington*, ed. N. Gash (Manchester, 1990), pp. 230–1; *Russell's early correspondence*, II, 132, 139.

16. *Greville memoirs*, IV, 201–2.

17. Foster, 'Class and county government', 55; see also Russell's non-partisan behaviour over Birmingham Justices, discussed in F.C. Mather, *Public order in the age of the Chartists* (Manchester, 1959), p. 67.

18. Ibid., pp. 40–1.

19. Beales, 'Peel, Russell and reform', 879.
20. Russell, *English government and constitution*, p. 250.
21. See G.C. Lewis, 'Secondary punishments', *The Law Magazine*, VII (Jan. 1832), 14.
22. C. Grey, 'Secondary punishments – transportation', *E.R.*, LVIII (Jan. 1834), 336–60; Brougham, *Hansard*, XXIV, 620, 20 June 1834.
23. Russell, *English government and constitution* (new edn, 1865), p. lvi.
24. Russell, 'Earls Grey and Spencer', 265.
25. Mitchell and Deane, *British historical statistics*, pp. 6, 410.
26. Sir H. Maxwell, *The life and letters of George William Frederick fourth earl of Clarendon* (2 vols., 1913), I, 86–7.
27. D. Roberts, *Victorian origins of the British welfare state* (New Haven, 1960), p. 287.

Chapter 6

1. Spring Rice, in R.M. Bacon, *A memoir of the life of Edward, third Baron Suffield* (Norwich, 1838), pp. 479–80; Duncannon, in Sanders, *Melbourne's papers*, pp. 228–31; *Russell's early correspondence*, II, 97–8; Bourne, *Palmerston*, p. 523.
2. The voting is analysed in Gash, *Reaction and reconstruction*, pp. 214–16.
3. R. Stewart, *The foundation of the Conservative party* (1978), p. 117.
4. Moore, *Politics of deference*, pp. 249–50.
5. E. Jaggard, 'The 1841 British general election; a reconsideration', *Australian Journal of Politics and History*, XXX (1984), 101, 103.
6. The figures for borough splits are mine. For split voting itself, see T.J. Nossiter, 'Aspects of electoral behavior in English constituencies, 1832–1868', in *Mass politics: studies in political sociology*, ed. E. Allardt and S. Rokkan (New York, 1970), p. 165; Phillips, 'Many faces of Reform', 123–5, 128.
7. Estimates suggest that the independent radical element declined from 50 in 1835 to 20 in 1836 and 8 in 1840: Gash, *Reaction and reconstruction*, pp. 167–8.
8. Parkes, quoted in Thomas, *Philosophical radicals*, p. 445.
9. J.R. Vincent. *Pollbooks: how Victorians voted* (Cambridge, 1968 edn), 14–15, 20–1. C.E. Brent identified the same pattern for a later period: 'The immediate impact of the Second Reform Act on a southern county town: voting patterns at Lewes borough in 1865 and 1868', *Southern History*, II (1980), 129–77.
10. Newbould, 'Whiggery and the growth of party', 148. The evidence presented in this article is very useful, but its negative conclusions about whig leadership are the result, it seems to me, of unrealistic expectations on the author's part.
11. Brougham used it in 1834, and Althorp in 1835, at which date Melbourne talked of the 'Whig and Liberal party': see Gash, *Reaction and reconstruction*, p. 165. The *Annual Register* used the term 'Liberal' in writing of the party at the 1837 and 1841 election. E. Halévy, in *A history of the English people 1830–1841* (1927), p. 183, writes that 'Reform' party was still the official designation at the 1837 and 1841 elections, though 'Liberal' was used more in newspaper articles.
12. *Hansard*, L, 518, 23 August 1839.
13. T. Spring Rice, 'Present state and conduct of parties', *E.R.*, LXXI (April 1840), 281–2.
14. Henry, Lord Cockburn, *Life of Lord Jeffrey with a selection from his correspondence* (2 vols., Edinburgh, 1852), II, 282–3.
15. Kriegel, *Holland House diaries*, p. 348.
16. See e.g. *Russell's early correspondence*, II, 46 (Sept. 1834).
17. Broughton, *Recollections*, VI, 88.
18. Ziegler, *Melbourne*, p. 129.
19. Maxwell, *Clarendon*, I, 276.
20. At Liverpool, October 1838: H. Jephson, *The platform: its rise and progress* (2 vols., 1968 edn), II, 243–4.
21. *Hansard*, XLIX, 1159, 2 August 1839.
22. Victory speech, Stroud election 1837: S. Walpole, *The life of Lord John Russell* (2 vols., 1889), I, 284.
23. G.W.E. Russell, *Social silhouettes* (1906), p. 154.
24. Lord John Russell, *English government and constitution* (new edn, 1865), p. xcvii.
25. 1831: E. Hughes, 'The bishops and Reform, 1831–3: some fresh correspondence', *E.H.R.*, LVI (1941), 464.
26. Holland, in Kriegel, *Holland House*

diaries, p. 217.

27. Broughton, *Recollections*, v, 180.
28. Bacon, *Suffield*, p. 264.
29. Russell, *Recollections*, p. 150.
30. F. Smith, *The life and work of Sir James Kay-Shuttleworth* (1923), p. 86.
31. P.H. Bagenal, *The life of Ralph Bernal Osborne MP* (1884), pp. 22–5.
32. For figures for 1830–66, see *P.P.* 1871, LVI, 757. After 1868, Gladstone was nearly as prolific: see Morley, *Gladstone*, II, 429.
33. *Russell's early correspondence*, II, 185.
34. Kriegel, *Holland House diaries*, p. 357.
35. A. Macintyre, *The Liberator: Daniel O'Connell and the Irish party 1830–1847* (1965), pp. 51–73.
36. I. Gross, 'Parliament and the abolition of negro apprenticeship 1835–1838', *E.H.R.*, XCVI (1981), 569–70.
37. G.I.T. Machin, *Politics and the Churches in Great Britain 1832 to 1868* (Oxford, 1977), p. 40; Stewart, *Foundation of the Conservative party*, p. 163.
38. D. Hempton, *Methodism and politics in British society 1750–1850* (1987 edn), pp. 161–2.
39. *Erskine May's Treatise on the law, privileges, proceedings and usage of parliament*, ed. Sir C. Gordon (20th edn, 1983), p. 867.
40. Baring, *Hansard*, LII, 201–11, 13 February 1840, LIV, 130, 15 May 1840.
41. *Diary of Haydon*, IV, 493.
42. See e.g. Howick, *Hansard*, XXXVII, 52–3, 7 March 1837; Russell, ibid., XL, 1184, 15 February 1838.
43. Ibid., LI, 775, 781, 29 January 1840.
44. Kriegel, *Holland House diaries*, p. 410.
45. *A selection from the speeches and writings of the late Lord King with a short introductory memoir by Earl Fortescue* (1844), pp. 34, 36.
46. Davis, 'Whigs and electoral deference', 84.
47. On the status of the votes, see Russell, *Hansard*, XLV, 156, 6 February 1839, and the discussion in ibid., XLV, 585ff., 19 February 1839.
48. S. Buxton, *Finance and politics: an historical study 1783–1885* (2 vols., 1888), I, 48–9; L. Brown, *The Board of Trade and the free trade movement 1830–42* (Oxford, 1958), p. 203. Advocates of free trade differed wildly on the price cost of tariffs: estimates varied from £11 million to £90 million per year.
49. Sir C. Webster, *The foreign policy of Palmerston 1830–1841: Britain, the liberal movement and the Eastern question* (2 vols., 1951), II, 750–1.
50. Villiers, *Hansard*, XLV, 630, 19 February 1839; Baines, ibid, XLV, 217, 11 February 1839; Philips, ibid., XLV, 641, 19 February 1839 and XLVI, 738, 15 March 1839.
51. See e.g. W. Clay, ibid., XLVI, 516, 13 March 1839; T.B. Hobhouse, ibid., XLVI, 744, 15 March 1839.
52. Ibid., XLVI, 844, 18 March 1839.
53. W. Clay, ibid., XLVI, 519, 13 March 1839.
54. Howick, ibid., XLVI, 546, 550, 13 March 1839.
55. Russell, ibid., XLVI, 704, 14 March 1839.
56. Howick, ibid., XLVI, 524, 538, 13 March 1839; Russell, ibid., XLVI, 704, 14 March 1839.
57. I. Newbould, *Whiggery and reform, 1830–41: the politics of government* (Basingstoke, 1990), p. 304.
58. Wood to Stansfeld, 4 March, 6 May, 1841, Hickleton papers, Cambridge University Library, A 4 50A.
59. Gash, *Reaction and reconstruction*, pp. 181–2, 208, 211.
60. *Times*, 26 January 1839, p. 4.
61. *Hansard*, LIV, 631, 26 May 1840.
62. Morpeth, ibid., LVIII, 936, 28 May 1841.
63. Ibid., LVIII, 661, 18 May 1841.
64. Russell, ibid., LVIII, 41, 666–7, 7, 18 May 1841.
65. H.W. Tancred, cited in Trinder, *Victorian Banbury*, p. 58; *The annual register . . . 1841* (1842), p. 145; *Carlisle's viceregal speeches*, p. 262.
66. Russell, *Times*, 1 July 1841, p. 2.
67. *Letters from Lord Sydenham, Governor-general of Canada 1839–1841, to Lord John Russell*, ed. P. Knaplund (1931), p. 141. Ellice spoke of the beneficial effects of the free trade cry on the election results: Gash, *Reaction and reconstruction*, p. 182.
68. Jenkins, *Gladstone, whiggery*, p. 9.
69. Stanley, *Arnold*, II, 43.

Chapter 7

1. Graham 1837: D. Read, *Peel and the Victorians* (Oxford, 1987), p. 87.
2. Gash, *Politics in the age of Peel*, p. 441.
3. *Greville memoirs*, III, 194.

4. For what follows, see in particular: *A correct report of the speeches delivered by Sir Robert Peel ... at Glasgow January ... 1837* (1837), and his speech at the Merchant Taylors' Hall, reported in *Times*, 14 May 1838, pp. 5–6.
5. Davidoff and Hall, *Family fortunes*, p. 95.
6. (Wellington) *The autobiography and memoirs of Benjamin Robert Haydon (1786–1846)*, ed. T. Taylor (2 vols., 1926 edn), II, 661; Scarlett, *Abinger*, p. 174; (Graham) D.G. Paz, *The politics of working-class education in Britain, 1830–50* (Manchester, 1980), p. 85.
7. *The prime ministers' papers: W.E. Gladstone*, ed. J. Brooke and M. Sorensen (4 vols., 1977–81), II, 255.
8. *Hansard*, LIX, 555, 17 September 1841.
9. Ibid., LXXX, 734, 21 May 1845.
10. 1847: Read, *Peel and the Victorians*, p. 256.
11. Parker, *Peel*, II, 299–300.
12. Brooke and Sorensen, *Gladstone*, III, 28–9.
13. Mitchell and Deane, *British historical statistics*, p. 488.
14. Brooke and Sorensen, *Gladstone*, II, 267.
15. Ibid., II, 214.
16. Hardcastle, *Campbell*, II, 184 (Jan. 1844); *Greville memoirs*, V, 295–7 (Aug. 1845); *Letters of Queen Victoria 1837–1861*, II, 92 (Melbourne, Nov. 1845).
17. A. Briggs, *Chartist studies* (1959), p. 386.
18. Parker, *Sir James Graham*, I, 333–6.
19. Jennings, *Anecdotal history of parliament*, p. 268.
20. R.A. Soloway, *Prelates and people: ecclesiastical social thought in England 1783–1852* (1969), p. 298.
21. Scarlett, *Abinger*, p. 175.
22. C. Elizabeth [Tonna], *Personal recollections* (1841), pp. 28, 35–6.
23. C. Whibley, *Lord John Manners and his friends* (2 vols., Edinburgh, 1925), I, 107.
24. For Anglican clergymen's anguished reaction to Chartism, see Soloway, *Prelates and people*, pp. 255–62.
25. Jennings, *Croker*, II, 412.
26. A. Miall, *Life of Edward Miall* (1884), pp. 30–1, 67.
27. Morley, *Gladstone*, I, 304; R. Shannon, *Gladstone; I: 1809–1865* (1982), p. 127.
28. Brooke and Sorensen, *Gladstone*, II, 265.
29. Ibid., II, 238.
30. Parker, *Sir James Graham*, I, 422.
31. See e.g. *Greville memoirs*, V, 283–4.
32. Sanders, *Melbourne's papers*, p. 99.
33. G.H. Sumner, *Life of Charles Richard Sumner, bishop of Winchester* (1876), p. 163.
34. (Monteagle, the former Spring-Rice) Machin, *Politics and the Churches 1832–68*, p. 171.
35. Gladstone, quoted in Southgate, *Passing of the whigs*, p. 111.
36. A. Prentice, *History of the Anti-Corn Law League*, ed. W.H. Chaloner (2 vols., 1968 edn), I 197–9, 236–8; Richard, *Memoirs of Joseph Sturge*, pp. 274–6.
37. As Cobden admitted: R.G. Cowherd, *The politics of English Dissent* (1959), pp. 131–2.
38. Brooke and Sorensen, *Gladstone*, III, 11–12.
39. McCord, *Anti-Corn Law League*, pp. 122, 124, 130–1.
40. Peel, *Private letters of Peel*, pp. 285–6.
41. Aspinall, *Charles Arbuthnot*, p. 239. See the views of Buccleuch and Mahon in *Memoirs of Sir Robert Peel*, ed. Lord Mahon and E. Cardwell (2 vols., 1856–7), II, 255, 260–2.
42. Brooke and Sorensen, *Gladstone*, III, 79.
43. *Memoirs of Peel*, II, 163–6.
44. Parker, *Peel*, III, 478; Peel, *Private letters of Peel*, p. 273.
45. Graham's phrase: Parker, *Sir James Graham*, II, 41. But that Peel thought the same is implied in ibid., II, 42 and in Peel, *Private letters of Peel*, p. 282.
46. *Memoirs of Peel*, II, 288–9, 296–7.
47. Read, *Peel and the Victorians*, pp. 236–9.

Chapter 8

1. September 1852, quoted in A. Alison, *Our future policy* (1852), p. i.
2. At Manchester, *Times*, 7 November 1856, p. 7; at Pontefract, ibid., 29 October 1860, p. 10.
3. *Carlisle's viceregal speeches*, p. 245.
4. At Edinburgh, *Times*, 2 April 1863, p. 9.
5. Palmerston (Glasgow), ibid., 1 April 1863, p. 9; Gladstone (Wrexham), ibid., 23 October 1862, p. 7 and (Bolton) 12 October 1864, p. 9.

6. Ibid., 11 October 1862, p. 7.
7. Palmerston (Greenock), ibid., 1 April 1863, p. 9, and (Bradford) 10 August 1864, p. 9.
8. Ibid. (Greenock and Bradford).
9. Gladstone (South Shields), ibid., 9 October 1862, p. 8, (Sunderland) 11 October 1862, p. 8, and (Bolton) 12 October 1864, p. 9.
10. Ibid., 11 August 1862, p. 6, and 1 April 1863, p. 9.
11. Ibid., 11 August 1862, p. 6.
12. *The Palmerston papers: Gladstone and Palmerston . . . 1851–1865*, ed. P. Guedalla (1928), p. 210.
13. J. Curran, 'The press as an agency of social control: an historical perspective' in *Newspaper history from the seventeenth century to the present day*, ed. G. Boyce, J. Curran and P. Wingate (1978), p. 60.
14. A.J. Lee, *The origins of the popular press in England 1855–1914* (1976), p. 290.
15. W.R. Greg, 'The newspaper press', *E.R.*, CII (Oct. 1855), 470–98; *Regina v. Palmerston: the correspondence between Queen Victoria and her foreign and prime minister 1837–1865* ed. B. Connell (1962), p. 187.
16. One of the most striking of the many contexts in which this thinking appears is in the middle of a footnote on a constitutional question in Earl Grey's *Parliamentary government*, pp. 112–13: 'To be in a constant conflict with evil in some shape or other, is obviously the condition appointed by Providence both for men and nations, and the moment that struggles for improvement cease, corruption and decay commence'.
17. *Hansard* LXXXVII, 1178–9, 16 July 1846.
18. Maxwell, *Clarendon*, I, 265–7.
19. Machin, *Politics and the Churches 1832–68*, p. 192.
20. S. Palmer, *Politics, shipping and the repeal of the Navigation Laws* (Manchester, 1990), p. 88.
21. *Letters of Cornewall Lewis*, p. 206.
22. J. Prest, *Lord John Russell* (1972), p. 345.
23. Gash, *Reaction and reconstruction*, p. 197.
24. Shannon, *Gladstone I*, pp. 243–4.
25. A.G. Gardiner, *The life of Sir William Harcourt* (2 vols., 1923), I, 74, 88. See also P. Mandler, *Aristocratic government in the age of Reform: whigs and Liberals 1830–1852* (Oxford, 1990), pp. 77–80.
26. Carlisle, Grey and Labouchère were the three principal opponents of action in cabinet: Prest, *Russell*, pp. 322–3.
27. Walpole, *Russell*, II, 196–7.
28. Morley, *Gladstone*, I, 511, 649–50.
29. J.B. Conacher, *The Peelites and the party system 1846–52* (Newton Abbot, 1972), pp. 134–6.
30. Shannon, *Gladstone I*, p. 305.
31. Connell, *Regina v. Palmerston*, pp. 158–9.
32. Peel's son and heir Sir Robert remained in the government, as did a number of other junior ministers. For more detail on Peelite behaviour, see Gurowich, 'Continuation of war', 608n36.
33. *The parliamentary diaries of Sir John Trelawny, 1858–1865*, ed. T.A. Jenkins (1990), pp. 32, 37.
34. See Gurowich, 'Continuation of war', 621–7.
35. H. Parris, *Constitutional bureaucracy: the development of British central administration since the eighteenth century* (1969), p. 108; *Autobiographic recollections of George Pryme*, ed. A. Bayne (Cambridge, 1870), p. 196; D. Roberts, 'Lord Palmerston at the Home Office', *The Historian*, XXI (1958–9), 63–81.
36. 1856: Bagehot, *Collected works*, VI, 81–5.
37. J. Hart, 'Sir Charles Trevelyan at the Treasury', *E.H.R.*, LXXV (1960), 106. Normanby called for separate committees of MPs from each part of the Kingdom to prepare local legislation: Prest, *Russell*, pp. 288–9. Later suggestions for change included: Greg, 'Expected Reform Bill', 231; T.E. May, 'The machinery of parliamentary legislation', *E.R.*, XCIX (Jan. 1854), 243–82; and H. Brougham, 'The House of Commons and law amendment', *Quarterly Review*, XCV (Sept. 1854), 482.
38. G.C. Lewis, 'State of the nation: the ministry and the new parliament', *E.R.*, LXXXVII (Jan. 1848), 152, 154–5.
39. *Hansard*, CIII, 725, 14 March 1849; Parris, *Constitutional bureaucracy*, pp. 208–9. See also the views of Wood and his friend Nassau Senior in M.C.M. Simpson, *Many memories of many people* (1898), pp. 185–6, 222–4.

40. Clokie and Robinson, *Royal Commissions*, pp. 76–8.
41. G. Kitson Clark, *The making of Victorian England* (1962), p. 271.
42. Parris, *Constitutional bureaucracy*, p. 73.
43. See the tables in A.C. Howe, *The cotton masters 1830–1860* (Oxford, 1984), pp. 263, 264, 267, and in *P.P.*, 1871, LVI, 757.
44. Vincent, *Liberal party*, p. 127.
45. O.C. Williams, *The historical development of private bill procedure and standing orders in the House of Commons* (2 vols., 1948), I, 88.
46. Henry Grenfell, in B. Mallet, *Thomas George earl of Northbrook: a memoir* (1908), p. 228.
47. As Granville wrote in 1882: ibid., p. 35.
48. Lord Redesdale, *Memories* (2 vols., 1915), I, 136.
49. *Reminiscences by Goldwin Smith*, ed. A. Haultain (New York, 1910), pp. 301–2. For Lady Theresa Lewis's epitaph on Carlisle's intellectual inadequacy (despite a First at Christ Church College Oxford), see Maxwell, *Clarendon*, II, 296. For George Grey having to knock sense into his Cemeteries Bill, see Prest, *Russell*, p. 229.
50. Lowe, *Hansard*, CXL, 138, 1 February 1856.
51. Guedalla, *Palmerston papers*, p. 326.
52. Ibid., pp. 214–16; Lewis, *Hansard*, CXLIX, 2130–2, 3 May 1858.
53. Guedalla, *Palmerston papers*, pp. 214–16.
54. A.J.P. Taylor, *The trouble makers: dissent over foreign policy 1792–1939* (1957), p. 63.
55. On this, see also Clarendon, in *A century of diplomatic blue books 1814–1914*, ed. H. Temperley and L.M. Penson (Cambridge, 1938), p. 133.
56. See E.D. Steele, *Palmerston and Liberalism, 1855–1865* (Cambridge, 1991), pp. 191–214.
57. Temperley and Penson, *Diplomatic blue books*, pp. 162–3.
58. Jennings, *Anecdotal history of parliament*, pp. 296–7; Mandler, *Aristocratic government*, pp. 273–4.
59. *Hansard*, CLXVIII, 1103, 1 August 1862.
60. See H. Cunningham, 'The language of patriotism, 1750–1914', *History Workshop*, XII (Autumn 1981), 19.
61. Connell, *Regina v. Palmerston*, p. 279.
62. The queen's jibe is in *The letters of Queen Victoria second series: a selection from Her Majesty's correspondence and journal between the years 1862 and 1885*, ed. G.E. Buckle (3 vols., 1926–8), I, 168.
63. *Hansard*, CXII, 381–2, 389, 438, 25 June 1850; see also George Grey, ibid., CXII, 543, 27 June 1850.
64. *Speeches of Russell*, II, 328–32; Odo Russell in Walpole, *Russell*, II, 325–8.
65. *Hansard*, CLXIX, 932, 27 February 1863. The gushing quotation was Trelawny's: *Trelawny diaries*, p. 227.
66. See the material presented in *British Foreign Secretaries and foreign policy: from Crimean war to First World war*, ed. K.M. Wilson (1987), p. 35, and W. Harris, *The history of the radical party in parliament* (1885), pp. 402–3.
67. Chamberlain, *Lord Aberdeen*, p. 516.
68. As Cobden asserted at the time. See the references in D. Southgate, '*The most English minister . . .*': *the policies and politics of Palmerston* (1966), p. 518.
69. T.W. Reid, *Life of W.E. Forster* (New York, 1970 edn, 2 vols. in 1), I, 362. See also *Trelawny diaries*, p. 209.
70. See the debate, instigated by Forster, at *Hansard*, CLXXVII, 1850, 17 March 1865, and the opposition to him of pure-milk free-traders like Robert Lowe and James White. Dr G.R. Searle kindly drew my attention to this debate.
71. For the 1857 election, see Vincent, *Liberal party*, pp. 72–3, and A.B. Hawkins, *Parliament, party and the art of politics in Britain, 1855–59* (Basingstoke, 1987), pp. 65–8, 76–7.
72. Nine of these were during the Conservative government of 1858–9. Defeats averaged eleven per session even during the 'stable' years 1860–5. For detailed figures, see Lowell, *Government of England*, II, 79.
73. Maddyn, *Chiefs of parties*, II, 173.
74. Lord E. Fitzmaurice, *The life of Granville George Leveson Gower second Earl Granville 1815–1891* (2 vols., 1905), I, 407; *Trelawny diaries*, p. 187; Disraeli, in *Hansard*, CLXVI, 1883, 19 May 1862.
75. At Manchester, *Times*, 7 November 1856, p. 7; at Pontefract, ibid., 29 October 1860, p. 10.
76. Fraser, 'Growth of ministerial control', 456.
77. *Hansard*, CLXVIII, 1125, 1 August 1862.
78. Steele, *Palmerston and Liberalism*, pp.

126–7. For another radical's (qualified) praise of Palmerston, see *Trelawny diaries*, pp. 170, 221, 241.

79. Cox, *Efficient secret*, p. 103.

80. Moore, *Politics of deference*, pp. 262–9 (on South Leicestershire and North Warwickshire).

81. Figures are drawn from the tables in J.A. Thomas, *The House of Commons 1832–1901: a study of its economic and functional character* (Cardiff, 1939), pp. 4–7 (I have included a few 'Irish repealers' and 'radicals' whom Thomas counts separately).

82. Bagehot, *English constitution*, pp. 107, 173; May, *Constitutional history 1760–1860* (1861 edn), I, 430, II, 252–3, 622.

83. *Hansard*, CLIV, 334, 10 June 1859.

84. Morley, *Gladstone*, II, 151–2.

85. The phrase was Clarendon's: Fitzmaurice, *Granville*, I, 487.

Chapter 9

1. *Hansard*, LXXII, 684, 13 February 1844.

2. See Prest, *Russell*, pp. 236, 271. For Wood's greater zeal in unfolding these ideas, see *The later correspondence of Lord John Russell 1840–1878*, ed. G.P. Gooch (2 vols., 1925), I, 155, 161–2, and R.J. Moore, *Sir Charles Wood's Indian policy 1853–66* (Manchester, 1966), pp. 6–8.

3. *Russell's later correspondence*, I, 154.

4. J. Saville, *1848: the British state and the Chartist movement* (Cambridge, 1987), p. 34.

5. For Wood on this, see J. Lee, *The modernisation of Irish society 1848–1918* (Dublin, 1973), p. 37.

6. *Carlisle's viceregal speeches*, pp. 35, 42.

7. See R.D.C. Black, *Economic thought and the Irish question 1817–1870* (Cambridge, 1960), pp. 45–6.

8. *Carlisle's viceregal speeches*, p. 225.

9. *The personal papers of Lord Rendel* (1931), p. 120.

10. See C.P. Fortescue on this, in *Hansard*, CLXXXII, 1016–17, 10 April 1866.

11. G.F.A. Best, *Temporal pillars: Queen Anne's Bounty, the Ecclesiastical Commissioners, and the Church of England* (Cambridge, 1964), pp. 394–6.

12. Walpole, *Russell*, I, 77.

13. As George Grey said in defending the Ecclesiastical Titles Bill: *Hansard*, CXV, 606, 25 March 1851.

14. Fitzmaurice, *Granville*, I, 222.

15. J.P. Parry, *Democracy and religion: Gladstone and the Liberal party, 1867–1875* (Cambridge, 1986), p. 275.

16. B. Harrison, 'The Sunday trading riots of 1855', *H.J.*, VIII (1965), 219–45; *Greville memoirs*, VIII, 47. See also Connell, *Regina v. Palmerston*, pp. 201–3.

17. *Hansard*, XCI, 965–6, 19 April 1847.

18. Ibid., XCI, 958–9.

19. R. Johnson, 'Educational policy and social control in early Victorian England', *Past and Present*, XLIX (Nov. 1970), 117–18.

20. See Cowper, *Hansard*, CXLVIII, 1231, 11 February 1858.

21. J. Hurt, *Education in evolution: Church, state, society and popular education 1800–1870* (1971), pp. 70, 96.

22. J. Prest, *Liberty and locality: parliament, permissive legislation, and ratepayers' democracies in the nineteenth century* (Oxford, 1990), p. 5.

23. Ibid., p. 184.

24. A. Redford and I. Russell, *The history of local government in Manchester* (2 vols., 1939–40), II, 223.

25. *P.P.*, 1865, XLVII, 279; *P.P.*, 1884–5, LXI, 267.

26. W.L. Burn, *The age of equipoise: a study of the mid-Victorian generation* (1964), p. 219.

27. U. Henriques, *Before the welfare state: social administration in early industrial Britain* (1979), p. 145.

28. Bright, *Hansard*, CLVI, 243, 27 January 1860; Hodgkinson, ibid., CLXV, 310, 14 February 1862.

29. Burn, *Age of equipoise*, chapter 4.

30. R. Lowe, 'The past session and the new parliament', *E.R.*, CV (Apr. 1857), 552–78.

31. *Times*, 13 October 1858, p. 12.

32. A.P. Martin, *Life and letters of Robert Lowe Viscount Sherbrooke* (2 vols., 1893), II, 243.

33. James Bryce, in *Essays in Reform* (1867), p. 104. See e.g. J.S. Mill, *Considerations on representative government* (1861), ch. 3.

34. *Hansard*, CLXXXII, 1259–62, 13 April 1866.

35. From *On liberty* (1859): J.S. Mill, *Utilitarianism: Liberty: Representative government*, ed. H.B. Acton (1972 edn), p. 120.

36. *Trelawny diaries*, p. 256.
37. W.E. Gladstone, 'The declining efficiency of parliament', *Quarterly Review*, xcix (Sept. 1856), 546–7, 552–8; see *Trelawny diaries*, pp. 207, 265.
38. At Kilmarnock: *Times*, 1 November 1860, p. 10.
39. *Hansard*, clxviii, 1112, 1114, 1 August 1862.
40. Maddyn, *Chiefs of parties*, ii, 182.
41. Bagehot, *English constitution*, pp. 177–8.
42. Greg, 'Expected Reform Bill', 226, 231; J.F. Stephen, 'Parliamentary government', *Contemporary Review*, xxiii (1873–4), 1–19, 165–81. In 'Cost of party government', *Quarterly Review*, cxxvi (Apr. 1869), 394–413, Greg urged the systematic classification of paupers, education reform, the creation of a Ministry of Justice, an attack on the criminal classes, and effort to improve the dwellings of the metropolitan poor.
43. Greg, 'Expected Reform Bill', 236–7, 252.
44. See e.g. George Grey, 1852, quoted in McCord, 'Some difficulties of parliamentary reform', 382. The Peelite Graham noted an improvement in artisanal morals too: Parker, *Sir James Graham*, ii, 204–5.
45. There is interesting material on the tensions on the Reform question between one Liberal MP for a small borough (Banbury) and his radical supporters in *A Victorian MP and his constituents: the correspondence of H.W. Tancred, 1841–1859*, ed. B.S. Trinder (Banbury, 1969), pp. 38, 57, 71–3. In 1857, Palmerston complained of the problems of parliamentary management resulting from the 'pledges unguardedly and needlessly made [by various MPs] to some few radicals in his borough or county': Connell, *Regina v. Palmerston*, p. 229.
46. At the Guildhall: *Times*, 24 July 1861, p. 10.
47. E.P. Bouverie, ibid., 1 November 1860, p. 10.
48. *Hansard*, clxxv, 325, 11 May 1864.
49. See ibid., clxxxii, 179, 207, 1257, 1437, 13 March, 13, 16 April 1866 (Arthur Peel, Fawcett, Mill, Layard).
50. Forster, ibid., clxxxii, 1392, 16 April 1866; Goschen, ibid., clxxxii, 1966, 23 April 1866; Lord F. Cavendish,

ibid., clxxxiii, 1611, 31 March 1866.
51. Holyoake noted this sea-change with regret: E.C. Mack and W.H.G. Armytage, *Thomas Hughes: the life of the author of 'Tom Brown's schooldays'* (1952), p. 144.
52. Howe, *Cotton masters*, pp. 244–6.
53. Bagenal, *Osborne*, p. 149.
54. On 1866, see Seymour, *Electoral reform*, p. 247, and G. Himmelfarb, *Victorian minds* (1968), p. 344; on 1860, see H.C.F. Bell, 'Palmerston and parliamentary representation', *Journal of Modern History*, iv (1932), 186–213.
55. Fitzmaurice, *Granville*, i, 227–8.
56. G.M. Trevelyan, *The life of John Bright* (1913), pp. 366–7; Jephson, *The platform*, ii, 454.
57. J. Morley, *The life of Richard Cobden* (2 vols., 1881), ii, 363.
58. F.M.L. Thompson, 'Land and politics in England in the nineteenth century', *Transactions of the Royal Historical Society*, xv (1965), 23–44; Howe, *Cotton masters*, p. 235.
59. Steele, *Palmerston and Liberalism*, p. 232.
60. Morley, *Cobden*, ii, 219–20, 365.
61. Bernard Cracroft, in *Essays in Reform*, p. 165; J.D. Coleridge (1860) in E.H. Coleridge, *Life and correspondence of John Duke Lord Coleridge Lord Chief Justice of England* (2 vols., 1904), i, 259–60.
62. *The education of Henry Adams: an autobiography* (Boston, 1961 edn), p. 190.
63. Simpson, *Many memories*, pp. 242–5, 254.
64. *Disraeli, Derby and the Conservative party: journals and memoirs of Edward Henry, Lord Stanley 1849–1869*, ed. J. Vincent (Hassocks, 1978), p. 124; *George Douglas eighth duke of Argyll (1823–1900): autobiography and memoirs*, ed. Dowager duchess of Argyll (2 vols., 1906), ii, 76.
65. Jephson, *The platform*, ii, 435. This election needs more study.
66. W.E. Gladstone, 'Prospects political and financial', *Quarterly Review*, ci (Jan. 1857), 268.
67. *Times*, 15 October 1864. p. 7.
68. See G.I.T. Machin, 'Gladstone and nonconformity in the 1860s: the formation of an alliance', *H.J.*, xvii (1974), 347–64.
69. Moore, *Politics of deference*, p. 382.
70. Bagehot, *English constitution*, p. 174.

71. Locke King, Cobden: *Hansard*, CXIV, 850, 867, 20 February 1851.
72. Lewis, ibid., CLVII, 2185–6, 23 April 1860; Russell, ibid., CLVIII, 201, 26 April 1860.
73. Connell, *Regina v. Palmerston*, p. 229; Moore, *Wood's Indian policy*, p. 17.
74. Gladstone, *Hansard*, CLIII, 1058–9, 29 March 1859; Russell, ibid., CLVI, 2058–9, 1 March 1860.
75. Ibid., CXIV, 1039–40, 28 February 1851, and CXIX, 258, 9 February 1852.
76. Ibid., CLXXXIII, 486, 904, 1567, 1884, 7, 14, 31 May, 4 June 1866 (Gladstone, Cardwell, Goschen, Gladstone).
77. Argyll, 1858: *Argyll's autobiography*, II, 125–6.
78. *Hansard*, CLXXXII, 1970, 23 April 1866.
79. Ibid., CLXXXII, 38, 12 March 1866.
80. R. Lowe, *Speeches and letters on Reform* (1867), passim. See e.g. that of 15 July 1867: *Hansard*, CLXXXVIII, 1539–50.
81. Maxwell, *Clarendon*, II, 314; M. Cowling, *1867: Disraeli, Gladstone and revolution: the passing of the second Reform Bill* (Cambridge, 1967), pp. 102–5.
82. Reid, *W.E. Forster*, I, 380.
83. Seymour, *Electoral reform*, pp. 260–1.
84. As e.g. Gladstone and Amberley said: *Hansard*, CLXXXVI, 39–45, 534, 18, 25 March 1867.
85. Cowling, *1867*, pp. 72, 344–5.
86. H.J. Hanham, *Elections and party management: politics in the time of Disraeli and Gladstone* (Hassocks, 1978 edn), p. 404; *P.P.*, 1872, XLVII, 383.
87. Seymour, *Electoral reform*, p. 303.
88. *English constitution*, p. 281 (introduction to 2nd edn, 1872).
89. Clarendon's phrase: Maxwell, *Clarendon*, II, 330.

PART IV: INTRODUCTORY

1. T. Lloyd, 'Uncontested seats in British general elections, 1852–1910', *H.J.*, VIII (1965), 260–5.
2. T. Lloyd, *The general election of 1880* (Oxford, 1968), p. 105.
3. Jennings, *Anecdotal history of parliament*, p. 361.
4. *The political correspondence of Mr Gladstone and Lord Granville 1868–1876* ed. A. Ramm (2 vols., 1952), II, 266, 274.
5. See T.J. Nossiter, *Influence, opinion and political idioms in Reformed England: case studies from the North-east 1832–74*

(Hassocks, 1975), pp. 181–3.
6. D.A. Hamer, *The politics of electoral pressure: a study in the history of Victorian reform agitations* (Hassocks, 1977), pp. 98–116, 165–78; D.M. Thompson, 'The Liberation Society, 1844–1868', in *Pressure from without in early Victorian England*, ed. P. Hollis (1974), p. 225.
7. K.O. Morgan, *Wales in British politics 1868–1922* (Cardiff, 1980 edn), pp. 22–7.
8. *P.P.*, 1872, XLVII, 67. See also the figures in *Erskine May's Treatise on the law of parliament*, p. 867.
9. *Rectorial addresses delivered before the University of Edinburgh 1859–1899*, ed. A. Stodart-Walker (1900), p. 193.
10. *Why I am a Liberal*, ed. A. Reid (1885), p. 114.
11. See Hamer, *Liberal politics*. For the debate about the 1886 crisis, see chapter 10, note 40, p. 361 below. There are, of course, exceptions to these standard interpretations, of which two are particularly noteworthy: A.B. Cooke and J.R. Vincent, *The governing passion: cabinet government and party politics in Britain 1885–86* (Brighton, 1974), and Jenkins, *Gladstone, whiggery*. However, Jenkins is often in strident disagreement with Cooke and Vincent, and both books are weak on the political principles of the defecting whig-Liberals.
12. For more detailed figures, see Jenkins, *Gladstone, whiggery*, pp. 5–6.
13. W.C. Lubenow, *Parliamentary politics and the Home Rule crisis: the British House of Commons in 1886* (Oxford, 1988), p. 183.

Chapter 10

1. Duke of Argyll, *The reign of law* (1867), p. 428.
2. *Letters and other writings of the late Edward Denison*, ed. Sir B. Leighton (1872), pp. 167–74. See L.N. Goldman, 'The Social Science Association, 1857–1886: a context for mid-Victorian Liberalism', *E.H.R.*, CI (1986), 95–134.
3. 1869: *Letters of Denison*, p. 105.
4. *Hansard*, CLXXX, 185, 227–9, 14 June 1866.
5. A.D. Elliot, *The life of George Joachim*

Goschen 1st Viscount Goschen 1831–1907 (2 vols., 1911), I, 8.

6. English constitution, p. 142.
7. E. Hodder, The life of Samuel Morley (3rd edn, 1887), p. 347.
8. These figures are compiled from annual returns in P.P. from 1869 onwards, except for the 1864 figure, which I have computed from the index to Hansard.
9. The pleasures of life (1891 edn), pp. 89–93.
10. Mack and Armytage, Thomas Hughes, pp. 166–7.
11. J. Morley, 'The Liberal programme', Fortnightly Review, II (n.s.) (Sept. 1867), 359–69.
12. Parliamentary buff book: being an analysis of the divisions of the House of Commons, ed. T.N. Roberts (1869, 1870 et seq.).
13. See Lowell, Government of England, II, 76–7, and H. Berrington, 'Partisanship and dissidence in the nineteenth-century House of Commons', Parliamentary Affairs, XXI (1967–8), 338–74.
14. Thomas, House of Commons 1832–1901, pp. 14, 16.
15. The most detailed revisionist account of this complicated issue is J. Spain, 'Trade unionists, Gladstonian Liberals and the labour law reforms of 1875', in Currents of radicalism: popular radicalism, organised labour and party politics in Britain, 1850–1914, ed. E.F. Biagini and A.J. Reid (Cambridge, 1991), pp. 109–33.
16. P.W.J. Bartrip, 'State intervention in mid-nineteenth century Britain: fact or fiction?', Journal of British Studies, XXIII (1983–4), 76.
17. P.P., 1872, XLVII, 403.
18. Speeches of Jacob Bright, M.P., 1869 to 1884, ed. Mrs J. Bright (1885), pp. 186–7; Winterbotham, Hansard, CXCVI, 1758–9, 14 June 1869.
19. Ibid., CCV, 1852, 28 April 1871.
20. For figures, see F. Clifford, A history of private bill legislation (2 vols., 1885–7), II, 678.
21. L.T. Hobhouse, Liberalism (1911), pp. 122–3.
22. Mack and Armytage, Thomas Hughes, p. 159.
23. M. Cruickshank, Church and state in English education 1870 to the present day (1963), pp. 47, 190.
24. J.W. Adamson, English education,

1789–1902 (Cambridge, 1930), p. 372.
25. See Gladstone at Blackheath, 1871, in Gladstone's speeches, ed. A.T. Bassett (1916), p. 413, and Stansfeld, Hansard, CCVIII, 78, 20 July 1871.
26. Clifford, Private bill legislation, II, 507.
27. P.J. Waller, Town, city, and nation: England 1850–1914 (Oxford, 1983), pp. 301, 304.
28. P.P., 1884–5, LXI, 267.
29. See Hennock, Fit and proper persons, pp. 313–21.
30. E.P. Hennock, 'Finance and politics in urban local government in England, 1835–1900', H.J., VI (1963), 221.
31. Hennock, Fit and proper persons, pp. 75, 161–2.
32. D. Fraser, The evolution of the British welfare state: a history of social policy since the Industrial Revolution (Basingstoke, 1984 edn), p. 144.
33. Burn, Age of equipoise, p. 193.
34. Hartington, cited in Southgate, Passing of the whigs, p. 414; Mr Chamberlain's speeches, ed. C.W. Boyd (2 vols., 1914), I, 165.
35. Marquess of Hartington, Election speeches in 1879 and 1880 with address to the electors of North-east Lancashire (1880), p. 136.
36. The findings were summarised and popularised in The acre-ocracy of England: a list of all owners of three thousand acres and upwards, ed. J. Bateman (1876).
37. Hartington, Election speeches in 1879 and 1880, pp. 118–19, 195–6.
38. Hansard, CCLII, 1632, 10 June 1880.
39. See E. Bristow, 'The Liberty and Property Defence League and individualism', H.J., XVIII (1975), 761–89.
40. These assumptions are very widespread. Particular examples which have caught my attention recently (in addition to Bristow, ibid.) are: G. Alderman, The railway interest (Leicester, 1973), pp. 77–9, 108–17; Southgate, Passing of the whigs, p. 372; and Bradley, Optimists, p. 223. G.L. Goodman, 'Liberal Unionism: the revolt of the whigs', Victorian Studies, III (1959–60), 173–89, sees Liberal Unionism as a class movement.
41. G.D. Phillips, 'The whig lords and Liberalism, 1886–1893', H.J., XXIV (1981), 169–70.
42. Lymington, Fowler, Hansard, CCLII, 1693, 1726, 10 June 1880.

43. H.M. Lynd, *England in the eighteen-eighties: toward a social basis for freedom* (1968 edn), p. 107.
44. Gladstone and Shaw-Lefevre: *Hansard*, CCLXXIX, 1111, 1126, 10 May 1883.
45. W.E. Gladstone, *Midlothian speeches 1879*, ed. M.R.D. Foot (Leicester, 1971 edn), p. 95.
46. *Argyll's autobiography*, II, 398; see also Jenkins, *Gladstone, whiggery*, p. 220.
47. Goschen, *Hansard*, CCCII, 497–504, 26 January 1886.

Chapter 11

1. At Bolton, *Times*, 12 October 1864, p. 9; see also at Liverpool, ibid., 13 October, p. 7.
2. Parry, *Democracy and religion*, p. 153.
3. Gladstone, *Midlothian speeches*, p. 90.
4. *Gladstone's Boswell: late Victorian conversations by Lionel A. Tollemache and other documents*, ed. A. Briggs (Brighton, 1984), p. 201; Parry, *Democracy and religion*, p. 167; *Gladstone diaries*, X, 130–1.
5. F.D. Maurice, cited in G.W.E. Russell, *Prime ministers and some others: a book of reminiscences* (1918), p. 43.
6. W.E. Gladstone, *The Church of England and ritualism* (1875), p. 52.
7. *Correspondence on Church and religion of William Ewart Gladstone*, ed. D.C. Lathbury (2 vols., 1910), I, 168.
8. Morley, *Gladstone*, I, 304.
9. Ibid., I, 191.
10. *Gladstone on Church and religion*, II, 86.
11. W.E. Gladstone, 'The county franchise and Mr Lowe thereon', *Nineteenth Century*, II (Nov. 1877), 554–8; *Gladstone's Boswell*, p. 93; and the material cited in Parry, *Democracy and religion*, p. 168n116.
12. Address, 1868, in *Speeches of William Ewart Gladstone M.P. in South-west Lancashire, October 1868* (1868), p. iii.
13. Coleridge, *Coleridge*, II, 322.
14. *Gladstone-Granville correspondence 1868–76*, I, 56–7.
15. Ibid., I, 171.
16. 'Notes and queries on the Irish demand', *Nineteenth Century*, XXI (Feb. 1887), 177–8.
17. At Sunderland, *Times*, 11 October 1862, p. 8.
18. See J.P. Parry, 'Gladstone and the disintegration of the Liberal party', *Parliamentary History*, X (1991), 396–7.
19. *Gladstone diaries*, XI, 294–5, 302, 408, 444.
20. Ibid., VII, xxxiiin.
21. E.S. Purcell, *Life and letters of Ambrose Phillips de Lisle* (2 vols., 1900), II, 79.
22. Circa 1896: Brooke and Sorensen, *Gladstone*, I, 136.
23. Parry, *Democracy and religion*, pp. 170, 172.
24. This distinction is apparent in a famous speech of 1886, cited in *Gladstone diaries*, X, xliii.
25. The quotation is from R.W. Dale, *The politics of nonconformity: a lecture delivered in the Free Trade Hall, Manchester, November 21st 1871* (Manchester, 1871), p. 32. For Gladstone's confidence in the moral and ethical power of such preaching, see 'Universitas Hominum', 601–2; for his habit of scoring Dissenting sermons, see Parry, *Democracy and religion*, p. 163.
26. 'Universitas Hominum', 601.
27. *Pall Mall Gazette*, 29 June 1886, p. 1.
28. Parry, *Democracy and religion*, pp. 241–2.
29. *Gladstone's Boswell*, p. 193.
30. *Hansard*, CLXXXVII, 714, 17 May 1867.
31. Russell, *Prime ministers*, p. 44; on the Irish Church Bill, see Morley, *Gladstone*, II, 264, 266.
32. *The political correspondence of Mr. Gladstone and Lord Granville 1876–1886*, ed. A. Ramm (2 vols., Oxford, 1962), I, 40.
33. *Stanley diary 1849–69*, p. 230.
34. *The Red Earl: the papers of the fifth Earl Spencer 1835–1910*, ed. P. Gordon (2 vols., Northampton, 1981–6), I, 129.
35. *Gladstone diaries*, XI, 518n8.
36. Gladstone, 'County franchise and Mr Lowe', 538, 560.
37. [W.E. Gladstone,] 'Germany, France, and England', *E.R.*, CXXXII (Oct. 1870), 592.
38. W.A. Hayes, *The background and passage of the Third Reform Act* (New York, 1982), p. 92.
39. Gardiner, *Harcourt*, I, 495.
40. E. Hughes, 'The changes in parliamentary procedure, 1880–1882', in *Essays presented to Sir Lewis Namier*, ed. Pares and Taylor, p. 308.
41. *Hansard*, CLIII, 1066, 29 March 1859.
42. *Gladstone diaries*, X, 238, 451.
43. Gladstone, *Speeches in October 1868*,

pp. iv, xv, 14.

44. *Times*, 20 December 1867, p. 6.

45. Gladstone, *Speeches in October 1868*, p. x; Parry, *Democracy and religion*, pp. 178–9, 181.

46. See e.g. A. Austin, 'Character and ability in politics', *National Review*, IX (July 1887), 676–7.

47. Ashwell and Wilberforce, *Samuel Wilberforce*, III, 241.

48. *Gladstone diaries*, XI, 193–4, 213; Hayes, *Third Reform Act*, pp. 193–4.

49. See Morley, *Gladstone*, II, 227–32, and Parry, *Democracy and religion*, pp. 261–2, 266.

50. *Greville memoirs*, VIII, 297.

51. Gladstone, 'County franchise and Mr Lowe', 560.

52. Ibid., 542.

53. *Lord Carlingford's journal: reflections of a cabinet minister 1885*, ed. A.B. Cooke and J.R. Vincent (Oxford, 1971), p. 134.

54. *Memoir and letters of Sir Thomas Dyke Acland*, ed. A.H.D. Acland (1902), p. 346.

55. See e.g. E. Akroyd, *On the present attitude of political parties* (1874).

56. On the importance of parliament, see e.g. W.H. Fremantle, 'Convocation, parliament and the prayer-book', *E.R.*, CXL (Oct. 1874), 427–61.

57. G.C. Brodrick, *Political studies* (1879), p. 240.

58. Ibid., p. 224; H. Reeve, 'Plain whig principles', *E.R.*, CLI (Jan. 1880), 259.

59. Parry, *Democracy and religion*, pp. 92–7, 417.

60. Morley, *Gladstone*, II, 155, 171–2; *Stanley diary 1849–69*, pp. 228–9; *Extracts from journals kept by George Howard, earl of Carlisle*, ed. Lady C. Lascelles (1871), p. 342; O.W. Hewett, *Strawberry Fair: a biography of Frances, Countess Waldegrave 1821–1879* (1956), p. 240.

61. 1858: Fitzmaurice, *Granville*, I, 307.

62. Robert Ferguson, 1857, in Maxwell, *Clarendon*, II, 145.

63. Parry, *Democracy and religion*, pp. 141–3.

64. T.W. Reid, *The life, letters, and friendships of Richard Monckton Milnes, first Lord Houghton* (2 vols., 1890 edn), II, 361.

65. R. Palmer, earl of Selborne, *Memorials, Part II: personal and political 1865–1895* (2 vols., 1898), II, 349.

66. Coleridge, *Coleridge*, II, 203, 240.

67. *Argyll's autobiography*, I, 481.

68. Gardiner, *Harcourt*, I, 260.

69. Cowling, *1867*, p. 102.

70. See F.H. Hill, in *Gladstone's Boswell*, pp. 220–1; Hawkins, *Parliament, party*, p. 40; and the material cited in Parry, *Democracy and religion*, p. 142.

71. See the material cited in ibid., p. 141; and *Gladstone diaries*, X, 425n8.

72. *Stanley diary 1849–69*, pp. 228–9.

73. John, earl of Kimberley, *A journal of events during the Gladstone ministry 1868–1874*, ed. E. Drus (1958), p. 37.

74. Selborne, *Memorials 1865–95*, I, 334.

75. Cowling, *1867*, p. 101.

76. Maxwell, *Clarendon*, II, 224.

77. B. Holland, *The life of Spencer Compton eighth duke of Devonshire* (2 vols., 1911), I, 30.

78. Reginald, Viscount Esher, *Cloud-capp'd towers* (1927), p. 115.

79. R. Jenkins, *Sir Charles Dilke: a Victorian tragedy* (1958), p. 101.

80. Duke of Portland, *Men, women and things: memories* (1937), pp. 188–9.

81. Esher, *Cloud-capp'd towers*, p. 98.

82. *The Vanity Fair album*, I (1869), no. 8.

83. *Journals and letters of Esher*, p. 125.

84. *Parl. Deb. 4*, CLXXXVI, 1231, 24 March 1908; see also J. Buchan, in *The Graphic*, CXXXIII, 18, 18 July 1931.

85. More information on this whole section can be found, with effort, in Parry, *Democracy and religion*, Part II (for the 1874 election, see ibid., pp. 381–410). On the strength of the church in the 1870s, see G. Kitson Clark, *Churchmen and the condition of England 1832–1885* (1973), p. 146, and also Clark, *Making of Victorian England*, p. 170.

86. See those writers cited in Parry, *Democracy and religion*, p. 396n129.

87. G.W.E. Russell, *Sir Wilfrid Lawson: a memoir* (1909), p. 106.

88. Parry, *Democracy and religion*, p. 383.

89. Dale, *Politics of nonconformity*, p. 32.

90. *Argyll's autobiography*, II, 319–20.

91. *Stanley diary 1849–69*, p. 229.

92. Parry, *Democracy and religion*, pp. 136–7.

93. Russell, *Recollections*, pp. 312–13.

94. B. Disraeli, *Addresses on education, finances, and politics* (1873), pp. 29–30.

95. *The correspondence of Lord Overstone*, ed. D.P. O'Brien (3 vols., Cambridge, 1971), III, 1165.

96. J. Winter, *Robert Lowe* (Toronto,

1976), p. 248.

97. *Gladstone's Boswell*, p. 135.

98. 'Letter on the alarming state of public affairs, December 1871' (unpub.), 3rd Earl Grey papers, Department of Paleography and Diplomatic, University of Durham.

99. Grey, *Hansard*, CCVII, 1598, 13 July 1871; Russell, ibid., CCVIII, 513, 31 July 1871.

100. Lyveden and Somerset: ibid., CCVIII, 1276, 1290, 10 August 1871.

101. For this doctrine see C.C. Weston, 'Salisbury and the Lords, 1868– 1895', *H.J.*, XXV (1982), 120–1.

102. *Gladstone-Granville correspondence 1868–76*, II, 438.

103. See Parry, *Democracy and religion*, pp. 322–4.

104. The quotation is Layard's. For this and some other examples, see ibid., p. 409.

105. S. Collini, *Public moralists: political thought and intellectual life in Britain 1850–1930* (Oxford, 1991), pp. 273–5.

106. Stephen, 'Parliamentary government', 170.

107. Akroyd, *Present attitude of political parties*.

108. Morley, *Gladstone*, II, 494. At this time, the Liberal academic T.H. Green admitted to having overestimated the extent of working-class 'moral progress' in 1866–7. He was also appalled by agricultural labourers' selfishness in striking at harvest-time. See M. Richter, *The politics of conscience: T.H. Green and his age* (1964), pp. 328–9.

109. Gardiner, *Harcourt*, I, 240, 265–70, 285–6, 290.

110. Ibid., I, 270.

111. The quotations are from the *Leeds Mercury* and from Cowper-Temple: Jenkins, *Gladstone, whiggery*, pp. 44, 47. See Parry, *Democracy and religion*, pp. 401–2, 408–9.

112. Brodrick, *Political studies*, pp. 233–8. See also Reeve's 'Plain whig principles', 279: 'the first and plainest of Whig principles is to maintain the authority of Parliament'.

Chapter 12

1. Even Hartington invoked popular power, admitting that his parliamentary speeches sought to appeal to an extra-parliamentary audience, which alone could overthrow Disraeli: *Election speeches in 1879 and 1880*, pp. 226–7. Later, he suggested that parliament would achieve nothing on difficult questions like redistribution without 'some pressure and compulsion' from outside: *Times*, 28 July 1884, p. 7.

2. Lowell, *Government of England*, I, 502.

3. J. Chamberlain, 'A new political organization', *Fortnightly Review*, XXII (July 1877), 131.

4. Brodrick, *Political Studies*, pp. 257–77; Reeve, 'Plain whig principles', 279; E.D.J. Wilson, 'The caucus and its consequences', *Nineteenth Century*, IV (Oct. 1878), 695–712; W.T. Marriott, 'The Birmingham caucus', ibid., XI (June 1882), 949–65; J. Tulloch, 'The Liberal party and the Church of Scotland', *Blackwood's Magazine*, CXXIV (Sept. 1878), 260.

5. Hamer, *Politics of electoral pressure*, pp. 49–52, 155, 218–26.

6. Hanham, *Elections and party management*, pp. 142–3.

7. Esher, *Cloud-capp'd towers*, p. 110; *Times*, 7 February 1879, p. 10.

8. For Hartington on this, see Jenkins, *Gladstone, whiggery*, pp. 79–80.

9. *Gladstone-Granville correspondence 1876–86*, I, 38–47.

10. Morley, *Gladstone*, II, 587; *Gladstone-Granville correspondence 1876–86*, I, 3.

11. Shannon, *Bulgarian agitation*, ch. 6; R.E. Prothero, *The life and correspondence of Arthur Penrhyn Stanley* (2 vols., 1893), II, 486, 502; Brodrick, *Political Studies*, p. 246. Hartington had no time for the agitation and its 'innumerable parsons': Holland, *Devonshire*, I, 184.

12. H.A.L. Fisher, *James Bryce (Viscount Bryce of Dechmont)* (2 vols., 1927), I, 215; *Life and letters of Dean Church*, ed. M.C. Church (1895 edn), p. 280. For the activities of the Patriotic Association, see H. Cunningham, 'The Conservative party and patriotism', in *Englishness: politics and culture 1880–1920*, ed. R. Colls and P. Dodd (1986), p. 285.

13. Gladstone, *Midlothian speeches*, p. 50; G.W.E. Russell, *One look back* (1912), pp. 178–9, 192–3.

14. See those cited in Parry, *Democracy and religion*, pp. 436–7.

15. Gladstone, *Midlothian speeches*, pp. 91–2.
16. Disraeli's comment on defeat was that, 'like Napoleon, I have been beaten by the elements': Lord R. Gower, *Records and reminiscences* (1903), p. 349.
17. Hartington, *Election speeches in 1879 and 1880*, pp. 60, 69; Lloyd, *1880 election*, pp. 55–9, 154; Reeve, 'Plain whig principles', 275; Gladstone, *Midlothian speeches*, p. 136.
18. Lowell, *Government of England*, II, 79–80; see also the sharp decline in the number of amendments passed to government bills at this time, set out in ibid., I, 317.
19. *Election speeches in 1879 and 1880*, pp. 33, 36, 39, 69.
20. Bagehot, *Collected works*, VII, 233–7.
21. Hartington: *Times*, 7 February 1879, p. 10.
22. R. Lowe, 'The docility of an "imperial" parliament', *Nineteenth Century*, VII (Apr. 1880), 557–66; P.J. Durrans, 'A two-edged sword: the Liberal attack on Disraelian imperialism', *Journal of Imperial and Commonwealth History*, X (1981–2), 270.
23. *Election speeches in 1879 and 1880*, p. 229.
24. Lowe, 'Docility', 565.
25. Harcourt: *Times*, 15 January 1879, p. 6; Gardiner, *Harcourt*, I, 328–9.
26. Durrans, 'A two-edged sword', 269.
27. The tone was set by Harcourt and Hartington: *Times*, 8 February 1879, pp. 6, 10.
28. Gardiner, *Harcourt*, I, 350. Childers and Lowe complained of Tory vacillation on foreign policy: S. Childers, *The life and correspondence of Hugh C.E. Childers* (2 vols., 1901), I, 251; Gordon, *Red Earl*, I, 147.
29. *Election speeches in 1879 and 1880*, p. 218.
30. Ibid., p. 224; Hartington at Liverpool, *Times*, 8 February 1879, p. 10.
31. Gladstone, *Midlothian speeches*, pp. 57–8, 163; Hartington, *Election speeches in 1879 and 1880*, p. 88.
32. J. Howarth, 'The Liberal revival in Northamptonshire, 1880–1895: a case study in late nineteenth century elections', *H.J.*, XII (1969), 78–118, esp. 87; Olney, *Lincolnshire politics*, pp. 246–8.
33. Jenkins, *Gladstone, whiggery*, p. 144.
34. C.C. O'Leary, *The elimination of cor-*rupt *practices in British elections 1868–1911* (Oxford, 1962), p. 231.
35. Burt, *Hansard*, CCXIX, 222, 13 May 1874.
36. Ibid., CCXVII, 809, 23 July 1873.
37. Gladstone recognised this in 1872: ibid., CCX, 1908, 26 April 1872.
38. Selborne, *Memorials 1865–95*, II, 98–9.
39. Trevelyan, *Hansard*, CCXVII, 814–20, 23 July 1873 and ibid., CCXIX, 206, 13 May 1874; Forster, ibid., CCXIX, 244, 13 May 1874; *Speeches of Jacob Bright*, p. 20.
40. John Bright, cited in Hayes, *Third Reform Act*, p. 47; Hartington, in Seymour, *Electoral reform*, pp. 298–9.
41. Trevelyan, *Hansard*, CCXVII, 816, 23 July 1873.
42. Hartington, *Election speeches in 1879 and 1880*, pp. 210–11.
43. *Speeches of Jacob Bright*, pp. 144–5, 251.
44. Goschen, *Hansard*, CCXXXVIII, 231, 22 February 1878.
45. See p. 80 and p. 175 above; Trevelyan, *Hansard*, CCXVII, 808, 23 July 1873; Campbell-Bannerman, ibid., CCXIX, 230, 13 May 1874.
46. *Speeches of Jacob Bright*, pp. 13, 17.
47. *Election speeches in 1879 and 1880*, p. 123.
48. Lubbock, *Hansard*, CCXCIV, 1806, 2 March 1885.
49. Lubbock and Courtney: ibid., CCXCIV, 1815, 1926, 2, 3 March 1885.
50. Seymour, *Electoral reform*, p. 502.
51. Ibid., p. 501.
52. C.T.D. Acland and Leatham: *Hansard*, CCXCIV, 1845–6, 1823–4, 2 March 1885.
53. Acland, Leatham, Shaw-Lefevre: ibid., CCXCIV, 1845, 1823–6, 1833, 2 March 1885.
54. Gladstone: ibid., CCII, 147, 15 June 1870.
55. Ibid., CCLXXXVI, 711, 24 March 1884. In fact, Hartington had fought in cabinet to shield Ireland from franchise extension, and had toyed with the idea of minority representation there, but the rest of the cabinet did not think this practicable or necessary.
56. Holland, *Devonshire*, I, 393.
57. See e.g. J.S. Morrill, 'Cheshire politics, 1832–1974', in *A history of the county of Chester*, ed. B.E. Harris (3 vols., 1979–87), II, 144, 146.

58. See H. Reeve, 'The redistribution of seats', *E.R.*, CLXI (Jan. 1885), 272–96.

59. M.E.J. Chadwick, 'The role of redistribution in the making of the Third Reform Act', *H.J.*, XIX (1976), 676.

60. Gladstone, *Hansard*, CCXCIV, 380, 1 December 1884.

61. See Boundary Commission report, *P.P.*, 1884–5, XIX, 1.

62. H. Pelling, *Social geography of British elections 1885–1910* (1967), pp. 133–4, 149–51, 215–18.

63. Cooke and Vincent, *Governing passion*, p. 3.

64. 1886: *Salisbury-Balfour correspondence: letters exchanged between the third marquess of Salisbury and his nephew Arthur James Balfour 1869–1892*, ed. R. Harcourt Williams (Ware, 1988), p. 137.

65. See e.g. *The radical platform: speeches by J. Chamberlain, M.P.: autumn 1885* (Edinburgh, 1885), pp. 3–4, 23, 36.

66. For this view in 1886, see G.D. Goodlad, 'Gladstone and his rivals: popular Liberal perceptions of the party leadership in the political crisis of 1885–1886', in *Currents of radicalism*, ed. Biagini and Reid, pp. 177–8. For Chamberlain and religion, see Parry, *Democracy and religion*, pp. 224–5.

67. A. Simon, 'Church disestablishment as a factor in the general election of 1885', *H.J.*, XVIII (1975), 806–7, 816–17.

68. *Times*, 4 November 1885, pp. 9–10.

69. *Argyll's autobiography*, II, 395–8.

70. Cooke and Vincent, *Governing passion*, pp. 16–17.

71. (Hartington) Holland, *Devonshire*, I, 399; (Chamberlain) Viscount Gladstone, *After thirty years* (1929), p. 197.

72. Evelyn Baring: see Marquess of Zetland, *Lord Cromer* (1932), p. 123.

73. *The diary of Sir Edward Walter Hamilton 1880–1885*, ed. D.W.R. Bahlman (2 vols., Oxford, 1972), I, 190; *Gladstone diaries*, X, 69.

74. P. Magnus *Gladstone: a biography* (1954), p. 287.

75. Morley, *Gladstone*, III, 144.

76. *Lord Carlingford's journal*, p. 74.

77. E.D. Steele, 'Ireland for the Irish', *History*, LVII (1972), 240–2.

78. Jenkins, *Gladstone, whiggery*, p. 150; Lansdowne, *Hansard*, CCLII, 1870, 2 August 1880.

79. C. Dewey, 'Celtic agrarian legislation and the Celtic revival: historicist implications of Gladstone's Irish and Scottish Land Acts 1870–1886', *Past and Present*, LXIV (1974), 63; see e.g. *Speeches of Jacob Bright*, p. 257.

80. In 1882, Forster denied the Parnellites' claim to be 'the leaders and representatives of the Irish people': *Florence Arnold-Forster's Irish journal*, ed. T.W. Moody and R. Hawkins (Oxford, 1988), 467. So did Goschen, if they agitated against law: *Hansard*, CCCIV, 1460–1, 13 April 1886.

81. July 1886: Mallet, *Northbrook*, p. 233.

82. *Gladstone diaries*, XI, 394, 467.

83. J.L. Garvin, *The life of Joseph Chamberlain II: 1885–1895* (1933), pp. 135–6.

84. J. Loughlin, *Gladstone, Home Rule and the Ulster question 1882–93* (Dublin, 1986), pp. 39–42, 172–96.

85. *Hansard*, CCCV, 601, 16 May 1886.

86. Charles Russell, ibid., CCCIV, 1359, 12 April 1886.

87. Morley, ibid., CCCIV, 1275, 9 April 1886; Campbell-Bannerman, ibid., CCCV, 933, 13 May 1886.

88. Morley, ibid., CCCIV, 1275, 9 April 1886; Whitbread, ibid., CCCIV, 1404–5, 12 April 1886.

89. Morley, ibid., CCCIV, 1275, 9 April 1886; Bryce, ibid., CCCV, 1215, 17 May 1886.

90. Gladstone, ibid., CCCV, 598–9, 16 May 1886; C. Russell, ibid., CCCIV, 1362, 12 April 1886.

91. Burt, ibid., CCCIV, 1372, 12 April 1886; Cowen, ibid., CCCVI, 306, 7 June 1886.

92. Gladstone, ibid., CCCIV, 1084, 8 April 1886.

93. As Chamberlain said: *Salisbury-Balfour correspondence*, p. 135.

94. Henry James, *Hansard*, CCCV, 929, 13 May 1886; Hobhouse, ibid., CCCV, 1204, 17 May 1886.

95. Goschen, ibid., CCCIV, 1458, 13 April 1886.

96. Ibid., CCCIV, 1238, 9 April 1886.

97. See e.g. Goschen, ibid., CCCIV, 1475–6, 13 April 1886, and Parry, *Democracy and religion*, pp. 443–4.

98. Goschen, *Hansard*, CCCIV, 1463, 13 April 1886; Lymington, ibid., CCCVI, 49, 25 May 1886.

99. Ibid., CCCIV, 1262–3, 9 April 1886.

100. Leatham, ibid., CCCV, 1018, 13 May 1886.

101. Ibid., 1011–12.

102. Ibid., CCCV, 916, 13 May 1886.

103. Goschen, ibid., CCCIV, 1458, 13 April 1886, and CCCVI, 1167, 7 June 1886.
104. A.C. Sellar, 'The contest for the Union', *E.R.* CLXV (Apr. 1887), 579.
105. Hartington, *Hansard*, CCCIV, 1250, 9 April 1886; see also Selborne, *Memorials 1865-95*, II, 204.
106. Holland, *Devonshire*, I, 98-104.
107. See Garvin, *Joseph Chamberlain II*, pp. 145, 188, 192, 222.
108. Leatham, *Hansard*, CCCV, 1011, 13 May 1886.
109. Selborne, *Memorials 1865-95*, II, 226; Holland, *Devonshire*, II, 253.
110. *Gladstone diaries*, XI, 451, 486.
111. Holland, *Devonshire*, II, 110.
112. *Gladstone diaries*, X, cxlv-cxlvi.
113. Morley, *Gladstone*, III, 287-8.
114. *Gladstone diaries*, XI, 535-6, 541, 547-8. For Gladstone's suggestion that Chamberlain was not a gentleman, see *Gladstone-Granville correspondence 1876-86*, II, 458. For his behaviour during the 1886 negotiations, see P.T. Marsh, 'Tearing the bonds; Chamberlain's separation from the Gladstonian Liberals, 1885-6', in *The Gladstonian turn of mind: essays presented to J.B. Conacher*, ed. B.L. Kinzer (Toronto, 1985), pp. 123-53.
115. *Times*, 24 June 1886, p. 9, and 2 July 1886, p. 10.
116. At Truro, ibid., 1 November 1887, p. 10.
117. Lubbock and Hartington: *Hansard*, CCCIV, 1234, 1244, 9 April 1886.
118. Leatham, ibid., CCCV, 1016, 13 May 1886.
119. See those cited in Parry, *Democracy and religion*, p. 443.
120. Hartington, *Hansard*, CCCIV, 1238, 9 April 1886, and CCCV, 605, 10 May 1886.
121. Gladstone, ibid., CCXIII, 1203, 18 April 1887. For criticism, see Selborne, *Memorials 1865-95*, II, 261-2, 277, 354-5, and Hartington at Inverness, *Times*, 4 October 1888, p. 7.
122. G.W.E. Russell, *One look back*, p. 262.
123. *Gladstone diaries*, X, xliii, XI, 576.
124. Trevelyan, *Bright*, pp. 453, 456.
125. The phrase belongs to R.E. Prothero, a typical Broad Church Unionist: 'The national party of the future', *Quarterly Review*, CLXIX (Oct. 1889), 558.

Epilogue

1. The phrase (critical) is T.H. Huxley's: Parry, *Democracy and religion*, p. 442.
2. J. Buchan, 'A lucid interval', *Blackwood's Magazine*, CLXXXVII (Feb. 1910), 165-86.
3. K.O. Morgan, 'Gladstone and Wales', *Welsh History Review*, I (1960-3), 82.
4. For no-popery in Welsh and Scottish politics, see David Bebbington, 'Religion and national feeling in nineteenth-century Wales and Scotland', in *Religion and national identity*, ed. S. Mews (Oxford, 1982), p. 502.
5. Thomas, *House of Commons 1832-1901*, p. 14.
6. B. McGill, 'Francis Schnadhorst and Liberal party organisation', *Journal of Modern History*, XXXIV (1962), 32; (1892) *The letters of Queen Victoria third series: a selection from Her Majesty's correspondence and journal between the years 1886 and 1901*, ed. G.E. Buckle (3 vols., 1930-2), II, 173.
7. J.M. Lee, 'Parliament and the appointment of magistrates: the origins of advisory committees', *Parliamentary Affairs*, XIII (1959-60), 85-94.
8. G. Searle, *Corruption in British politics 1895-1930* (Oxford, 1987), pp. 85-7.
9. Berrington, 'Partisanship and dissidence', 371; J.D. Fair, 'Party voting behaviour in the British House of Commons, 1886-1918', *Parliamentary History*, V (1986), 67.
10. Lowell, *Government of England*, I, 477.
11. T.W. Heyck, 'Home rule, radicalism and the Liberal party, 1886-1895', *Journal of British Studies*, XIII (1973-4), 89.
12. Earl of Portsmouth, 'Executive government and the Unionists', *Quarterly Review*, CLXXIII (Oct. 1891), 542, 552-3.
13. T.E. Kebbel, 'Is the party system breaking up?', *Nineteenth Century*, XLV (Mar. 1899), 511; third Earl Grey, 'In peril from parliament II', ibid., XXVIII (Dec. 1890), 1012-13; A. Milman, 'The peril of parliament', *Quarterly Review*, CLXXVIII (Jan. 1894), 267; R. Brett 1886, cited in Lubenow, *Parliamentary politics*, p. 325.
14. Portsmouth, 'Executive government', 536-7; L.J. Jennings, 'Parliamentary and election prospects', *Quarterly Re-*

view, CLXXIV (Jan. 1892), 269–71.

15. From a Conservative pamphlet of 1895, quoted in Cunningham, 'Conservative party and patriotism', 294–5.

16. *Parl. Deb. 4*, XXVII, 1225, 30 July 1894.

17. G.H.L. Le May, *The Victorian constitution: conventions, usages and contingencies* (1979), p. 190.

18. See e.g. J. Campbell, *F.E. Smith first earl of Birkenhead* (1983), p. 133.

19. E.J. Bristow, *Vice and vigilance: purity movements in Britain since 1700* (Dublin, 1977), pp. 117, 120, 154, 160–3, 205, 211–13.

20. His daughter Violet's phrase: see *H.H.*

Asquith: letters to Venetia Stanley, ed. M. and E. Brock (Oxford, 1985 edn), p. 117.

21. Lowell, *Government of England*, I, 523–34; Proceedings of the NLF, 1898, cited in *The nineteenth-century constitution 1815–1914: documents and commentary*, ed. H.J. Hanham (Cambridge, 1969), pp. 220–1.

22. For example, the Liberal Unionist Cromer charged that higher social expenditure was weakening fiscal reserves and so threatening Britain's ability to fight a war. See D. French, *British economic and strategic planning 1905–1915* (1982), p. 15.

Further reading

General and biographical

The best bibliographies for this period are *Bibliography of British history 1789–1851*, ed. L. Brown and I. Christie (Oxford, 1977), and *Bibliography of British history 1851–1914*, ed. H.J. Hanham (Oxford, 1976), a marvellous achievement. Handy collections of statistics are available in: *Abstract of British historical statistics*, ed. B.R. Mitchell and P. Deane (Cambridge, 1962), from which most of the unattributed details about population, prices, taxation and government expenditure which appear in the text are taken; *British historical facts 1830–1900*, ed. C. Cook and B. Keith (1975); and *British parliamentary election results 1832–1885*, ed. F.W.S. Craig (1977).

Prime among the many sources for nineteenth-century political debate are *Hansard's parliamentary debates*, puzzlingly underused by historians. Of the many periodicals consulted, the *Edinburgh Review* is the most instructive for whig/Liberal thinking, with competition from the 1860s from the radical *Fortnightly Review* and from the 1870s from *The Nineteenth Century*. *The Wellesley index to Victorian periodicals 1824–1900*, ed. W.E. Houghton, E.R. Houghton and J.H. Slingerland (Toronto, 5 vols., 1966–89) breaks the code of anonymity which most journals imposed on their contributors.

This book could not have been written without the Victorian and Edwardian craving for lengthy *Lives and Letters*. Almost all politicians included in the *Biographical notes* above were honoured with one (many are cited in the Notes). Some modern editions of nineteenth-century diaries are also important, like *The Holland House diaries 1831–1840*, ed. A.D. Kriegel (1977).

Academic historians tend to find political biography problematic. There are a number of good biographies of Canning (such as those by P.J.V. Rolo, Wendy Hinde and Peter Dixon), but no systematic treatment of his political impact. E.A. Smith's *Lord Grey 1764–1845* (Oxford, 1990), and Donald Southgate's *'The most English minister...': the policies and politics of Palmerston* (1966), are the best available *Lives* of their subjects, full of information, but both figures have perhaps eluded all their biographers to date. Philip Ziegler's *Melbourne: a biography of William Lamb 2nd Viscount Melbourne* (1978 edn) is an entertaining read, as is the chapter on Hartington in John Pearson's *Stags and serpents: the story of the House of Cavendish and the dukes of Devonshire* (1983). Hartington deserves a much fuller survey. Both Colin Matthew and Richard Shannon are working on double-volume lives of that most problematic of characters, Gladstone; the first volumes of each, reaching 1874 and 1865 respectively, present him in very different lights, but both are important. A foretaste of Professor Matthew's second volume is available in the long, perceptive and subtle 'Introduction' to volume x of his edition of *The*

Gladstone diaries (Oxford, 1990), covering the years 1881–6. The best single-volume life probably remains Philip Magnus's *Gladstone: a biography* (1954). John Prest's *Lord John Russell* (1972) is useful in parts, but a powerful discussion of Russell's central role in Liberal history is overdue.

Recent treatments of other important Liberal figures include E.A. Wasson, *Whig renaissance: Lord Althorp and the whig party 1782–1845* (New York, 1987), and D.D. Olien, *Morpeth: a Victorian public career* (Washington D.C., 1983). William Harcourt is in need of a modern biographer. So are George Grey and Charles Wood, though R.J. Moore's *Sir Charles Wood's Indian policy 1853–66* (Manchester, 1966), is excellent, and there is helpful material in D. Smith, 'Sir George Grey at the mid-Victorian Home Office', *Canadian Journal of History*, XIX (1984), 361–86.

Leslie Mitchell recreates an aristocratic milieu in *Holland House* (1980). There are a number of analyses of the characteristics of Liberal MPs: the most recent, and interesting, is W.C. Lubenow, *Parliamentary politics and the Home Rule crisis: the British House of Commons in 1886* (Oxford, 1988).

Much good work is being done on the intellectual context of Liberal politics, among which should be singled out: B. Hilton, *The age of atonement: the influence of evangelicalism on social and economic thought, 1785–1865* (Oxford, 1988); L.N. Goldman, 'The Social Science Association, 1857–1886; a context for mid-Victorian Liberalism', *English Historical Review*, CI (1986), 95–134; and J. Morrell and A. Thackray, *Gentlemen of science: early years of the British Association for the Advancement of Science* (Oxford, 1981).

The history of the parliamentary party

The lack of general books on parliamentary Liberalism is remarkable. The nearest is D. Southgate, *The passing of the whigs, 1832–1886* (1962), though this book takes a very different approach. The reader is best referred to general political history textbooks by those with an interest in Liberalism, such as Richard Shannon, *The crisis of imperialism, 1865–1915* (1974), and the old multi-volume *History of the English people* by E. Halévy.

More detailed works on particular periods are more plentiful, and often of very high quality. Austin Mitchell's *The whigs in opposition, 1815–1830* (Oxford, 1967) is one such. E.A. Wasson's article, 'The coalitions of 1827 and the crisis of whig leadership', *Historical Journal*, XX (1977), 587–606, is suggestive. The 1830s have recently been subjected to a dazzling variety of revisionist interpretations, which have comprehensively seen off the Peelite dismissiveness of Norman Gash's *Reaction and reconstruction in English politics, 1832–1852* (Oxford, 1965), chapter 6. Ian Newbould's *Whiggery and reform, 1830–1841: the politics of government* (Basingstoke, 1990) is the most sober of these interpretations, and Peter Mandler's *Aristocratic government in the age of reform: whigs and Liberals, 1830–1852* (Oxford, 1990) the most creative and flamboyant, though unkind critics would say that it is about the 1980s as much as the 1830s. Richard Brent's *Liberal Anglican politics: whiggery, religion and reform 1830–1841* (Oxford, 1987), is a stimulating and lucid essay which says much of significance beyond its ostensible confines of religious policy.

Intelligent analysis of the period after 1846 is still scarce, and in a way the most interesting remains W.L. Burn's idiosyncratic but impressively learned *The age of equipoise: a study of the mid-Victorian generation* (1964). E.D. Steele's *Palmerston and Liberalism, 1855–1865* (Cambridge, 1991), has recently added significant depth to our understanding. Paul Gurowich's 'The continuation of war by other means: party and politics, 1855–1865', *Historical Journal*, XXVII (1984), 603–31, has an interesting approach that should be developed further. The classic work on the 1860s remains

John Vincent's incomparable, brilliant and magnificently flawed *The formation of the Liberal party, 1857–1868* (1966). That this was a Ph.D. thesis should be a sobering thought to blinkered, unambitious or concept-crazy research supervisors everywhere. Another model Ph.D., of a different kind, was Richard Shannon's *Gladstone and the Bulgarian agitation, 1876* (1963), a thought-provoking book with far-reaching implications. The only general account of Gladstone's Liberal party, D.A. Hamer's *Liberal politics in the age of Gladstone and Rosebery: a study in leadership and policy* (Oxford, 1972), has a very different definition of both leadership and policy to that of this book, concentrating on internal party conflict and on the minority which advocated a programmatic approach. T.A. Jenkins, *Gladstone, whiggery and the Liberal party 1874–1886* (Oxford, 1988), is important: it is the first book to take non-Gladstonian Liberalism during its period seriously. A.B. Cooke and John Vincent, *The governing passion: cabinet government and party politics in Britain, 1885–86* (Brighton, 1974), is a most stimulating book, archivally idiosyncratic, but much misunderstood and underrated by those who reduce it to a work of mere 'high political' manoeuvre.

Radicals and pressure groups

The 1830s are well served. There is William Thomas, *The Philosophical radicals: nine studies in theory and practice 1817–1841* (Oxford, 1979). On anti-slavery, the most suggestive articles are: R. Anstey, 'Parliamentary reform, Methodism and anti-slavery politics, 1829–1833', *Slavery and abolition*, II (1981), 209–26; D.B. Davis, 'The emergence of immediatism in British and American anti-slavery thought', *Mississippi Valley Historical Review*, XLIX (1962–3), 209–30; I. Gross, 'The abolition of negro slavery and British parliamentary politics, 1832–3', *Historical Journal*, XXIII (1980), 63–85, and idem, 'Parliament and the abolition of negro apprenticeship 1835–1838', *English Historical Review*, XCVI (1981), 560–76. Also important is A. Tyrrell, *Joseph Sturge and the moral radical party in early Victorian Britain* (1987). Norman McCord's splendid debunking of the myth of *The Anti-Corn Law League 1838–1846* (1958) is still fresh. F.M.L. Thompson treats the land reform movement similarly in 'Land and politics in England in the nineteenth century', *Transactions of the Royal Historical Society*, XV (1965), 23–44. Richard Edsall has written an interesting biography of *Richard Cobden: independent radical* (Cambridge, Mass., 1986).

On the religious radicalism of mid- and late-Victorian England, Brian Harrison's *Drink and the Victorians: the temperance question in England 1815–1872* (1971) is still essential, well complemented by A.E. Dingle, *The campaign for prohibition in Victorian England: the United Kingdom Alliance, 1872–1895* (1980). D.A. Hamer, *The politics of electoral pressure: a study in the history of Victorian reform agitations* (Hassocks, 1977), is useful on both temperance and disestablishment campaigners. For the latter, see also D.W. Bebbington, *The nonconformist conscience: chapel and politics, 1870–1914* (1982), and D.M. Thompson, 'The Liberation Society, 1844–1868', in *Pressure from without in early Victorian England*, ed. P. Hollis (1974), pp. 210–38. Eugenio Biagini has presented much interesting material from working-class Liberal newspapers in his *Liberty, retrenchment and reform: popular Liberalism in the age of Gladstone, 1860–1880* (Cambridge, 1992).

Parliamentary reform and the constitution

J.B. Conacher has produced a helpful collection of documents on the three Reform Acts: *The emergence of British parliamentary democracy in the nineteenth century* (New

371

York, 1971). Still the best book on the Reform process is Charles Seymour, *Electoral reform in England and Wales* (1915; reprinted, Newton Abbot, 1970), though students will not entertain the idea. K.T. Hoppen makes some important comparative points in 'The franchise and electoral politics in England and Ireland, 1832–1885', *History*, LXX (1985), 202–17.

The definitive Nuffield account of the 1832 Act is Michael Brock's *The Great Reform Act* (1973). John Cannon's *Parliamentary reform, 1640–1832* (Cambridge, 1973), provides a valuable longer-term perspective, and some perceptive ideas. There is also an extensive article literature. Much computer-literate work has recently been done on the interstices of the unreformed electoral system: the analyses are headed by Frank O'Gorman, *Voters, patrons and parties: the unreformed electoral system of Hanoverian England 1734–1832* (Oxford, 1989) and John A. Phillips, *The Great Reform Bill in the boroughs: English electoral behaviour, 1818–1841* (Oxford, 1992). But the material in the text on electoral contests before 1832 comes from my own work. Peter Fraser's 'Public petitioning and parliament before 1832', *History*, XLVI (1961), 195–211, is suggestive.

Since the historical profession showed its flexibility by absorbing F.B. Smith's *The making of the Second Reform Bill* (Cambridge, 1966) and Maurice Cowling's 'high-political' *1867: Disraeli, Gladstone and revolution: the passing of the Second Reform Bill* (Cambridge, 1967) in successive years, little new has been said, or needed saying, on that topic.

The 1884–5 settlement, though more important, has been studied less, but a similar division exists in the literature: Andrew Jones, *The politics of Reform 1884* (Cambridge, 1972), takes the high road, and W.A. Hayes, *The background and passage of the Third Reform Act* (New York, 1982), a rather lower one.

Bruce Kinzer, *The ballot question in nineteenth-century English politics* (New York, 1982), treats its subject with impressive thoroughness. So does C.C. O'Leary, *The elimination of corrupt practices in British elections, 1868–1911* (Oxford, 1962).

The great works on nineteenth-century constitutional history are now of a certain age. A.L. Lowell, *The government of England* (2 vols., 1908) remains as unread as it is seminal. Erskine May, *The constitutional history of England since the accession of George the Third 1760–1860* (2 vols., 1861), and Walter Bagehot, *The English constitution* (1867), are a better guide to mid-Victorian Liberal assumptions than to previous history, but are still a better historical guide than most twentieth-century works. G.H.L. Le May, *The Victorian constitution: conventions, usages and contingencies* (1979) is thin for this period. *The nineteenth-century constitution 1815–1914: documents and commentary*, ed. H.J. Hanham (Cambridge, 1969), is always interesting and often outstanding.

On the development of the cabinet there is A. Aspinall, 'The cabinet council, 1783–1835', *Proceedings of the British Academy*, XXXVII (1952), 145–252, and J.P. Mackintosh, *The British cabinet* (1962). Despite its title, the utility of G.W. Cox, *The efficient secret: the cabinet and the development of political parties in Victorian England* (Cambridge, 1987), lies in its statistical investigations into parliamentary voting. The best works on parliament and legislation are venerable: J. Redlich, *The procedure of the House of Commons: a study of its history and present form* (3 vols., 1908), and F. Clifford, *A history of private bill legislation* (2 vols., 1885–7). Peter Fraser, 'The growth of ministerial control in the nineteenth-century House of Commons', *English Historical Review*, LXXV (1960), 444–63, is important. So is Hugh Berrington, 'Partisanship and dissidence in the nineteenth-century House of Commons', *Parliamentary Affairs*, XXI (1967–8), 338–74. There is useful material in B. Chubb, *The control of public expenditure: financial committees of the House of Commons* (Oxford, 1952), and in H.D. Clokie and J.W. Robinson, *Royal Commissions of Inquiry: the significance of investigations in British politics* (Stanford, 1937). Angus Hawkins,

' "Parliamentary government" and Victorian political parties, c.1830–c.1880', *English Historical Review*, CIV (1989), 638–69, offers a general overview of the period.

The best book on government administration is H. Parris, *Constitutional bureaucracy: the development of British central administration since the eighteenth century* (1969). R.A. Chapman and J.R. Greenaway's *The dynamics of administrative reform* (1980) offers an interesting modern perspective. Specific articles of note include J.R. Torrance, 'Sir George Harrison and the growth of bureaucracy in the early nineteenth century', *English Historical Review*, LXXXIII (1968), 52–88, and J.R. Breihan, 'The abolition of sinecures, 1780–1834', *Proceedings of the Consortium on Revolutionary Europe*, XI (1981), 141–9.

The standard work on criminal law reform is L. Radzinowicz, *A history of English criminal law and its administration from 1750* (5 vols., 1948–86).

Local government and politics

No modern scholar has yet replaced two classic works: J. Redlich and F.W. Hirst, *Local government in England* (2 vols., 1903), and S. and B. Webb, *English local government from the Revolution to the Municipal Corporations Act* (9 vols., 1906–29). But there is one outstanding recent book: E.P. Hennock, *Fit and proper persons: ideal and reality in nineteenth-century urban government* (1973). See also his 'Central/local government relations in England: an outline 1800–1950', *Urban History Yearbook 1982*, pp. 38–49. Of value also is B. Keith-Lucas, *The English local government franchise: a short history* (Oxford, 1952). Though modern work tends to be highly specialised, there have been some significant studies: Avner Offer, *Property and politics, 1870–1914: landownership, law, ideology and urban development in England* (Cambridge, 1981); Christine Bellamy, *Administering central-local relations 1871–1919: the Local Government Board in its fiscal and cultural context* (Manchester, 1988); and John Prest, *Liberty and locality: parliament, permissive legislation, and ratepayers' democracies in the nineteenth century* (Oxford, 1990).

Work on local politics is without end. Derek Fraser provides an overview, for the big towns, in *Urban politics in Victorian cities: the structure of politics in Victorian cities* (Leicester, 1976). R.J. Morris has much to say on 'Voluntary societies and British urban elites, 1780–1850: an analysis' in *Historical Journal*, XXVI (1983), 95–118. Impressive local studies include: Barrie Trinder, *Victorian Banbury* (Banbury, 1982); Sir Francis Hill, *Georgian Lincoln* (Cambridge, 1966) and *Victorian Lincoln* (Cambridge, 1974); F.W.H. Sheppard, *London 1808–70: the infernal wen* (1971); *A history of modern Leeds*, ed. D. Fraser (Manchester, 1980); and R.J. Olney, *Lincolnshire politics, 1832–1885* (Oxford, 1973).

Social policy

The best general accounts include: U. Henriques, *Before the welfare state: social administration in early industrial Britain* (1979); Derek Fraser, *The evolution of the British welfare state* (Basingstoke, 1984); and D. Roberts, *Victorian origins of the British welfare state* (New Haven, 1960). Peter Bartrip offers salutary reflections on the ineffectiveness of many measures, in 'British government inspection, 1832–1875: some observations', *Historical Journal*, XXV (1982), 605–26, and 'State intervention in mid-nineteenth century Britain: fact or fiction?', *Journal of British Studies*, XXIII (1983–4), 63–83.

The literature on the Poor Law alone is massive. See Anthony Brundage, *The making of the New Poor Law 1832–39* (1978), Peter Dunkley, *The crisis of the Old Poor Law in England 1795–1834: an interpretive essay* (New York, 1982), and Peter Mandler, 'The making of the New Poor Law *redivivus*', *Past and Present* CXVII (1987), 131–57. Each writer has also been involved in debates on the subject in learned journals. J.R. Poynter's *Society and pauperism: English ideas on poor relief, 1795–1834* (1969), is an important survey.

Other suggestive books on aspects of social policy include: Martin Wiener, *Reconstructing the criminal: culture, law and policy in England, 1830–1914* (Cambridge, 1990), which is also an entry into a vast literature on crime, policing and punishment; P.B. Munsche, *Gentlemen and poachers: the English game laws, 1671–1831* (Cambridge, 1981); and Royston Lambert, *Sir John Simon, 1816–1904, and English social administration* (1963), a pioneering study of Victorian public health administration. See also his 'A Victorian national health service: state vaccination 1855–71', *Historical Journal*, V (1962), 1–18, and 'Central and local relations in mid-Victorian England: the Local Government Act Office, 1858–71', *Victorian Studies*, VI (1962), 121–50. The history of the open spaces movement has been neglected, but is a good subject. There is valuable information on it in Lord Eversley's *Commons, forests and footpaths* (1910).

Religion and education

Owen Chadwick, *The Victorian Church* (2 vols., 1966–70) is still an indispensable starting-point. G.I.T. Machin's *Politics and the Churches in Great Britain 1832 to 1868* (Oxford, 1977), and *Politics and the Churches in Great Britain 1869 to 1921* (Oxford, 1987), are standard for religious policy. Hilton, *Age of atonement*, and Brent, *Liberal Anglican politics*, listed above, are strong on the intellectual ramifications of policy. Two important articles are Geoffrey Best, 'The whigs and the Church Establishment in the age of Grey and Holland', *History*, XLV (1960), 103–18, and J.P. Ellens, 'Lord John Russell and the Church rate conflict: the struggle for a Broad Church, 1834–1868', *Journal of British Studies*, XXVI (1987), 232–57.

The history of education, as of the constitution, has been best served by historians of the pre-1970 vintage. Still the most useful work in the field is J.W. Adamson, *English education 1789–1902* (Cambridge, 1930). There is valuable material in R.L. Archer, *Secondary education in the nineteenth century* (Cambridge, 1921). Marjorie Cruickshank, *Church and state in English education 1870 to the present day* (1963) is also important. J. Murphy, *Church, state and schools in Britain, 1800–1970* (1971) is a handy brief guide. Among the best of the modern books are: D.G. Paz, *The politics of working-class education in Britain, 1830–50* (Manchester, 1980); D.I. Allsobrook, *Schools for the shires: the reform of middle-class education in mid-Victorian England* (Manchester, 1986); and S. Fletcher, *Feminists and bureaucrats: a study in the development of girls' education in the nineteenth century* (Cambridge, 1980).

Ireland

Three splendid recent general histories are available: Roy Foster, *Modern Ireland 1600–1972* (1988); K, Theodore Hoppen, *Ireland since 1800: conflict and conformity* (1989); and J. Lee, *The modernisation of Irish society 1848–1918* (Dublin, 1973). K.T. Hoppen's *Elections, politics and society in Ireland, 1832–1885* (Oxford, 1984) is also a fund of information, with added light relief.

Particular episodes are well covered in: G. Broeker, *Rural disorder and police reform in Ireland, 1812–36* (1970); G.I.T. Machin, *The Catholic question in English politics, 1820–1830* (Oxford, 1964); A. Macintyre, *The Liberator: Daniel O'Connell and the Irish party 1830–1847* (1965); R.D.C. Black, *Economic thought and the Irish question, 1817–1870* (Cambridge, 1960); A.D. Kriegel, 'The Irish policy of Lord Grey's government', *English Historical Review*, LXXXVI (1971), 22–45, and 'The politics of the whigs in opposition, 1834–1835', *Journal of British Studies*, VII (1967–8), 65–91; K.B. Nowlan, *The politics of repeal: a study in the relations between Great Britain and Ireland, 1841–50* (1965); J.H. Whyte, *The Independent Irish party, 1850–9* (Oxford, 1958); A. Warren, 'Gladstone, land and social reconstruction in Ireland, 1881–1887', *Parliamentary History*, II (1983), 153–73; and J. Loughlin, *Gladstone, Home Rule and the Ulster question, 1882–93* (Dublin, 1986).

Foreign, imperial and economic policy

Good general overviews include: M. Chamberlain, *'Pax Britannica'? British foreign policy 1789–1914* (1988); P. Hayes, *The nineteenth century, 1814–80* (1975); and K. Bourne, *The foreign policy of Victorian England, 1830–1902* (Oxford, 1970). A.J.P. Taylor, *The trouble makers: dissent over foreign policy 1792–1939* (1957) is scintillating and irreverent. B. Porter, *The refugee question in mid-Victorian politics* (Cambridge, 1979) is an impressive study, centring on the Orsini affair, but with much wider ramifications.

As for the empire, C.A. Bayly, *Imperial meridian: the British empire and the world, 1780–1830* (1989), is a marvellous synthesis-cum-creation on the early part of the period. J.M. Ward, *Colonial self-government: the British experience 1759–1856* (1979), is important. So, still, is W.P. Morrell, *British colonial policy in the age of Peel and Russell* (Oxford, 1930). For an earlier period, H.J.M. Johnston, *British emigration policy 1815–1830: 'shovelling out paupers'* (Oxford, 1972), and Peter Burroughs, *The Canadian crisis and British colonial policy, 1828–1841* (1972), are both useful. A.G.L. Shaw, *Convicts and the colonies* (1966) is a study of penal transportation.

Peter Cain offers a good succinct survey of economic policy in its global aspect in *Economic foundations of British overseas expansion, 1815–1914* (1980), and some inspired speculation, with A.G. Hopkins, in 'Gentlemanly capitalism and British expansion overseas', *Economic History Review*, XXXIX (1986), 501–25, and ibid., XL (1987), 1–26. More sober studies of major incidents are Lucy Brown, *The Board of Trade and the free trade movement 1830–42* (Oxford, 1958), and Sarah Palmer, *Politics, shipping and the repeal of the Navigation Laws* (Manchester, 1990).

The history of free trade in Britain, a glorious subject, has long awaited its student. An important work by A.C. Howe is forthcoming. Similarly neglected are large chunks of pre-Gladstonian Liberal financial policy, which historians do not seem disposed to take seriously. Unfortunately, Sydney Buxton, *Finance and politics: a historical study 1783–1885* (2 vols., 1888) was not much different; but his work is very useful on Gladstone. So is H.C.G. Matthew, 'Disraeli, Gladstone, and the politics of mid-Victorian budgets', *Historical Journal*, XXII (1979), 615–43; the story of Gladstonian finance is continued in introductions to successive volumes of his edition of *The Gladstone diaries*.

Index